# Time Out

# Berlin Guide

**Penguin Books**

KATIH

PENGUIN BOOKS

Published by the Penguin Group
Penguin Books Ltd, 27 Wright's Lane, London W8 5TZ, England
Penguin Books USA Inc., 375 Hudson Street, New York, New York 10014, USA
Penguin Books Australia Ltd, Ringwood, Victoria, Australia
Penguin Books Canada Ltd, 10 Alcorn Avenue, Toronto, Ontario, Canada M4V 3B2
Penguin Books (NZ) Ltd, 182-190 Wairau Road, Auckland 10, New Zealand

Penguin Books Ltd, Registered Offices: Harmondsworth, Middlesex, England

First published 1993
Second edition 1995
10 9 8 7 6 5 4 3 2 1

Colour reprographics by Argent, 32 Paul Street, London EC2A 4LB
Mono reprographics, printed and bound by William Clowes Ltd, Beccles, Suffolk NR34 9QE

## Edited and designed by

Time Out Magazine Limited
Universal House
251 Tottenham Court Road
London W1P OAB
Tel: 0171 813 3000
Fax: 0171 813 6001

## Editorial

**Managing Editor**
Peter Fiennes
**Editor**
Dave Rimmer
**Executive Editor**
Julie Emery
**Deputy Editor**
Nicholas Royle
**Researcher/Writer**
Chris Bohn
**Indexer**
Rosamund Sales

## Design

**Art Director**
Warren Beeby
**Art Editor**
John Oakey
**Designers**
Paul Tansley, Elroy Toney
**Picture Editor**
Fiona Seres

## Advertising

**Group Advertisement Director**
Lesley Gill
**Sales Director**
Mark Phillips
**Advertisement Sales (Berlin)**
Runze & Casper Verlagsservice

## Administration

**Publisher**
Tony Elliott
**Managing Director**
Mike Hardwick
**Financial Director**
Kevin Ellis
**Marketing Director**
Gillian Auld
**Production Manager**
Mark Lamond

**Features in this guide were written and researched by**:
**Introduction** Dave Rimmer. **Essential Information** Chris Bohn, Stephen Taylor. **Getting Around** Stephen Taylor, Ed Ward. **Accommodation** Lori Anderson. **Berlin by Season** Julie Wedow. **Sightseeing** Julie Emery, Karen Nickel, Dave Rimmer. **History** Frederick Stüdemann-Schulenberg. **Berlin by Area** Ed Ward. **Berlin Today** Kevin Cote. **Eating & Drinking** Lori Anderson, Kevin Cote, Julie Emery, Joanne Fowler, Jerold James Gordon, Karen Nickel, Dave Rimmer, Ed Ward. **Shopping** Melissa Drier, Zakiah Omar, Julie Wedow. **Services** Julie Wedow. **Art Galleries** Albrecht Thiemann, Neal Wach. **Museums** Chris Bohn, Joanne Fowler, Karen Nickel. **Media** Kevin Cote. **Cabaret** Neal Wach. **Clubs** Annie Lloyd, Dave Rimmer. **Dance** Julie Wedow. **Film** Dirk Schäfer, Ken Stillman. **Music: Classical & Opera** Jerold James Gordon. **Music: Rock, Folk & Jazz** Biba Kopf, Dave Rimmer. **Sport & Fitness** Thekla Ahlrichs. **Theatre** Julian Eaves, Neal Wach. **After Hours** Dave Rimmer. **Business** Kevin Cote. **Children** Jody Goodman, Cheryl Tlam. **Gay & Lesbian Berlin** Thekla Ahlrichs, Ken Stillman. **Students** Thekla Ahlrichs, Susanne Kitlitscho. **Women's Berlin** Thekla Ahlrichs. **Trips Out Of Town** Julian Eaves, Ed Ward. **Survival** Chris Bohn, Stephen Taylor. **Further Reading** Chris Bohn, Dave Rimmer.

The Editor would like to thank the following individuals for help, information and moral support:
Thekla Ahlrichs, Lori Anderson, Gosto Babka von Gostomski, Chris Bohn, Kevin Cote, Volker Hauptvogel, Annie Lloyd, Patrick Lonergan, Klaus Maeck, Mark Reeder, Neal Wach, Trevor Wilson.

**Photography** by Wolfgang Brückner except for:
**Hulton Deutsch** pages 49, 50, 52, 54, 55, 56, 58, 59, 63, 65, 66, 67; **Wolfgang Tillmans** page 195; **Barry J Holmes** page 265; **Robert Harding** page 267; **Image Bank** pages 189, 190; **German Tourist Board** pages 245, 247, 249, 250, 251.

# Contents

# About the Guide

This is the second edition of the *Time Out Berlin Guide*, one in series of city guides that includes London, Amsterdam, Paris, New York, Prague, Madrid and Rome. This latest edition has been thoroughly revised, updated and, where necessary, rewritten. We've laboured to make it as useful as possible. Addresses, telephone numbers, transport details, opening times, admission prices and credit card details are all included in our listings.

Although it covers all the major sights, attractions and museums, the *Berlin Guide* is much more than a book for tourists and casual visitors. We also point you towards hundreds of the city's more obscure and eccentric venues, bars, clubs and happenings. We tell you both what to see and what to avoid. Written and researched by people who live in the city, this *Guide* offers an informed, insider's view: Berlin as the Berliners know it.

## CHECKED & CORRECT

All information was checked and correct at the time of writing, but please bear in mind that, especially in a city such as Berlin, still adjusting to reunification, things are liable to sudden and unpredictable change. This is particularly true of nightlife, and of ventures on the east side of town, where things tend to wink in and out of existence. This state of flux is one of the things that makes Berlin so exciting, but it may be as well to phone before you set out, to check opening times, dates of exhibitions, admission prices and other important details.

## ADDRESSES

Since the last *Berlin Guide*, the German system of postcodes has changed. In our listings we've included both the Postleitzahl (postcode, always five digits beginning with a '1') and the district name, eg Schöneberg. Bear in mind that while you don't need the district name to address a letter, very few people are going to be able to direct you to 'Berlin 10783'.

## PRICES

The prices listed throughout this *Guide* should be used as guidelines. Fluctuating exchange rates and inflation can cause prices, in shops and restaurants especially, to change rapidly. If prices and services somewhere vary wildly from those we've quoted, ask if there's a good reason. If there's not, take your custom elsewhere and, then, please let us know. We try to give the best and most up-to-date advice, so we always want to hear if you've been overcharged, badly treated or otherwise given the runaround.

## CREDIT CARDS

Compared to the UK or US, credit cards are still not widely used in Berlin, although this is slowly changing. The following abbreviations have been used for credit cards: AmEx – American Express; DC – Diners Club; EC – Eurocard; JCB – Japanese credit cards; MC – Mastercard/Access; V – Visa.

## RIGHT TO REPLY

It should be stressed that the information we give is impartial. No organisation or enterprise has been included in this guide because its owner or manager has advertised in our publications. Impartiality is the reason our guides are so successful and well respected. We trust you will enjoy the *Time Out Berlin Guide* and that it helps you make the most of your stay. But if you disagree with any of our assessments, let us know; your comments on places you have visited are always welcome. You'll find a reader's reply card at the back of this book.

# Introduction

Berlin, Berlin. It's taken every punch the twentieth century could find to throw at it, and proudly bears the scars. Like the old buildings still pock-marked with holes from Russian bullets. Or the concrete Nazi bunkers still standing here and there. Or the narrow strip of land where the Wall once ran, snaking its way across the city like a jagged knife wound, only just beginning to heal.

They're glamorous scars – the kind that if worn on a face would make it maybe less beautiful, but a whole lot more arresting. And Berlin's is a dark glamour. It might no longer star Sally Bowles, or Michael Caine as Harry Palmer, but it's still a place where the outrageous has space to happen, and sooner or later always does.

In the mid-nineties we might think of that space as no-man's land. Not just the physical variety, though there's certainly still plenty of that. Look around Potsdamer Platz, the once and future cen-

tre of town, and you can see the shape of it. Tower cranes employed in the construction of prestige corporate headquarters now loom above the wasteland where once stood watchtowers and rolls of barbed wire. To the north, the Reichstag awaits renovation by Norman Foster and the eventual arrival of the Federal parliament. And around the edges, from abandoned bank vaults, derelict power stations and converted bunkers now occupied by the army of nightlife, booms an insistent dancefloor thud.

And while physical no-man's land gets re-developed, Berlin remains in a no-man's land of history – no longer the divided Cold War city it was, not yet the capital of unified Germany it will become. The only rule in this historical lacuna is that nothing will stay the same. As the city spreads out its grandiose plans for the future, odd pockets of alternative culture flourish among the ruins. But despite the social tensions and eco-nomic pain attendant on reunification, Berlin also remains an amiable city: large but intimate, well serviced and easy to get around in, liberal and open, fringed with lake and forest and full of pave-ment life in the summer.

Amiable, but a bit mixed up. Berlin is still two cities, although the line between them grows ever more blurred. East and West have met and min-gled and remain largely unimpressed with one another. While the subsidy squeeze has meant west Berlin growing poorer and tattier, east Berlin has been getting not just a facelift, but a whole new lease of life. The formerly communist side of town is still short of services compared to the west – a shortage reflected in the listings in this guide – but a new energy is these days firing up areas such as Prenzlauer Berg or the northern part of Mitte. Just take a walk around. You can feel it on the streets.

And spread out across both sides of the city are thriving music, film, theatre and art scenes. Berlin also offers, between the bars which never close and the clubs which occupy the strangest post-indus-trial spaces, some of Europe's wildest and weird-est nightlife, and certainly its longest nights.

A unified city that's still divided, a capital that isn't a capital, somewhere you can still expect the unexpected – the Berlin of the mid-nineties is a place like no other. It won't last for ever. Catch it now, before it's too late. *Dave Rimmer*

# Essential Information

*Facts to help you find your feet in Berlin.*

There are some things you need to know right at the start of your visit to Berlin, however long you might be staying. We cover the essentials here, but for more detailed information *see chapter* **Survival.**

## Visas

A valid passport is all that you need for a stay of up to three months in Germany, if you are an EC national. Officially, within a week of arriving in Germany you are supposed to register your address at the **Anmeldungsamt** (local registration office). To find the one in your district, phone the **Landeseinwohneramt** (state registration office) on *783 85 04*. Take your passport and expect to queue.

However, your passport probably won't be stamped when you arrive in the country, so unless you need to register to enrol as a student or extend your stay beyond three months, don't worry about registering.

### Residence Permits

For stays of longer than three months, you'll need a residence permit. EC citizens, EFTA citizens (from Finland, Austria, Sweden, Norway, Switzerland) and citizens of Andorra, Australia, Israel, Japan, Canada, Malta, New Zealand, the US and Cyprus, can obtain this from the **Landeseinwohneramt Berlin** (*see below*).

A residence permit is free of charge and can normally be obtained on the day of application. Appointments are not required but queues start at around 6am and you can expect a wait of up to two hours. Once you have queued it only takes a few minutes for the interviewer to process your application and grant you a visa.

You will need to take with you your passport, two passport-size photos and proof of an address in Germany (your **Anmeldebestätigung** – an official form confirming that you have registered at the **Anmeldungsamt**, or registration office). If you have a work contract, take that along too and you may be granted a longer stay than you would otherwise.

### Landeseinwohneramt Berlin

*Dominicusstraße 12, Schöneberg, 10823 (783 85 04) U4 Innsbrucker Platz, S6 Schöneberg.* **Open** 7.30am-1pm Mon, Tue, Thur; 7.30am-noon Fri. **Closed** Wed.
If you are unsure about your status, contact the German Embassy in your home country. If you are already in Berlin, contact your embassy or consulate, listed under 'Botschaften' in the Gelbe Seiten (Yellow Pages), or *see chapter* **Survival.**

## Customs

Since the Single European Market agreement came into force at the beginning of 1993, EC nationals over the age of 17 have been able to import limitless goods for their personal use, if bought tax-paid. But if you decide to bring vast quantities of alcohol into or out of Germany, you may have to convince customs officials that you are, say, planning to throw a party.

For citizens of non-EC countries and for duty-free goods, the old limits still apply:
• 200 cigarettes **or** 50 cigars **or** 250 grams (8.82 ounces) of tobacco.
• 1 litre of spirits (over 22 per cent alcohol), **or** 2 litres of fortified wine (under 22 per cent alcohol), **or** 2 litres of non-sparkling and sparkling wine.
• 50 grams (1.76 ounces) of perfume.
• 500 grams (1.1lb) coffee.
• 100 grams (3.52 ounces) tea.
• Other goods to the value of DM125 for non-commercial use.
• The import of meat, meat products, fruit, plants, flowers and protected animals is restricted or forbidden.

There are no restrictions on the import and export of currency.

## Insurance

EC countries have reciprocal medical treatment arrangements with Germany. All EC citizens will need form E111. British citizens can get this by filling in the application form in leaflet SA30, available in all Department of Social Security (DSS) offices or over the post office counter. You should get your E111 at least two weeks before you leave. Make sure you read the small print on

*Shop hours are strictly regulated – 3pm on a Saturday could see you tramping the streets.*

the back of form E111 so that you know exactly how to obtain medical or dental treatment at a reduced charge.

You should be aware that the E111 does not cover all medical costs (for example, dental treatment) and that it is therefore best to take out private insurance before leaving for Germany.

Citizens from non-EC countries should take out private medical insurance before their visit. German medical treatment is expensive: the minimum charge for a visit to the doctor will be DM40. For more information *see chapter* **Survival: Health**. The British Embassy (*see above*) publishes a list of English-speaking doctors, dentists and other medical professionals, as well as lawyers and interpreters.

As always when travelling abroad, it would be in visitors' best interests to take out insurance on personal belongings before leaving for Berlin. Such insurance is usually included in package holidays, but be sure to check.

## Money

The unit of German currency is the Deutsche Mark, abbreviated to DM. The DM is divided into 100 Pfennigs (pfg). Coins in use are 1 pfennig, 5 pfennigs, 10 pfennigs, 20 pfennigs, 50 pfennigs, DM1, DM2 and DM5. Notes come in DM5, DM10,

DM20, DM50, DM100, DM200, DM500 and DM1,000 denominations.

Berliners prefer to use cash for most transactions, although the larger hotels, shops and most restaurants will accept one or more of the major credit cards (Access/Mastercard, American Express, Diners' Club, Visa) and many will take Eurocheques with guarantee cards, and travellers' cheques with ID. In general, the German banking and retail systems are less enthusiastic about credit than their UK and US equivalents, though this is slowly changing.

If you want to take out cash on your credit card, banks will give an advance against Visa and Mastercard (Access) cards. But you may not be able to withdraw less than the equivalent of US$100. Automatic tellers around the city displaying the appropriate symbols will give you smaller amounts of cash, but beware of the charges involved. German cash machines are surprisingly temperamental, so you shouldn't rely on them. In the east, credit cards, Eurocheques and travellers' cheques are occasionally accepted, but cash is best.

### American Express

*Kurfürstendamm 11 (2nd Floor), Charlottenburg, 10719 (882 75 75). S3, S5, S6, S7, S9/U2, U9 Zoologischer Garten.* **Open** 9am-5pm Mon-Fri; 9am-noon Sat.
Holders of an American Express card can use the company's facilities here, including the cash advance service.

# Banks

Most banks are open from 9am to noon Monday to Friday, from 1-3pm three afternoons a week, and from 2-6pm on the other two afternoons a week (days vary). German banks are notoriously bureaucratic. If you are staying long enough to warrant opening a German bank account, the Sparkasse (with branches all over the city) is much less trouble than arranging transfers. Otherwise, **Wechselstuben** (bureaux de change) are open outside normal banking hours and generally give better rates than banks. If you want to phone around, look under Wechselstuben in the Gelbe Seiten (Yellow Pages).

### Deutsche Verkehrsbank
*In Zoo Station, Hardenbergplatz, Charlottenburg, 10623 (881 71 17). U2, U9, S3, S5, S6, S7, S9 Zoologischer Garten.* **Open** 7.30am-10pm Mon-Fri; 8am-7pm Sun, public holidays.

### Deutsche Verkehrsbank
*In Hauptbahnhof, Friedrichshain, off Stralauer Platz, 10243 (428 70 29). S3, S5, S6, S7, S9 Hauptbahnhof.* **Open** 7am-10pm Mon-Fri; 7am-6pm Sat; 8am-4pm Sun, holidays.
The *Wechselstuben* of the Deutsche Verkehrsbank offer among the best rates of exchange in the city.

## German Time

Germany is one hour ahead of Greenwich Mean Time, except between the end of September and the end of October (when it's the same). Clocks are turned forward an hour at the end of March, and back an hour at the end of September.

In Germany 'am' and 'pm' are not used; instead, time is based on the 24-hour system. Thus 8am is 8 Uhr (or 8h), noon is 12 Uhr Mittags, 5pm is 17 Uhr and midnight is 12 Uhr Mitternachts.

## Climate

Berlin has a Continental climate, hot in the summer and cold in the winter, especially when the wind blows in from the surrounding lowlands. At the end of October temperatures can be below zero and in January and February Berlin often ices over. Spring begins in late March or April. The average range of temperatures is: January to February -3°C to 4°C; March to May 8°C to 19°C; June to July 21°C to 24°C; August to September 22°C to 19°C; October to December 13°C to 3°C.

## Public Holidays

On public holidays (Feiertagen) you will find it difficult to get things done, but most cafés, bars and restaurants stay open. Public holidays are: New Year's Day, January 1; Good Friday; May Day May 1; Ascension Day; Whitsun; Day of German Unity June 17; Reunification Day October 3; Day of Prayer and National Repentance, third Wednesday in November; Christmas Eve, December 24; Christmas Day, December 25; Boxing Day, 26 December.

## Opening Times
### Shops

Shop opening hours are strictly regulated. Standard opening hours are from 9am-6.30pm Monday to Friday and from 9am-2pm on Saturday. The first Saturday of each month is known as Langer Samstag (long Saturday). On this day some of the larger shops open until 6pm from October to April, and until 4pm during the summer.

The late shopping law allows people to continue trading until 8.30pm on Thursdays, although few but the bigger stores do so. A recent change in the law allows family businesses to stay open later than 6.30pm providing a family member staffs the shop, and some corner newsagents and tobacconists are beginning to take advantage of this. Most Turkish shops in Kreuzberg and Neukölln are open on Saturday afternoons and on Sundays from 1-5pm. Many bakers open to sell cakes on Sundays from 2-4pm. If you run out of food, some shops keep long hours, but they are expensive. *See chapter* **After Hours**.

### Edeka
*in Schloßstraße Station, Steglitz, 12163 (794 40 45). U9 Schloßstraße.* **Open** 3-10pm Mon-Fri; 1-10pm Sat; 10am-8pm Sun, public holidays.

### Metro
*in Fehrbelliner Platz Station, Wilmersdorf, 10707 (861 70 10). U2, U7 Fehrbelliner Platz.* **Open** 11am-10.30pm daily.

### Metro
*in Kurfürstendamm Station, Charlottenburg, 10719 (883 41 41). U3, U15 Kurfürstendamm.* **Open** 11am-11pm Mon-Fri, Sun; 11am-midnight Sat.

### Bars

Bar opening times vary considerably, but most start serving around 6pm and stay open until at least 1am, if not through until the morning. If the bar you happen to be in does close, there's plenty of opportunity to continue partying in cafés and clubs until dawn breaks. *See chapters* **Cafés & Bars** *and* **After Hours**.

## Tipping

The standard tip in restaurants is 10 per cent, but it is not obligatory. Check for the words *Bedienung Inclusiv* on your bill, which means that service has already been included.

In a taxi, it's a good idea to round up the bill to the nearest Mark.

In Berlin, as elsewhere in Germany, jaywalking is an offence for which you can be fined. Even Berliners obey the little red man on the traffic light; ignore it and you can be fined DM10 on the spot.

### Berliner Schnauze (Berlin's Wit)

Berliners are renowned for their wit. Karl Marx defined it as 'a curious mixture of a small dose of irony with a little measure of scepticism and a large one of vulgarity'. The un-German qualities of Berliners – their tolerance and openness – are in this sardonic vein.

Unlike the British, Berliners are not prepared to stand sheepishly in queues for hour upon hour; sometimes you'll have to use your elbows.

### Tourist Offices

If you need to know anything about anything, telephone the offices listed below. The staff are friendly, even if you can't speak German.

### Berlin Tourist Information (Verkehrsamt)

*Europa-Center, Budapesterstraße, Tiergarten, 10787 (262 60 31). U2, U9, S3, S5, S6, S7, S9 Zoologischer Garten.* **Open** 8am-10.30pm Mon-Sat; 9am-9pm Sun.

### Verkehrsamt im Bahnhof Zoo

*Main Hall, Zoologischer Garten, Hardenbergplatz, Charlottenburg, 10623 (313 90 63). U2, U9, S3, S5, S6, S7, S9 Zoologischer Garten.* **Open** 8am-11pm Mon-Sat.

### Verkehrsamt am Flughafen Tegel

*Main Hall, Tegel Airport (4101 31 45). U7 Jacob-Kaiser-Platz, then bus 109, X9 or both buses run direct from Zoologischer Garten.* **Open** 8am-11pm daily.

# Vocabulary

Most west Berliners will have at least a smattering of English. In the east, however, Russian was the first language learned at school; although English is rapidly being acquired, it is very useful – and polite – to have at least basic German, especially if you intend to venture out of the city.

German may be a little more complicated grammatically than French, but it is still closely related to English in its etymology. Thus once you have mastered the basics, it is relatively easy to pick up.

## Pronunciation

z – pronounced ts
w – like English v
v – pronounced somewhere between f and v
s – like English z, but softer
r – like French r, throaty
a – as in father
e – as in day
i – as in seek
o – as in bottom
u – as in loot
ä – combination of a and e, sometimes pronounced like **ai** in p**ai**d and sometimes pronounced like **e** in s**e**t
ö – combination of o and e, as in French **eu**
ü – combination of u and e, like tr**ue**
ai – like p**ie**
au – like h**ou**se
ie – like fr**ee**
ei – like f**i**ne
eu – like c**oi**l

## Useful Phrases

hello – *guten Tag*
goodbye – *aufwiedersehen, tschüss* or *tschau*
yes – *ja; jawohl* (formal)

no – *nee; nein* (formal)
please – *bitte*
thank you – *danke schön*
excuse me – *entschuldigen Sie mir bitte*
sorry – *pardon*
I'm sorry, I don't speak German – *entschuldigung, ich kann kein Deutsch*
do you speak English? – *sprechen Sie Englisch?*
sir – *Herr*
madam – *Frau*
waiter – *Kellner*
open – *offen*
closed – *geschlossen*
I would like… – *Ich möchte…*
how much is…? – *wieviel kostet…?*
could I have a receipt? – *darf ich bitte eine Quittung haben?*
how do I get to…? – *wie komme ich nach…?*
how far is it to…? – *wie weit ist es nach…?*
left – *links*
right – *rechts*
straight ahead – *gerade-hinaus*
far – *weit*
near – *nah*
street – *die Straße*
square – *der Platz*
gate – *das Tor*
good – *gut*
bad – *schlecht*
big – *groß*
small – *klein*

## Numbers

0 *null*; 1 *eins*; 2 *zwei*; 3 *drei*; 4 *vier*; 5 *fünf*; 6 *sechs*; 7 *sieben*; 8 *acht*; 9 *neun*; 10 *zehn*; 11 *elf*; 12 *zwölf*; 13 *dreizehn*; 14 *vierzehn*; 15 *fünfzehn*; 16 *sechszehn*; 17 *siebzehn*; 18 *achtzehn*; 19 *neunzehn*; 20 *zwanzig*; 21 *einundzwanzig*; 22 *zweiundzwanzig*; 30 *dreissig*; 31 *einunddreissig*; 32 *zweiunddreissig*; 40 *vierzig*; 50 *fünfzig*; 60 *sechzig*; 70 *siebzig*; 80 *achtzig*; 90 *neunzig*; 100 *hundert*; 101 *hunderteins*; 110 *hundertzehn*; 200 *zweihundert*; 201 *zweihunderteins*; 1,000 *tausend*.

# Getting Around

*Steering a path through the city, by boat, train, car and bike.*

Even the alleged German efficiency has been sorely tested by the job of reuniting Berlin's transport systems. But, with the job finally done, and the transit ring around Berlin half complete (the southern half), it's possible to get around this sprawling city with a minimum of fuss – unless, of course, you get stuck in some of the new construction that's currently underway.

## Arriving in Berlin

### From Tegel Airport

*Airport Information (41 01 23 06).* **Open** 6am-11pm daily.
Take bus 109 to the Zoologischer Garten (known as Zoo Station or just Zoo) in the centre of the city. This costs DM3.70. From Zoo you can connect by bus, U-Bahn (underground) or S-Bahn (surface rail) to anywhere in the city. You will also find rail and tourist information offices at Zoo (*see below*). Alternatively, you can take the 109 bus to Jacob-Kaiser-Platz U-Bahn, or the 128 bus to Kurt-Schumacher-Platz and transfer to the underground system, for which your bus ticket is valid (*see below* **Tickets & Travel Passes**); whether you use Kurt-Schumacher-Platz (U6) or Jacob-Kaiser-Platz (U7), depends on your ultimate destination, so pick up a free transport map at the airport (*see below* **Maps**). A taxi into the city centre will cost about DM30.

### From Berlin Tempelhof Airport

*Airport Information (69510).* **Open** 5am-11pm daily.
Berlin Tempelhof is just south of the city centre on the U6 line. Connections to the rest of Berlin are easy. The U-Bahn station (Platz der Luftbrücke) is a short walk from the terminal building, as are bus connections.

### From Schönefeld Airport

*Airport Information (60910).* **Open** 24 hours daily.
The airport of east Berlin is a long way to the south-east of the city. All officials are trained in the old east German way and can sometimes be a little over-scrupulous. A taxi to Zoo Station will cost about DM55. The 171 bus takes you to the S-Bahn, which provides easy access to the east and west, with S9 going to Haputbahnhof, Alexanderplatz, Friedrichstraße and Zoo, and the S45 taking a southern route to Westend. If you are heading for Zoo take the 171 bus to U-Bahn station Rudow and catch a U7 train in the Rathaus Spandau direction. For Zoo station change at Möckernbrücke onto the U2, direction Krumme Lanke, and change again to the U1, direction Ruhleben, at Wittenbergplatz.

### From Train Stations

*Zoologischer Garten (Bahnhof Zoo), Hardenbergplatz, Charlottenburg, 10623 (297 613 41).* **Open** 5.30am-11pm daily.
The main station from most destinations to the west is Zoo, although if you are heading for the south-west of the city you should disembark at Berlin-Wannsee. Hauptbahnhof (27916 62) is the former GDR main station, and connects to many points south and east, including Vienna, Warsaw, Prague and Budapest.

### From Bus Stations

*Information (3 01 80 28).* **Open** 5.30am-9.30pm Mon-Sat.
Buses arrive in west Berlin at the Central Bus Station on the Messedamm 8, Charlottenburg, 14057 opposite the radio tower (Funkturm) and the ICC (International Congress Centrum). From there, continue by U-Bahn line U2, direction Vinetastraße (station Kaiserdamm), to the centre.

## Public Transport

The two former transport administrations, the BVB in east Berlin and BVG in west Berlin, have now merged and become the Berliner Verkehrs-Betriebe, which is abbreviated, somewhat illogically, to **BVG**.

Since July 1990, the BVG has implemented its new tariff system, appropriately named Unbegrenzte Berlin (Unbounded Berlin). The underground (**U-Bahn:** parts of which run above ground) and the surface rail network (**S-Bahn:** parts of which run underground) are connected to the bus, tram and even ship lines on the same tariff system administered by the BVG. A single ticket is valid for all lines on the network for two hours. For prices, *see below* **Tickets & Travel Passes**.

Unified Berlin is well served by the U- and S-Bahn which, together with stretches of **Regionalbahn** (regional railway), form the Schnellbahnnetz (the express train network) for the Berlin region. There has been constant renovation work on the S-Bahn in the west since 1984, when it was purchased back from East Germany. Much of the renovation necessary to complete the network in the eastern half of the city has been done. New stretches are being built, including a northern ring, and the S-Bahn lines are affected by Deutsche

Reisebahn's restructuring of their Berlin operations, causing some temporary disruptions, which are usually announced on small flyers in stations bearing the figure of Max the mole.

## U-Bahn

The first stretch of Berlin's U-Bahn was opened in 1902 and the network now consists of nine lines and 163 stations. The first trains run shortly after 4am; the last between midnight and 1am, except on weekends on the U1/15 and U9 lines. Each direction is named after the last stop on the line. You can take a bicycle on the U-Bahn (but not in the first carriage) from 9am to 2pm, and after 5.30pm on weekdays (all day at weekends and holidays), at the concessionary rate. With a yearly or monthly ticket, a Berlin ticket or a Kombi-Tages-karte (*see below* **Tickets & Travel Passes**), you can take your bicycle for free. The U1 from Gleisdreieck to Schlesi-sches Tor is elevated and is an unusual way to see some of Berlin's sights. Also worthy of exploration is the elevated stretch of the U2 between Senefelderplatz and Pankow, where it is known as the Magistratsschirm (council umbrella), providing pedestrians with cover from Berlin showers.

## S-Bahn

Now that much of the renovation on the S-Bahn network has been completed it is an efficient means of transport, especially in the east of the city. Some of the original rolling stock fitted with wood remains, but is increasingly being used only on the weekend Historische S-Bahn excursions. On the S-Bahn, bicycles may only be taken in carriages that display the bicycle symbol.

## Regionalbahn (Regional Railway)

At the extremities of the city the regional railway presents an opportunity to circumnavigate the whole of Berlin for the price of an Unbounded Berlin single fare (*see above*). Make sure you renew your ticket after two hours.

## Buses

Berlin has a dense network of bus lines (numbering 155), and a restricted number (45) run in the early hours (*see below* **Travelling at Night**). The day lines run from 4.30am to about 1am the next morning. Enter at the front of the bus and exit in the middle. The driver sells only individual tickets, but all tickets from the orange or yellow machines on the U-Bahn are valid. Bus route 100, running double-deckers from Zoo to beyond Alexanderplatz, passes several of the major sights and is well worth a trip. Each bus has a three-digit number: the first indicates where the bus originates, the second shows which part of the city it crosses, and the third marks its destination.

## Tram

At the moment there are only 38 tram lines, all of them in east Berlin. The BVG is currently considering plans to extend the tram network into the west.

## Maps

The best overview of the public transport network is provided by the Liniennetz, a map of all BVG route networks for Berlin, including Potsdam. It costs DM3 and includes an enlarged map of the city centre and a map of the U- and S-Bahn. If you're travelling in the early hours (*see below* **Travelling at Night**) you'll need the **Nacht-liniennetz**, a free map of all BVG night routes. The handy map of the **Schnellbahnnetz** (express train network, consisting of U-Bahn, S-Bahn and Regionbahn) is invaluable, as the maps below

ground are often illegible. These are available for free from the grey-uniformed Customer Assistance personnel who can be found in most of the larger U-Bahn and S-Bahn stations.

For more money (DM9) you can buy the **Falkplan**, an excellent, combined street plan and transport network map. If you love timetables, and in Berlin things tend to happen on time, the BVG also sells a large **Kursbuch** for DM5.

## Tickets & Travel Passes

Apart from the Zeitkarten (longer-term tickets, *see below*), tickets for Berlin's public transport system can be bought from the yellow or orange-coloured machines at the entrances to U-Bahn stations. These take coins and sometimes notes, give change and have a limited explanation of the ticket system in English. Once you've purchased your ticket, you must validate it in the small red box next to the machine. If you're caught without a valid ticket you will be fined DM60 on the spot. Ticket inspections are fairly frequent, particularly on weekends.

**Note**: In the current subsidy squeeze, public transport prices are rising and will continue to do so. At the time of this guide going to press, fare increases for 1995 had been announced but not specified, except for the new single ticket price of DM3.70. The other prices below are those current in 1994. We have included these as a rough guide to the fare structure, but they are all expected to rise by around seven per cent. Furthermore a zone system similar to London's is under consideration, so if the copy of this book you are holding is not brand new, be prepared to fork out even more.

## Single Ticket (Normaltarif)

Single, normal-fare tickets cost DM3.70 (DM2.30 for children between the ages of 6 and 14, the unemployed, and students studying in Berlin). This ticket allows you to use the entire BVG network for two hours, with as many changes between bus, U-Bahn and S-Bahn and with as many breaks as you like.

## Short-Distance Fare (Kurzstreckentarif)

The Kurzstreckentarif (ask for a Kurzstrecke) costs DM2.30 (DM1.80 concessions). It is valid for three U- or S-Bahn stops, or six bus stops. No transfers are allowed.

## Multiple Tickets (Sammelkarten)

The short-distance Sammelkarte with four fares costs DM7.80 (DM6 concessions). The normal Sammelkarte with four fares costs DM12 (DM7.80 concessions). The Unbounded Berlin conditions for single tickets apply to Sammelkarten (*see above* **Public Transport**), but the card must be stamped before each use in the red franking machines on buses, trams and at U-Bahn and S-Bahn stations.

## Berlin Ticket

The Berlin ticket is valid for 24 hours and permits unlimited travel on the entire BVG network and on the BVG ship line. It costs DM13 (DM6.50 concessions). You can even take along a child between the ages of 6 and 14 for the same price, or, failing that, a bicycle or a dog.

## Combination Day-Ticket (Kombi-Tageskarte)

The combination day-ticket costs DM18.50 (DM9.30 children). It provides the same entitlements as the Berlin ticket, but is only valid for one person. In addition, it offers the opportunity to explore Berlin's waters on the boats of the Stern and Kreisschiffahrt Company between April and October (*see below* **Boat Trips**). But for the rest of the year, it's better value to buy a Berlin ticket (*see above*).

## Family Day Cards (Familien-Tageskarten)

If you are in Berlin with your children on weekends and public holidays (Feiertagen), you can buy a family card for DM10. Berlin is then yours for the day. Children must be under 16, but there's no limit to the number of children eligible.

## Longer-Term Cards (Zeitkarten)

If you're staying in Berlin for several days, it makes sense to buy a **sechs-Tage-Karte** (six-day-card), valid from Monday to Saturday across the entire network for DM33 (no concessions available). A stay of over two weeks makes an **Umweltkarte** (environment card) economical. This is free, available at numerous U- and S-Bahn stations during the working week, but the validating sticker (available in most machines) costs DM82 (DM38 students, DM47 apprentices, DM70 seniors). This works for one calendar month across the network, and is transferable to other users. If you decide to settle in Berlin, buy a **Jahreskarte** (year card) for DM700 (DM650 seniors). These are only available at ticket-windows in stations, and at BVG Customer Service.

## Lost Property & Customer Services

### BVG Fundbüro

*Lorenzweg 5, Tempelhof, 10773 (lost property 751 80 21; customer services 752 70 20). U6 Ullsteinstraße.* **Open** 9am-3pm Mon, Tue, Thur; 9am-6pm Wed; 9am-2pm Fri.
The Fundbüro is the lost and found office of the BVG. The building also houses the BVG's Kundendienst (customer service department). Some of the staff speak English.

## Travelling at Night

Berlin has a comprehensive **Nachtliniennetz** (night-line network) that covers all parts of town and consists of 60 bus and tram routes. It operates between 1-4am. Before and after these times the regular timetable for bus and tram routes applies.

Ticket prices for the night-line network are the same as for the day. Services are run along all the routes at least every 30 minutes and at weekends as often as every 15 minutes. Buses and trams that run at night are distinguished by an N in front of the number.

**Note**: The N16 to Potsdam runs only once an hour; the U1 and U9 run all night only on Friday and Saturday. S-Bahn lines 3 to 10 provide an hourly service. On lines N11 and N41 taxis are used and (as BVG boasts) will deliver you to your front door for the regular price.

Night-line network maps and timetables are available from the BVG information kiosks at all stations.

The BVG also operates a **Taxi-Ruf-System** (taxi calling service) on the U-Bahn for people with disabilities, and for female passengers from 8pm every evening until the network closes down for the night. Just ask the station master (the person in the booth in the middle of the platform) to phone, giving your destination and method of payment, since you will have to pay the full taxi fare. *See also below* **Disabled Travellers**.

## Boat Trips

Besides the BVG there are several private companies operating on Berlin's waterways.

### Stern und Kreisschiffahrt GmbH

*Puschkinallee 16-17, Treptow, 12435 (61 73 90-0). S6, S8, S9 S10 Treptower Park.* **Open** 7.30am-4pm daily.
The White Fleet (Die Weisse Flotte) was East Germany's ship company. It is now part of the Stern and Kreisschiffahrt Company, which offers various cruises along the Spree and the Dahme as well as around the lakes in the area. Departure points and times vary, but timetables are available from the company. A round trip will cost about DM15.

### Kultur-Kontor

*Savignyplatz 9-10, Charlottenburg, 10623 (313 08 88). S3, S5, S6, S9 Savignyplatz.* **Open** *May-Sept* Sat.
Trips along the Spree and Landwehrkanal. The details vary from season to season, so phone the company or pick up a copy of its timetable. A round-trip costs about DM18.

### Reederei Heinz Riedel

*Planufer 78, Kreuzberg, 10967 (691 37 82). U8 Schönleinstraße.* **Open** *Oct-Apr* 8am-5pm Mon-Fri; 8am-1pm Sat; *May-Sept* (also fair weather days in October) daily.
Fascinating excursions are offered which start in the city and pass through industrial suburbs into rural Berlin. Tours also leave in the other direction and explore Neukölln's waterways. A tour through the city costs about DM15.

## Taxis

If you're feeling stressed or simply want to get somewhere fast, take a ride in one of Berlin's fleet of comfortable and reliable Mercedes taxis. But remember, Berlin taxi drivers are frustratingly lackadaisical. Often they cruise in the outside lane and can't stop even if they see you.

The starting fee is DM4 and thereafter the fare is DM2.10 per kilometre (about DM3.36 per mile) for the first six kilometres. At night this rises to DM2.30 per kilometre (about DM3.68 per mile). An increasing number of taxis are now accepting credit cards. There are many taxi stands in the centre of Berlin, including those listed below.

Alternatively, phone the 24-hour radio cab service (*26 10 26/69 02/24 00 24/36 44*). In Treptow, Köpenick, Marzahn, Hellersdorf and at Schönefeld airport the phone number is (*33 66*).

There is a DM6 fee for cabs ordered by telephone. Most taxi firms can transport the disabled but require advance notice.

### Taxi Stands

**Zoo Station**, *Hardenbergplatz, Charlottenburg, 10623*.
**Alexanderplatz**, *at the entrance to the S-Bahn station, Mitte, 10178*.
**Savignyplatz**, *Charlottenburg, 10623*.

## Car Hire

Car hire in Germany is not generally expensive. The major firms are represented in Berlin. Look under Autovermietung in the Gelbe Seiten (Yellow Pages) and be sure to shop around.

## Bicycle Hire

Cycling in Germany is a joy. The authorities have invested millions of Deutschmarks in cycle lanes throughout the country. Berlin is no exception, but in the east of the city, despite rapid work, a network of cycle lanes is only just beginning to blossom; and anyway, because of the manic rate of reconstruction, the streets are often torn up. A wonderful guide to Berlin's best bike routes is the **ADFC Fahrradstadtplan**, available in most bike shops for DM12. The companies below are reliable, cheap bicycle-hire firms. Or look under Fahrradverleih in the Gelbe Seiten (Yellow Pages).

### Bikes & Jeans

*Albrechtstraße 18, Mitte, 10117* (281-6687). *S3, S5, S6, S9/U6 Friedrichstraße*. **Open** 10am-9pm daily. **Rates** DM15-DM20 per day; DM30-DM40 Fri-Sun.

### Fahrradstation

*Möckernstraße 92, Kreuzberg, 10963* (216 91 77). *U1, U7 Möckernbrücke/U7 Yorckstraße*. **Open** 10am-2pm, 3-6pm, Mon-Fri; 10am-2pm Sat. **Rates** DM15-DM25 per day; DM50-DM65 for three days.

### Zweirad-Bardt

*Kantstraße 88, Charlottenburg, 10627* (323 8129). *U7 Wilmersdorfer Straße/S3, S5, S6, S9 Charlottenburg*. **Open** 9am-6pm Mon-Fri; 9am-1pm Sat. **Rates** DM15 per day; DM300 deposit.

## Disabled Travellers

### Telebus-Zentrale

*Esplanade 17, Pankow, 13187* (478 820). *U2 Vinetastraße*. **Open** (office hours) 9am-3pm Mon-Fri.
The Telebus service, a bus service for disabled people (*see chapter* **Survival**), is available to tourists. You may be able to use this service at short notice if it's not too busy, but it's best to contact the office two weeks before your arrival in Berlin so that you can be issued with a pass that will guarantee you use of Telebus. The service itself runs from about 5am to 1am.

# Accommodation

**The best beds, the ritziest rooms and the cheapest campsites.**

The **Radisson Plaza Hotel**: East German architecture for western businessmen. See page 17.

In Berlin, even more so than other European cities, finding accommodation can be nightmarish. It's advisable to contact hotels and reservation agencies a month ahead, especially during major holidays and festivals (the Berlinale Film Festival is a particularly bad time to try to find a room, but *see also chapter* **Berlin by Season**). To book a room before you arrive, either contact one of the hotels we list, or the main tourist office at the address below, well in advance of your arrival. If you haven't booked ahead, you can try to book a hotel room through any tourist office (Verkehrsamt) for a fee of DM5. Be sure to pick up a copy of the tourist information leaflet *Berlin Hotel Register* while you're there.

Hotels are concentrated in two areas of the city: around Zoologischer Garten in the west and Mitte in the east. We have organised the listings below accordingly. Since reunification, the hotel trade in the east has only expanded slowly. We've concentrated on some of the better hotels in the east around Unter den Linden and Friedrichstraße; if

you stay here, many of Berlin's sights and museums will be on your doorstep.

Budget hotels are mainly in the west of the city. Staying in a budget hotel will mean paying between DM50 and DM100 a night, and these cheaper places are often fully booked. It's worth trying the **Mitwohnzentrale** listed below first. If you're adventurous and really want to get a feel for life in the former GDR, then buy *Übernachten in den neuen Bundesländern*, published by Grafit (DM24.80) and available from any German bookseller or from Grant and Cutler's in London. This book lists families in east Berlin and the former GDR who will take you in for about DM25 a night.

If you decide to stay longer in Berlin, your best source, besides word of mouth, is either a Mitwohnzentrale or the classified ads in *Zitty*, *Tip* or the *Berliner Morgenpost* (*see chapter* **Media**). The Wohnungsnot (housing shortage) in Berlin is extreme, and while the two halves of the city grow back together, anyone who owns property in the east is hanging on to it while prices rise. Many peo-

# SPREEHOTEL

*The Spree Hotel is an oasis of tranquility in the heart of the city. Our hotel has 158 rooms and offers a high standard of luxury.*

*Staying with us means*
*· being close to historic Berlin*
*· being close to the theatre*
*· having the Underground, S-Bahn and boat landing- stage at your doorstep*

*The **Hotel Palace**, in all its sixties splendour. See page 16.*

ple are already cashing in and sub-letting rooms for up to three times the current rent. Expect to pay between DM600-DM800 a month (bills extra) for a two-room flat in the more central districts of Prenzlauer Berg, Kreuzberg and Schöneberg.

The listings below aim to give a rounded idea of what to expect from each establishment. Each has been visited by *Time Out* staff and judged according to its overall appeal. Unless otherwise stated, breakfast is included. A typical German breakfast consists of rolls (known in Berlin as Schrippe), salami, cheese, and tea or coffee.

Our price categories work as follows: a De Luxe hotel is one in which a double room costs DM350 or more; an Expensive hotel is DM220 or more; Moderate is DM125 or more; and the rest are Budget. All prices given are room prices. *See also chapters* **Gay Berlin**, **Students** *and* **Women's Berlin** *and*, for a list of facilities and sights in each area, *page 264* **Area Index**.

## Tourist Information

The following will help you find a room in Berlin:

### Verkehrsamt Berlin (Central Tourist Office Berlin)

*Martin-Luther-Straße 105, Schöneberg, 10820 (21 234 for hotels or 262 6011 for private rooms/fax21232520). U4 Rathaus Schöneberg.* **Open** *7am-3pm Mon-Thur; 7am-2pm Fri.*
This is the only office that will book your hotel and rooms in private homes in advance. (The others can only book rooms on the day you want them.) Write or call and they'll happily send you a list of every hotel in Berlin.

### Berlin Tourist Information (Verkehrsamt)

*Europa-Center, Budapesterstraße, Charlottenburg, 10787 (262 60 31). U2, U9, U12/S3, S5, S6, S7, S9 Zoologischer Garten.* **Open** 8am-10.30pm Mon-Sat; 9am-9pm Sun.

### Verkehrsamt im Bahnhof Zoo

*tourist office in Zoo Station, main hall (313 90 63). U2, U9, U12/S3, S5, S6, S7, S9 Zoologischer Garten.* **Open** 8am-10.30pm Mon-Sat; 9am-9pm Sun.

### Verkehrsamt im Flughafen Tegel

*tourist office in Tegel Airport, main hall (4101 31 45). U7 Jakob Kaiser Platz, then bus 109 or X9.* **Open** 8am-11pm daily.

### Verkehrsamt im Hauptbahnhof

*tourist office in Hauptbahnhof, main hall (279 52 09). S3, S5, S6, S7, S9 Hauptbahnhof.* **Open** 8am-8pm daily.

## De Luxe

## West Berlin

### Bristol Hotel Kempinski Berlin

*Kurfürstendamm 27, Charlottenburg, 10719 (884 340/fax 883 6075). U15, U9 Kurfürstendamm.* **Rates** *single DM420-480; double DM470-530; suite DM600-2,800; breakfast DM30.* **Credit** AmEx, DC, MC, V.
Perhaps Berlin's most famous hotel, if not its best, the Kempinski exudes a faded charm. But even though the rooms are plush, you never really feel you're living in the lap of luxury, as you certainly should for this price. The staff tend to be less than pleasant. The Bristol Bar on the ground floor with its fat leather sofas and lots of old, dark wood, has a long cocktail list and snooty waiters. The Kempinski Eck restaurant is nothing special; but then, neither is the Kempinski Grill.

**Hotel Transit**: see page 23.

**Hotel services** *Bar. Conference services. Cosmetic salon. Laundry service. Lift. Sauna. Solarium. Swimming pool. Restaurants (3).* **Room services** *Minibar. Room service. Telephone. TV.*

### Grand Hotel Esplanade

*Lützowufer 15, Tiergarten, 10785 (261 011/fax 265 1171/telex 185986). U2, U4, U15 Nollendorfplatz.* **Rates** *single DM380-470; double DM430-520; suite DM650-1150; breakfast DM29.* **Credit** AmEx, DC, MC, V.
A relatively new (1988) addition to Berlin's glut of luxury hotels and easily one of the best. The entrance is rather grand, with a huge, gushing wall of water across from the door and hundreds of lights glittering above your head. The lobby is spacious and beautifully decorated, and there are art exhibitions adorning some of the walls on the ground floor. The well-tended rooms are sparkling white and 30 have been set aside for non-smokers. If you decide to stay here, you get the added benefit of being within stumbling-back-to-bed distance of the excellent Harry's New York Bar on the ground floor. Plush, but not intimidating, Harry's features a long, long cocktail list, nightly jazz, and wonderful, welcoming red sofas.
**Hotel services** *Bar. Conference facilities. Laundry service. Lift. Parking. Restaurant. Sauna. Swimming pool. Wheelchair access.* **Room services** *Radio. Room service. Telephone. TV.*

### Hotel Inter-Continental

*Budapester Straße 2, Tiergarten, 10787 (26020/fax 2602 80760/telex 184 380). S3, S5, S6, S7, S9/U2, U9 Zoologischer Garten.* **Rates** *single DM335-445; double DM385-495; suite DM495-2500; breakfast DM29.* **Credit** AmEx, DC, EC, MC, V.
If you're on a generous expense account, this is the place to stay. Extraordinarily plush and spacious, the Inter-Continental exudes luxurious living. The rooms are large,

tastefully decorated and blessed with elegant bathrooms. The lobby is huge and airy; its soft leather chairs are the ideal place to read the morning paper or wait for your next appointment. The staff are relatively friendly, but not the best in town.
**Hotel services** *Bar. Conference facilities. Laundry service. Lift. Parking. Sauna. Swimming pool.* **Room services** *Room service. Radio. Telephone. TV.*

### Hotel Palace

*Im Europa-Center, Charlottenburg, 10789 (250 20/fax 262 6577/telex 184 825). S3, S5, S6, S7, S9/U2, U9 Zoologischer Garten.* **Rates** *single DM280-450; double DM330-500; suites DM650-2600; breakfast DM27.* **Credit** AmEx, DC, EC, V, MC.
Recent renovations haven't altered the fact that this place is located in the middle of the hideous Europa-Center. That said, the rooms of this Best Western hotel are luxurious, reasonably roomy and complete with all the amenities.
**Hotel services** *Bar. Conference facilities. Laundry service. Lift. Parking. Restaurant (special diets catered to).* **Room services** *Minibar. Radio. Room service. Telephone. TV.*

### Hotel Schweizerhof Berlin

*Budapester Straße 21-31, Tiergarten, 10787 (269 60/telex 185 507/fax 269 6900). S3, S5, S6, S7,S9/U2, U9 Zoologischer Garten.* **Rates** *single or double DM345-495; suites DM650-1200; breakfast DM29.* **Credit** AmEx, DC, EC, MC, JCB, V.
The Schweizerhof doesn't look like much from the outside, but once inside the large, elegant lobby, it becomes clear that you're in one of Berlin's ritzier hotels. Actually the lobby and the friendly staff are the Schweizerhof's strong points: the rooms themselves can be elbow-banging tight and the bathrooms are often more generously designed than many of the somewhat cramped bedrooms.
**Hotel services** *Bar. Conference facilities. Laundry service. Lift. Parking. Restaurant. Sauna. Swimming pool.* **Room services** *Minibar. Radio. Room service. Telephone. TV.*

## East Berlin

### Berlin Hilton

*Mohrenstraße 30, Mitte, 10117 (238 20/telex 305 776/fax 2382 4269). U2, U6 Stadtmitte.* **Rates** *single DM295-475; double DM345-525; suites from DM700-3000; breakfast DM29.50.* **Credit** AmEx, DC, EC, JCB, MC, V.
Originally called the Dom Hotel when the foundations were laid in 1988, it was taken over by Hilton and opened in January 1991. It's supremely well-placed on the Gendarmenmarkt across from the German and French Cathedrals, and a U-Bahn stop, and offers top-quality rooms and services in a pleasant atmosphere. The lobby is huge and airy, full of plants and with a restaurant bang in the middle. Standard rooms are blue, gray and rattan, including 14 non-smoking rooms; 14 suites include the art deco, two-storey Maisonette Suite with a working gramophone (a snip at DM3000 a night). The concierge will sell you a chunk of the Wall.
**Hotel services** *Bar. Bicycle Rental. Disco. Fitness Centre. Laundry service. Lift. Parking. Restaurants (3). Sauna. Solarium. Squash court. Swimming pool. Whirlpool.* **Room services** *Hairdryer. Minibar. Radio. Room service. Telephone. TV.*

### Maritim Grand Hotel Berlin

*Friedrichstraße 158-164, Mitte, 10117 (232 70/fax 232 73362). U6 Französische Straße.* **Rates** *single DM355-535; double DM480-660; suites DM730-3400; breakfast DM28.* **Credit** AmEx, DC, EC, JCB, V.
In the heart of the future business centre of Berlin, at the corners of Unter den Linden and Friedrichstraße, lies the grat-

The **Hotel California**: *check in any time you like. See page 20.*

ifyingly elegant Grand Hotel, which somehow manages to live up to its name. Its 35 suites are individually furnished with period décor, according to whoever they are named after (try the Schinkel or Lessing suites), and its 350 rooms exude traditional taste, design and comfort. There's a hotel garden with a sun patio and atrium as well as ten bars and restaurants and a non-smoking floor. But best of all is the bombastic staircase and foyer.
**Hotel services** *Bar. Conference services. Laundry service. Lift. Restaurant. Sauna. Swimming pool.* **Room services** *Minibar. Radio. Room service. Telephone. TV.*

### Hotel Metropol

*Friedrichstraße 150-153, Mitte, 10117 (238 75/fax 238 74209). S1, S2, S3, S5, S6, S7, S9/U6 Friedrichstraße.* **Rates** *single* DM300-350; *double* DM330-410; *suites* DM600-1,200; *breakfast* DM25. **Credit** AmEx, DC, EC, JCB, MC, V.
Don't be put off by the dreary brown exterior of this yellow-windowed building – the 340 rooms inside offer a comfortable stay in light, natural surroundings and the interior has recently been completely renovated. There are three non-smoking floors as well as executive rooms in the quieter part of the hotel, plus four restaurants and a bar. This area around Friedrichstraße station is becoming the new commercial and shopping centre of Berlin, and the hotel is just minutes away from Unter den Linden and the Brandenburg Gate.
**Hotel services** *Bar. Conference services. Laundry service. Lift. Parking. Restaurants (4). Sauna. Swimming pool. Fitness centre.* **Room services** *Minibar. Radio. Room service. Safe. Telephone. TV.*

### Radisson Plaza Hotel

*Karl Liebknecht Straße 5, Mitte, 10178 (238 28/telex 304 754/fax 238 27590). S3, S5, S6, S7, S9 Hackescher Markt/Alexanderplatz.* **Rates** *single* DM250-520; *double* DM290-570; *suites* DM450-2,500; *breakfast buffet* DM27. **Credit** AmEx, DC, EC, JCB, V.

The Radisson Plaza is surrounded by new restaurants and shops. The architecture may look suspiciously east German (because it is), but its 600 rooms are modern and comfortable. The hotel is mostly popular with Japanese and American business people, who like to gather in the gold-, black- and maroon-leathered lobby. If they need more room, they simply move into the Conference Centre. The recently opened Thank God It's Friday restaurant offers American and Cajun foods as well as a stunning view of Museum Island. There is live entertainment in the bar every evening, and plenty of sightseeing in the area: Museum Island, the State Opera House, Berlin Cathedral and the Nikolaiviertel.
**Hotel services** *Bar. Conference services. Laundry service. Lift. Parking. Restaurant. Swimming pool. Sauna.* **Room services** *Minibar. Radio. Room service. Safe. Telephone. TV.*

## Expensive

## West Berlin

### Hotel Alexander

*Pariser Straße 37, Wilmersdorf, 10707 (881 6091/fax 881 6094) U7 Adenauerplatz.* **Rates** *single* DM160-260; *double* DM260-360; *extra bed* DM60. **Credit** AmEx, DC, EC, JCB, MC, V
On a lively street south of the Ku'damm, this self-styled 'art hotel' has rooms with ultra-modern furnishings. The double rooms are spacious, the single ones small but cosy. If you don't like the grey marbled wallpaper and metal trimmings of the opulent-looking 'café-bistro', the surrounding area is packed with bars and restaurants. Staff speak English and are helpful.
**Hotel services** *Bar. Restaurant. Fax facilities.* **Room services** *Room service. Radio. Telephone. TV with cable. Mini-bar. Safe.*

## Berlin Plaza Hotel

*Knesebeckstraße 62, Charlottenburg, 10719 (884130/telex 184 181/fax 884 13754). U15 Uhlandstraße.* **Rates** *single* DM148-198; *double* DM198-260; *triple* DM310. **Credit** AmEx, DC, EC, JCB, MC, V.

Get ready to be dazzled by the Berlin Plaza's mirror and brass foyer, which mixes well with several pink sofas and various pieces of modern art from local galleries. The hotel has seven floors (one of which is non-smoking), and was renovated in 1989. Its 131 rooms are tastefully decorated in pink maroon and white, but are rather small and plain. All the double rooms and some of the singles have both shower and bath. You can mix your own muesli at the breakfast buffet (included in room price): the food is freshly made and bread is baked on the premises. German specialities are served in the restaurant and bar. As for the hotel's prices – you're paying for its central location just off the Kufürstendamm. **Hotel services** *Bar. Conference facilities. Laundry service. Lift. Parking (DM20 a day). Restaurant.* **Room services** *Hairdryer. Minibar. Radio. Safe. Telephone. TV.*

## Hotel Berliner Hof

*Tauentzienstraße 8, Schöneberg, 10789 (254 950/fax 262 3065). U1, U2, U15 Wittenbergplatz.* **Rates** *single* DM150-225; *double* DM180-280; *extra bed* DM60. **Credit** AmEx, DC, EC, MC, V.

You won't get much more central than this: the Europa-Center is next door, the Ku'damm's round the corner and all the public transport you could want is on your doorstep. The Berliner Hof's rooms all face the back of the hotel and are quiet, spacious and pleasantly decorated. **Hotel services** *Lift. Parking (DM10).* **Room services** *Minibar. Radio. Telephone. TV.*

## Hotel Bremen

*Bleibtreustraße 25, Charlottenburg, 10707 (881 4076/fax 882 4685). S3, S5, S6, S7, S9 Savignyplatz.* **Rates** *single* DM250-280; *double* DM310-340; *suite* DM340-420; children under-12 free. **Credit** AmEx, DC, JCB, MC, V.

'Small' is the key-word at this quiet, charming hotel just off the Ku'damm. The 53 rooms and suites were renovated in 1989 and, though cramped, are tastefully decorated. The bathrooms, also a bit tight, are bright and clean. The glass-enclosed breakfast room on the fifth floor offers stunning views. The tiny lobby bar stays open around the clock. There are a few tables and chairs in the light, elegant lobby. **Hotel services** *Bar. Conference facilities. Laundry service. Lift. Parking.* **Room services** *Minibar. Radio. Room service. Telephone. TV.*

## Hotel Consul

*Knesebeckstraße 8-9, Charlottenburg, 10623 (311 060/fax 312 2060). U2 Ernst-Reuter-Platz.* **Rates** *single* DM169; *double* DM215; *suite* DM360. **Credit** AmEx, DC, EC, JCB, MC, V.

When this was known as the Hotel Windsor, it was a place of some note; now the Consul's owners are trying to reinject some of its former glory. But at the moment the place is sadly delapidated and only some of the otherwise spacious and comfortable rooms have been renovated. The hotel offers guests special deals on public transport: you can buy a day pass (valid on all buses, trams, U-Bahn, and S-Bahn lines) for only DM5 (it's normally DM12, though prices are set to change as we go to press, *see chapter* **Getting Around**). **Hotel services** *Laundry service. Lift. Parking. TV room. Bicycle rentals.* **Room services** *Minibar and TV in most rooms. Room service. Radio. Telephone.*

## Curator Hotel

*Grolmanstraße 41-43, Charlottenburg, 10623 (884 26-0/telex 18 33 89/fax 884 26-500). S3, S5, S6, S7, S9 Savignyplatz.* **Rates** *single* DM240; *double* DM300; *suite* DM350-550. **Credit** AmEx, DC, EC, JCB, MC, V.

The quiet, elegant Curator Hotel has 100 spacious rooms, in which not a single detail has been overlooked, right down to the extra-long beds and the phone in the bathroom. The staff are friendly and helpful. Unwind in the sauna and tan yourself in the solarium or on the roof terrace when the weather permits it. The elegant bar just off the lobby is an excellent meeting place. **Hotel services** *Bar. Conference facilities. Parking, Sauna. Solarium.* **Room services** *Minibar. Radio. Safe. Telephone. TV. Two rooms equipped for disabled guests.*

## Hecker's Hotel

*Grolmanstraße 35, Charlottenburg, 10623 (8890-0/telex 184954 hhblnd/fax 8890 260). U15 Uhlandstraße.* **Rates** *single* DM260; *double* DM310; *extra bed* DM60; children under-12 free; *breakfast* DM15. **Credit** AmEx, EC, DC, JCB, MC, V.

Unremarkable on the outside, quite pleasant inside. They have recently added 27 rooms. Although there's not much of a lobby, the bar/restaurant off the entrance has just been renovated and is a fine place to sit and wait. Rooms are a good size and comfortable, with lots of nice little touches – pencil sharpeners, for example, and fresh fruit. Bathrooms are smaller, but clean and well-lit. The walk-in closets are easily the best in Berlin. **Hotel services** *Bar. Parking.* **Room services** *Minibar. No-smoking rooms. Radio. Telephone. TV.*

## Hotel Riehmers Hofgarten

*Yorckstraße 83, Kreuzberg, 10965 (781 011/fax 786 6059). U6, U7 Mehringdamm.* **Rates** *single* DM200-240; *double* DM240-280. **Credit** AmEx, DC, EC, MC, V.

Housed in a historically listed turn-of-the-century building, Riehmers is well located in the city end of Kreuzberg and a wise choice for those who want value for money. Double rooms are large and bright although the singles are a bit cramped. The ample breakfasts are served in a small dining room and the staff are friendly and helpful. Take a look at the beautiful courtyard out the back, which was used as a location in the movie *Just A Gigolo*. Popular with music biz and media types. **Hotel services** *Bar. Conference facilities. Laundry service. Lift. Restaurant.* **Room services** *Minibar. Radio. Room service. Safe. Telephone. TV.*

# East Berlin

## Berliner Congress Center

*Märkisches Ufer 54, Mitte, 10179 (27580/fax 2758 2170). S3, S5, S6, S7, S9 Jannowitzbrücke.* **Rates** *single* DM 190; *double* DM240; *extra bed* DM40; children under-12 free. **Credit** AmEx, DC, EC, JCB, MC, V.

As the name suggests, an ideal hotel for business guests who need conference facilities. There are 13 conference rooms, three restaurants and a banquet room, as well as 110 bedrooms. The airy Wintergarden is a splendid place for a meal. The rooms are comfortable, if a bit dull, the baths lovely. **Hotel services** *Bar. Laundry. Lift. Parking (DM20).* **Room services** *Minibar. Radio. Telephone. TV.*

## Berlin Hilton Krone

*Mohrenstraße 30, Mitte, 10117 (238 20/fax 2382 4269). U2, U6 Stadtmitte.* **Rates** *single* DM205-315; *double* DM255-265; *breakfast* DM24.50. **Credit** AmEx, DC, EC, MC, JCB, V.

The Krone is part of the same building as its parent, the Berlin Hilton (*see above* **De Luxe: East Berlin**). This is the affordable, less grand part of the complex: the rooms are cheaper, but you can still use all of the Hilton services. **Hotel services** *Bowling. Laundry service. Lift. Parking (DM22 a day). Squash court. Swimming pool. Whirlpool. Fitness centre. Sauna. Solarium. Bicycle rental.* **Room services** *Minibar. Safe. Telephone. TV.*

### Hotel Luisenhof

*Koepenicker Straße 92, Mitte, 10179 (279 1109/fax279 2983). U8 Heinrich-Heine-Straße.* **Rates** *single* DM187-230; *double* DM230-320; *suite* DM380. **Credit** AmEx, DC, EC, JCB, V.

The beautiful building housing the Luisenhof dates from the late nineteenth century and was the headquarters and stables of a Berlin coaching company. When the Communists held sway, it was home to the party training centre of the SED. It was re-opened after renovation in early 1993 and both interior and exterior have been tastefully restored in original town-house style. It's in the middle of old Berlin, close to the major cultural sights and what is fast becoming the city's business district.

**Hotel services** *Conference facilities. Fax. Flowers. Laundry service. Lift. Restaurants (2). Photocopying.* **Room services** *Minibar. Fax connection. Radio. Safe. Telephone. TV.*

### Hotel Unter den Linden

*Unter den Linden 14, Mitte, 10117 (238 110/fax 238 11100/telex 112109). S3, S5, S6, S7, S9/U6 Friedrichstraße.* **Rates** *single* DM150-190; *double* DM220-240; *suite* DM320. **Credit** AmEx, EC, DC, MC, V.

The sprawling, old-fashioned lobby looks onto one of the busiest intersections in east Berlin, the corner of Friedrichstraße and Unter den Linden. The rooms are small and the furniture plain, but the staff are friendly. The bathrooms are also rather small – some of them need a few contortions to get into – but are immaculately clean. Anyway, you can't get much more central than this.

**Hotel services** *Bar. Bistro. Conference facilities. Laundry service. Lift.* **Room services** *Minibar. Radio. Telephone. TV.*

---

**Moderate**

## West Berlin

### Alpenland Hotel

*Carmerstraße 8, Charlottenburg, 10623 (312 3970/fax 313 8444). S3, S5, S6, S7, S9 Savignyplatz.* **Rates** *single* DM 80-120; *double* DM 100-200; *extra bed* DM50. **Credit** AmEx, DC, EC, MC, V.

The Alpenland is a no-frills, friendly hotel in Charlottenburg. Renovations were completed in 1993, so the rooms are fresh and clean, as well as reasonably spacious. The large, pristine bathrooms are especially fine, although not every room has its own. Communal toilets are on every floor. Breakfast is taken in the restaurant downstairs, which also has a pleasant bar.

**Hotel services** *Bar. Restaurant.* **Room services** *Telephone. TV.*

### Hotel Bogota

*Schlüterstraße 45, Charlottenburg, 10707 (881 5001/telex 184 946/fax 883 5887). S3, S5, S6, S7, S9 Savignyplatz.* **Rates** *single* DM68-125; *double* DM110-180; *extra bed* DM50. **Credit** AmEx, DC, EC, MC, V.

A pleasant, 130-bedroom hotel with good service and very good prices. It's slightly to the south of Kurfürstendamm and is frequented by an unlikely melange of backpackers, businessmen and tourists. This is made possible by the range of rooms and prices available. About half of the double rooms have showers and toilets and most of them, though plainly furnished, are comfortable. If there are four of you on a small budget, you can take a double room and pay an extra DM50 per person (including breakfast) for the two extra beds. The place is more functional than fancy, but it's clean, friendly and reasonably central.

**Hotel services** *Lift. TV room.* **Room services** *Telephone.*

### Hotel California

*Kurfürstendamm 35, Charlottenburg, 10719 (883 011/fax 883 016). U15 Uhlandstraße.* **Rates** *single* DM155-175; *double* DM185-225; *extra bed* DM50-60; *breakfast buffet* DM18. **Credit** AmEx, DC, EC, MC, V.

The California is smack in the middle of some of Berlin's best shops and right next to a new McDonald's. The lobby sports a small fountain and a large piece of the Wall, as well as some deep sofas to sink into after a hard day's sightseeing. The rooms are basic and comfortable. The lift stops only on every half floor, so there are still 12 stairs to climb to your room. The hotel can hire you a bicycle in the summer.

**Hotel services** *Bar. Conference facilities. Lift. Solarium (DM5 for ten minutes). TV room.* **Room services** *Minibar. Radio. Safe. Telephone. TV. Hairdryer.*

### Hotel Pension Castell

*Wielandstraße 24, Charlottenburg, 10707 (882 7181/fax 881 5548). U7 Adenauer Platz.* **Rates** *single* DM80-110; *double* DM110-160.* **No credit cards.**

Tucked away just off of the Kufürstendamm and near many designer shops, this 22-room pension also has friendly staff and good-sized rooms. Only a few have a toilet and shower in the room, and the furniture is sparse but not unattractive.

**Hotel services** *Lift. TV room.* **Room services** *Telephone.*

### Hotel Charlot am Kurfürstendamm

*Giesebrechtstraße 17, Charlottenburg, 10629 (323 4051/52/fax 324 0819). U7 Adenauerplatz or S3, S5, S6, S7, S9 Charlottenburg.* **Rates** *single* DM70-145; *double* DM116-210. **Credit** AmEx, EC, V.

There aren't many better Berlin hotels in this price range. It's in a beautiful residential area full of chic shops and great cafés; the historical Jugendstil building has been well restored; it has a friendly management; and the 24 bedrooms are spotlessly clean. Only about half have showers and toilets, but the communal ones are quite clean. Despite its name, the hotel is actually five minutes away from the Ku'damm.

**Hotel services** *Bar. Lift. Parking. TV room.* **Room services** *Telephone. TV.*

### Hotel Clausewitz

*Clausewitzstraße 9, Charlottenburg, 10629 (882 1129/fax 883 4903). U7 Adenauerplatz.* **Rates** *single* DM130; *double* DM170.* **No credit cards.**

If the Charlot (*see above*) is full, you might want to try this place just across the street. It's on the first floor of a pea-green building and has only nine rooms and no lobby. The rooms are small and plain with a shower and toilet, and the breakfast room is fairly new. There are great things just outside the door – it's a short walk to the Ku'damm, and to the Kurbel cinema across the street, which has films in English.

**Hotel services** *Pets permitted.* **Room services** *Radio. TV.*

### Hotel-Pension Elba

*Bleibtreustraße 26, Charlottenburg, 10707 (881 7504/fax 882 3246). S3, S5, S6, S7, S9 Savignyplatz.* **Rates** *single* DM95-150; *double* DM150-175. **Credit** AmEx, MC, V.

The Elba is closer to a hotel in atmosphere and size, which is reflected in the prices. But it's known for the friendliness of its staff and is housed in a splendid townhouse in a prime location. Its 18 rooms range from the cramped to the capacious, but all are well equipped with showers and toilets, and have recently been redecorated in plain white and wood.

**Hotel services** *Lift.* **Room services** *Minibar. Radio. Telephone. TV.*

### Hotel-Pension Funk

*Fasanenstraße 69, Charlottenburg, 10719 (882 7193/fax883 3329). U2, U9 Spichernstraße.* **Rates** *single* DM60-75; *double* DM100-135.* **No credit cards.**

*The impossibly opulent* **Hotel Inter-Continental**. *See page 16.*

The Funk is housed in the former apartment of the Danish silent movie star Asta Nielsen. The proprietor does his best to maintain the ambience of a pre-war flat, and the rooms are furnished with pieces from the twenties and thirties. The effect is very cosy, and the 15 rooms are comfortable and large, even if not all of them have their own showers. For an extra DM40 per person (including breakfast) you can fit another two people into a double room.
**Hotel services** *Lift.* **Room services** *Telephone.*

### Hotel-Pension Großmann
*Bleibtreustraße 17, Charlottenburg, 10623 (881 6462). S3, S5, S6, S7, S9 Savignyplatz.* **Rates** *single* DM110-120; *double* DM140-160. **No credit cards.**
The rooms in this palatial landmark building aren't quite as lovely as the building's exterior suggests, but they are very big and comfortable. This is an excellent spot for a small group travelling together. The rooms have sinks and showers, but toilets are in the hall.
**Hotel services** *TV room.* **Room services** *Telephone.*

### Pension Kettler
*Bleibtreustraße 19, Charlottenburg, 10623 (883 4949 or 8835676/fax 882 4228). S3, S5, S6, S7, S9 Savignyplatz or U15 Uhlandstraße.* **Rates** *single* DM110-145; *double* DM120-180; *breakfast* DM15. **No credit cards.**
The seven quiet and light bedrooms in this grand old building overlook an impressive courtyard. Most of the double rooms and some of the single rooms (rather small for the price) have showers. Breakfast is relatively expensive for a pension, and if you stay here you would do better to seek nourishment in one of the many cafés around Savignyplatz.
**Room services** *Room service. Telephone.*

### Hotel Heidelberg
*Knesebeckstraße 15, Charlottenburg, 10623 (313 0103/fax 313 5870). S3, S5, S6, S7, S9 Savignyplatz.* **Rates** *single* DM148-168; *double* DM178-198; *suite* DM218. **Credit** AmEx, EC, MC, V.
Those responsible for decorating the Hotel Heidelberg obviously got lost somewhere back in the sixties. The dining room fronts the street and its open door seems to be inviting the public to step in. Except nobody does, and even the guests all seem to dine in the café next door. The rooms, though small and plain, are comfortable enough, with their own showers and toilets. In any event, the Heidelberg's location is central.
**Hotel services** *Bar. Lift. Parking. TV room.* **Room services** *Safe. Telephone.*

### Pension Silvia
*Knesebeckstraße 29, Charlottenburg, 10623 (881 2129/fax885 0435). S3, S5, S6, S7, S9 Savignyplatz.* **Rates** *single* DM55; *double* DM100-200; rooms for three and four can be made up for an extra DM50 per person; *breakfast* DM9.50. **No credit cards.**
This pension has been in business for 100 years and its present owner, Silvia, is an abrasive Saxon with a story or two to tell about the hotel trade. The 15 rooms range in price from the cheap to the moderate, but they are all large, white and airy and have modern bathrooms. The location's convenient and don't be put off by the shabby dining room. You can get a decent breakfast for little more in many of the nearby cafés.
**Hotel services** *TV room.*

### Pension Viola Nova
*Kantstraße 146, Charlottenburg, 10623 (313 457/fax 312 3314). S3, S5, S6, S7, S9 Savignyplatz.* **Rates** *single* DM85-130; *double* DM110-150; *breakfast buffet* DM9.50. **Credit** AmEx, DC, EC, MC, V.
This is a popular tourist area – close to Kurfürstendamm and the Savignyplatz nightlife – and the Viola Nova is one of many similar pensions in the district. Like the others, this is an old, converted Berlin house; the Viola Nova is notable for its very friendly owners, its pleasant breakfast room and its value for money.
**Room services** *Telephone. TV.*

### Hotel-Pension Waizennegger
*Mommsenstraße 6, Charlottenburg, 10629 (881 4528). S3, S5, S6, S7, S9 Savignyplatz.* **Rates** *single* DM75-125; *double* DM120-160. **No credit cards.**

**Grand Hotel Esplanade**. *See page 16.*

The Waizennegger is in a delightful residential area, slightly off the beaten track, but still close enough to Savignyplatz to be convenient. The owners have made a real effort to make this a home away from home: six cosy rooms, most with shower and toilet, are all filled with overstuffed furniture. **Hotel services** *Lift.* **Room services** *TV.*

### Hotel Westerland

*Knesebeckstraße 10, Charlottenburg, 10623 (312 1004/fax 313 6489). S3, S5, S6, S7, S9 Savignyplatz.* **Rates** *single* DM115-135; *double* DM185-205; *triple* DM275. **Credit** EC, V.
Despite the forbidding exterior (a seedy-looking sign adorns an even seedier burgundy façade), the interior is really very pleasant. The beautiful wooden reception desk is quite stunning, and the breakfast room and bedrooms keep up the standard. Rooms are provided with either a bath or a shower and are very comfortable – if there were anything good on German TV it would almost be worth forgoing the sights of Berlin to luxuriate in some of their armchairs.
**Hotel services** *Lift. Parking.* **Room services** *Minibar. Radio.* **Room service** *Safe. Telephone. TV.*

## East Berlin

### Hotel Berolina

*Karl-Marx-Allee 31, Mitte, 10178 (238 130/fax 242 3409). U5 Schilling Straße.* **Rates** *single* DM130-160; *double* DM160-220; *suite* DM270-330. **Credit** AmEx, DC, EC, JCB, V.
A huge, monolithic building, and a good choice for lovers of Communist pomp. Built during the Krushchev era on East Berlin's biggest strip, the Berolina has been renovated and now offers the usual range of services associated with any large modern hotel, including courteous and efficient staff. The lower-priced double rooms, though spotless, are hutch-

like and impersonal. The breakfast and dining rooms are, however, beautifully furnished.
**Hotel services** *Bar. Conference facilities. Lift. Parking.* **Room services** *Radio. Telephone. TV.*

### Hotel Fischer Insel

*Neue Roßstraße 11, Mitte, 10179 (238 07700/fax238 07800). U2 Märkisches Museum.* **Rates** *single* DM120-150; *double* DM160-180; *extra bed* DM60. **Credit** AmEx, DC, EC, MC, V.
Probably the cheapest hotel in the middle of east Berlin and although the furniture is a wee bit on the cheesy side, it is comfortable enough. The bathrooms are large, but the showers are not unlike those you might find at a public swimming pool. Still, for the price and location, you can't do better and the staff are extraordinarily helpful and friendly. Stop in the restaurant upstairs for one of the cheapest hotel meals around and a stunning view of east Berlin.
**Hotel services** *Conference facilities. Lift.* **Room services** *Minibar. Radio. Telephone. TV.*

### Hotel Märkischer Hof

*Linienstraße 133, Mitte, 10115 (282 7155/fax282 4331). U6 Oranienburger Tor.* **Rates** *single* DM125-165; *double* DM155-195; *triple* DM225. **Credit** AmEx, EC, V.
A family-run hotel that's well placed at the top end of Friedrichstraße at the crossing with Oranienburger Straße. You'll be within walking distance of some of Berlin's main attractions – the Berliner Ensemble, the Metropoltheater and the Staatsoper – and some of the city's most beautiful districts. The hotel is quiet and intimate, with extremely friendly staff, comfortable rooms and a pension atmosphere. Recommended.
**Hotel services** *Parking.* **Room services** *Minibar. Radio. Telephone. TV.*

### Spreehotel

*Wallstraße 59, Mitte, 10179 (273 60/fax 200 2109). U2 Märkisches Museum.* **Rates** *single* DM170-230; *double* 200-260; *suite* DM250-350; *extra bed* DM35; children under six free. **Credit** AmEx, EC, MC, V.
One of the best hotels in the eastern part of the city, the Spreehotel is near the heart of Berlin, but bordered by a quiet tree-lined street and an arm of the River Spree. The rooms are quite spacious and tastefully decorated – there's no sense of being in an overcrowded city here. The view from the breakfast room over the Spree and out to the city is superb. There is no restaurant but there are plenty of comfortable places to meet people: either the large airy lobby, the bar or the breakfast room. Friendly staff add to the appeal.
**Hotel services** *Bar. Conference facilities. Laundry facilities. Lift. Parking.* **Room services** *Minibar. Radio. Telephone (no surcharge). TV. No-smoking rooms.*

## Budget

### Hotel-Pension am Lehniner Platz

*Damaschkestraße 4, Charlottenburg, 10711 (323 4282/fax 323 9359). U7 Adenauerplatz.* **Rates** *single* DM90; *double* DM110-120; *extra bed* DM40. **No credit cards**.
This 30-bed pension on a quiet street just off the Ku'damm has rooms which are bright and light. The decor is nice but nothing special. Breakfasts are hearty and the dining room is enlivened with art exhibitions.
**Hotel services** *Lift.*

### Hotel-Pension Bialas

*Carmerstraße 16, Charlottenburg, 10623 (312 5025/fax213 4396). S3, S5, S6, S7, S9 Savignyplatz.* **Rates** *single* DM65-95; *double* DM95-150; *extra bed* DM40-50; children under 12 DM20-25. **Credit** EC, V.
The location is good, on a quiet side street off the bustling

Savignyplatz, and you get the basics. There are 30 rooms, some with shower and toilet, all reasonably clean, with a pleasant breakfast room. Packed lunches available for daytrippers.
**Hotel services** *TV room.*

### Hotel-Pension Charlottenburg

*Grolmannstraße 32-33, Charlottenburg, 10623 (881 5254). S3, S5, S6, S7, S9 Savignyplatz.* **Rates** *single* DM65-95; *double* DM100-150. **No credit cards.**
The Charlottenburg is on one of the many roads fanning out from the Savignyplatz. It's small and modern, with 19 adequate rooms, but lacks character.
**Hotel services** *TV room.*

### Hotel-Pension Elfert

*Knesebeckstraße 13-14, Charlottenburg, 10623 (312 1236/fax 312 1236). S3, S5, S6, S7, S9 Savignyplatz.* **Rates** *single* DM85-95; *double* DM130-150. **No credit cards.**
A homely pension in a quiet, old Berlin block just south of Savignyplatz. The rooms are delightful, beautifully furnished and some come complete with shower, but unfortunately none have a toilet. If you want a soothing stay in a modestly priced hotel with flowery wallpaper in the lobby, then this would suit you fine.
**Room services** *Telephone. TV.*

### Hotel-Pension Imperator

*Meinekestraße 5, Charlottenburg, 10719 (881 4181/fax 882 5185). S3, S5, S6, S7, S9/U2, U9 Zoologischer Garten.* **Rates** *single* DM70-100; *double* DM120-160; *breakfast* DM12-20. **No credit cards.**
One of the best places to stay in Berlin. The building is a huge townhouse and the Imperator occupies the second floor. Its 11 bedrooms are all vast and stylishly furnished with a mixture of antique and modern furniture, and all have modern showers. The breakfast and television rooms are gorgeous and the proprietor's taste in paintings is exquisite. Take a look in the kitchen and you'll find one wall plastered with photos of the jazz musicians and artists who have stayed here, Cecil Taylor and John Cage among them. Hugely enjoyable and atmospheric.
**Hotel services** *Conference facilities. Laundry service. Lift. TV room.* **Room services** *Room service.*

### Hotel Pension München

*Güntzelstraße 62, Wilmersdorf, 10717 (854 2226/fax853 2744). U9 Güntzelstraße.* **Rates** *single* DM60-100; *double* DM78-125; *breakfast* DM9. **Credit** EC, V.
Even though the lift looks suspiciously antiquated, it's much better to venture into this cage than to hike up the stairs to the third floor of this residential building. Owned by artists, this pension features lots of natural wood, modern art, and eight bright, cheerful rooms decorated in red, white and bright floral with modern furniture. It makes a welcome change from the average pension, as does its helpful and friendly owner. A five-minute walk will connect you to the U-Bahn. Recommended.
**Hotel services** *Garage. Lift.* **Room services** *Telephone. TV.*

### Hotel-Pension Trautenau

*Trautenaustraße 14, Wilmersdorf, 10717 (861 3514). U9 Güntzelstraße.* **Rates** *single* DM40; *double* DM70-95. **No credit cards.**
A cheap pension in a residential neighbourhood, with 12 reasonable rooms at more than reasonable prices. The décor is uniquely tasteless: checkerboard floors in the hallways, mismatched floral themes in the rooms, and framed pictures of kittens on the walls. The rooms are small but clean, and some have a shower in the room. The neurotic proprietress only speaks German and hates it when Anglophone tourists start

chatting to her in English. You have been warned. Still, it's very cheap and only a brisk five-minute walk to the U-Bahn station.
**Hotel services** *Lift.*

### Hotel Transit

*Hagelbergerstraße 53-54, Kreuzberg, 10965 (785 5051/fax 785 9619). U6, U7 Mehringdamm.* **Rates** *single* DM80; *double* DM99. **Credit** AmEx, EC, MC, V.
A converted factory houses this unexpectedly bright, airy hotel. It's in an ideal location for sampling Kreuzberg nightlife and the young, friendly, English-speaking staff are always on hand. The rooms are basic but clean and the DM33 dormitory bed is the best value in town. There's also a 24-hour shower/bag deposit service for early arrivals. Three-bed rooms cost DM130, four-bed rooms DM170, five-bed rooms DM210 and six-bed rooms DM250. All rooms have showers. An excellent place to stay.
**Hotel services** *Bar. Laundry service. Lift. TV room.* **Room services** *Safe.*

### Pension-City Galerie

*Leibnizstraße 48, Charlottenburg, 10629 (324 2658/fax 324 2658). U7 Adenauer Platz.* **Rates** *single* DM80; *double* DM110-120. **Credit** V.
A pleasant place that offers the amenities of a small bar and a TV room – rare for a pension of its size. The 11 good-sized rooms are located on the first floor of a pretty, tan-coloured building and three of them have showers. It's a cosy place on a busy street in between Kantstraße and the Ku'damm. Convenient for both shopping and bar-hopping.
**Hotel services** *Bar. TV room.*

### Pension Finck

*Güntzelstraße 54, Wilmersdorf, 10717 (861 2940/fax861 8158). U9 Güntzelstraße.* **Rates** *single* DM55; *double* DM100-110. **No credit cards.**
Pension Finck is on the third floor of a residential building, and directly above another pension, so make sure you get the right one. It's a homely jumble, with lots of knick-knacks hanging on the walls of the lobby and breakfast room. The 14 good-sized rooms are decorated in the same eclectic fashion as the rest of the place, and eight of them have a shower in the room. The toilets are on the hallway. The friendly owner will let you use her telephone at the main desk. The place is right next to a U-Bahn station.
**Hotel services** *Lift.*

### Pension Kreuzberg

*Grossbeerenstraße 64, Kreuzberg, 10963 (251 1362). U7 Mehringdamm.* **Rates** *single* DM40-65; *double* DM70-95; *extra bed* DM30-40. **Credit** EC.
A small, friendly pension in a typical, old Berlin building. It's not for the unfit, as there are four very steep flights of stairs to the reception. None of the rooms have their own bathroom: there's a communal one on each floor, so be prepared to wait in the mornings. The reception has a phone, which you may be allowed to use, and there's a very small breakfast room. Cheap and in a good location.

### Studentenhotel Hubertusalle

*Delbrückstraße 24, Wilmersdorf, 14193 (891 9718/fax 892 8698). S3 ,S7 Grunewald.* **Open** March-Oct. **Rates** *single* DM45-80; *double* DM70-110; *triple* DM90-126. **No credit cards.**
The Studentenhotel is right by the Hubertus lake and a good place to stay in the summer (indeed, it's only open March to October). The building is an ugly eighties construction, the 60 rooms are plain and functional and you'll be sharing a bathroom on the corridor. You can get a meal in the cafeteria until 10pm. The place is packed all the time, so you'll have to book in advance, but it's worth it for prices like these. It's only a ten-minute ride to the centre of town.
**Hotel services** *TV room.*

## Mitwohnzentrale

Mitwohnzentrale are a sure way to save some money in your search for accommodation. The agencies listed below will find you anything from a room in a shared house for a week, to a flat to rent for a couple of years. During the summer months, when Berlin is less crowded, they are a good place to start looking for short-term accommodation. But it may be more difficult at other times of the year, especially during the Berlin Film Festival in February. Most of the agencies accept advance bookings, so book ahead.

If you're staying for a couple of weeks and you manage to find something through a Mitwohnzentrale, you will probably pay DM40-80 a night. For longer stays, the agencies charge between three and four per cent of the monthly rent, which will usually be less than the outrageous fees often charged by other private agents (known as Makler in German), who should be avoided if possible. Private rooms can also be booked through the Verkehrsamt Berlin (*see above*).

### Erste Mitwohnzentrale
*Sybelstraße 53, Charlottenburg, 10629 (324 3031/fax324 9977). U7 Adenauer Platz.* **Open** 9am-8pm Mon-Fri; 10am-6pm Sat, Sun.

### Mitwohnzentrale
*Ku'damm Eck, Kurfürstendamm 227-8, third floor, Charlottenburg, 10719 (88 3051/fax882 6694). U15, U9 Kurfürstendamm.* **Open** 9am-7pm Mon-Fri; 11am-3pm Sat, Sun.

### Mitwohnzentrale Wohnwitz
*Holsteinischestraße 55, Wilmersdorf, 10717 (861 8222/fax861 8272). U7 Blissestraße.* **Open** 10am-7pm Mon-Fri; 10am-1pm Sat; 1-2pm Sun.

### Mitwohnzentrale Kreuzberg
*Mehringdamm 72, Kreuzberg, 10961 (786 6002/fax785 0614). U6, U7 Mehringdamm.* **Open** 10am-7pm Mon-Fri.

### Zeitraum Wohnkonzepte
*Horstweg 7, Charlottenburg, 14059 (325 61 81/fax321 9546). U2 Sophie-Charlotte-Platz.* **Open** 10am-1pm and 3pm-7pm Mon-Fri.

## Youth Hostels

Youth hostels in Berlin are crammed most of the year round, so if you're hoping to make use of them, book ahead, or be prepared to try a few before you find one that has vacancies. You have to be a member of the YHA. The hostels listed below all have midnight curfews and single-sex dormitories. If you're hoping to enjoy the nightlife, you'd be better off trying one of the cheaper Pensionen in Kreuzberg.

### Jugend Zentrale
*Tempelhofer Ufer 32, Kreuzberg, 10963 (264 9520 or 262 3024-25/fax262 9529). U2, U7 Möckernbrucke.* **Open** 10am-4pm Mon, Wed, Fri; 1-6pm Tue, Thur.

Here's where you get your YHA membership card. Bring your passport and a passport-sized photo.

### Jugendgästehaus
*Kluckstraße 3, Schöneberg, 10785 (261 1097 or 261 1098). U2 Kurfürstenstraße.* **Rates** DM28 a night members.
Phone for reservations at least two weeks in advance. Sleep in four- to eight-bed dorms.

### Jugendherberge Wannsee
*Badeweg 1, Zehlendorf, 14129 (803 2034 or 803 2035). S3 Nikolassee.* **Rates** DM28 a night members.
Phone to reserve as early as possible; the rooms all have four beds.

### Jugendberge Ernst Reuter
*Hermsdorfer Damm 48-50, Wedding, 13467 (404 1610). U6 Alt-Tegel, then bus 125.* **Rates** DM23 a night members.
Sleep in four- to six-bed dorms.

### Jugendgästehaus am Zoo
*Hardenbergstraße 9a, Charlottenburg, 10623 (312 9410/fax401 5283). S3, S5, S6, S7, S9/U2, U9 Zoologischer Garten.* **Rates** DM35 a night. No membership required.
Rooms are four-to eight-bed dorms.

## Camp Sites

If you want to explore the camp sites of surrounding Brandenburg, ask for a camping map from any tourist office (Verkehrsamt) in Berlin (*see above* **Tourist Information**). Below we list those within Berlin. For group reservations, contact the Deutscher Camping Club (*listed below*). Prices don't vary that much between sites: for tents, expect to pay between DM5.50 and DM7.50 for rent, plus DM7.50 per person per night: for caravans it's DM8.50 for rent, plus DM7.50 per person per night.

### Deutscher Camping Club
*Geisbergstraße 11, Schöneberg, 10777 (218 6071/fax213 4416). U4 Viktoria-Luise-Platz.* **Open** 10.30am-6pm Mon; 8am-4pm Wed; 8am-1pm Fri.

### Krampnitzer Weg
*Kladow, 14089 (365 27 97). U7 Rathaus Spandau and then bus 135.*
**Services** *children's playground, food shop, restaurant, shower, handicapped toilet, sportsground, swimming and bathing in open water.*

### Dreilinden
*Kremnitz-Ufer 44, Zehlendorf, 14109 (805 12 01). R3 Griebnitzsee.*
**Services** *children's playground, restaurant, shower.*

### Kohlhasenbrück
*Neue Kreisstrasse 36, Zehlendorf, 14109 (805 1737). R3 Griebnitzsee.*
**Services** *children's playground, showers, laundry facilities, restaurant.*

### Krossinsee
*Wernsdorfer Straße 45, Köpenick, 12527 (675 8687). S6 Grünau, tram 68 to Schmöckwitz and then bus 463.*
**Services** *chalets for rent, children's playground, fishing, food shop, restaurant, shower, swimming and bathing in open water, bicycle, boat and surf board rental, surf school.*

# Berlin by Season

*From tennis to tattoos, jazz to Jeunesses Musicales, Berlin offers a variety of in- and outdoor shows and activities.*

Berlin's liberal licensing laws have created the impression that its citizens do nothing but party all year round. But a look at their calendar shows nothing of the sort. Cultural events, covering the spectrum of classical music, jazz, theatre and film, take up most of the space in anyone's festival diary. Berliners are serious about their sports, and turn out in large numbers to support international marathon runners, German tennis stars or American football players.

Berlin by season is a tale of two cities: in winter the weather forces everyone behind closed doors; summer is the season Berliners save for fun – at festivals such as the gay community's Christopher Street Day, at district festival drink-ups and weekend lakeside laze-abouts.

## Information

### Verkehrsamt Berlin
*Main office: Martin-Luther-Straße 105, Schöneberg, 10825 (2123-4).* **Open** 9am-3pm. Branch offices at Bahnhof Zoo or Tegel Airport. Europa-Center office open until 10pm.
The tourist office publishes annual and seasonal *Berlin Turns On* guides to events throughout Berlin, including most annual events. The staff are usually helpful about more off-beat happenings. *See chapter* **Essential Information**.

### Messe Berlin Trade Fair and Exhibition Grounds
*Messedamm 22, Charlottenburg, 14055 (3038-0). U2 Kaiserdamm.* **Open** 24-hour telephone information. Helpful, multi-lingual staff provide details on trade fairs.

## Spring

### Musik Biennale Berlin
*Philharmonie, Matthäikirchstraße 1, Schöneberg, 10785 (254 88-0). U1 Kurfürstenstraße/bus 148.*
*Schauspielhaus, Gendarmenmarkt, Mitte, 10117 (209 0215-7). U6 Französische Straße.* Contact: *Berliner Festspiele, Budapester Straße 50, Tiergarten, 10787 (25 48 90).* **Dates** 1995 and every other year in March. **Admission** varies.
After unification, this former East German festival highlighting trends in contemporary serious music was spared extinction and put on the west Berlin life support system. Held every other year, the ten-day event invites international avant garde and modern composers and musicians to present music that is anything but harmonious.

### International Tourism Trade Fair Berlin
*Messe Berlin Trade Fair and Exhibition Grounds, Messedamm 22, Charlottenburg, 14055 (3038 0). U2 Kaiserdamm.* **Open** 10am-6pm. **Dates** early March. **Admission** DM15; DM10 concs.

Berliners dub this enormous tourism and travel trade fair 'the world's biggest travel agency'. Although you can't make bookings during the six-day fair, you can pick up enough brochures to open a recycling plant, and get first-hand information on the world's most popular or obscure destinations.

### Urbane Aboriginale
*Ballhaus Naunynstrasse, Naunynstraße 27, Kreuzberg, 10997 (2588 66 44). U8 Moritzplatz.*
*Hebbel Theater, Stresemannstraße 29, Kreuzberg, 10963 (251 0144). U1, U6 Hallesches Tor.*
*Podewil, Klosterstraße 68, Mitte, 10179 (24 74 96). U2 Klosterstraße.*
Contact: *Freunde Guter Musik e V, Erkelenzdamm 11-13, Kreuzberg, 10999 (615 2702).* **Dates** spring.
**Admission** DM15 per performance.
This festival of iconoclastic music and performance has been introducing experimental, avant garde artists from different nations to Berlin since 1985. Between ten and 40 musicians, theatre, dance and performance groups and soloists spend about a week demonstrating that the world's underground art world is a strange beast indeed.

### Berliner Halbmarathon
Contact: *Berlin Marathon, Alt-Moabit 92, Moabit, 10559 (392 1102).* **Date** first Sun in April. **Admission** participants DM25; free spectators.
As its name suggests, this 21-kilometre (13-mile) run is half the stretch of the summer marathon. The starting point is on the wide, majestic Karl-Marx-Allee. The organisers are aiming to develop this event, perhaps even to the size of the Göteburg or Milan half-marathons, which, with some 36,000 and 40,000 participants respectively, have more than twice as many runners.

### May Day Riots
*Traditionally beginning on Oranienstraße, Kreuzberg, 10997.* **Date** afternoon of May 1. **Admission** free.
On May Day you can usually count on Berlin's black-clad Autonomen to swarm out of their squats and clash with hordes of police during their traditional march through Kreuzberg.

### Theatertreffen Berlin
Contact: *Berliner Festspiele, Budapester Straße 50, Tiergarten, 10787 (254 890).* **Dates** two weeks in May. **Admission** varies.
The best that German-speaking theatre has to offer. A jury of experts picks about a dozen of the most intriguing new theatrical productions from theatres in Germany, Austria and Switzerland. The winning companies get a trip to Berlin where they perform their piece two or three times during the fortnightly meeting. There's a smaller Youth Theatre Meeting at the end of May that runs along much the same principles. Venues vary each year, so check local press for details.

**Opposite:** *In Berlin, as soon as the sun comes out so do the street parties.*

*One of the great misnomers – **Oktoberfest** starts at the end of September. See page 30.*

## German Open

*LTTC Rot Weiss e V, Gottfried-von-Cramm-Weg 47-55, Grunewald, 14193 (826 2207). S3 Grunewald/bus 119, 186 Hagenplatz.* **Dates** 19th week of the year, in May. **Admission** DM30-DM100 for seats; DM25 for day ticket with access to all courts except centre court.

The fifth largest international women's tennis championship in the world is not just a chance for Steffi to bag another $900,000, it's also a week-long get-together of Germany's rich and famous. Mortals have a hard time getting tickets – centre court games are sold out at least a year in advance. Day tickets with access to all eight courts except centre court are affordable, available and generally worthwhile during the first few days.

## Freie Berliner Kunstausstellung

*Funkturm Exhibition Halls, Hammarskjöld Platz, Charlottenburg, 14055 (3038-0). U2 Kaiserdamm.* **Dates** spring. **Admission** DM6; DM4 concs; DM3 per person in groups of ten.

Europe's largest show of professional and amateur art, this jury-free exhibition of 2,500 Berlin artists covers 9,800 square metres (11,721 sq yards) in three halls.

## Deutsche Pokalendspiele (German Football Cup)

*Olympiastadion, Charlottenburg, 14053 (30 06 33). U2 Olympia-Stadion.* **Tickets & information** *Berliner Fußball Verband, Humboldtstraße 8a, Grunewald, 13407 (896 9940).* **Date** May/June. **Admission** DM20-DM110.

Berlin's football frenzy, when 65,000 fans drink and dance in the aisles of a sold-out Olympic stadium.

## Import Messe Berlin

*Messe Berlin Fair and Exhibition Grounds, Messedamm 22, Charlottenburg, 14055 (3038 0). U2 Kaiserdamm.* **Open** 10am-6pm. **Dates** early June. **Admission** DM20; DM45 for four days.

A four-day trade fair for the world's importers, exporters, and producers of textiles, leather wear, accessories, jewellery, glass, ceramics, carpets and furniture.

## Summer

### Berlin Philharmonic Orchestra at the Waldbühne

*Waldbühne, Glockenturmstraße/cr Passenheimer Straße, Charlottenburg, 14053. U2 Olympia Stadion, shuttle buses run for major events.* **Date** June. **Admission** DM27-DM32.

The Berlin Philharmonic ends its season with an open-air concert at the Waldbühne. The event marks the arrival of summer for 22,500 Berliners, who, once darkness sets in, light up the venue with thousands of lighters. The Waldbühne is one of Berlin's best summer venues for big-name rock bands. It hosts an Oldie Night (DM48-58) each Aug or Sept. Films are shown on the huge screen. Check local press.

### Deutsch-Französisches Volksfest (The German-French Festival)

*Kurt-Schumacher-Damm, Tegel, 13405 (401 3889). U6 Kurt-Schumacher-Platz.* **Dates** mid-June until mid-July. **Admission** DM2.

Berlin's largest Volksfest features Europe's biggest travelling rollercoaster, and lots of wine, frogs' legs, snails etc.

### Christopher Street Day Parade

*In 1994 the parade for the first time followed a west-east axis, beginning at Adenauerplatz, marching through the Brandenburg Gate and finishing at the Rotes Rathaus.* **Date** June. **Admission** free; DM10-DM25 evening parties at different venues.

Commemorating the 1969 riots at the Stonewall Bar in Christopher Steet, New York, which marked the beginning of modern gay liberation. The Saturday parade and week-long festival are a celebration of Berlin's lesbian and gay community and have developed into one of the most flamboyant tourist attractions. *See also chapter* **Gay Berlin**.

### Love Parade

*Traditionally follows a route from Wittenbergplatz along Kurfürstendamm to Adenauerplatz and back.* **Date** first Sat in July. **Admission** free for parade, varies for raves.

A kind of techno/house Mardi Gras. Dozens of floats, each

with its own DJs and sound system sponsored by clubs from all over Europe, provide the soundtrack for tens of thousands of ravers. In a way, it's a political demonstration, and has so far been licensed as such, though this may change. Love Paraders are campaigning for 'Peace, Joy, Sponge Cakes'.

## Bach Days Berlin

*Philharmonie, Matthäikirchstraße 1, Schöneberg, 10785, (254 88-0). U1 Kurfürstenstraße/bus 148.*
*Schloß Charlottenburg, Spandauerdamm, Charlottenburg, 14059 (329 911). U1 Sophie-Charlotte-Platz/U7 Richard Wagner-Platz.*
*Schauspielhaus, Gendarmenmarkt, Mitte, 10117 (209 0215-7). U6 Französische Straße.*
*Plus various churches throughout Berlin.*
Contact: *VDMK, Kaiserdamm 31, Charlottenburg, 14057 (301 5518).* **Dates** first two weeks of July. **Admission** DM10-DM42.
Despite a series of hot summers since 1970, this nine-day festival paying tribute to the work of Bach and other baroque composers has lured 16,000-20,000 classical music buffs indoors each year. They come to hear top international baroque orchestras and soloists perform. Since the fall of the Wall the festival has expanded to classical music venues in eastern Berlin, and sites outside Berlin, such as Schloß Sanssoucci in Potsdam (*see chapter* **Trips out of Town**).

## Jazz in July

*Quasimodo, Kantstraße 12a, 10623 (312 8086). U2, U9 Zoologischer Garten.* **Dates** two to three weeks beginning early July. **Admission** DM20-DM30.
More summertime music, this time in the smoky cellar of the Quasimodo. Organisers pick up top jazz acts already on their way to large European festivals. Recent headliners have included Arturo Sandoval, Michael Brecker, Ruben Blades, and the Yellow Jackets. This excellent venue is in tune with seasonal trends, and concerts are usually packed out.

## Deutsch-Amerikanischer Volksfest (The German-American Festival)

*Around Trumanplaza, Zehlendorf, 14195 (401 3889). U2 Oskar-Helene-Heim.* **Dates** late July-mid Aug. **Admission** DM2.
The allies may be gone, but the German/American festival they established in 1961 continues. There are rides, gambling and stalls selling alcohol, German specialities and authentic American junk food. It's tacky, but Berliners love it.

## Heimatklänge (World Wide Festival of Urban Roots and Dance Music)

*At the Tempodrom, In den Zelten, Tiergarten, 10557 (39 440 45; fax 394 61 73). S3, S5, S6, S9 Lehrter Stadtbahnhof.* **Dates** July, Aug (phone for details). **Admission** free.
Berlin's biggest world music event. Through July and August, for four nights a week plus Sunday afternoons, the Tempodrom tent-venue in the Tiergarten hosts acts from all over the globe. Expect anything from a chanting Mongolian shaman to an orchestra of Patagonian nose flautists.

## Hofkonzerte

*Schultheiss Brauerei, Schmiedehof, Methfesselstraße 28-48, Kreuzberg, 10965 (780 030). U6 Platz der Luftbrücke.*
*Podewil, Klosterstraße 68, Mitte, 10179 (24 74 96). U2 Klosterstraße.*
**Dates** every weekend in July, Aug. **Admission** DM12; DM10 concs.
Inside the redbrick Schultheiss brewery next to the Kreuzberg, there's jazz on Friday and classical concerts on Saturday evenings. While the Schultheiss concerts present local musicians, Podewil schedules primarily eastern European artists. If it rains, concerts move indoors. At both there's veggie food and wurst, wine and beer.

## Classic Open Air

*Gendarmenmarkt, Mitte, 10117. U6 Französische Straße.* Contact: *Media On-Line May-July (20 90 24 88).* **Date** four days (Thur-Sun) in July. **Admission** DM25-DM115.
Established in 1990, this four-day festival is already a fixture in the calendars of classical music lovers. Organisers schedule big names such as José Carreras or Montserrat Caballé for the opening concert and fill up the rest with lighter but nonetheless quality talent. Set in one of the city's most beautiful squares, tree-lined and flanked by the Schauspielhaus, and the French and German cathedrals, the festival provides a perfect place to sit beneath the setting sun and rising stars and enjoy the music. Many Berlin orchestras take part, and soloists are engaged from all over Europe.

## Internationale Funkaustellung (International Electronics Exhibition)

*Messe Berlin Trade Fair Grounds, Messedamm 22, Charlottenburg, 14055 (3038-0). U2 Kaiserdamm.* **Open** 10am-7pm. **Dates** late Aug 1995 and every other year. **Admission** DM16.
All that is new and up-and-coming in the world of consumer electronics comes to town during this nine-day trade fair. World market leaders present the latest, from audio, hifi, TV, video and camcorders, to antennae, satellite reception stations and mobile communications. It's an amazing display of modernity, visited by upwards of 370,000 people.

# Autumn

## Berliner Festwochen (Berlin Festival Weeks)

*Philharmonie, Matthäikirchstraße 1, Schöneberg, 10785, (254 88-0). U2 Kurfürstenstraße/bus 148.*
*Schauspielhaus, Gendarmenmarkt, Mitte, 10117 (209 0215-7). U6 Französische Straße.*
*Plus various other venues.*
Contact: *Berliner Festspiele, Budapester Straße 50, Tiergarten, 10787 (254 890).* **Dates** through Sept. **Admission** varies.
The cultural summer closes with a month of events, concerts and performances highlighting a different nation or artistic theme. The emphasis is on classical music and international theatre, accompanied by exhibitions, readings and seminars.

## Medieval Fortress Festival

*Spandauer Zitadelle, Am Juliusturm, Spandau, 13599. U7 Zitadelle.* **Date** 2nd weekend in Sept. **Admission** DM3.
The Middle Ages are revived for 20,000 Berliners at the grounds of the historic citadel in Spandau by jesters, theatre troupes, musicians and animals. While the Juliusturm probably dates back to the twelfth century, most of the citadel is not medieval – it was built by an Italian between 1560-1590.

## Berliner Marathon

*Finishing point at Kaiser Wilhem Memorial Church, Breitscheidplatz, 10789. U2, U9 Zoologischer Garten.* Information: *Berlin Marathon, Alt-Moabit 92, Moabit, 10559 (392 1102).* **Date** last Sunday in Sept.
**Admission** participants DM55 residents of Germany; DM60 foreign residents; spectators free.
Berlin's biggest sporting event is also the world's third largest marathon after New York and London. Sprinters are led past most of Berlin's landmarks on their 42km (26-mile) trek through ten districts, including the Brandenburg Gate, Unter den Linden, the Berlin Cathedral, Philharmonie and Kaiser Wilhem Memorial Church. About 20,000 runners take part, cheered on by a million spectators. Two thirds of the participants come from Germany, the remainder from all over the world, so finding a hotel room over the weekend is next to impossible. Don't plan on leaving the city – traffic is re-routed into an incomprehensible labyrinth.

## Nachtbogen

*Oderberger Straße, between Kastanienalle and Schönhauser Allee. U2 Eberswalder Straße.* **Date** early Sept. **Admission** free.

A one-day arts festival that closes Oderberger Straße to traffic and allows Berlin and international artists to place their site-specific work in public and private spaces. Sculpture, light installations, paintings, theatre, live music and readings are placed out in the street as well as indoors.

## Internationale ADAC
## Avus-Rennen für Wagen (Auto Race)

*Avus Race Course, at the Funkturm next to the Messe Berlin Trade Fair Grounds, Messedamm 22, Charlottenburg, 14055 (3038-0). U2 Kaiserdamm.* **Date** end Sept. **Admission** DM20-DM50.

The most important race in the German Touring Car Championships speeds along a 2.64km portion of the Autobahn towards Wannsee; also held in May.

## Oktoberfest

*(Information 213 3290).* **Dates** end Sept-first ten days in Oct. **Admission** DM1.50 adults; children free.

Nothing like being at Bavaria's bash, but Berlin's version provides a good excuse to guzzle beer until it doesn't matter where you are. Partake of the charcoal-grilled sausages.

## International Film and Video Festival Interfilm/Vipfilm

*Babylon Mitte, Rosa-Luxemburg-Straße 30, Mitte, 10178 (organiser 693 2959). U2 Rosa-Luxemburg-Platz. Plus various venues, check local press for details.* **Dates** Oct-Dec. **Admission** DM7-10.

No glitzy cocktail parties or star-studded receptions here: the capital's second largest film festival after the Berlinale focuses on international independent and alternative films and videos, presenting work that never makes it to Cannes or the Berlinale. Interfilm started off underground in 1982 as a Super 8 festival. Senate funding was granted in 1983, only to be cut back by two thirds a year later. They've been struggling ever since, but the festival still returns.

## JazzFest Berlin

*Haus der Kulturen der Welt, John-Foster-Dulles-Allee 10, Tiergarten, 10557 (397 87-0). Bus 100.*
*Philharmonie, Matthäikirchstraße 1, Tiergarten, 10785 (254 88-0). U2 Kurfürstenstraße/bus 148.*
*Musikinstrumenten-Museum, Tiergartenstraße 1, Tiergarten, 10785. U2 Kurfürstenstraße/bus 148.*
Contact: *Berliner Festspielen (254 890).* **Dates** Oct or Nov. **Admission** varies.

Jazz dominates the cultural scene for four days each autumn. The whole jazz spectrum is on offer, performed by a mixed bag of internationally renowned artists and the originators of local jazz projects. Going strong since 1964, the festival is often accompanied by sub-festivals highlighting specific categories of contemporary music and photo exhibitions.

## AVE

*Straßenbahndepot Moabit, Wiebestraße 29-39, Moabit, 10553 (345 1350). U7 Mierendorffplatz.* **Date** three days (Fri-Sun) in Nov. **Admission** DM20.

Berlin's avant-garde 'Fashion Fair for Believers', as organisers call it, has been struggling since it started in 1988, but has assumed an important position in the local scene. Some 25 up-and-coming local young designers are showcased.

## Jüdische Kulturtage
## (Jewish Culture Days)

*Various venues. Contact: Jüdisches Gemeindehaus, Fasanenstraße 79/80, Charlottenburg, 10623 (884 72150).* **Date** three weeks in Nov. **Admission** varies.

The annual arts and cultural festival of the city's principal Jewish organisation, the Jüdisches Gemeindehaus. Numerous venues provide space for an extensive programme of theatre, music, film, readings, panel discussions, dance and workshops. Past themes have included 'Jewish Life in Eastern Europe' and, in 1993, 'Jewishness from California'.

# Winter

## German Tattoo Convention

*Huxley's Neue Welt, Hasenheide 108-114, Kreuzberg, 10967 (788 1401). U7, U8 Hermannplatz.* **Date** three days in Dec. **Admission** DM25 for day ticket.

Hundreds of long-haired, leather-wearing Lemmy lookalikes perform their art on whatever flesh you choose to have done.

## Menschen Tiere Sensationen

*Deutschlandhalle, Messedamm 26, Charlottenburg, 14055 (3038 1). U2 Kaiserdamm.* **Dates** two weeks mid-end Dec. **Admission** DM25-DM80.

The largest oldest circus held outside of a big top in Europe.

## Christmas Markets

**Dates** last week of Nov to Dec 27. **Admission** free.

Yuletide markets speckle the capital throughout the holiday season. Handicrafts, decorations and traditional gingerbread, roasted candied almonds, cinnamon stars, piping-hot spiced Glühwein and good cheer. The largest markets are at **Marx-Engels-Platz** (*S-Bahn Hackescher Markt; 1-9pm Mon-Fri, Sun; 1-10pm Sat*), including rides and games; **Kaiser Wilhelm Memorial Church**, Breitscheidplatz (*U2/U9 Zoologischer Garten; 11am-9pm Sun-Thur, 11am-10pm Fri, Sat*); and a traditional market in the old city centre of Spandau (*U7 Altstadt Spandau; 10am-7pm Sat, Sun*).

## New Year's Eve on the Rocks

Thousands of Berliners of all ages climb the heights to watch the firework spectacle that explodes over the city as church bells ring in the new year. Popping champagne corks make about as much noise as the pyrotechnics on the Teufelsberg (Devil's Mountain) at the northern tip of the Grunewald, and the Kreuzberg, the hill after which that area is named.

## Internationale Grüne Woche
## (Green Week)

*Messe Berlin Trade Fair Grounds, Messedamm 22, Charlottenburg, 10455 (3038 0). U2 Kaiserdamm.* **Open** 9am-6pm. **Dates** Jan. **Admission** DM15; DM45 for ten days; DM12 per person for groups of 20.

The annual farm show is actually a ten-day orgy celebrating food and drink from Germany and the world. Hordes of Berliners and visitors flock to the exhibition halls to sample German gastronomic specialities and exotic foods.

## Jeunesses Musicales World Orchestra Concert

*Venue changes (information 80 33 91 22).* **Date** early Jan. **Admission** DM12-DM35; DM8 students.

On December 27 each year, orchestra members of the world's largest international youth cultural association meet to rehearse before their winter tour. Berlin has often served as starting point for the orchestra's European tour since 1988.

## Berlin International Film Festival

*See chapter* **Film.**

## VideoFest

*Podewil Klosterstraße 68, Mitte, 10179 (240-3209). U6 Klosterstraße.* Contact: *Mediopolis (262 8714).* **Date** mid-Feb. **Admission** DM15-DM10; DM12-DM8 concs.

Some 200 videos from 40 countries are shown during one of the world's largest video events. The festival presents productions in video art, documentary, fiction, video clip and computer animation. Nightflight at 11pm offers a different, off-beat menu each evening.

# Sightseeing

*Memorials and museums, checkpoints and chunks of Wall, public parks and nasty Nazi buildings: what to see and where to see it.*

Sculptor Friedrich Drake's Goddess of Victory atop the **Siegessäule**. See page 45.

Although Berlin is a difficult city to get to know quickly, it's well structured for visitors because the main sights tend to be clustered together. The Brandenburg Gate is next to the Reichstag and a minute's walk from one of the Soviet War Memorials; Schloß Charlottenburg is across the road from the Egyptian Museum (home of the bust of Nefertiti); east Berlin's major museums are all on Museuminsel (Museum Island), west Berlin's are mainly to be found in the south-western suburb of Dahlem or in the central district of Charlottenburg.

The key to really getting to know Berlin is not by its sights, but by its people and atmosphere. Riding around on the U-Bahn won't give you an idea of how the city fits together, or indeed where the Wall was. A better approach is to walk around, and maybe get lost occasionally. Or you could sit in the top of a double-decker bus and sightsee in cheap comfort. Board bus 129 at Wittenbergplatz, across from **KaDeWe** (*listed below under* **The Sights**), for a ride up the Kurfürstendamm (known universally as the Ku'damm) to the lush section of Grunewald, where it terminates. Get back on and stay on until you're in the groovier parts of Kreuzberg for a good introduction to what makes Berlin so vital. There are guided bus tours if you prefer to see all the sights on one ride: *see below* **Tours**.

Use this chapter as a quick reference to Berlin's major sights (and some of the less well known ones too). Many of the places listed are to be found elsewhere in the Guide, covered in greater detail. In the **Berlin by Area** chapter we have investigated the most interesting districts of Berlin. Unless otherwise specified, 'children' in our listings implies schoolchildren. Most places demand an ID card, so it makes sense to get an ISIC card (available at travel agents) before you leave the UK.

If you're planning a day's sightseeing and don't want to spend your time criss-crossing the city, consult the **Area Index** on page 264.

## Focal Points

### Alexanderplatz
*Mitte, 10178, S3, S5, S6, S7, S9/U2, U5, U8*
*Alexanderplatz.*
Once the traffic hub of Berlin, Alexanderplatz was rebuilt in wonderfully tasteless style by the GDR government after the war. If you like Communist architectural kitsch, you'll love this place. Check out the dinky plastic façade of Kaufhof, once the Centrum department store, best-stocked

emporium in the old East. Alexanderplatz station is also worth a look, both inside and out, for those who want to catch an echo of the Cold War (and we defy you not to get lost should you venture inside). Alexanderplatz is home to the **Fernsehturm** (television tower), and is only a short walk from the **Nikolaiviertel** and the **Rotes Rathaus** (*see below for all three*). Despite Alexanderplatz's undoubted aesthetic shortcomings, it's a good place to sit in or wander around and soak up the unique atmosphere of Berlin Mitte. The area has been changing fast since reunification in 1989 but decent bars and restaurants are still fairly thin on the ground and most of them tend to shut earlier than elsewhere in the city.

## Bahnhof Zoo/Zoo Station

*Charlottenburg, 10623. U2, U9, S3, S5, S6, S7, S9 Zoologischer Garten.*

All self-respecting cities have areas that are known to be favourite haunts of tourists, drop-outs and punks long past their sell-by date; Berlin has Zoologischer Garten, its main train station. Zoo Station has gained notoriety. There's even a book/film (*Christiane F: Wir Kinder Vom Bahnhof Zoo*) and a U2 song (*Zoo Station* from *Achtung Baby*) named after it. As you emerge from the underground station you will be immediately struck by the seediness: Polish and Russian cigarette-sellers vie for your attention and down-and-outs ask you for Kleingeld (small change). Before the Wall came down, and although it was in the West, Zoo was controlled by the Eastern authorities, who ran the railway lines. Western police were not allowed in, which partly explains how it became a hangout for junkies. Today you'll see transport police (who police the U- and S-Bahn all day) with large and ferocious dogs (the same ones, incidentally, which used to police the Wall), arguing with the people hanging around the S-Bahn entrance. But don't let this put you off, for the area around Zoo Station is Tourist City. You want bright lights, tacky souvenirs and McDonald's? Well, here they are. You could be in any other major capital city in the western world.

## Dahlem Museums

*Arnimallee 27, Zehlendorf, 14195 (830 11). U1 Dahlem-Dorf.* **Open** 9am-5pm Tue-Fri; 10am-5pm Sat, Sun.
**Admission** DM4; DM2 children, students; free Sun.
The affluent south-western suburb of Dahlem – just a short trip out of the city centre – houses Berlin's largest and densest concentration of museums. The complex includes the **Gemäldegalerie** (Picture Gallery); the **Skulpturengalerie** (Sculpture Gallery); the **Museum für Islamische Kunst** (Islamic Art); the **Museum für Indische Kunst** (Indian Art); the **Museum für Ostasiatische Kunst** (Far Eastern Art); and the **Museum für Völkerkunde** (Anthropology). The **Museum für Deutsche Volkskunde** (German Ethnology) is in a different complex nearby, as is the **Brücke Museum** (The Bridge Museum), which is devoted to the works of The Bridge movement, a collection of artists who saw themselves as a bridge between the artistic values they each represented. The sheer volume of the collections at Dahlem means that you can't possibly see everything in one day. Be selective or risk a cultural overdose. *See chapter* **Museums** for reviews.

## Gendarmenmarkt

*Mitte, 10117. U6 Französische Straße.*
This is truly one of Berlin's grandest and most impressive squares, yet it was left in ruins after World War II and restoration work didn't begin until 1977. The Gendarmenmarkt was renamed the **Platz der Akademie** by the GDR in 1950 to commemorate the 250th anniversary of the Academy of Sciences, but it reverted to its former name in 1992. It is called after the Gen d'armes regiment of cuirassiers, which had its stables and guardhouse here from 1735-82. The **Konzerthaus** (formerly the

Schauspielhaus), a major venue for classical music, sits in the centre, with the **Französischer Dom** (Cathedral) and the **Deutscher Dom**, on its north and south flanks. The Französischer Dom was re-opened in 1987, but is no longer a place of worship. There is a great wine restaurant, the **Weingaststätte Turmstuben** (*see chapter* **Restaurants**), upstairs and a Huguenot Museum near the entrance. Unter den Linden and along it most of the other grand sights of the Mitte district are within a short walk of this square.

## The Kurfürstendamm

*Charlottenburg, Wilmersdorf, 10707, 10719, 10709, 10711. U9, U15 Kurfürstendamm, U7 Adenauerplatz.*
Two miles (3km) of pure consumerism, the Ku'damm was built up after the construction of the Wall, when Berlin's main drags – Leipziger Straße and Unter den Linden – were left in the East. It's glitzy and showy and great for strolling along, but for more interesting shops you need to stray just off the beaten track (try Budapester Straße or Bleibtreustraße, for instance). The showcases on the street are fascinating. During the squatters' riots in the early eighties, people smash-and-grabbed the stuff inside them and they remained boarded up for months. And the grand old cafés (such as Café Möhring and its younger rival Café Kranzler) are superb – order a bowl of *milchkaffee* and a hefty portion of *apfel strudel*. Some 500,000 East Berliners came here on November 10, 1989 and caused a colossal traffic jam. The congestion hasn't eased much since. *See also chapter* **By Area**.

## Oranienburger Straße

*Mitte, 10178. U6 Oranienburger Tor. S1, S2 Oranienburger Straße.*
This is the old Jewish quarter and currently the central thoroughfare of Bohemian east Berlin – an area of contrasts between ruin, restoration and all points in between. New fashion shops such as **Karl Faktor** and **Nix** (*see chapter* **Shopping**) jostle with bars and restaurants such as **Tacheles, Obst & Gemüse, Café Orange, Café Oren, VEB OZ** and **Silberstein** (*see chapters* **Restaurants** *and* **Cafés & Bars**). The 'art mile' of Auguststraße runs right off it (*see chapter* **Galleries**). Slap bang in the middle is the **New Synagogue** (*see below*) and round the corner on Tucholskystraße the Adass Yisroel congregation has been revived. Next door to it is **Beth Café** (*see chapter* **Cafés & Bars**), east Berlin's only kosher restaurant. There's always plenty to see by day and it's exceedingly lively at night, though the 'alternative' scene which moved in here after the Wall came down is these days beginning to seem a little jaded. Be warned: the restaurants around here are always packed and few offer any kind of system by which you can queue for a table or be appraised of how long you might have to wait. Book ahead or be prepared for a free-for-all. *See also chapter* **By Area**.

## Museumsinsel (Museum Island)

*Mitte, 10178. S3, S5, S6, S9 Hackescher Markt.*
At the heart of Berlin, an island in the middle of the Spree, this is the oldest museum complex in the city. Friedrich Wilhelm III initiated the construction so that the public could see the treasures collected by the royal family. The **Pergamon Museum, Altes Museum, Bode Museum** and **Nationalgalerie** are all here. The **Neue Museum** is being restored and should have reopened by the time you read this. The Pergamon is home to the superb Ishtar Gate, as well as numerous other Islamic and Byzantine treasures. Other Byzantine, as well as Egyptian, artefacts can be found in the Bode Museum, whereas nineteenth- and early-twentieth-century works of art are held in the National-

*Restoration of the **Gendarmenmarkt**, ruined in World War II, didn't begin until 1977.*

galerie. The Altes Museum was designed by Schinkel and is a venue for temporary exhibitions. *See chapter* **Museums** for museum details and reviews.

## Savignyplatz
*Charlottenburg, 10623. S3, S5, S6, S9 Savignyplatz.*
Although long past its trendy heyday in the sixties, Savignyplatz is still a good place to explore bars, restaurants and shops. The pretty square has plenty of green hedges, and seats on which to bill and coo with the one you love. Several famous Berlin cafés and bars are on nearby side-streets: **Shell**, **Café Savigny**, **Dieners**, **Schwarzes Café** and **Florian** (*see chapters* **Restaurants** and **Cafés & Bars**). The arches around the S-Bahn are good for shopping. Bookstores such as **Bücherbogen** and gift shops such as **Genious-Group** (*see chapter* **Shopping**) are among the highlights.

## Unter den Linden
*Mitte, 10117. S1, S2 Unter den Linden.*
A splendidly pompous Prussian boulevard, later to become a splendidly pompous showcase for the GDR, Unter den Linden was named after the lush lime trees that lined it. Hitler ordered the trees to be cut down to make more room for his military parades, but they have since been replanted. The street is once again becoming an excellent place for a Sunday stroll. Much of Unter den Linden didn't survive World War II, but several old buildings were rebuilt under the GDR regime, including the **Alte Bibliothek** (Old Library) once the Royal library; **St Hedwigs-Kathedrale**, seat of the Catholic bishop in Berlin; and the **Deutsche Staatsoper** on nearby Bebelplatz. The Nazis began their book-burning here at the Alte Bibliothek by throwing volumes out of the library window into a huge bonfire on May 11, 1933. The **Humboldt University** across the street was founded by statesman Wilhelm von Humboldt in 1810. Statues of him and his geographer brother, Alexander von Humboldt, grace the entrance to the main building. Don't let the lovely façade fool you: inside it's hideously institutional. Next door is Schinkel's first work, the **Neue Wache** (new guard house), where the Tombs of the Unknown Soldier and the Anti-Fascist Resistance Fighter, as well as an Eternal Flame, were to be found. It was first made into a war memorial in 1931, for soldiers who fell in World War I, but has been in its present incarnation since 1969. The **Deutsches Historisches Museum**, in the Zeughaus, partially designed by Germany's most famous Baroque architect Andreas Schlüter and the oldest building on Unter den Linden, is next door. The Zeughaus will be used as a government building when parliament moves to Berlin by the year 2000. Also on Unter den Linden are the **Lustgarten** (pleasure garden) and the **Schloßbrücke**. The Lustgarten is *the* place for demonstrations, festivals, and the like; the Schloßbrücke is the most beautiful bridge in Berlin – which is saying something, as Berlin has more bridges than Venice. Eight marble goddesses, representing Athene and Nike escorting the Warrior, line the bridge which connects Unter den Linden with Karl-Liebknecht-Straße. The bridge is yet another one of the masterworks of Karl Friedrich Schinkel, this one completed in 1824. The sculptures were based on his designs, but completed by students in 1857; they were removed for safety during World War II, which is the only reason they have managed to survive intact. West Berlin kept the sculptures until 1981, when they were returned.

The **New Synagogue**, set on fire by the Nazis on Kristallnacht, 1938. See page 42.

## The Sights

### Berliner Dom (Berlin Cathedral)
*Lustgarten, Mitte, 10178 (246 90). S3, S5, S6, S9 Hackescher Markt.* **Open** 9am-7.30pm Mon-Sat; 11.30am-7.30pm Sun. **Admission** free, but into the dome itself DM3; DM1.50 children, students, pensioners, groups. Photo permission DM3.
The dramatic Berliner Dom is now more or less healed of its war wounds. Built at the turn of the century in Italian Renaissance style, it was destroyed during World War II and remained a ruin until 1973, when restoration work began. It's always looked fine from the outside and the internal work is almost complete, apart from the crypt containing about 90 sarcophagi of the Hohenzollern dynasty. Crammed with Victorian detail, including dozens of statues of eminent German Protestants, the Dom serves as a house of worship and venue for frequent musical events such as Sunday afternoon organ recitals. Acoustics aren't too hot, though.

### Berliner Rathaus (Berlin Town Hall)
*Rathausstraße 10, Mitte, 10178 (240 10). S3, S5, S6, S7, S9/U2, U5, U8 Alexanderplatz.* **Open** 8am-6pm Mon-Fri. **Admission** free.
Berlin's town hall sits just off Alexanderplatz. This magnificent building was built during the 1860s of terracotta brick. The history of Berlin up to that point is illustrated in a series of 36 reliefs on the façade. During GDR times, it served as East Berlin's town hall – which made its nickname, 'Red Town Hall' (because of the colour of the façade), especially fitting. West Berlin's city government workers moved here from their town hall, Rathaus Schöneberg, in 1991. Guided tours are run by arrangement, phone (*24 010*) for details.

*A welcome splash of colour in former East Berlin's architectural showcase of commie kitsch, **Alexanderplatz**. See page 31.*

## Botanischer Garten (Botanical Garden)

*Königin-Luise-Straße 6-8, Zehlendorf, 14195. S1
Botanischer Garten, U9 Rathaus Steglitz.* **Open** 9am until
sunset daily. **Admission** DM4; DM2 children, students.
The Botanical Garden was landscaped at the beginning of
this century on a 42-hectare (104-acre) plot of land. Today it
is home to approximately 18,000 species of plant, and
includes 16 greenhouses and a museum with special displays
on herbs and dioramas of flowers. *See chapter* **Museums**.

## Brandenburger Tor (Brandenburg Gate)

*Pariser Platz, Mitte, 10117. S1, S2 Unter den Linden.*
Berlin's famous gate was the scene of much partying after
the Wall came down. It had been sandwiched between the
East and West walls for nearly 30 years. Constructed in 1791
and designed by Langhans, the Gate was built as a triumphal
arch celebrating the Prussian capital city. It was first called
the Friedenstor (Gate of Peace) and is the only remaining city
gate left from Berlin's original 18. (Today U-Bahn stations
are named after some of the other city gates, such as
Hallesches Tor and Schlesisches Tor.) The Quadriga statue,
designed by Schadow, that sits on top of the gate has had a
turbulent history. When Napoleon conquered the city in 1806
he decided to take the statue home with him and held it
hostage until his defeat in 1814. The Tor was later a favourite
place for Nazi rallies. It was badly damaged during World
War II and repaired in 1956-7, but then was damaged again
after everyone had partied around it in 1990.

## Charlottenburg Museums

*Schloßstraße, Charlottenburg, 10585 (32 09 12 61). U2
Sophie-Charlotte-Platz or Richard-Wagner-Platz.* **Open**
*Ägyptisches Museum and Antikenmuseum* 9am-5pm
Mon-Thur; 10am-5pm Sat, Sun. *Bröhan Museum* 10am-
6pm Tue-Sun. **Admission** DM4; DM2 children, students,
unemployed; free Sun and public holidays; free under-
sixes and school classes.
As if there weren't enough to see in Schloß Charlottenburg
across the street (*see below*), these three museums offer a
wealth of art and artefacts to look at. The **Ägyptisches
Museum** (Egyptian Museum) is dominated by the breathtaking bust of Nefertiti (the Germans call her *Nofretete*); but
other delightful treasures, like a real mummy, are also on
display. The **Antikenmuseum** (Museum of Antiquities)
keeps a wide assortment of Greek, Roman, and Etruscan
artefacts. The **Bröhan Museum** houses a medium-sized
collection of art nouveau and art deco pieces. *See chapter*
**Museums** for reviews.

## Checkpoint Charlie

*Friedrichstraße, Mitte, 10117. U6 Kochstraße or U2, U6
Stadtmitte.*
The world's most famous border crossing is now a large
carpark frequented by hawkers of Wall chunks, toy Trabis
and Commie badges. There is nothing left of the border post
except an old barrier and watchtower preserved for poster-
ity. The American Business Center at Checkpoint Charlie is
scheduled to be built here, as soon as the last landowner in
the area accepts the offer by the property developers. Just
down Friedrichstraße from where the border used to be
is the **Haus am Checkpoint Charlie**, a museum documenting the history of the Wall. *See chapter* **Museums**.

## Europa-Center

*Breitscheidplatz 5, Charlottenburg, 10789. S3, S5, S6,
S7, S9/U2, U9 Zoologischer Garten.*
The Europa-Center, a skyscraper attached to a shopping area
and cultural centre, was built in the mid-sixties and looks it.
Tacky and nasty, it houses a tourist information centre,
around 100 stores, restaurants, the largest of Berlin's many
Irish pubs, cinemas, a hotel (**Hotel Palace**, *see chapter*
**Accommodation**) and Die Stachelschweine, a cabaret. It
even contains a very posh (and expensive) swimming pool
and sauna. If you're completely mad, you can swim outside,

*The sixties-styled* **Fernsehturm**.

even in winter, as the pool is constructed so you can swim
outside and back in again. Head up to the observation platform for a dizzying look at the area. The strange sculpture
in front of the Center was erected in 1983 and has become a
congregating place for tourists, punks and others. It is officially called Weltenbornen (Fountain of the Worlds), but like
almost everything else in Berlin, it has a nickname:
Wasserklops (water meatball).

## Fernsehturm (TV Tower)

*on Alexanderplatz, Mitte, 10178 (213 33 33). S3, S5,
S6, S7, S9/U2, U5, U8 Alexanderplatz.* **Open** *Apr-Oct*
9am-11pm daily; *Nov-Mar* 8am-11pm daily; 1-11pm 2nd
and 4th Tue of the month. **Admission** DM5.
The TV Tower rises up from the space-age architecture of
Alexanderplatz. It took four years to erect the thing at the
end of the sixties. A ride to the top (DM5) gives you a great
view of the city centre. The view at night is especially fine,
particularly of the sparkling Unter den Linden, feeding into
the Brandenburg Gate. If heights make you hungry, have a
twirl in the revolving restaurant above the observation area.

## Friedrichswerdersche Kirche

*Werderscher Markt, Mitte, 10117 (208 13 23). U2
Hausvogteiplatz.* **Open** 10am-6pm Wed-Sun. **Admission**
DM4; DM2 children, students, unemployed; free Sun.
Built according to a design by Schinkel during the 1820s, the
Friedrichwerdersche church currently houses the Schinkel-

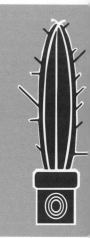

# Train Stations

Berlin's U- and S-Bahn stations offer a whole underground landscape. Märkisches Museum station on the U2 line in Mitte shows the history of Berlin in a series of relief maps, from the thirteenth-century medieval settlement until, well... not quite the present. The last map, commissioned before the Wall came down, is of Berlin in the 1980s – that is to say, East Berlin. The government only allowed their side of the city to be depicted.

Both the S- and U-Bahn stations at **Alexanderplatz** are worth a look. The S-Bahn station has a huge curving glass canopy which reaches from floor to ceiling, through which you can glimpse the trunk of the Fernsehturm (television tower, *see above*) and pieces of Alexanderplatz. The underground station, biggest on the network, has shops and stalls and art on the walls instead of ads.

Much of the western stretch of the U1 line is worth exploring. The building at **Dahlem-Dorf**, stop for all the Dahlem museums on the U2 line, is a pun: *Dorf* means small village and the station resembles a thatched country house. Strange benches on the platform are modelled as male and female forms. The **Wittenbergplatz** stop, near KaDeWe, was renovated to look like it did in the twenties, right down to the glazed-tile and art deco adverts. Many of the stations in between these two are distinctly gothic.

The stop near Schloß Charlottenburg and the nearby art museums is a work of art itself: a row of mosaics line the walls at **Richard-Wagner-Platz**, on the U7. These were salvaged from a turn-of-the-century hotel on Potsdamer Straße, the Bayernhof, shortly before it was torn down in 1975. One depicts the Tannhäuser, from Wagner's opera of the same name.

At the Spandau end of U7 things get quite postmodern. The **Zitadelle** stop is a space-age

*Trainspotting* at **Anhalter Bahnhof.**

interpretation of the nearby medieval citadel. At **Rathaus Spandau** ornate lamps hang from a very high ceiling above incredibly wide platforms. Twenty-seven stops eastwards, on a stretch which dates from the thirties, **Hermannplatz** is magnificent with its blocky pillars and lofty ceilings.

**Anhalter Bahnhof** used to be Berlin's largest train station. Now there is nothing left of the old station above ground save a small chunk of pitted façade – first it was wrecked by bombs, then blown up by city planners – and now only the S1 and S2 trains stop underground.

Museum, a collection of the artist/architect's sculptures. The neo-Gothic structure was, like almost everything else in the area, destroyed during World War II, but was successfully restored and re-opened in 1987. *See chapter* **Museums.**

### Funkturm (Radio Tower)
*Messedamm, 14055 (303 80). U2 Theodor-Heuss-Platz.* **Open** 10am-11pm daily. **Admission** DM5; DM3 children, students. DM3; DM1 students to restaurant only. The 150-metre (164-yd) Funkturm was built in 1926 and looks not unlike a smaller version of the Eiffel Tower. The Observation deck is at 126 metres (138 yds). Vertigo-sufferers should seek solace in the restaurant, which is only 55 metres (60 yds) from the ground. At the foot of the tower

is the Deutsches Rundfunkmuseum (German Broadcasting Museum): *see chapter* **Museums.**

### Gedenkstätte Deutscher Widerstand (Memorial of the German Resistance)
*Stauffenbergstraße 13-14, Tiergarten, 10785 (26 540). U2 Kurfürstenstraße.* **Open** 9am-6pm Mon-Fri; 9am-1pm Sat, Sun. **Admission** free.
An exhibition chronicling the German resistance to National Socialism is housed here. The building is part of a complex known as the Bendlerblock, which was owned by the German military from its construction in 1911 until 1945. At the back is a memorial to the conspirators killed during their attempt to assassinate Hitler at this site on July 20, 1944.

The **Berliner Dom**, *badly damaged in WWII and now almost fully restored. See page 34.*

### Gedenkstätte Plötzensee (Plötzensee Memorial)

*Hüttigpfad, Charlottenburg, 13627 (344 32 26). Bus 123.* **Open** *Mar-Sept* 8am-6pm daily; *Oct, Feb* 8.30am-5.30pm; *Nov, Jan* 9.30am-4.30pm; *Dec* 9.30am-4pm. **Admission** free.

The Nazis executed 2,500 political prisoners here. In a single night in 1943, 186 people were hanged in groups of eight. In 1952 it was declared a memorial to the victims of Fascism. There is little to see today, apart from the execution area with its meat hooks upon which victims were hung, and a small room with an exhibition of death warrants and pictures of some of the leading members of the resistance. Booklets in English are available from the information office. The stone urn near the entrance is filled with earth from National Socialist concentration camps. Today the rest of the prison is a juvenile corrective centre.

### Haus der Kulturen der Welt

*John-Foster-Dulles-Allee 10, Tiergarten, 10557 (397 87-0).* **Admission** free.

Haus der Kulturen der Welt (House of World Cultures) used to be the Kongresshalle, which was the American contribution to an international architectural exhibition held in 1957. Its roof duly collapsed in 1980, but was subsequently rebuilt. Berliners provided a nickname for the odd thing (as is their penchant): the 'pregnant oyster'. Have a bite downstairs in the café or check out one of their excellent exhibitions themed around obscure corners of global culture.

### Kaiser-Wilhelm-Gedächtniskirche (Kaiser-Wilhelm-Memorial-Church)

*Breitscheidplatz, Charlottenburg, 10789 (24 50 23). S3, S5, S6, S9/U2, U9 Zoologischer Garten.* **Open** 9am-7pm Mon-Sat; *the old tower* 9am-4pm Mon-Sat. Guided tours 1.15pm Wed-Fri. **Admission** free.

One of Berlin's best-known sights, at its most dramatic by night. The neo-Romanesque church was built at the end of the nineteenth century in honour of Kaiser Wilhelm I. Much of the structure was destroyed during an air raid in 1943. Today it serves as a stark reminder of the damage done by the war, although some might argue that the bombing has improved what was orginally a profoundly ugly structure. The ruin of the tower is flanked on either side by modern extensions made of stunning blue stained-glass windows that glow eerily at night. The square around the church, Breitscheidplatz, is a favourite hangout for punks, the homeless and more beggars wanting Kleingeld (small change).

### Karl-Marx-Allee

*Mitte, Friedrichshain, 10178, 10243. U5 Schillingstraße, Strausberger Platz, Weberwiese or Rathaus Friedrichshain.*

The GDR began building this boulevard with all due pomp in 1951, when it was known as Stalinallee, and it was workers on this project who downed tools and provoked the June 1953 uprising. Rather tatty buildings in the then current Stalinist style now line this exhilaratingly broad shopping street: it's a must for connoisseurs of Communist architecture. Western stores now have their premises here, where, in GDR times, relatively swanky eastern shops held sway.

### Kaufhaus des Westens (KaDeWe)

*Wittenbergplatz, Schöneberg, 10789 (212 10). U1, U2 Wittenbergplatz.* **Open** 9am-6.30pm Mon-Fri; 9am-2pm Sat.

'The Department Store of the West' is Germany's largest luxury department store, and is reputed to be the biggest on the Continent. It's most famous for its food hall on the sixth floor, and rightly so, even if the show of opulence is a little overpowering. The array and variety of food is mind-boggling: *Wurst*-lovers will think they have died and gone to heaven, but vegetarians should make a point of steering clear of the

# Cemeteries

Where should you leave that single red rose for Marlene Dietrich? In the Friedenauer Friedhof, a tiny cemetery in a quiet neighbourhood (*U9 Friedrich-Wilhelm-Platz*). Marlene's grave in the far right corner is so understated that it nearly fades into the background. A copper angel turned blue with age fittingly marks the row where she lies. The gravestone reads simply 'Here I stand on the marker of my days'; with the name 'Marlene' and the years 1901-1992. Berlin still seems ambivalent, at best, about the return of the star. Marlene hasn't yet been added to the list of the cemetery's famous interred – officially that is. One fan wrote on the list of the cemetery's famous dead at the entrance, 'Marlene Dietrich, the most beautiful woman in the world'. But someone else has added, 'not including her face and figure'.

Heinrich Mann, author of *Professor Unrath*, on which *The Blue Angel* was based, lies in east Berlin, in the **Friedhof der Dorotheenstädtischen und Friedrich-Werderschen Gemeinden** (*U6 Zinnowitzerstraße*). A bronze bust of Mann tops his headstone. A characteristic cigar stub can sometimes be seen balanced on the simple stone marking the grave of Bertolt Brecht and his wife Helene Weigel. Philosopher GWF Hegel and Carl Friedrich Schinkel, the architect of the Schauspielhaus (now the Konzerthaus) and the Altes Museum are also buried here.

Europe's largest Jewish cemetery is deep in east Berlin: the **Neuer Jüdischer Friedhof** in Weißensee (*U2 Schönhauser Allee, transfer to S8, S85; or S86 to Ernst Thälmann Park, then transfer to Tram 28 or 58 to Smetanastraße*). Magnificent mausoleums, some inlaid with mosaics, line the inside wall. While strolling among the shroud-like trees and ivy-entangled black gravestones, packed tightly together, look out for the grave of the Mendel family. The asymmetric white-stone memorial was designed in 1923 by Bauhaus king Walter Gropius. In Große Hamburger Straße are the remains of another Jewish cemetery, the **Alter Jüdischer Friedhof**, which was destroyed by the Nazis in 1938. A marker to the philosopher **Moses Mendelssohn** is one of the few that can still be seen.

**Haus der Kulturen der Welt** – *see page 40.*

meat departments. There are numerous places to stop, eat and drink when the sight of all that food makes you hungry; *see chapter* **Restaurants**.

## The Kreuzberg
*Kreuzberg, 10965. U6 Platz der Luftbrücke.*
Berlin's bohemian area was named after this hill (Kreuz means cross, Berg means hill), which is in turn named after the cross on the top of the monument at the summit. The **Viktoria Park** was built here at the end of the nineteenth century, complete with artificial waterfall (turned on only in the daytime and not always in winter). The memorial was designed by Schinkel to commemorate victories in the Napoleonic Wars and the summit is one of the few places where you can find a view of this flat city. It's wonderful on a sunny afternoon (although you can see more when the trees lose their leaves in winter) and a brilliant place to watch the dawn. On summer nights, the beer garden in the park, Golgotha (*see chapter* **Cafés & Bars**), can be a lot of fun.

## Marx-Engels Platz
*Mitte, 10178. S3, S5, S6, S9 Hackescher Markt.*
One of the few remaining monuments to the old boys; the

# Schinkel

Karl Friedrich Schinkel, born in 1781, was responsible for trying to give Berlin a complete and distinctive look. Schooled in the ideals of Greek architecture, he developed his own neoclassical style after principles of monumental simplicity and geometrical clarity. His journeys to Italy formed the basis for many of his designs: he would paint during his stays there and return to Berlin brimming with ideas. But the occupation of Berlin in 1806 by French troops stopped nearly all building activity and Schinkel had to work as a restaurateur.

After the French left, Friedrich Wilhelm III made Schinkel curator of monuments. In this capacity he was commissioned to build the Neue Wache on Unter den Linden, the Altes Museum (1824-30) and the Schauspielhaus (now called the Konzerthaus). The latter was built on the foundations and six Ionic columns of Langham's earlier state theatre (1800-1802), which had burned down. Designed and built from 1818-21, the Schauspielhaus is characterised by a classical simplicity in an early German neoclassical style. For the Friedrich Werder church, Schinkel proposed a classical design, but the Crown Prince argued successfully for a gothic style.

Other places to see Schinkel's work include his pavilion at Schloß Charlottenburg (1824), Viktoria Park in Kreuzberg, Schloß Glienicke and the Nikolaikirche (1830-37) in Potsdam. He died in 1841.

huge statue of Karl and Fred should be visited while it's still there. Take a seat on Karl's big lap. Surrounding the statue are bronze reliefs of members of the proletariat freeing themselves from their oppressors, and steel bars with photographic images of more of the same.

## The New Synagogue
*Oranienburger Straße 30, Mitte, 10178. S1, S2 Oranienburger Straße.*
Built during 1857-66, set on fire by the Nazis on Kristallnacht and later further destroyed by bombs, the New Synagogue is now receiving a new lease of life. The façade and wonderful dome can be viewed from the street while renovations scheduled for completion in 1995 (though still not finished as we went to press), include plans for a museum, library and exhibition inside. Although the New Synagogue is no longer a place of worship, the Adass Yisroel congregation has been revived just around the corner on Tucholskystraße. *See above* **Oranienburger Straße**, *also chapter* **By Area**.

## Nikolaiviertel
*Mitte, 10178. S3, S5, S6, S7, S9/U2, U5, U8 Alexanderplatz.*
The oldest area in Berlin, restored – some of it pretty badly – by the GDR and turned into a tourist spot full of (mostly) nasty shops and restaurants. You can visit Berlin's oldest parish church, the **Nikolaikirche**, built around 1230, or try your luck at **Zum Nußbaum**, which tends to be either very full or shut. A few yuppie restaurants and bars have opened recently in the Nikolaiviertel, including **Otello's**, a closet-sized bar with accordions covering the ceiling. The times, they have a' changed in Berlin: even Benetton has moved in, for example.

## Olympiastadion (Olympic Stadium)
*Charlottenburg, 14053 (305 81 23/304 06 76). U1 Olympia-Stadion.* **Open** 10am-5.30pm daily, except event days. **Closed** Nov to Apr. **Admission** DM3; DM1.50 children; DM2.50 concs, groups.
Built from 1934-36 for Hitler's 1936 Olympic Games (an attempt at Aryan propaganda that was gloriously sunk by Jesse Owens and other record-breaking black US athletes), the 76,000-seat stadium still hosts football games and track and field athletics, as well as rock concerts. *See box* **Nazi Architecture**; *also chapter* **By Area**.

## Palast der Republik
## (Palace of the Republic)
*Marx-Engels-Platz, Mitte, 10178. S3, S5, S6, S9 Hackescher Markt.*
Don't even think of going into this asbestos-contaminated relic of the GDR: it has been closed to the public since 1990. Built in the mid-seventies (a sadly obvious fact) as the main parliamentary chamber of the GDR, it also contained discos, bars and a bowling alley. The Palast der Republik replaced what was left of the war-ravaged Prussian castle, residence of the Kaisers. Arguments continue about whether to rebuild this Stadtschloß, as it was called, or grace the sight with some new postmodernist structure. One way or another, though, the communist Palast will soon be gone.

## Pfaueninsel (Peacock Island)
*in der Havel, Zehlendorf, 14109 (805 30 42). Bus 216 or 316 to ferry at Nikolskoer Weg.* **Ferries** run hourly from 8am-6pm daily.
This 98-hectare (242-acre) non-smoking island in the Havel River is part of the Potsdam complex (though within Berlin's borders) and was developed at the behest of Friedrich Great and his successors in the eighteenth and nineteenth

*The* **Reichstag***: waiting for the arrival of the government. See page 44.*

*Lime trees once lined east Berlin's Prussian boulevard* **Unter den Linden***. See page 34.*

centuries. It's a peaceful place for a walk, landscaped in the English fashion, complete with fake ruins and odd fountains. Once a menagerie, now only a few peacocks remain. It is reached by Berlin's shortest ferry ride. *See chapter* **Trips Out Of Town**.

## Philharmonie

*Matthäikirchstraße 1, Tiergarten, 10785 (25 48 80). S1, S2, U2 Potsdamer Platz.*
A bizarre architectural wonder, the Philharmonie is home to the world-renowned Berlin Philharmonic Orchestra and is famous for offering near-perfect acoustics and views from all of its 2,200 seats. Free guided tours (in German only) can be arranged (phone 25 48 81 24 for details). *See chapter* **Music: Classical & Opera**.

## Reichstag

*Platz der Republik, Tiergarten, 10557 (397 70). S1, S2 Unter den Linden.* **Open** 10am-5pm Tue-Sun.
**Admission** free (for exhibition and Plenarsaal). Tours of the Reichstag must be arranged in advance.
Designed by Frankfurt architect Paul Wallot, in Italian High Renaissance style, the Reichstag was completed in 1894 to house the government of Bismarck's united Germany. It was burned on February 17, 1933 – an event the Nazis may or may not have organised themselves, but nonetheless blamed on the Dutchman Marius van der Lubbe and certainly used as an excuse to clamp down on Communists and suspend basic freedoms. The war left the building a ruin, which it remained until 1970. If the current building doesn't resemble its old photographs, that's because it still remains bare both of much elaborate ornamentation and the dome, which was blown up in 1957 and never rebuilt. Today it is still home to the interesting exhibition Questions of German History.

The parliament will move here when it finally leaves Bonn, by which time it will have been revamped and extended by Norman Foster. *See chapter* **Museums**.

## Schloß Charlottenburg

*Luisenplatz, 10585 (32 09 11). U2 Sophie-Charlotte-Platz or U7 Richard-Wagner-Platz.* **Open** 10am-5pm Tue-Sun.
**Admission** *multiple ticket* (palace, pavilion, Belvedere) DM8; DM3 students; DM4 groups of 15 or more; *single tickets* (palace only) DM4; DM1.50 students; DM2.50 groups; free under-14s.
Schloß Charlottenburg is the most important surviving Prussian palace. It was built in many phases from 1695-1790 and is now the site of a number of exhibitions. The **Schinkel-Pavilion**, containing an exhibition on the architect, was designed by him and completed in 1825. The **Belvedere** was designed as a teahouse in 1788 and houses an exhibition of KPM porcelain. Interred in the Mausoleum are the remains of Kaiser Wilhelm I and assorted other Hohenzollerns (only open from April to October). *See also chapter* **Museums**.

## Schlösser & Park Glienicke (Glienicke Palaces)

*on the Königstraße, Zehlendorf, 14109 (805 30 41). Bus 116.* **The palace is closed to the public at time of writing; phone for details.**
Glienicke Palace was built from 1826-32 from designs by Schinkel for Prince Carl of Prussia. It was closed at the time of writing and its reopening date is unknown. However, the park is open and the Palace can be viewed from the Italianate gardens. The **Glienicker Brücke**, a bridge built in 1909, was famous as the location for East-West spy exchanges. *See also chapter* **Trips Out of Town**.

### Shell House

*corner of Reichpietschufer and Stauffenbergstraße,*
*Tiergarten, 10785. U1 Kurfürstenstraße.*
Designed by Emil Fahrenkamp in 1932, the Shell House,
these days offices for the electricity company BEWAG, is a
curvaceous architectural masterpiece. It somehow managed
to survive the war, but is not standing up to the march of
time too well. The undulating façade is currently being
restored. Essential viewing for fans of twentieth-century
architecture.

### Siegessäule

*Straße des 17 Juni, Tiergarten, 10785 (391 29 61). S3,*
*S5, S6, S9 Bellevue.* **Open** 1-5.30pm Mon; 9am-6pm Tue-
Sat; last admission 5.30pm. **Admission** DM1.50; DM1
students.
The Siegessäule (victory column) was built from 1871-73 to
commemorate the Prussian campaigns against Denmark
(1864), Austria (1866) and France (1870-71). On top of the column is an eight-metre (26-foot) high gilded Goddess of
Victory by sculptor Friedrich Drake. Until 1938 the statue

# Nazi Architecture

Hitler and his pet architect Albert Speer had
grandiose plans for Berlin – or Germania, as
it was to be renamed. Once the rest of the
world had been subjugated, the capital of the
Thousand Year Reich would be equipped with
dinky features such as a monstrous hall with a
dome 16 times the size of St Peter's in Rome,
a triumphal arch three times as tall as the one in
Paris, a chancellery that would require visiting
diplomats to take a chastening quarter-
mile hike once inside the building, and a
Führer's palace no less than 150 times the size
of Bismarck's.

Well, war put a stop to all that and Allied
bombs demolished much of what the Nazis
actually did build. Some fine examples of fancy
fascist architecture did, however, survive. Fans
of tyrannical town-planning might start with
**Flughafen Tempelhof** (*Tempelhofer Damm,*
*U6 Platz der Luftbrücke*). Originally opened in
1923, this was greatly expanded by the Nazis
and had its place in Speer's plan for Germania.
Not only the largest building in Berlin but
one of the largest in the world, its 400-metre
quarter-circle form is probably best appreciated
from the air. At ground level it's impossible to
take in all at once.

Somehow the **Luftfahrtsministerium** – the
Nazi air ministry (*corner of Leipziger Straße and*
*Wilhelm Straße, U2, S1, S2 Potsdamer Platz*) –
survived wartime bombardment and went on to
house various East German ministries until the
Wall came down and the Treuhand moved in.
Overbearing and bureaucratic, this is totalitari-
an architecture at its bleakest. The finance ministry is now scheduled to set up house here when
it arrives from Bonn.

The **Olympiastadion** in Neu-Westend (*see*
*listing*), the set for Leni Riefenstahl's least boring film *Olympiad*, orchestrates height, space
and enclosure in a way that is both chilling and
thrilling. Built as a Nazi showpiece for the world
on the occasion of the 1936 Olympics, this
actually does what fascist architecture was
intended to do: impress.

**Flughafen Tempelhof** *– opened in 1923.*

Other remants of the Third Reich include
offices around Fehrbelliner Platz (*U1, U7*
*Fehrbelliner Platz*) which are now used by the
city Senate; the Finanzamt at Bismarkstraße 48
(*U2 Bismarckstraße*), where the Nazi eagle now
clutches the street number instead of a swastika;
the Reichsbank building at Werderscher Markt
in Mitte (*U2 Hausvogteiplatz*); and the ruins of
the Gestapo HQ at the **Topography of Terror**
(*see listing*).

There are also assorted blank, grey concrete
Nazi bunkers around town, including one on
Pallasstraße near the junction with Potsdamer
Straße which Wim Wenders used in *Wings Of*
*Desire*, and one in Mitte which is now a techno
club called... Bunker (*see chapter* **Clubs**).

was in the Platz der Republik, but was moved to the round-about on Hitler's orders. He had plans to knock down the Reichstag and build a new complex of buildings. The Großer Stern (big star) is the name given to the star-shaped round-about which circles the column. Climb the 285-step spiral staircase to the viewing platform for a glorious panoramic view. The monument was used to great cinematic effect in Wim Wenders' last halfway decent movie *Wings Of Desire*.

### Sowjetisches Ehrenmal im Tiergarten (Soviet War Memorial)

*Straße des 17 Juni, Tiergarten, 10557. S1, S2 Unter den Linden.*
Built during 1945-6 from marble that came from Hitler's Reich chancellery, the Soviet War Memorial is crowned with a bronze Soviet soldier. The two tanks on either side were supposedly the first Soviet tanks to reach Berlin in World War II. Until recently, it was guarded by two Russian soldiers who were in turn guarded by two Allied soldiers.

### Stadtmauer (City Wall)

*Littenstraße/Waisenstraße, Mitte, 10179. U2 Klosterstraße.*
Long before the infamous Wall, Berlin had another wall; the medieval city wall of the original thirteenth- to fourteenth-century settlement. There's almost as much left of this wall as there is of the more recent one. Built along the wall is the old (and extremely popular) restaurant **Zur Letzten Instanz**. There has been a restaurant on this site since 1525.

### Tiergarten

*Tiergarten, 10785. S3, S5, S6, S7, S9 Tiergarten.*
Hunting grounds of the Prussian electors since the sixteenth century, the Tiergarten was turned into a park in the eighteenth century. During the war, bombs damaged much of it, and in the desperate winter of 1945-6 almost all the trees that were left were cut down for firewood. The park was left as a depressing collection of wrecked monuments and sorry-looking shrubbery interspersed with vegetable plots. Rehabilitation began in 1949 with the symbolic planting of a young lime tree by then mayor Ernst Reuter. Some of the trees were donated by Queen Elizabeth II. A stone on the Großer Weg, the large path in the park, is inscribed with names of the German towns that contributed trees. Today the Tiergarten is one of the largest city parks in Europe. Take a stroll on the lovely Löwenbrücke (Lion Bridge), which is marked by four huge iron lions, or just get lost roaming through the 167-hectare (412-acre) park. *See also chapter* **By Area**.

### Treptower Park

*Treptow, 12435. S6, S8, S9, S10 Treptower Park.*
Treptower Park is home to a huge, sobering monument to the Soviet soldiers who died in the war against Hitler, as well as a mass grave for 5,000 of them. As you walk down the tree-lined avenue you arrive at a statue of Mother Russia, weeping for her dead children. Fascinating if heavy-handed white stone reliefs, set up almost as stations of the cross and bearing quotations from Stalin, depict the story of how the Soviets triumphed over Fascism. On top of the tomb at the far end of the park is a huge statue of a valiant, square-jawed Soviet soldier, clasping a child in one arm, and with the other smashing a swastika.

### Volkspark Friedrichshain

*Friedrichshain, 10249. S8, S10 Landsberger Allee.*
A huge park with assorted bits of socialist realist art, an open-air stage and an early twentieth-century fountain of fairy tale characters among lush greenery. The graves of the fighters who fell in March 1848 in the battle for German Unity are here.

### Zitadelle Spandau

*Am Juliusturm, Spandau, 13599 (339 11). U7 Zitadelle.* **Open** 9am-5pm Tue-Sun. **Admission** DM1.50.

Spandau's old citadel was constructed from 1560-94. The Julius tower, a romantic Italian Renaissance-style tower on the banks of the Havel, remains today. Make it a day trip: *see chapter* **Trips Out Of Town**.

### Zoologischer Garten (Zoo)

*Hardenbergplatz 8, Tiergarten, 10787 (25 40 10). S3, S5, S6, S7, S9/U2, U9 Zoologischer Garten.* **Open** *zoo* 9am-6.30pm daily summer, 9am-dusk winter; *aquarium* 9am-6pm daily. **Admission** *zoo* DM10, DM5 children, DM8 students; *aquarium* DM9, DM4.50 children, DM7.50 students; *combined* DM15, DM7 children, DM12 students.
The Zoological Garden, Germany's oldest zoo, opened in 1844. With 16,000 animals from 1,700 species, it is by some way the largest in the world. It is also one of the most important. The aquarium is also one of the world's most varied, including more than 500 species displayed in four sections: Oceanic, Freshwater, a Crocodile Hall and an Insectarium.

## Tours

If you feel overwhelmed by the scope of Berlin's offerings, you could let someone do the tourist planning for you. Three big agencies that can help are **Severin + Kuhn, Berolina Berlin** and **Berliner Bären Stadtrundfahrt**. Tours are pretty much the same and take you to all of Berlin's greatest hits. Two-hour tours cost DM30, three-hour tours cost DM41 and four-hour tours cost DM45.

Nightclub tours are another option. Severin + Kuhn offers a four-hour evening for DM99 that includes the cost of the show and a drink. At Berolina there are two options: three and a half hours for DM90 or four and a half hours for DM108. Berliner Bären has the biggest: two nightclubs in five and a half hours for DM95. All three also offer day-trips to Potsdam for DM49. Summertime trips to places such as Dresden and the Spreewald are also offered.

**Severin + Kuhn** *Kurfürstendamm 216, Wilmersdorf, 10719 (883 1015). U15 Uhlandstraße.* **Open** 9am-6pm daily. **No credit cards.**
**Berolina Berlin** *Meineckestraße 3, Charlottenburg 17219 (883 3131). U9, U15 Kurfürstendamm.* **Open** 8am-6pm Mon-Fri; 8.30am-11.30am Sat. **Credit** AmEx, V.
**Berliner Bären Stadtrundfahrt** *Rankestraße 35, Charlottenburg, 10789 (213 4077). U9, U15 Kurfürstendamm.* **Open** 8.30am-6pm Mon-Fri. **Credit** AmEx, DC, EC, MC, V.

## Boat and Walking Tours

For a different view of Berlin, see it from its many canals. Being flat, it is also a very good walking city and pedestrian-paced tours are ideal for taking in the city's history.

Two firms offer boat trips, **Horst Duggen** and **Stern und Kreisschifffahrt.** Trips can last from three to 12 hours and go all over the city. Most interesting are the longer trips, such as the four-hour tour from Charlottenburg to Spandau or from the Kongresshalle out to the Müggelsee.

**Treptower Park** – *monument to Soviet dead.*

Prices start at DM10 and range up to DM50. Boat tours are offered between April and October. Boats leave from Jannowitzbrücke, Treptow, Wannsee, Tegel, Spandau and Potsdam.

'Discover Berlin' walking tours (DM10, DM8 students) with an English-speaking guide are run twice weekly – 10.30am, 2.30pm, Mon, Fri – by **Berlin Walks**, who offer a two-and-a-half-hour route from the Gedächtniskirche to Alexanderplatz and all historic points in between, including the Reichstag and the site of Hitler's bunker. The same company offers more specialised routes – 'Infamous Third Reich Sites' (Mon, Thur, Sat), 'Where Was The Wall'? (Tue, Fri, Sun) – at around DM15, with reductions for students from April through October. Other options include private or motorised tours.

**Horst Duggen** *An der Kongresshalle, Moabit, 10557 (394 4954/218 9933). S3, S5, S6, S9 Lehrter Stadtbahnhof/S1, S2 Unter den Linden.* **Open** *Mar-Oct* 9am-6pm Mon-Fri. **No credit cards.**

**Stern und Kreisschifffahrt** *Puschkinallee 16-17, Treptow, 12435 (61 73 90-0). S6, S8, S9, S10 Treptower Park.* **Open** 7.30am-4pm daily. **No credit cards.**

**Berlin Walks** *Eislebenerstraße 1, Charlottenburg, 10789 (211 66 63).* Contact Nick Gay or any Berlin Tourist Office for further information (*Apr-Oct*). **No credit cards.**

**Unter den Linden** – *thou shalt not jaywalk.*

# Die Mauer (The Wall)

In East German officialese it was known as the 'Anti-Fascist Protection Barrier'; in West Berlin it was simply Die Mauer; to the rest of the world it was the Berlin Wall. A historical reality made implacably concrete, for 28 years it snaked 97 miles (155km) around the perimeter of West Berlin. Eighty people were shot trying to get over it, one of the most secure frontiers in the world. Star of stage, screen and radio, and handy backdrop for visiting politicians, it achieved the status of global symbol long before it was breached on November 9, 1989.

And now there is bugger all left of it.

Five years later, you still occasionally get those jarring moments when you realise you've slipped from west to east. The lampposts change shape. There are fewer people on the streets, fewer bars and shops. But as time goes by and Berlin slowly knits together, the border gets harder to notice, the transition becomes ever more seamless.

As for actual bits of Wall, the most central surviving stretch runs along Niederkirchner Straße, just off Wilhelmstraße (*U2, S1, S2 Potsdamer Platz*), between the Luftfahrtsministerium and the Topograpy of Terror (*see chapter* **Museums**). It's a pock-marked piece, a block or two long, much of it chipped away by tourists with hammers, and now protected by a wire fence.

A longer stretch, now known as the East Side Gallery and commemorating the Wall's traditional function as graffiti canvas, can be found along Mühlenstraße by the river Spree (*S3, S5, S6, S9 Berlin Hauptbahnhof*). This is decked by mostly political work from various international artists and is billed as the world's largest outdoor picture gallery.

From the S-Bahn lines running across the Spree west of Friedrichstraße, you can see a length of Wall, graphically divided into 28 segments, each of them representing a year from 1961-1989. For each year there is a body count of people killed trying to get over. If you want to view this at ground level, it's at the corner of Reinhardstraße and Schiffsbauerdamm (*S1, S2 Unter Den Linden*).

There are also small hunks of Wall all over town. A few displaced slabs are still lying around on Potsdamer Platz. There's a piece at one of the Tauentzienstraße entrances to the Europa-Center and another in Pariser Platz outside the Akademie der Kunst building. Various hotel lobbies also boast their very own chunks of Wall. Lo, how the mighty has fallen.

# History

# Key Events

## Ascanians to Prussians

**1237** Cölln first mentioned in a church document.
**1307** The towns of Berlin and Cölln officially united under the rule of the Ascanian family.
**1319** Last of the Ascanians dies.
**1359** Berlin joins the Hanseatic League.
**1411** Friedrich of Hohenzollern is sent by the Holy Roman Emperor to bring peace to the region.
**1447-48** The 'Berlin Indignation'. The population rebels and locks Friedrich II and his courtiers out of the city.
**1535** Accession of Joachim I Nestor, the first Elector to embrace Protestantism. The Reformation arrives in Berlin.
**1538** Work begins on the Stadtschloß.
**1618-48** Berlin and Brandenburg are ravaged by the Thirty Years War – the population is halved.
**1640-88** Reign of Friedrich Wilhelm, the Grand Elector.
**1662-68** Construction of the Oder-Spree canal.
**1672** Jewish and Huguenot refugees begin to arrive in Berlin.
**1695** Work begins on Schloß Charlottenburg.
**1701** Elector Friedrich III, son of the Grand Elector, has himself crowned Friedrich I, King of Prussia. Work begins on the German and French cathedrals at the Gendarmenmarkt.
**1713-40** Reign of King Friedrich Wilhelm, who expands the army and gives Berlin the character of a garrison city.
**1740-86** Reign of Friedrich II – Frederick the Great – a time of construction, military expansion and administrative reform.
**1788-91** Construction of the Brandenburg Gate by Karl Gottfried Langhans for King Friedrich Wilhelm II. Johann Schadow adds the Quadriga.
**1806** Napoleon marches into Berlin on October 27. Two years of French occupation. The Quadriga is shipped to Paris.
**1810** Wilhelm von Humboldt founds the university.
**1813** Napoleon is defeated at Grossbeeren and Leipzig.
**1814** General Blücher brings the Quadriga back to Berlin and restores it on the Brandenburg Gate.

## Biedermeier to Bismarck

**1837** Foundation of the Borsig Werke marks the beginning of Berlin's expansion into Continental Europe's largest industrial city.
**1838** First railway line, from Berlin to Potsdam.
**1840** Friedrich Wilhelm IV accedes to the throne. With a population of around 400,000, Berlin is the fourth largest city in Europe.
**1848** The 'March Revolution' breaks out. Berlin briefly in the hands of the revolutionaries.
**1861** Accession of King Wilhelm I.
**1862** Appointment of Otto von Bismarck as Prime Minister of Prussia.
**1871** Following victory in the Franco-Prussian war, King Wilhelm I is proclaimed German Emperor and Berlin becomes the Imperial capital.

## The Fall of Empire

**1879** Electric lighting comes to Berlin, which also boasts the world's first electric railway. Three years later telephone services are introduced. The city emerges as Europe's most modern metropolis.
**1888** Kaiser Wilhelm II comes to the throne.
**1890** Kaiser Wilhelm II sacks Bismarck.

*Berlin, June 1939, on the eve of war.*

**1894** Completion of the Reichstag.
**1902** First underground line is opened.
**1914-18** World War I.
**1918** On November 9, Kaiser Wilhelm abdicates, Philip Scheidemann proclaims Germany a republic and Karl Liebknecht declares Germany a socialist republic. Chaos ensues.
**1919** Spartacist uprising is suppressed by the Freikorps.
**1920** Attempted right-wing coup lead by Wolfgang Kapp.
**1923** Hyperinflation – one dollar is worth 4.2 billion marks.
**1926** Joseph Goebbels comes to Berlin to take charge of the local Nazi party organisation.
**1927** Berlin boasts more than 70 cabarets and nightclubs.
**1933** Hitler takes power.

## The Nazi Years

**1936** The 11th Olympic Games are held in Berlin.
**1938** Kristallnacht, November 9. Jewish homes, businesses and synagogues in Berlin are stoned, looted and set ablaze.
**1939** Outbreak of World War II, during which Berlin suffers appalling devastation.
**1944** A group around Colonel Count von Stauffenberg attempts to assassinate Hitler. Most are subsequently executed at Plötzensee prison.
**1945** Germany signs unconditional surrender on May 8.

## Post-War Berlin

**1948-49** The Berlin Blockade. The Soviets cut off all transport links to west Berlin. For 11 months the city is supplied by the Allied Airlift.
**1949** Foundation of Federal Republic in May and of the German Democratic Republic on October 7.
**1953** The June 17 uprising in East Berlin is suppressed.
**1958** Krushchev issues the 'Berlin Ultimatum'.
**1961** The Wall goes up on August 13.
**1965** Students stage a sit-down protest on the Ku'damm.
**1968** Student leader Rudi Dutschke is shot.
**1971** Erich Honecker succeeds Walter Ulbricht as East German head of state. Signing of the Quadrapartite Agreement formalises Berlin's divided status.
**1980-81** The 'Hot Winter' of violent protest by squatters.
**1987** East and West celebrate Berlin's 750th birthday.
**1989** On November 9, the Wall comes down.

# Ascanians to Prussians

**Rising out of a swamp in the Middle Ages, Berlin thrived as a trading post, switched on to the Enlightenment and finally became the centre of an Empire.**

Berlin's origins are neither remarkable nor auspicious. It emerged some time in the twelfth century from swamp-lands that pioneering German knights had wrested from the Slavs. The name Berlin is believed to be derived from the Slav word *birl*, meaning swamp.

Located on either side of the Spree river, Berlin and its twin settlement Cölln (on what is now Museum Island) were founded as trading posts half-way between the older fortress towns of Spandau and Köpenick. Today the borough of Mitte embraces Cölln and old Berlin, and Spandau and Köpenick are outlying suburbs. The town's existence was first recorded in 1237, when Cölln was mentioned in a church document.

The Ascanian family, who held the title of Margraves of Brandenburg, ruled over the twin towns and the surrounding region. Eager to encourage trade, they granted special rights to merchants with the result that Berlin and Cölln emerged as prosperous trading centres linking east and west Europe. In 1307 the two towns were officially united. In the thirteenth century, construction began on the **Marienkirche** and **Nikolaikirche**, both of which still stand. The latter gave its name to the **Nikolaiviertel**.

The early years of prosperity came to an end in 1319 with the death of the last Ascanian ruler. This opened the way for robber barons from the outlying regions, eager to take control. However, despite political upheaval and the threat of invasion, Berlin's merchants did manage to continue business. In 1359 the city joined the Hanseatic League of free-trading European cities (more prominent members were Hamburg and London).

## ROMAN AROUND

The threat of invasion remained. Towards the end of the fourteenth century two powerful families, the Dukes of Pommerania and the notoriously brutal von Quitzow brothers, began to vie for control of the city. Salvation came with Friedrich of Hohenzollern, a nobleman from southern Germany sent by the Holy Roman Emperor in 1411 to bring peace to the region. Initially, Friedrich was well received. The bells of the Marienkirche were melted down to be made into weapons for the fight against the aggressors. (In a strange echo of history, the bells were again transformed into tools of war in 1917, in the reign of Kaiser Wilhelm II, the last of the Hohenzollerns to rule.) Having defeated the Quitzow brothers, Friedrich officially became Margrave. In 1416 he took the title of Elector of Brandenburg, denoting his right to vote in the election of the Holy Roman Emperor.

But with peace and stability came the gradual loss of Berlin's independent traditions as Friedrich consolidated his power. In 1442 foundations were laid for the Berlin castle and a royal court was founded. Disputes began to erupt between the patrician classes (representing trade) and the guilds (representing crafts).

Increasing social friction culminated in the 'Berlin Indignation' of 1447-48 when the population rose up in rebellion. Friedrich's son (Friedrich II) and his courtiers were locked out of the city and the foundations of the castle were flooded. But the uprising collapsed and the Hohenzollerns returned triumphant. While merchants were forced to shoulder new restrictions, courtiers were exempted from communal jurisdiction. The city began to lose economic impetus and Berlin was transformed from an outlying trading post to a small-sized capital (in 1450 the population was 6,000).

## Reformation & Debauchery

The Reformation arrived in Berlin and Brandenburg under the reign of Joachim I Nestor (1535-71), the first Elector to embrace Protestantism. Joachim strove to improve the cultural standing of Berlin by inviting artists, architects and theologians to work in the city. In 1538 Caspar Theyss and Konrad Krebbs, two master-builders from Saxony, began work on a Renaissance-style palace. The building took a hundred years to complete and evolved into the bombastic Stadtschloß which stood on the Spree island until the East German government demolished it in 1950.

Joachim's studious nature was not reflected in the behaviour of his subjects. In a foretaste of Berlin's later reputation for debauchery and decadence, self-indulgence characterised life in the late sixteenth-century city. Repeated attempts to clamp down on excessive drinking, gambling and loose morals had little effect. Visiting the city, Abbot Trittenheim remarked that 'the people are good, but rough and unpolished, they prefer stuffing themselves to good science'.

After stuffing itself with another 6,000 people, Berlin left the sixteenth century with a population of 12,000 – double that of a hundred years earlier.

## War & Reconstruction

The outbreak of the Thirty Years War in 1618 dragged Berlin on to the wider political stage. Although initially unaffected by the conflict between Catholic forces loyal to the Holy Roman Empire and the Swedish-backed Protestant armies, Berlin was eventually caught up in the war which was to leave the German-speaking states ravaged, divided and weakened for over two centuries. In 1626 Imperial troops occupied Berlin and plundered the city. In the following years Berlin was repeatedly sacked and forced to pay taxes to the occupying forces. Trade collapsed and its hinterland was laid waste. To top it all, there were four epidemics between 1626 and 1631 which claimed thousands of lives. By the time the war ended in 1648, Berlin had lost a third of its housing stock, the population had fallen to less than 6,000 and municipal coffers were greatly depleted.

### GOING DUTCH

Painstaking reconstruction was carried out under the reign of Friedrich Wilhelm (later known as the Grand Elector). He succeeded his father in 1640, but chose to see out the war in exile. Influenced by Dutch ideas on town-planning and architecture, Friedrich Wilhelm embarked on a policy that linked urban regeneration, economic expansion and solid defence. New fortifications around the city were built and a garrison of 2,000 soldiers set up. In the centre of town, the **Lustgarten** was laid out opposite the palace. Running west from the palace the first Lindenallee (avenue of lime trees: Unter den Linden) was created. To revive the economy, housing and property taxes were abolished in favour of a modern-style sales tax. With the money raised, three new towns – Friedrichswerder, Dorotheenstadt and Friedrichstadt – were built. (Together with Berlin and Cölln these now make up the Mitte borough.) In the late 1660s a canal linked the Spree and Oder rivers, confirming Berlin's position as an east-west trading centre.

But Friedrich Wilhelm's most inspired policy

**Friedrich the Great** – *Voltaire's patron.*

was to encourage refugees to settle in the city. First to arrive were over 50 Jewish families from Vienna. In 1672 Protestant Huguenot settlers arrived from France. The influence of the new arrivals was pronounced, bringing new skills and industries.

### A LA FRANÇAISE

The growing cosmopolitan mix laid the foundations for a flowering of intellectual and artistic life. By the time the Grand Elector's son Friedrich III took the throne in 1688 one fifth of Berlin's population spoke French. This legacy can be seen in the many French words that pepper Berlin dialect, such as *Boulette* (hamburger) and *Etage* (floor).

In 1695 work began on **Schloß Charlottenburg** to the west of Berlin. A year later the Academy of Arts was founded. And in 1700, intellectual life was further stimulated by the founding of the Academy of Sciences under Gottfried Leibniz. The construction of the German and French cathedrals at the **Gendarmenmarkt** in 1701 gave Berlin one of its most beautiful squares. Five years later the **Zeughaus** (Armoury) on Unter den Linden was completed.

In 1701 Elector Friedrich III took a step up the hierarchy of European nobility when he had himself crowned Prussian King Friedrich I (not to be confused with the earlier Elector). In little more than half a century, Berlin had progressed from a devastated town to a thriving commercial centre with a population of nearly 30,000.

## Enlightened Despotism

The association of Prussia with militarism can broadly be traced back to the eighteenth century and the efforts of two men: King Friedrich Wilhelm I and his son Friedrich II, also known as Friedrich the Great. Although they hated each other and had vastly different sensibilities (Friedrich Wilhelm was boorish and mean, his son sensitive and philosophical), together they launched Prussia as a major military power and in the process gave Berlin the character of a garrison city.

King Friedrich Wilhelm (1713-40) made parsimony and militarism state policy – and almost succeeded in driving Berlin's economy into the ground. The only thing that grew was the army, which by 1740 numbered 80,000 troops. Many of these were deployed in Berlin and billeted in the houses of ordinary citizens.

With a king more interested in keeping the books than reading them, intellectual life suffered. Friedrich had no use for art, so he closed down the Academy of Arts: a collector of soldiers he swopped rare Oriental vases with the King of Saxony for a regiment. The Tsar got a small gold ship in exchange for 150 Russian giants.

The obsession with all things military did, however, have some positive effects. The king needed competent soldiers, so he made school attendance compulsory; the army needed doctors, so he set up medical institutes. Eventually Berlin's economy also picked up on the back of demand from the military. City administration was reformed. Skilled immigrants (this time mostly from Saxony) met the increased demands. The result was a population boom (from 60,000 in 1713 to 90,000 in 1740) and a growth in trade and manufacturing.

### RUSSIAN ABOUT

While his father collected soldiers, Friedrich the Great deployed them in a series of wars with Austria and Russia (from 1740-42, 1744-45 and 1756-63, the Seven Years War) in a bid to win territory in Silesia in the east. Initially, the wars proved disastrous. The Austrians occupied the city in 1757, the Russians in 1760. But with a mixture of luck and military genius, Friedrich finally emerged victorious from the Seven Years War.

When not fighting, the king devoted his time to forging a modern state apparatus (he called himself 'first servant of the state'; Berliners called him 'Old Fritz') and transforming Berlin and Potsdam. This was partly due to conviction – the king was friends with Voltaire and brought him to live at Potsdam, and Old Fritz saw himself very much as an aesthetically minded Enlightenment figure – but was also a political necessity. He needed to convince enemies and subjects that even in times of national crisis he was able to afford grand projects.

So Unter den Linden was made into a grand boulevard. At the palace end, the Forum Fredericianum, constructed by the architect von Knobelsdorff, comprised the St Hedwigskathedrale, the opera house, the Prince Heinrich Palace (now the Humboldt University) and the state library. Although never completed, the Forum remains one of Berlin's main attractions.

To the west of Berlin, the Tiergarten was landscaped and a new palace, the Schloß Bellevue (now the Berlin residence of the German president), was built. Friedrich also decided to replace a set of barracks at the Gendarmenmarkt by a theatre, now called the **Schauspielhaus**.

To encourage manufacturing and industry, advantageous excise laws were introduced. Businesses such as the KPM (Königliche Porzellan-Manufacture) porcelain works were nationalised and turned into prestigious, lucrative enterprises. Legal and administrative reforms also characterised Friedrich's reign. Religious freedom was enshrined in law; torture was abolished; and Berlin became a centre of the Enlightenment. Cultural and intellectual life blossomed around figures such as Moses Mendelssohn the philosopher and Gottfried Lessing the poet. By the time Friedrich died in 1786, Berlin had a population of 150,000 and was the capital of one of Europe's grand powers.

## Overture to Empire

The death of Friedrich the Great also marked the end of the Enlightenment in Prussia. His successor, Friedrich Wilhelm II, was more interested in spending money on architecture than wasting his time with political thought. Censorship was stepped up and the king's extravagance plunged the state into an economic and financial crisis. By 1788 over 14,000 people in the city were dependent on state and church aid. The state apparatus began to crumble under the weight of incompetent and greedy administrators. When he died in 1797, Friedrich Wilhelm II left his son with huge debts.

However, the old king's expensive love of classicism left Berlin with its most famous monument: the **Brandenburg Gate**. It was built by Karl Gottfried Langhans in 1789, the year of the French Revolution. Two years later, Johann Schadow added the Quadriga, a sculpture of a bare-chested

Victoria riding a chariot drawn by four horses. Originally one of 14 gates marking Berlin's boundaries, the Brandenburg Gate is now the geographical and symbolic centre of the city.

If the king did not care for intellect, then the emerging bourgeoisie did. Towards the turn of the century, Berlin became a centre of German Romanticism. Literary salons flourished, and remained a feature of Berlin's cultural life into the middle of the nineteenth century. Despite censorship, Berlin still had a platform for liberal expression. The city's newspapers welcomed the French Revolution so enthusiastically that in the southern German states Jacobins were referred to as 'Berliners'.

**The Brandenburg Gate** – *built in 1789.*

## Invasion & Reform

In 1806 Berlin came face to face with the effects of revolution in France: following the defeat of the Prussian forces in the battles of Jena and Auerstadt on October 14, Napoleon's army headed for Berlin. The king and queen fled to Königsberg and the garrison was removed from the city. On October 27 Napoleon marched through the Brandenburg Gate. Once again Berlin was an occupied city.

Almost immediately, Napoleon set about changing the political and administrative structure. He called together 2,000 prominent citizens and told them to elect a new administration, the *Comité Administratif*, which oversaw the city's day-to-day administration until the French troops left in 1808.

Napoleon decreed that property belonging to the state, the Hohenzollerns and many aristocratic families be expropriated. Works of art were removed from palaces in Berlin and Potsdam and sent to France: even the Quadriga was taken from the Brandenburg Gate and shipped to Paris. The city also suffered financially. With nearly 30,000 French troops stationed in the city, Berliners had no choice but to supply them with accommodation and food. On top of this came war reparations.

When the French left, reform-minded aristocrats seized the opportunity to introduce a series of wide-ranging reforms in a bid to modernise the Prussian state. One key aspect was the clear separation of state and civic responsibility, which gave Berlin independence to manage its own affairs. A new council, based loosely on the *Comité Administratif*, was elected (though only property owners and the wealthy were entitled to vote). In 1810 the philosopher Wilhelm von Humboldt (*see* chapter **Students**) founded the university. Remaining restrictions on the Jewish population were removed. Other reforms included the introduction of a simplified sales tax. A 'trade police' was established to monitor trading standards. Generals Scharnhorst and Gneisenau overhauled the army.

Although the French occupied Berlin again in 1812 on their way home from the Russian campaign, they were met with stiff resistance. A year later the Prussian king joined the anti-Napoleon coalition. Thousands of Berliners signed up. When Napoleon tried to capture the city once more, he was defeated at Grossbeeren. This, together with a defeat for the French in the Battle of Leipzig, marked the end of Napoleonic rule in Germany.

In August 1814, General Blücher brought the Quadriga back to Berlin, and restored it to its place on the Brandenburg Gate. One symbolic addition was made: an Iron Cross and a Prussian eagle were added to the staff in Victoria's hand.

### Brandenburger Tor (Brandenburg Gate)
*Pariser Platz, Mitte, 10117. S1, S2 Unter den Linden.*

### Gendarmenmarkt
*Mitte, 10117. U6 Französische Straße.*

### Konzerthaus
*Gendarmenmarkt, Mitte, 10117 (203 0921). U6 Französische Straße.* **Open** for tours, by arrangement.

### Lustgarten
*Unter den Linden, Mitte, 10178. S1, S3, S5, S6, S9/U6 Friedrichstraße.*

### Marienkirche
*Karl-Liebknecht-Straße 8, Mitte, 10178 (242 44 67). S3, S5, S6, S7, S9/U2, U8 Hackescher Markt.* **Open** 10am-5pm Mon-Thur, Sat. **Admission** free. **Tours** 1pm Mon-Thur.

### Nikolaikirche
*Nikolaikirchplatz, Mitte, 10178 (23 80 90 81). U2 Klosterstraße.* **Open** 10am-5.30pm Tue-Sun. **Admission** DM3; DM1 concs.

### Nikolaiviertel
*Mitte, 10178. S3, S5, S6, S7, S9/U2, U5, U8 Alexanderplatz.*

### Schloß Charlottenburg
*Luisenplatz, Charlottenburg, 10585 (32 09 11). U2 Sophie-Charlotte-Platz or Richard-Wagner-Platz.* **Open** 10am-5pm Tue-Sun. **Admission** *multiple ticket* (palace, pavilion, Belvedere) DM8; DM3 students; DM4 groups of 15 or more; *single tickets* (palace only) DM4; DM1.50 students; DM2.50 groups; free under-14s.

### Zeughaus (The Armoury)
*Deutsches Historisches Museum, Unter den Linden 2, Mitte, 10117 (21 50 20). S3, S5, S6, S9/U6 Friedrichstraße.* **Open** 10am-6pm Mon, Tue, Thur-Sun. **Admission** DM4; DM2 concs.

# Biedermeier to Bismarck

**Revolutions came and went, but the Industrial Revolution was here to stay – industrialists August Borsig and Werner Siemens named their own suburbs to make sure of that.**

**Otto von Bismarck** *dictates the terms of peace at Versailles in February 1871.*

The reform initiated in 1810 was short-lived. Following the Congress of Vienna (1814-15), which established a new order for post-Napoleonic Europe, King Friedrich Wilhelm III reneged on promises of constitutional reform. Instead of a greater unity among the German states, a loose alliance came into being: dominated by Austria, the German Confederation was distinctly anti-liberal.

In Prussia itself, state power increased. Alongside the police, a secret service and vice squad were set up. The police president had the power to issue directives to the city council. Book and newspaper censorship increased. The authorities sacked Humboldt from the university he had set up.

With their hopes for lasting change frustrated, the bourgeoisie withdrew to their salons. It is one of the ironies of this time that although political opposition was quashed, a vibrant cultural movement flourished. Academics such as Hegel and Ranke lectured at the university and enhanced Berlin's reputation as an intellectual centre. The period became known as *Biedermeier* after a fictional character embodying bourgeois taste, created by Swabian comic writer Ludwig Eichrodt.

Another legacy of this period is the range of neo-classical buildings designed by Karl Friedrich Schinkel, such as the **Neue Wache** on Unter den Linden and the Bauakademie (building academy) which was demolished in the sixties. (For more on Schinkel, *see chapter* **Sightseeing**.) For the majority, however, the post-Napoleonic era was a period of frustrated hopes and bitter poverty.

Industrialisation swelled the ranks of the working class. Between 1810 and 1840, the city's population doubled to around 400,000, making Berlin the fourth largest city in Europe. But most of the new arrivals lived in slums, in conditions which would later lead to riots and revolution.

## Industrial Revolution

Prussia was ideally equipped for the industrial age. By the nineteenth century it had grown dramatically and boasted one of the greatest abundances of raw materials in Europe. The founding of the Borsig Werke in the Chausseestraße in 1837 established Berlin as the workshop of Continental Europe. August Borsig was Berlin's first big industrialist. His factories turned out locomotives for the new railway which had started with the opening of the Berlin to Potsdam line in 1838. Borsig also left his mark through the establishment of a suburb (Borsigwalde) that still carries his name.

The other great pioneering industrialist, Werner Siemens, set up his electrical engineering business in a small house near Anhalter Bahnhof. The first to manufacture telegraph equipment in Europe, Siemens personified the German industrial ideal with his combination of technical genius and business savvy. The Siemens company also left a permanent imprint on Berlin through the building of a new suburb (Siemensstadt) to house its workers. With the growth of such companies, Berlin became Continental Europe's largest industrial city.

## 1848 and All That

Friedrich Wilhelm IV's accession to the throne in 1840 raised hopes of an end to repression; and initially, the new king appeared to want genuine change. He declared an amnesty for political prisoners, relaxed censorship, sacked the hated justice minister and granted asylum to political refugees.

Political debate thrived in coffee houses and wine bars. The university was another focal point. In the late 1830s, Karl Marx spent a term there, just missing Otto von Bismarck. In the early 1840s Friedrich Engels came to Berlin to do his military service. The thaw didn't last long. Friedrich Wilhelm IV shared his father's opposition to constitutional reform. Living and working conditions for most Berliners worsened. Rapid industrialisation had also brought sweat-shops, 17-hour days and child labour. This was compounded in 1844 by harvest failure which drove up prices for potatoes and wheat. Food riots broke out on the Gendarmenmarkt when a crowd stormed the market stalls. It took the army three days to restore order.

Things came to a head in 1848, year of revolution across Europe. Berliners seized the moment. Political meetings were held in beer-gardens and in the Tiergarten, and demands made for internal reform and a unification of the German-speaking states. At the end of one demonstration in the Tiergarten, there was a running battle between police and demonstrators on Unter den Linden.

On March 18, the king finally conceded to allowing a new parliament to be set up, and made vague

**Napoleon III** *(left) and* **Bismarck** *on the morning after the French surrender at Sedan.*

promises about other reforms. Later that day, a crowd of 10,000 which had gathered to celebrate the victory were set upon by soldiers. Shots were fired and the revolution began. Barricades went up throughout Berlin and demonstrators fought with police for 14 hours. Finally the king backed down (again). In exchange for the dismantling of barricades, the king ordered his troops out of Berlin. Days later, he took part in the funeral service for the 'March dead' – the 183 revolutionaries who had been killed – and promised more freedoms.

Berlin was now ostensibly in the hands of the revolutionaries. The city was patrolled by a Civil Guard, the king rode through the streets wearing the revolutionary colours (black, red, gold) and seemed to embrace liberalism and nationalism. Prussia, he said, should 'merge into Germany'. But the revolution was short-lived. Pressed on unification, the king merely suggested that the other German states send representatives to the Prussian National Assembly. The offer was rebuffed. Liberals instead convened a German National Assembly in Frankfurt in May 1848. At the same time, a new Prussian Assembly met in the Schauspielhaus on the Gendarmenmarkt to debate a new constitution. Throughout the summer and autumn of 1848, reforming fervour took over Berlin.

### MOOD SWING

The onset of winter, however, brought a change of mood to the city. Using continuing street violence as a pretext, the king ordered the National Assembly to be moved to Brandenburg. In early November he brought troops back into the city and declared a state of siege. Press freedom was restricted. The Civil Guard was dissolved, followed shortly by the National Assembly. On December 5 the king delivered his final blow to the liberals by unveiling a new constitution fashioned to his own tastes. Throughout the winter of 1848/49 thousands of liberals were arrested or expelled. A new city constitution, drawn up in 1850, reduced the number of eligible voters to five per cent of the population, around 21,000 people. Increased police powers meant the position of police president was more important than that of mayor.

By 1857 the increasingly senile Friedrich Wilhelm had gone quite literally mad. His brother Wilhelm acted as regent until becoming king on Friedrich's death in 1861. Once again, the people's hopes were raised: the new monarch began his reign by appointing liberals to the cabinet. The building of the **Rotes Rathaus** (Red Town Hall) gave the city council a headquarters to match the size of the royal palace. Built between 1861-1869, the Rathaus was named for the colour of its bricks, not (yet) the political persuasion of its members.

By 1861, the king found himself in dispute with parliament around proposed army reforms. The king wanted to strengthen his direct control of the forces. Parliament wouldn't accept this, so the king went over its members' heads and appointed a new prime minister: Otto von Bismarck.

## The Iron Chancellor

An arrogant genius who began his career as a diplomat, Bismarck was well able to deal with unruly parliamentarians. Using a constitutional loophole, he quickly pushed through the army reforms. Extra-parliamentary opposition was dealt with by oppression and censorship, and Bismarck turned his mind to German unification.

Unlike the bourgeois revolutionaries of 1848 who desired a Germany united by popular will and endowed with political reforms, Bismarck strove to bring the German states together under the authoritarian dominance of Prussia. His methods involved astute foreign policy and outright aggression. Wars against Denmark (1864) and Austria (1866) brought the post-Napoleonic order to an abrupt end. Prussia was no longer the smallest of the Great Powers but an initiator of geo-political change. The defeat of Austria confirmed the primacy of Prussia among the German-speaking states. Victory on the battlefield boosted Bismarck's popularity across Prussia, but not in Berlin. He was defeated in his Berlin constituency in the 1867 election to the North German League (a Prussian-dominated body linking the northern states and a stepping stone to overall unification).

Bismarck's third war – against France in 1870 – revealed his scope for intrigue and opportunism. He exploited a dispute over the succession to the Spanish throne to provoke France into declaring war on Prussia. Citing the North German League and treaties with the southern German states, Bismarck brought together a united German army under Prussian leadership. Following the defeat of the French army on September 2, Bismarck moved quickly to turn a unified military campaign into the basis for a unified nation. The Prussian king would be German emperor: beneath him would be four kings, 18 grand-dukes and assorted princes from the German states which would retain some regional powers. (This arrangement formed the basis for the modern federal system of *Länder*.)

On January 18, 1871 King Wilhelm was proclaimed German Kaiser (emperor) in the Hall of Mirrors in Versailles. In just nine years, Bismarck had united Germany, forging an empire that dominated central Europe. The political, economic and social centre of this new creation was Berlin.

### Neue Wache

*Unter den Linden, Mitte, 10178. S1, S2, S3, S5, S6, S9/U6 Friedrichstraße.*

### Rotes Rathaus (Berlin Town Hall)

*Rathausstraße 10, Mitte, 10178 (240 10). S3, S5, S6, S7, S9/U2, U5, U8 Alexanderplatz.* **Open** 8am-6pm Mon-Fri. **Admission** free.

# The Fall of Empire

*For 40 years after unification, Germany steamed ahead, with Berlin at the helm. Then came World War I and the slide into the abyss.*

The coming of empire threw Berlin into one of its greatest periods of expansion and change. The economic boom (greatly helped by five billion gold francs extracted from France as war reparations) led to a wave of speculation. Farmers in Wilmersdorf and Schöneberg became millionaires overnight as they sold off their fields to developers.

During the decades following unification, Berlin emerged as Europe's most modern metropolis. This period was later dubbed the Gründerzeit (foundation years). The Gründerzeit was marked by a move away from traditional Prussian values of thrift and modesty, towards the gaudy and bombastic. In Berlin, the change of mood manifested itself in monuments and buildings. Of these the **Reichstag**, the **Siegessäule** (Victory Column), the **Berliner Dom** and the **Kaiser-Wilhelm-Memorial Church** are the most prominent.

Superficially, the Reichstag (designed by Paul Wallot and completed in 1894) represented a commitment to parliamentary democracy, but in reality Germany was still in the grip of conservative forces. The authoritarian power of the Kaiser remained intact, as was demonstrated by the decision of Kaiser Wilhelm II to sack Bismarck in 1890 following disagreements over policy.

## GROWTH AREA

When Bismarck began his premiership in 1861, his offices in the Wilhemstraße overlooked potato fields. By the time he lost his job in 1890, they were in the centre of Europe's newest and most congested city. Economic boom and growing political and social importance attracted hundreds of thousands of new inhabitants to the city. At the time of unification in 1871, 820,000 people lived in Berlin; by 1890 the population had nearly doubled.

The growing numbers of the working class were shoved into hastily built Mietskasernen tenements (rental barracks) which mushroomed across the city – particularly in Kreuzberg, Wedding and Prenzlauer Berg. Poorly ventilated and overcrowded, the Mietskasernen (many of which still stand) are characterised by a series of interlinked backyards. They became both a symbol of Berlin and a breeding ground for social unrest.

The Social Democratic Party (SPD), founded in 1869, quickly became the voice for the city's havenots. In the 1877 general election it won over 40 per cent of the vote in Berlin. The left-wing reputation (Rotes Berlin) which has followed the city into the late twentieth century was born.

In 1878 two assassination attempts on the

**Kaiser Wilhelm II**'s *epoch is associated with showy militarism and foreign policy bungles.*

Kaiser gave Bismarck an excuse to classify Socialists as enemies of the state. He introduced a series of restrictive laws to curb the 'red menace', and outlawed the SPD and two other progressive parties. The ban existed until 1890 – the year of Bismarck's sacking – but did little to stem support for the SPD. In the general election held that year, the SPD dominated the vote in Berlin. And in 1912 it won over 70 per cent of the Berlin vote to become the largest party in the Reichstag.

## Kaiser Bill

Famed for his moustache, Kaiser Wilhelm II came to the throne in 1888 and quickly became (in many people's eyes) the personification of the new Germany: bombastic, awkward and unpredictable. Like his grandmother Queen Victoria he gave his name to an era. Wilhelm's epoch is associated with showy militarism and foreign policy bungles leading to a world war that cost the Kaiser his throne.

The Wilhemine years were also characterised by further explosive growth in Berlin (the population rose to two million by 1910 and by 1914 had doubled again) and a blossoming of the city's cultural and intellectual life. The **Bode Museum** was built in 1904 and in 1912 work began next door on the **Pergamon Museum**. In 1912 a new opera house was unveiled in Charlottenburg (later destroyed by wartime bombing; the Deutsche Oper now stands on the same site). Expressionism took off in 1910 and the Kurfürstendamm became the location for many new art galleries. Although Paris still remained ahead of Berlin in the arts, the German city was fast catching up.

By the time of his abdication in 1918, Wilhelm's reign had also seen the emergence of Berlin as a centre of scientific and intellectual development. Six Berlin scientists (including Albert Einstein and Max Planck) were awarded Nobel Prizes.

In the years preceding World War I, Berlin appeared to be loosening its stiff collar of pomposity. Tangoing became all the rage in new clubs around the Friedrichstraße. Yet despite the progressive changes, growing militarism and international tension overshadowed the period.

Germany was not alone in its preparedness for war. By 1914 Europe was armed and waiting to tear itself apart. In June 1914 the assassination of Archduke Franz Ferdinand provided the excuse. On August 1, war was declared on Russia and the Kaiser appeared on a balcony of the royal palace to tell a jubilant crowd that from that moment on, he would recognise no parties, only Germans. At the Reichstag the deputies, who had virtually unanimously voted in support of the war, agreed.

No one was prepared for the disaster of World War I. After Bismarck, the Germans had come to expect quick, sweeping victories. The armies on the western front settled into their trenches for a

**Kaiser Wilhelm II** *reigned from 1880-1918.*

war of attrition that would cost over a million German lives. Meanwhile, the civilian population began to adapt to austerity and shortages. After the 1917 harvest failed, there were outbreaks of famine. Dog and cat meat started to appear on the menus in the capital's restaurants. The SPD's initial enthusiasm for war evaporated and in 1916 the party refused to pass the Berlin budget. A year later, members of the party's radical wing broke away to form the Spartacus League. Anti-war feeling was voiced in strikes in April 1917 and January 1918. These were brutally suppressed, but when the Imperial Marines in Kiel mutinied on November 2, 1918 the authorities were unable to stop the force of the anti-war movement.

The mutiny spread to Berlin where members of the Guards Regiment came out against the war. On November 9 the Kaiser was forced into abdication and subsequent exile. This date has a weird significance in German history; it's the anniversary of the establishment of the Weimar Republic (1918); Kristallnacht (1938); and the fall of the Wall (1989). It was on this day that Philip Scheidemann, leading SPD MP and proponent of republicanism, broke off his lunch in the Reichstag, walked over to a window overlooking Konigsplatz (now Platz der Republik) where a crowd had massed, and declared: 'The old and the rotten have broken down. Long live the new! Long live the German Republic!'.

At the other end of Unter den Linden, Karl Liebknecht, who together with Rosa Luxemburg headed the Spartacus League, declared Germany a Socialist republic from a balcony of the occupied royal palace. (The balcony was the same one the Kaiser used when he spoke to Berliners on the eve of war, and has been preserved as part of the **Staatsratsgebaude**, State Council building, of the East German government.)

Liebknecht and the Spartacists wanted a Communist Germany similar to Soviet Russia; Scheidemann and the SPD wanted a parliamentary democracy. Between them stood those still loyal to the vanished monarchy. All were prepared to fight their respective corners. Barricades were erected in the city centre and street battles ensued. It was in this climate of turmoil and violence that Germany's first attempt at republican democracy – later known as the Weimar Republic – was born.

## Chaos

The revolution in Berlin may have brought peace to the Western Front, where hostilities were ended on November 11, but in Germany it unleashed a wave of political terror and instability. The new masters in Berlin, the SPD under the leadership of Friedrich Ebert, ordered renegade battalions of soldiers returning from the front (known as the Freikorps) to quash the Spartacists who launched a concerted bid for power in January 1919.

Within days, the uprising had been bloodily suppressed and Liebknecht and Luxemburg went into hiding. On January 15, Freikorps officers traced them to a house in Wilmersdorf and took them under arrest. They were then taken to a hotel near Zoo station for interrogation. Between the hotel and Moabit prison, the officers murdered both of them and dumped Luxemburg's body over the Liechtenstein Bridge into the Landwehr Canal. Today a plaque marks the spot.

Four days later, the national elections returned the SPD as the largest party: the social democrats' victory over the extreme left was complete. Berlin was deemed too dangerous for parliamentary business, so the government swiftly decamped to the quaint provincial town of Weimar from which the first German republic took its name.

Germany's new constitution ended up being full of good liberal intentions but riddled with technical flaws. And this left the country wide open to weak coalition government and quasi-dictatorial presidential rule.

Another crippling blow to the new Republic was the Versailles Treaty, which set the terms of peace. Reparation payments (set to run until 1988) blew a hole in a fragile economy already weakened by war. Support for the right-wing nationalist lobby was fuelled by the loss of territories in both east and west. And restrictions placed on the German military led some right-wingers to claim that Germany's soldiers had been 'stabbed in the back' by Jews and left-wingers at home.

In March 1920, a right-wing coup was staged in Berlin under the leadership of Wolfgang Kapp, a civil servant from east Prussia. The recently returned government once again fled the city. For four days Berlin was besieged by Freikorps. Some of them had taken to adorning their helmets with a new symbol, the *Hakenkreuz* or swastika.

Ultimately a general strike and the refusal of the army (the *Reichwehr*) to join Kapp brought an end to the putsch. But the political and economic chaos in the city remained. Political assassinations were commonplace. Food shortages lead to bouts of famine. Inflation started to escalate.

There were two main reasons for the precipitate devaluation of the Reichsmark. To pay for the war, the increasingly desperate imperial government had resorted to simply printing more money – a policy continued by the new republican rulers. The burden of reparations also lead to an outflow of foreign currency. In 1914 one dollar bought just over four Reichmarks; by 1922 it was worth over seven thousand. And one hyperinflationary year later, one dollar was worth 4.2 billion marks. Workers needed suitcases to carry the bundles of notes that made up their salaries.

In the same year, 1923, the French government sent troops into the Ruhr industrial region to take by force reparation goods which the German government said it could no longer afford to pay. The Communists planned an uprising in Berlin for October but lost their nerve. In November a young ex-corporal called Adolf Hitler, who lead the tiny National Socialist Party (NSDAP or Nazi), launched an attempted coup from a beer-hall in Munich. His programme called for armed resistance against the French, an end to the 'dictatorship of Versailles' and punishment for all those – especially the Jews – who had 'betrayed' Germany at the end of the war.

Hitler's first attempt at power came to nothing. Instead of marching on Berlin, he went to prison. Inflation was finally brought down with the introduction of a new currency (one new mark was worth one trillion old ones). But the overall decline of moral and social values that had taken place in the five years since 1918 was not so easy to restore.

## The Golden Twenties

When Joseph Goebbels came to Berlin in 1926 to take charge of the local Nazi party organisation, he observed: 'This city is a melting-pot of everything that is evil – prostitution, drinking houses, cinemas, Marxism, Jews, strippers, negroes dancing and all the off-shoots of modern art.' The term 'evil' is better applied to Goebbels himself, but his description of twenties Berlin was not far wrong.

The city overtook Paris as Continental Europe's arts and entertainment capital and in the process added its own decadent twist. By 1927 Berlin boasted over 70 cabarets and nightclubs. At the Theater des Westens cabaret artist Josephine Baker danced to a packed house. Baker also danced naked at parties thrown by playwright Karl Volmoeller in his flat on Pariser Platz.

While Brecht's *Threepenny Opera* played at the Theater am Schiffbauerdamm, Berlin's Dadaists gathered at the Romanisches Café on Tauentzienstraße (later destroyed by bombing – the Europa-Center now stands on the site). There was a proliferation of avant-garde magazines reflecting new ideas in art and literature. But the flipside was an underbelly of raw poverty and glaring social tension reflected in the works of painters such as George Grosz and Otto Dix. In the music halls, Brecht and Weill used a popular medium to ram home points about social injustices.

In architecture and design the revolutionary ideas emanating from the Bauhaus school in Dessau (it briefly moved to Berlin in 1932 but was closed down by the Nazis a year later) were taking concrete form in building projects such as the Shell House (now BeWag) building on the Landwehr canal, the Siemensstadt new town, and the model housing project Hufeisensiedlung (Horse Shoe Estate) in Britz. Furniture, ceramics, sculptures and sketches created in the Bauhaus workshop from 1919-1933 are kept in the **Bauhaus Archiv-Museum für Gestaltung**.

## EXTREME REACTIONS

The stock market crash on Wall Street and the onset of depression in 1929 ushered in the brutal end of the Weimar Republic. The fractious coalition governments that had just managed to hold on to power in the brief years of prosperity in the late twenties were no match for rocketing unemployment and a surge in support for extremists.

Already by the end of 1929 nearly one in four Berliners were out of work. The city's streets became a battleground for clashes between Nazis, Communists and social democrats. Police relied on water cannons, armoured vehicles and guns to quell street-fighting across the city. One May Day demonstration left 30 dead and hundreds wounded. At Bülowplatz (now Rosa-Luxemburg-Platz) where the Communist party, the KPD, had its headquarters, there were battles between Communists, police and Nazi stormtroopers (the SA). In August 1931 two police officers were murdered on Bülowplatz. One of the men accused of the murders (and later found guilty by a Nazi court) was Erich Mielke, a young Communist, later to become the head of East Germany's secret police, the Stasi.

In 1932 the violence in Berlin reached crisis level. In just six weeks over the summer, 300 street battles left 70 dead. In the general election in July,

the Nazis took 40 per cent of the vote and Hermann Göring was appointed Reichstag president. But the prize of government still eluded the Nazis. At the elections in November, the Nazis lost two million votes across Germany and 37,000 in Berlin where the Communists emerged as the strongest party. In Wedding, over 60 per cent voted for the KPD.

The election had been held against the backdrop of a strike by 20,000 public transport employees. A survey recorded that almost half of Berlin's inhabitants were living four to a room and that a large proportion of the housing stock was unfit for human habitation.

General Kurt von Schleicher's government ruled by presidential decree. Schleicher had promised President von Hindenburg he could tame the Nazis into a coalition. When he failed, his rival Franz von Papen overcame Hindenburg's dislike for Hitler and manoeuvred the Nazi leader into power. On January 30, 1933, Hitler was named Chancellor. That evening, the SA staged a torchlight parade through the Brandenburg Gate to the Chancellery. Looking out from the window of his house, the artist Max Liebermann remarked to his dinner guests: 'I cannot eat as much as I'd like to puke.'

### Bauhaus Archiv-Museum für Gestaltung
*Klingelhöferstraße 13-14, Tiergarten, 10785 (25 40 020). Bus 109, 116, 124, 129.* **Open** 10am-5pm Mon, Wed-Sun. **Admission** DM4; DM2 concs.

### Berliner Dom (Berlin Cathedral)
*Lustgarten, Mitte, 10178 (246 90). S3, S5, S6, S9 Hackescher Markt.* **Open** 9am-7.30pm Mon-Sat; 11.30am-7.30pm Sun. **Admission** free; *dome* DM3; DM1.50 children, students, pensioners, groups. *Photo permit* DM3.

### Bodemuseum
*Museumsinsel, entrance Monbijoubrücke, Mitte, 10178 (203 55 508). S3, S5, S6, S9/U6 Friedrichstraße.* **Open** 9am-5pm Tue-Sun. **Admission** DM4; DM2 concs.

### Kaiser-Wilhelm-Gedächtniskirche (Kaiser Wilhelm Memorial Church)
*Breitscheidplatz, Charlottenburg, 10789 (24 50 23). S3, S5, S6, S9/U2, U9 Zoologischer Garten.* **Open** 9am-7pm Mon-Sat; *old tower* 9am-4pm Mon-Sat. **Tours** 1.15pm Wed-Fri. **Admission** free.

### Pergamon Museum
*Bodestraße 1-3 (enter on Kupfergraben), Mitte, 10178 (2035 5444). S3, S5, S6, S9 Hackescher Markt.* **Open** 9am-5pm Tue-Sun. **Admission** DM4; DM2 concs.

### Reichstag
*Platz der Republik, Tiergarten, 10557 (397 70). S1, S2 Unter den Linden.* **Open** 10am-5pm Tue-Sun. **Admission** free (for exhibition and Plenarsaal). Tours of the Reichstag must be arranged in advance.

### Siegessäule
*Straße des 17 Juni, Tiergarten, 10785 (391 29 61). S3, S5, S6, S9 Bellevue.* **Open** 1-5.30pm Mon; 9am-6pm Tue-Sat (last admission 5.30pm). **Admission** DM1.50; DM1 students.

### Staatratsgebaude
*Marx-Engels-Platz, Mitte, 10178. S3, S5, S6, S9 Hackescher Markt.*

# The Nazi Years

**Hitler elects himself dictator, concentration camps open on the edge of the city and Albert Speer prepares to transform Berlin. The Allies and the Red Army beat him to it.**

The government Hitler now led was a coalition of Nazis and German Nationalists led by the media magnate Alfred Hugenberg. Together their votes fell just short of a parliamentary majority, so another election was called for March. In the meantime, Hitler continued to rule by decree.

The last relatively free election of the Republic was also the most violent, marked by open persecution of Communists. The Nazis banned meetings of the KPD, shut down Communist newspapers and broke up SPD election rallies.

On February 27, a fire broke out in the Reichstag. It was almost certainly started by the Nazis, who used it as an excuse to step up the persecution of opponents. Over 12,000 Communists were arrested. Spelling it out in a speech at the Sportspalast two days before the election, Goebbels said: 'It's not my job to practise justice. Instead I have to destroy and exterminate – nothing else.'

The Nazis still didn't achieve an absolute majority (in Berlin they polled 34 per cent), but that no longer mattered. With the support of his allies in the coalition, Hitler pushed through an Enabling Law giving him dictatorial powers. By summer, Germany had been declared a one-party state.

Already *ad hoc* concentration camps – known as brown houses after the colour of the SA uniforms – had sprung up around the city. The SS established itself in the **Prinz Albrecht Palais** where it was later joined by the secret police, the Gestapo. Just to the north of Berlin near Oranienburg, a concentration camp, **Sachsenhausen**, was set up (*see chapter* **Trips Out of Town**).

Along the Kurfürstendamm squads of SA stormtroopers would go 'Jew baiting' and on April 1, 1933, the first boycott of Jewish shops began. On May 10, Goebbels, who became Minister for Propaganda, organised a book-burning, which took place on Bebelplatz opposite the University of Berlin. Books by Jews or writers deemed degenerate or traitors were thrown on to a huge bonfire.

Berlin's unemployment problem was tackled through a series of public works programmes, growing militarisation, which drew new recruits to the army, and the 'encouragement' of women to leave the workplace. Following the policy of *Gleichschaltung* (co-ordination) the Nazis began to bring all aspects of public life under their control. With a few exceptions, party membership became obligatory for doctors, lawyers, professors and journalists. During the Night of the Long Knives in July 1934, Hitler settled old scores with opponents within the SA and Nazi party. At Lichterfelde barracks, officers of the SS shot over 150 SA members. Hitler's predecessor as Chancellor, General von Schleicher, was shot together with his wife at their home in Wannsee.

After the death of President Hindenburg in August 1934, Hitler had himself named Führer (leader) and made the armed forces swear a personal oath of allegiance to him. Within less than two years, the Nazis had subjugated Germany to their will.

## BIG JESSE

A brief respite came with the Olympic Games in August 1936. In a bid to persuade foreign participants and spectators that all was well in the Reich, Goebbels ordered the removal of anti-Semitic slogans from shops. 'Undesirables' were also moved out of the city and the pavement-side display cases that held copies of the racist Nazi newspaper *Der Stürmer* (the Stormtrooper) were dismantled.

The Games themselves, which were mainly held at the newly built **Olympic Stadium** in Charlottenburg, were not such a success for the Nazis, who had to watch the black American Jesse Owens clock up medals and records. Had Hitler been in the stadium on the occasions when Owens won, he would almost certainly have refused to present him with his medals, as in the case of black high-jumpers Cornelius Johnson and David Albritton. But the Games did work as a public relations exercise. Observers left Berlin glowing with reports about a strident and healthy nation. But had any of the foreign visitors stayed, they would have seen the reality of Hitler's policy of co-ordinating all facets of life in Berlin within the Nazi doctrine.

As part of a campaign to remove what the Nazis considered to be *entartete Kunst* (degenerate art) from German cultural life, works of modern art were collected in a touring exhibition designed to show the depth of depravity in contemporary ('Jewish-dominated') culture. But Nazi hopes that these 'degenerate' works would repulse the German people fell flat. When the exhibition

**Jesse Owens** *broke five world records and equalled a sixth in the 1936 Olympic Games.*

arrived at the Zeughaus in Berlin in 1938, thousands queued for admission. The people loved the paintings. After the exhibition, the paintings were sent to auction in Switzerland. Those that remained unsold were burnt in the fire station in Köpenickerstraße. More than 1,000 oil paintings and 4,000 watercolours were destroyed.

## SLICED LIMES
Shortly after taking power, Hitler ordered that the lime trees on Unter den Linden be chopped down to give Berlin's boulevard a cleaner, more sanitised form. This was just the first step taken in Nazi urban planning.

Hitler's plans for the redesign of Berlin reflected the hatred the Nazis felt for the city. Hitler entrusted young architect Albert Speer with the job of recreating Berlin as a metropolis to 'outtrump Paris and Vienna'. The heart of old Berlin was to be demolished and its small streets replaced by two highways stretching 37 km (23 miles) from north to south and 50 km (30 miles) from east to west. Each axis would be 90 metres (100 yards) wide. Crowning the northern axis would be a huge Volkshalle (People's Hall) nearly 300 metres (328 yards) high with space for over 150,000 people. Speer and Hitler also had plans for a triumphal arch three times the size of the Arc de Triomphe and a new Führer's palace 150 times bigger than the one occupied by Bismarck. The new city was to be called Germania.

The onset of war meant that Speer only built a fraction of what was intended. Hitler's new Chancellery was constructed in under a year, finished in early 1939. It was demolished after the war. On the proposed east-west axis, a small section around the **Siegessäule** was widened for Hitler's fiftieth birthday in April 1939. For other surviving examples of Nazi architecture, *see chapter* **Sightseeing**.

## Persecution
Of the half a million Jews living in Germany in 1933 over a third lived in Berlin. The Jewish community had played an important role in Berlin's development and their influence was especially prevalent in the financial, artistic and intellectual circles of the city.

The Nazis wiped out these centuries-old traditions in 12 years of persecution and murder. Arrests soon followed the initial boycotts and acts of intimidation. From 1933 to 1934, many of Berlin's Jews fled to exile abroad. Those who stayed were to be subjected to legislation (the Nuremberg Laws of 1935) that banned Jews from public office, forbade them to marry Aryan Germans and stripped them of citizenship. Jewish cemeteries were desecrated and the names of Jews chipped off war memorials.

Berlin business institutions that had been owned by Jews – such as the Ullstein newspaper group and the Tietz and Wertheim department stores on Alexander and Potsdamerplatz – were

'Aryanised'. The Nazis either expropriated the shops or forced the owners to sell at ridiculously low prices.

On November 9, 1938, a wave of 'spontaneous' acts of vandalism and violence against Jews and their property began in response to the assassination of a German diplomat in Paris by a young Jewish emigré. Jewish businesses and houses across Berlin were stoned, looted and set ablaze. A total of 24 synagogues were set on fire. The Nazis rounded up 12,000 Jews and took them to Sachsenhausen concentration camp.

## War & Destruction

Since 1935, Berliners had been taking part in practice air raid drills, but it was not until the Sudeten crisis of 1938 that the possibility of war became real. At that juncture Hitler was able to get his way and persuade France and Britain to let him take over the German-speaking areas of northern Czechoslovakia. But a year later, his plans to repeat the exercise in Poland were met with resistance in London and Paris. Following Germany's invasion of Poland on September 1, 1939, Britain and France declared war on the Reich. Despite a huge Nazi propaganda exercise and spectacular early victories, most Berliners were horrified by the war. The first air raids came in early 1940 when the RAF bombed Pankow and Lichtenberg.

In 1941 following the German invasion of the Soviet Union, the 75,000 Jews remaining in Berlin were required to wear a yellow Star of David and the first large-scale and systematic deportations to concentration camps began. By the end of the war in May 1945, only 5,000 Jews remained in Berlin.

Notorious assembly points for the deportations were Putlitzstraße in Wedding, Große Hamburgerstraße and Rosenstraße in Mitte. On January 20, 1942, a meeting of the leaders of the various Nazi security organisations in the suburb of Wannsee agreed on a 'final solution' to the Jewish question. They joked and drank brandy as they sat around discussing mass murder.

The turning-point in the war came with the surrender of the German army at Stalingrad on January 31, 1943. In a bid to grab some advantage from this crushing defeat, Goebbels held a rally in the Sportpalast where he announced that Germany had now moved into a state of 'total war'. By summer, women and children were being evacuated from Berlin and schools were shut down. By the end of 1943, over 700,000 people had fled Berlin.

The 'Battle of Berlin', which the RAF launched in November 1943, began to reduce much of the city centre to rubble. Between then and February 1944, over 10,000 tonnes of bombs were dropped on the city. Nearly 5,000 people were killed and around a quarter of a million made homeless.

## BUNKER MENTALITY

On July 20, 1944, a group of officers, civil servants and former trade unionists launched a last ditch attempt to remove Hitler through assassination and bring an end to war. But Hitler survived the explosion of a bomb placed at his eastern command post in East Prussia by Colonel Count von Stauffenberg. That evening Stauffenberg was killed by firing squad in the courtyard of army headquarters in Bendlerstraße, now **Stauffenbergstraße**. The other members of the plot were rounded up and put on trial at the People's Court and subsequently executed at **Plötzensee Prison**.

In early January 1945, the Red Army launched a major offensive that carried it on to German soil. On February 12, the heaviest bombing raid killed over 23,000 people in little more than an hour. As the Red Army moved into Berlin's suburbs, Hitler celebrated his last birthday on April 20 in his bunker behind Wilhelmstraße. Three days later, Neukölln and Tempelhof fell. By April 28, Alexanderplatz and Hallesches Tor were in the hands of the Red Army. The next day Hitler called his last war conference. He then married his long-time companion Eva Braun and committed suicide with her the next day. As their bodies were being burnt by loyal SS officers, a few streets away a red flag was raised over the Reichstag. The city officially surrendered on May 2. Germany's unconditional surrender was signed on May 8 at the Red Army command centre in **Karlshorst**.

### Gedenkstätte Plötzensee (Plötzensee Memorial)
*Hüttigpfad, Charlottenburg, 13627 (344 32 26). Bus 123.* **Open** *Mar-Sept* 8am-6pm daily; *Oct, Feb* 8.30am-5.30pm; *Nov, Jan* 9.30am-4.30pm; *Dec* 9.30am-4pm. **Admission** free. *Brochure available in English.*

### KZ Sachsenhausen
*Straße der Nationen 22, Oranienburg, 16515 (033 01 35 16). S1 Oranienburg.* **Open** 8.30am-6pm Tue-Sun. **Admission** free.

### Olympiastadion (Olympic Stadium)
*Charlottenburg, 14053 (305 81 23/304 06 76). U2 Olympia-Stadion.* **Open** 10am-5.30pm daily, except event days. Closed Nov-Apr. **Admission** DM3; DM2.50 concs, groups; DM1.50 children.

### Siegessäule
*Straße des 17 Juni, Tiergarten, 10785 (391 29 61). S3, S5, S6, S9 Bellevue.* **Open** 1-6pm Mon; 9am-6pm Tue-Sat (last admission 5.30pm). **Admission** DM1.50; DM1 students.

### Stauffenbergstraße
*Tiergarten, 10785. S1, S2 Potsdamer Platz.*

### Topographie des Terrors
*Stresemannstraße 110, Kreuzberg, 10963 (25 48 67 03). S1, S2 Anhalter Bahnhof.* **Open** 10am-6pm Tue-Sun. **Admission** free. *Located in what used to be the Prinz Albrecht Palais.*

**Opposite:** *with war just around the corner, Hitler presides at a mass rally of Nazis.*

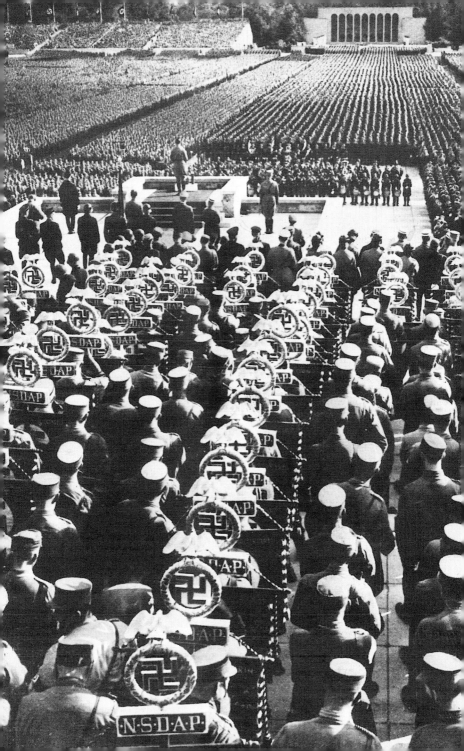

# Post-War Berlin

**Split in half, Berlin became two separate cities, but 29 years of political crisis and popular pressure would lead to reunification.**

When Bertolt Brecht returned to Berlin in 1948 he encountered 'a pile of rubble next to Potsdam'. Nearly a quarter of all buildings in the city had been destroyed. The human cost of the war was equally startling – around 80,000 Berliners had been killed, thousands more, mostly Jews, would not return from the concentration camps.

There was no gas or electricity and only the suburbs had running water. Public transport had all but completely broken down. In the first weeks following capitulation, Red Army soldiers went on a rampage of random killings and rapes. Thousands of men were rounded up and transported to labour camps in the Soviet Union. Food supplies were used up and later the harvest in the war-scarred land around the city failed. Come winter, the few remaining trees in the Tiergarten and other city parks were chopped down for firewood.

Clearing the rubble was to take years of dull, painstaking work. The *Trümmerfrauen* or 'rubble women' cleared the streets and created mountains of brick and junk – such as the Teufelsberg, one of seven such hills which still exist today.

The Soviets stripped factories across the city as part of a programme to dismantle German industry and carry it back to the Soviet Union. As reparation, whole factories were moved to Russia.

Under the terms of the Yalta agreement which divided Germany into four zones of Allied control, Berlin was also split into four sectors, with the Soviets in the east and the Americans, British and French in the west. A *Kommandatura*, made up of each army's commander and based in the building of the People's Court in Elßholzstraße, administered the city. Initially the administration worked well in getting basics, such as the transport network, back to some form of running order. But tensions between the Soviets and the western Allies began to rise as civilian government of city affairs returned. In the eastern sector, a merger of the Communist and Social Democratic parties (which had both been refounded in summer 1945) was pushed through to form the Socialist Unity Party (SED). In the western sector, however, the SPD continued as a separate party.

Events came to a head after elections for a new city government in 1946. The SED failed to get

**Opposite:** *An East German child chips away at the Berlin Wall, New Year's Eve 1989.*

*Eighty people died trying to flee East Berlin.*

more than 20 per cent of the vote, while the SPD won nearly 50 per cent of all votes cast across the city. The Soviets vetoed the appointment to office of the SPD's mayoral candidate, Ernst Reuter, who was a committed anti-Communist.

## The Berlin Airlift

The situation worsened in Spring 1948. In response to the decision by the Western Allies to merge their respective zones in western Germany into one administrative and financial entity and introduce a new currency, the Soviets walked out of the *Kommandatura*. In late June, all transport links to west Berlin were cut off and the blockade of the city by Soviet forces began. Three 'air-corridors' linking west Berlin with western Germany became life-lines as Allied aircraft transported thousands of tonnes of food, coal and industrial components to the beleaguered city.

Within Berlin, the future division of the city began to take permanent shape as city councillors from the west were drummed out of the town hall. They moved to Schöneberg Town Hall in the west. Fresh elections in the western sector returned Reuter as mayor. The Free University was set up in response to Communist dominance of the Humboldt University in the East.

Having failed to starve west Berlin into submission, the Soviets called off the blockade after 11 months. The blockade also convinced the Western Allies that they should maintain a presence in Berlin and that their sectors of the city should be linked with the Federal Republic which had been founded in May 1949. The response from the East was the founding of the German Democratic Republic on October 7. With the birth of the 'first workers' and peasants' state on German soil' the formal division of Germany into two states was complete.

## Cold War

During the Cold War, Berlin was the focal point for stand-offs between the US and USSR. Far from having any control over its own affairs, Berlin was wholly at the mercy of geopolitical developments. Throughout the fifties the Berlin question remained high on the international agenda.

Technically the city was still under Four Power control, but since the Soviet departure from the *Kommandatura* and the setting up of East Germany with its capital in East Berlin (a breach of the wartime agreement on the future of the city), this counted for little in practice.

In principle the Western Allies adhered to these agreements by retaining ultimate authority in West Berlin while allowing the city to be integrated as far as possible into the West German system. (There were notable exceptions such as the exemption of West Berliners from conscription and the barring of city MPs from voting in the West German parliament.)

Throughout the fifties the two halves of Berlin began to develop separately as the political systems in East and West evolved. In the East, Communist leader Walter Ulbricht set about creating Moscow's most hard-line ally in eastern Europe. Work began on a Moscow-style boulevard – called Stalinallee – running east from Alexanderplatz. Industry was nationalised and subjected to rigid central planning. Opposition was kept in check by the newly formed Ministry for State Security: the Stasi.

West Berlin landed the role of 'Last Outpost of the Free World' and as such was developed into a showcase for capitalism. As well as the Marshall Plan, which paid for much of the reconstruction of western Germany, the Americans poured millions of dollars into West Berlin to maintain it as a counterpoint to Communism. The West German government, which at the time refused to recognise East Germany as a legitimate state, demonstrated its commitment to seeing Berlin reinstated as the German capital by holding occasional parliamentary sessions there. The prominence accorded West Berlin was later reflected in the high profile of its politicians (Willy Brandt for instance) who were received abroad by Prime Ministers and Presidents – unusual for mere mayors.

Yet despite the emerging divisions, the two halves of the city continued to co-exist in some abnormal fashion. City planners on both sides of the sectoral boundaries initially drew up plans with the whole city in mind. The transport system crossed between East and West, with the underground network being controlled by the West and the S-Bahn by the East.

Movement between the sectors (despite 'border' checks) was relatively normal as Westerners went East to watch a Brecht play or buy cheap books. Easterners went West to work, shop or see the latest Hollywood films.

The secret services of both sides kept a high presence in the city, and there were frequent acts of sabotage on either side. Berlin earned itself the title of espionage capital of the world.

### MONEY TALKS

As the effects of US dollars and the West German 'economic miracle' took hold, West Berlin began to recover. A municipal housing programme meant that 200,000 new flats had been built by 1963. Unemployment dropped from over 30 per cent in 1950 to virtually zero by 1961. The labour force also included about 50,000 East Berliners who commuted over the inter-sector borders. In the East reconstruction was slower. Until the mid-fifties East Germany paid reparations to the Soviet Union. And to begin with, there seemed to be more acts of wilful destruction than positive construction. The old palace, slightly damaged by bombing, was blown up in 1950 to make way for a parade ground which later evolved into a car park. Now a debate is raging over whether or not it should be reconstructed from old plans.

### MOVING STORY

In 1952 the East Germans sealed off the border with West Germany. The only way out of the 'zone' was through West Berlin and the number of refugees from the East rose dramatically from 50,000 in 1950 to over 300,000 in 1953. Over the decade, one million refugees from the East came through West Berlin.

In June 1953, partly in response to the rapid loss of skilled manpower, the East German government announced a 10 per cent increase in working 'norms' – the number of hours and volume of output that workers were required to fulfil each day. In protest, building workers on the Stalinallee (now Karl-Marx-Allee) downed tools on June 16 and marched towards the government offices in the old Air Ministry on Leipziger Straße. The government refused to relent and by the next day strikes had broken out across the city. Communist party offices were stormed and red flags torn from public buildings. By mid-day the government had lost control of the city and it was left to the Red Army to restore order. Soviet tanks rolled into the centre of East Berlin where they were met by stones thrown by demonstrators. By nightfall the uprising was crushed. According to official figures 23 people died, though other estimates put the figure at over 200. There followed a wave of arrests across East Berlin with more than four thousand people being detained. The majority went on to receive stiff prison sentences. The June 17 uprising only furthered the wave of emigration. By the end of the fifties it was almost possible to calculate the moment when East Germany would cease to function as an industrial state through the loss of skilled labour. Estimates put the loss to the East German economy through emigration at around DM100 billion. Ulbricht stepped up his demands on Moscow to take dramatic action.

In 1958, the Soviet leader Nikita Khruschev tried to bully the Allies into relinquishing West Berlin with an ultimatum calling for an end to the military occupation of the city and a 'normalisation of the situation in the capital of the GDR', by which he meant Berlin as a whole. The ultimatum was rejected and the Allies made clear their commitment to West Berlin. Unwilling to provoke a world war over Berlin, but needing to prop up his ally, Khruschev backed down and sanctioned Ulbricht's alternative plan for a solution.

## BARRIER METHOD

Throughout the early summer of 1961 rumours began to spread in the city that Ulbricht intended to seal off West Berlin with some form of barrier or reinforced border. Emigration had reached a highpoint as 1,500 East Germans fled West each day and it became clear that events had reached a crisis point. However, when, in the early hours of August 13, units of the People's Police (assisted by 'Working Class Combat Groups') began to drag bales of barbed wire across Potsdamer Platz, Berlin and the world were caught by surprise.

In a finely planned and executed operation (overseen by Erich Honecker, then Politburo member in charge of security affairs), West Berlin was sealed off within 24 hours. As well as a fence of barbed wire, trenches were dug, the windows in houses lining or straddling the new border were bricked up, and tram and railway lines were interrupted: all this under the watchful eyes of armed

guards. Anyone trying to flee West risked being shot, and in the 29 years the Wall stood, nearly 80 people died trying to escape. Justifying their actions, the East Germans later claimed they had erected an 'Anti-Fascist Protection Barrier' to prevent a world war.

Days later the construction of a brick wall began. When it was completed, the concrete part of the 100-mile (160km) fortification ran to 70 miles (112km); 23 miles (37km) of the Wall ran through the city centre. Previously innocuous streets such as Bernauerstraße (where houses on one side were in the East, those on the other in the West) suddenly became the location for the world's most sophisticated and deadly border fortifications.

The initial stunned disbelief of Berliners turned into despair as it became clear that (as with the June 17 uprising) the Western Allies could do little more than make a show of strength. President Kennedy dispatched American reinforcements to Berlin and, for a few tense weeks, American and Soviet tanks squared off at Checkpoint Charlie.

Moral support from the Americans came with the visit of Vice President Lyndon Johnson a week after the Wall was built. And two years later Kennedy himself arrived and spoke to a crowd of half a million people in front of the Schöneberg Town Hall. His speech linked the fate of West Berlin with that of the free world and ended with the now famous statement 'Ich bin ein Berliner' (literally, alas, 'I am a doughnut').

In the early years the Wall became the scene of many daring escape attempts (all documented in the **Museum Haus Am Checkpoint Charlie**, *see chapter* **Museums**) as people abseiled off buildings, swam across the Spree river, waded through sewers or simply tried to climb over the Wall. But as the fortifications were improved with mines, searchlights and guard dogs, and as the guards were given orders to shoot, escape became nearly impossible. (By the time the Wall fell in November 1989 it had been 'updated' four times to incorporate every conceivable deterrent.)

In 1971, the Four Powers met and signed the Quadrapartite Agreement which formally recognised the city's divided status. Border posts (such as the infamous Checkpoint Charlie) were introduced and designated to particular categories of visitors – one for foreigners, another for West Germans and so on.

## CIVIC COUNTERPARTS

During the sixties, with the Wall as infamous and ugly backdrop, the cityscape of modern Berlin (both East and West) began to take shape. On Tauenzienstraße in the West the Europa-Center was built and the bomb-damaged Gedächtniskirche was given a partner – a new church made up of a glass-clad tower and squat bunker. In the Tiergarten, Hans Scharoun laid out the Kulturforum as West Berlin's answer to the Museuminsel complex in the East. The first building to go up was Scharoun's Philharmonie which was completed in 1963. Mies van der Rohe's Neue National Gallerie (which he had originally designed as a Bacardi factory in Havana) was finished in 1968. In the suburbs work began on concrete mini-towns, Gropiusstadt and Maerkisches Viertel. Conceived as modern-day solutions to housing shortages, they would later develop into alienating ghettos.

In the East, the **Alexanderplatz** was rebuilt (though in such a horrific way that the Senate has now made its redesign a priority) and the **Fernsehturm** (television tower) was finished (*see chapter* **Sightseeing** for both). The historic core of Berlin was mostly cleared to make way for parks (such as the Marx-Engels Forum) or new office and housing developments. On the eastern outskirts of the city in Marzahn and Hohenschönhausen work began on mass-scale housing projects.

In 1965, the first sit-down was staged on the Kurfürstendamm by students protesting against low grants and expensive accommodation. This was followed by political demonstrations as students took to the streets to protest against the State in general and the Vietnam war in particular. The first communes were set up in Kreuzberg, thereby sowing the seeds of a counter-culture which was to make that district famous.

In 1967 and 1968, the student protest movement came into increasingly violent confrontation with the police. One student, Benno Ohnesorg, was shot dead by police at a demonstration against the Shah of Iran, who visited the city in June 1967. A year later the students' leader, Rudi Dutschke, was shot by a right-winger. Demonstrations were held outside the offices of the newspaper group Springer whose papers were blamed for inciting the shooting. It was out of this movement that the Red Army Faction (also known as the Baader-Meinhof group) was to emerge. It was often to make headlines in the seventies, not least through a series of kidnappings of high-profile city officials.

## ABNORMAL NORMALITY

The signing of the Quadrapartite Agreement confirmed West Berlin's abnormal status and ushered in an era of decline as the frisson of Cold War excitement and sixties rebellion petered out. More than ever, West Berlin depended on huge subsidies from West Germany to keep it going.

Development schemes and tax-release programmes were introduced to encourage business to move to the city (to keep the population in the city, Berliners also paid less income tax) but still the economy and the population declined.

At the same time there was growth in the number of *Gastarbeiter* (guest workers) who arrived from southern Europe and particularly Turkey, to take on jobs (mostly menial and low-paid) which

most Germans shunned. Today there are 120,000 Turks in the city, concentrated in Kreuzberg.

By the late seventies, Berlin seemed to have reached the depths of decline. The city government was discredited by an increasing number of scandals, mostly connected with the property world. In East Berlin Erich Honecker's regime (he succeeded Ulbricht in 1971), which had begun in a mood of reform and change, became increasingly repressive. Some of East Germany's best writers and artists, who had previously been willing to support socialism, left the country. The Communists were glad to be rid of them. From its headquarters in Normannenstraße (now a museum, *see chapter* **Museums: Ministerium für Staatssicherheit**) the Stasi directed its policy of mass observation and increasingly succeeded in permeating every part of East German society. Between East and West there were squalid exchanges of political prisoners for hard currency.

The late seventies and early eighties saw the rise of the squatter movement (centred in Kreuzberg), which brought violent political protest back to the streets. The problem was diffused after the Senate caved in and gave squatters rent contracts.

In 1987 Berlin celebrated its 750th birthday twice, as East and West vied to outdo each other with exhibitions and festivities. In the East the Nikolaiviertel was restored and Honecker began a programme to do the same for the few remaining historical sites which had survived bombing and post-war planning. The statue of Frederick the Great riding his horse was returned to Unter den Linden. But restored monuments were not enough to stem the growing dissatisfaction of East Berliners. The development of *perestroika* in the Soviet Union had been ignored by Honecker who stuck hard to his Stalinist instincts. Protest was increasingly vocal. By the Spring of 1989, the East German state was no longer able to withstand the pressure of a population fed up with Communism. Throughout the summer, thousands fled the city and the country via Hungary, which had opened its borders to the West. Those who stayed began demonstrating for reforms.

By the time Honecker was hosting the celebrations in the Volkskammer (People's Chamber) to mark the fortieth anniversary of the GDR on October 7, 1989, crowds were demonstrating outside and chanting 'Gorby! Gorby!' to register their opposition. Honecker was ousted days later. His successor, Egon Krenz, could do little to stem the tide of opposition. In a desperate bid to defend through attack, he decided to grant the concession East Germans wanted most – freedom to travel. On November 9, 1989 the Berlin Wall was opened, just over 29 years after it had been built. As thousands of East Berliners raced through to the sound of popping corks, the end of East Germany and the unification of Berlin and Germany had begun.

# Berlin Today

**With neo-Nazi propaganda on the increase and east Berliners voting for their old leaders, stores closing down and investors looking elsewhere, the reunified city faces a stiff challenge.**

Take a train east on the U2 line. After leaving Gleisdreieck station, you swoop over the logistics centre for the largest construction site in Europe. A few minutes later you plunge into the bowels of the future city centre at Potsdamer Platz. The scale of Berlin's building boom dwarfs just about every other activity in town, and will continue to do so until the end of the century.

Berlin's pre-war nucleus is not being restored. After devastation by Allied bombing and decades as a stretch of no-man's land between East and West, it is being built from the ground up. The logistics centre will be in operation night and day until the last inner-city block is complete – some time around the year 2000. Each hour a steady stream of railway wagons carries away thousands of tons of sand, removed to build foundations. At the same time, incoming trains deliver the ingredients for the millions of tons of concrete that will be mixed here before Berlin regains its hub.

Meanwhile, Berlin finds itself in a weird wrinkle in time: no longer the divided, spy-infested capital of the Cold War, but not yet the bustling capital of Central Europe it is destined to become once all this construction is finished and the government arrives from Bonn.

Through the grime and dust of the building boom, Berlin's future has never looked brighter. War-ravaged buildings are being carefully restored. Universities are once again attracting distinguished faculties. Fortunes are being made selling goods and services in outlying regions of eastern Germany and beyond. A new generation of young Berliners dances till dawn in techno clubs that were once bunkers, bank vaults or power stations. Many of them were barely teenagers when the Wall was breached in 1989.

## CH-CH-CH-CH-CHANGES

Though unification has vouchsafed a future for Berlin, the problem today is holding out until that future arrives. Ironically, just at the point when Berliners are more in control of their own destiny than ever before, their faith in the future is at an all-time low. In the summer of 1994, as the French, British, American and Soviet forces marched out of town to end nearly half a century of occupation, many Berliners were sentimental. Rather than

*Trendy Ku'damm housing for the new Berlin.*

being jubilant about getting rid of foreign troops, they seemed more concerned about their city losing its international flair. And when the German Bundestag voted by a narrow margin in the summer of 1991 to move the seat of government from Bonn to Berlin, instead of seeing the eventual arrival of thousands of dull but well-heeled civil servants as sheep waiting to be fleeced, locals viewed the eventual influx with trepidation. The Berliners' first concern: government employees would ruin the market for low-cost housing.

Lack of enthusiasm at regaining capital-city status played right into the hands of conservative forces in Bonn that over the next few years argued to reconsider the move to Berlin, or at least postpone it indefinitely. The discussion ended with legislation in 1994 that set a moving-in deadline of 1998. But for over two years it proved disastrous for the city, holding up badly needed investment.

In the meantime, Berliners' worst post-unification nightmares have come true. East Berliners have indeed gained the freedoms for which they demonstrated in the autumn of 1989. But along with them they got rising rents, unemployment, and crime rates in derelict neighbourhoods which approach those in the slums of urban America.

## SCARY MONSTERS

Disillusioned youth is susceptible to neo-Nazi propaganda, and there have been isolated attacks on Asian and black foreigners in eastern districts. If the number of violent attacks on immigrants has decreased recently, it may only be a reflection of Germany's stringent new asylum laws.

West Berliners, on the other hand, spoiled by four fat decades of huge subsidies and tax breaks from Bonn, plus extraordinary public services, have been hit hard by the huge costs of unification. Funding for municipal projects and maintenance has been cut to the bone, and what's left over is being transferred to east Berlin.

At the European Parliament elections in June, 1994 – the first Euro elections ever to take place in Berlin, east or west – residents of east Berlin overwhelmingly voted for candidates representing their former Communist leaders. The Party of Democratic Socialism (PDS), the post-unification name of Erich Honecker's old Socialist Unity Party of Germany, swept east Berlin wards with a total of 40 per cent of the vote. Mainstream political parties still hold sway in united Berlin. But the PDS victory in east Berlin shows, four years after unification, that people on that side of town are clinging to old visions of the future in the absence of meaningful new ones.

But, although east Berliners like to complain, their lot is beginning to improve. Downtown façades are being restored after years of Socialist neglect, retail stores are becoming nearly as plentiful as they are in west Berlin, and in 1995 a huge shopping mall complex will be completed on Friedrichstraße. Young east Berliners in Mitte and Prenzlauer Berg have discovered they are living near some of the trendiest nightclubs and bars in town. And middle-aged residents have found easy jobs as sales reps that come with company cars and mobile telephones. Unemployment, at about 13 per cent in east and west Berlin, remains a problem.

## GOLDEN YEARS

For all the work that remains, you can't help but notice progress on the march in east Berlin. Tower cranes dominate the city centre skyline while industrial estates spring up on the outskirts of town. The behemoth structures being built on Potsdamer Platz by Daimler-Benz (a headquarters for its Debis division) and Sony (a new home for its European headquarters, currently in Cologne) were controversial from the start.

First opposition politicians in the Berlin Senate claimed the investors acquired the land far below its true value. Then there was a huge brawl over master planning for the area: how high could the builders go and what percentage of space had to contain flats and shops?

World class architects who were once attracted here now say city planners have put so many restrictions on new construction projects in Berlin's Mitte district that the result will be structures robbed of vitality and urban sophistication; blocks and blocks of squat, boring buildings. City planning and building officials counter that they want no part of a downtown jungle of postmodern architecture. Their aim is to preserve the city's original dimensions, and its unique mix of neighbourhoods where people live, work, shop and entertain themselves in the same immediate area.

But, although the scale of construction is huge, the amount of building is less than initially anticipated. Some potential investors have been stung by the recession in Europe. Others have been put off by the shortage of capital in Germany caused by unification. Still others are already seeing over-capacity in the market for office space.

## REBEL REBEL

Bertelsmann announced it was withdrawing plans for a huge media complex at the end of Leipziger Straße. Swedish conglomerate Skanska scrapped plans for an elegant shopping mall at the north end of Friedrichstraße near Oranienburger Straße. A number of other large investors are extending options to acquire property, or letting them expire.

It's not only builders and developers who are reappraising their commitment to Berlin. International retailers are discovering the city is falling short of their initial expectations. Japan's up-market department store Mitsukoshi closed down its elegant location on the Kurfürstendamm after waiting for two years for more Japanese tourists to materialise. The Virgin Megastore just down the street also opted to shut down, after not finding the same conditions in this metropolis which make it successful elsewhere.

Also, as subsidies to industry in west Berlin are being cut back, major industrial employers are shutting down local operations and opening in cheaper locations just outside the city, or transferring them to their factories in western Germany. Siemens and AEG, both electrical companies with a long tradition in Berlin, have made thousands of workers redundant in the last few years.

International airlines are cutting services to Berlin. TWA and American Airlines no longer fly from Berlin across the Atlantic, citing unprofitability on the routes. And Conti-Flug, which had a convenient and cheap service between City Airport in London and Tempelhof Airport, has suspended operations.

West Berlin's cultural scene was once supported to the tune of 210 million marks annually by the government in Bonn. That budget has been cut, forcing the city to close down theatres. Other projects are running out of funding. Renovations to Berlin's magnificent Protestant cathedral, the

*East Berlin's Socialist chic architectural showcase **Alexanderplatz** is up for redevelopment.*

Berlin Dom, have been delayed due to shortage of funds.

Many Berliners are frankly concerned that with funds from Bonn being diverted to help finance the 70 billion mark move of the government here by the end of the decade, there might be little of substance left in the capital by the time it arrives.

In one bid to save money, the Berlin Senate has agreed to give up the city's state status in Germany's federal system through a political merger with Brandenburg, the state surrounding Berlin. This would streamline administration and consolidate useful joint activities such as economic development promotion. But in relinquishing its city-state status, Berlin would also no longer qualify for the funds which are transferred from wealthy German states to less well-off states through a federal compensation programme. As a result, the inevitable fusion between Berlin and Brandenburg has become a poker game, with Berlin holding out for final approval of the scheme until Bonn agrees to a graduated schedule of reducing compensation funds over time.

There have also been damaging delays in other important decisions. Berlin has three civilian airports, but none of them is a true international airport with the hub capacity of Heathrow or Frankfurt am Main. Key investment projects in the Berlin region, particularly for foreign companies, depend on the availability of a large international airport near the city. Three locations have been investigated south of the city, as well as an option to expand the Schönefeld airport on the border of southern east Berlin. But haggling over costs for the locations, and pressure from citizens' groups, have turned the airport into a political issue.

## ASHES TO ASHES

Many of Berlin's problems today stem from a second-rate political and business class which is bland and uncomfortable with change. In west Berlin these people rose to their positions during the Cold War era by maintaining the status quo. Money continued to flow into West Berlin from Bonn, and politicians and civil servants simply had to manage it. Now that the city has been thrust into the free market economy, the bureaucrats are floundering. The cry for competent leadership in local politics is great. Edzard Reuter, the retiring chairman of Daimler-Benz and widely respected son of Berlin's first post-war mayor, Ernst Reuter, is expected to play the role of a white knight.

But Berlin's long-term salvation lies in a younger generation of savvy business and political leaders. The upside of the city's current lack of sustained vision and commitment to genuine renewal is that new and unique ideas can theoretically move into the vacuum. But even here Berlin's recent track record has been dubious. Rather than encouraging the arrival of the young people who could eventually form a leadership class, Berlin appears to be discouraging them. Instead of expanding the city's three universities, there are plans to save money by reducing the student body, which today numbers over 100,000, by some 30,000 students.

**Essen mit Verstand!
Genießen Sie einen gesunden
Imbiß im Bistro oder speisen
Sie im Nichtraucherbereich des
Restaurants.**

Grunewaldstraße 10
Nähe U-Bahnhof Kleistpark
10823 Berlin - Schöneberg
Telefon: 215 58 38

Öffnungszeiten:
Mo - Fr: 11 - ? Uhr

## Vollwert-Restaurant

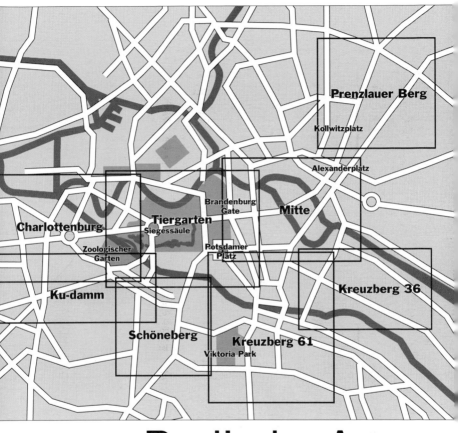

# Berlin by Area

# Berlin by Area

**Whether your heroes are Brecht and Weill or you want to hang out with Wenders' angels, you'll need to know how Berlin breaks down into districts.**

Berlin is a big, sprawling city, cut up by rivers and canals, interspersed with pockets of green. During its rapid growth in the nineteenth century, it gobbled up a number of small communities and then, in the mid-twentieth century, became two cities with a Wall between them. Today, the Wall is down, the small towns exist mostly as names on the map, but there are still big changes from one part of town to another.

From beginnings as a small fortified enclave on an island in the Spree (now Museuminsel), Berlin soon expanded into what is today approximately the *Bezirk* (borough) of Mitte. For many years, that's where the city stayed: the court preferred the pleasures of Potsdam or Königsberg, and Berlin was merely a river town. But towards the end of the seventeenth century, Kaiser Friedrich Wilhelm took a town that had been devastated by war and disease and started shaping it into a modern metropolis, establishing a harbour, building Schloß Charlottenburg, and encouraging immigration,

particularly of Jews and French Huguenots.

Within a century, Berlin had been transformed into one of Europe's great cities: a military, commercial and cultural centre. This expansion was in turn dwarfed by the enormous boom that started in 1871, when Berlin was named the capital of the united German Reich. By the 1920s, Berlin had become a world city, ranked with New York, London, and its great rival, Paris. *Groß Berlin* (Greater Berlin) was officially subdivided into 20 *Bezirken*. Today, there are 23, three having been added to East Berlin in 1949.

Hitler hated Berlin (and, it must be noted, Berlin largely returned the enmity), and hired Alfred Speer to transform it into something closer to his taste, the megalopolis of Germania, capital of the Thousand Year Reich. World War II slowed these plans down, and only a few buildings (notably Tempelhof Airport) and some grandiose street plans (the traffic circle of the *Großer Stern*) were completed.

*The* **International Conference Centre**, *for pop concerts and power lunches. See page 80.*

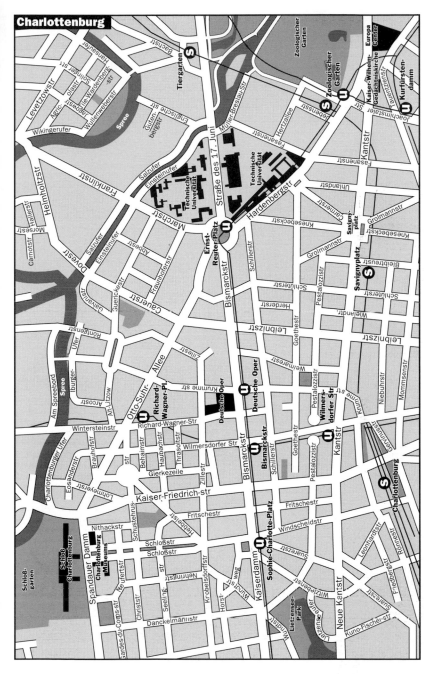

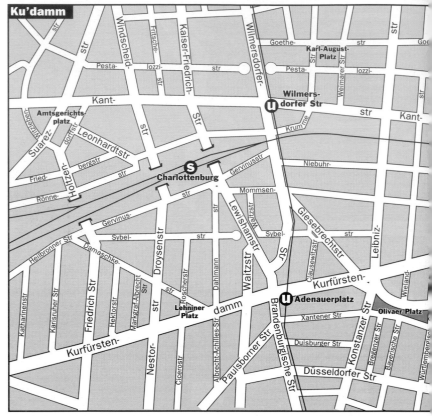

The Allies then bombed the city into submission, leaving a good half of it completely uninhabitable. Massive rebuilding was necessary on both East and West sides. As an island in the middle of East Germany, West Berlin had to come up with novel solutions, since there was nowhere for it to expand. This explains the number of modern Dachbau, or top-floor, extensions of old buildings. East Berlin was under heavy pressure to serve as a showcase for the glories of Communism, so what little money there was mostly went into architectural centrepieces that were both cheap and overblown (eg Alexanderplatz). The rest either remained soot-encrusted and bullet-pocked, or else was flattened and flat-blocked.

Here, we focus on Mitte, Prenzlauer Berg, Kreuzberg, Schöneberg, Tiergarten, and Charlottenburg, with a short section on other neighbourhoods of interest. Any restaurants, cafés, museums, venues, or sights mentioned can be found in their respective chapters.

## Charlottenburg

Once upon a time before the Wall fell, Charlottenburg was Berlin to most tourists. They stayed in Kurfürstendamm hotels, did their shopping there and, if they were museum-goers, went to the complex around Schloß Charlottenburg. There's more Berlin to see now, but Charlottenburg maintains a central position in the cultural and commercial life of the city.

## Around the Kurfürstendamm

The huge steel sculpture by the Urania (no, we've never seen anybody skateboard it), with its grim monument to children killed in traffic by Berlin's drivers, marks the start of 'downtown', where the stores, cinemas and big hotels were concentrated in divided Berlin. **Wittenbergplatz** has a wonderful restored U-Bahn station with old ads on the walls, and outside stands a memorial to those who died in concentration camps, looking eerily like a

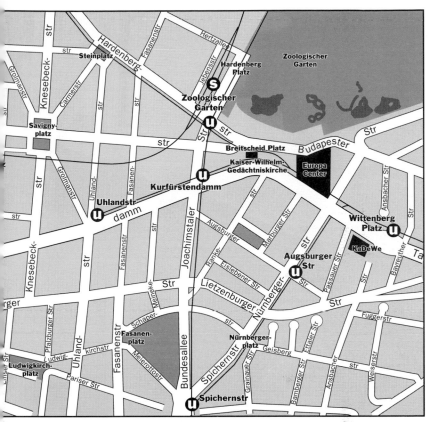

departure board in a train station. The huge department store, KaDeWe stands here, and is worth a visit if only for its food floor, which some say rivals Harrods.

The tubular steel sculpture in the divider on **Tauentzienstraße** was commissioned for the city's 750th anniversary in 1987 and nicely represents the then divided city in that the two halves twine around each other but never meet. Just up the road is the Europa-Center, whose revolving Mercedes star is visible from just about anywhere in the city. For all its height, there's little inside of interest: it's Berlin's answer to a mid-American shopping mall, although its sauna is one of the city's best, and there are also car-hire agencies, a hotel and a tourist office. Next to it stands one of the city's main symbols, the Kaiser-Wilhelm-Gedächtniskirche (Memorial Church), a not-very-attractive 1899 church made spectacular by being bombed in 1943, and left in reinforced ruins as a reminder of war in the middle of the glitz.

**Bahnhof Zoologischer Garten** is, for the moment, still the central train station for Berlin, although a massive construction project at the Lehrter Stadtbahnhof will change this by the turn of the century. Some of the folks hanging around there will doubtless call attention to the appropriateness of calling this place Bahnhof Zoo, but since this is a major meeting-place of U-Bahn, S-Bahn, and bus lines (including the all-important night buses), it is also well-patrolled.

Walking south on **Joachimstaler Straße** brings you back to the **Kurfürstendamm**, or **Ku'damm**, as the locals call it. Named for the Prussian Kurfürst (Elector), who was one of the princes responsible for electing the Holy Roman Emperor, it has long been a popular street, the hangout of the demi-monde in the twenties, lined with trees and plenty of surviving old buildings. With cinemas (mostly showing dubbed Hollywood fare), restaurants (from the venerable Bovril to Burger King), chic shops and offices, it's a street dedicated

*Sleazy **Savignyplatz**: once a training ground for British spies.*

to separating you from your Deutsche Marks. The side streets to the south are a bit quieter, albeit even more up-market, and **Bleibtreustraße** to the north has more shops and some of the most outrageous examples of nineteenth-century 'Gründerzeit' architecture in Berlin. **Kantstraße** more or less parallels the Ku'damm to the north, and has more shops to look in. **Savignyplatz**, once a training ground for British spies thanks to its small red-light district, has numerous foreign-correspondent offices, and more chic places, particularly the restaurants and cafés on **Grolmannstraße** and the shops in **Savigny-passage**.

## Concerts & Conferences

The International Conference Centre (ICC) at the top of **Neue Kantstraße** looks like something out of Raumschiffe Enterprise (Star Trek), and is used for large gatherings from pop concerts to political rallies. Next door, the even larger Messe- und Ausstellungsgelände (Trade Fair and Exhibition Area) plays host to trade fairs ranging from electronics to food to aerospace, and from the Funkturm (Radio Tower) on top, you can get a panoramic view of western Berlin. The nearby Deutschlandhalle is another major concert venue, and Hitler's impressive Olympic Stadium is home turf for the useless Hertha BSC football club and other sports and concert events. Its swimming pool is popular in the summertime. The Maifeld, once the parade ground for the British Army, is now open to the public again for concerts and other large gatherings, and the Waldbühne beyond is Berlin's most popular outdoor concert and cinema venue in the summer.

## Around Schloß Charlottenburg

Impressive though a lot of the buildings on the long street variously named **Bismarckstraße** or **Kaiserdamm** are, the building that brought Charlottenburg into being is still the ruler here. Coming into view as you walk up **Schloßstraße**, Queen Sophie Charlotte's summer palace was intended to be Berlin's answer to Versailles. Today, the Schloß is most interesting as a park: the guided tours are conducted only in German, and the museums on the grounds proper are mostly of interest to specialists, but the grounds easily transport the visitor back to the eighteenth century.

The museums across the street are another matter, though: the star attraction of the Ägyptisches Museum is of course Queen Nefertiti, although the rest of the museum and the occasional travelling shows that stop there shouldn't be ignored either. The Museum of Greek and Roman Antiquities pales next to the Pergamon, although the collection of pornographic potsherds is remarkable. The surrounding area also contains the Bröhan Museum (art deco and art nouveau) and the Primeval and Early History Museum.

For those who like to wander, the streets just south of Bismarckstraße, particularly those named for philosophers (Leibnitz, Goethe, etc) have a lot of interesting small shops selling antiques, books, and the fashions that the well-to-do residents of Charlottenburg sport in the cafés and restaurants in this area.

## Kreuzberg

Kreuzberg is divided into two distinct areas, known as **36** and **61** after the old Berlin postcodes. These were replaced in 1993, but you're unlikely to hear anyone saying they live in Kreuzberg 10999.

## Kreuzberg 36

Running north from the Landwerkanal to the Spree, 36 was the Children's Paradise in the seventies, turned into a hard-to-reach pocket by the Wall, forgotten by the rest of the city, filled with decaying old tenements that were soon filled with squatters. For years, 36 meant left-wing youth avoiding the draft, and Turks who gravitated there because of the cheap rent and because people left them alone. The air was filled with the smell of hashish, the sound of Turkish pop music and the noise of political activity. Punk and Anatolia set the styles, and graffiti displayed contempt for the ruling class and sympathy in Turkish for the Kurds.

It's the graffiti, in fact, that's the tip-off: sometimes it includes dates, as for demonstrations. Some of it is five or six years old. Although the traditional Mayday riot still happens, with the 13-year-old children of the original demonstrators now in its van, 36 isn't what it used to be. The Wall came down, and suddenly this pocket found itself very attractively situated, midway between the business centres of the East and West. Those tenements weren't legally inhabited, those warehouses on the Spree were empty. 'Nice' restaurants started to appear, along with graffiti urging us to kill yuppies, or at least throw them in the Spree.

Gentrification reared its well-coiffed head. These days a Kreuzberg bar crawl can still be fun – some of the restaurants, such as Abendmahl, are among the city's best, and Henne on Leuschnerdamm has been serving the definitive roast chicken for ages.

The anarchistic Autonomen, long changed from political activists to a thuggish semi-criminal presence, will still mess up the paint-job of your Mercedes if you seem to live in the neighbourhood (and aren't Turkish: the Turks fight back), but heroin and beer, two great stunners of action, have taken their toll. Kreuzberg 36 seems like a place where time has stopped for the German population. No longer young, they live in punk dreams while the real alternative culture has moved on to Mitte and Prenzlauer Berg, and the political activists are fighting the proposed Tiergarten tunnel and defending the rights of asylum-seekers from offices all over town. The open-air Turkish market still lines the Maybachufer, and 36 is still the capital of Turkish Berlin, alive with activity. Old 36 still has an edge, but there's something sad about it, a living warning about the transience of Bohemia. It gave its gift to Berlin style, and Berlin moved on.

Nonetheless, if only as a trip through an open-air museum, a stroll around 36 is worth taking. **Oranienstraße** is its main street, and a walk from one end to the other nicely encapsulates the changes the neighbourhood is going through. Across **Skalitzer Straße**, it changes to **Wiener Straße**, where bars such as Madonna still welcome the old crowd, and the mammoth Görlitzer Park turns into the world's largest outdoor

*The streets around* **Chamissoplatz** *were spared much of the Allied bombing. See page 83.*

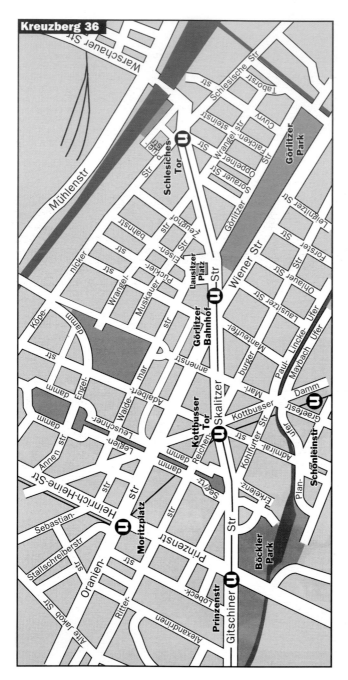

Kreuzberg 36

*The open-air Turkish market on* **Maybachufer**. *See page 81.*

Turkish barbeque on weekends. South of here is the **Paul-Lincke-Ufer**, lined with restaurants offering Sunday brunch, one of which inhabits the ground floor of a spectacular house owned by retired members of Morgenrot, one of the more successful Neue Deutsche Welle rock bands.

More daily life can be seen in the streets around the well-restored **Schlesisches Tor** U-Bahn station, with its onion domes, a sometime café in its ground floor, and a bustling trade in windscreen-washing punks. Nearby, the spooky old **Oberbaumbrücke** is being restored, having fallen into disrepair during the years it was used for spy exchanges, but a temporary pedestrian bridge stands nearby, and is the best way to get to the East Side Gallery, the longest remaining stretch of Wall, painted on commission by artists who decorated parts of the original and featuring a souvenir shop filled with the sorts of things your friends will expect you to bring from Berlin. Back across in 36, more transition into gentrification can be seen on **Köpenicker Straße**, and fans of art deco in the service of commerce are urged to check out the gigantic warehouse on **Pfuelstraße**, which runs for a block towards the Spree.

## Kreuzberg 61

The other Kreuzberg, the one that actually has the 'cross hill' for which the area is named, is Kreuzberg 61, again named after the old post codes. The **Landwehrkanal** is Kreuzberg's Rubicon: on the north side, it's 36, on the south 61. The change, however, is more than that of a mere postcode.

Somehow, this is an area that took the old Kreuzberg energy and made it work. Here, you can actually see painters painting, jewellery-makers making jewellery, and political action committees working on issues closer to home than the Maoist revolution in Peru.

The natural way to enter 61 is via **Viktoriapark**, with its cheery fake waterfall cascading down the hill, its large outdoor beer-garden Golgotha, and the commanding view from the monument at the hill's summit, from which you can see this relatively flat city spread out below – and, on one side, the Schultheiss brewery making its awful beer. Back at ground-level, walk down **Kreuzbergstraße** until it crosses **Mehringdamm** and you'll be on **Bergmannstraße**, one of the hubs of neighbourhood activity, with cafés, junk shops and galleries. The Markthalle on **Marheinekeplatz** is one of three in the city (the others are in 36, and the Moabit section of Tiergarten) and definitely worth a stroll for food-lovers.

Given 61's political leanings, you might be surprised to wander the streets above **Chamissoplatz** (just up **Nostitzstraße** off **Bergmannstraße**) some day and see swastikas hanging everywhere, while happy people line the sidewalks, cheering and waving Nazi flags, but don't be alarmed: even more than in 36, the old buildings here escaped the bombing, and there are whole blocks which can be turned into 1937 with minimal outlay by any film company; if you've ever seen 'old Berlin' in the cinema, chances are it was filmed here. With a decent imagination, you can set the scene yourself, setting the clock back even further, if it makes you more comfortable, although the hulking presence of the Columbushaus, a red-brick monster currently used by the Police for automobile registration, stands as a reminder that the Nazis once had a prison in its basement. The old water-tower on **Fidicinstraße** has been restored, and now features gigs by local bands.

**Bergmannstraße** continues east to **Sudstern**, past several large cemeteries, and eventually comes

to the **Hasenheide**, the other of the neighbourhood's large parks, with its famous outdoor cinema in summertime, and another good view from atop the **Rixdorfer Höhe**. From here, you can see Tempelhof Airport, Berlin's downtown air facility. Once the central airport for the city, it was begun in the twenties, but substantially redone by Albert Speer, who saw it as one of the main axis points of Germania, and the curving buildings loom with a definite Nazi menace. Tempelhof was where

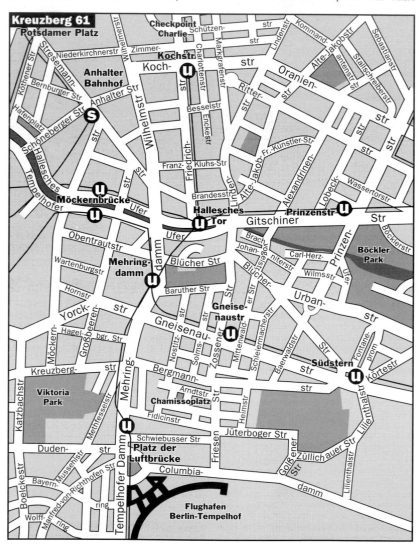

*The monumental* **Unter den Linden**.

Lufthansa Airlines started, but its place in the city's affections was cemented during the Berlin Airlift of 1948-9, when it served as the base for the 'raisin-bombers' which flew in and out at a rate of one a minute, bringing needed supplies to the blockaded city and tossing boxes of candy and raisins to kids waiting nearby as the planes taxied in. The monument in the nearby **Platz der Luftbrücke** commemorates the pilots who flew these missions, as does a photo-realist painting stuck up in a corner of the terminal building.

After commercial flights to Tempelhof were discontinued in the early seventies, it became the centre of the US air operation here. Today operations are split between small airlines like Air Croatia and Conti-Flug and the smaller equipment of larger lines like SAS, Sabena and Lufthansa, all flying to European destinations. With three airports serving the city, it is likely that something will have to give, but the building itself, the largest in Berlin and one of the largest in the world, is likely to survive whatever changes are on their way.

One other part of Kreuzberg 61 deserves mention, although it is diametrically across the Bezirk from Tempelhof, and that is the part, once made an island by the Wall, around **Anhalter Bahnhof**. Once the city's main rail terminus, only a tiny piece of façade remains today, preserved in its bombed state near the S-Bahn station that bears

its name. Another ruin near the station is a section of the eighteenth-century city wall that was excavated and reconstructed for the city's 750th birthday celebration. On **Stresemannstraße**, the Bauhaus-designed Europahaus was heavily bombed during the War, but the lower stories remain, and the Café Stresemann on the corner is a popular local hangout.

Continuing up Stresemannstraße, you will reach the Martin-Gropius-Bau, one of the city's best museums, which is home to some of the most innovative exhibitions that come to Berlin, as well as a good collection of Futurist and Dadaist art and a nice basement café that spills out on to the terrace in summer. Next to it is a deserted patch of ground that once held the Prinz Heinrich Palais, which the Gestapo took over as its headquarters. In the basement, thousands of political prisoners were held and tortured to death, and the land was flattened after the War. In 1985, during an acrimonious debate over the design of a memorial to be placed on the land, a group of citizens cut the wire surrounding it and staged a symbolic 'excavation' of the site. To their surprise, they hit the Gestapo's basement, and immediately plans were made to reclaim the site. Today, there's an exhibition, Topographie des Terrors, with a ground-level photographic display of the site's history, and railings over which you can look down into the cells. Debate continues as to the site's eventual disposition: one architect submitted a plan by which the cells would be exposed to the elements and eventually rot away, but plans now call for a more formal visitors' centre and permanent display.

## Mitte

When the Wall was up, the idea of this part of town calling itself Mitte, or middle, seemed just a bit ludicrous. True, it was the place where the city was born on the sand islands in the Spree, and before World War II it had been the hub of the city. But it was not central to East Berlin, and, despite international-quality hotels and the International Business Centre at Friedrichstraße Station, it didn't seem too important. In the reunited city, though, Mitte has regained its title as centre of the city in every way possible: culturally, scenically, administratively. With the historic old buildings scrubbed until they shine, an influx of capital promoting new construction, and a new energy from youthful settlers, Mitte is back in the middle again.

## Unter den Linden

This legendary boulevard begins at the **Brandenburg Gate**, the symbol of Berlin. Modelled on the Propylaeus gateway into ancient Athens, it is topped by the Quadriga, added in 1795. The four-horse chariot with Victory driving has had the iron

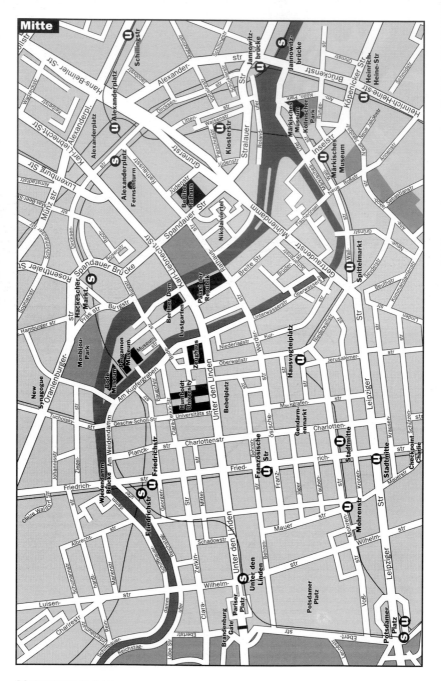

# Mitte

**Palast der Republik:** *the old East German legislature, saturated in asbestos. See page 88.*

cross in her hand restored after some controversy, and the Quadriga you see may be a replica: the original is sometimes taken down for repairs and restoration. Once, only the monarch could use the central arch of the Gate; today it's available only to those royalty of the streets, taxi drivers and the number 100 bus.

Immediately to the east of the Gate is **Pariser Platz**, site of the 1994 visit by US President Clinton, but more usually host to hawkers of DDR and USSR souvenirs and Bratwurst stands. On the south side, a stone commemorates the once and future site of the US Embassy, and, a little further on, a graffiti-splashed Wall segment stands outside the Akademie der Kunst.

Originally laid out to connect the town centre with the Tiergarten, **Unter den Linden** got its name from the Linden (lime trees) that shaded its sidewalks. Hitler, concerned that they obscured the view of his parades, had them felled, but they've been replanted. Between the Gate and the Spree, the side streets were laid out in a grid by Frederick the Great for his Friedrichstadt, which he hoped would provide the model for Berlin's continued growth. The western end of Unter den Linden is all recent, having been badly bombed, and among the glories of Soviet-influenced architecture is the Russian and Ukrainian Embassy (formerly the Soviet Embassy) with its large bust of Lenin (who, as a student, worked in the nearby Staatsbibliothek) remaining as a vestige of the old days.

Humboldt University is now integrated into Berlin's university system, and its grand old façade has been restored, as have the two statues of Humboldt, between which booksellers set up their tables in good weather. Across the street, **Bebelplatz**, the site of the huge Nazi book-burning (noted by a plaque on the west wall), is framed by the Kommodie and the Staatsoper, whose cafés and restaurants are appropriately glitzy. Just a few blocks south of here lies the **Gendarmenmarkt**, one of the high-points of Frederick the Great's vision for the city. Here, the two cathedrals, the Französischer Dom (now a museum dedicated to the Huguenots, who fled here from persecution in France in the seventeenth century) and the Deutscher Dom, frame the Konzerthaus Berlin (formerly the Schauspielhaus), once a theatre and now home to the superb Deutsches Symphonie-Orchester Berlin.

Back on Unter den Linden, the statue of Frederick the Great (taken down by the DDR, it suddenly and mysteriously reappeared one night when the party line on him changed) points towards the river. The Mahnmal was once known as the Neue Wache when it served as a guardhouse for the royal residences in the area, and is today a memorial to the German dead in the last war. The police presence is in case someone takes exception (as some did at its rededication in 1993) to the inclusion of the Jews in that number. Next to it stands the Zeughaus, the former armoury that cur-

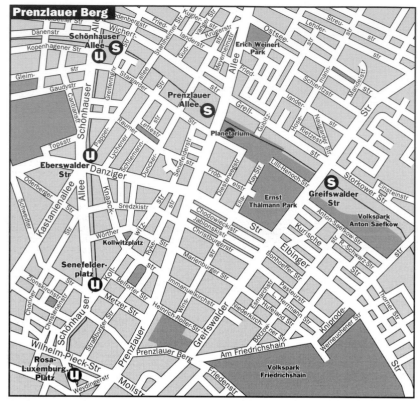

rently houses the Museum for German History. Its exhibitions no longer have the peculiar slant that made the place a favourite for Western tourists to visit in DDR times, and it will have to find a new home when the government arrives from Bonn and uses the Zeughaus for offices.

## Museuminsel & Fischerinsel

The island where Berlin started is divided in half, with **Werder Straße** being the actual line of division. The northern part has a collection of museums, and is therefore known as Museuminsel, while the southern half was once a neighbourhood for the city's fishermen.

For the most part, the museums are more impressive seen from the outside than the inside. The exception is the Pergamon-Museum, a showcase for three important pieces of ancient architecture, the Great Altar of Pergamon (a Greek temple complex in what is now Turkey), the Blue Gate of Babylon, and the Market of Augustus from Caesarium. The Alte Nationalgalerie has, with uni-

fication, been made the repository of the earlier half of the city's collection of art and is particularly strong in German painters up to the start of World War I. The Bode Museum is a strange assortment of displays in serious need of rationalisation, the Neues Museum is finally having its severe bomb-damage repaired (although opening has not yet been scheduled), and the Altes Museum, from 1830, plays host to a succession of travelling exhibitions.

Across the **Lustgarten** (Pleasure Garden) from the Altes Museum stands the Berliner Dom, fully restored and holding weekly services after many years of existing in spite of the displeasure of the DDR. Its lush nineteenth-century interior is hardly the perfect acoustic space for the frequent concerts held there, but it's definitely worth a visit to see the outrageous gilded sarcophagi of Sophie-Charlotte and Frederick I.

Directly across Unter den Linden stands the Palast der Republik, home of the East German legislature, the Volkskammer, which was condemned after unification for asbestos contamination and closed. It stands on the site of the Berliner Schloß, built in 1699 and used as a royal residence until 1918, which was heavily bombed and lay in ruins until 1952, when the DDR levelled it. Moves to rebuild it (the original plans are still on file) have continued since then, although there is opposition from people who see it as a symbol of Prussian aggression. In 1993, a French artist drew the entire façade on sheets of plastic and erected them around the closed Palast, making for an impressive trompe d'oeil that got the pro-Schloß forces clamouring once again. Inside, they mounted an exhibition of the building's former glories in hopes of finally tilting public opinion their way, but it came down in September 1994, and now the future of the site is once again undecided.

Fischerinsel, while hardly as spectacular as the other half of the island, is still a charming, quiet area with a number of hotels, seafood restaurants, and, across from the Märkisches Museum (which houses an exhibition of circus history), **Köllnischer Park**, in which you can visit Maxi and Tilo, the official Berlin bears.

## Alexanderplatz

Visitors who have read Alfred Döblin's classic *Berlin Alexanderplatz* or seen the multi-part television film by Fassbinder may arrive here and wonder what happened. What happened was that in the early seventies Erich Honecker decided this historic square should reflect the glories of Socialism, and tore it all down, replacing it with a masterpiece of commie kitsch: wide boulevards, monotonous white buildings filled with cafés and shops, and, of course, the impressive golf-ball-on-a-knitting-needle, the Fernsehturm (Television Tower), from whose observation deck and revolving restaurant there's a fantastic view of the city on a clear day. At ground level, capitalism's neon icons sit incongruously on Honecker's erections, the goofy clock with the fifties-style atom design on the top tells the time all over the world, and at the new Markthalle, you can sip an Alexanderbräu at the brew-pub or get a Big Mac at McDonald's. Plans are afoot to raze Alexanderplatz once again, which will doubtless result in an equally ugly collection of non-Communist architecture. Even the Fernsehturm is scheduled to fall in this latest vision for the square.

The Rotes Rathaus (Red Town Hall) is so called because of the colour of its bricks, not, as some will wryly tell you, for the goings-on inside. Built in the 1860s, it is once again the Mayor's seat and city administrative centre. The nearby Marienkirche is one of Berlin's few remaining medieval buildings. Just inside the door, a wonderful Berlinish Dance of Death fresco dating from the fourteenth century is being painstakingly restored, and fans of organ music shouldn't miss a concert on the eighteenth-century organ.

The Marienkirche hit the headlines in 1989 when the new civil-rights movement chose it for one of the first sit-ins in the city, since churches were one of the few places in the old East Germany where large numbers of people could congregate without state permission. Facing the church is the Marx-Engels Forum, with its large statue of those two gentlemen and aluminum stelae etched with photographs of the workers' plight around the world. No one, of course, is quite sure how long the statue will remain.

Down **Spandauer Straße**, past the Rotes Rathaus, is the Nikolaiviertel, centred on the Nikolaikirche with its awful DDR reconstruction and odd collection of artefacts that purports to tell the ancient history of Berlin. The eighteenth-century neighbourhood was completely destroyed during the War, and the reconstruction job here isn't too bad, though obviously prefabricated, with a good selection of restaurants, cafés, and overpriced shops, and an old-time European feeling that's rare in Berlin.

## Friedrichstraße

What post-War West Berlin pretended the Kurfürstendamm was, Friedrichstraße had been and will be again: Berlin's answer to the Champs Élysées or Fifth Avenue. It starts at Hallesches Tor in Kreuzberg and ends at Orianienburger Tor in Mitte, but the best way to explore it is to take the U-Bahn to Kochstraße and realise that the big open space that exists to the north of where you're standing used to be **Checkpoint Charlie**. The original checkpoint is in storage at the moment, waiting for a place to be exhibited, but the Haus am Checkpoint Charlie is a fascinating museum of the ways people got across the Wall, legally or not, in the old days. An adjoining courtyard holds an old watch-tower, and a section of Wall. Walking north towards Friedrichstraße Bahnhof, you'll notice that the whole area is a welter of construction sites as companies strive to put up offices and upmarket shops.

The black and white skyscraper near the station is the Internationale Handelzentrum (International Trade Centre), the building from which East Germany conducted its trade in cheap consumer durables and coal, getting technology, raw materials and hard currency in return. The state held the monopoly in this trade, of course, and shortly after the government fell most of the officials in this building were indicted for extortion. The station interior is notable mostly for its ability to confuse, since this was the main East-West gateway for all categories of people (East and West German and foreigners) and necessitated a warren of passageways and interior spaces to maintain

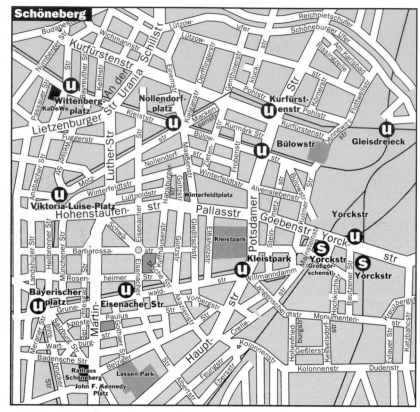

security. Changing trains here requires more than a little maze-solving ability. The building just to the north is known as the Tränenpalast (Palace of Tears), since it was where departing visitors left their Eastern friends and relations who could not follow them back home. Today, it's a concert and circus venue, and has a cinema. Following the train tracks to the east, you arrive at a succession of antique stores, bookshops and cafés in the Bogen, or arches, ending at Museuminsel with the resolutely Americanophile Lucky Strike club.

North on Friedrichstraße, the Metropol Theatre is a survivor of the bombing, now putting on musical revues. Crossing the river on the newly restored wrought iron **Weidendammerbrücke**, turn left towards the Berliner Ensemble theatre, with its bronze statue of Brecht, who directed the company from 1948-56. Behind it, at **Schumannplatz**, stands the Deutsches Theatre, another of the city's important companies.

Back on Friedrichstraße is the Friedrichstadt-palast, a large cabaret that was one of the enter-

tainment hot-spots of the DDR, and still pulls the crowds today. Just beyond is the Oscar Wilde, an Irish pub that is distinguished from the many others in town by being the social centre for the many Irish workers who are involved in the construction boom currently going on.

## Oranienburgerstraße

If the area below the station is the new upmarket face of Mitte, Oranienburgerstraße is the face of its new bohemia. Historically it was the centre of Berlin's Jewish community, which celebrated its central position in the city's life by building the New Synagogue here in 1866. This was the synagogue that was attacked during Kristallnacht in 1939 (50 years to the day before unification), and Allied bombs damaged the rest of the interior in 1945. The façade remained intact, however, and the Moorish dome has been reconstructed and given a spanking new gilding, although visitors to the interior (which will be open in May 1995) will instead see grass and a glassed-in area pro-

**Prenzlauer Berg**'s *planetarium.*

tecting the ruins, a reminder for the ages of what has been lost.

This important piece of Jewish history drew a lot of young people to Berlin in the early nineties, many of them American Jews. As a result, a significant renaissance occurred here: cafés, Jewish restaurants, shops and galleries opened and, at the street's western end, Tacheles, a squatted alternative arts centre, became the hub of local activity in the ruins of an old department store. Operating a bar, gallery, cinema and a music venue, Tacheles' importance can be judged by the many imitations it has spawned in the surrounding streets, identifiable by their graffiti-strewn exteriors and manic alternative energy. Check the scrap metal sculpture collection in their backyard.

Further down Oranienburgerstraße is **Monbijou Park**, the former gardens of a long-gone royal residence, in which Germany's first potatoes were planted (with catastrophic results for the national cuisine). At the street's end, on the site of a former synagogue and Jewish cemetery on **Großer-Hamburger-Straße**, there is a memorial to the thousands of Berlin Jews who were forced to congregate there before being shipped off to die in the concentration camps.

## Sophienstraße and beyond

Sophienstraße is a jewel in Mitte: an eighteenth-century street restored in 1987 for the city's 750th anniversary, and lined with handcrafts ateliers which have replicas of old merchants' metal signs hanging outside. The small Museum in Mitte features exhibitions about the neighbourhood's history, including such vanished glories as Potsdamer Platz and the Jewish quarter on Oranienburgerstraße, and a bit further up the street is the Sophienkirche from which the street gets its name, sitting behind wrought-iron fences and much better looking from the outside than inside.

A few other pockets of old Berlin survive in Mitte: the old St Hedwig's Hospital at the corner of Großer-Hamburger-Straße and **Krausnickstraße**, the quiet residential areas around **Arkonaplatz** and **Zionkirchsplatz**, and surrounding **Koppenplatz**, but you have to seek them out amidst the daunting blandness of post-War East German architecture.

## Prenzlauer Berg

If the fall of the Wall has precipitated a renaissance in any neighbourhood in Berlin, it is surely Prenzlauer Berg. Long described as grey and

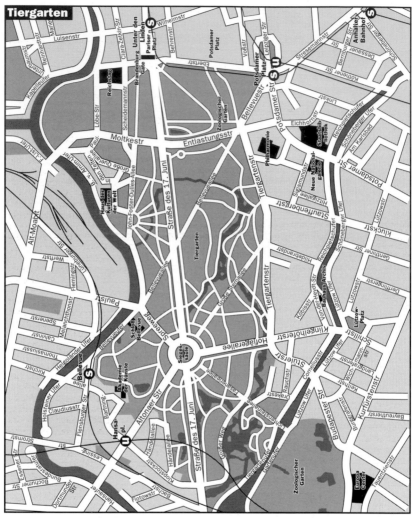

depressing, an area of workers' houses unrelieved
by any sites of historical or touristic interest,
these days the east Berlin district is having its
façades renovated, its streets cleaned and its
buildings newly inhabited by everyone from
artists to yuppies. Galleries and cafés are spring-
ing up, and hundred-year-old buildings are having central heating, bathrooms and telephones
installed for the very first time.

Built around the turn of the century during the
construction boom, Prenzlauer Berg seems to have
had more visionary social planners than some of

the other neighbourhoods that date from the same
period. It has wider streets and sidewalks, giving
the area a distinctive, open look that is unique in
Berlin. Although the majority of the buildings
await restoration, looking down a street in which
some have been scrubbed and painted gives the
feeling of a nineteenth-century boulevard.

The hot centre of Prenz'lberg, as its inhabitants
call it, is the triangular section bounded by
**Schonhauser Allee** on the west and **Greifswalder Straße** on the east, with the S-Bahn
tracks forming the northern boundary. Starting at

the Senefelder Platz U-Bahn station, walk up Schonhauser Allee, noting the old Jewish graveyard, Berlin's oldest, and fairly gloomy even by local standards because of the closely packed stones and canopy of trees. At **Sredzkistraße** stands an old brewery that houses not only a huge furniture store, but the Franz Club, Kesselhaus, and Kulturbraueri, a club complex that's one of the best in town. The streets to the east of here are alive with other clubs, restaurants, and shops. One block of **Husemannstraße** was lovingly restored by the DDR for the city's 750th birthday and is today lined with boutiques, cafés, two museums (one of hairdressing), and an agency that hires horse-and-buggy rigs for special events.

Husemannstraße feeds into **Kollwitz Platz**, one of the prettiest spots in the area, a small park dedicated to the painter and social reformer Käthe Kollwitz, whose statue stands in the park. It was in some of the cafés around here that the first meetings of the dissidents in East Berlin were held in the early '80s, until they got too big and had to be moved to the nearby Gethsemanekirche. Taking **Knaackstraße** off Kollwitz Platz brings you past a nicely restored synagogue to another square containing a small park with a watertower in it. Again, this park is bounded by cafés, and is one of the centres of artistic life in Prenzlauer Berg.

Heading north on **Prenzlauer Allee**, you arrive at Ernst Thällman Park, named for the leader of the pre-1933 Communist Party in Germany and, perhaps, scheduled for renaming. In its north-west corner stands the Zeiss Planetarium, a great DDR interior space that once hymned Soviet cosmonauts and still runs programmes on what's up there in space. Considering the wide expanse of sky visible from most streets in Prenz'lberg, it seems a fitting symbol for the whole neighbourhood.

Prenzlauer Berg is undergoing such rapid change at the moment that new places to visit and things to do appear almost daily. Like the more bohemian parts of Mitte, it hums with energy and creativity, much of it generated by the same artists, writers and musicians who lived here before the Wall came down. Whether you're gallery-hopping, seeing a band at the Franz Club, or eating in one of its inexpensive restaurants, you're sure to catch a whiff of it.

## Schöneberg

It seems more than a coincidence that the old post code for Schöneberg was 62: it seems to go Kreuzberg 61 one better in trendiness and chic. Its old buildings are just a bit more upmarket, its cafés and bars just a bit hipper. If it sometimes seems a bit much, even the worst cynic has to admit that the diversity of this part of town ensures there's something for nearly everybody here.

Schöneberg's northern boundary can be found where **Potsdamer Straße** crosses Kufürstenstraße, but the neighbourhood identity doesn't kick in until you cross **Bülowstraße**. At Nollendorfplatz U-Bahn station, the memorial to the homosexuals killed in concentration camps is a reminder of the immediate area's history: Christopher Isherwood chronicled Berlin from his rooming house at **Nollendorfstraße 17**, and today **Motzstraße** is one of the hot centres of Berlin's gay life. Walking up **Maaßenstraße**, you arrive at **Winterfeldplatz**, site of a lively twice-weekly market where the locals come to pose and occasionally buy things. If you don't get lost in the antiquarian bookshops on Winterfeltdplatz, walk straight on to **Goltzstraße**, and watch Schöneberg's café society watch you from the trendy places that mingle with the pricey, fascinating shops. This is pretty much the scene as Goltzstraße crosses **Grünewaldstraße** and turns into **Akazienstraße**, which ends at another of the area's main thoroughfares, **Hauptstraße**.

A right turn off Akazienstraße on **Belzigerstraße** brings you eventually to Rathaus Schöneberg, from whose steps John F Kennedy announced that he was a Berliner in 1963, and Berlin mayor Walter Momper welcomed the East Berliners in 1989. Nearby streets bear an audacious art-project in the form of signs hanging from lampposts with excerpts taken from the anti-Jewish laws of the 1930s, progressively demonstrating the loss of Jews' rights to the Nazis. At this end, Hauptstraße starts with the Dominicuskirche, one of the city's few Baroque churches, and continues north-east, lined with buildings from the nineteenth-century building boom, when newly wealthy farmers built villas along it. This is also a major area for department-stores. David Bowie and Iggy Pop once resided at number 152 (Bowie in a big first-floor apartment at the front, Pop in a more modest Hinterhof flat). Hauptstraße becomes Potsdamer Straße at Kleist Park, which is entered through a double colonnade moved from the Unter den Linden palace in the eighteenth century, where it was getting in the way. The mansion in the park was used by the Nazis for their law courts, and after the War it was the headquarters for the Allied occupying forces. After the signing of the Ost-Verträge in 1972, which recognised the separate status of East and West Germany, the building stood virtually unused save for occasional meetings, at which the Americans, British and French would observe a ritual pause, as if expecting the Soviet representative, who had last attended in 1948, to show up. In 1990, a Soviet finally did wander along and the Allies held a last meeting here to formalise their withdrawal from the city in 1994. This may be the place where the Cold War ended.

A few blocks further down, past some of the chillier examples of thirties German architecture, is a block of flats on **Pallasstraße**, built atop an air-raid bunker the planners were unable to destroy. It, along with some of the used-furniture shops on nearby **Goebenstraße**, showed up in Wim Wenders' *Wings of Desire*. On the north-west corner of the intersection with Potsdamer Straße stood the Sportpalast, site of many Nazi speeches including Goebbels' 'Total War' speech of 1944.

Perhaps the best way to get to know Schöneberg, though, is through its many restaurants, bars and cafés, sipping a cappuccino at the Café Berio, Café Einstein, or Café M, or a beer at the Pinguin, the Zoulou or the Screwy Club. The locals won't mind: after all, most of them were once strangers here themselves.

## Tiergarten

Originally a hunting preserve for the local princes, the park for which this Bezirk is named is surely one of the nicest in Europe. It was opened to the public when the Brandenburg Gate was dedicated, and they're still coming: on a sunny summer's day it hosts thousands of nature-lovers, joggers, kids, football players and Turkish barbecues. It's so lovely there you may be tempted to pitch a tent, but don't: it's illegal.

Its biggest monument is the Siegessäule, a column celebrating victory in the last war the Germans won: the Franco-Prussian War. It's topped with a golden statue of Nike, with captured French cannons and cannon-balls, sawn in half and gilded, providing the decoration of the column proper. Fans of Wim Wenders' *Wings of Desire* can climb to the top for a fine view. The Siegessäule stands in the middle of the **Großer Stern**, a large traffic roundabout that, with the roads that feed into it, was part of Hitler's grand plan for the capital city of Germania. The column itself was moved there from in front of the Reichstag, where Hitler complained that it spoiled his view. The main east-west street passing through is the **Straße des 17er Juni**, whose name commemorates the East Berlin workers' uprising in 1953. To the east, it runs into the Brandenburg Gate (on the other side it becomes Unter den Linden), with a couple of small monuments in the divider strip proclaiming freedom for those behind the Wall, and the impressive Soviet War Memorial, the only piece of Soviet property in West Berlin, standing on the north side of the street just across **Entlastungsstraße**. Once, this posed quite a problem: built in the British Zone, it was surrounded by a British military enclosure, which was guarded by the Berlin Police, all to protect the monument and the two Soviet soldiers who stood 24-hour guard. Today, anyone can walk right up to the memorial

and read its Russian inscriptions. The two tanks flanking it are alleged to have been the first two Soviet tanks into Berlin, but this is probably legend.

Just down Entlastungsstraße is the Reichstag, hugely imposing with its grand lawn stretching towards the Tiergarten. Most people know it from the fire that destroyed it in 1933, which the Nazis (who were almost certainly the culprits) blamed on a mentally-ill Dutchman named Van der Lubbe. Today, it is used for ceremonial purposes and houses an exhibition entitled Questions of German History and, after a wrapping by Christo in spring 1995, will become the house of the German Parliament when the government moves from Bonn. An eerily understated new monument on the lawn commemorates left-wing legislators removed by the Nazis and sent to concentration camps.

Across Entlastungsstraße, **John-Foster-Dulles Allee** leads back into the park, and past the Haus der Kulturen der Welt (formerly the Kongreßhalle), an impressive bit of modern architecture whose reflecting pool contains a Henry Moore sculpture. The Haus, along with the carillon next to it, was designed by Oscar Niemeyer who also designed Brasilia. A gift from the Americans known to the locals as the 'pregnant oyster', it collapsed shortly after being opened – an event that gave the name to one of Berlin's best-known bands, Einstürzende Neubauten. Today, it houses superb exhibits of world culture and hosts musical ensembles and cinema screenings from far-off lands. Alongside the building runs **In den Zelten**, a street with a history as long as it is short, having been a campground for Huguenot refugees, the site of Berlin's first coffee-house, and for a short time in the thirties, Dr Magnus Hirschfeld's groundbreaking Institute for Sexual Research.

Dulles Allee ends at **Spreeweg**, in front of Schloß Bellevue, a minor palace from 1705 that now houses the German President when he's in town: the flag flying from its roof is the signal he's in. When he is, there are a few more soldiers in the **Englischer Garten** than make for a comfortable stroll. Like its more famous cousin in Munich, this garden came about because King Ludwig I of Bavaria decided that the fact that there weren't constant revolutions in England was due to the plentiful green open spaces in the cities. The idea caught on, and these gardens became such an integral part of German life that Lenin once commented that revolution in Germany was impossible because it would require people to step on the grass.

Back at the Großer Stern, there is a monumental statue of Bismarck set back from the road, flanked by statues of Prussian generals Moltke and Roon, reminders of the past that, judging from the constantly reappearing graffiti, seem to have a few people worried. Continuing along the circle, following Straße der 17er Juni to the west will bring you to the Technisches Universität. Starting at the

*More cranes than buildings: construction around Friedrichstraße. See page 89.*

Tiergarten S-Bahn station and continuing along the road on Saturdays and Sundays is a popular and pricey flea market and crafts market. And following **Klopstock Straße** off 17er Juni will bring you into the Hansa Viertel, a postwar housing project whose buildings were designed by a Who's Who of architects, which still draws busloads of architecture students from around the world.

Another street coming off the Großer Stern, **Hofjägerallee**, heads towards the city centre. At the park's edge, **Tiergartenstraße** has a few of the buildings left over from when this was Embassy Row, most notably the former (and maybe future) Japanese and Italian embassies. The street ends at the Kulturforum complex, with the Philharmonie, home of the overrated Berlin Philharmonic Orchestra, the Kammermusiksaal, where smaller ensembles play, and, hidden away in a corner, the delightful Musikinstrumentenmuseum, where visitors can sometimes hear ensembles of music students playing, and tour the innards of a genuine Mighty Wurlitzer organ. Nearby is the Staatsbibliothek, the West Berlin central library, and Mies van der Rohe's Neuenationalgalerie, which contains the later half of the national collection and hosts touring exhibits.

To the east lies **Potsdamer Platz**, which is today a chaotic construction site best avoided in a car. Once a major hub, Potsdamer Platz had swanky hotels and restaurants, and a traffic problem that caused the erection of the world's first traffic signal, but the proximity of Hitler's headquarters caused the area to be bombed flat, and the passing of the East-West border through its middle left it desolate for most of the postwar era. Today, the land has been acquired by Daimler-Benz, Sony and other companies, and office buildings are going up. The whole area is swathed with mystery: allegedly, interesting finds have been made, and hushed up, during excavation, and in the wasteland between **Pariser Platz** and Potsdamer Platz a small hill of rubble was long rumoured to be the closed-up entrance to Hitler's vast underground bunker. Recently, however, historians have established it to be the Fahrerbunker, used by chauffeurs, rather than the Führerbunker.

Walking down **Potsdamer Straße**, you come to **Reichpietschufer**, and here a left turn will bring you to **Stauffenburgstraße**, where the Gedenkstätte der Deutsche Widerstand (Memorial to the German Resistance) memorialises the plotters who tried to blow Hitler up on July 20, 1944. Continuing down the canal bank, Emil Fahrenkanp's Shell building is a modern architectural masterpiece (best seen from the bridge) that almost fell apart before the current restoration work started. On past the Grand Hotel Esplanade is the Bauhaus Archiv, which documents the influential Saxon school through exhibits of objects, drawings and an interactive computer program in English, and several other languages, explaining the whole thing.

## Other Hoods

Because Berlin's underlying soil is sandy, until recently large buildings haven't been built here, which means that the city sprawls. The U-Bahn and S-Bahn system, however, can take you to some of its lesser-known neighbourhoods in minutes. Here are some suggestions for further exploration.

### West Berlin

To the north, the city eventually gives itself up to block after block of industrial works and housing for the people who work there, and while the Moabit section of Tiergarten has some charm, particularly along the river, it's harder to defend areas such as Wedding and Reinickendorf. One sight in Wedding, though, is worth the trip: the Gedenks-stätte Berliner Mauer, a section of the Wall without graffiti (it was on the east side) that has been preserved by the Berliner Museum. It lies between **Bernauer Straße** and **Invalidenstraße** near the Nordbahnhof S-Bahn station.

Southern West Berlin was the American Sector, and sections such as Steglitz, Dahlem and Zehlendorf contain some of the city's wealthiest residences. Besides the museum complex (*see chapter* **Museums**), Dahlem is the home of the Freie Universität, some of whose departments occupy former villas seized by the Nazis from their Jewish owners. In Zehlendorf, Mexikoplatz is a beautifully preserved plaza with one of the city's best-known left-wing book-stores in its S-Bahn station. Elsewhere in Zehlendorf, the Onkel-Toms-Hütte development is a historically important collection of workers' houses designed in the twenties and thirties by architects Bruno Taut, Hugo Häring and Otto Rudolf Solvisberg, painted in unique colours only available from one firm in Germany, and today lived in by workers in professions that are a far cry from those of the original inhabitants. Take the U-Bahn to Onkel-Toms-Hütte and walk down **Onkel-Tom-Straße** towards the woods. Other than this, Zehlendorf's main claim to fame these days is the many empty buildings left by the departing American troops, the future of which is undecided at the time of writing.

Perhaps the best way to ogle the mansions in Steglitz and Dahlem is by auto or bicycle, wandering down the streets wondering at the mélange of architectural styles and trying to guess which Steglitz mansion is the one Helmut Kohl has bought in anticipation of the government moving to Berlin in 1999.

Another southern district, Neukölln, was a pocket south-east of Kreuzberg until the Wall came down, and now is the most direct neighbour of Schönefeld Airport. **Karl-Marx-Straße** here is a major shopping district, but the Rixdorf sec-tion around **Richard-Schadoma-Platz** is charming because of the many old buildings that remain there. Further south, at Britz-Sud, the Bruno-Taut-Ring, a horseshoe-shaped housing estate, is a fine example of Bauhaus architecture.

One other tourist attraction in a seldom-visited neighbourhood should be mentioned: in a tiny graveyard just off the **Südwest Korso** in Friedenau, south-west of Schöneberg, is Marlene Dietrich's grave. Like most graveyards here, this one has a card marking the location of some of its more prominent residents at the gateway, giving their names and occupations. La Dietrich has not been formally added to this list, but a fan has scrawled her name and 'Most Beautiful Woman in the World', so she's easy to find.

South of Charlottenburg and west of Schöne-berg lies Wilmersdorf. This is a mostly boring district of smart apartments that nonetheless has many bars and cafés and a lot of streetlife at night in the area around **Ludwig-Kirch-Platz**.

### East Berlin

The obscure New York songwriter David Ackles once wrote a song called 'Subway to the Country' about wishing he could jump on the underground and get out where the land was green. Well, David, come to Berlin: at termini such as Königs Wusterhausen and Strausberg Nord you can do just that, particularly if you take a bicycle and are willing to pedal for 30 minutes or so. Even some of the closer-in stations can offer pleasant surroundings of two-family houses with backyards filled with fruit-trees. Not all of the neighbourhoods here are universally attractive: it's best to avoid Marzahn after dark, although its Biesdorf district is quite nice and has a small park and castle. Another park worth a visit is **Treptower Park**, with its immense Soviet war memorial and pleasant picnic area. From here, several excursion boats leave in the summer for trips along the Spree, and there are other boats with on-board restaurants. The park continues to the south, where it becomes the **Plänterwald**, site of a big amusement park.

Fans of urban living can see plenty of examples of Eastern bloc apartment buildings in the east, built on a plan that is echoed in the outlying areas of any major former Warsaw Pact city. Of particular note is the long string of Soviet-style Zuckerbäcker apartment buildings lining **Frank-furter Allee** (formerly **Marx-Lenin Allee**), con-structed along a utopian scheme that made each a miniature model of ideal Communist society, with all classes of workers included in each building. Artists were given the top floors. These buildings, although somewhat ratty today, are listed as having architectural and historical value, and are presently being restored. As for Frankfurter Allee, it is a street that continues in a straight line almost to the Polish border.

**Opposite:** *Treptower Park.*

# Eating & Drinking

# Restaurants

**It's not all meat and two veg – neue deutsche Küche and moves to blend German food with international cuisine are spicing up Berlin's restaurant-going.**

Berlin boasts a greater variety of cuisines than any other German city, for which it can thank its relatively large immigrant community. For example, some of the best Turkish food outside Turkey can be found in Kreuzberg, and Italian cuisine at its best can be sampled at some of the many Italian restaurants dotted around the city.

Traditional German cooking (gutbürgerliche Küche) can be splendid, but is often hearty, unhealthy stuff, especially since so many dishes revolve around some version of pork. The neue deutsche Küche, or new German cuisine, offers some relief. Dishes are lighter, and more interesting, than traditional food, although still far inferior to French nouvelle cuisine.

Breakfast is a much-loved tradition here, and it's served until well into the afternoon. In fact some cafés even offer breakfast from noon (*see also* chapter **Cafés & Bars**). Traditionally, lunch is the main meal in Germany, but in Berlin anything goes: whatever you want in the evening, a take-away snack, a light supper (Abendbrot) or a gigantic dinner, you can have it. Things are of course a little trickier if you're vegetarian. *See box* **Berlin for Vegheads.**

The options for eating out in east Berlin used to be slim but are steadily improving, especially in the Mitte and Prenzlauer Berg areas, where new restaurants seem to spring up every day. Though you'll find some excellent eastern restaurants in our listings, generally the standards of food and service still lag behind the west and restaurants tend to close earlier on that side of the city.

The average prices listed below are for a starter and a main course. We've organised the restaurants according to price: Inexpensive means an average of less than DM25, Moderate is DM25 to DM39, and Expensive is anything over DM40. We've also included a selection of the better Imbißes (snack bars) as another way to find good, cheap eats.

In restaurants a service charge of 17 per cent is included in the price of a meal, but, unless the service is very poor, diners generally add an extra tip by rounding up the bill. So, if the bill is DM7.50, pay DM8; if it's DM48, pay DM50, although some people simply add 10 per cent. Tips are handed to the server when paying, not

left on the table. Be warned: when you hand over the cash, take care not to say 'danke' unless you want them to keep the change.

**If you want to find a restaurant in a particular area of the city, *see page 264* Area Index.**

## Expensive

DM40 and over.

### Abendmahl
*Muskauer Straße 9, Kreuzberg, 10997 (612 5170). U1 Görlitzer Bahnhof.* **Open** 6pm-1am daily. **Average** DM40. **No credit cards.**
The name means 'Last Supper' and the warm decor is enlivened with a little religious kitsch: religious statues about the bar, red velvet curtains, and menus decorated with 3D religious postcards. The menu changes regularly and all dishes are given wacky names: recent examples included Sussi And The Couch Potatoes and The World Of Suzie Wong. What you get are inventive and wonderfully presented fish and vegetarian dishes followed by spectacular desserts. Service is charming, efficient and laid-back. An ideal place to linger with friends. Book at weekends.

### Altes Zollhaus
*Carl-Herz-Ufer 30, Kreuzberg, 10961 (692 3300). U1 Prinzenstraße.* **Open** 6-11.30pm Tue-Sat. **Average** menus at DM70-100. **Credit** AmEx, DC, EC, JBC, V.
This former customs house on the Landwehrkanal does a brilliant job of modernising German cuisine, using only the freshest locally grown ingredients, many of them organically raised. The superb wine list and attentive service in pleasant surroundings – plus the healthy-sized portions – make this a value-for-money splurge, if that's not a contradiction. Reservations essential.

### Bamberger Reiter
*Regensburgerstraße 7, Schöneberg, 10777 (2 18 42 82; bistro 2 13 67 33). U4 Viktoria-Luise-Platz.* **Open** 1am (kitchen closes 10pm) Tue-Sat. **Average** DM140; *bistro* DM60. **Credit** AmEx, DC, V; *bistro* **no credit cards.**
Outstanding French cuisine earned Bamberger Reiter a very official Michelin star. The décor in the main restaurant – dark wood, mirrors and elaborate flower arrangements – provides a pleasant backdrop. The food is also excellent in the cheaper and equally pleasant bistro next door which is part of the same concern. Booking is recommended.

### Biberbau
*Durlacherstraße 15, Wilmersdorf, 10715 (853 2390). U9 Bundesplatz.* **Open** 6pm-1am Wed-Mon. **Average** DM50. **No credit cards.**
Biberbau's agreeable but pricey German-French cuisine attracts a bourgeois crowd. Booking is a must.

## Bovril

*Kurfürstendamm 184, Charlottenburg, 10707 (881 84 61). U7 Adenauer Platz.* **Open** noon-2am Mon-Sat. **Average** DM50. **Credit** AmEx, DC, EC, JCB, V.
A bright bistro, popular with business, intellectual and artistic types for its selection of light, German-French meals, exquisitely prepared. The menu changes daily. Celebs hang out here during the film festival. Superb soups.

## Café Einstein

*Kurfürstenstraße 58, Tiergarten, 10785 (261 5096). U1, U2, U4 Nollendorfplatz.* **Open** 10am-2am daily. **Average** DM42. **Credit** AmEx, DC, JCB, V.
Café Einstein models itself on a Viennese coffee shop, and the efficient-but-aloof waiters wear tuxedos. Enjoy anything from one of the wonderful cappuccinos to an expensive if exquisite full-blown meal, and sit and watch the rest of the customers. The high-ceilinged main room is always loud and busy, particularly on Sundays, when Berlin's finest come out first to sample the famous breakfasts and later to sup melange and scoff strudel. In the summertime you can eat in the leafy garden. *See also chapter* **Cafés & Bars**.

## Diekmann

*Meineckestraße 7, Wilmersdorf, 10719 (883 33 21). U9, U15 Kurfürstendamm.* **Open** noon-1am Mon-Sat; 6pm-1am public holidays. **Average** DM50. **No credit cards.**
A former shop that has been remodelled into a comely restaurant offering venison, fish and a small but good wine selection. Service is friendly and multilingual.

## Don Camillo

*Schloßstraße 7, Charlottenburg, 14059 (322 35 72). U2 Sophie-Charlotte-Platz.* **Open** noon-3pm, 6-11.30pm, Thur-Tue. **Average** DM80. **No credit cards.**
One of the best Italian restaurants in town. Food is prepared at the table. The home-made pasta comes in ten varieties and can be accompanied by any one of a range of sauces. Seasonings are minimal to let the delicate flavour of the meats shine through; garlic is added only upon request. Reservations are essential.

## Dschungel

*Nürnberger Straße 53, Schöneberg, 10789 (218 6698). U1 Augsburger Straße.* **Open** 11am-1am Mon-Sat. **Average** DM40. **Credit** AmEx, EC, V.
The Dschungel was a nightclub which prided itself on never having changed the decor since the mid-seventies when Bowie used to hang out there. Now it's a restaurant and they still haven't done much to the decor. Result: it feels like a disco with a few tables dragged in. The menu is oddly cosmopolitan: every dish from a different cuisine. Our vegetable tempura was excellent, though.

## Florian

*Grolmanstraße 52, Charlottenburg, 10623 (313 91 84). S3, S5, S6, S9 Savignyplatz.* **Open** 6pm-3am daily, kitchen closes at 1am. **Average** DM40. **No credit cards.**
A light, white restaurant in the attractive area around Savignyplatz. A sprinkling of celebrities can often be spotted among the members of the film, media and art scene who cluster around the bar sipping sparkling wine, before sitting down to order from a small menu of nouvelle European dishes. Nice ambience but overpriced. Useless for vegetarians.

## Französischer Hof

*Jägerstraße 36, Mitte, 10117 (229 3152). U2, U6 Stadtmitte.* **Open** 11am-midnight daily. **Average** DM45. **Credit** DC, EC, V.
On the splendid Gendarmenmarkt and close to the Hilton Hotel, the Französischer Hof offers classic German and French meals. Dress up a bit for this spot; it draws a theatre and classical music crowd in the evenings.

## Franzotti

*Kreuzbergstraße 71, Kreuzberg, 10965 (785 3850). U6, U7 Mehringdamm.* **Open** 6pm-2am daily. **Average** DM40. **No credit cards.**
This newish place next to well established Osteria No 1 (*see below*) bills itself as a 'vineria' rather than a restaurant. The menu offers a small selection of Italian food and 31 pages of fine wines. Don't worry if you find the choice mind-boggling: the waiters are helpful and know their stuff. The excellent vegetable antipasto platter costs DM26 and is enough appetiser for three. Follow it with pennini with mushrooms and chicken liver (DM16) or the fillet of lamb with garlic and rosemary (DM26), washed down by one of their 11 Chiantis. Roomy, relaxing and recommended.

## Hakuin

*Martin-Luther-Straße 1, Schöneberg, 10777 (218 2027). U2, U3 Wittenbergplatz.* **Open** 6-11.30pm Mon-Wed, Fri except Buddhist holidays; noon-3pm, 6-11.30pm, Sat, Sun, public holidays. **Average** DM40. **No credit cards.**
Hakuin provides excellent but expensive Buddhist vegetarian food. In the beautiful no-smoking room people eat quietly amid a jungle of plants and a large fish pool with a gentle fountain. Fruit curries are often served on bamboo serving plates, in tune with the décor. Smokers are exiled to a small, much more boring room next door. A extremely peaceful place.

## La Riva

*Spreeufer 2, Mitte, 10178 (242 5183). U2 Klosterstraße.* **Open** noon-midnight daily. **Average** DM50. **Credit** AmEx, DC, EC, V.
On the edge of the Nikolaiviertel and with a very nice terrace overlooking the Spree river, La Riva offers original Italian cuisine and specialities from Tuscany.

## Lubitsch

*Bleibtreustraße 47, Charlottenburg, 10623 (882 3756). S3, S5, S6, S9 Savignyplatz.* **Open** from 10am, kitchen closes midnight. **Average** DM55. **No credit cards.**
Lubitsch is a new and currently fashionable feeding trough for the Charlottenburg art crowd – on our visit the long, narrow dining area was dominated by an enormous table of architects. Decor is sleek, service unhurried but professional, food is excellent neue deutsche Küche, perhaps a little overpriced. You are not advised to sit near the door on a cold evening, though – opening it wide seems to be their only means of ventilation.

## Lutter & Wegner

*Schlüterstraße 55, Charlottenburg, 10629 (881 3440). S3, S5, S6, S9 Savignyplatz.* **Open** 6.30pm-2am daily. **Average** DM40. **Credit** AmEx.
Nouvelle cuisine is served elegantly at this Berlin landmark, established in 1811. It was first a wine cellar in eastern Berlin, but after World War II re-opened as a restaurant in the West serving food and selected wines. The enormous wooden bar and background jazz evoke an Old World atmosphere that attracts a mixed crowd of young and old. Arrogant service isn't always made up for by the good food and beautiful ambience: this place definitely has its off nights. But worth visiting, if only for a drink.

## Opern Palais

*Unter den Linden 5, Mitte, 10117 (200 2269). U6, S3, S5, S6, S7, S9 Friedrichstraße.* **Open** 8.30am-midnight daily. **Average** DM35 in Fredericus; DM60 in Könige Luise. **Credit** AmEx, EC, V.
Take your pick of two restaurants and two cafés in this large, smart villa next to the Staatsoper. The Fredericus restaurant offers hearty traditional German food. The expensive and somewhat stiff Könige Luise serves up top-class French-derived international cuisine. The cafés serve very hearty breakfasts and a selection of 70 cakes.

# The Menu

## Meals
**Fruhstück** breakfast
**Mittagessen** lunch
**Abendessen** evening meal

## Basics
**Vorspeise** starter
**Hauptgericht** main course
**Nachspeise** dessert
**Speisekarte** menu
**Brötchen** bread roll
**Butter** butter
**Eier** eggs
**Gemüse** vegetables
**Käse** cheese
**Knoblauch** garlic
**Fleisch** meat
**Fisch** fish
**Gekochte Ei** boiled egg
**Obst** fruit
**Nudeln** noodles
**Omelett** omelette
**Pfeffer** pepper
**Pochierteier** poached eggs
**Ruhreier** scrambled eggs
**Salz** salt
**Scharf** hot
**Soße** sauce
**Speigeleier** fried eggs
**Zucker** sugar

## Soups (Suppen)
**Bohnensuppe** bean soup
**Erbsensuppe** pea soup
**Fleischsuppe** clear soup with meat dumplings
**Hühnersuppe** chicken soup
**Leberknödelsuppe** clear soup with liver dumplings
**Linsensuppe** lentil soup
**Kartoffelsuppe** potato soup
**Zweibelsuppe** onion soup

## Starters (Vorspeise)
**Fleichsalat** sausage salad with onion
**Gemischter Salat** mixed salad
**Grüner Salat** green salad
**Leberpaste** liver paté
**Melone mit Schinken** melon with ham

## Meat (Fleisch)
**Bockwurst** fat boiled sausage
**Bratwurst** grilled sausage
**Currywurst** sausage served with curry sauce
**Eisbein** pigs' trotters
**Hackfleisch** mincemeat
**Hirsch** venison
**Huhn, Hänchen** chicken
**Kanninchen** rabbit
**Kotelett** cutlet
**Krautwickerl** cabbage leaves stuffed with mincemeat
**Lamm** lamb
**Leber** liver
**Nieren** kidneys
**Rindfleisch** beef
**Sauerbraten** beef marinated, then roasted
**Schinken** ham

**Schweinebraten** roast pork
**Schweinefleisch** pork
**Truthahn** turkey
**Weisswurst** white sausage
**Wienerwurst** boiled sausage
**Wurst** sausage

## Fish (Fisch)
**Aal** eel
**Forelle** trout
**Hering** herring
**Hummer** lobster
**Kabeljau** cod
**Karpfen** carp
**Kaviar** caviar
**Krabben** prawns or shrimps
**Lachs** salmon
**Makrele** mackerel
**Muscheln** mussels
**Schellfisch** haddock
**Scholle** plaice; **seezunge** sole
**Tintenfisch** squid
**Thunfisch** tuna
**Zander** pike perch

## Vegetables (Gemüse)
**Bohnen** beans
**Bratkartoffeln** fried potatoes
**Brokkoli** broccoli
**Champignons** mushrooms
**Erbsen** peas
**Gurke** cucumber
**Karotten** carrots
**Kartoffelbrei** mashed potatoes
**Kartoffelpuree** creamed potatoes
**Kartoffelsalat** potato salad
**Knoblauch** garlic
**Knödel** dumpling
**Kopfsalat** lettuce
**Linsen** lentils
**Paprika** peppers
**Pommes Frites** chips
**Rosenkohl** Brussels sprouts
**Rote Rübe** beetroot
**Rotkohl** red cabbage
**Salzkartoffeln** boiled potatoes
**Sauerkraut** pickled cabbage
**Spargel** asparagus
**Tomaten** tomatoes
**Zweibeln** onions

*A mixed crowd of young and old are drawn to **Lutter & Wegner**. See page 102.*

## Paris Bar

*Kantstraße 152, Charlottenburg, 10623 (313 8052). S3, S5, S6, S9 Savignyplatz.* **Open** noon-1am daily. **Average** DM45. **Credit** AmEx.

A classic French bistro that locals either love or hate. The Paris Bar menu has standard, competently cooked French dishes, such as rack of lamb or venison with berry sauce. Art adorns the walls: some good, some laughable. The waiters tend to be snooty but can sometimes turn on the charm. Overrated and expensive – 12 Belon oysters will set you back a swingeing DM90 – it can nevertheless be a lot of fun when you get a showbiz crowd in there: during the Filmfest, for example.

## Paris Moskau

*Alt-Moabit 141, Tiergarten-Moabit, 10557 (394 2081). S3, S5, S6, S9 Lehrter Stadtbahnhof.* **Open** 6-11.30pm daily. **Average** DM60, set menu DM70-100. **No credit cards.**

Once a railway linesmen's canteen on the tracks between Paris and Moscow, this place always has at least one fish dish, and often poultry and venison with Russian-French influences. Beautiful location and fine food and wine, but all save the most dedicated nouvelle cuisine fans will blanche at the tiny portions.

## Restaurant am Fasanenplatz

*Fasanenstraße 42, Wilmersdorf, 10719 (883 97 23). U1, U9 Spichernstraße.* **Open** noon-2pm Wed-Sat; 5.30-11.30pm Sun. **Average** DM60; **set meals** DM48 lunch; DM58-95 dinner. **Credit** AmEx, EC, V.

A treat in the idyllic area around Fasanenplatz. Paintings exploding with colour, lots of small halogen lights, fine wines and friendly service make this a quiet and extremely relaxing place for German cuisine with a twist. Reservations are definitely advisable.

## Sabu

*Salzburger Straße 19, Schöneberg, 10825 (787 4483). U4, U7 Bayerischer Platz.* **Open** noon-2pm Mon-Fri; 6pm-midnight daily. **Average** DM40. **Credit** AmEx, EC, MC, V.

Probably the best Japanese restaurant in Berlin. A smart, white place with a calm atmosphere and traditional dishes given an individual slant. The tempura is heavenly, noodle soups the stuff of legend, and the sushi is so good that this is the restaurant of choice for sushi chefs from other Japanese places. Extravagant set menus hover around DM75. It's on a quiet street and there's a tiny veranda with only a table for two that's wonderful on summer nights, if you can get it.

## Shell

*Knesebeckstraße 22, Charlottenburg, 10623 (312 8310). S3, S5, S6, S9 Savignyplatz.* **Open** 9am-2am Mon-Sat; 10am-1am Sun. **Average** DM40. **Credit** AmEx, EC, V.

A former petrol station turned chic restaurant, Shell has a reputation for snooty service and overpriced new German cuisine. On our last visit, though, everything had greatly improved: the waiter was sweet and helpful, the food was delicious and in portions so big they were hard to finish. The brunches here are always excellent.

## Toto

*Bleibtreustraße 55, Charlottenburg, 10627 (312 5449). S3, S5, S6, S9 Savignyplatz.* **Open** noon-midnight daily. **Average** DM40. **No credit cards.**

A smart Italian place near Savignyplatz, with higher-than-average prices and a short menu. The food is excellent and beautifully prepared. Freshly made tomato soup and fettuccine with wild mushrooms are both worth spending your Deutsche Marks on, and the tiramisu and zabaglione come highly recommended. Service can be chaotic, but it all fits in well with the mood of the place.

## Moderate

Average DM25-39.

### Astir's

*Grolmanstraße 56, Charlottenburg, 10623 (313 63 20).*
*S3, S5, S6, S9 Savignyplatz.* **Open** noon-1am Mon-Sat;
6pm-1am Sun. **Average** DM35. **Credit** AmEx, MC.
Astir's could be just another trendy place in the Savignyplatz area, but its friendly service sets it apart. Eat fine
new German cuisine dishes under arty posters and try to
leave room for dessert. The set menus, which are available
until 6pm and start at about DM16.50, are usually a good
deal. Soups are a speciality and the salads and fish selections
tend to be reliable choices. Don't miss the warm salmon over
salad greens.

### Ax Bax

*Leibnitzstraße 34, Charlottenburg, 10625 (313 85 94).*
*U7 Wilmersdorfer Straße.* **Open** 6pm-4am daily, kitchen
closes 1am. **Average** DM35. **No credit cards.**
The German-Austrian food is good and good value, and the
subdued interior is pleasant, but hope that you don't catch
Amadeus, the tailcoat-clad waiter, on a bad day. You can
also just stop by for a drink at the bar.

### Café Addis

*Tempelhofer Ufer 6, Kreuzberg, 10963 (251 6730). U1,*
*U6 Hallesches Tor.* **Open** 4pm-1am Wed-Mon. **Average**
DM27. **No credit cards.**
Berlin's small Ethiopian community has turned a funky
neighbourhood bar into a first-rate showpiece for its exotic
cuisine, spicy stews served on *injera*, a towel-like bread.
Scoop up bits of the hearty food with your hands from the
tray in the centre of your table, and make sure there's a beer
(or some homemade Ethiopian honey wine) nearby.

### Café Aroma

*Hochkirchstraße 8, Schöneberg, 10829 (782 5821).*
*U7/S1, S2 Yorckstraße.* **Open** 6pm-midnight Mon-Sat;
4pm-midnight Sun. **Average** DM30. **No credit cards.**
Run by ever so slightly spaced-out young Italians, Aroma is
always a hubbub of activity and conversation. It's crowded
and a little chaotic, but the food here is always excellent. The
salads and pasta sauces are inventive and lovingly prepared
and the wine list is interesting. It's situated on a quiet, leafy
street and there are tables outside in summer. You would be
best advised to book.

### Café Oren

*Oranienburger Straße 28, Mitte, 10117 (282 8228). S1,*
*S2 Oranienburger Straße.* **Open** 10am-1am daily,
kitchen closes midnight daily, except 12.30am Sat.
**Average** DM25. **No credit cards.**
A Jewish (not kosher) restaurant that is right next to the New
Synagogue and offers inventive fish and vegetable dishes.
Everything, including the service, was perfect on our visit.
The garlic cream soup was thick and tasty; the salad fresh
and crispy; and the soya cutlet breaded with sesame, in a
light curry sauce served with fried banana and rice, was
heavenly. There is excellent vegetarian borscht and the
Orient Express platter, a large selection of Meze, is good
value at DM16.50. As bustling as Oranienburger Straße
outside, so it's best to book.

### Café Restaurant Jolesch

*Muskauerstraße 1, Kreuzberg, 10997 (612 3581). U1*
*Schlesisches Tor.* **Open** 10am-1am daily, kitchen closes
11.30pm. **Average** DM28. **No credit cards.**
Deservedly popular spot serving brilliant interpretations of
Austrian cuisine: the goulash is thick with hot paprika and
caraway, and the Tafelspitz is tender. Always a couple of
inventive vegetarian entrées on the daily menu, and the
soups, too, can be ingenious. Dinner reservations suggested.

### Candela

*Grunewaldstraße 81, Schöneberg, 10823 (782 1409).*
*U7 Eisenacher Straße.* **Open** 5pm-1am daily. **Average**
DM25. **Credit** V.
Excellently prepared Italian food, with large selections of
both pizza and pasta and an inventive day menu are on offer
at Candela. The service is good and unobtrusive.

### Carpe Diem

*Savigny Passage 577, Charlottenburg, 10623*
*(313 2728). S3, S5, S6, S9 Savignyplatz.* **Open** noon-
midnight Tue-Sat. **Average** DM32, set lunch DM18. **No
credit cards.**
Tapas and other Mediterranean specialities are served under
the S-Bahn arches in this imaginatively designed restaurant.
The tables are a little too close together for comfort, but it's
a lively place with loud music and effusive service.

### Ginetun

*Schiffbauerdamm 8, Mitte, 10117 (282 3965). U6, S1,*
*S2, S3, S5, S6, S7, S9 Friedrichstraße.* **Open** 5pm-1am
Mon; noon-1am Tue-Sun. **Average** DM28. **Credit**
AmEx, MC, V.
A busy Armenian restaurant offering a good mix of well-
prepared meat and vegetarian dishes. Starters include yogurt
soup, bortsch and talma (vine leaves stuffed with meat,
served with a yogurt sauce and a surprisingly good side
salad topped with garlicky grated carrot, DM12.50). Follow
up with lamb kebab (DM21.50) or the mushrooms stuffed
with feta cheese (DM18.50).

### Hard Rock Café

*Meinekestraße 21, Charlottenburg, 10623 (88 46 20).*
*U9, U15 Kurfürstendamm.* **Open** noon-2am daily.
**Average** DM30. **Credit** AmEx, DC, JCB, V.
Very loud, very air-conditioned and very pricey, the Hard
Rock can at least boast authentic hamburgers, dozens of
cocktails and good desserts.

### Hardtke

*Meinekestraße 27, Charlottenburg, 10623 (881 98 27).*
*U3 Uhlandstraße.* **Open** 11am-12.30am daily. **Average**
DM35. **No credit cards.**
Meat-and-potato loving tourists from all over Germany flock
to this 40-year-old Berlin institution. The menu is full of
typically heavy German dishes such as Sauerbraten with
red cabbage and potato dumplings. Hardtke's home-made
sausages are also popular. Too many tourists, though, spoil
the atmosphere.

### Heinrich

*Sophie-Charlotte-Straße 88, Charlottenburg, 14059 (321*
*6517). U2 Sophie-Charlotte-Platz.* **Open** noon-1am daily.
**Average** DM28. **Credit** EC, V.
Named after satirist and illustrator Heinrich Zille, who
used to live at this address, this is the only place in Berlin
where you'll find horse ragout on the same menu as buck-
wheat pancakes. Vegetarian options rub shoulders with
traditional German standbys, and original wooden fittings
are interspersed with Zille's photographs of the area at the
turn of the century. Service is courteous and unhurried,
the wine list is long, the cheese soup and dandelion salads
particularly good.

### Hitit

*Corner of Danckelmannstraße/Knobelsdorffstraße,*
*Charlottenburg, 14059 (322 45 57). U2 Sophie-*
*Charlotte-Platz.* **Open** noon-1am daily. **Average** DM38.
**No credit cards.**
Completely different from most other Turkish restaurants
in the city, Hitit serves excellent Anatolian/Turkish food
in an elegant setting, complete with Hittite wall reliefs,
stylish high-backed chairs and pale walls. Choose from over
150 dishes listed, with ample options for vegetarians. The

Turkish wines are recommended, as are all the dishes our party of ten tried. Service is extremely friendly and the atmosphere calm and soothing, aided by the small waterfall running down the wall at the front of the restaurant.

### India Haus
*Feurigstraße 38 (corner Dominicusstraße), Schöneberg, 10827 (781 2546). U4 Rathaus Schöneberg.* **Open** 5pm-midnight Mon-Fri; noon-1am Sat, Sun. **Average** DM25. **Credit** DC, EC, V.
Though more and more places are opening, Berlin is not a great town for Indian food. India Haus is a cut above the rest. Just off Schöneberg's Hauptstraße, it offers a long menu, with wide choices for vegetarians. The almond soup is excellent and the malay kofta delicious, but we didn't fare as well with the chicken tikka – the bird was dry and the sauce too hot. In the Imbiß part you can stand and eat cheaply from a smaller menu, before nipping round the corner to catch a movie in English at the Odeon.

### Istanbul
*Knesebeckstraße 77, Charlottenburg, 10623 (883 2777). S3, S5, S6, S9 Savignyplatz.* **Open** noon-midnight daily. **Average** DM40. **Credit** AmEx, DC, EC, JBC, MC, V.
The oldest Turkish restaurant in Berlin serves well cooked meals at inflated prices. The menu is extensive, offering a wide selection of starters, meat and fish dishes: veggies can opt for a selection of hot and cold *meze*. From the street you can't see inside: open the door and you could almost be in Constantinople. The interior is dark and lavishly decorated with Islamic and Turkish paraphernalia. At the weekends belly-dancers perform in the room at the back.

### Kellerrestaurant im Brecht Haus
*Chaussestraße 125, Mitte, 10115 (282 3843). U6 Oranienburger Tor.* **Open** daily 5pm-2am. **Average** DM30. **Credit** AmEx, DC, EC, V.
A small restaurant in the cellar of the house where Brecht lived before his death in 1956. The dark brown wooden interior is covered with model stage sets and photographs of Brecht. Some of the dishes (designated on the menu by an asterix) are taken from the cookbook of Helene Weigel, the actress and Brecht's wife. These include roast beef with horseradish sauce, coated in an egg pancake, and fried pork and beef patties, served with green beans and bacon dumplings. Vegetarians will find little, but the creamy cheese soup is recommended. Nice salads too. The wine cellar offers a good selection of French, Italian, German, Portuguese and Californian wines, with prices ranging from DM24 to DM480 for a 1943 Château la Caillon.

### Kien-du
*Kaiser-Friedrich-Straße 89, Charlottenburg, 10585 (341 14 47). U2 Sophie-Charlotte-Platz.* **Open** 6pm-midnight Mon-Fri; 4.30pm-midnight Sat, Sun. **Average** DM30. **No credit cards.**
It doesn't look much – fairly drab decor enlivened by the usual Buddhist bits and pieces – but, without a shadow of a doubt, Kien-du serves the best Thai curries in town. There's a huge selection of them too, although only a small choice for vegetarians. Try the beef, potatoes and peanuts in hot yellow sauce or the curried pineapple, bamboo and peppers – then take the edge off with a Singha beer. They're extremely flexible here, and happy to prepare things to your specifications.

### Kyoto
*Wilmersdorfer Straße 94, Charlottenburg, 10629 (883 2733). U7 Adenauerplatz.* **Open** 6pm-midnight Tue-Sun. **Average** DM35. **No credit cards.**
Light, pleasant, traditional Japanese joint with sushi à la carte and tatami rooms in the back. There's a selection of set dinners (sukiyaki with all the trimmings costs DM48) and specialities such as Kyoto Bento: pieces of sushi and sashimi decoratively arranged in a black lacquer box. For the price, the best Japanese food in this part of town and it's usually no problem getting a table.

### Lusiada
*Kurfürstendamm 132a, Halensee, 10711 (891 5869). U7 Adenauerplatz.* **Open** 5pm-2am Mon-Wed; 5pm-3am Thur-Sat; 5pm-midnight Sun. **Average** DM25. **No credit cards.**
A chaotic but nonetheless welcoming restaurant, appealing to prominent Berliners. They come for the laid-back atmosphere and fine Portuguese fish dishes. Great when it's late: you can still eat at 3am.

### Marjellchen
*Mommsenstraße 9, Charlottenburg, 10629 (883 2676). S3, S5, S6, S9 Savignyplatz.* **Open** noon-1am Mon-Fri, Sun; 5pm-midnight Sat. **Average** DM35. **Credit** DC, EC, JCB, MC, V.
Specialities from East Prussia, Pomerania and Silesia are served here. The atmosphere is one of German Gemütlichkeit (comfort and conviviality): there's an excellent bar, service is great and the larger-than-life owner likes to recite verse.

### Merhaba
*Hasenheide 39, Kreuzberg, 10967 (692 1713). U7 Südstern.* **Open** 4pm-midnight Mon-Fri, Sun; noon-midnight Sat. **Average** DM35. **Credit** AmEx, MC, V.
A Turkish hot-spot heavy on authentic wines and traditional food. Ignore the main courses and share a selection of spicy appetisers instead. Effusive service but uninspiring decor of mirrors and chrome.

### Mesa
*Paretzer Straße 5, Wilmersdorf, 10713 (822 5364). U1 Heidelberger Platz.* **Open** 4pm-midnight daily. **Average** DM30. **No credit cards.**
Out of the way but worth the effort: this classy Lebanese restaurant serves up neat variations on the usual Middle East staples. There are lots of lamb and chicken dishes, couscous, and plenty for vegetarians. Try the vegetable rosti that comes with three dipping sauces (DM15) and the spicy lentil soup. Egyptian cigarettes are on sale and free Lebanese Chiclets arrive with the bill.

### Meyhane
*Kantstraße 143, Charlottenburg, 10623 (313 9460). S3, S5, S6, S9 Savignyplatz.* **Open** noon-2am Mon-Thur, Sun; noon-4am Fri, Sat. **Average** DM25. **No credit cards.**
Although the décor is hideous, the service and standard of food is exceptional; many of the customers are Turks. The iskender and yogurtlu kebabs here are especially recommended, though there's plenty for vegetarians too. Fresh quince sprinkled with salt and a glass or two of raki (if you can face it) round off the meal nicely. Service is typically Turkish, and efficient. Open late, too.

### Offenbach-Stuben
*Stubbenkammerstraße 8, Prenzlauer Berg, 10437 (445 85 02). S8, S10 Prenzlauer Allee.* **Open** 6pm-2am daily. **Average** DM39. **Credit** AmEx, DC, EC, JBC, MC, V.
For a long time Offenbach-Stuben was considered the most desirable place in which to be seen eating in Prenzlauer Berg. The cuisine is fairly international (roasts and the like); the décor is fifties in style. You're best advised to book in advance to avoid disappointment.

**Opposite:** *Stop by the bar for a drink at* **Ax Bax** *or take a chance on Amadeus, the tailcoat-clad waiter who has good days and bad days. See page 105.*

## Osteria No 1

*Kreuzbergstraße 71, Kreuzberg, 10965 (786 9162). U6 Platz der Luftbrücke.* **Open** noon-midnight daily. **Average** DM35. **No credit cards.**

Crowded in the evenings, but nonetheless pleasant, Osteria looks a bit like a wine cellar inside. A young, groovy crowd tuck into delicious, if a mite overpriced Italian food. The selection of pasta sauces is particularly good. It has its off nights, depending on your waiter. Reservations are crucial.

## Petit Chinois

*Spandauer Damm 82, Charlottenburg, 14059 (322 5157). U2 Kaiserdamm.* **Open** noon-2.30pm, 6-11pm, Mon-Fri, Sun; 6-11pm Sat. **Average** DM28, Rijstafel DM26. **No credit cards.**

This restaurant-cum-Kneipe-with-food has achieved an enviable status. Go along and sample the freshest, tastiest Chinese-Indonesian-style food in town.

## Primo

*Südstern 3, Kreuzberg, 10967 (691 4597). U7 Südstern.* **Open** 5pm-1am daily. **Average** DM25. **No credit cards.**

This friendly, Italian-run place is always full. It's strong on pasta, traditional thin-base Italian pizzas and wine.

## Publique

*Yorckstraße 62, Kreuzberg, 10965 (786 9469). U7/S1, S2 Yorckstraße.* **Open** 6pm-2am daily, kitchen closes 1am. **Average** DM32. **No credit cards.**

Part restaurant, part bar, Publique serves reasonably priced dishes with a French touch. Daily specials are chalked up on a board. The atmosphere is laid-back and no one cares what you're wearing.

## Ristorante Chamisso

*Willibald-Alexis-Straße 25, Kreuzberg, 10965 (691 5642). U6 Platz der Luftbrücke.* **Open** 6pm-1am daily. **Average** DM28. **No credit cards.**

This excellent Italian restaurant with lots of charm situated on picturesque Chamissoplatz – wonderful to sit outside in summer – offers a varying selection of fresh pastas with interesting sauces, vegetable dishes, inventive salads and meat-based dishes with a strong Italian accent. Reservations advisable but not essential.

## Restauration 1900

*Husemannstraße 1, Prenzlauer Berg, 10435 (442 2494).* **Open** daily noon-2am. **Average** DM25. **Credit** AmEx, EC.

Long gone are the days when you could have a satisfying meal at Restauration 1900 and pay for it with cheapo Eastmarks, but this landmark private business from the GDR days is still going strong. The food (basically German with Italian touches) is mediocre, but 1900 is still very much a place in which to see and be seen, and the art exhibited inside changes regularly.

## Reinhard's

*Poststraße 28, Mitte, 10178 (242 5295). U2, U5, U8/S3, S5, S6, S7, S9, S75 Alexanderplatz.* **Open** 9am-2am daily, kitchen closes midnight. **Average** DM33. **Credit** AmEx, DC, EC, JBC, MC, V.

A large, busy American-style bistro in the restored medieval Nikolaiviertel near Alexanderplatz. It sounds like a clash of cultures, but is interesting nevertheless. Popular with the business set. One of their waitresses was recently dubbed the very best in Berlin. Reservations essential.

## Santiago

*Wörtherstraße 36, Prenzlauer Berg, 10435 (441 2555). U2 Senefelder Platz.* **Open** 6pm-2am at least, Mon-Fri; 10am-3am Sat, Sun. **Average** DM27. **No credit cards.**

Restauration 1900, next door (*see above*), was started by a German woman and her Chilean husband, and this sister restaurant/bar is his baby. Typically, the menu is grilled steaks and chops, but it's got a better wine list than 1900, and as a lunch stop it's good value: try the empanada (South American meat pie) with its zingy chilli sauce, or one of the big baguette sandwiches.

*The cafés at the* **Opern Palais** *serve breakfasts and a range of 70 cakes. See page 102.*

## Skales

*Rosenthaler Straße 12, Mitte, 10119 (283 3006). U8*
*Weinmeisterstraße.* **Open** from 5pm daily. **Average**
DM28. **No credit cards**.
The name means stairs in Greek, and there's a massive concrete staircase leading nowhere in the middle of this Greek
restaurant on the edge of Mitte's nightlife district. Service
can be snooty and uninformed about the menu, but the Greek
dishes are good value and tasty. The artsy crowd blends well
with the pastel-washed walls and high ceilings.

## Storch

*Wartburgstraße 54, Schöneberg, 10823 (784 2059). U7*
*Eisenacher Straße.* **Open** 6pm-1am daily, kitchen closes
11.30pm. **Average** DM35. **No credit cards**.
It's hard to recommend Storch too highly. The Alsatian food
– one soup starter, varying meat and fish dishes from the
place where German and French cuisines rub shoulders – is
both finely prepared and generously proportioned. The
cheese board is excellent and so is the house speciality – tarte
flambée, a sort of crispy cross between pizza and quiche that
comes sweet or savoury and costs DM13-DM15. The cosmopolitan front of house staff are probably the best and nicest
crew in Berlin. Long wooden tables are shared by different
parties and the atmosphere nearly always buzzes. Not the
place for a quiet chat and occasionally you get stuck next to
someone you don't like but the only real drawback here is
that there's rarely much for vegetarians. Booking essential
and no reservations accepted for after 8pm.

## Tandoory

*Prinz-Georg-Straße 10, Schöneberg, 10827 (782 7927).*
*S1 Schöneberg.* **Open** 3pm-midnight daily. **Average**
DM28. **Credit** AmEx, EC, V.
Most Berlin Indian places have similar menus, but this one
is different: dairy-based dishes with rich sauces. Try the
kofta dilkush, vegetable balls in a mouth-wateringly spicy
tomato sauce (DM15), or the paneer pasanda, filled Indian
cheese in a cashew nut sauce (DM19). The imported Indian
decor is well over the top and the music, last time we were
there, sounded like New Delhi honky-tonk.

## TGI Friday's

*Karl-Liebknecht-Straße 5, Mitte, 10178 (2382 7960). S3,*
*S5, S6, S7, S9 Hackescher Markt/Alexanderplatz.* **Open**
noon-midnight Mon-Thur, Sun; noon-1am Fri, Sat.
**Average** DM35. **Credit** AmEx, DC, EC, V.
An enormous branch of the American chain, TGI Friday's
serves up a wide selection of American dishes: burgers, Tex-
Mex, steaks, sandwiches and so on. We were not impressed.
The tables for two are minuscule, the 'large' portion of
nachos is tiny for DM14.80, the fettuccine alfredo at DM16.50
wasn't so much bland as tasteless, the fries were soggy, the
spinach salad (DM13.80) was limp. The drinks were even
more overpriced than the food, the service was dizzy and the
main courses arrived as we were tucking into our starter.
Add to that, distracting televisions tuned to sports, humdrum AOR in the background, and exceedingly slim pick-
ings for vegetarians, and TGI Friday's is one place you can
safely give a miss.

## Thai Palace

*Meierottostraße 1, Wilmersdorf, 10179 (883 2823). U1,*
*U9 Spichernstraße.* **Open** 5pm-midnight Mon-Fri, Sun;
noon-11pm Sat. **Average** DM33. **Credit** AmEx, DC, EC,
JBC, MC, V.
A large, beautifully decorated restaurant with immaculately dressed staff. The menu at the Thai Palace divides into
meat and fish dishes, and even though the English trans-
lations are bad, at least they help you choose. Anything
hot is marked *scharf*. The yellow chicken curry in coconut
milk is delicious, and the mixed starter recommended. The
house wine is passable.

*Step inside* **Reinhard's**. *See page 108.*

## Thürnagel

*Gneisenaustraße 53, Kreuzberg, 10961 (691 48 00). U7*
*Südstern.* **Open** 6pm-midnight daily. **Average** DM33.
**No credit cards**.
Pricey, fussy fish and vegetarian food is placed before
Kreuzberg trendies at Thürnagel. Décor is understated (beige
walls and gentle lighting); while the menu gives incredibly
complicated descriptions of the food.

## Trattoria da Enzo

*Großbeerenstraße 60, Kreuzberg, 10965 (785 8372). U6,*
*U7 Mehringdamm.* **Open** 6pm-midnight daily. **Average**
DM32. **No credit cards**.
A bustling little place that serves up authentic pizzas
and good pasta dishes as well as commendable meat and
chicken. Wash it all down with an excellent Salentino,
philanthropically priced at DM10.

## Tres Kilos

*Marheinekeplatz 3, Kreuzberg, 10961 (693 6044). U7*
*Gneisenaustraße.* **Open** 6pm-2am daily. **Average** DM30.
**No credit cards**.
Popular with the young and hip of Berlin, Tres Kilos serves
(mainly) quality Mexican food. The décor is pure Tex-Mex
meets Berlin, and diners get a pot of crayons to draw on the
paper tablecloths. The vegetarian quesadillo is always good,
and the guacamole is heavenly. The margaritas are excellent, but stick to the plain ones (frozen or on the rocks) and
avoid the sickly strawberry variety. Service is both good and
good-looking and there's a wide selection of tequilas and the
usual imported Mexican beers which can also be imbibed at
the bar. Free monkey nuts with drinks. Booking essential.

## Tuk Tuk

*Großgörschenstraße 2, Schöneberg, 10827 (781 1588). U7*
*Kleistpark.* **Open** 5.30pm-1am daily, kitchen closes
11.30pm. **Average** DM30. **Credit** EC, MC, V.
Tuk Tuk's cosy interior resembles a bamboo hut, with
Indonesian bric-à-brac all over the place. The menu is very
long, with a separate section for vegetarians. The gado
gado is humdrum, although you get a lot of it, while the rice
platter at DM70 for two is excellent value.

## Turmstuben

*Gendarmenmarkt 5 (in the Französischer Dom), Mitte,*
*10117 (229 9313). U6 Französische Straße.* **Open** noon-
1am daily. **Average** DM39. **Credit** AmEx, EC, V.
The international menu here is reasonable, and items range
from small salads to large meat and fish dishes, but the real
reasons to dine here are the huge selection of wines and the
lovely view. Drop in after a concert at the Schauspielhaus,
or to wind up a long day of sightseeing.

### Wohlbold

*Vorbergstraße 10, Schöneberg, 10823 (784 6735). U7 Eisenacher Straße.* **Open** 6pm-1am daily. **Average** DM30. **No credit cards.**
Superb and well priced south-west German cooking arrives at your table in vast quantities at Wohlbold. Good Baden wines assist the convivial atmosphere.

### XII Apostoli

*Bleibtreustraße 49 (Savigny Passage), Charlottenburg, 10623 (312 1433). S3, S5, S6, S9 Savignyplatz.* **Open** 24 hours daily. **Average** DM38. **No credit cards.**
Overrated and overpriced, this glorified pizzeria is cramped and impersonal, with rude service, humdrum food and trad jazz doodling irritatingly in the background. Only good news: it's open 24 hours. *See chapter* **After Hours.**

### Zur Nolle

*Georgenstraße, S-Bahnbogen 203, Mitte, 10117 (208 2655). U6, S1, S2, S3, S5, S6, S7, S9 Friedrichstraße.* **Open** 10am-midnight daily. **Average** DM26. **Credit** AmEx, MC, V.
Located in a cavernous space under the overhead railway by

# KaDeWe Food Halls

Instead of sitting in a restaurant or queuing at an Imbiß, the Feinschmecker-Etage (Gourmet Food Hall) on the sixth floor of KaDeWe (*see chapter* **Shopping** and pictures opposite) offers a different approach to dining. You can stop off for anything from a nibble to a full meal at one of the many food stalls that dot the shopping floor. Really it's up to you and your wallet. You can shell out DM135 on 50g of Sevruga caviar or snack on sausage for DM4. Six Belon oysters will cost you DM26 and there are prawn cocktails no one could finish for DM15. Nouvelle cuisine specialities at the Paul Bocuse stand come in the region of DM30 while sushi is reasonably priced at around DM5 per piece. The choice of cuisine is extraordinary and the quality high.

Perhaps the best approach is to browse around, taking an hors d'oeuvres here and a main course there. Try some of the savoury canapés at DM2.50 apiece, washed down with a glass of champagne for DM13. Follow it with a brimming bowl of bouillabaisse for DM12.50. Assorted schnitzels are served up for between DM12-18 and vegetarian pasta dishes cost around DM10. If you've got any room after sampling some of that little lot, KaDeWe has an extraordinary selection of cakes.

One big plus, or minus, depending on your predilection: there is no smoking allowed.

Friedrichstraße station that was formerly a briefing room for border guards, and before that a twenties beerhall, Zur Nolle serves German standbys and international food to an interesting mix of travellers and local businesspeople. There's a beer garden out back and excellent jazz brunches on Sundays.

## Inexpensive

Less than DM25.

### Altberliner Bierstuben

*Saarbrückerstraße 16, Prenzlauer Berg, 10405 (442 6130). U2 Senefelderplatz.* **Open** noon-2am daily. **Average** DM22. **No credit cards.**
You'll often have to wait a few minutes for a table at this busy restaurant, but fear not, there's also a small bar. Cheap, traditional Berlin food is served in an old Berlin atmosphere. Recommended.

### Ambrosius

*Bergmannstraße 11, Kreuzberg, 10961 (692 7182). U6, U7 Mehringdamm.* **Open** 8am-midnight Mon-Sat. **Average** DM12. **No credit cards.**
Basic German food and local colour at bargain basement prices: hearty soup of the day for DM4.50, half a pig's leg, boiled potatoes and sauerkraut for DM8.50. We defy you to manage both in one sitting. They also serve their own beer. Watch out for the name – Ambrosius – they have one or two branches around town.

### Angkor

*Seelingstraße 36, Charlottenburg, 14059 (325 59 94). U2 Sophie-Charlotte-Platz.* **Open** 6-11.30pm Mon-Thur, Sun; noon-11.30pm Fri, Sat. **Average** DM25. **No credit cards.**
Extraordinarily friendly service and exotic décor make Angkor a good spot for dinner. The Cambodian food tends towards the spicy, so think twice before asking for extra hot. Have the cold ricepaper rolls stuffed with shrimp to get the meal off to a flying start; move on to beef with Asian aubergine and coconut sauce; then try the fried bananas.

### Athener Grill

*Kurfürstendamm 156, Charlottenburg, 10709 (892 10 39). U7 Adenauerplatz.* **Open** 11am-4am Mon-Thur, Sun; 11am-5am Fri, Sat. **Average** DM10. **Credit** AmEx, DC, MC, V.
This self-service restaurant is popular, and not only with the late-night crowd, for its cheap, filling Greek food. The gyros are excellent but vegetarians ill-served.

### Brazil

*Gormannstraße 22, Mitte, 10119 (208 6313). U8 Weinmeisterstraße.* **Open** 5pm-2am daily. **Average** DM22. **No credit cards.**
Just like the Terry Gilliam movie of the same name, this bar and restaurant has nothing to do with Brazil the country, save for the odd palm heart in the salads. Most of the main courses, meat or vegetarian (small selection), are based around polenta or pancakes: heavy and filling but not terribly inspiring.

### Café Clara

*Clara-Zetkin-Straße 90, Mitte, 10117 (229 2909). U6, S1, S2, S3, S5, S6, S7, S9 Friedrichstraße.* **Open** 9.30am-midnight Mon-Fri; 11am-midnight Sat, Sun. **Average** DM15. **No credit cards.**
A popular lunch spot for local businessmen and tourists, the menu changes daily but usually features reasonably priced pasta, and meat and fish dishes. In summertime you can eat outside in the garden.

*Excellent Thai food at the friendly Mahachai.*

## Café Hardenberg
*Hardenbergstraße 10, Charlottenburg, 10623 (312 26 44). U2 Ernst-Reuter-Platz.* **Open** 9am-1am daily. **Average** DM12. **No credit cards.**
Located across from the Technical University and next to the Goethe Institute, this trendy café is usually packed with students discussing philosophy over coffee. Simple, decent plates of spaghetti, omelettes, salads and sandwiches are sold at reasonable prices. It's also a good place for cheap vegetarian food.

## Café Nola
*Dortmunder Straße 9, Tiergarten, 10555 (399 69 69). U9 Turmstraße.* **Open** 6pm-2am daily, kitchen until 11.30pm. **Average** DM20. **No credit cards.**
Two Swiss chefs bravely attempt California cuisine in this uncharacteristically picturesque corner of Moabit and, more often than not, succeed. A light hand on the sauces, with fruit and chillies providing some of the flavour, an emphasis on fish and vegetarian entrées, and a well chosen wine list with unusual Chilean, Californian and South African bottles, and you've got a refreshingly un-Berlinisch dining experience.

## Café Orange
*Oranienburger Straße 32, Mitte, 10117 (282 0028). S1, S2 Oranienburger Straße.* **Open** 10am-1am daily. **Average** DM22. **No credit cards.**
High ceilings, with beautiful mouldings and light orange walls, Café Orange is a delight for the eyes as well as the palate. It tends to be terribly crowded at night, so try it for lunch. The fresh pizzas are tasty and the salads large enough to feed a small army of rabbits. Also a great place for breakfast or just coffee when exploring this lively part of town.

## Chandra Kumari
*Gneisenaustraße 4, Kreuzberg, 10961 (694 3056). U6, U7 Mehringdamm.* **Open** noon-midnight daily. **Average** DM15. **No credit cards.**
This very small restaurant serves scrumptious, superb-value

Sri Lankan cuisine. Try the astonishing jackfruit curry. Spicing is on the mild side, but the cooks who work frantically in the open-plan kitchen turn out some of the best, freshest and most reasonably priced Ceylonese delights in town. Always crowded, but worth the wait.

## Dodge
*Dunkerstraße 80a, Prenzlauer Berg, 10437 (no phone). U2 Eberswalder Straße.* **Open** 9am-4am Mon-Sat; 8am-4am Sun. **Average** DM12. **No credit cards.**
Americanophilia runs wild in Prenzlauer Berg. Scrupulously authentic charcoal-broiled hamburgers – they've even got the pickles right – and Buffalo chicken wings (plus less scrupulously authentic 'Mexican' food) for dinner, or pancakes with maple syrup and a variety of omelettes for breakfast (which is served until 5pm) will make you think you've stumbled into a California luncheonette in 1961.

## Großbeerenkeller
*Großbeerenstraße 90, Kreuzberg, 10963 (251 3064). U1, U7 Möckernbrücke.* **Open** 4pm-2am Mon-Fri; 6pm-2am Sat. **Average** DM22. **No credit cards.**
Going strong since 1862, this cellar Kneipe is a real Berlin institution among insiders. Berliners from all walks of life come for the substantial 'Hoppel-Poppel' breakfast, homemade dishes and, of course, beers.

## Jimmy's Diner
*Pariser Straße 41, Wilmersdorf, 10707 (882 3141). U2 Hohenzollernplatz.* **Open** 4pm-4am Mon-Thur, Sun; 4pm-6am Fri, Sat. **Average** DM18. **No credit cards.**
This clean and self-conscious recreation of a fifties diner, complete with red plastic booths and soda pop posters, serves generous portions of Mexican food and burgers at a good price. The burgers are almost too big to finish, and Americans vouch for their authenticity. But there's nothing for vegetarians and the place sometimes gets a little too full. *See also chapter* **Early Hours.**

## La Culinaria
*Kantstraße 32, Charlottenburg, 10625 (312 86 80). S3, S5, S6, S9 Savignyplatz.* **Open** 6pm-3am daily. **Average** DM28. **No credit cards.**
Great penne à la vodka and other unique pasta variations are the trademark of Culinaria. Don't be surprised if you're handed a free grappa at the end of the meal: it's common practice in Italian restaurants here. The staff are attentive and polite.

## Luisen-Bräu Brauerei
*Luisenplatz 1, Charlottenburg, 10585 (341 9388). U1 Richard-Wagner-Platz.* **Open** 9am-1am Mon-Thur, Sun; 9am-2am Fri, Sat. **Average** DM17. **No credit cards.**
Waitresses serve up armfuls of cloudy home brew at this modern pub-brewery across the street from Charlottenburg Palace. Huge beer vats stand at the back of the room behind rows of long wooden benches and tables. Meats are priced by the kilo; stews and salads are doled out at the buffet.

## Mahachai
*Schlüterstraße 60, Charlottenburg, 10625 (313 0879). S3, S5, S6, S9 Savignyplatz.* **Open** 5pm-1am Tue-Fri; noon-1am Sat, Sun.* **Average** DM22. **No credit cards.**
Walking into this friendly Thai restaurant you feel you're on a visit to an enchanted island. Excellent food comes prettily displayed, and the staff are helpful.

## Marché
*Kurfürstendamm 14, 10719 (882 7578). U9, U15 Kurfürstendamm.* **Open** 8am-midnight daily. **Average** DM17. **Credit** V.
Healthy and freshly prepared food is what you'll find at the Marché, not ambience. Located on the most tourist-ridden stretch of the Ku'damm, this Swiss-owned chain offers

*Vegetarians, not hugely well catered for in Berlin, get a good choice in **Petite Europe**.*

vegetables, meats and desserts at various stands, buffet-fashion. The mood livens in summer when tables are set outside on the pavement.

### Mare e Mondo/Da Gino
*Kirchstraße 20, Moabit, 10557 (392 5486). U9 Turmstraße/S5, S6, S7, S9 Bellevue.* **Open** noon-midnight Mon-Sat. **Average** DM23. **No credit cards.**
A neighbourhood Italian place like many others, except for a slew of home-made pasta specialities, which include a stunning vegetarian pasta roll, cheese-and-basil-filled ravioli and black pasta with shellfish. Other offerings are above average, too. Now if they'd just make up their minds about the name of the place…

### Noodle Company
*Yorckstraße 84, Kreuzberg, 10965 (785 2736). U6, U7 Mehringdamm.* **Open** 5pm-1am Mon-Sat; noon-1am Sun. **Average** DM18. **No credit cards.**
A welcoming spot, the Noodle Company serves up a wide variety of pasta and noodle dishes, from excellent spaghetti with pesto to more exotic Indonesian noodles and an appetising salad bar.

### Pasternak
*Knaackstraße 22-24, Prenzlauer Berg, 10405 (441 3399). U2 Senefelder Platz.* **Open** noon-2am Mon-Sat; 10am-2am Sun. **Average** DM21. **No credit cards.**
Book at least a day in advance if you want to dine in this small bar and Russian restaurant on Prenzl'berg's chicest corner: it's always crammed to the gunnels, which can be irritating as people constantly brush past you looking for places. Try for a table in the small back room. They also let buskers in to play, so avoid if you don't want ancient Neil Young songs strummed in your left ear. But the atmosphere is friendly and the food fine and filling. Kick off with the borscht (DM7) or the ample fish plate (smoked salmon, trout, mussels and sprats, DM11). Then broach the Pelmeni or Wareniki (DM12) – sort of Russki ravioli filled with either meat or potatoes – or the hearty Beef Stroganoff (DM18.50).

### Petite Europe
*Langenscheidtstraße 1, Schöneberg, 10827 (781 2964). U7 Kleistpark.* **Open** 5pm-1am daily. **Average** DM20. **No credit cards.**
A rough-and-ready, welcoming neighbourhood Italian joint, serving decent, well-priced nosh. Vegetarians get a wide

choice for once, and all diners get a free bruschetta while they're waiting and a free grappa after the meal. We defy you to finish the calzone.

### Restaurant Jagdhütte
*Eisenzahnstraße 66, Wilmersdorf, 10709 (892 5949). U7 Adenauerplatz.* **Open** 11.30am-midnight daily. **Average** DM20; daily special (11.30am-7pm) DM9.80. **No credit cards.**
Typical Berlin restaurant on a Ku'damm corner specialising in game dishes: venison goulash with noodles and redcurrant sauce, for example, at DM15. Run by a Scot (all the staff speak English) its dark-wood interior is usually full of pensioners tucking into the cheap three-course daily special.

### Tegernseer Tönnchen
*Berliner Straße 118, Wilmersdorf, 10715 (323 3827). U7 Wilmersdorfer Straße.* **Open** 11.30am-midnight daily. **Average** DM23. **No credit cards.**
The old-fashioned décor of this Bavarian-style restaurant lacks polish, but feesl authentically German. Heaped portions of Wiener Schnitzel, Eisbein, Bavarian meatloaf and mounds of potatoes fill most tables.

### Tiergarten Quelle
*Stadtbahnbogen 482, Bachstraße, near Haydnstraße (392 76 15). S3, S5, S6, S9 Tiergarten.* **Open** 11am-midnight Mon-Fri; 11am-1am Sat, Sun; kitchen opens 5pm. **Average** DM15. **No credit cards.**
TU students jam this funky bar for huge servings of the food Grandma made: potatoes with quark and linseed oil, pork medallions with melted cheese with Käsespätzle, mixed grill with sauerkraut, Maultaschen with spinach, stone litre mugs of (unfortunately) Schultheiss beer. The Kaiserschmarren (minced pancakes with rum-soaked raisins and cherries topped with whipped cream) at DM9.50 is a meal in itself. You'll wonder where they buy the giant plates. Go when school's out of session or you'll never get a table.

### Weltrestaurant Markthalle
*Pücklerstraße 34, Kreuzberg, 10977 (617 5502). U1 Görlitzer Bahnhof.* **Open** 8am-2am Mon-Thur, Sun; 8am-4am Fri, Sat; kitchen closes midnight. **Average** DM20. **No credit cards.**
Known locally as Markthalle, this unpretentious restaurant and bar, with big chunky tables and wood-panelled walls,

is fast becoming a Kreuzberg institution. They serve great breakfasts until 6pm, a lunch menu from noon, and in the evening a selection of filling and reasonably priced meals: poached eggs in a mustard sauce with spinach and boiled potatoes, for example, at DM10.50. The soups are excellent and the daily specials always include at least one veggie option. Afterwards pop down into the basement for one of the events at the Mingus club (*see chapter* **Clubs**) or nip over the road for a drink at Der Goldene Hahn (*see chapter* **Cafés & Bars**).

## Imbiß & Fast Food

All over Berlin you'll see the sign **Imbiß** – a catch-all term embracing just about anywhere you get food but not table service, from stand-up street corner Currywurst or Döner Kebab stalls, to self-service snack bars offering all manner of exotic cuisine. The quality varies wildly, but some excellent cheap food can be found in these places. Here's a selection of the more interesting ones.

### Ashoka

*Grolmanstraße 51, Charlottenburg, 10623 (313 2066). S3, S5, S6, S9 Savignyplatz.* **Open** 11am-1am daily.
A friendly Indian snack bar where good-value, no-frills food is served with plenty of choice for vegetarians – try the banana curry with basmati rice. If Ashoka's full, this street also has two other Indian Imbißes and one Indian restaurant.

### Freßco

*Oranienburger Straße 47, Mitte, 10117 (282 9647). U6 Oranienburger Tor.* **Open** *winter* noon-midnight daily; *summer* noon-2am daily.
Right next to Obst & Gemüse and over the road from Tacheles, this is a popular spot to snack for all those bar-crawling the Oranienburger Straße area. Soups, salads,

baguettes, tapas, doughnuts, pasta, Calzone – this Imbiß has it all, in both carnivorous and veghead versions. Be prepared to queue a little, though.

### Habibi

*Goltzstraße 24, Schöneberg, 10781 (215 33 32). U1, U4 Nollendorfplatz.* **Open** 11am-3am Mon-Fri, Sun; 11am-5am Sat.
Freshly made Arab specialities are what draw ravenous night owls to this snack bar handy for the many bars and clubs of the Schöneberg area. They also have a branch at Akazienstraße 9 which is open until 2am.

### Konnopke's Imbiß

*Beneath the U2 tracks, corner of Dimitroff Straße and Schönhauser Allee, Prenzlauer Berg, 10435 (no phone). U2 Eberswalder Straße.* **Open** 5am-7pm Mon-Sat.
The quintessential Berlin Imbiß, going strong under family management since 1930, Konnopke's makes its own Wurst, and serves a large variety of sandwiches, including several vegetarian offerings, which people eat in a sort of Biergarten under the tracks.

### Ku'damm 195

*Kurfürstendamm 195, Wilmersdorf, 10707 (no phone). S3, S5, S6, S9 Savignyplatz.* **Open** noon-2am daily.
Berlin's best-known Imbiß, and one that's not frequented by tourists. Buy Russian shashlik kebab and Currywurst fresh from the grill.

### Kulinarische Delikatessen

*Oppelner Straße 4, Kreuzberg, 10997 (618 6758). U1 Schlesisches Tor.* **Open** 8am-2am daily.
Why do Berliners tend to eat such bad Turkish food? Probably because they know deep in their hearts that some day they'll come upon a place like this, where the same old selections are done to a Platonic ideal. The Döner's not bad, but it's the vegetarian offerings that make it really special: try an aubergine-falafal combo kebab, a zucchini kebab, or even one of the salads.

*Night owls gather until 3am at* **Habibi** *for their range of freshly made Arab specialities.*

## Kwang-Ju-Grill
*Emser Straße 24, Wilmersdorf, 10707 (883 9794). U2
Hohenzollernplatz.* **Open** noon-midnight Mon-Thur, Sun;
noon-2am Fri, Sat.
There's a hundred different items on the menu of this excellent Korean Imbiß: starters and soups at around DM3, every
kind of meat and fish dish for between DM8-DM16, and a
small selection of vegetarian options. Order at the counter
and sit at one of the tables inside or (in the summer) out.
Wash it down with a hot sake or Chinese beer.

## Joseph Lange
*Wilmersdorfer Straße 118, Charlottenburg, 10627 (31
67 80). U7 Wilmersdorfer Straße.* **Open** 8.30am-6.30pm
Mon-Fri; 8.30am-2pm Sat.
Most savvy Wurstwaren have a small Imbiß in them so
customers can check out the goods, and what Lange has
going for him is not only some fine Wurst, but a Currywurst
that could be Berlin's best. Ask for a Wurst mit Kraut, and
specify Scharfketchup, and better get a drink while you're
at it: that ketchup *is* spicy. Wurst and ketchup are both
available to take home.

## McKebap City
*across from taxi stand, north side of Bahnhof
Friedrichstraße, Mitte, 10117 (no phone). U6, S3, S5,
S6, S7, S9 Friedrichstraße.* **Open** 8am-1am daily.
If you're going to enter the Döner wars, you'd better have
your marketing down. From the faked Camel logo to the
clever name – McKebap City – the line outside this little
joint says that these guys are doing it right. And, taking
a key element from the more famous fast-food chain, the
'secret sauce' on the excellent kebabs seems to contain a
healthy dose of sugar.

## Mr Hot Dog
*Schönhauser Allee 124, Prenzlauer Berg, 10437 (no
phone). U2 Schönhauser Allee.* **Open** 10am-11pm daily.
The American owner of Mr Hot Dog left a career in the New
York advertising business to cash in on the fall of the Wall
and bring the hot dog to east Berlin. The hot dogs are genuine and delicious, but avoid the fake chilli sauce.

## Pagoda
*Bergmannstraße 88, Kreuzberg, 10961 (691 2640). U7
Gneisenaustraße.* **Open** noon-midnight daily.
This lovely Imbiß is easily as good as some of the costlier
Thai restaurants in town, and, in fact, with nothing over
DM13.50 on the menu, you could make a decent dinner at
the Pagoda. Dozens of menu selections, the proper amount
of chillis already in the dish, making a dip into the hot-sauce
jar only minimally necessary, and fast, friendly service add
up to a lunch-stop worth making. There's nothing here for
vegetarians, though.

## Spätzle
*Lüneberger Straße, S-Bahnbogen 390, Tiergarten, 10557
(no phone). S5, S6, S7, S9 Bellevue.* **Open** 9am-8pm
Mon-Sat; 11am-8pm Sun.
A lovely little place serving the pastas of Swabia, including,
of course, Spätzle (with Bratwurst, lentils, or meatballs),
Kasespätzle (with cheese), Maultaschen (like giant ravioli),
and Schupfenknudle (a cross between pasta and chips).
Wash it down with a brown Berg beer.

## Sushi
*Pariser Straße 44, Wilmersdorf, 10707 (881 2790). U2
Hohenzollernplatz.* **Open** noon-3pm, 5pm-midnight, Mon-
Fri; 6pm-midnight Sat; 4pm-10pm Sun.
Excellent stand-up sushi in this Imbiß handy for all the
bars of the Ludwig-Kirch-Platz area. You can buy it à la carte
at an average of DM4 per piece, or a complete sushi dinner
for DM18-25.

## Die Tofuerei
*Krefelderstraße 2, Tiergarten, 10555 (no phone). U9
Turmstraße.* **Open** 11am-6pm Mon-Fri; 11am-1pm Sat.
Not only a vegetarian Imbiß, but some of the best vegetarian
food in Berlin at this former butcher's shop, which is packed
at noontime. The daily specials are superb, but so are the
takeaways, the Orient burger for example.

## Vietnam Imbiß
*Damaschkestraße 30, Charlottenburg, 10711 (324 9344).
U7 Adenauerplatz.* **Open** 10am-9pm Mon-Fri.
Berlin is thin on Vietnamese food, but this popular little place
serves up healthy, filling hybrid. The daily special is the star
of the show, but most things on the menu (the sickly-sweet
'sweet-sour' items excepted) are top-notch. Expect to wait if
you arrive around noon: the neighbourhood loves this place.

# Berlin for Vegheads

Germany is notoriously tough for vegetarians,
but Berlin is big and cosmopolitan enough to
offer meat-free dishes in all price ranges.

First, though, forget traditional German
restaurants. If you're lucky you might find an
omelette or Gemüseplatte – an uninspiring
plate of boiled vegetables, occasionally topped
off with a slimy boiled egg – but the former
will likely be fried in lard and the latter boiled
in meat stock. There is also a tendency to
sprinkle Speck – pieces of fatty bacon – in
anything otherwise meat-free. Ham, for many
in this country, just doesn't 'count' as meat.

Neue deutsche Küche places are just as bad.
Some of the best and most expensive restaurants in Berlin can offer nothing but asparagus or wild mushroom dishes, and those only
when said vegetables are in season (June and
September/October respectively).

The best bet is to stick to non-German
cuisines: Italian, Greek, Turkish, Indian,
Japanese, Lebanese, Mexican, Thai and
Indonesian places should all have something
more interesting than a salad. So should most
of the cooler cafés. Some handy phrases to
remember are 'Ich bin (Wir sind) Vegetarier'
(I am/we are vegetarian); 'Ich möchte kein
Fleisch/keinen Fisch essen' (I don't want to
eat any meat/fish); 'Gibt es Fleisch darin?' (Is
there meat in it?); and 'Keine Fleischbrühe'
(No meat stock). Bear in mind, though, that
in a lot of places, especially on the east side,
you may be met with blank stares and be
taken for a raving lunatic.

Finally, there are one or two top-notch
vegetarian places in Berlin: check the listings
for **Abendmahl** and **Hakuin**, or the Imbiß
**Die Tofuerei**.

# Cafés & Bars

**From dour, smoky corner pubs to Bugs Bunny carrot barstools and mutant poetry readings, Berlin offers an intoxicating range of drinking experiences.**

Berlin is a city of bars and cafés. There's one on nearly every street corner, and by choosing your corners carefully, you can snack, drink, smoke, chat and sup coffee right around the clock. Here the distinction between bars and cafés is nowhere near as rigid as it is in the UK: in Berlin you could have breakfast, lunch, afternoon coffee, dinner and get horribly drunk all in the same place. But while there is this overlap, and while many establishments work as cafés in the daytime and as bars in the evening, distinctions between the two remain.

In a café you might sit for hours nursing a cup of coffee with your head stuck into a book or newspaper – there's no pressure to go once you've had your coffee and no minimum charge. Sitting at a pavement café, people-watching, is a great way to get to know the life of the town.

A favourite pastime and a well-established tradition is afternoon Kaffee und Kuchen, the German equivalent of English tea. Ice-cream is another passion with the Germans, and many cafés have a separate ice-cream menu with all manner of exotic concoctions on offer: berries, fruits, chocolate and nuts. The one thing they all have in common is too much whipped cream (Schlagsahne) ladled on top.

Bars have a different kind of life. While there is still quiet conversation around tables, people also stand around or perch on stools, eye each other up, harass the barstaff. Berlin bars go out of their way to establish their identity in terms of decor, mood, atmosphere, style of service, volume of music and nature of crowd – which leads both to some pretty cool places and to some very crazy dives. The best bars are something between institutions and families, and have a life of their own. Especially when it's late, late, late, you never know when something might happen to bring the whole place together into some spontaneous event. Maybe the staff will suddenly provide drinks for the house, or everyone will start dancing on the bar.

The best bars and cafés tend to be clustered in certain areas (and we're not talking about the characterless Ku'damm here); although some superb bars can be found down seemingly sleepy streets. We've listed places by area, and also suggested a few districts that are well suited for bar-crawling.

Bars and cafés vary wildly, from the Eck-Kneipe (corner bars), which are dark, smoky, unwelcoming and full of locals (usually male), through slick bars in Charlottenburg, to rough and ready, noisy dives in Kreuzberg. One thing most places have in common, however, is the never-ending flow of people trying to sell you something: roses, newspapers, magazines, jewellery, even scarves and oriental fans. On a long night's drinking you can encounter the same rose-seller several times. At the end of the night, when they just want to go home, they can be very persistent and you can sometimes barter them down considerably. So if you wake up in the morning next to a huge bunch of red roses, don't say we didn't warn you.

Many bars in Berlin don't have strict opening times: by law (unique in Germany to Berlin) bars only have to close for one hour a day, and that's for cleaning purposes (although some of them don't close at all). For those partial to a drink or two, and oppressed by restrictive licensing laws, going to Berlin is rather like going to heaven. On the other hand, because there are some places that stay open until 7am, certain boozers feel they have to keep on going until the bitter end – downing drinks at a speed learnt to achieve that certain glow by 11pm. The lesson here is: pace yourself.

Though some bars close at the same time every night, many of them are open-ended. They'll keep on serving as long as there are enough people to make it worth their while, or if the staff themselves are still having a good time. Many of the closing times we have given are therefore approximate, and places may stay open later. But if the barstaff have started piling the chairs on the tables around you and are giving 'time you went home, matey' looks from across the room, there's bound to be somewhere else in walking distance that's still open. Ask the people behind the bar: that's probably where they're going.

## Charlottenburg

### Aschinger
*Kurfürstendamm 26, Charlottenburg, 12719 (882 55 58). U9, U15 Kurfürstendamm.* **Open** 11am-1am daily.
The refreshing, light beer at Aschinger goes down so easily you can drink a lot before realising it: the waitress will keep bringing you a fresh beer unless you put your coaster on top of your glass. Pretzels, salads, sausages and pea soup are among the snacks at the buffet. One of the few pubs where you aren't greeted by a cloud of smoke.

## Café Aedes
*under the S-Bahn bridge on Savignyplatz,
Charlottenburg, 10623 (312 55 04). S3, S5, S6, S9
Savignyplatz.* **Open** 9am-midnight daily; *breakfast* 9am-
3pm.
A small, trendy café tucked under the S-Bahn line at
Savignyplatz. A steady flow of fashionable types pop in and
out for a cappuccino, a late breakfast, or to look at the other
fashionable types.

## Café Bleibtreu
*Bleibtreustraße 45, Charlottenburg, 10623 (881 47 56).
S3, S5, S6, S9 Savignyplatz.* **Open** 9.30am-1am Sun-
Thur; 9.30am-2.30am Fri, Sat.
Welcoming and laid-back, the durable Café Bleibtreu has
remained popular since Charlottenburg's sixties heyday. The
musty furnishings haven't changed much since then either.

## Café Hardenberg
*Hardenbergstraße 10, Charlottenburg, 10623 (312 26
44). U2 Ernst-Reuter-Platz.* **Open** 9am-1am daily.
Witness students in their natural habitat, day or night, at
the spacious and relaxing Hardenberg, next to the Goethe
Institut and opposite the Technical University. Most nurse
a drink for hours, listening to classical music or chatting.
Others come for cheap eats, usually less than DM10. Furnishings include museum posters, plants and ceiling fans.

## Café Konditerei Richter
*Giesebrechtstraße 22, Charlottenburg, 10629 (324 37
22). U7 Adenauerplatz.* **Open** 7am-8pm Mon-Sat;
9.30am-8pm Sun.
Walking into this luxurious yet cosy café is like walking into
your rich grandma's parlour. You sit on slightly worn, green
velvet chairs at tables with starched linen tablecloths under
ornate chandeliers. The unhurried pace of the place is relaxing. There's soup and spaghetti but the stars of the menu are
the scrumptious pastries and cakes.

## Café Kranzler
*Kurfürstendamm 18, Charlottenburg, 10719 (882 69
11). U9, U15 Kurfürstendamm.* **Open** 8am-midnight
daily.
Dominating a corner of Berlin's Piccadilly Circus (Ku'damm
Eck, with its huge electronic wall newspaper), Kranzler is
one of the city's oldest and most popular coffee houses. The
hard-to-miss, three-storey café is a magnet for tourists, mainly because of its location. The apple strudel is disappointing;
come here instead for the popular people-watching terrace
overlooking the Ku'damm.

## Café Möhring
*Kurfürstendamm 213, Charlottenburg, 10719 (881 20
75). U15 Uhlandstraße.* **Open** 7am-midnight daily.
An original art nouveau coffee house that was once a haunt
for men and women of letters, intellectuals and politicians.
Today, regulars come for the breakfasts and homemade
cakes, served to the accompaniment of a background waltz.

## Café Savigny
*Grolmanstraße 53-54, Charlottenburg, 10623 (312 81
95). S3, S5, S6, S9 Savignyplatz.* **Open** 10am-2am daily.
It's hard to find a table at this small but airy café. Sparsely
decorated, painted nearly entirely white with round arched
doorways, the Savigny has a Mediterranean feel to it. It's
popular with the media, fashion and art crowd.

## Dicker Wirt
*Danckelmannstraße 43, Charlottenburg, 14059 (321 99
42). U2 Sophie-Charlotte-Platz.* **Open** 4pm-4am daily.
The picture of the fat bartender, or Dicker Wirt, hanging
just outside, is your first encounter with this hanging-on
student hang-out, which has changed little since the sixties.
It's full of people playing cards or reading the paper while

**Café Savigny** *– popular with media types.*

drinking mugs of Guinness. A female version of the place,
Dicke Wirtin (Fat Barmaid), is located near Savignyplatz on
Carmerstraße.

## Diener
*Grolmannstraße 47, Charlottenburg, 10623 (881 53 29).
S3, S5, S6, S9 Savignyplatz.* **Open** 6pm-2am Mon, Wed-
Sun.
An old-style Berlin bar, named after a famous German boxer.
The walls are adorned with faded hunting murals and photos of famous Germans you won't recognise. The atmosphere
is soothing, perhaps because there's no music (a rarity in this
city), although Diener does boast one waiter, Andreas, who
is well known for being rude to the customers. A haunt of
the theatre crowd. You could almost be in twenties Berlin.

## Dollinger
*Stuttgarter Platz 21, Charlottenburg, 10627 (323 87 83).
S3, S5, S6, S7, S9 Charlottenburg.* **Open** 9am-2am daily;
*breakfast* 9am-2pm daily.
Plenty of windows make this corner bar a key spot for perus-
ing the action on Stuttgarter Platz. The viewing gets even
better in summer when drinking moves outdoors and joins
up with the tables from bars nearby.

## Dralle's
*Schlüterstraße 69, Charlottenburg, 10629, (313 50 38).
S3, S5, S6, S9 Savignyplatz.* **Open** 3pm-2am Mon-Thur,
Sun; 3pm-3am Fri, Sat.
Trendy hang-out for an oldish crowd. Staff are efficient,
drinks pricey and snacks are served.

## Gasthaus Lentz
*Stuttgarter Platz 20, Charlottenburg, 10627 (324 16 19).
S3, S5, S6, S7, S9 Charlottenburg.* **Open** 10am-2am
daily; *breakfast* 10am-11.30am daily.
An older crowd is drawn to this unpretentious, spacious
café nestled in the cluster of bars on Stuttgarter Platz.
Cigarette-smoking intellectuals pack the place day and night.
*Guardian*-reading thirtysomethings will feel at home here.

## Klo
*Leibnizstraße 57, Charlottenburg, 10629 (324 22 99).
S3, S5, S6, S9 Savignyplatz/U7 Adenauer Platz.* **Open**
7pm-3am Mon-Thur, Sun; 6pm-5am Fri-Sat.
It's Hallowe'en every night at this corner bar designed like
a haunted house. Lights go out suddenly, giant foam stalac-
tites drop down from the ceiling and brush your head, while
the sound of eerie laughter fills the room. Litres of beer are
served in glass bed-pans. Although it gets tedious, Klo
(meaning toilet) is worth visiting if only for the experience.

## Ku'dorf
*Joachimstaler Straße 15, Charlottenburg, 10719 (883 66
66). U9, U15 Kurfürstendamm.* **Open** from 8pm daily.
Even though it costs DM5 to get in the door, this underground

*If it's good enough for Pico of Zoulou Bar (centre), it's good enough for you – **Bar**.*

village just off the Ku'damm attracts up to 2,000 at weekends. There are 18 bars, two discos, a food kiosk and souvenir/T-shirt shop. The enormous quantity of booze, combined with hordes of teenagers, makes for a rowdy joint as it nears 5am. Bouncers frisk guests to ensure things don't get out of hand. Not recommended in the slightest.

### Leysieffer
*Kurfürstendamm 218, Wilmersdorf, 10719 (882 78 20). U15 Uhlandstraße.* **Open** 9am-7pm Mon-Wed, Fri, Sat; 9am-8.30pm Thur; 10am-8pm Sun.
Indulge yourself in style at this recently refurbished café housed in what used to be the Chinese Embassy. Exquisite tortes and fruitcakes are served upstairs in the high-ceilinged café resembling an art gallery. Mounds of truffles and bonbons, beautifully presented, are sold downstairs in the shop.

### Rosalinde
*Knesebeckstraße 16, Charlottenburg, 10623 (881 95 01). S3, S5, S6, S9 Savignyplatz.* **Open** 10am-2am daily; *breakfast* 10am-4pm daily.
An abundance of flowers and classical music create a feeling of intimacy at this small café near Savignyplatz. Share a quiet breakfast at one of the tables for two, or nibble on cake and coffee at the triangular bar.

### Rost
*Knesebeckstraße 29, Charlottenburg, 10623 (881 95 01). S3, S5, S6, S9 Savignyplatz.* **Open** 9am-2am daily.
The name of this bar means 'rust', but the only thing remotely rusty here is the sign. The interior is designed simply with pale apricot walls and odd white lights extending from the ceiling. Cool, collected and catering to an older crowd, this is also a haunt of the theatre world.

### Schwarzes Café
*Kantstraße 148, Charlottenburg, 10623 (313 8038). S3, S5, S6, S7, S9 Savignyplatz.* **Open** 24 hours Mon, Wed-Sun.
Centrally located, and open around the clock for breakfasts and meals. It used to be all black (hence the name) but some of the décor has been brightened up, although one of the rooms upstairs and the toilets retain their overpowering blackness. Service can be slow.

### Wintergarten im Literaturhaus
*Fasanenstraße 23, Charlottenburg, 10719 (882 54 14). U15 Uhlandstraße.* **Open** 9.30am-1am daily.
The Wintergarten is the café in the Literaturhaus, which has lectures, readings, exhibitions and an excellent bookshop in the basement. The greenhouse-like sunny winter garden or salon rooms of the café are great for ducking into a book or scribbling out postcards. Breakfast, snacks and desserts.

### Zillemarkt
*Bleibtreustraße 48a, Charlottenburg, 10623 (881 70 40). S3, S5, S6, S9 Savignyplatz.* **Open** 8.30am-midnight daily.
Dark wood tables lit by candles and stone floors give this former antiques market a warm feeling, making it ideal for long rambling conversations over foamy glasses of beer. In summer, you can dine in the outdoor garden or on the pavement, if you dare brave the rumble of the overhead trains.

### Zwiebelfisch
*Savignyplatz 7-8, Charlottenburg, 10623 (312 73 63). S3, S5, S6, S7, S9 Savignyplatz.* **Open** noon-6.30am daily.
Zwiebelfisch means 'onion fish', after a German printing term for a type-setting mistake. The obscure literary reference suits this café, which is filled with beer-drinking philosophers. It's a little on the expensive side, but the atmosphere is unpretentious – dark and smoky with worn wooden tables – and can get really weird around 2-3am. The French onion soup is excellent.

## Kreuzberg

## Kreuzberg 36

### Anton
*Oranienstraße 170, Kreuzberg, 10999 (615 7102). U1, U8 Kottbusser Tor.* **Open** 10am-2am Mon-Thur, Sun; 10am-4.30am Fri, Sat.
Don't be put off by the orange walls, they're surprisingly inoffensive once you get used to them. A pleasant, airy café, with reasonable prices.

### Bar
*Skalitzerstraße 64 (corner of Wrangelstraße), Kreuzberg, 10997 (612 43 88). U1 Schlesisches Tor.* **Open** 10am-5am daily.
The perfect place to unwind into the early hours in a friendly local bar atmosphere, friendly to all and local to anyone.

### Bierhimmel
*Oranienstraße 183, Kreuzberg, 10997 (615 31 22). U1, U8 Kottbusser Tor.* **Open** 3pm-3am daily; *cocktail bar* 3pm-3am Wed-Sat.
From the outside, Bierhimmel is just another Kreuzberg bar, but its secret lies through the swing doors. Inside is a cosy, fifties-style cocktail bar bathed in red. Popular with the local drag queens.

### Café Altenberg
*Görlitzer Straße 53, Kreuzberg, 10997 (612 67 66). U1 Görlitzer Bahnhof.* **Open** 10am-1am daily.
A successful attempt to bring a bit of Vienna to Berlin. Recline on the leather-backed sofas and indulge in intellectual conversation.

## Café Bar Morena
*Wienerstraße 60, Kreuzberg, 10999 (611 47 16). U1 Görlitzer Bahnhof.* **Open** *from 9am-5am daily.*
Famous breakfasts, from bacon and eggs to pancakes, are served to people who wake up at all hours. In the evening it's a crucial meeting place, although the service can be rather slow. The music isn't overpowering like most of the other bars around here, and the half-tiled walls and parquet flooring give it an art deco feel.

## Café Übersee
*Paul-Lincke-Ufer 44, Kreuzberg, 10555 (618 87 65). U1 Kottbusser Tor.* **Open** *10am-2am daily; breakfast until 4pm daily.*
Vines cover the outside, and the inside is crawling with arty Kreuzbergers. In other words, a classic Kreuzberg café.

## Elefant
*Oranienstraße 12, Kreuzberg, 10999 (612 30 13). U1, U8 Kottbusser Tor.* **Open** *3pm-4am daily.*
A small, seedy bar that draws in a young Kreuzberg crowd; most of them spend their time at the pinball machines.

## Der Goldene Hahn
*Pücklerstraße 20, Kreuzberg, 10997 (618 8098). U1 Görlitzer Bahnhof.* **Open** *9pm-3am daily.*
A newish small bar with unpretentious brick walls, old wooden pharmacist's fittings and lots of stuffed chickens, Der Goldene Hahn is relaxed and smart and seems to indicate the direction in which Kreuzberg is heading. Nice place for a drink or a bite at the Weltrestaurant Markthalle.

## Henne Alt-Berliner Wirtshaus
*Leuschnerdamm 25, Kreuzberg, 10999 (614 7730). U8 Moritzplatz.* **Open** *7pm-12.30am Wed-Sun.*
Right next to where the Wall used to be, Henne serves up the best fried chicken in town. It's a traditional old Berlin bar, on two floors, with efficient, friendly staff and pretty reasonable prices.

## Madonna
*Wienerstraße 22, Kreuzberg, 10999 (611 69 43). U1 Görlitzer Bahnhof.* **Open** *11am-3am daily.*
Nasty, loud and loved by the Kreuzberg rock crowd, Madonna has been an institution for years but latterly seems past its best.

## Maureen Bar
*Ohlauer Straße 3, Kreuzberg, 10999 (612 7065). U1 Görlitzer Bahnhof.* **Open** *9pm-4am daily.*
Small and sort of ambiguous – is it gay? is it straight? is it either? – this newish bar just around the corner from Madonna has a family feel, a large selection of drinks and a wonderfully peculiar taste in music.

## Max und Moritz
*Oranienstraße 162, Kreuzberg, 10969 (614 10 45). U1, U8 Kottbusser Tor.* **Open** *6pm-1am daily.*
A traditional bar-restaurant serving reasonably priced, basic, Berlin food, though drinks veer towards the expensive. Wooden tables and chairs, designer spit and sawdust. Recommended.

## Milchbar
*Manteuffelstraße 41, Kreuzberg, 10997 (611 70 06). U1 Görlitzer Bahnhof.* **Open** *8pm-5am daily.*
Loud, smoky and bursting at the seams, the Milchbar has long been the 'in' place in Kreuzberg for punky/rocker types.

## Mini Café
*Spreewaldplatz 14, Kreuzberg, 10999 (611 55 82). U1 Görlitzer Bahnhof.* **Open** *7pm-open-ended daily.* Things wind down between 5am-8am.
The Mini Café definitely has to be seen to be believed. The

décor consists of Gary Glitter cast-offs: the padded silver ceiling is especially groovy. It's next door to the Café Bar Morena (*see above*).

## Morgenland
*Skalitzerstraße 35, Kreuzberg, 10999 (611 32 91). U1 Görlitzer Bahnhof.* **Open** *10am-2am daily; meals served 4pm-midnight daily.*
This carefully styled, soft peach café represents the current trend towards sophistication in this otherwise run-down part of Berlin. Great breakfasts till 3pm.

## Die Rote Harfe
*Oranienstraße 13, Kreuzberg, 10999 (618 44 46). U1, U8 Kottbusser Tor.* **Open** *10am-3am Tue-Sun.*
Next door to the Elefant (*see above*), but definitely more upmarket than the usual Kreuzberg dive, Die Rote Harfe is more of a cross between a traditional English pub and a wine bar. Cheap beer.

## Schnabelbar
*Oranienstraße 31, Kreuzberg, 10999 (no phone). U1, U8 Kottbusser Tor.* **Open** *from 10pm.*
An essential stop on any Oranienstraße crawl and open all night, this place is recognisable by the metal beak (Schnabel) which pokes out over the door. Inside there's a long bar and a tiny dancefloor, over which some of Berlin's better DJs can be found spinning funk, soul, rare groove and reggae.

## Wiener Blut
*Wienerstraße 14, Kreuzberg, 10999 (618 9023). U1, U8 Görlitzer Bahnhof.* **Open** *4pm-5am daily.*
A hot, smoky, narrow, blood-red bar that is often packed with people wearing leather trousers. Best stay away if you dislike very loud rock music.

# Kreuzberg 61

## Arcanoa
*Zossener Straße 48, Kreuzberg, 10961 (691 24 64). U7 Gneisenaustraße.* **Open** *6pm-4am Mon-Thur, Sun; 6pm-5am Fri, Sat.*
Like a remnant of a *Mad Max* set, Arcanoa is a fairly good example of Berlin at its weirdest. The bar consists of a slab of stone with grooves cut into it, through which run streams of water. Upstairs people perch on strange tree-things made of scaffolding and netting. Bar food served up until 4am, good fruit shakes and non-alcoholic drinks.

## Café Adler
*Friedrichstraße 206, Kreuzberg, 10969 (251 8965). U6 Kochstraße.* **Open** *8.30am-1am Mon-Fri; 10am-1am Sat, Sun.*
Right next to what used be Checkpoint Charlie, you could once watch history in the making from the large windows of this elegant corner café. Today you're more likely to see tower cranes, traffic congestion and hawkers of Wall chunks. A good stop for coffee or a light meal after a visit to the British Bookshop (*see chapter* **Shopping**).

## Café Anfall
*Gneisenaustraße 64, Kreuzberg, 10961 (693 68 98). U7 Südstern.* **Open** *5pm-5am Tue-Sun; from 10pm Mon.*
A great punk/bohemian mixture of décor (furry leopard-skin wallpaper and silver foil) and clientèle, Anfall is loud, friendly and often kind of strange.

## Café Atlantic
*Bergmannstraße 100, Kreuzberg, 10961 (691 92 92). U7 Gneisenaustraße.* **Open** *10am-3am daily; meals served until midnight daily.*
A popular, spacious and smoky place for coffee, Atlantic gets loud and crowded fast. Halogen lights and large canvases add the arty touch. Breakfast is a must (served until 4pm).

*There may be an entrance fee at weekends, but **Boudoir** is always packed. See page 121.*

### Café Milagro

*Bergmannstraße 12, Kreuzberg, 10961 (692 23 03). U7 Gneisenaustraße.* **Open** 9am-1am Mon-Thur; 9am-2am Fri, Sat; 10am-1am Sun.

Light and friendly café, famous for its breakfasts, served up until 4pm. There are also meals served in the evening from 9pm to midnight. A whole room is reserved for non-smokers. Disorientating stairs lead to the hospital-like toilets.

### Café Mistral

*Gneisenaustraße 90, Kreuzberg, 10961 (693 06 66). U7 Gneisenaustraße.* **Open** 4pm-3am Mon-Fri; from noon Sat, Sun.

A tiny, dark cellar with a tomb-like atmosphere. It feels like a catacomb.

### Café Mora

*Großbeerenstraße 57a, Kreuzberg, 10965 (785 05 85). U6, U7 Mehringdamm.* **Open** 11am-2am daily.

Although usually full of arty types, and occasionally offering music, the black and white Café Mora lacks atmosphere.

### Café Rampenlicht

*Körtestraße 33, Kreuzberg, 10967 (692 13 01). U7 Südstern.* **Open** 9am-2am daily; *breakfast* 9am-4pm daily; *meals served* 10am-midnight daily.

A spacious, light and comfortable café furnished in woody colours. Good, cheap snacks and breakfasts.

### Café Turandot

*Bergmannstraße 92 (cnr Solmsstraße), Kreuzberg, 10961 (692 5186). U7 Gneisenaustraße.* **Open** 10am-2am daily.

Laid-back dive, usually full of doped-out locals playing pool.

### Ex

*Im Mehringhof, Gneisenaustraße 2, Kreuzberg, 10961 (693 58 00). U6, U7 Mehringdamm.* **Open** noon-midnight Mon-Thur; 8pm-1am Fri, Sat; 7pm-midnight Sun.

This large, airy café run by the infamous Alternative Mehringhof collective offers cheap beer and occasional music

– skateboard punk hardcore sort of stuff. If you haven't got at least five earrings and a couple of studs in your nose, people will stare at you as if you're some kind of freak.

### Golgotha

*Auf dem Kreuzberg, Kreuzberg, 10965 (785 24 53). S1, S2/U7 Yorckstraße.* **Open** *Apr-Sept* 11pm-6am daily.

In the middle of Viktoria Park with a dancefloor inside and a beer garden outside, all human life – or as much of it as can be found in Kreuzberg 61 – hangs out here on summer nights. In wintertime, with the action confined to quarters, it's little more than a meat market.

### Kookaburra

*Chamissoplatz 4, Kreuzberg, 10965 (691 2021). U6 Platz der Luftbrücke.* **Open** 6pm-4am daily.

On a quiet corner of beautiful Chamissoplatz, this spacious, friendly bar is a good place for an aperitif before, or a digestif after, a meal at the nearby Ristorante Chamisso (*see chapter* **Restaurants**).

### Malheur

*Gneisenaustraße 17, Kreuzberg, 10961 (692 86 28). U6, U7 Mehringdamm.* **Open** 4pm-3.30am Mon-Thur, Sun; 4pm-5am Fri, Sat.

Unlike most Kreuzberg watering holes, Malheur is roomy enough to sit on something other than a complete stranger's knee. Can get very crowded in the evening, though. Nibble on tortilla chips and salsa to soak up the alcohol.

### Niagara

*Gneisenaustraße 58, Kreuzberg, 10961 (692 61 72). U7 Südstern.* **Open** 6pm-6am daily.

A very dark and small late-night joint. Niagara is very loud and usually full of extremely drunk people.

### Yorckschlößchen

*Yorckstraße 15 (cnr Großbeerenstraße), Kreuzberg, 10965 (215 80 70). U6, U7 Mehringdamm.* **Open** 9am-3am Mon-Thur, Sun; 9am-4am Fri, Sat.

The great collection of jazz memorabilia goes towards making Yorckschlößchen popular with everyone in this part of Kreuzberg. Take a late Sunday breakfast and be entertained by the free live jazz from 2pm. In autumn there's live blues and the like from 9pm Wednesdays.

# Mitte

### Bärenschänke
*Friedrichstraße 124, Mitte, 10178 (282 90 78). U6 Oranienburger Tor.* **Open** 11am-1am daily.
A delightfully nasty old dive that has retained that wonderful, no-frills GDR quality. Barmaids with peroxided hair, and delicious, greasy and salty food, provide the perfect antidote to too much hipness on the nearby Oranienburger Straße.

### Boudoir
*Brunnenstraße 192, Mitte, 10119 (282 8674). U8 Rosenthaler Platz.* **Open** 10pm-2am Mon-Thur; 10pm-3am Fri, Sat; 4pm-8pm Sun.
A generous space, mostly painted red, with strange sixties plastic furniture and an enormous oval bed set in one corner – Boudoir, as the name suggests, and unusually for east Berlin, is kind of sexy. It's a fun place. Even the monthly art exhibitions, though not always good, are a cut above most of those in east Berlin bars. At the weekend, when DJs play jazzy stuff, there's a DM10 entrance fee.

### Café Beth
*Tucholskystraße 60, Mitte, (281 8135). S1, S2 Oranienburger Straße.* **Open** 10am-6pm Mon-Thur; 10am-3pm Fri.
Meeting place for the Berlin Jewish community in a bistro atmosphere. American and British Jews may puzzle over what gets delivered when they order familiar Kosher favourites here, since the knishes and 'Gefüllte Fisch Amerikaner Art' bear little resemblance to what they get at home, but this café wing of the Congregation Adass Jisroel guarantees *kashruth* and everything is tasty and well-made. Don't be put off by the machine-gun-toting police currently in front of all of Berlin's Jewish-orientated businesses: they're friendly.

### Café Silberstein
*Oranienburger Straße 27, Mitte, 10117 (281 20 95). S1, S2 Oranienburger Straße.* **Open** 4pm-4am daily.
The high-backed metal chairs and sculptures hanging off the wall from all angles make this arty bar popular with visitors to east Berlin, but the bar staff are, um, less than eager to please, shall we say?

### Hackbarths
*Auguststraße 49a, Mitte, 10119 (282 77 06). U8 Weinmeisterstraße.* **Open** 9am-3am daily; *breakfast* 9am-2pm.
Local trendies and squatters enjoy their coffee here. Good (though microwaved) quiche and vegetable rolls plus a selection of interesting cakes, such as chocolate pear, make it a popular stop for lunchtime snacks.

### Ici
*Auguststraße 61, Mitte, 10117 (281 4064). U6 Oranienburger Tor.* **Open** 3pm-3am daily.
Featuring original painting and sculpture from local artists; a copy of a Camus will help you feel at home among the self-consciously literary set that inhabits this quiet café. Good selection of wines by the glass, though.

### Obst & Gemüse
*Oranienburger Straße 48, Mitte, 10117 (no phone). U6 Oranienburger Tor.* **Open** from noon.
This former greengrocer's (Obst und Gemüse means fruit and veg) is opposite Tacheles and has large windows through which you can watch the wildlife on Oranienburger Straße. Nothing much else special about it, though.

### Opern Café
*Unter den Linden 5, Mitte, 10117 (200 22 69). U6 Französische Straße.* **Open** 8.30am-midnight daily.
The café in the elaborately decorated palatial villa next to the Staatsoper is a favoured coffee-stop for Berliners and visitors. Choose from a huge selection of beautifully displayed cakes. It's an excellent place to sit outside in the summer and watch the world go by.

### Oscar Wilde
*Friedrichstraße 112a, Mitte, 10117 (282 8166). U6 Oranienburger Tor.* **Open** 11am-2am Mon-Thur, Sun; 11am-3am Fri, Sat; *music* 10.30pm Thur-Sat.
Favourite watering hole of Berlin's Irish – particularly people working on the many construction sites in this area – it offers the obligatory ingredients of Guinness, Eurosport and plates of egg and chips. Music at the weekends.

### Tacheles
*Oranienburger Straße 53-56, Mitte, 10117 (312 10 77). U6 Oranienburger Tor.* **Open** 10am-5am daily.
This former department store turned alternative arts beehive is a favourite on the 'let's go to east Berlin' trail. The ground-floor bar is purposely scruffy in an arty way; the bar staff are moody and experts in the art of not catching customers' eyes, and the music is usually far too loud. The artists' workshops are worth a look, though, if they feel like letting you in, and the performance spaces are splendid. The building itself, latterly clad in riotous neon, is spectacular in its own way, as are the scrap metal sculptures out back. Go and have a look, and then spend some time in a decent bar. Tacheles' future is permanently in doubt, but don't worry if they have managed to close the place down by the time you read this – there's plenty more to see and do in the area.

### Village Voice
*Ackerstraße 1a, Mitte, 10115 (282 4550). U8 Rosenthaler Platz.* **Open** 10am-2am Mon-Sat; 11am-2am Sun.
Café/bookstore and culture centre with a good selection of English-language books and a changing programme of poetry readings. There's a film club on Tuesdays and Thursdays, showing movies in the original. The food is standard fare.

### VEB OZ
*Auguststraße 92, Mitte, 10117 (no phone). S1, S2 Oranienburger Tor.* **Open** from 9pm daily.
A small bar just near Tacheles, bizarrely furnished with seats made out of sawn-off Trabant cars, and a bar constructed from old GDR petrol pumps. Nice place for a quiet drink on week nights, it can get uncomfortably crowded at the weekends.

# Prenzlauer Berg

### Bibo Ergo Sum
*Lychener Straße 12, Prenzlauer Berg, 10437 (442 8890). U2 Eberswalder Straße.* **Open** 5pm-5am.
If René Descartes had indeed been a drunken fart, this might have been the place for him. Certainly a couple of glasses of the unpronounceable Czech black beer on tap here would floor any but the most robustly constituted of philosophers. A friendly pub-style place, with dark-wood fittings and exposed electrics.

### Bla-Bla
*Sredzkistraße 19a, Prenzlauer Berg, 13581 (442 35 81). U2 Eberswalder Straße.* **Open** 6pm-8am daily.
Having built a bar in the front room of their ground-floor flat, the owners of this house lowered the lights and opened up their very comfortable living room to the public. It's a great place to start off an evening, read a paper, sink into a sofa or have a sober conversation.

## Café Anita Wronski

*Knaackstraße 26-28, Prenzlauer Berg, 10405 (442 8483). U2 Senefelderplatz.* **Open** 10am-3am daily.
A friendly café on two levels with scrubbed floors, beige walls, hard-working staff and as many tables crammed into the space as the laws of physics allow. Watch out for the waiter carting around a small, ribbon-bedecked toboggan and then try and figure out why he's doing it. We couldn't. Excellent brunches at around DM10.

## Café November

*Husemannstraße 15, Prenzlauer Berg, 10435 (442 8425). U2 Eberswalder Straße.* **Open** 10am-2am at least.
Especially nice during the day, when light floods into this bright, white café through show windows that also offer views of the beautifully restored Husemannstraße. It's a friendly place and, unusual for this district and frankly something of a relief, there isn't much art on the walls. Breakfasts are served all day from 10am-6pm.

## Café Westphal

*Kollwitzstraße 64, Prenzlauer Berg, 10435 (442 76 48). U2 Senefelderplatz.* **Open** 9am-3am daily.
Café Westphal grew out of a squat and became a centre for dissident activities before the revolution. After some difficult times and a threat of closure, it is now a legitimate café and a meeting place for a mixed bag of students, artists and, to the chagrin of the local anarchists, the occasional coachload of tourists. But it's still a great place to be.

## Galerie-Café Eisenwerk

*Sredzkistraße 33, 1058 (448 09 61). U2 Eberswalder Straße.* **Open** 10am-6am daily.
Like most of Prenzlauer Berg's cafés, this place serves as a gallery for local artists. The art is surprisingly good too, and gives the café a unique ambience. Eisenwerk is a small place with barstools unsuitable for vertigo sufferers.

## Kommandatur

*Knaackstraße 20, Prenzlauer Berg, 10405 (no phone). U2 Senefelderplatz.* **Open** 2pm-7am daily.
A small, smoky place heaving with trendy and often unfriendly Prenzlauer Bergers who are reluctant to share their bar with anyone else. There isn't much room for newcomers, anyway. The charged atmosphere here, though, does have a certain spark lacking in some of the area's nicer cafés.

## Krähe

*Kollwitzstraße 84, Prenzlauer Berg, 10435 (442 8291). U2 Eberswalder Straße.* **Open** 10am-2am Tue-Sat; 5pm-2am Mon.
The Krähe (which means 'crow') has distressed walls, a huge wall-hanging depicting bird life in sort of day-glo pastels, and a large marble-topped bar with plenty of places to perch. This is nice, as in most Prenzlauer Berg cafés you're pretty much confined to tables. At the bottom of the rickety basement stairs there is a small cinema, which on our last visit had a programme of Terry Gilliam movies.

## Lampion

*Knaackstraße 54, Prenzlauer Berg, 10435 (442 6026). U2 Eberswalder Straße.* **Open** 4pm-3am daily.
Small bar with dozens of umbrellas hanging from the ceiling, bar staff with a penchant for strange martial music and occasional puppet shows in the small theatre at the back.

## Metzer-Eck

*Metzer Straße 33, Prenzlauer Berg, 10405 (442 7656). U2 Senefelderplatz.* **Open** 4pm-1am daily.
Now a normal Berlin corner pub, back in the communist days this was one of the few privately owned places in the area. One-time Reuters correspondent in East Berlin Peter Millar wrote a book about the bar and its regulars, *Tomorrow Belongs To Me* (*see chapter* **Further Reading**).

Things have changed greatly since then, but this remains a friendly local and vastly different from the new arty-style Prenzl'berg bar. Cheap, too.

## Tantalus

*Knaackstraße 26, Prenzlauer Berg, 10405 (no phone). U2 Senefelderplatz.* **Open** 2pm-2am Mon-Thur, Sun; 2pm-4am Fri, Sat.
Instead of art on the walls, this place has insects. Well, painted insects: lines of giant ants crawl down from holes in the gilded plasterwork. Tantalus isn't usually as crowded as the other bars by the Wasserturm, and it can be a relief to settle at a table here after being elbowed around in, say, Kommandatur.

## Seife und Kosmetik

*Schliemannstraße 21, Prenzlauer Berg, 10437 (no phone). U2 Eberswalder Straße.* **Open** 24 hours daily.
In the grand Berlin tradition of bars named after the shops which once occupied the premises: Seife und Kosmetik means 'soap and cosmetics'. Ironic, because a lot of the local fauna in this nicely sleazy late-night dive look pretty unwashed. The walls could do with a scrub too, but at least all the scribbled graffiti makes a change from the usual Prenzl'berg paintings. Arty, it ain't.

## Titanic

*Winsstraße 30, Prenzlauer Berg, 10405 (436 31 87). U2 Eberswalder Straße.* **Open** 10am-between 2am and 4am daily.
The ventilation pipes, models, the moss-green walls and ceiling, natural wood, extraordinarily friendly staff and similarly talkative customers make Titanic one of the best bars in Prenzlauer Berg. It's always busy and serves dishes of Italian and German peasant food.

## Torpedo Käfer

*Dunckerstraße 69, Prenzlauer Berg, 10437 (444 5763). U2 Eberswalder Straße.* **Open** 11am-2am.
Bright, roomy bar that also serves breakfast until 6pm, basic bar food thereafter (chilli con carne, mozarella and tomato salad and so on, for around DM7). In classic Prenzl'berg fashion, the menu lists as Ausser Haus (takeaway) a sculpture costing DM16,000 and a painting for DM2,500. The coffee is especially good here.

# Schöneberg

## Belmundo

*Winterfeldtstraße 36, Schöneberg, 10781 (215 20 70) U1, U2, U4 Nollendorfplatz.* **Open** 9am-1am Mon-Sat. 10am-midnight Sun.
Round the corner from the always bustling Berio, Belmundo provides a pleasant low-key escape from the hustle of the area's busier cafés.

## Café Berio

*Maaßenstraße 7, Schöneberg, 10777 (216 19 46). U1, U2, U4 Nollendorfplatz.* **Open** 9am-midnight daily.
The locals' choice for breakfasts, it also has plenty of homemade cakes and excellent ice cream. Café Berio has been an institution since the thirties and the tables outside are a prime people-watching spot in summer.

## Café Kleisther

*Hauptstraße 5, Schöneberg, 10827 (784 67 38). U7 Kleistpark.* **Open** 10am-5am daily; *breakfast* 10am-4pm daily; *meals served* noon-2am daily.
A large, bright place with art exhibitions that change monthly and where the people behind the bar are usually livelier than the ones in front of it. There's little atmosphere, but at least you can always get a seat.

## Café M

*Goltzstraße 33, Schöneberg, 10781 (216 70 92). U7 Eisenacher Straße.* **Open** 8am-1am daily; *non-stop breakfast* daily.
A place with terrible music, rude staff and young Berliners desperately trying to be hip. Avoid.

## Ex 'n' Pop

*Mansteinstraße 14, Schöneberg, 10783 (no phone). U7/S1, S2 Yorckstraße.* **Open** from 9pm Tue-Sun.
Once the wild heart of alternative West Berlin and still a hangout for survivors from the crazy mid-eighties, Ex 'n' Pop is quieter these days, but remains a place where the unexpected always stands a chance of happening. The Thursday 'Night Of The Living Words' event – a kind of mutant poetry reading – is always a blast and bands often take to the small stage. Spacious, scruffy, loud and full of characters.

## Fischlabor

*Frankenstraße 13, Schöneberg, 10781 (216 26 35). U7 Eisenacher Straße.* **Open** 9pm-5am daily.
Fischlabor is difficult to find and certainly looks nothing special from the street, but once inside you'll find two rooms of weird, space-agey décor and occasionally DJs playing a mix of funk, soul and rare groove.

## Mutter

*Hohenstaufenstraße 4, Schöneberg, 10781 (216 4990). U1, U2, U4 Nollendorfplatz.* **Open** 9am-4am.
Mutter tries to do everything at once: two bars, an enormous selection of wines, beers and cocktails, breakfasts from 9am-4pm, a sushi bar from 6pm plus a lot of other snacks on offer. As our barman said, when we discovered you could only buy wine in the front bar: 'It's a bit complicated here.' It's roomy, the decor is heavy on gold paint and the spectacular corridor to the toilets has to be walked to be believed.

## Pinguin Club

*Wartburgstraße 54, Schöneberg, 10823 (781 3005). U7 Eisenacherstraße.* **Open** 9pm-4am daily.
Small Anglo-German bar, decorated with fifties' Americana and assorted kitsch bits and pieces, complete with sparkling disco ball. Staff are a mixture of rock 'n' roll-mad Germans and dance-crazy English eccentrics (as are the punters). It's a music biz hangout as well as being a brilliant neighbourhood bar, and the music varies wildly, depending on who's working, ranging from Die Toten Hosen to the Pet Shop Boys. Take your pick from 156 spirits and don't be surprised at the end of the night if everyone starts waltzing.

## Screwy Club

*Frankenstraße 2, Schöneberg, 10781 (215 4441). U7 Eisenacher Straße.* **Open** 9pm-2am Tue-Thur; 9pm-4am Fri, Sat.
Small, friendly bar decorated with artwork by Chuck Jones and Tex Avery. The barstools, for example, are set on giant cartoon-style Bugs Bunny carrots.

## Strüdel

*Grunewaldstraße 21, Schöneberg, 10823 (218 7516). U7 Eisenacher Straße.* **Open** 9pm-3am daily.
A small bar, decorated with wonderful eccentricity, that offers 19 Belgian beers, 15 tequilas, 12 fruit juices and scores of cocktails all served with great care and attention. Excellent place for a tête-à-tête, but not much room for large groups.

## Turbine Rosenheim

*Rosenheimer Straße 4, Schöneberg, 10823 (218 8788). U7 Eisenacher Straße.* **Open** 3pm-2am Mon-Thur, Sun; from 10am Fri, Sat.
Roomy and relaxed, with basic bar food (chilli con carne at DM7, for example, or insalata caprese for DM9), Turbine offers a good selection of drinks, usually tasteful music and is a nice place to stretch out and chat.

# Berlin by Bar Crawl

Few big cities can beat Berlin for the time-honoured pastime of bar crawling. It's not just that there are so many of them, or that they stay open so uncommonly late. It's also that the best of the city's watering holes tend to cluster in distinct areas and a night out drinking, with a short walk between bars, offers as good a way as any of getting to know Berlin's neighbourhoods.

Take Oranienstraße in Kreuzberg. We've listed some of the better places, but if you started at Oranienplatz and had one drink in every bar you passed – gay bars, Turkish bars, hip hop bars, black leather trouser rock 'n' roll bars – you'd keel into the gutter long before you reached Skalitzer Straße, and miss the further merriment to be had in the hangouts of Wiener Straße beyond.

Leafy Schöneberg seems quiet by comparison, but in and around the area between Winterfeldtplatz and Hauptstraße lurks an extraordinary assortment of bars to perch at or prop up. Start out at a cool cocktail bar, move on to a place where they're all smashing bottles on the wall, stop somewhere in between where the stools are giant 3D cartoon carrots.

Along Mitte's Oranienburger Straße, up and down Auguststraße, round the corner into Rosenthaler Straße, flows a ceaseless current of night-crawling humanity. It seems as if every place is some kind of art exhibit, with paintings for decor and sculpture for seats, each trying to outdo the others in cheek and originality.

In Prenzlauer Berg, the corner of Knaackstraße and Rykestraße buzzes with nightlife. Cafés bunch below the Wasserturm. A brief walk through grand and tatty streets brings you to further hostelries on Kollwitzplatz and up Husemannstraße. Quiet conversation at the tables of gallery cafés is here the order of the night.

Particularly in summer, there's a special Berlin feeling to be had, strolling down a quiet, gas lit boulevard beneath fragant trees, maybe two or three in the morning, and at every corner the light and warmth, clatter, chatter and possibility of refreshment at another neighbourhood bar.

### Zoulou Bar

*Hauptstraße 4, Schöneberg, 10728 (784 68 94). U7 Kleistpark.* **Open** 8pm-6am Mon-Thur, Sun; 10pm-9am Fri, Sat.
A small, atmospheric bar that's very crowded between 10pm and 2am; after that the crowd thins out and it's best to pay a visit then. Usually full of staff from nearby bars until the morning.

## Tiergarten

### Bar am Lützowplatz

*Lützowplatz 7, Tiergarten, 10785 (262 6807). U1, U2, U4 Nollendorfplatz.* **Open** 5pm-3am Sun-Thur; 5am-4am Fri, Sat; *happy hour* 5pm-9pm daily.
The longest bar in Berlin with a drinks list to match. Classy customers in Chanel suits and furs sip expensive, well made cocktails and no doubt spend the evening comparing bank balances.

### Café Einstein

*Kurfürstenstraße 58, Tiergarten, 10785 (261 5096). U1, U2, U4 Nollendorfplatz.* **Open** 10am-2am daily; *breakfast* until 2pm daily; *meals served* until midnight daily.
Café Einstein is a Viennese-style coffee house with hectic, tuxedo-clad waiters, international papers and magazines, and a renowned apple strudel. In summer you can sit in the garden at the back and enjoy a leisurely breakfast. *See also chapter* **Restaurants**.

### Caracas

*Kurfürstenstraße 9, Tiergarten, 10785 (261 56 18). U1 Kurfürstenstraße.* **Open** from 10pm daily.
A wild, wacky Brazilian-run cellar bar decked in pink plastic flowers. A small alcove has tatty sofas to sink into when you've worked your way through the 20 kinds of rum, or jigged around on the tiny dancefloor.

### Harry's New York Bar

*Lützowufer 15, Tiergarten, 10785 (26 10 11). U1, U2, U4 Nollendorfplatz.* **Open** from 6pm daily.
A pricey cocktail bar in the Grand Hotel Esplanade, Harry's is sister to the famous American hangout of the Lost Generation in Paris in the twenties. Berlin's more modern version, started in 1988, is sleek and sophisticated, with a jazz singer at the piano. Just behind the musician is a wall of pictures featuring US presidents. Cocktails are expertly mixed and worth splashing out on.

### Kumpelnest 3000

*Lützowstraße 23, Tiergarten, 10785 (261 69 18). U1 Kurfürstenstraße.* **Open** 5pm-5am daily, later at weekends.
Kumpelnest is the place many Berliners end their evening, or morning. It used to be a brothel, the walls are carpeted and one of the barmen is deaf (which can make ordering drinks interesting). You'll find it at its best at the end of a long Saturday night: crowded, chaotic and with people attempting to dance to disco classics.

## Wilmersdorf

### Berlin Bar

*Uhlandstraße 145, Wilmersdorf, 10719 (883 79 36). U1 Hohenzollerndamm.* **Open** 10pm-7am daily.
Small and thin (if there's someone standing at the bar, it's hard to squeeze by between them and the wall) Berlin Bar goes on serving when all else around here has closed. You pay for the privilege, though. After 4am it's full of people who've finished working in other places.

### Café Kronenbourg

*Pfalzburger Straße 11, Wilmersdorf, 10719 (881 77 93). U1 Hohenzollernplatz.* **Open** 9am-1am Mon-Thur, Sun; 9am-4am Fri, Sat; *breakfast* until 4pm daily.
Good-looking and slightly scruffy Berliners are found in this mellow hangout around Ludwig-Kirch-Platz. Friendly waiters join guests at their table for a chat or a cigarette. Racks packed with *Time* and *Der Spiegel* are found in each room.

### Galerie Bremer

*Fasanenstraße 37, Wilmersdorf, 10719 (881 4908). U3 Uhlandstraße.* **Open** 8pm-3am Mon-Sat.
In the front there's an art gallery that's open between noon and six; in the back there's a quiet cocktail bar. Pricey, but an excellent place for a tête-à-tête or romantic rendezvous.

### Zur Weißen Maus

*Ludwigkirchplatz 12, Wilmersdorf, 10719 (882 22 64). U1, U9 Spichernstraße.* **Open** 6pm-4am Mon-Thur, Sun; 6pm-5am Fri, Sat.
The entrance bell and pricey drinks list at the White Mouse lend a feeling of exclusivity to this civilised twenties-style bar. It's decorated in black and orange, with a painting by Berlin's own Otto Dix on the wall. Zur Weißen Maus is quiet, making it a good spot to bring an intimate date. It's on the south-east corner of the impressive Ludwigkirchplatz.

# Inside the Eck-Kneipe

On many corners, down certain streets, especially in the less fashionable quarters, you'll run across the typical Berlin Eck-Kneipe – corner pub. Looking for a little local colour, you may be tempted to wander in. Be pepared.

Inside it'll probably be smoky. Strange German pop music with oom-pah-pah undertones caroms from a juke box in the corner. Indigenous fruit machines with rules comprehensible only to the locals click and whirr to themselves as someone absently feeds in coins from time to time. The locals are mostly male, and mostly drunk out of their faces. They all know each other and bellow in thick, barely intelligible Berlinisch, following arcane native rituals it would take an anthropolgist to unravel and downing huge quantities of Schnapps and Schultheiss beer.

Then you walk in. You are a stranger. You have invaded their inner sanctum. Be prepared. At the worst, you can expect outright hostility. At best, they might try to talk to you. If you're British, expect daft conversational openings about the Royal Family (a German obsession), World War II, English food, or that fact that in Britain, as everyone in Berlin knows, it is always raining cats and dogs.

If you're looking for a quiet drink, forget it.

# Shops & Services

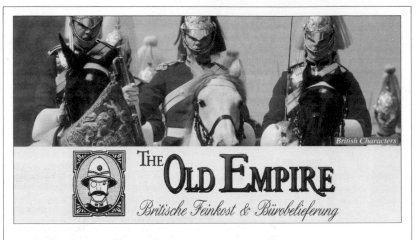

# Shopping

*From tin soldiers to life-size James Deans, Berlin's bizarre bazaars offer a unique shopping experience.*

Berlin was once an elegant shopping centre to rival Paris and New York. And it could be again. Paris department store Galeries Lafayette is moving into the new Friedrichstadt Passagen shopping arcade in 1995, and many retailers are waiting for them to set standards in the area. In the meantime, however, Berlin is still somewhat backward in the ways of commerce. Decades of division not only turned East Berlin into a retail desert, but left the West isolated from consumerism's cutting edge. Although reunification has ushered in much-needed improvements, there's still a long way to go. Sales assistance, for example, is still generally pushy and often downright nasty.

Things worth investing your money in are few and far between in Berlin. Clothes shops, on the whole, are terrible and many of those worth visiting feature clothes by designers you can buy at home anyway. Both new and antiquarian bookshops are excellent, if you read German (we list some shops that also stock books in English). Meissen porcelain is popular with visitors, but very expensive. Second-hand clothes freaks are in luck, though, as are flea- and junk-market junkies. Lovers of Cold War memorabilia will also find themselves with lots to choose from: don't go home without some Russian badges, a Russian hat, a toy Trabi and an alleged piece of the Wall.

For more shops, *see chapters* **Art Galleries** and **Early Hours**. For made-to-measure clothing and more florists, *see chapter* **Services**.

## OPENING HOURS

Any move to reform Germany's restrictive opening hours is blocked by the public service unions on the one hand, and the retailers on the other. Under present law, shops may not sell goods after 6.30pm on weekdays, or 2pm on Saturdays (except every first Saturday in the month, when retailers can open until 6pm in the winter and 4pm in the summer, known as Langer Samstag). The only compromise recently was to allow family businesses to stay open after 6.30pm provided a family member is manning the shop.

The Langer Donnerstag, or long Thursday, was introduced in the early nineties and permits shops to stay open until 8.30pm on that day. All large department stores and most shops in downtown western Berlin take advantage of this, but retailers in other parts of town have been slow to take up the idea. If you want to go on a shopping spree in a particular area, *see* **Area Index** *page 264.*

## Fashion

### Anna von Griesheim
*Pariser Straße 44, Wilmersdorf, 10707 (885 44 06). U2, U9 Spichernstraße.* **Open** 10am-6pm Mon-Fri; 11.30am-1.30pm Sat. **Credit** AmEx, DC, EC, JCB, V.
A charming shop aimed at yuppies. The stock consists of fine city suits and simple dresses by this couture-trained designer.

### Biscuit
*Windscheidstraße 25, Charlottenburg, 10627 (323 4488). U7 Wilmersdorfer Straße.* **Open** noon-6.30pm Mon-Fri; 10am-2pm Sat. **Credit** AmEx, EC, V.
A small, neighbourhood shop filled with playfully patterned and generously cut men's shirts by Berlin shirtmaker Peitscher. But Biscuit's crisp cottons and soft rayons are not just for men. Prices are from around DM150-DM200. Their gallery with 'shirt installations' is located at *Grunewaldstraße 89, Schöneberg (781 61 12). U7 Eisenacherstraße.*

### Blue Moon
*Wilmersdorfer Straße 80, Charlottenburg, 10629 (323 7088). U7 Adenauerplatz.* **Open** 11.30am-6.30pm Mon-Fri; 10am-2pm Sat. **Credit** AmEx, EC, MC, V.
Long a favourite clothing supply house for casual trendies and clubbers. Wide selection of jeans and wacky shoes (the highest platforms in town) plus Doc Martens.

### Bramigk Design
*Savigny Passage, S-Bahnbogen 598, Charlottenburg, 10623 (313 51 25). S3, S5, S6, S9 Savignyplatz.* **Open** 11am-6.30pm Mon-Fri; 11am-2pm Sat. **No credit cards.**
Berlin's resident minimalist Nicola Bramigk specialises in quietly distinctive womenswear and hand-picked Italian fabrics (for sale by the metre). She also sells the best shoes of the season, to finish off the look.

### Brown's
*Nürnbergerstraße 50, Charlottenburg, 10789 (211 74 32). U1, U2, U15 Wittenbergplatz.* **Open** 10am-6.30pm Mon-Fri; 10am-2pm Sat. **Credit** AmEx, DC, EC, JCB, MC, V.
A smart haberdashery for young male fashion traditionalists. The clothes are immaculately presented, and include everything from Swedish shirts by Stenstrom's, clothes by CP Company, John Smedley, and hand-loomed British scarves by Susan Hirsh.

### Durchbruch
*Schlüterstraße 54, Charlottenburg, 10629 (881 55 68). S3, S5, S6, S9 Savignyplatz or U7 Adenauerplatz.* **Open** 11am-6.30pm Mon-Fri; 10am-2pm Sat. **Credit** AmEx, EC, V.
A Berlin fashion landmark, renowned for its rubble-like brick walls (and poorly presented clothes). Going strong for a decade with offbeat designer collections from highly

recommendable local designers such as Lisa D, Studio Ito, Sybilla Pavenstedt and the Durchbruch team. International guests include Yoneda Kausuko and Michael Klein d'Oeil.

## Ermenegildo Zegna

*Bleibtreustraße 24, Charlottenburg, 10707 (882 37 86). U15 Uhlandstraße.* **Open** 9.30am-6.30pm Mon-Fri; 9.30am-2pm Sat. **Credit** AmEx, DC, EC, V.
The Italian luxury menswear-maker's first franchise operation in Germany was opened with help from leading Berlin retailer Mientus. Everything you'd expect from a leading men's collection: socks, shirts, ties, jackets and so on.

## Evento

*Grolmanstraße 53-54, Charlottenburg, 10623 (313 32 17). S3, S5, S6, S9 Savignyplatz.* **Open** 11am-6.30pm Mon-Fri; 11am-2pm Sat. **Credit** AmEx, DC, EC, V.
The selection is limited but to the point in Berlin designer Christina Breuer's Evento boutique. A few key shapes per season can be made to order in your choice of colours and fabrics. Or try your luck off the racks.

## Karl Faktor

*Oranienburger Straße 7, Mitte, 10178 (281 9838). S3, S5, S6, S9 Hackescher Markt.* **Open** 11am-6.30pm Tue-Fri; 11am-2pm Sat. **Credit** AmEx, EC, V.
Katja Dathe has courageously opened a boutique in the fashion wasteland of Mitte, featuring her unusual, body-conscious designs in mute tones of brown, grey and cream. Jewellery and shoes by local craftspeople also sold.

## Lisa D

*Brunnenstraße 192, Mitte, 10119 (282 84 92). U8 Rosenthaler Platz.* **Open** noon-6pm Mon-Fri (or ring for an appointment). **No credit cards.**
Berlin-based avant garde designer Lisa D holds court in the atelier she shares with hat-maker Fiona Bennett (*see below* **Fashion Accessories**) in a delapidated east Berlin soap factory turned design centre. Her clothes tend to be long and flowing, recently featuring a lot of string-tying techniques.

## Max Mara

*Kurfürstendamm 178, Charlottenburg, 10707 (885 2545). U7 Adenauerplatz.* **Open** 10am-6.30pm Mon-Fri; 10am-2pm Sat. **Credit** AmEx, DC, EC, MC, V.
A sleek new store on the Ku'damm, this elegant Italian label provides women with leisure wear, classy coats and jackets, and evening wear.

## Mike's Laden

*Nürnberger Straße 50-56, Schöneberg, 10789 (218 80 20). U1, U2, U15 Wittenbergplatz.* **Open** 10am-6.30pm Mon-Fri; 10am-2pm Sat. **Credit** AmEx, EC, V.
Gaultier Junior, Dolce & Gabbana, Ann Demeulemeester, Paul Smith, Dries Van Noten and other up-to-the-minute selections for trendy young things with cash to spare.

## New Noise/Scenario

*Schönleinstraße 31, Kreuzberg, 10967 (691 5063). U8 Schönleinstraße.* **Open** 11am-6.30pm Mon-Fri; 10am-2pm Sat. **No credit cards.**
A record shop with a good selection of hip-hop, acid jazz, house and rarities, plus togs to match the sounds you're dancing to by X-Large, Komodo and Hysteric Glamour.

## Nix

*Auguststraße 86, Mitte, 10117 (208 83 59). U6 Oranienburger Tor.* **Open** noon-6.30pm Tue, Fri; noon-8.30pm Thur; noon-2.30pm Sat. **No credit cards.**
Young designers Barbara Gebhardt and Angela Herb have taken up residence in the middle of the East Side's bar/gallery scene with their New Individual X-tras (NIX). Unusual in cut, not extravagantly priced and with a dash of humour, though they do use materials that looked washed and worn.

**Galerie Extra** *for classic design. See p137.*

## Ozone

*Knesebeckstraße 27, Charlottenburg, 10623 (883 1124). S3, S5, S6, S9 Savignyplatz.* **Open** 10am-2pm, 3-6.30pm Mon-Fri; 10am-2pm Sat. **Credit** EC, MC, V.
Ozone is two shops in one. The first offers an excellent selection of imported designer sportswear; the second, everything you need for every kind of dance and aerobics, from tutus to tap shoes. The staff are really nice, too.

## Patrick Hellmann Pour Elle

*Fasanenstraße 26, Charlottenburg, 10719 (882 42 01). U3, U9 Kurfürstendamm.* **Open** 9.30am-6.30pm Mon-Fri; 9.30am-2pm Sat. **Credit** AmEx, DC, EC, V.
A prolific upmarket retailer with five shops to his name, Hellmann opened his womenswear shop to specialise in contemporary chic from international fashion makers. The latest from Alaia, Dolce & Gabbana, Sitbon, Gaultier, Calvin Klein, shoes by Kelian, bags from Prada. Sales assistants are somewhat snobby here.

## Patrick Hellmann Sport

*Bleibtreustraße 20, Charlottenburg, 10623 (882 29 66). S3, S5, S6, S9 Savignyplatz.* **Open** 9.30am-6.30pm Mon-Fri; 9.30am-2pm Sat. **Credit** AmEx, DC, EC, MC, V.
Purveyors of the American idea of sportswear – for him and for her – from Ralph Lauren and Calvin Klein, plus Armani Sport. Toiletries from Trumper and Czech & Speake.

## Ralf Setzer Fashion for Women

*Bleibtreustraße 19, Charlottenburg, 10623 (883 13 50). S3, S5, S6, S9 Savignyplatz.* **Open** 10am-6.30pm Mon-Fri; 10am-2pm Sat. **Credit** AmEx, DC, EC, V.
Intelligent selections from Strenesse, G Gigli, Katherine Hamnett, Kenzo and others. For fashion minimalists.

### Schwarze Mode
*Grunewaldstraße 91, Schöneberg, 10823 (784 59 22).*
*U7 Kleistpark or Eisenacherstraße.* **Open** noon-6.30pm
Mon-Fri; 11am-4pm Sat. **Credit** AmEx, DC, EC, V.
Warm leatherette, rubber and vinyl are among the particular delicacies stocked here for Gummi (rubber) enthusiasts.
Clothes come in all sizes and shapes, to be worn under, over
and around.

### Seven Ups
*Bleibtreustraße 48, Charlottenburg, 10623 (883
5108). S3, S5, S6, S9 Savignyplatz.* **Open** 10.30am-
6.30pm Mon-Fri; 10.30am-2pm Sat. **Credit** AmEx, DC,
EC, MC, V.
An idiosyncratic assortment of styles by local designers and
others, worth a browse as some items are quite unusual and
often reasonable.

### Skoda Attendance
*Kurfürstendamm 50, Charlottenburg, 10707 (885 10
09). U15 Uhlandstraße.* **Open** 11am-6.30pm Mon-Fri;
11am-2pm Sat. **Credit** AmEx, DC, EC, MC, V.
Claudia Skoda is Berlin's only designer who has made it on
an international scale. She calls her style 'progressively feminine' and uses her own techniques of knitting and weaving,
often incorporating stretch materials, to create unusual fabrics that rarely look like knitwear.

### Toni Gard
*Schlüterstraße 38, Charlottenburg, 10629 (885 25 85).*
*U15 Uhlandstraße.* **Open** 10am-6.30pm Mon-Fri; 10am-
2pm Sat. **Credit** AmEx, DC, EC, MC, V.
A Düsseldorf label that is sweeping the nation with its understated, purist approach to apparel.

### Wicked Garden
*Grunewaldstraße 71, Schöneberg, 10823 (782 0455). U7
Eisenacher Straße.* **Open** 11am-6.30pm Mon-Fri; 10am-
2pm Sat. **Credit** AmEx, EC, MC, V.
Fabulous new shop featuring the latest styles from clubland
– everything from punk through grunge to techno. Owner
Katherina Deeken regularly replenishes her supply from
designers in London and the US as well as Berlin, and
stocks promising, unestablished designers. A selection of
raver T-shirts, caps and hats.

### Windsurfing Chiemsee and Friends
*Pariser Strasse 15, Charlottenburg, 10719 (883 85 96).*
*U1 Hohenzollernplatz.* **Open** 10am-6pm Mon-Fri; 10am-
1.30pm Sat. **No credit cards.**
Stussy clothes and other surf-dude/club culture attire, including a good selection of Stussy hats.

## Vintage & Second-hand Clothes

### Colours, Kaufrausch
*Bergmannstraße 102, Kreuzberg, 10961 (694 33 48).*
*U7 Gneisenaustraße.* **Open** 11am-6.30pm Mon-Fri; 10am-
2pm Sat. **No credit cards.**
The price tags are colour-coded (with nothing higher
than DM59), as are the vintage offerings which range from
forties to seventies party frocks, to last week's discarded
T-shirts and jeans. Patience and a good eye will be well
rewarded.

### Checkpoint
*Mehringdamm 57, Kreuzberg, 10961 (694 4344). U7
Mehringdamm.* **Open** 10am-6.30pm Mon-Fri; 10am-2pm
Sat. **No credit cards.**
The crayon-coloured walls should immediately grab your
attention, but once you start rummaging through Checkpoint's huge selection of seventies gear, you'll be lost in the
mists of time. Printed bellbottoms, striped, ribbed sweaters,

*Feel the weight at* **Garage** *– second-hand
clothing at DM25 a kilo.*

leather coats and jackets (DM100-DM150) and other unforgettable stuff from the era of *Charlie's Angels* and *Starsky
and Hutch*.

### Falbala
*Ludwigkirchstraße 9a, Wilmersdorf, 10719 (881 32 55).*
*U1, U9 Spichernstraße.* **Open** 1-6pm Mon-Fri. **No credit
cards.**
Former East Berlin theatre-costume designer Josefine Edle
von Krepl has been collecting vintage clothes and accessories
for many years. Her shop is jam-packed with forgotten
German treasures.

### Garage
*Ahornstraße 2, Tiergarten, 10787 (211 27 60). U1, U2,
U4, U15 Nollendorfplatz.* **Open** 11am-6.30pm Mon-Fri;
11am-6pm Sat. **Credit** EC, MC, V.
The best of Berlin's second-hand shops, where clothes are
priced by the kilo (DM25). It's surprisingly well-organised,
given the barracks-like nature of the place, but be prepared
to wait for a dressing room. Particularly good for a cheap,
last-minute party outfit. Huge selection of leather and furry
jackets and coats.

### Made in Berlin
*Potsdamer Straße 106, Tiergarten, 10785 (262 24 31).*
*U1 Kurfürstenstraße.* **Open** 11am-6.30pm Mon-Fri;
10am-2pm Sat. **Credit** EC, MC, V.
Garage's (*see above*) sister store, where all the 'better stuff'
supposedly goes. Dresses and jackets are in the DM40-DM50
range. It's still very cheap and cheerful, and you *still* have to
wait an eternity for a changing room.

### Spitze
*Weimarer Straße 19, Charlottenburg, 10625 (31 60 68).*
*U7 Wilmersdorfer Straße.* **Open** 2-6.30pm Mon-Fri;
11am-2pm Sat. **Credit** DC, EC, MC, V.
Clothes, accessories and handicrafts from 1860 to 1960, and
certainly Berlin's best address for men's and women's clothing from the forties. Spitze also stocks a lovely assortment
of old table- and bed-linen.

## Shoes & Fashion Accessories

### Birkenstock Shop
*Krumme Straße 41, Charlottenburg, 10627 (313 4996).*
*U2 Deutsche Oper.* **Open** 9am-6pm Mon-Fri; 9am-2pm
Sat. **No credit cards.**
It takes a lot of walking around to get to know Berlin, which
is possibly one reason why the Birkenstock chain has such
a strong following here. These clumpy sandals are comfortable, and, what with the grunge scene, have even become
vaguely fashionable.

### Bleibgrün
*Bleibtreustraße 29/30, Charlottenburg, 10707 (882 1689). U15 Uhlandstraße.* **Open** 11am-6.30pm Mon-Fri; 11am-2pm. **Credit** AmEx, EC, DC, V.
Berlin's best designer shoe shop, with a good selection from Jan Jansen, Lagerfeld, Montana and Maud Frizon. Bags and knitwear also for sale.

### Bree
*Kurfürstendamm 44, Charlottenburg, 10719 (883 7462). U15 Uhlandstraße.* **Open** 9.30am-6.30pm Mon-Fri; 9.30am-2pm Sat. **Credit** AmEx, DC, EC, MC, V.
This German leather goods company must have a patent on practicality; their durable and easy-to-organise handbags, briefcases, wallets, rucksacks and suitcases are toted by many a yuppy professional.

### Brilliant
*Schlüterstraße 30, Charlottenburg, 10629 (324 19 91). S3, S5, S6, S9 Savignyplatz.* **Open** 10am-6.30pm Mon-Fri; 10am-2pm Sat. **Credit** AmEx, DC, EC, V.
Just the idea of housing jewellery and glasses in one shop makes Brilliant worthy of note, but it also has some of the snappiest frames to be found anywhere in this eyewear-conscious town. There are horn frames from Munich painter Franz Rizicka, super plastic numbers from Proksch's, as well as frames designed by the owners, in bamboo and other woods.

### Budapester Schuhe
*Kurfürstendamm 199, Charlottenburg, 10719 (881 17 07). U3 Uhlandstraße.* **Open** 9.30am-6.30pm Mon-Fri; 9.30am-2pm Sat. **Credit** AmEx, DC, EC, V.
For once, men are blessed with the best shoe shop in Berlin: Budapester Schuhe. Superbly made classics from Austria, America and Britain and some incredible bargains during the sales.

### Chapeau Claudette!
*Wielandstraße 36, Charlottenburg, 10629 (323 48 65). S3, S5, S6, S9 Savignyplatz.* **Open** 10am-6pm Mon-Fri. **No credit cards.**
A gem of a shop, Chapeau Claudette! has delightful hats for men and women to match the memorable décor, and a place to sit down and sip tea while you decide what and whether or not to buy.

### Fiona Bennett
*Brunnenstraße 192, Mitte, 10119 (282 84 92). U8 Rosenthaler Platz.* **Open** noon-6pm Mon-Fri (or ring to make an appointment). **No credit cards.**
Fiona Bennett is a truly mad hatter. Her creations have been admired by, among others, Vivienne Westwood (first lady of English fashion and a guest lecturer at the Hochschule der Künste) and they range in style from romantic to wild. Her bright and roomy, red-carpeted studio in the crumbling soap factory premises she shares with Lisa D (*see above*) is worth a visit.

### Kaufhaus Schrill
*Bleibtreustraße 46, Charlottenburg, 10623 (882 40 48). S3, S5, S6, S9 Savignyplatz.* **Open** 11am-6.30pm Mon-Fri; 10am-4pm Sat. **Credit** EC, V.
Kaufhaus Schrill has every kind of outrageous accessory. Lots and lots of fun.

### Les Dessous
*Fasanenstraße 42, Wilmersdorf, 10719 (883 36 32). U1 Spichernstraße.* **Open** 10am-6.30pm Mon-Fri; 10am-2pm Sat. **Credit** AmEx, DC, EC, V.
A beautiful shop with friendly sales assistants, featuring luxurious lingerie, silk dressing gowns and fabulous swimwear by Capucine Puerarari, La Perla, Malizia, Armani and André Sardá.

### Rio
*Bleibtreustraße 52, Charlottenburg, 10623 (313 31 52). S3, S5, S6, S9 Savignyplatz.* **Open** 10am-6.30pm Mon-Fri; 10am-2pm Sat. **Credit** EC, V.
Baubles and beads from New York, Paris – and wherever there's a feeling for colour, contour and design. Huge and well-chosen earring selection.

### Mandarina Duck
*Kurfürstendamm 36, Charlottenburg, 10719 (885 24 27). U15 Uhlandstraße.* **Open** 9.30am-6.30pm Mon-Fri; 10am-2pm Sat. **Credit** AmEx, DC, EC, V.
Sleek, Italian handbag and luggage collections schlepped by well-travelled media types. Characteristic design elements include a special finishing treatment that makes the calf-leather wallets, bags and briefcases scratch-resistant and waterproof; sand-blasted steel clasps; and quirky but durable corrugated rubber for luggage.

### Marc & Bengels
*Grunewaldstraße 92, Schöneberg, 10823 (784 84 64). U7 Kleistpark.* **Open** 11am-6.30pm Mon-Fri; 10am-2pm Sat. **Credit** AmEx, DC, EC, MC, V.
Spectacular underwear for men: boxers, slips, all-in-ones. Playful, sultry and sensational. The selection includes Versace, L'Homme Invisible, Cerutti and Kirtos.

### Stellina
*Schlüterstraße 30, 10629 (323 7997). S3, S5, S6, S9 Savignyplatz.* **Open** 10am-6pm Mon-Fri; 10am-2pm Sat. **Credit** AmEx, DC, EC, MC, V.
A small shop jam-packed with jewellery by Gaultier, Lagerfeld, Christian Lacroix and Kenzo, plus a few unique handbags and beautiful gift cards.

### Zapato
*Maaßenstraße 14, Schöneberg, 10777 (215 20 27). U1, U2, U4 Nollendorfplatz, and branches.* **Open** 10am-6pm Mon-Fri; 10am-2pm Sat. **Credit** AmEx, EC, V.
Funky, unusual shoes are sold here – they end up adorning the feet of Berlin's young and hip.

### Zoé
*Bleibtreustraße 50a, Charlottenburg, 10623 (312 64 53). S3, S5, S6, S9 Savignyplatz.* **Open** 11am-6.30pm Mon-Fri; 10.30am-2pm Sat. **No credit cards.**
A fine selection of antique jewellery and accessories. Art deco fans are in for a treat.

## Handmade Jewellery

There are several interesting, contemporary jewellery workshops and galleries. The designers work with a variety of materials, including metal and stone. Their work doesn't come cheap.

### Feinschmiede
*Windscheidstraße 24, Charlottenburg, 10627 (323 40 48). U2 Sophie-Charlotte-Platz.* **Open** 11am-6pm Tue-Fri; 11am-2pm Sat. **No credit cards.**
Unusual, hand-crafted metalwork brooches, earrings and necklaces. Some pieces are made with silk or even paper. Also on display are steel chairs (from DM600), and candlesticks by a Berlin-based designer, available by order.

### Schmuckgalerie Fritz & Fillmann
*Dresdener Straße 20, Kreuzberg, 10999 (615 17 00). U1, U8 Kotthusser Tor.* **Open** 1-6pm Tue-Fri; 11am-2pm Sat. **No credit cards.**
The Schmuckgalerie Fritz & Fillman features highly original designs from the workshop of these two Berliners, and goldsmiths from all over Germany. A large selection of very unusual rings is on display, making this place popular

among brides and grooms-to-be. Prices range from the lower hundreds to the thousands of marks. They make designs to order and offer courses.

### Treykon Schmuckwerkstatt

*Savignyplatz 13, Charlottenburg, 10623 (312 42 75). S3, S5, S6, S9 Savignyplatz.* **Open** 10am-6.30pm Tue-Fri; 10am-2pm Sat. **Credit** AmEx, DC, EC, MC, V.
The designs of metal- and stone-worked jewellery kept here vary from the ultra-modern to the classic. Treykon holds about three major exhibitions a year.

## Antiques

## Antiques & Flea Markets

It's also worth checking out *Zitty* and *Tip* for the most up-to-date market listings. Don't bother trying to pay for anything by credit card.

### Berliner Antik & Flohmarkt

*Bahnhof Friedrichstraße, S-Bahnbögen 190-203, Mitte, 10117 (215 02 129). S1, S2, S3, S5, S6, S9/U6 Friedrichstraße.* **Open** 11am-6pm Mon, Wed-Sun.
Berlin's only indoor antique centre, and a welcome new addition to the Friedrichstraße area. About 60 dealers have taken up residence in the renovated arch spaces under the S-Bahn tracks, as has the Zille Museum, a private collection of memorabilia and artwork by Berlin's foremost street artist, Heinrich Zille. The market is in two sections.

### Flea Market Am Humboldthain

*Gustav-Meyer-Allee, Wedding, 13355 (323 35 99/463 20 78) U8 Voltastraße.* **Open** 8am-4pm Sat, Sun.
A good, if slightly out of the way general flea market in a traditional working class district of Wedding. You might come across the odd rare German-language copy of Bowie's 'Heroes', for example.

### Flea Market at Askanierring/Ecke Flankenschanze

*Askanierring, Spandau, 13585 (371 4412). U7 Altstadt Spandau.* **Open** 8am-4pm Sat, Sun.
Reminiscent of London's Portobello Road before it went upmarket.

### Flea Market on Fehrbelliner Platz

*Fehrbelliner Platz, Wilmersdorf, 10707. U1, U7 Fehrbelliner Platz.* **Open** 8am-4pm Sat, Sun.
Long a Sundays-only affair, the Fehrbelliner Platz market has now expanded to a two-day run. It's a bit of a hodge-podge, with a few very good dealers sprinkled between mountains of useless bric-à-brac.

### Flea Market on Straße des 17 Juni

*Straße des 17 Juni, Charlottenburg, 10787. U2 Ernst-Reuter-Platz/S3, S5, S6, S9 Tiergarten.* **Open** 8am-3pm Sat, Sun.
Early twentieth-century *objets*, high-quality with prices to match, are among the jumble of vintage and alternative clothing, second-hand records and books, and tasty French fries sold at this Charlottenburg flea market. Arts and crafts further along the street.

### Pariser Platz Market

*Pariser Platz, at Brandenburg Gate, Mitte, 10117. S1, S2 Unter den Linden.* **Open** 9am-dusk daily.
The Pariser Platz Market at Brandenburg Gate is one of the best places in Berlin to look for 'Commie kitsch' stuff – Russian toy cars, Communist Party membership cards, and Soviet army uniforms and equipment, including binoculars and watches.

### Zille Hof

*Fasanenstraße 14, Charlottenburg, 10623. U15 Uhlandstraße.* **Open** 8.30am-5pm Mon-Fri; 8.30am-1pm Sat.
Zille Hof is a neat and tidy junk market located almost next door to the highly exclusive Kempinski Hotel. You'll find the better bric-à-brac indoors, while the real bargains lurk in the courtyard outside.

## Antiques & Collectors' Shops

Collectors, admirers and browsers with an interest in the eighteenth and nineteenth centuries will find many of the better dealers clustered on Keithstraße and around Eisenacher Straße and Goltzstraße in Schöneberg. The streets surrounding Fasanenplatz (Wilmersdorf) are worth exploring, as is Suarezstraße (Charlottenburg).

### Das Alte Bureau

*Goltzstraße 18, Schöneberg, 10781 (216 59 50). U7 Eisenacher Straße.* **Open** 3-6pm Mon-Fri; 11am-2pm Sat. **No credit cards**.
Antique desks, filing cabinets, chairs and bookshelves for romantic workaholics.

### Jukeland

*Crellestraße 13, Schöneberg, 10827 (782 33 35). U7 Kleistpark.* **Open** 2-6pm Tue-Fri; 11am-2pm Sat. **No credit cards**.
Everything you need to turn your place into an American diner, from neon signs, jukeboxes and Cadillac couches, to diner-style tables and seatings. There are plenty of forties and fifties adverts and signs, and you can even pick up a life-size James Dean should you so desire.

### Klaus Rachner Raumausstattung

*Zillestraße 105, Charlottenburg, 10585 (341 97 15). U2, U7 Bismarckstraße.* **Open** 9am-1pm Mon-Fri; 3-6pm Sat. **No credit cards**.
Only for those interested in large pieces of antique furniture: beautifully preserved chairs, tables, and cupboards; together with chests of drawers and writing tables in mahogany, walnut and oak. There are some smaller pieces, such as mirrors and picture frames.

### Knopf Paul

*Zossener Straße 10, Kreuzberg, 10961 (692 12 12). U7 Gneisenaustraße.* **Open** 9am-6pm Tue, Fri; 2-6pm Wed, Thu, Sat. **No credit cards**.
Buttons, buttons and more buttons: antique and contemporary buttons made from glass, horn, bone, fabric, plastic and metal, in every conceivable size, shape and colour. Collectors should ask about rarities kept hidden away in the backroom.

### Kontor für Antike Öfen

*Pariser Strasse 20, Wilmersdorf, 10707 (881 38 39). U2 Spichernstraße.* **Open** 3-6.30pm Mon-Fri; 10am-2pm Sat. **Credit** EC.
Berliners are used to the large tiled ovens that stand in the middle of rooms, as many of the city's apartments are still heated by coal. Nevertheless, it's difficult not to be awed by the exquisite antique heating systems on sale here.

### Odeon Art Deco

*Uhlandstraße 20-25, Charlottenburg, 10623 (883 6021). U15 Uhlandstraße.* **Open** 1-6.30pm Mon-Fri; 11am-2pm Sat. **No credit cards**.
At Odeon Art Deco you can rummage through furniture, lamps, mirrors, carpets, accessories and jewellery from the twenties and thirties – most of it original.

### Schöne Alte Spitzen

*Suarezstraße 6, Charlottenburg, 14057 (321 67 91). U2 Sophie-Charlotte-Platz.* **Open** noon-6pm Mon-Fri; 11am-2pm Sat. **No credit cards.**
An ideal antique shop for those with an interest in old granny stuff, Schöne Alte Spitzen has lace collars, lace-edged linen and cotton tablecloths, napkins, pillow-covers, and so on. A few clothes, old hats and parasols, and beautiful silver-mesh purses and gloves.

### Timmermann's Indian Supply

*Berliner Straße 88, Potsdam, 14467 (0331 220 76). S1, S3 Wannsee, then bus 116 to Glienicker Brücke.* **Open** 10am-6pm Mon-Fri; 11am-3pm Sat. **Credit** EC, MC.
Timmermann's vintage Indian motorcycles are in tip-top condition and make really big toys for really big kids. The beautifully restored thirties gas station where the machines are sold is worth the trip in itself.

### Ubu

*Bleibtreustraße 55, Charlottenburg, 10623 (313 51 15). S3, S5, S6, S9 Savignyplatz.* **Open** 3-6.30pm Mon-Fri; 11am-2pm Sat. **No credit cards.**
Early Baedekers in a variety of languages, plus other vintage travel literature, antique trunks and travelling cases, toiletry, smoking kits and model ships.

### Wolfgang Haas

*Suarezstraße 3, Charlottenburg, 14057 (321 45 70/825 83 66). U2 Sophie-Charlotte-Platz/204 bus.* **Open** 3-6pm Mon-Fri; 11am-2pm Sat. **Credit** AmEx, DC, EC, MC, V.
Period, lacquered-timber furniture, glassware, ceramics and other small antique pieces dating from 1800 to 1960 are collected together at Wolfgang Haas. There are classic tables, chairs and cabinets, as well as art nouveau pieces. The selection of German crystal from the nineteenth and twentieth centuries is particularly good; the paintings are all post-1945.

### Woytnik

*Beifußweg 68a, Rudow, 12357 (662 53 51). Bus 141.* **Open** 9am-6pm Mon-Fri. **No credit cards.**
Actually a model shop, but worth visiting if you happen to be looking for East German street-car models.

## Bookshops

### The British Bookshop

*Mauerstraße 83-84, Mitte, 10117 (238 46 80). U2, U6 Stadtmitte.* **Open** 9.30am-6.30pm Mon-Fri; 9.30am-2pm Sat. **No credit cards.**
A big shop with a large stock of contemporary and classic fiction, the British Bookshop also boasts comprehensive English language teaching, travel and children's sections. It tends to be pricier than some other shops. There are frequent readings and signing-sessions and a good selection of newspapers and magazines.

### Bücherbogen am Savigny Platz

*Savignyplatz Bogen 593, Charlottenburg, 10623 (312 19 32, fax, 313 72 37). S3, S5, S6, S9 Savignyplatz.* **Open** 9.30am-6.30pm Mon-Fri; 9.30am-2pm Sat. **Credit** V.
A great art-book store, with painting, sculpture, architecture and photography departments on the Savignyplatz premises. People interested in fashion and film are directed to the nearby Tattersall/Savigny Passage Bücherbogen. The Kochstraße branch concentrates on architecture, Berlin culture, twentieth-century art, photography and design.
**Branches** am Tattersall, S-Bahnbogen 585, Charlottenburg, 10623 (fax 313 25 15). In der Nationalgalerie, Potsdamer Straße 50, Tiergarten, 10785 (fax 261 10 90) Kochstraße 19, Kreuzberg, 10969 (251 13 45, fax 251 11 73).

### Dharma Buchladen

*Akazienstraße 17, Schöneberg, 10823 (784 50 80). U7 Eisenacherstraße.* **Open** 9.30am-6pm Mon-Fri; 9.30am-2pm Sat. **No credit cards.**
Schöneberg's Dharma Buchladen has a selection of books on Buddhism, plus Tarot cards and lots of New Age paraphernalia. The sales assistants, however, seem to be somewhat lacking in cosmic love.

### Kiepert

*Knesbeckstraße 20, Charlottenburg, 10623 (311 0 090). U2 Ernst-Reuter-Platz.* **Open** 9am-6.30pm Mon-Fri; 9am-2pm Sat. **Credit** AmEx, EC, MC, V.
A large bookshop opposite the Technical University, Kiepert has a wide selection of fiction and non-fiction, worldwide travel guides in German and English, and a pretty good English section.

### Kohlhaas & Co

*Fasanenstraße 23, Charlottenburg, 10719 (882 50 44). U15 Uhlandstraße.* **Open** 10am-6.30pm Mon-Fri; 10am-2pm Sat. **Credit** (over DM50 only) EC, MC, V.
Housed in the cellar beneath Literaturhaus, this small, well-run bookshop goes against the general Berlin bookstore trend of nasty, unfriendly service. German literature in German is what's for sale.

### Marga Schoeller Bücherstube

*Knesebeckstraße 33, Charlottenburg, 10623 (881 11 12/881 11 22). S3, S5, S6, S9 Savignyplatz.* **Open** 9am-6.30pm Mon-Fri; 9am-2am Sat. **Credit** AmEx, EC, V.
Cooperatively owned general bookstore with an excellent selection of new English books which, if not the biggest in Berlin, is certainly the best in this part of town and it beats the opposition in many subject areas – for example, New Age and psychology. Staff generally know their stuff and are very helpful.

### The (Original Version)

*Sesenheimer Straße 17, Charlottenburg, 10627 (313 76 22). U2, U7 Bismarck Straße.* **Open** noon-9pm daily. **No credit cards.**
If you're looking for cheap, second-hand English and American literature, or you want to unload some of your books for cash, this is the place to visit. The selection isn't huge but it's well-stocked with literature, crime and science fiction, and overall it's an interesting place. They also rent videos in English and if you're in Berlin for a while, it would be worth joining the video club (*see chapter* **Film**).

### One World Books

*Grolmanstraße 22, Charlottenburg, 10623 (313 37 70). S3, S5, S6, S9 Savignyplatz.* **Open** 10am-6.30pm Mon-Fri; 10am-2pm Sat. **No credit cards.**
One World is a remainder bookshop which deals in hardbacks in English and other languages at half or even a third of the original published price. The selection of books on the arts and literature in English is wide. There's also a section for those with an interest in eastern European literature.

### Wiens Laden & Verlag

*Gleditschstraße 37, Schöneberg, 10781 (217 08 37). U7 Kleistpark.* **Open** 1-6pm Tue-Fri; 11am-2pm Sat. **No credit cards.**
Artists' books and volumes by and about artists are sold in editions from small presses such as Edition Hundertmark, Cologne or, indeed, the house publisher Wiens Verlag.

## Antiquarian Books

If you're particularly interested in second-hand books you should take a walk down Winterfeldt Straße (near U-Bahn Nollendorfplatz). Otherwise,

just look up 'Buchhandel' and the sub-heading 'Antiquariats-Buchhandel' in the *Gelbe Seiten* (Yellow Pages).

### Antiquariat

*Schönhauser Allee 126, Prenzlauer Berg, 10437 (449 78 53). U2 Schönhauser Allee.* **Open** 10am-6.30pm Mon-Fri; 10am-1am Sat. **No credit cards.**
This bookshop sells quality second-hand books covering all subject areas and has a particularly good collection of literature from the GDR.

### Antiquariat Kiepert

*Knesebeckstraße 20, Charlottenburg, 10623 (313 50 00). U2 Ernst-Reuter-Platz.* **Open** 9am-6.30pm Mon-Fri; 10am-2pm Sat. **Credit** AmEx, EC, MC, V.
Specialists in books, maps and graphics, dating from 1500 onwards. Many areas are covered, but particularly extensive is the collection of antique books on natural sciences and architecture. Lithographs, dating back to the fifteenth century, cost from DM150.

### Antiquariat Senzel

*Knesebeckstraße 113-114, Charlottenburg, 10623 (312 58 87). U2 Ernst-Reuter-Platz.* **Open** noon-6.30pm Mon-Fri; 11am-2pm Sat. **No credit cards.**
You can have a seat in Antiquariat Senzel and enjoy a leisurely read. Most of the antiquarian books are in German, but you will find the odd volume in English. You can also unearth beautiful leather-bound publications, a selection of old maps and some second-hand books in English and French. Well worth a browse – you never know what you might turn up.

### Das Arabische Buch

*Knesebeckstraße 16, Charlottenburg, 10623 (313 80 21). U2 Ernst-Reuter-Platz.* **Open** 10am-6pm Mon-Fri; 10am-2pm Sat. **Credit** EC.
Das Arabische Buch has new books from the Middle and Far East, and a few cabinets of precious old editions. There are handwritten Korans and other antique books in English, French and German.

### Düwal

*Schlüterstraße 17, Charlottenburg, 10625 (313 30 30). S3, S5, S6, S9 Savignyplatz.* **Open** 3-6.30pm Mon-Fri; 11am-2pm Sat. **No credit cards.**
A sizeable bookstore sporting shelves of German, French and English books. Some date back to the sixteenth century, but most are from the eighteenth to the twentieth centuries. Prices can run to thousands of marks.

### Fair Exchange

*Dieffenbachstraße 58, Kreuzberg, 10967 (694 46 75). U8 Schönleinstraße.* **Open** 11am-6.30pm Mon-Fri; 10am-1pm Sat. **No credit cards.**
Fair Exchange stocks a large selection of English-language books, and concentrates on literature.

### Grober Unfug

*Zossener Straße, 32-33, Kreuzberg, 10961 (693 64 13). U7 Gneisenaustraße.* **Open** 11am-6pm Mon-Fri; 10am-2pm Sat. **No credit cards.**
Stockists of comics in all languages, including annuals, and comic art from *Viz* to arty French stuff.

### Schropp

*Lauterstraße 14-15, Schöneberg, 12159 (859 4911). U9 Friedrich-Wilhelm-Platz.* **Open** 9am-6pm Mon-Fri; 9am-1pm Sat. **Credit** AmEx, EC, V.

**Opposite: Wicked Garden***, wicked gear. See page 129.*

The best selection in Berlin of books, new maps, and prints of antique maps. Illuminated globes are also sold.

## Children

Children's merchandise tends to be extremely expensive in Germany, so it's probably best for the visiting shopper to steer clear of clothes and shoes. Wooden toys, however, are a German speciality and, though pricey, are often original enough to warrant the expense. Whimsical hanging clowns and birds that swing from the ceiling, push-and-pull toys for toddlers, trains, dolls' houses and furniture for older children are among the most popular examples of the genre. Beautiful picture-books for young children and handmade puppets also make charming gifts. If you're determined to buy clothing, department stores are your best bet. **KaDeWe** (*see box below* **The Ku'damm**) is expensive, but does have an extensive children's department. Cheaper clothes can be found at any Hertie, C&A or Hennes and Mauritz store.

### Berliner Zinnfiguren Kabinet

*Knesebeckstraße 88, Charlottenburg, 10623 (31 08 02). S3, S5, S6, S9 Savignyplatz.* **Open** 10am-noon, 1-6pm, Mon-Fri; 10am-1pm Sat. **Credit** AmEx, EC, MC, V.
Tin soldiers, Biedermeier figures in frock coats, animals for the farm, zoo or Noah's ark – all these models are made from tin and are tiny, terrific and easy to transport.

### Heidi's Spielzeugladen

*Kantstraße 61, Charlottenburg, 10623 (323 75 56). U7 Wilmersdorferstraße.* **Open** 9.30am-6pm Mon-Fri; 9.30am-2pm Sat. **No credit cards.**
Lots of small wooden toys, including wooden cookery utensils and dolls' houses, are the attraction at Heidi's Spielzeugladen. You'll also find a selection of wall-hangings, books and puppets.

### Hennes & Mauritz

*Kurfürstendamm 234, 10719 (882 3844). U15 Kurfürstendamm.* **Open** 10am-6.30pm Mon-Fri; 10am-2pm Sat. **Credit** AmEx, DC, EC, MC, V.
H&M has taken over the art nouveau rooms of the former Berlin coffee house establishment Café Möhring with good value, happy clothes for kids.

### Klein-Holz

*Stuttgarter Platz 21, Charlottenburg, 10627 (323 86 81). S3, S5, S6, S9 Charlottenburg.* **Open** 10am-6pm Mon-Fri; 9am-2pm Sat. **Credit** EC, V.
The examples of handcrafted wooden toys at Klein-Holz reflect both a naive and refined sensibility. The mid-sized animals are especially appealing.

### Michas Bahnhof

*Nürnberger Straße 21, Schöneberg, 10789 (218 66 11). U1 Augsburger Straße.* **Open** 2-6.30pm Mon-Fri. **Credit** AmEx, EC, DC, V.
One block south of the Ku'damm, this small shop is packed with model trains, both old and new, and everything that goes with them. Whatever you do, don't miss the antique miniature cars.

### Modellautos

*Leibnitzstraße 42, Charlottenburg, 10629 (324 42 13). U7 Adenauer Straße.* **Open** 9.30am-6pm Mon-Fri; 10am-*

The 600 square metres of floorspace at **Katakomben** are filled with the latest Italian designs.

2pm Sat. **Credit** AmEx, DC, EC, V.
Hundreds of modern model cars can be purchased here, but none of them are radio-controlled.

### Ria's Kinderstube
*Ansbacher Straße 8, Schöneberg, 10787 (214 28 88).*
*U1, U2, U15 Wittenbergplatz.* **Open** 10am-6pm Mon-Fri;
10am-2pm Sat. **No credit cards.**
You'll get a good overview of the baby-wear market by browsing through Ria's. The stock also includes clothes and gear for younger children, together with a selection of toys.

### Spiele Shop
*Berliner Straße 132, Wilmersdorf, 10715 (87 15 35). U7*
*Blissestraße.* **Open** 9.30am-6pm Mon-Fri; 9.30am-2pm
Sat. **No credit cards.**
Educational toys, and toys with no didactic raison d'être, fill the shelves at the Spiele Shop.

### Spiel Vogel
*Uhlandstraße 137, Wilmersdorf, 10717 (87 23 77/87 82*
*96). U1 Hohenzollernplatz.* **Open** 9am-6pm Mon-Fri;
9am-1pm Sat. **No credit cards.**
A standard selection of toys and books is stocked here, along with models and kits for making dolls' furniture.

### Tam-Tam
*Lietzenburger Straße 92, Charlottenburg, 10719 (882 14*
*54). U15 Uhlandstraße.* **Open** 10am-6pm Mon-Fri; 10am-
2pm Sat. **No credit cards.**
A bright, charming shop with a large selection of wooden toys, including building blocks, trains, trucks, dolls' houses and furniture, plus child-sized wooden stoves, cupboards and household appliances. You'll also find puppets and a stuffed menagerie.

### Übermuth
*Mommsenstraße 64, Charlottenburg, 10629 (881 39 50).*
*S3, S5, S6, S9 Savignyplatz.* **Open** 10am-1pm, 3-6pm,
Tue-Fri; 10am-1pm Sat. **No credit cards.**
The cutest kids' wear you could hope to find anywhere. Lots

of navy and white sailors' looks by French firms and Über-muth's own designs. The hand-embroidered alphabet bibs are particularly endearing.

### Vom Winde Verweht
*Eisenacherstraße 81, Schöneberg, 10823 (784 77 69).*
*U7 Eisenacher Straße.* **Open** 10am-6pm Mon-Fri; 10am-
2pm Sat. **Credit** EC, MC, V.
Kites, Frisbees, boomerangs, balls and marbles.

## Cosmetics & Healthcare

### Calla
*Winterfeldstraße 38, Schöneberg, 10781 (215 43 21).*
*U1, U2, U4 Nollendorfplatz.* **Open** 10am-6pm Mon-Fri;
10am-2pm Sat. **No credit cards.**
All the natural cosmetics, soaps, lotions and scents sold at Calla are produced by homoeopathic and herbal specialists.

### Condomi
*Kantstraße 38, Charlottenburg, 10625 (313 50 51). S3,*
*S5, S6, S9/U2, U9 Zoologischer Garten.* **Open** 10.30am-
6.30pm Mon-Fri; 10.30am-2pm Sat. **No credit cards.**
While you can buy condoms everywhere in Berlin (in vend-ing machines in the subway, on the street and in many bars), you'll have more fun choosing from the mind-boggling selec-tion of coloured or plain, patterned or textured, animal-shaped or fruit-flavoured rubbers at this store.

### Friseur Bedarf von Malachinski
*Mommsenstraße 62, Charlottenburg, 10629 (881 8081).*
*U15 Uhlandstraße.* **Open** 9am-6pm Mon-Fri; 10am-1pm
Sat. **No credit cards.**
Wholesale hair cosmetics and accessories normally available only at hairdressers, at up to 30 per cent discount rates.

### Harry Lehmann
*Kantstraße 106, Charlottenburg, 10627 (324 35 82). U7*
*Wilmersdorfer Straße/S3, S5, S6, S9 Charlottenburg.*

**Open** 9am-6.30pm Mon-Fri; 9am-2pm Sat. **Credit** AmEx, EC, MC, V.

A Berlin original that has been selling perfume by weight since 1928. There's a wide range of floral essences, or olfactory cocktails such as 'Lambada', 'Point Of No Return', or 'Eau de Berlin'. The old-fashioned bottles and labels are sure to make you smile.

### Mekkanische Rose

*Leibnizstraße 47, Charlottenburg, 10629 (323 1419). U7 Adenauerplatz.* **Open** 10.30am-6.30pm Mon-Fri; 10.30am-2pm Sat. **No credit cards.**

Over 100 oriental perfumes and essential oils.

### Rosewater's

*Knesebeckstraße 5, Charlottenburg, 10623 (313 42 42). U2 Ernst-Reuter-Platz.* **Open** 10am-6.15pm Mon-Fri; 10am-2pm Sat. **No credit cards.**

A beautiful bath shop, stocked with soaps and body-care products, to soothe the skin and please the eye.

## Design & Household Goods

### Antik und Kerzen

*Kurfürstendamm 188 (entrance Schlüterstraße), Charlottenburg, 10707 (883 89 86). U7 Adenauerplatz.* **Open** 11am-6.30pm Mon-Fri; 10am-2pm Sat. **Credit** AmEx, DC, EC, V.

Germany is a candle-loving nation, and, in her tallow-lined shop, Sylvia Magnus stocks them in every colour and shape.

### Bale Möbel & Decoration

*Savignyplatz 6, 10623 (312 90 66). S3, S5, S7, S9 Savignyplatz.* **Open** 10am-6pm Mon-Wed, Fri; 10am-8pm Thur; 10am-2pm Sat. **No credit cards.**

You'll find no better place in Berlin for bamboo furniture, exotic-looking futons, beds, armchairs, sofas and floor cushions. There's a collection of glassware and ceramics, and a lovely selection of kimonos from DM119.

### Depot

*Bleibtreustraße 48, Charlottenburg, 10623 (883 37 62). S3, S5, S6, S9 Savignyplatz.* **Open** 11am-6.30pm Mon-Fri; 10am-2pm Sat. **No credit cards.**

Imported goodies such as French dish-towels, divine picnic baskets, iron baskets, cobalt blue glasses and garden chairs.

### Fingers

*Nollendorfstraße 35, Schöneberg, 10777 (215 34 41). U1, U2, U4 Nollendorfplatz.* **Open** 2.30-6.30pm Mon-Fri; 11am-2pm Sat. **No credit cards.**

Fingers houses super finds from the forties, fifties and sixties. Stock includes lipstick-shaped cigarette lighters, vintage American and German toasters, weird lighting fixtures and all sorts of splendidly eccentric china and glassware.

### Firlefanz

*Eisenacherstraße 75, Schöneberg, 10823 (781 74 75). U7 Eisenacherstraße.* **Open** 2.30-6.30pm Mon-Fri. **No credit cards.**

A treasure trove for collectors of post-war bric-à-brac, occasional furniture, and (some very good) toys. Don't overlook the shoes, bags and other accessories.

### Galerie Extra

*Bleibtreustraße 41 (entrance Mommsenstraße), Charlottenburg, 10623 (882 16 12). S3, S5, S6, S9 Savignyplatz.* **Open** 2-6.30pm Mon-Fri; 11am-2pm Sat. **Credit** AmEx, DC, EC, MC, V.

Classics of twentieth-century design are Galerie Extra's speciality. You might find a 1945 Charles Eames chair, say, a Mies Van Der Rohe chair from 1927 or a Gaetano Pesce couch from 1969.

### Genious-Group

*Savigny Passage, S-Bahnbogen 574-575, Charlottenburg, 10623 (313 11 82). S3, S5, S6, S9 Savignyplatz.* **Open** 10am-6.30pm Mon-Fri; 10am-2pm Sat. **Credit** AmEx, DC, EC, V.

Genious-Group's array of ingenious gifts somehow manages to tempt those who already have everything into acquiring something else. The fine wines and comestibles are equally alluring. You are unlikely to go away empty-handed.

### Galerie Weinand

*Oranienplatz 5, Kreuzberg, 10999 (614 25 45). Bus 129.* **Open** 1-7pm Tue-Fri; 11am-2pm Sat. **No credit cards.**

This gallery's owner and founder, Herbert Jakob Weinand, is Berlin's star interior designer. The objects for the home that are displayed here are made by an international group of contemporary interior designers and, indeed, by Herbert Jakob Weinand himself.

### Katakomben

*Monumentenstraße 24, Kreuzberg, 10829 (785 5995). U7 Yorckstraße.* **Open** noon-6.30pm Mon-Fri; 10am-2pm Sat. **No credit cards.**

The 'catacombs' in the cellar of a very ordinary-looking building house a design and lighting showroom that is worth a visit just to see the space. The showroom functions as a gallery for artful interior design, with new exhibits every two months, and also features hip Italian companies such as Arfelx, Edra, and Moroso. Uncluttered and dramatically lit, the catacombs are an underground empire with towering ceilings and parquet floors that cover 600 square metres.

### KPM (Königliche Porzellan Manufaktur)

*Wegelystraße 1, Tiergarten, 10623 (390 09 90). S3, S5, S6, S9 Tiergarten.* **Open** 9am-6pm Mon-Fri; 9am-2pm Sat. **Credit** AmEx, DC, EC, JCB, MC, V.

Königliche Porzellan Manufaktur (KPM) sell hand-crafted and hand-painted tableware, vases and figurines in various designs ranging from Frederick the Great's favourite rococo patterns, to elegant neo-classical and Bauhaus designs. This shop, located on the KPM factory premises, sells seconds at reduced prices.

### Lichthaus Mösch

*Tauentzienstrasse 7a, Schöneberg, 10789 (213 6028). U1, U2, U15 Wittenbergplatz.* **Open** 9.30am-6.30pm Mon-Fri; 9.30am-2pm Sat. **Credit** AmEx, EC, MC, V.

Besides selling every imaginable type of modern lighting fixture, Lichthaus Mösch features Italian fantasy and function: the latest Allessi range of products at a glance, from a range of teapots, through clocks and picture frames, to silverware.

### Magazin

*Suarezstraße 12, Charlottenburg, 14057 (321 57 09). U2 Sophie-Charlotte-Platz.* **Open** 11am-6.30pm Mon-Fri; 10am-2pm Sat. **No credit cards.**

Great gift ideas, plus accessories for the home or office. Designs are modern and classic: the colourful ceramic goods include cups, plates, bowls and vases. There are plenty of sleek-looking items for desks, such as Bauhaus lamps.

### Seidlein & Seidlein

*Bleibtreustraße 49, Charlottenburg, 10623 (312 44 80). S3, S5, S6, S9 Savignyplatz.* **Open** 10am-6.30pm Mon-Fri; 10am-2pm Sat. **No credit cards.**

Come to Seidlein & Seidlein for natural-looking household fabrics, charming ceramics and – in the holiday season at least – woollen mice.

### Wohnart

*Uhlandstraße 179/180, Charlottenburg, 10623 (882 52 52). U15 Uhlandstraße.* **Open** 10am-6.30pm Mon-Fri; 10am-2pm Sat. **Credit** AmEx, EC, MC, V.

*So-called Department Store of the West,* **KaDeWe** *outstrips many of its rivals. See page 137.*

If the slick, modern, large- and small-scale kitchen and glassware and furniture of Wohnart do not appeal, go to the shop next door for state-of-the-art paper supplies for home and office.

## Glass & Ceramics

### Ceramica Atelier
*Fraenkelufer 46, Kreuzberg, 10999 (614 49 37). U1 Kottbusser Tor.* **Open** *10am-7pm Mon-Fri; 11am-5pm Sat.* **No credit cards.**
Fernando Marquina makes sculptural ceramics for the floor and the wall. His work is nature-inspired and costs from DM200 for a small shell-like bowl or a sea-creature, to DM10,000 for a wall-relief. His studio also has some vases and bowls for daily use.

### Galerie Glaswerk
*Kantstraße 138, corner of Schlüterstraße, Charlottenburg, 10623 (315 97 52). S3, S5, S6, S9 Savignyplatz.* **Credit** *AmEx, DC, EC, MC, V.*
Everything here is made from glass – clear and stained – from the tiniest baubles and car-rings to oil-lamps, candle-sticks, carafes, bowls and vases. More interesting is the basement gallery, where glass sculptures and pricey decorative-functional goods can be found.

### Glasklar Glaeser
*Knesebeckstraße 13/14, corner of Goethestraße, Charlottenburg, 10623 (31 60 37). U2 Ernst-Reuter-Platz.* **Open** *11am-6.30pm Mon-Fri; 11am-2pm Sat.* **No credit cards.**
Glassware for daily use is the key to Glasklar Glaeser. Choose from vases, oil-lamps, carafes, and clear glass tea-pots with glass warmer-stands to match. A few monochrome-coloured pieces also in stock.

### Galerei Theis
*Neuferstraße 6, Charlottenburg, 14059 (321 23 22). Bus 145, 204.* **Open** *2.30-6.30pm Tue-Fri; for special exhibitions in May, Sept, Dec 2.30-6.30pm Tue-Sun.* **Closed** *Feb, July.* **No credit cards.**
Telephone first to find out who's currently exhibiting at

Galerei Theis, designer ceramics gallery (also because this place keeps irregular hours). There are about 20 artists on permanent display.

**Florists**

### Eberhard Bohnstedt
*Ludwigkirchstraße 11, Wilmersdorf, 10719 (881 93 63). U1 Hohenzollernplatz.* **Open** *9am-6pm Mon-Fri; 9am-2pm Sat.* **No credit cards.**
The city's star florist. Seasonal and unusual arrangements, such as green tomatoes, wild roses and begonias.

**Food**

### Brotgarten
*Seelingstraße 30, off Schloßstraße, Charlottenburg, 14059 (322 88 80). U2 Sophie-Charlotte-Platz.* **Open** *9am-6pm Mon-Fri; 9am-1.30pm Sat.* **No credit cards.**
Health-food store Brotgarten is notable for its mixes of muesli, dried fruits and nuts, and its good selection of wholesome breads, made with a variety of nuts and seeds. Natural-product sweets also available.

### Fuchs Rabe
*Ludwigkirchstraße 3, Charlottenburg, 10719 (882 39 84). U1 Hohenzollernplatz.* **Open** *8.30am-6pm Mon-Fri; 8am-2pm Sat.* **No credit cards.**
Superb selection of cheeses, as good or better than KaDeWe's (*see below*). There's also far less hassle involved in purchasing the foodstuffs, especially if you want to pay for your Poilane bread and your chèvre at the same time.

### KaDeWe (Kaufhaus des Westens)
*Wittenbergplatz, Schöneberg, 10789 (212 10). U1, U2, U15 Wittenbergplatz.* **Open** *9am-6.30pm Mon-Fri; 9am-2pm Sat.* **Credit** *AmEx, DC, EC, MC, V.*
'The Department Store of the West' is Germany's largest luxury department store and reputed to be Europe's biggest. It's most famous for its lavish food hall on the sixth floor, although it's also a decent enough place for clothes and home furnishings. Wurst-lovers will think they have died and gone to heaven, but vegetarians should make a point of steering

# Sending Goods back to the UK/USA

If you couldn't resist buying that beautiful Biedermeier armchair, a four-and-a-half-foot section of the Berlin Wall, or any other bulky goods, and you want to get them back to the UK or the USA, try one of the following firms. Alternatively, look in the Gelbe Seiten (Yellow Pages) under Umzüge (Removals). Rates may be lower than you think.

## To the UK

### Avanti
*Köpenicker Straße 8b, Kreuzberg, 10997 (612 56 72). U8 Heinrich-Heine-Straße.* **Open** 9am-6pm Mon-Fri; 9am-2pm Sat, Sun. **No credit cards**.

### F+N
*Alsenstraße 14, Steglitz, 12163 (03320 8845). U9 Walther-Schreiber-Platz/S1 Feuerbachstraße.* **Open** 8am-5pm Mon-Fri. **No credit cards**.

## To the USA

### Atege
*Quitzowstraße 11-17, Tiergarten, 10559 (390 00 40). U9 Birkenstraße.* **Open** 9am-6pm Mon-Fri. **No credit cards**.

### Franzkowiak, Internationale Transporte
*Uhlandstraße 83/84, Wilmersdorf, 10717 (87 03 61). U7 Blissestraße.* **Open** 8am-4.30pm Mon-Thur; 8am-4pm Fri. **Credit** AmEx, DC, EC, MC, V.

---

clear of the meat department. There are numerous places to stop, eat and drink, some of them quite reasonable (*see also* chapter **Restaurants**).

### Kolbo
*Auguststraße 77/78, Mitte, 10117 (no phone). U6 Oranienburger Tor.* **Open** 10am-6pm Mon-Thu; 10am-3pm Fri. **Credit** AmEx, EC, MC, V.
Kosher meat, cheese, bread, wine and meaty snacks, plus ritual objects in the heart of the old Jewish quarter.

### Leysieffer
*Kurfürstendamm 218, Charlottenburg, 10719 (882 78 20). U15 Uhlandstraße.* **Open** 9am-8pm Mon-Fri; 10am-7pm Sun, holidays. **No credit cards**.
Leysieffer is the place to buy Rote Grütze, a delicious compote of red berries, and the even more delectable custard that accompanies it. Or try out the famous champagne truffles, the spiced chocolate bars, or any of the other high-calorie treats on offer.

### Mekong
*Krummestraße 51, Charlottenburg, 10627 (313 1247). U2 Deutsche Oper.* **Open** 9am-6.30pm Mon-Fri; 9am-2pm Sat. **No credit cards**.
There is no Chinatown in Berlin, so for Asian foodstuffs this is the best one-stop shop. You'll find everything from Indian to Chinese, Indo-Chinese to South-East Asian vegetables, roots, spices, herbs, plus a selection of reasonably priced frozen seafood.

### Salumeria
*Windscheidstraße 20, Charlottenburg, 10627 (324 33 18). U2 Sophie-Charlotte-Platz.* **Open** 10.30am-6.30pm Mon-Fri; 9am-2pm Sat. **Credit** AmEx, DC, EC, MC, V.
A pricey deli that stocks all the requisites for a good Italian meal: wines and cheeses, grappa and meats, biscuits, cakes, and pasta. There's a café serving drinks and light meals.

### The Old Empire
*Kantstraße 22, Charlottenburg, 10623 (313 22 27; orders 315 2493). S3, S5, S6, S9 Savignyplatz.* **Open** 8am-6.30pm Mon-Fri; 9am-2pm Sat. **Credit** V.
The owner of this new shop was in the British Army until his unit pulled out of Berlin. He stayed and opened this British delicatessen, where, apart from a menu of fresh sand-

wiches and baguettes with names such as Big Ben, Churchill and Eurotunnel, you can pick up Marmite or Walker's biscuits. Day-time deliveries made on a three-wheeler (*see* **Services**), and a gift parcel service that will put the best of Britain in a basket.

### The Turkish Market
*on Maybachufer, Neukölln, 120457. U1, U8 Kottbusser Tor.* **Open** noon-6.30pm Tue, Fri. **No credit cards**.
A noisy, crowded street market just across the canal from Kreuzberg, catering for the culinary needs of the neighbourhood's many Turkish residents. There are good buys and great tastes to be found.

### Winterfeldt Market
*Winterfeldtplatz, Schöneberg, 10781. U1, U2, U4 Nollendorfplatz.* **Open** 8am-2pm Wed, Sat. **No credit cards**.
Come to the Winterfeldt Market on Saturdays to experience the multi-cultural, young-old Berliner mix. Everybody shows up to buy their vegetables, cheese, wholegrain breads, olives, meat, wursts, herring, flowers, clothes, pet supplies and toys; or simply to meet up over a coffee, beer or falafel at one of the many cafés.

## Records, Tapes & CDs

*See also* **New Noise/Scenario** *above, listed under* **Fashion**.

### Canzone Importschallplatten
*Savigny Passage, S-Bahnbogen 583, Charlottenburg, 10623 (312 40 27). S3, S5, S6, S9 Savignyplatz.* **Open** 10.30am-6.30pm Mon-Fri; 10am-2pm Sat. **No credit cards**.
Canzone's stock of world music includes hard-to-find discs that will move you to an oriental, Latin, tango, Brazilian, or African beat.

### Delirium
*Krumme Straße 58, Charlottenburg, 10627 (313 95 08). U2 Deutsche Oper.* **Open** noon-6.30pm Mon-Fri; 10am-2pm Sat. **No credit cards**.
With DJ Kid Paul on the staff roster, Delirium is easily the

# The Ku'damm

For all the fuss that's made over Berlin's 'grand boulevard' and 'liveliest avenue', the Kurfürstendamm could never be described as stylish. Its humdrum merchandising and artless visual display is enough to repel the discerning window-shopper, despite the high concentration of designer names on the stretch. It's as if Bond Street had mutated into Oxford Street. Nevertheless, once in Berlin there's no avoiding the Ku'damm: it's the nearest the city comes to a magnificent mile.

There are, indeed, some notable stores on the Ku'damm. **Kramberg**, for men and women (no 56) is Berlin's 'home-away-from-home' for the major Italian designers – Armani, Versace et al – plus Vivienne Westwood and Donna Karan. **Versace** recently moved to town with his own boutique (no 185), and quickly became popular with members of the Russian mafia as a place to spend their hard-earned marks. Fashion freaks with money have lots of choice: **Yves Saint Laurent** holds court at no 52, **Jil Sander** at no 48, **Escada** is on the opposite side of the street at no 186, joined by **Harvey's** (no 186, entrance around the corner) where men will find a hand-picked selection of trendy designer gear.

**Ralf Setzer for Men** (no 46) features hip, classic, casual and city apparel from Kenzo, Stone Island and others. **Kookai** (no 205) and **Esprit** (no 26) are among Berlin's more attractive young fashion outlets, even if their style is familiar across Europe. **Mey & Edlich** (no 217) is geared towards an older and preppier customer, with its tastefully tailored and sporting selections for men and women: respected German fashion firms such as Windsor and Toni Gard are represented. **H&M** (Hennes & Mauritz, no 20) offers fashion at more affordable prices. The lingerie corner is highly valued by stylish bargain hunters, and the children's department in this branch offers happy, durable clothes for babies and children up to age eight. **Hallhuber** (no 27) combines its own in-house brand with favourite German and European mid-price men's and women's collections.

And then to finish – or start – the Ku'damm, there's Berlin's most famous flagship store, **KaDeWe** (*see page 138* **Food** *and chapter* **Restaurants**), a fairly uninspired and uninspiring department store, despite its reputation. Even so, the food hall on the sixth floor does hold an awe-inspiring collection of ham, sausage and salami, plus the freshest fish in town. Sample a shrimp salad or smoked-salmon sandwich if you get hungry.

## Escada
*Kurfürstendamm 186, 10707 (881 16 36).* U7 *Adenauerplatz.* **Open** 9.30am-6.30pm Mon-Fri; 9.30am-2pm Sat. **Credit** AmEx, DC, EC, JCB, MC, V.

## Esprit
*Kurfürstendamm 26, 10719 (882 51 25).* U3, U9 *Kurfürstendamm.* **Open** 10am-6.30pm Mon-Fri; 9am-2pm Sat. **Credit** AmEx, DC, EC, V.

## Hallhuber
*Kurfürstendamm 237, 10719 (881 44 77).* U3, U9 *Kurfürstendamm.* **Open** 9.30am-6.30pm Mon-Fri; 9.30am-2pm Sat. **Credit** AmEx, DC, EC, MC, V.

## Harvey's
*Kurfürstendamm 186, 10707 (883 38 03).* U3, U9 *Kurfürstendamm.* **Open** 10am-6.30pm Mon-Fri; 10am-2pm Sat. **Credit** AmEx, DC, EC, V.

## H & M (Hennes und Mauritz)
*Kurfürstendamm 20, 10719 (882 62 99).* U3, U9 *Kurfürstendamm.* **Open** 9.30am-6.30pm Mon-Fri; 9am-2pm Sat. **Credit** AmEx, EC, V.

## Jil Sander
*Kurfürstendamm 48, 10707 (883 37 30).* U3, U9 *Kurfürstendamm.* **Open** 10am-6.30pm Mon-Fri; 10am-2pm Sat. **Credit** AmEx, DC, EC, MC, V.

## Kookai
*Kurfürstendamm 205, 10719 (881 87 83).* U3 *Uhlandstraße.* **Open** 9.30am-6.30pm Mon-Fri; 9am-2pm Sat. **Credit** AmEx, EC, V.

## Kramberg
*Kurfürstendamm 56, 10707 (327 9010).* U7 *Adenauerplatz.* **Open** 9.30am-6.30pm Mon-Fri; 10am-2pm Sat. **Credit** AmEx, DC, EC, MC, V.

## Mey & Edlich
*Kurfürstendamm 217, 10719 (885 43 75).* U3, U9 *Kurfürstendamm.* **Open** 9.30am-6.30pm Mon-Fri; 9.30am-2pm Sat. **Credit** AmEx, DC, EC, MC, V.

## Ralf Setzer Men's
*Kurfürstendamm 46, 10707 (883 83 32).* U3, U9 *Kurfürstendamm.* **Open** 10am-6.30pm Mon-Fri; 10am-2pm Sat. **Credit** AmEx, DC, EC, JCB, MC, V.

## Gianni Versace
*Kurfürstendamm 185, 10707 (885 74 60).* U3, U9 *Kurfürstendamm.* **Open** 9.30am-6.30pm Mon-Fri; 9.30am-2pm Sat. **Credit** AmEx, DC, EC, JCB, MC, V.

## Yves St Laurent
*Kurfürstendamm 52, 10707 (883 39 18).* U3, U9 *Kurfürstendamm.* **Open** 9.30am-6.30pm Mon-Fri; 9.30am-2pm Sat. **Credit** AmEx, DC, EC, JCB, MC, V.

West End rival to Hardwax when it comes to techno, dance and clubwear. Its try-out turntables are an extra attraction.

### Gelbe Musik

*Schaperstraße 11, Wilmersdorf, 10719 (211 39 62). U1, Augsburger Straße/U1, U2 Spichernstraße.* **Open** 1-6pm Mon-Fri; 11am-2pm Sat. **No credit cards.**
Contemporary, minimalism, world, electronic, industrial and extreme noise fill the racks at Gelbe Musik. Rare vinyl and rare import CDs, audio magazines and sound objects make for absorbing browsing.

### Hardwax

*Reichenbergerstraße 75, Kreuzberg, 10999 (618 8846). U1 Görlitzer Bahnhof.* **Open** 10am-6.30pm Mon-Fri; 10am-2pm Sat. **No credit cards.**
Hardwax is the leading dance and techno record shop in Berlin. Records are not filed by artist but by record label. See Berlin's DJs buying their records on Tuesdays and Fridays when new stock comes in. Staff are a mite taciturn, but it's a good place to pick up club flyers.

### FNAC

*Meineckestraße 23, Charlottenburg, 10719 (884 720). U15, U9 Kurfürstendamm.* **Open** 10am-6.30pm Mon-Fri; 10am-2pm Sat. **Credit** AmEx, EC, DC, V.
A branch of the French chain, selling CDs and records, as well as videos and books.

### Logo

*Bergmannstraße 10, Kreuzberg, 10961 (693 1998). U6, U7 Mehringdamm.* **Open** noon-6.30pm Mon-Fri; 11am-2pm Sat. **No credit cards.**
There's a broad selection of secondhand vinyl and CDs at Logo, with a lot of jazz and blues as well as rock. Bergmannstraße and the surrounding area is full of interesting secondhand shops.

### Mr Dead and Mrs Free

*Bülowstraße 5, Schöneberg, 10783 (215 14 49). U1, U2 Nollendorfplatz.* **Open** noon-6.30pm Mon-Fri; noon-2pm Sat. **No credit cards.**
The best place for indie and obscure underground rock records, with lots of UK and American imports.

## Stationery

### Art Store

*Savigny Passage, S-Bahnbogen 584, Charlottenburg, 10623 (313 22 82). S3, S5, S6, S9 Savignyplatz.* **Open** 11am-6.30pm Mon-Fri; 10am-2pm Sat. **No credit cards.**
Art Store in Savigny Passage has notebooks, posters, postcards, pins, plates and puzzles based on original works by Keith Haring, Andy Warhol, Cindy Sherman and Joseph Beuys, among others.

### Papeterie

*Grunewaldstraße 83, Schöneberg, 10823 (782 00 78). U7 Eisenacherstraße.* **Open** 10am-6.30pm Mon-Fri; 10am-2pm Sat. **Credit** EC, V.
Notebooks, diaries, photo albums, daybooks, agendas, boxes, organisers, wrapping paper, as well as pens, pencils, striped paper clips and Wolfgang Riebesehl leather goods are all available at Papeterie.

### Washi

*Grolmanstraße 59, Charlottenburg, 10623 (313 86 76). U2 Ernst-Reuter-Platz.* **Open** 10am-6pm Mon-Fri; 10am-2pm Sat. **No credit cards.**
The Japanese paper connection, Washi in Charlottenburg offers a wide assortment of writing utensils and attractive handmade paper.

## Supermarkets

These are the central Berlin branches of the major German chains. If you're looking for value for money, go to **Aldi**, **Plus** or **Penny Markt**. **Kaisers** and **Bolle** have a greater range, but are slightly more expensive. If you want to drool, go to **KaDeWe** (*see page 138* **Food**).

### Aldi

*Martin-Luther-Straße 14-18, Schöneberg, 10777 (central office 779 9058). U4, U7 Bayrischerplatz.* **Open** 9am-6.30pm Mon-Fri; 8am-1pm Sat. **No credit cards.**

### Bolle

*Nürnbergerstraße 25, Charlottenburg, 10789 (218 79 75). U1, U2, U15 Wittenbergplatz.* **Open** 8am-6pm Mon-Fri; 8am-1pm Sat. **No credit cards.**

### Kaiser's

*Wittenbergplatz 4, Schöneberg, 10789 (218 10 70). U1, U2, U15 Wittenbergplatz.* **Open** 8am-6pm Mon-Fri; 8am-1pm Sat. **No credit cards.**

### Penny Markt

*Winterfeldtstraße 74, Schöneberg, 10781 (211 20 75). U1, U2, U4 Nollendorfplatz.* **Open** 9am-6pm Mon-Fri; 8am-1pm Sat. **No credit cards.**

### Plus

*Bülowstraße 19, Schöneberg, 10783 (216 30 06). U1, U2, U4 Nollendorfplatz.* **Open** 8.30am-6pm Mon-Fri; 8am-1pm Sat. **No credit cards.**

### Reichelt

*Potsdamer Straße 152, Schöneberg, 10783 (311 89-0). U1 Kufürstenstraße.* **Open** 9am-6.30pm Mon-Fri; 9am-2pm Sat. **No credit cards.**

## Department Stores

### Hertie

*Wilmersdorfer Straße 118, Charlottenburg, 10627 (31 10 50). U7 Wilmersdorfer Straße.* **Open** 9.30am-6.30pm Mon-Fri; 9am-2pm Sat. **Credit** AmEx, DC, EC, MC, V.

### KaDeWe

*Tauentzienstraße 21, Schöneberg, 10789 (212 10). U1, U2, U15 Wittenbergplatz.* **Open** 9am-6.30pm Mon-Fri; 9am-2pm Sat. **Credit** AmEx, DC, EC, MC, V.

### Karstadt

*Wilmersdorfer Straße 109, Charlottenburg, 10627 (318 90). U7 Wilmersdorfer Straße.* **Open** 9.30am-6.30pm Mon-Fri; 9am-2pm Sat. **Credit** AmEx, DC, EC, MC, V.

### Kaufhof

*Alexanderplatz 9, Mitte, 10178 (246 40). S3, S5, S6, S9/U2, U8 Alexanderplatz.* **Open** 9am-6pm Mon-Fri; 9am-2pm Sat. **Credit** AmEx, DC, EC, MC, V.

### Wertheim

*Kurfürstendamm 231, Charlottenburg, 10719 (88 20 61). U15, U9 Kurfürstendamm.* **Open** 9am-6.30pm Mon-Fri; 9am-2pm Sat. **Credit** AmEx, DC, EC, MC, V.

### Woolworth

*Wilmersdorfer Straße 113, Charlottenburg, 10627 (313 40 95). U7 Wilmersdorfer Straße.* **Open** 9.15am-6.30pm Mon-Fri; 9am-2pm Sat. **No credit cards.**

# Services

*While service may not be top of the bill in Berlin, there's still plenty of choice – get your pubes trimmed in Kreuzberg or Nigri-sushi delivered to your door in Wilmersdorf.*

Ask any Briton, Australian or American settled in Berlin about service in the city and it will be all they can do not to laugh in your face. Truth is, you are telling a joke only they understand. Service is a foreign word in Berlin. Not because it's English – Germans use the same word to describe the same thing – but because there isn't very much of it. Competitive entrepreneurs of other First World countries make it their business to come up with new strategies to make consumers' lives easier. But delivery service in Berlin is limited to the efforts of neighbourhood Italians, Chinese, Indians and pizzerias, who clutter residents' mailboxes with takeaway menus. Berliners keep stacks of these in a kitchen drawer, sorted into the good, the acceptable and the awful. Free and fast home delivery is virtually

unknown for the most basic needs in life, but couriers will pick up and deliver almost anything in the city (*see also chapter* **Business**).

As Berlin grows into its new role as a major European capital, Berliners are likely to become more acquainted with cosmopolitan standards of efficiency and the thing they call service. Until then, it's do-it-yourself business as usual.

## Information

### Berlin Tourismus Marketing
*Martin-Luther-Straße 105, Schöneberg, 10825 (212 34). U4 Rathaus Schöneberg.* **Open** 9am-3pm Mon-Fri.
Staff here can answer most questions concerning travellers' needs. There are branches at Bahnhof Zoo, Tegel Airport and Europa-Center (which is open until 10pm).

## Fashion

## Costume Hire

### Theaterkunst GmbH

*Eisenzahnstraße 43/44, Grunewald, 10709 (86 02 34).*
*U1/U7 Fehrbellinerplatz.* **Open** 8am-4.45pm Mon-Thur,
Fri; 8am-3.30pm. **No credit cards.**
Three warehouse floors are piled to the ceiling with attire to
clothe any man, woman or monster of your historical fancy.
Founded in 1908, the collection was wiped out in the wars
and started up again in 1951. Outfits are on loan for a week.
Elaborate Baroque or Rococo costumes cost up to DM800;
costumes from more recent times are about DM250.

## Dry Cleaning and Alteration

### Änderungsschneiderei Özsan

*Bleibtreustraße 45, Charlottenburg, 10623. S5*
*Savignyplatz.* **Open** 9am-6.30pm Mon-Fri; 9am-2pm Sat.
**No credit cards.**
A fast and friendly seamstress will repair rips, zippers etc
in two to three days. One-day service on request.

### Nantes

*Uhlandstraße 20-25, Charlottenburg, 10623 (883 5746).*
*U3 Uhlandstraße.* **Open** 8am-6pm Mon-Fri; 9am-1pm Sat.
**No credit cards.**
Recommended by designer boutiques, they charge more than
most and take at least four days, but it's worth the wait for
valuable items. Everything comes back well ironed.

## Formal Wear Hire

### Graichen

*Klosterstraße 32, Spandau, 13581 (331 3587). U7*
*Rathaus Spandau.* **Open** 10am-6pm Mon-Fri. **No credit**
**cards.**
Tuxedoes, short and long women's attire and bridal gowns
for formal events. Rental fees for black ties run from DM120-
DM200, women's evening wear can be had for DM90-DM400.

### Junge

*Enzianstraße 3, Lichterfelde, 12203 (831 1400). S1*
*Botanischer Garten.* Private residence, call ahead.
An unofficial hat rental operation run out of a retired couple's flat – they closed their costume shop but couldn't part
with their collection of Father Christmas outfits, bowlers and
top hats. Hats cost DM20 a day (plus DM50 deposit).

### Spitze

*Weimarer Straße 19, Charlottenburg, 10625 (313 1068*
*60 68). U7 Wilmersdorfer Straße.* **Open** 2-6.30pm Mon-
Fri; 11am-2pm Sat. **Credit** DC, EC, V.
Spitze – a gold mine for glamorous clothes and accessories
from 1860 to 1960 – will rent out most of its nuggets for a
third of the sale price. Period suits, tuxes and top hats, or
evening- and ball gowns, can be hired for an average cost of
DM100 for a few days (or 30 per cent of the sale price for a
fortnight). Evening gloves, handbags, shoes and other accessories also for hire. *See also chapter* **Shopping.**

## General Services

## Detectives & Security

### ABD Allgemeiner Bewachungsdienst

*Stralauer Allee 1-16, Friedrichshain, 10245 (589 1114).*
*S86 Warschauer Straße.* **Open** 24 hours. **Credit** AmEx,
EC, V.
Bodyguards, transport of money and valuables, security at
large functions and other security services.

### Detektei Grützmacher

*Düsseldorfer Straße 32, Wilmersdorf, 10707 (883 4068).*
*U7 Konstanzer Straße.* **Open** 9am-4pm Mon-Fri. **No**
**credit cards.**
A family business since 1889, these sleuths specialise in commercial investigation, but will also check out spouses and
deal with other private affairs.

## Luggage Repair

### Kofferhaus Meinecke

*Meineckestraße 25, Wilmersdorf, 10719 (882 2262).*
*U15, U9 Kurfürstendamm.* **Open** 9.30am-6.30pm Mon,
Wed, Fri; 9.30am-8.30pm Thur; 9.30am-2pm Sat. **Credit**
AmEx, D, EC, JCB, MC, V.
Specialises in Samsonite, Delsey, Airline, Traveller, Rimova
and Picard, and will repair all types of baggage within two
or three days. Repairs are not delivered, but a new suitcase
can be delivered in the city area.

### Witt

*Hauptstraße 9, Schöneberg, 10827 (781 4937). U7*
*Kleistpark.* **Open** 9am-6pm Mon-Fri; 9am-1pm Sat.
**Credit** AmEx, D, EC, JCB, MC, V.
Luggage repairs can be completed in a day, and if damage
has resulted during a flight, the cost will be billed to the airline. Probably Berlin's most extensive suitcase spare parts
assortment, including patches. Evening delivery possible.

## Shoe Repair

### Artur Plagwitz

*Pestalozzistraße 99, Charlottenburg, 10625 (313 9609).*
*U2 Ernst-Reuter-Platz.* **Open** 8.30am-6pm Mon-Fri; 9am-
noon Sat.
Sturdy repairs and next-day service by this genuine cobbler.

### Picobello

*in KaDeWe, Tauentzienstraße 21, Schöneberg, 10789*
*(21 21 0). U1, U2, U15 Wittenbergplatz.* **Open** 9am-
6.30pm Mon-Fri; 9am-8.30pm Thur; 9am-2pm Sun. **No**
**credit cards.**
New heels and soles while you wait. Keys also cut.

## Shoe Maker

### Michael Oeler

*Am Tempelhofer Berg 6 (Aufgang 3), Kreuzberg, 10965*
*(692 2198). U7 Mehringdamm.* **Open** 11am-6pm Mon-
Fri. **No credit cards.**
Michael Oeler's Trippen label is sold by only a few, daring
shoe shops in town. His original creations range from clunky
wooden clogs that tie-up Roman style, to sky-high platforms.
Will make almost any shoe to fit within one to three weeks.

## Telephone Services

Operated by the Deutsche Bundespost Telekom.
**Alarm Call (Weckauftrag)** *(0 11 41).* **Open** 24 hours.
**Fee** DM2.30 per wake-up call. Ring up and give the time you
want to be buzzed. When you are, your rude awakening is a
recording of the time.
**Answering Service (Abwesenheitsauftrag)** *(0 11 41).*
**Open** 24 hours. **Fee** DM7 per day for noted messages from
callers; DM5 per day for a message to callers.
**Message Call (Benachrichtigungsauftrag)** *(0 11 41).*
**Open** 24 hours. A message to someone in Berlin. **Fee** DM4.30
per message; DM5.30 per message for a specific person.
**Reminder Call (Erinnerungsauftrag)** *(0 11 41).* **Open**
24 hours daily. A message to yourself. **Fee** DM3 per
reminder call; DM4 per call for a specific person.

**Udo Walz:** *a snip at DM95 for a wash, cut and dry.*

## Hair and Beauty

For fitness studios and swimming pools, *see chapter* **Sport and Fitness**. *See also chapters* **Women** *and* **Gay and Lesbian**.

## Baths and Saunas

### Schokofabrik

*Naunynstraße 72, Kreuzberg, 10997 (615 1464). U1 Kotbusser Tor.* **Open** 5-10pm Mon; 1-10pm Tue-Sun. Closed for eight weeks in summer. **Admission** call for details.

The Turkish bath in this former chocolate factory breaks with tradition – it's only for women and it's heavenly. To ensure maximum relaxation, there's a crèche to stow kids and a café offering refreshments. The whole complex is women-only, with two floors for dance and sport that hold weekend workshops. *See also chapter* **Women**.

### Thermen

*Europa-Center, Nürnberger Straße 7, Charlottenburg, 10787 (65 1464). U2, U9 Zoologischer Garten.* **Open** 10am-midnight Mon-Sat; 10am-9pm Sun. **Admission** DM32 adults, three hours for DM27; DM15 children. **No credit cards**.

One of the most popular places to sweat and swim in Berlin is atop the Europa-Center, offering a grand view of the western city centre. There are five saunas, three Roman steam baths, a huge indoor-outdoor heated pool and a sun terrace.

## Beauty Salons

### Classic Nails

*Bundesallee 81, Friedenau, 12161 (859 4268). U9 Friedrich-Wilhelm-Platz.* **Open** 10am-7pm Mon–Fri; by appointment only Sat. **No credit cards**.

Manicures and nail extensions. Very reasonable rates.

### Creative Nails

*Nürnberger Straße 28, Schöneberg, 10789 (217 6286). U1 Augsburger Straße.* **Open** 10am-6.30pm Mon-Fri. **No credit cards**.

Highly professional repairs and extensions for nail biters or long claw lovers. Those looking for more than just a French manicure can try elaborate nail paintings that will put butterflies and flowers at their fingertips, or real gold nails, with or without gems.

### Kosmetik Studio in KaDeWe

*Ansbacher Straße 30, Schöneberg, 10789 (213 4657). U1, U2, U15 Wittenberg Platz.* **Open** 10am-7pm Mon-Fri. **Credit** AmEx, EC, DC, JCB, V.

Beauty services for pretty faces and, for tired feet, a 25-minute pedicure. There's a highly relaxing private tanning cabin for palefaces looking to avoid the sweaty stench of sun studios.

### Marie France

*Fasanenstraße 42, Charlottenburg, 10719 (881 6555). U1, U9 Spichernstraße.* **Open** 9am-6pm Tue, Wed, Fri; 9am-8.30pm Thur; 9am-2pm Sat. **No credit cards**.

The four cosmeticians at this clean, pleasant salon speak English with a French accent and use French-only products (Mességué and Lancray). They specialise in hot wax depilation, at DM65 for full leg, DM40 for half leg. A DM74 basic fee for face and dekolleté facials can be expanded to include a peeling, lymph drainage, eye, neck and hand masks, and electro-acupuncture treatment or a very soothing foot reflex massage.

## Condoms

### Dublosan

*Mühlenfeldstraße 22, Hermsdorf, 13467 (404 6996). U6 Alt-Tegel.* **Open** 9am-3pm, answering machine takes orders until 6pm, Mon-Fri. **No credit cards**.

Private customers can order a minimum of 100 condoms from DM30. Deliveries until 8pm, so plan ahead.

# Hair Salons

## Kaiserschnitt

*Wiener Straße 20, Kreuzberg, 10999 (611 6387). U1 Görlitzer Bahnhof.* **Open** 11am-6pm Mon-Fri; 11am-5pm Sat. **No credit cards.**
The name, meaning Ceasarian, reveals their fetish for below-the-belt cuts. The salon's claim to fame came with its exclusive pubic hairstyling service. Heads of hair also cut; at around DM50 for men, DM60 for women.

## Mod's Hair

*Meineckestraße 6, 10719 (883 6687). U15, U9 Kurfürstenstraße.* **Open** 9am-6.30pm Mon-Fri; 9am-8.30pm Thur; 9am-1pm Sat. **Credit** AmEx, EC, MC, V.
This Parisian chain, with 50 salons in France, has spread its franchise into Austria, Belgium, Italy, Canada, Switzerland, Japan and 25 German cities. Women with DM80-DM90 to spare may acquire something short and round, like a nineties bob. Men's cuts cost from DM50-DM60.

## Udo Walz

*Kurfürstendamm 200, Charlottenburg, 10719 (882 7457). U15 Uhlandstraße/bus 109, 119,129, 219.* **Open** 9am-6pm Mon-Fri; 9am-2pm Sat. **Credit** AmEx, DC, EC, MC, V.
Udo likes to have his picture taken with Claudia Schiffer – whether he actually cuts her hair is another matter. The stylists know what they're doing – wash, cut and dry for DM95.

# Optician

## Ruhnke Optik

*Tauentzienstraße 16, Charlottenburg, 10789 (213 2045, contact lens department 213 2046).* **Open** 9.30-6.30pm Mon-Fri; 9am-2pm Sat. **Credit** AmEx, DC, EC, V.
Main branch of 19 shops throughout the city. On the spot small repairs and adjustments; for more complicated repairs allow a couple of days. Allow three days for prescriptions.

# Sun Studio

## City-Sun

*Tauentzienstraße 16, Charlottenburg, 10789 (218 8037). U2, U9 Zoologischer Garten.* **Open** 8am-10pm Mon-Sat; 10am-10pm Sun, holidays. **Credit** AmEx, DC, EC, MC, V.
Sun factory buzzing with bronzed, towel-clad Venuses and Adonises at all times of the year. Fifteen minutes in the frying coffin (panic button for claustrophobics) costs DM9.90.

# Leisure

# Auctions and Appraisals

## Leo Spik

*Kurfürstendamm 66, Wilmersdorf, 10707 (883 6170). U7 Adenauerplatz.* **Open** 9.30am-1pm, 2.30-6pm, Mon-Fri. **No credit cards.**
Berlin's only auction house to survive the war specialises in art and antiques from the Renaissance to classical modern art. Four annual auctions put paintings, silver, jewellery, furniture and carpets under the hammer. The emphasis is on Berlin and German art from local collections, but international valuables are also on offer.

## Villa Griesebach

*Fasanenstraße 25, Charlottenburg, 10719 (882 6811) U15 Uhlandstraße.* **Open** 10am-6.30pm Mon-Fri; 10am-2pm Sat. **No credit cards.**
This elegant villa on Berlin's Bond Street points to its turnover when supporting its claim to be the world's leading auctioneer for twentieth century German fine art. In 1993 its bi-annual auctions raked in over DM23.6 million. The collection up for grabs tours seven German cities before it goes on display one week before the auctions in November and late May or early June. Free appraisals on paintings or sculptures that could be considered for a Griesebach auction.

# Books

## Kiepert

*Hardenbergstraße 4-5, Charlottenburg, 10623 (311 009-0). U2 Ernst-Reuter-Platz.* **Open** 9am-6.30pm Mon-Fri; 9am-2pm Sat.
This large bookshop does same-day free delivery in the city centre. It has a wide selection of fiction and non-fiction, worldwide travel guides and a reasonable English section. The switchboard will put you through to the appropriate department for you to place your order. Pay the driver by cheque, or transfer money within three weeks.
*Delivery service.*

# Flower Delivery

## Fleurop

*National head office (713 710).* **Open** 7.30am-6pm Mon-Fri; 7.30am-1.30pm Sat. **Credit** varies.
Call for the nearest member florist in your area. The cheapest bouquet will cost you DM25, but there's a special fee of DM15 for modest lovers who want to send just one rose to someone, somewhere in Germany. Same-day delivery in Berlin, Germany or the rest of the world can only be provided if no personal note is attached. Dictated messages can be typed or handwritten at the receiver's end. Personally written messages with arrangements go via normal postal route.
*Delivery service.*

## Total Floral

*Pestalozzistraße 3, Charlottenburg, 10625 (313 9026). U2 Ernst-Reuter-Platz/S5 Savignyplatz.* **Open** 9am-6.30pm Mon-Fri; 9am-2pm Sat. **No credit cards.**
Exquisite arrangements of garden and field flowers in summer, and exotic photosynthesisers in winter, can be couriered to any city address for an additional DM8-DM30, depending on destination. Caller and florist agree on colour and price and payment is made by posting a cheque.
*Delivery service.*

# Food & Drink

## Banchetto

*Prinz-Eugen-Straße 17a, Wedding, 13347 (461 9794).* Orders taken daily 9am-10pm. **No credit cards.**
Home-made northern Italian specialities delivered for orders over DM150. Final preparations are made in your home. The menu offers various dishes for warm meals with antipasti, main course, salad and dessert; cold buffets and snacks for parties. Banchetto Vini *(462 7727)* will deliver wines.
*Delivery service.*

## Call-a-Pizza

**Charlottenburg** *(321 10755);* **Kreuzberg/Neukölln** *(624 1081);* **Schöneberg** *(784 1092);* **Mitte** *(229 1204) or consult Gelbe Seiten (under Gaststätten) for branches.*

## Halong

*Linienstraße 94, Mitte, 10115 (282 3765). U8 Weinmeister Straße.* **Open** noon-11pm daily. **No credit cards.**
Good Chinese grub delivered for free for orders over DM20 in Mitte, Prenzlauer Berg and Friedrichshain.
*Delivery service.*

Clip your talons into shape at **Creative Nails**. See page 144.

### KaDeWe
*Tauentzienstraße 21, Tiergarten, 10789 (2121-0). U1, U2, U15 Wittenbergplatz.* **Open** 9am-6.30pm Mon-Wed, Fri; 9am-8.30pm Thur; 9am-2pm Sat. **Credit** AmEx, DC, EC, JCB, MC, V.
The delicatessen is famous for its specialities from all continents. Special wishes are catered for, so if you crave something more exotic than what's already on offer at one of the gourmet bars, you need only call. While these can take up to three days to be fulfilled, same-day delivery is possible until 4pm in Berlin and Potsdam, with a DM10 fee for orders under DM200. Allow three days for delivery of large drinks orders.
*Delivery service.*

### The Old Empire
*Kantstraße 22, Charlottenburg, 10623 (313 22 27; orders 315 2493). S3, S5, S6, S9 Savignyplatz.* **Open** 8am-6.30pm Mon-Fri; 9am-2pm Sat. **Credit** V.
This British delicatessen makes free lunchtime deliveries (11am-4.30pm) on a conspicuous three-wheeler for a minimum order of DM25. Sandwiches and baguettes with names such as Princess Di (egg mayonnaise), Country Life (bacon & eggs), Shakespeare (cheese & salad) and Star of India (chicken tikka), range between DM3.50-DM6.
*Delivery service.*

### Rack
*Hohenzollerndamm 92, Dahlem, 14199 (826 4021). Bus 115, 249, 129.* **Open** 8am-6pm Tue-Fri; 8am-1pm Sat. **No credit cards.**
The food and wine delivery service requires two weeks' notice, deliveries for orders over DM250 are free of charge. There's a good selection of wine, champagne and spirits. The party service caters for up to 2,000 people.
*Delivery service.*

### Rogacki
*Wilmersdorfer Straße 145, Charlottenburg, 10585 (341 4091). U7 Wilmersdorfer Straße.* **Open** 9am-6pm Mon-Fri; 9am-2pm Sat. **No credit cards.**
Established in 1928, Berlin's fish institution provides salads, smoked eel, sandwiches, wurst and meat dishes. Call for details of the party service. Delivery charge DM10-30.
*Delivery service.*

### Sushi
*Pariser Straße 44, Wilmersdorf, 10707 (881 2790). U1 Spichernstraße.* **Open** *for deliveries* 6pm-11pm Mon-Sat; 5-10pm Sun. **No credit cards.**
The chefs at this popular sushi Imbiss deliver their fish and seaweed specialities free of charge for orders over DM30. Maki-sushi, Nigri-sushi, sashimi and vegetarian alternatives in Charlottenburg and Wilmersdorf are brought to your door within an hour. Deliveries to other districts take longer. Orders for over 20 people need a day's notice.
*Delivery service.*

## Photography
## Processing & Passport Photos

### Photo Huber
*Europa-Center, Charlottenburg, 10789 (262 4666). U15 Kurfürstendamm.* **Open** 10am-6.30pm/9pm.
Passport photos until 6.30pm, photo processing until 9pm.

### Drogerie Mehlhase
*Schlüter Straße 12, Charlottenburg, 10625 (312 4915). U2 Ernst-Reuter-Platz.* **Open** 9am-6pm Mon-Fri; 9am-1pm Sat. **No credit cards.**
The staff inside this chemist's will take your photo in the small photo cabin and deliver a set of four colour or black and white pictures (DM11.94 for both) in five minutes.

## Camera Hire

### PPS
*Hirtenstraße 19, Mitte, 10178 (23 27 57 58) U5, U8, S7 Alexanderplatz.* **Open** 8am-9pm Mon-Fri; 10am-6pm Sat, Sun.
Nikons, Hasselblads and professional equipment for hire.

# Galleries & Museums

# Art Galleries

*From Expressionists to Mutoids: the best of Berlin's contemporary art scene.*

The **Galerie Brusberg** was one of the first to promote East German painting. See page 151.

With nearly 800 exhibitions a year, Berlin is undoubtedly one of the most intriguing art centres in Europe. The wide range of contemporary painting and sculpture on display (and for sale) in more than 300 private galleries make the city a fascinating place for art fans.

Berlin's art world has been undergoing change ever since the Wall was dismantled. Whereas some established galleries had to close recently because of outrageous rent increases and declining sales, new spaces keep popping up elsewhere. Most typical of the current transition period is the art mile on Auguststraße in east Berlin, where you're likely to meet the most unusual and adventurous of Berlin's young gallery owners.

The district of Kreuzberg, on the other hand, is the centre of west Berlin's alternative galleries. Most of the establishment galleries are still found in Charlottenburg, the city's most densely populated gallery district. As the character of Berlin art varies so much according to district, we've organised them below by area.

An indispensible tool for anyone wishing to explore Berlin's art life is the *Berliner Kunstkalender* which is available at galleries and museums. It is published every month and contains comprehensive information on all temporary exhibitions, including addresses, hours and phone numbers of venues. The art pages of Berlin's listings magazines (*Tip* or *Zitty*) also provide current listings of exhibitions at museums and galleries.

*See also chapter* **Museums** *and page 264* **Area Index.**

## Public Galleries

### Akademie der Künste

*Hanseatenweg 10, Tiergarten, 10557 (390 0070). U9 Hansaplatz/S3, S5, S6, S7, S9 Bellevue.* **Open** *1-7pm Mon; 10am-7pm Tue-Sun.* **Admission** *DM6 adults; DM4 students, pensioners, disabled.*
Founded by the Prussian Prince Friedrich III in 1696, the Akademie der Künste is one of the oldest cultural institutions in Berlin. By 1938, however, the Nazis had forced virtually all of its prominent members into exile. Re-established in 1954 to serve as 'a community of exceptional artists' from

the world over, its multi-faceted programme now offers a great variety of events ranging from free jazz concerts and poetry readings to performances and film screenings. The Akademie also has a reputation for landmark exhibitions. An inspiring venue.
*Café. Group discounts. Wheelchair access.*

## DAAD Galerie

*Kurfürstenstraße 58, Tiergarten, 10785 (261 3640). U2, U4, U15 Nollendorfplatz/U1, U2, U3 Wittenbergplatz.* **Open** 12.30-7pm daily. **Admission** free.
When, in 1965, the German Academic Exchange Service (DAAD) initiated an Artists-in-Residence programme in West Berlin, no one would have expected the profound impact it was to have on cultural life in Berlin. The list of DAAD-sponsored artists reads like a *Who's Who* of the international art world: Armando, John Armleder, Daniel Buren, James Lee Byars, Edward Kienholz, Mario Merz, Nam June Paik, George Rickey – to mention just a few of those who've displayed here over the past 30 years. But the gallery also promotes the local avant garde, once a year filling its beautiful upstairs rooms with the work of such up-and-coming artists as Martin Assig.

## Haus am Lützowplatz

*Lützowplatz 9, Tiergarten, 10785 (261 3805). U2, U4, U15 Nollendorfplatz.* **Open** 11am-6pm Tue-Sun. **Admission** free.
One of the first non-commercial, private galleries to re-open in West Berlin after World War II, the Haus am Lützowplatz shows mostly figurative work of Berlin neo-realists and, more recently, paintings, sculpture and photography from Hungary, Bulgaria, Russia and Poland. There are two spaces for exhibitions – one on the raised ground floor (access from street level by way of a conspicuous staircase designed by Berlin artist Volkmar Haase), the other on the second floor.
*Wheelchair access from parking lot in the back of the house.*

## Haus am Waldsee

*Argentinische Allee 30, Zehlendorf, 14163 (807 2234). U1 Krumme Lanke.* **Open** 10am-6pm Tue-Sun. **Admission** DM4 adults; DM2 students, pensioners, disabled.
The Haus am Waldsee was founded in 1946 by the local arts council, in a villa in the wealthy suburb of Zehlendorf. During the first two decades after World War II the Haus mounted a series of pioneering exhibitions which presented the work of artists who had been banned by the Nazis and, as a result, were almost unknown in Germany at the time: Käthe Kollwitz (in 1946), Hermann Blumenthal (1947), Karl Schmidt-Rottluff (1948) and Max Ernst (1951). But even as late as 1980, with its show Heftige Malerei (violent painting), the gallery knew no ground for those neo-Expressionist Junge Wilde painters who – just three years later – were to be the main attraction of the international Zeitgeist show at Martin-Gropius-Bau (*see below*).
*Group discounts.*

## Haus der Kulturen der Welt (Kongreßhalle)

*John-Foster-Dulles-Allee 10, Tiergarten, 10557 (39 7870). 100, 248 bus.* **Open** usually 11am-7pm Tue-Sun. **Admission** DM4-8 adults; DM2-4 students, pensioners, disabled.
A unique institution and an important addition to Berlin's cultural life. Funded by the Federal Government and the Berlin Senate, the House of World Cultures was set up in January 1989 to promote artists from so-called Third World countries, mounting spectacular large-scale exhibitions such as contemporary Indian art, Bedouin culture in North Africa and the avant garde in China. The programme also features film festivals, readings, lectures, panel discussions, concerts and dance performances. Hugh A Stubbins' striking Kon-

greßhalle was erected in 1957/58 as America's contribution to Berlin's first international building exhibition. When the original structure collapsed in 1980, the building was rebuilt almost from the ground.
*Restaurant. Bookshop. Wheelchair access. Toilets for the disabled.*

## Hochschule der Künste (Highschool of Art)

*Hardenbergstraße 33, Charlottenburg, 10623 (31850). U2, U9/S3, S5, S6, S7, S9 Zoologischer Garten/U2 Ernst-Reuter-Platz.* **Open** 10am-7pm Mon-Sat. **Admission** free.
Enter the main lobby from Hardenbergstraße and you'll find a colourful diversity of student displays ranging from traditional painting to video installations and computer graphics. Most of the Junge Wilde painters are in some way connected with the HdK – either as teachers (Karl-Horst Hödicke, Georg Baselitz) or as former students (Salomé, Helmut Middendorf, Rainer Fetting).
*Wheelchair access.*

## Internationales Design Zentrum

*Kurfürstendamm 66, Wilmersdorf, 10707 (882 30 51). U7 Adenauerplatz.* **Open** 10am-5pm Mon-Fri. **Admission** free.
Berlin's only institution exclusively devoted to international design. The IDZ's first floor premises are located in a fancy nineteenth-century building on the Ku'damm which houses a gallery space, library and staff offices. Some of the exhibitions are mounted here, others at various unusual places such as the Zoo. Phone for up-to-date information.

## Kunsthalle Am Zoo

*Budapester Straße 42-46, Tiergarten, 10787 (251 0102). U2, U9/S3, S5, S6, S7, S9 Zoologischer Garten.* **Open** 10am-6pm Tue-Sun; 10am-10pm Wed. **Admission** DM4.50 adults; DM2 students, pensioners, disabled.
Although this remarkably busy exhibition hall couldn't be more central (near Zoo Station), its ground floor entrance is easy to miss. You'll find it right opposite the striking fountain (created by Berlin sculptor Joachim Schmettau) which dominates the plaza between Gedächtniskirche and the Europa-Center. The Kunsthalle serves as both a venue for big national and international art shows and a forum for new names of the local art scene (twice a year). In addition, the gallery regularly mounts historical and documentary exhibitions, for instance, on the French Revolution or American working class culture.
*Café. Wheelchair access.*

## Künstlerhaus Bethanien

*Mariannenplatz 2, Kreuzberg, 10997 (616 9030). U1, U15 Kottbusser Tor or Görlitzer Bahnhof.* **Open** 2-7pm Tue-Sun. **Admission** free.
The Künstlerhaus is housed in a nineteenth-century complex of former hospital buildings, and is mainly a workshop for contemporary art. Managed and funded by the Akademie der Künste and the DAAD (*see above*), it also provides one-year grants to artists. There are 21 artists' studios as well as three spaces for exhibitions, installations and performances (Studios I, II and III on the first floor). Bruce McLean was one of numerous international artists-in-residence to work here.
*Wheelchair access (ask porter for key to elevator).*

## Martin-Gropius-Bau

*Stresemannstraße 110, Kreuzberg, 10963 (254 86-0). U7, U15 Möckernbrücke/S1, S2 Anhalter Bahnhof.* **Open** 10am-8pm Tue-Sun. **Admission** DM8 adults; DM4 students, pensioners, disabled. **Credit** accepted at bookstands during special exhibitions only.
This is the top venue for large-scale international art exhibitions such as the 1982 Zeitgeist or 1991 Metropolis shows. But you may also find spectacular thematic exhibitions, for

example on the colonisation of the Americas. An absolute must is the permanent collection of the Berlinische Galerie, an overview of Berlin art since 1870.
*Bookshop. Film screenings. Guided tours. Lectures. Restaurant. Wheelchair access.*

## Neue Gesellschaft für Bildende Kunst (NGBK)

*Oranienstraße 25, Kreuzberg, 10999 (615 3031). U1, U8, U15 Kottbusser Tor.* **Open** noon-6.30pm daily. **Admission** free.
An offshoot of the late sixties student movement, the NBK has for more than 20 years produced a highly diversified and ambitious programme featuring photography, ethnic art, Berlin art and documentary shows. While the emphasis is on social realism, you can also find representatives of recent conceptual developments, such as Berlin artist Katharina Karrenberg. Enter via the ground floor bookshop.
*Bookshop. Wheelchair access.*

## Neue Nationalgalerie

*Potsdamer Straße 50, Tiergarten, 10785 (266 26 51). U15 Kurfürstenstraße.* **Open** 9am-5pm Tue-Fri; 10am-5pm Sat, Sun. **Admission** DM4 for permanent collection; varies for special exhibitions.
Housed in a classic building designed by Mies van der Rohe, the Neue Nationalgalerie offers an outstanding variety of (predominantly German) painting and sculpture ranging from early twentieth-century masterworks by Dix, Grosz and Beckmann to major pieces by contemporary stars such as AR Penck, Georg Baselitz or Anselm Kiefer. American art since 1945 (seminal canvases by Barnett Newman, Mark Rothko, Morris Louis and Frank Stella as well as works by sculptors Richard Serra and Sol LeWitt) are other highlights of the permanent collection. The gallery has a reputation for its superb temporary exhibitions of classic and contemporary modernists, including Francis Bacon, Lucien Freud, Pablo Picasso and Sandro Chia.
*Bookshop. Café. Guided tours. Wheelchair access.*

## Galerie Weißer Elefant

*Almstadtstraße 11, Mitte, 10119 (282 3908). U2, U5, U8/S3, S5, S6, S7, S75, S9 Alexanderplatz/U2 Rosa-Luxemburg-Platz.* **Open** 11am-7pm Tue-Fri; 3-6pm Sat. **Admission** free.
The oldest independent gallery in east Berlin, it now features a varied programme of painting, sculpture and photography by new German artists.
*Wheelchair access.*

# Commercial Galleries

## West

## Art Communication

*Pariser Straße 7, Wilmersdorf, 10719 (883 7186). U1, U9 Spichernstraße.* **Open** 2-7pm Tue, Wed, Fri; 2-8pm Thur; 11am-2pm Sat. **No credit cards.**
One of the many recent additions to Berlin's gallery scene. Art Communication specialises in young German and French painting, publishing excellent catalogues of its major shows. Artists featured include Jean-François Guzranyi, Thibaut de Reimpre, Bettina van Haaren and Frank Schult.
*Wheelchair access with assistance.*

## Galerie Brusberg

*Kurfürstendamm 213, Charlottenberg, 10719 (882 7682/83). U15 Uhlandstraße.* **Open** 10am-6.30pm Tue-Fri; 10am-2pm Sat. **No credit cards.**

**Opposite:** *another fund-raising drive at* **Akademie der Künste.** *See page 148.*

By the time Dieter Brusberg moved to Berlin in 1982, he was one of the most successful art dealers in Germany. Concentrating on Dadaism (Schwitters) and Surrealism (Magritte, Ernst) in the early days, Brusberg was among the first to display the vanguard of East German painting (Bernhard Heisig, Wolfgang Mattheuer and Werner Tübke). Recent exhibits have included Americans Jim Lawrence, Milo Reice and Muriel Kalish, along with German artists Harald Metzke and Jürgen Brodwulf.

## Galerie Volker Diehl

*Niebuhrstraße 2, Charlottenburg, 10629 (881 8280). U15 Uhlandstraße/S3, S5, S6, S7, S9 Savignyplatz.* **Open** 2-6.30pm Tue-Fri; 11am-2pm Sat. **No credit cards.**
A high-quality collection of contemporary German, Italian and American painters of the post-War generation are shown at this gallery, but you may also find Arte Povera objects by Mario Merz or minimal sculpture by Donald Judd. Volker Diehl helped to organise the seminal Zeitgeist show in 1982 and has been a prominent figure in the Berlin art world for many years.
*Wheelchair access.*

## Galerie Anselm Dreher

*Pfalzburger Straße 80, Wilmersdorf, 16719 (883 5249). U1 Hohenzollernplatz.* **Open** 2-6.30pm Tue-Fri; 11am-2pm Sat. **No credit cards.**
Anselm Dreher's unique gallery has been around for more than 25 years now, uncompromisingly promoting the concrete, minimal and conceptual tendencies in contemporary art. He was the first – and for quite some time the only one – to show the work of Carl André, Joseph Kosuth, Jochen Gerz and Ange Leccia in Berlin.
*Wheelchair access.*

## Galerie Franck + Schulte

*Mommsenstraße 56, Charlottenburg, 10629 (324 0044). U7 Adenauerplatz/S3, S5, S6, S7, S9 Savignyplatz.* **Open** 11am-6pm Mon-Fri; 11am-3pm Sat. **No credit cards.**
Eric Franck came from Geneva and Thomas Schulte all the way from New York to challenge the Berlin market with fresh ideas and an extremely ambitious programme. Although they started only in April 1991, they've already managed to become the talk of the town with exhibitions of Rebecca Horn, Robert Mapplethorpe, Nam June Paik, Ulrich Rückriem and other prominent figures.

## Galerie Bodo Niemann

*Knesebeckstraße 30, Charlottenburg, 10623 (882 2620). U15 Uhlandstraße/S3, S5, S6, S7, S9 Savignyplatz.* **Open** noon-6pm Tue-Fri; 11am-2pm Sat. **No credit cards.**
This gallery is first of all known for its startling exhibitions of photography and figurative and abstract art from the twenties, mostly by German artists such as Hannah Höch, Emil Orlik, Kurt Scheele or photographer August Sander. Niemann has an unerring eye for the neglected or forgotten works of that period and is responsible for numerous historical discoveries. He also shows contemporary artists including Heribert Ottersbach.
*Wheelchair access with assistance.*

## Galerie Nierendorf

*Hardenbergstraße 19, Charlottenburg, 10623 (785 6060). U2, U9/S3, S5, S6, S7, S9 Zoologischer Garten.* **Open** 11am-5pm Tue-Fri. **No credit cards.**
Established in 1923, Nierendorf is the oldest commercial gallery in town, and it has somehow managed to conserve the spirit of the good old days. The first floor showrooms look more like a twenties collector's flat than a modern gallery space, and what you'll see on the walls is definitely not of recent make either. But if you like German Expressionism or the hard-edged social realism of George Grosz and Otto Dix, this is the place to go. Some prints are still less than DM500.

**Galerie Nierendorf**: *the oldest commercial gallery in town. See page 151.*

## Galerie Georg Nothelfer

*Uhlandstraße 184, Charlottenberg, 10623 (881 4405).*
*U15 Uhlandstraße.* **Open** 2-6.30pm Tue-Fri; 10am-2pm
Sat. **No credit cards**.
Undisputedly one of the top galleries in town, Nothelfer
excels in German Informel (a post-War abstract movement),
Tachism, Lyrical Abstraction as well as gestural, scriptural
and narrative painting. While concentrating on well established European artists such as Pierre Alechinsky, Arnulf
Rainer, Antoni Tàpies and Cy Twombly, this longtime doyen
of the Berlin art world also has a weakness for Japanese
action painter Katzuo Shiraga, who creates large, relief-like
pictures by swinging across the canvas on a rope and apply-
ing the colours with his feet. Virtually all of Nothelfer's
artists today are considered first-rate in contemporary
abstract painting.

## Galerie Eva Poll

*Lützowplatz 7, Tiergarten, 10785 (261 7091). U2, U4,*
*U15 Nollendorfplatz.* **Open** 10am-3pm Mon; 11am-7pm,
4-7pm, Tue-Fri; 11am-3pm Sat. **No credit cards**.
When Eva Poll established her gallery in 1968, it was with
the intention of supporting a local group of young 'critical'
realists who had emerged in the mid-sixties. Since then, however, she's expanded the programme to include a colourful
diversity of contemporary European figurative painters.
Among the younger artists represented are GL Gabriel,
Sabine Grzimek, as well as Hans Scheib, whose painted wood
sculptures are very approachable.

## Galerie Pommersfelde

*Knesebeckstraße 97, Charlottenburg, 10623 (313 8005).*
*U2 Ernst-Reuter-Platz.* **Open** 2-6pm Tue-Fri; 11am-2pm
Sat. **No credit cards**.
Owner Werner Meyke, who opened this gallery in 1983, is
as much interested in language and literature as he is in art.
So some of the artists he represents explore the two media
simultaneously, such as painter-writer Split whose powerful Dubuffet-like canvases are matched by his equally disturbing poems and short stories. Constantly on the look-out

for new talent, Meyke was among the first to display the
beautifully balanced collages by Reneé Strecker and the
expressive abstracts by Gerd Wandrer.
*Wheelchair access.*

## Raab Galerie

*Potsdamer Straße 58, Tiergarten, 10785 (261 9217/18).*
*U15 Kurfürstenstraße/129, 148, 248, 348 bus.* **Open**
10am-6.30pm Mon-Fri; 10am-2pm Sat; 10am-4pm first Sat
of the month. **No credit cards**.
Ingrid Raab's spacious gallery is one of the top places for
contemporary expressive and figurative trends. Among the
artists represented are Elvira Bach, Luciano Castelli, Ken
Currie, Karl Horst Hödicke, Daniel Spoerri and, exclusively,
Rainer Fetting. More recently, Raab has also shown avant
garde work from St Petersburg. A generous supporter of
young talent on both sides of the Channel, she also runs two
galleries in London. Make sure you don't miss the exhibits
on the first floor.
*Wheelchair access.*

## Galerie Redmann

*Lutzowufer 33, Tiergarten, 10787 (261 9425). U2,*
*U9/S3, S5, S6, S7, S9 Zoologischer Garten.* **Open** 11am-
6pm Tue-Fri; 11am-2pm Sat. **No credit cards**.
'I show what I like myself,' says gallery owner Hans
Redmann. The gallery offers works from a wide variety of
styles and materials. While there is a propensity for figurative American painters such as Gaylen C Hansen, it is the
large-scale, fragile paper sculptures of Greek artist Pavlos
which are most striking.

## Galerie Nikolaus Sonne

*Kantstraße 138, Charlottenburg, 10623 (312 2355). S3,*
*S5, S6, S7, S9 Savignyplatz.* **Open** 11am-1pm, 3-6.30pm,
Tue-Fri; 11am-2pm Sat. **No credit cards**.
Juxtaposing extreme styles and traditions is the speciality

**'Opposite**: *student exhibit or the tutor's bike*
*at the* **Hochschule der Künste**? *See page*

of this young gallery. Its postmodern cornerstones are Warhol and Beuys, Keith Haring left some graffiti on the door, and the walls are hung with newcomers such as Martin von Ostrowski or Thomas Ruff.

### Galerie Springer
*Fasanenstraße 13, Charlottenberg, 10623 (317 063). U2, U9/S3, S5, S6, S7, S9 Zoologischer Garten.* **Open** 2-7pm Mon-Fri; 11am-2pm Sat. **No credit cards.**
Rudolf Springer is one of the grand old men of Berlin's art world. He opened his first gallery as early as 1948, and has produced a series of memorable exhibitions since then. Among the all-time greats he managed to present are Alexander Calder, Joan Miró, André Masson, Max Ernst and Henri Laurens. But he's also had a continuous passion for German post-War artists (Wols, Ernst Wilhelm Nay, AR Penck, Jörg Immendorf and Markus Lüpertz) and a never-fading interest in newcomers.
*Wheelchair access.*

### Zellermayer Galerie
*Ludwigkirchstraße 14, Wilmersdorf, 10719 (883 4144). U1 Hohenzollernplatz.* **Open** 11am-2pm Mon; 1-6pm Tue-Fri; 11am-2pm Sat. **No credit cards.**
A bright gallery space usually filled with contemporary figurative and abstract painting from the US, Eastern Europe and Germany. Occasionally, you may also find large-scale photography.
*Wheelchair access with assistance.*

## Kreuzberg

### Galerie am Chamissoplatz
*Chamissoplatz 6, Kreuzberg, 10965 (692 53 81). U7 Gneisenaustraße/U6 Platz der Luftbrücke.* **Open** 1-6.30pm Tue-Sun. **No credit cards.**
The first – and still leading – gallery for bitingly sardonic, well-crafted caricatures and cartoons. In addition, figurative painting and sculpture by east German and local artists (including Turkish-born painter Hanefi Yeter) are shown here. *See also below* **Galerie Tammen & Busch.**
*Readings. Wheelchair access with assistance.*

### Galerie Mainz
*Blücherstraße 66a, Kreuzberg, 10961 (693 8018). U7 Gneisenaustraße or Südstern.* **Open** 3-6pm Tue-Fri; 10am-1pm Sat. **Credit** AmEx, DC, V.
Another recent addition to Berlin's expanding art market. Although the quality of the work shown in this tiny gallery is varied (most of it is provided by local newcomers), it's an interesting address for moderately priced 'discoveries'. You can get (unsigned) original prints, etchings and engravings by Miró, Dale and other stars for less than DM500.
*Wheelchair access.*

### Galerie Neue Räume
*Lindenstraße 39, Kreuzberg, 10969 (251 4812). U6 Kochstrasse.* **Open** 10am-7pm Mon-Fri. **No credit cards.**
This gallery-cum-café, which is in a backyard building near Axel-Springer-Publishing House, is the locale for art exhibitions, readings, performances and concerts of avant

garde music. Owner Heidi Springfeld has managed to surprise visitors time and again with mavericks and outsiders, such as the Austrian Franz Blaas whose miniature sketchbook drawings were on display recently.

### Stil und Bruch
*Admiralstraße 17, Kreuzberg, 10999 (65 5547). U1, U8 Kottbusser Tor.* **Open** 2-7pm Thur-Sun. **No credit cards.**
A beautiful gallery in a redeveloped side street, just a stone's throw from Kottbusser Tor. The name (a pun on the German word Stilbruch, stylistic inconsistency) alludes to the irreversible destruction (Abbruch) inflicted on the area's infrastructure by profit-greedy developers during the seventies and early eighties. Since it opened in 1984, Stil und Bruch has continually focused on new and unknown names many of whom are graduates of the **Hochschule der Künste** (*see above* **Public Galleries**).
*Wheelchair access.*

### Galerie Tammen & Busch
*Fidicinstraße 40, Kreuzberg, 10965 (694 5248). U6 Platz der Luftbrücke.* **Open** 1-6.30pm Tue-Fri; 11am-2pm Sat. **No credit cards.**
Werner Tammen and Bernd Busch, long-time directors of Galerie am Chamissoplatz, opened this new space in November 1991 to show large-scale painting and sculpture. Their first exhibition featured bronze sculpture by Trak Wendisch. The gallery is situated at the very end of a backyard complex which also houses two sculptors' studios, an English theatre company and various small businesses. Unmissable.
*Wheelchair access.*

### Zwinger Galerie
*Dresdener Straße 125, Kreuzberg, 10999 (65 4605). U1, U8 Kottbusser Tor.* **Open** 2-7pm Tue-Fri; 11am-2pm Sat. **No credit cards.**
This is probably the most important showcase for conceptual art made in Berlin. Intriguing work by former members of Die Tödliche Doris and SUSI POP is shown here.
*Wheelchair access with assistance.*

## East

### allgirls gallery
*Kleine Hamburger Straße 16, Mitte, 10117 (612 34 50/215 6335). S1,*

**Galerie Franck + Schulte**: *the current talk of the town. See page 151.*

*S2 Oranienburger Straße/U6 Oranienburger Tor.* **Open** 4-7pm Tue-Fri. **No credit cards.**
A small space off Auguststraße where you'll find anything from paintings and sculptures to installations and performances. Most of it is provided by local sources. *See also chapter* **Women.**

### Galerie Berlin
*Friedrichstraße 231, Mitte, 10969 (251 4420). U6 Kochstrasse.* **Open** 11am-6pm Tue-Fri; 11am-2pm Sat. **No credit cards.**
Formerly the international branch of the GDR's official art trade and since November 1990 a thriving private venture, Galerie Berlin is well on its way to becoming east Berlin's most prestigious gallery. The owners concentrate on expressive painting from eastern Germany, offering a carefully balanced mixture of figuratives and abstracts by long-time celebrities (including Bernhard Heisig, Wolfgang Mattheuer and Walter Libuda), and more recent luminaries such as Hubertus Giebe and Gerd Sonntag. Early twentieth-century German Expressionism and Impressionism (Max Beckmann, Käthe Kollwitz, Max Liebermann) are the other highlights. *Wheelchair access.*

### Galerie Leo Coppi
*Wallstraße 90, enter via Spreeufer, Mitte, 10179 (200 4129). U2 Spittelmarkt.* **Open** 1-6.30pm Tue-Fri; 10am-2pm Sat. **No credit cards.**
Doris Leo and Helle Coppi opened this attractive gallery in June 1991 to promote a number of outstanding painters and graphic artists, most of whom live and work in east Berlin and Dresden. Our favourite is Angela Hampel. *Wheelchair access with assistance; ring bell on Wallstraße.*

### Galerie EIGEN + ART
*Auguststraße 26, Mitte, 10117 (280 6605). S1, S2 Oranienburger Straße/U6 Oranienburger Tor.* Open 2-7pm Tue-Fri; 11am-2pm Sat. **No credit cards.**

Gerd Harry Lybke has been running an independent gallery in Leipzig for many years and, shortly after the collapse of the Wall, started his second venture in Auguststraße. And although he recently spent a few months in New York setting up a temporary gallery, he has remained true to his roots: discovering and supporting the young avant garde from the world over.
*Wheelchair access with assistance.*

### Galerie Inselstraße 13
*Inselstraße 13, Mitte, 10179 (279 1808). U2 Märkisches Museum/U8 Heinrich-Heine-Straße.* **Open** 11am-6pm Mon-Fri; 10am-2pm Sat. **No credit cards.**
One of the first private galleries to open in east Berlin after the Wall came down. The emphasis is on German post-War developments, art from eastern Europe and work by east German artists who, until 1989, were banned from the state-controlled GDR galleries and thus lacked any opportunity to exhibit. There's also an ambitious lecture programme involving both artists and art historians.

### Im Kabinett
*Schönhauser Allee 8, backyard, 1st floor, Mitte, 10119 (442 7577). U2 Rosa-Luxemburg-Platz.* **Open** 2-7pm Tue-Sat. **No credit cards.**
Once confined to a tiny room in the district of Kreuzberg, Im Kabinett now occupies a beautifully refurbished space on the first floor of an old factory building. Its first show was devoted to the painter Strawalde who, along with his contemporary Gerhard Altenbourg, is one of many major east German artists represented, as well as photographers of the International avant garde.

### Kunsthaus Tacheles
*Oranienburger Straße 54-56, Mitte, 10117 (282 6185). U6 Oranienburger Tor.* **Open** 2-8pm daily. **No credit cards.**
If you like the far-out and bizarre, this is definitely the first

# Street Scene

Outside of conventional gallery spaces, Berlin is spattered with art of every description. At one end of the spectrum are the usual garish chunks of municipal sculpture, such as the giant three-quarter hula-hoop thing at an der Urania, the tubular steel monstrosity that runs along Tauentzienstraße representing divided Berlin, or the car upended in a lump of concrete at the western extremity of the Ku'damm.

At street level, graffiti scrawl these days seems to cover every façade in the city. Mostly derivative of early New York hip hop, more elaborate work appears and disappears in the kind of places you'd expect. The art is canonised at the **East Side Gallery**, an extant stretch of Wall just across the Spree from Kreuzberg by the Oberbaumbrücke, where polemical work by artists from all over the world stretches for a few hundred metres along Mühlenstraße. It's reckoned to be the world's largest outdoor art gallery.

On both sides of the city, any number of bars and cafés exhibit art. Unconventional displays pop up in all sorts of spaces, such as the wacky 'shirt installations' at Ralf Peitscher's shop at Grunewaldstraße 89 in Schöneberg (*see chapter* **Shopping**). Much can be chanced upon while walking around the more fashionable districts of east Berlin.

Over in Prenzlauer Berg, a few doors down from the Café Galerie OM at Stargarder Straße 13, an artist has seemingly lifted the blinds of an old shop front studio to reveal beautiful, large-scale sculpture for passers-by. This is in fact the **Galerie Frank Hänel** and is connected to the Bar Galerie Stargarder 18.

At the corner of Auguststraße and Tucholskystraße in Mitte, around the corner from Oranienberger Straße S-Bahn station, a riotous collage marks the entrance to a former squat whose courtyard is festooned with brightly painted banners and recycled flotsam. Along the tiny Mulackstraße, an unmarked door at number 23 is occasionally open to reveal a stark, semi-sculptural work. It is in fact the **Mulack 23 Gallery**. Across the street from it is a small green plot where rusted metal shapes twist upward as if planted there. In the wasteland behind Tacheles on Oranienberger Straße, the Mutoid Waste Company have left behind an assortment of rusty scrap metal sculpture.

Change is the only constant on the Berlin street scene. Much of what's mentioned here may have disappeared by the time you read this. But the point of street art is the moment of surprise, when you turn a corner to find something completely unexpected.

---

place to go. Housed in the ruins of a war-battered department store building, Kunsthaus Tacheles is unquestionably the most chaotic cultural laboratory in town. An international artists' community is at work in a number of makeshift studios on the second floor (and some even in the junk-covered backyard). Virtually all of the pieces are for sale (at moderate prices).

### Galerie Wohnmaschine
*Tucholskystraße 34 & 36, Mitte, 10117 (282 0795). S1, S2 Oranienburger Straße.* **Open** 2-7pm Tue-Fri; 11am-2pm Sat. **No credit cards**.
While Friedrich Loock and Michaela Irmscher are probably the youngest (and, some say, also the hippest and hottest) gallery owners in town, they're no newcomers. Their first exhibition was mounted in Loock's flat in 1988. They show only young local artists, and are now mounting their exhibits internationally.

## Specialised Galleries

## Auctions

### Kunstkabinett Gerda Bassenge
*Bleibtreustraße 19, Charlottenburg, 10623 (881 8104). U15 Uhlandstraße/S3, S5, S6, S7, S9 Savignyplatz.* **Open** 2-6pm Mon-Fri; 11am-2pm Sat. **No credit cards**.
Gerda Bassenge, the *grande dame* among Berlin's gallery owners, deals in eighteenth- and nineteenth century engravings, prints and graphic works ranging from Art Nouveau

and the Berlin Seccessionists (Liebermann, Corinth) to German Expressionism (Kollwitz, Pechstein), and rare books. Auctions several times a year. Ring for details.

### Galerie Pels-Leusden
*Fasanenstraße 25 (at Villa Grisebach), Charlottenburg, 10719 (885 9150). U15 Uhlandstraße.* **Open** 10am-6.30pm Mon-Fri; 10am-2pm Sat. **No credit cards**.
There are two big auctions each year – one in June, the other in late November. The rest of the year you get to see a diversity of exhibitions with a focus on classic modern art.

### Auktionshaus Sotheby's
*Palais am Festungsgraben, Unter den Linden, behind Neue Wache, Mitte, 10117 (394 3060). S1, S2, S3, S5, S6, S7, S9/U6 Friedrichstraße.* **Open** 10am-1pm, 2-5pm, Mon-Fri. **No credit cards**.
The emphasis is on German Expressionism and contemporary painting and sculpture. Auctions are held in May and November.

## Photography

### Galerie Berinson
*Niebuhrstraße 2, Charlottenburg, 10629 (882 6464). S3, S5, S6, S7, S9 Savignyplatz.* **Open** by appointment only. **No credit cards**.
A superb collection of Vintage, Bauhaus, Constructivist, Dada and avant garde photography from the twenties.

# Museums

**From the National Gallery to the Topography of Terror via Wedding's
Sugar Museum, Berlin's museums offer rich variety.**

Berlin has an extraordinary number of museums, although visiting them isn't too daunting a task because they're mostly clustered in groups. For this reason, we've arranged the museums by area: the main collections at Dahlem and Museum Island (Museuminsel) are listed first, followed by the best of the rest in the east. The Charlottenburg palace and museums complex precedes the best of the west listings.

Since reunification the state museums, under the administratration of the Prussian Cultural Heritage Foundation (*Stiftung Preußischer Kulturbesitz*) have undergone – and are still undergoing – considerable reorganisation to cut back on duplication. Before the Wall came down there were 28 state museums across the city. Now there are 17. But actually that still entails much cross-city trekking, as many museums still have branches in the former east and west. Take the Egyptian Museum, which is located both in Charlottenburg and at the Bode Museum. In some instances, their respective collections have been more rationally arranged. For example the Alte Nationalgalerie (Mitte) houses nineteenth-century paintings formerly at the Neue Nationalgalerie, which now concentrates on the twentieth century.

But be warned: the biggest change is due to take place in early 1996, when the Neue Gemäldegalerie, Kemperplatz, Tiergarten is completed. The new gallery will bring together under one roof the European painting collections from the Gemäldegalerie in Dahlem and from the Museuminsel. This in turn will form part of a Tiergarten culture complex alongside the already existing Kunstgewerbe Museum (Museum of Applied Art *see below*) and the Art Library.

With the situation in such a state of flux, it makes sense to check with Tourist Information on the latest state of play so you don't miss anything you really want to see – especially if you're reading this in 1996. We have noted changes as they stand at the time of going to press.

**Guided Tours** in English of westside state museums and Pergamon and Bode Museums in the east can be arranged by appointment. For Dahlem, Charlottenburg, Tiergarten and so forth contact the *Besucherdienst* at Dahlem (*830 14 66*), open 8am-noon Mon-Fri. Pergamon and Bode Museums (*203 55 444/500*) are open 9am-5pm. In both cases give at least 14 days' notice. Tours, costing DM80 per person plus admission, last about an hour.

As a general rule, the larger museums have either booklets or information sheets in English. However, a lot of museums have little or no information in English available: where this may be a problem, we have indicated it in the review.

## Dahlem Museums

The largest concentration of museums in Berlin is currently to be found at Dahlem, a swish suburban area to the south-west of the city centre.

Take the U1 to Dahlem-Dorf. As you leave the station, you will see signs directing you to the museums, as well as to the Free University, which is also located in this area. You might visit the student café **Luise** (*see chapter* **Students**) for a coffee or a meal, or try one of the other places along Königen-Luise-Straße. The Dahlem Museum complex itself has an overpriced café in the basement for drinks, snacks and full meals. But it's worth having a look at the cabinets at the back of the café, which display old knives and forks.

**Admission** for the entire complex is DM4; DM2 for students and pensioners; entrance is free on Sundays. At museums within the complex, information sheets are available for various sections: pick them up as you go along, but be sure to pay 10 pfennigs for each sheet, into one of the boxes dotted around the place.

### Brücke-Museum (Bridge Museum)
*Bussardsteig 9, Zehlendorf, 14195 (831 20 29). U1 Dahlem-Dorf.* **Open** 11am-5pm Wed-Mon. **Admission** DM5; DM2.50 concs.
A museum dedicated to the art of *Die Brücke* (The Bridge), a movement of artists established in Dresden in 1905 and credited with introducing Expressionism to Germany. On display are oils, watercolours, drawings and sculptures by the main members of the movement: Schmidt-Rottluff, Heckel, Kirchner, Mueller and Pechstein. Although rather out of the way, the Brücke is worth seeing: it's a connoisseur's museum, small but satisfying and coherently arranged. The sculptures are particularly interesting. Wander through the fancy neighbourhoods of Dahlem to the museum's location on the edge of the Grunewald. *See also chapter* **Trips Out Of Town**.

### Gemäldegalerie (Picture Gallery)
*Arnimallee 23-37, Zehlendorf, 14195 (830 12 17). U1 Dahlem-Dorf.* **Open** 9am-5pm Tue-Fri; 10am-5pm Sat, Sun. **Admission** *see above*.
The Gemäldegalerie has an astonishing number of works by

**Opposite: Museum für Verkehr und Technik.** *See page 164.*

most of art history's big boys, including Rubens, Dürer, Breughel, Holbein, Raphael, Gainsborough, El Greco, Canaletto and Caravaggio. Room after room of paintings, over two floors, arranged chronologically and by artistic school, await exploration. On the ground floor are works by German, Dutch and Italian artists from the thirteenth- to the sixteenth century, together with French and English paintings from the eighteenth century. On the first floor you'll find Dutch, French and Flemish works from the seventeenth century, Italian Baroque and rococo, and Spanish paintings. Devotees of Rembrandt won't be disappointed by the 20 or so of his canvases displayed here, which constitute one of the world's largest collections of his works. Also on display is a version of Botticelli's famous *Venus Rising* (the complete painting is in Florence) and Correggio's brilliant *Leda With The Swan*. Look also for Lucas Cranach's *Fountain of Youth* (1546), depicting an old, haggard women entering a pool and emerging from the other side young and beautiful again.

## Museum für Indische Kunst (Museum of Indian Art)

*Lansstraße 8, Zehlendorf, 14195 (830 13 61). U1 Dahlem-Dorf.* **Open** 9am-5pm Tue-Fri; 10am-5pm Sat, Sun. **Admission** *see above.*

Wonderful Indian treasures, expertly and stunningly lit, are to be found in this museum on the ground floor of the Dahlem complex. It covers almost 4,000 years of art from Nepal, Thailand, Indonesia, Tibet, Burma and India. Displays are arranged geographically: in the first two rooms you'll find objects from the Indian sub-continent, in the third treasures from Nepal and Tibet, followed by a gallery of South-East Asian art, and art from Java and Indonesia. One of the highlights is a house temple – an intricately carved homage to Buddha – while the collection of art from Buddhist cave monasteries along the Silk Route is world-famous.

## Museum für Islamische Kunst (Museum of Islamic Art)

*Lansstraße 8, Zehlendorf, 14195 (830 13 92). U1 Dahlem-Dorf.* **Open** 9am-5pm Tue-Fri; 10am-5pm Sat, Sun. **Admission** *see above.*

Established in 1904, the Museum of Islamic Art features exhibits from all Muslim countries, and traces the development of Islamic art from the eighth to the eighteenth century. There is a stunningly intricate sixteenth-century Koran displayed at the entrance, while the rest of the museum is arranged chronologically. Beautiful Persian rugs dating from the sixteenth and seventeenth centuries and lovely Islamic tiles from Turkey are among the artefacts.

## Museum für Ostasiatische Kunst (Museum of Far Eastern Art)

*Lansstraße 8, Zehlendorf, 14195 (830 13 61). U1 Dahlem-Dorf.* **Open** 9am-5pm Tue-Fri; 10am-5pm Sat, Sun. **Admission** *see above.*

The most disappointing of the museums in the Dahlem-Dorf complex was also the first museum of Far Eastern art in Germany. Established in 1906, it once inhabited the Museum of Decorative Art, now the Martin Gropius building. World War II and post-war chaos depleted the collection, but it has since expanded and now focuses primarily on paintings. Among the displays are Chinese, Korean and Japanese art dating from 3000 BC. Divided into eight sections, the museum also includes Chinese archaeology and decorative art, Buddhist art, Japanese woodcuts, ceramics and lacquer. The displays don't match up to others in the complex, although the collection is apparently one of the finest in Europe.

## Museum für Völkerkunde (Ethnological Museum)

*Lansstraße 8, Zehlendorf,14195 (830 12 26). U1 Dahlem-Dorf.* **Open** 9am-5pm Tue-Fri; 10am-5pm Sat, Sun. **Admission** *see above.*

The Ethnological Museum is much too big to be covered in one visit. Eight regional departments cover two floors: Oceanian, American, African, East Asian, South Asian, West Asian and European, as well as Music Ethnology. There is also an educational department which includes a junior museum and museum for the blind. No need to bother with all the collection, though, as some sections are pretty tedious (the early American exhibits, for instance, can easily be bypassed). But the South Sea (*Südsee*) collection should not be missed, nor should the beaded artefacts from Cameroon: the beaded throne is quite amazing (although it looks less than comfy). The displays themselves are a joy – no doubt the curators had a lot of fun putting them together. The most interesting collection contains New Guinean masks and effigies suspended from the ceiling in well-lit cabinets; a large assortment of boats and canoes; a number of curious façades; even a fully intact men's clubhouse. The figure of a woman, suspended over the doorway with her legs wide open, just goes to show that boys have always been boys.

## Museum für Volkskunde (Museum of German Ethnology)

*Im Winkel 6-8, Zehlendorf, 14195 (83 90 101). U1 Dahlem-Dorf.* **Open** 9am-5pm Tue-Fri; 10am-5pm Sat, Sun. **Admission** *see above.*

Traditional clothes, jewellery, furniture, cooking utensils and toys of the Germanic people of Europe, from the Rhine to Silesia, are collected at the Volkskunde. Exhibits are artfully arranged and informative. Particularly worth seeing is the traditional clothing, much of which was still worn regularly up to the first half of this century, and the displays of weaving and spinning machines are also admirable. The museum is not a part of the immense Dahlem complex, but down the street and around the corner – just follow the sign at the U-Bahn station.

## Skulpturensammlung Standort Dahlem/Sculpture Collection Dahlem

*Arnimallee 23/27, Zehlendorf, 14195 (830 12 52). U1 Dahlem-Dorf.* **Open** 9am-5pm Tue-Fri; 10am-5pm Sat, Sun. **Admission** *see above.*

About 1,200 sculptures, of wood, ivory, marble and bronze, are spread over two floors, in this section of the Dahlem complex. The collection dates from the Great Elector's *Kunsthammer* (chamber of art), although many of the treasures were destroyed during World War II. One of the highlights of the early Christian-Byzantine sculptures on the ground floor is a stunning ivory diptych depicting Jesus and Mary and made in mid-sixth-century Constantinople. Watch also for works by the German master Tilman Riemenschneider on the first floor, particularly his series of evangelists. The Italian Collection features a gorgeous marble relief by Donatello, the *Madonna Pazzi* (from around 1420) and the *Madonna* by Presbyter Martinus (1199). *See also* **Bodemuseum.**

# Museuminsel (Museum Island)

Berlin's oldest collection of museums is on the Museuminsel, an island in the middle of the Spree. In the 1820s Friedrich Wilhelm III commissioned the complex to display the vast number of art treasures the royal family had amassed. The location was also handy for any royal who fancied a look at the collection: at the time, the royal palace (demolished by the GDR after World War II and

**Opposite**: *the* **Pergamon Museum** *is one of the world's best. See page 160.*

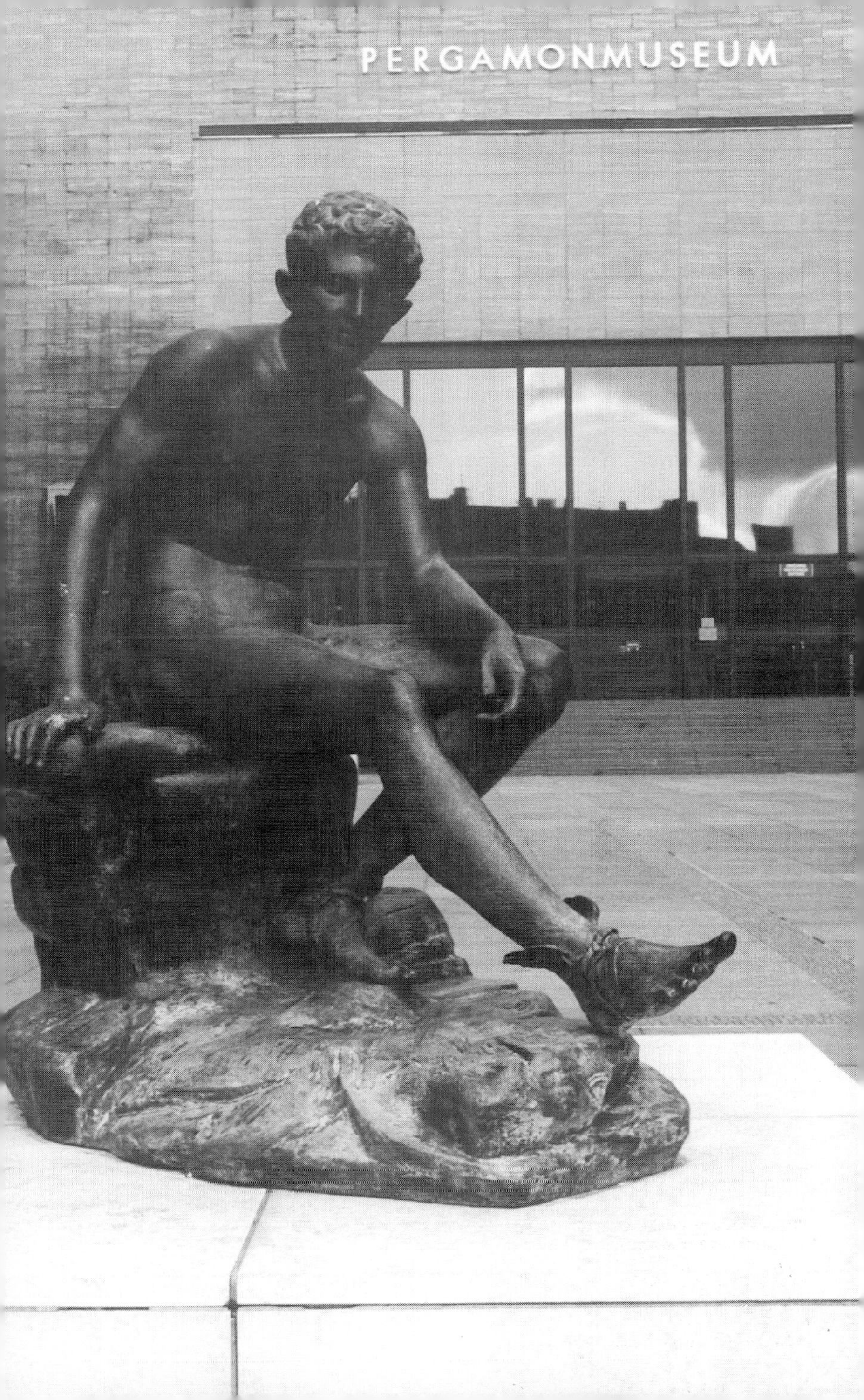
PERGAMONMUSEUM

replaced by the Palast der Republik) was just over the road.

**Admission:** day passes to the Museumsinsel (DM8) are economical if you plan to make a day of it; otherwise, you can pay as you go for DM4 a museum; DM2 for students and OAPs. Entrance is free on Sundays and public holidays.

### Alte Nationalgalerie (Old National Gallery)
*Bodestraße 1-3, Mitte, 10178 (20 35 55 30). S3, S5, S6, S9 Hackescher Markt.* **Open** 9am-5pm Tue-Sun.
**Admission** *see above.*
The Nationalgalerie collection includes nineteenth- and early twentieth-century works, mostly by German artists, with a few French canvases thrown in for good measure. Glorious sculptures by Gottfried Schadow grace the entrance hall; more of his works are displayed inside. French Impressionists feature alongside German Gothic. The collection itself is fascinating, but marred by the atrocious strip lighting. Expect to emerge with eye strain.

### Altes Museum
*Bodestraße 1-3, Mitte, 10178 (20 35 245). S3, S5, S6, S9 Hackescher Markt.* **Open** 9am-5pm Tue-Sun.
**Admission** *see above.*
The Altes Museum was opened as the Royal Museum in 1830 and originally housed all the art treasures on the island. The first of the museums, it was designed by the ubiquitous Karl Friedrich Schinkel and is considered one of his finest buildings. The entrance rotunda, in particular, is magnificent. Expect changing exhibitions on almost any subject.

### Bodemuseum
*Museumsinsel, entrance Monbijoubrücke, Mitte, 10178 (203 55 508). S3, S5, S6, S9/U6 Friedrichstraße.* **Open** 9am-5pm Tue-Sun.
The Kaiser Friedrich Museum opened here in 1904, but was renamed the Bode after Wilhelm von Bode, the former director responsible for bringing famous works of art to the Museumsinsel. The Bodemuseum is home to several different collections, among them paintings, sculpture, Byzantine art, coins and Egyptian art. The prized bust of Nefertiti, now housed in the **Egyptian Museum** in Charlottenburg (*see below*), resided here until the end of World War II, when the Allies spirited her away. Many notable works in the Dahlem Gemäldegalerie also came from the Bode. The coin cabinet has more than half a million coins, medallions and seals, making it one of the largest and most important such collections in the world. The main hall of lovely majolicas (Italian ceramics) leads to a magnificent central staircase and up to the paintings and Egyptian artefacts.

### Neues Museum (New Museum)
*Bodestraße 1-3, Mitte, 10178 (203 55 204). S3, S5, S6, S9 Hackescher Markt.*
The Neues Museum, built in 1859, is still a wartime ruin, and though work has begun in earnest to restore the structure, completion is a long way off. In the meantime, the museum runs the occasional exhibition, usually related to museum architecture. See press or tourist information for details.

### Pergamon Museum
*Bodestraße 1-3 (enter on Kupfergraben), Mitte, 10178 (2035 5444). S3, S5, S6, S9 Hackescher Markt.* **Open** 9am-5pm Tue-Sun. **Admission** *see above.*
The Pergamon Museum is dedicated to ancient spaces. Equipped with the gates, altars and gathering places of antiquity, it's the next best thing to being there. The vast Hellenistic Pergamon Altar (from which the museum takes its name) dates from 180-160 BC. It is made of white marble and carved with figures of the gods. The Market Gate of

Miletus, a two-storey Roman gate erected in 120 AD, once provided access to a public market and was large enough to contain a few shops of its own. In an adjoining room, the Babylonian Processional Street leads to The Gate of Ishtar, a striking cerulean and ochre tiled structure. It is the reconstruction of a street built during the reign of King Nebuchadnezzar (605-562 BC). Built between 1909 and 1930, the Pergamon is a relative newcomer to the island, but is one of the most significant architectural museums in the world.

## The Nikolai Quarter

### Hugenotten Museum
*Gendarmenmarkt, Mitte, 10117 (229 17 60). U6 Französische Straße.* **Open** noon-5pm Mon-Sat; 1-5pm Sun. **Admission** DM2; DM1 concs.
An exhibition on the history of the French Protestants in France and Berlin-Brandenburg is displayed in the Französischer Dom, the congregation's main church. The museum chronicles the religious persecution Calvinists suffered (note the bust of Calvin on the outside of the church) and their subsequent immigration to Berlin after 1685, at the invitation of the Hohenzollerns. The development of the Huguenot community is detailed with paintings, documents and artefacts. One part of the museum is devoted to the history of the church, in particular the effects of World War II. The church was bombed during a Sunday service in 1944 and remained a ruin until the mid-eighties. Other exports from France can be found in the wine restaurant upstairs.

### Märkisches Museum
*Am Köllnischen Park 5, Mitte, 10179 (270 05 14). U2 Märkisches Museum.* **Open** 10am-6pm Tue-Sun.
**Admission** DM3; DM1 concs.
Circus and variety show paraphernalia are displayed at the Märkisches Museum: old clown costumes, posters and brief histories of circuses and performers. In the back is a selection of programmes and newspaper articles from the scandalous variety shows and cabaret acts that made Berlin notorious in the twenties. The highlight is the stuffed body of a famous circus lion that gave up the ghost in 1987. The rest of the museum is a bit stuffy and static, but diehard circus-lovers won't be disappointed.

### Nikolaikirche
*Nikolaikirchplatz, Mitte, 10178 (23 80 90 81). U2 Klosterstraße.* **Open** 10am-5.30pm Tue-Sun. **Admission** DM3; DM1 concessions.
Inside Berlin's oldest congregational church, from which the Nikolai Quarter takes its name, is an interesting historical collection chronicling Berlin's development from its founding (c1230) until 1648. Old tiles, tapestries, stone and wood carvings – even old weapons and punishment devices – are on display. Part of the collection includes photographs of the extensive wartime damage, plus examples of how the stones melted together in the fiery heat of bombardment. Reconstruction of the church was completed in 1987, in time to celebrate Berlin's 750th anniversary.

### Otto-Nagel-Haus
*Märkisches Ufer 16-18, Mitte, 10179 (279 14 24). U2 Märkisches Museum.* **Open** 9am-5pm Tue-Sun.
**Admission** DM4; DM2 concs.
A moody, intimate museum of works by Nagel, Käthe Kollwitz, Max Lingner, and other Berlin artists active during the earlier part of this century. The Otto-Nagel-Haus first opened in 1982 as a permanent exhibition of 'proletarian-revolutionary and anti-Fascist art', according to its catalogue from the GDR days. It gives a fascinating look at life for

**Opposite:** *inside the* **Nikolaikirche.**

*There are over half a million coins stashed in the **Bodemuseum**. See page 160.*

Berlin's workers in the early twentieth century and touches on other artistic movements such as expressionism and cubism. This is the perfect-sized museum; not too big a collection to be overwhelming, and not too small to leave one unsatisfied. There's a small café on the ground floor.

### Schinkel-Museum

*Werderscher Markt (in the Friedrichswerdersche Kirche), Mitte, 10117 (208 13 23). U6 Französische Straße.* **Open** 9am-5pm Tue-Sun. **Admission** DM4; DM2 concs. The brick church was designed by Schinkel and completed in 1830. Its war wounds were repaired in the eighties and it reopened in 1987 as a homage to the architect that gave it life. Statues by Schinkel, Schadow and others stand inside, rubbing shoulders with the visitors in the soft light from the stained glass windows. Photographs and histories of those of his architectural masterworks that didn't survive the war (such as the Prinz-Albert-Schloß) are also on display.

## Husemannstraße

Apart from being home to two museums, this grand street in Prenzlauer Berg is something of a museum in itself. It was restored to its turn-of-the-century elegance as part of the city-wide celebration of Berlin's 750th anniversary in 1987. There are some great antique shops, clothing stores and gourmet food shops, as well as some fine bars and Restauration 1900, one of east Berlin's best-known restaurants (*see chapter* **Restaurants**).

### Friseurmuseum (Hairdressing Museum)

*Husemannstraße 8, Prenzlauer Berg, 10435 (4 42 25 81). U2 Eberswalder Straße.* **Open** 10am-5pm Tue-Thur; 10am-6pm Sat; 10am-4pm Sun. **Admission** DM2; DM1 concs.
Even if it does smell like old hair, this museum still warrants a visit. Ancient oriental hair accessories, barber's chairs, even a cup to wash the inside of your nose, are here. The most stomach-turning of the exhibits, though, is the jewellery made of hair: woven rings, bracelets, watch chains and brooches with hair landscapes.

### Museum Berliner Arbeiterleben (Museum of Berlin Working-Class Life)

*Husemannstraße 14, Prenzlauer Berg, 10435 (4 42 25 15). U2 Eberswalder Straße.* **Open** 10am-6pm Tue-Sun. **Admission** DM2; DM1 concs.
A reconstruction of a Berlin worker's flat, as it would have been at the turn of the century. It's an interesting way to tell the story of everyday life in Berlin, with all kinds of articles on display, ranging from a stove-heated curling iron to a weirdly shaped baby carriage. The front room is set aside for changing exhibitions.

## Elsewhere in the East

### Brecht-Haus

*Chausseestraße 125, Mitte, 10115 (282 99 16). U6 Zinnowitzer Straße, Oranienburger Tor.* **Open** 10am-noon Tue-Fri, every half hour; 5-6.30pm, Thur, every half hour; 9.30am-1.30pm Sat, every half hour (except noon). **Admission** DM4; DM2 concs.
Brecht's home, from 1948 until his death in 1953, has been preserved exactly as he left it. Tours of the house last about half an hour and give interesting insights into the life and reading habits of the playwright. The window at which he worked overlooked the grave of Hegel in the Dorotheenstädtische und Friedrichswerdersche Friedhof, which is where Brecht, too, is buried *(see chapter* **Sightseeing: Cemeteries**). His wife, the actress Helene Weigel, continued living here until she died in 1971. The Brecht archives are kept upstairs. Phone in advance for tours in English. The Kellerrestaurant near the exit serves 'select wines and fine beers and Viennese cooking in the style of Helene Weigel', in case you want to extend your Brecht-Weigel experience.

### Deutsches Historisches Museum

*Unter den Linden 2, Mitte, 10117 (21 50 20). S3, S5, S6, S9/U6 Friedrichstraße.* **Open** 10am-6pm Mon, Tue, Thur-Sun. **Admission** DM4; DMs concs.
The Zeughaus, where this is housed, was built as an arsenal in 1706 and is one of Berlin's most beautiful baroque buildings. During the latter half of the nineteenth century, it served as an army museum, and until the end of World War II possessed the largest historical collection of weapons in

Europe. During the GDR era, the museum made German history serve the needs of its incumbent rulers. Once the Wall came down, a sign went up on the door promising 'everything must be revised and seen in a new light', and a new curator was brought in from West Germany on the promise of staging themed exhibitions, such as The Art Of Memory about holocaust memorials, 'to make people think'. The GDR has not been forgotten, though. There's also a fine collection of the bizarre souvenirs representatives of socialist organisations used to present to each other – commemorative Sputnik plates and workers-of-the-world-unite paperweights.

## Ministerium für Staatssicherheit (Stasi Headquarters)/Forschungs- und Gedenkstätte Normannenstr.

*Ruschestraße 59, Lichtenberg, 10365 (553 68 54). U5 Magdalenenstraße.* **Open** 11am-6pm Tue-Fri; 2-6pm Sat, Sun. **Admission** DM5; DM2.50 concs.
As east Berlin grows to resemble the west more and more, one almost needs evidence that the GDR really happened. This museum, housed in part of what used to be the headquarters of the Ministerium für Staatssicherheit (East Germany's equivalent of the KGB), is the proof. You can look round the old offices of MFS boss Erich Mielke and view displays of bugging devices and spy cameras cannily concealed in books, plant pots and Trabant car doors. There's also a lot of communist kitsch: tasteless furniture, tacky medals, banners and busts of Karl and his cronies.

## Museum für Naturkunde (Museum of Natural History)

*Invalidenstraße 34, Mitte, 10115 (28 97 25 40). U6 Zinnowitzer Straße.* **Open** 9.30am-5pm Tue-Sun. **Admission** DM3; DM1.50 concs.
Berlin's Museum of Natural History is one of the world's largest and best organised. It's also one of the oldest: the kernel of the collection dates from 1716. A 12-metre (13-yard) tall skeleton of a brachiosaurus greets you in the first room, which is full of dinosaurs. Take a look at the archaeopteryx, perhaps the most perfectly preserved that has yet been unearthed. Even the feathers can be seen clearly. Another room has an enormous collection of fossils, from trilobites to lobsters. Other highlights include the skeleton of a giant armadillo and the vast insect collection (not for the squeamish). The animal collection, assembled in the twenties, almost makes you feel as if you're at the zoo – except that these critters are stuffed. And the immense mineralogical collection is a wonder: row upon row of rocks, set up exactly as they were when the building first opened in 1889. Don't miss the meteor chunks in the back of the room. The museum, which is a part of the Humboldt University, has over 60 million exhibits in its collection.

## Postmuseum

*corner of Leipziger- and Mauerstraße, Mitte, 10117 (22 85 47 01). U6 Stadtmitte.* **Open** 10am-6pm Tue-Sat. **Admission** DM1; 50pfg concs.
Although not as flashy and modern as its western branch in the Urania (*see below* **Postmuseum Berlin**), this museum has its own advantages – namely the neo-baroque building in which it's housed. The museum, built in the late nineteenth century by a former Postmaster General, is now under renovation, expected to be completed in 1995. The highlight of the museum is the large collection of stamps that mirror German history of the past 150 years. Among those on display are stamps from the first years of the GDR, with pictures of Mao during Chinese Friendship Month.

## Zille Museum

*Friedrichstraße Station in the S-Bahnbogen Arches 192-203, Mitte, 10117. S3, S5, S6, S9/U6 Friedrichstraße.* **Open** 11am-6pm Wed-Mon.
This small private museum is dedicated to photographer and cartoonist Heinrich Zille (1858-1929) – the compassionate,

funny and occasionally filthy chronicler of early twentieth-century working class Berlin lives. Pitched somewhere between the savagery of George Grosz and the sauciness of Donald McGill, his cartoons, captioned in Berlin dialect, capture the gallows humour of families often living in desperately impoverished circumstances. Rare among satirists, he achieved a fine balance of warmth and wit. His drawings of large-bottomed women, their bare-arsed, pissing kids, and his legless WWI vets might have offended Prussian propriety, but they were always popular within the milieux they recorded. The exhibition includes original drawings and photographs from his earliest works right up to his death.

## Charlottenburg

### Ägyptisches Museum

*Schloßstraße 70, Charlottenburg, 14059 (32 09 12 61/32 09 11). U2 Sophie-Charlotte-Platz or U7 Richard-Wagner-Platz.* **Open** 9am-5pm Sat-Thur. **Admission** DM8 combined ticket for Egyptian, antique, prehistoric, and romantic galleries, DM4 concs; DM4 single museum, DM2 concs; free Sundays.
The Egyptian Museum, just across the street from the Palace, is one of the most popular museums in Berlin, mainly because of the bust of Egyptian Queen Nefertiti. This piece of art, crafted in 1350 BC, was buried for more than 3,000 years until German archaeologists dug it up earlier this century. Nefertiti has a room to herself on the second floor. Also notable are a mummy and sarcophagi, a papyrus collection and the Kalabasha Gate. Despite the museum's popularity, no English booklets are available. But you could invest DM30 in a rather expensive hardback book which has full-colour pictures of the museum's main exhibits.

### Antiken Museum (Museum of Greek and Roman Antiquities)

*Schloßstraße 1, Charlottenburg, 14059 (32 09 12 15/6). U2 Sophie-Charlotte-Platz/U7 Richard-Wagner-Platz.* **Open** 9am-5pm Mon-Thur; 10am-5pm Sat, Sun. **Admission** DM4; DM2 concs; free Sun; combination card *see above.*
Across the street from the Egyptian Museum, the Antiken displays a wealth of antique treasures, from Ancient Greek pottery to Mediterranean jewellery and Egyptian mummy portraits. Outstanding exhibits include the exquisite collection of jewellery (in the basement) dating back to 2000 BC, and the marble bust of Cleopatra on the second floor. Slide shows featuring the jewellery and the Ancient Greek vases are held every two hours in German at no extra charge. Brochures in English are available.

**Schinkel** *'s very own museum.*

## Museum für Vor und Frühgeschichte (Primeval and Early History Museum)

*Spandauer Damm 20, Charlottenburg, 14059 (32 99 12 33). U2 Sophie-Charlotte-Platz/U7 Richard-Wagner-Platz.* **Open** 9am-5pm Mon-Thur; 10am-5pm Sat, Sun. **Admission** DM4; DM2 concs; free Sun; combination card *see above.*

The evolution of *Homo Sapiens* from one million BC to the Bronze Age is the subject of this museum next to the west wing of the palace. Keep an eye out for the sixth-century BC grave of a girl buried with a gold coin in her mouth. Beats Christmas pudding. Information is available in English.

### Schloß Charlottenburg

*Luisenplatz and Spandauer Damm, Charlottenburg, 14059 (32 09 11). U2 Sophie-Charlotte-Platz/U7 Richard-Wagner-Platz.* **Open** 9am-5pm Tue-Fri; 10am-5pm Sat, Sun. **Admission** DM8 combination ticket for all palace buildings; DM3 students, children; DM4 groups. Single admissions: *Historic rooms,* DM4; *Knobelsdorff Flügel* DM3; DM1.50 concs. *Neringbau, Schinkel or Belvedere* DM2.50; DM1.50 concs. *Mausoleum* DM1; 50pfg concs. *Galerie der Romantik* DM4; DM2 concs. Free Sundays and holidays. Mausoleum closed Nov-March.

Queen Sophie-Charlotte was the impetus behind this sprawling palace and garden. Sophie's husband built it in 1695 as a modest summer home for the 'philosophical Queen'. Later kings also summered here, tinkering with and adding to the buildings. Unless you have a whole day to spend, it's best to tackle only a part of the Schloß. The central and oldest section houses the bedrooms of its original residents, Sophie-Charlotte and her husband. The apartments can only be seen during guided tours in German. English group tours can be arranged several weeks in advance. Visitors may wander through the upper level unguided. Highlights of the newer west wing are the living quarters of Frederick the Great, including his collection of eighteenth-century paintings. The Romantic Gallery downstairs includes the beautifully bleak work of Caspar David Friedrich, alongside the paintings of Schinkel and lesser German romantics. The Schinkel Pavilion, named after the famous architect who designed it, used to be a small summer house. The house, built in 1825, contains sculpture, drawings, furniture, porcelain and paintings by Schinkel. The Belvedere, a former tea house, contains three storeys of porcelain from the eighteenth and nineteenth centuries, including some by KPM Berlin, once porcelain-makers to the kaiser. Carl Gotthard Langhans, architect of the Brandenburg Gate, designed the Belvedere in 1788. The Mausoleum contains the tombs of Queen Louise, King Friedrich Wilhelm III, Kaiser Wilhelm I and Kaiserin Augusta.

## Kreuzberg

### Martin-Gropius-Bau

*Stresemannstraße 110, Kreuzberg, 10963 (25 48 60). S1, S2 Anhalter Bahnhof.* **Open** 10am-8pm Tue-Sun. **Admission** DM6; DM4 concs.

The Martin-Gropius-Bau is named after its architect, uncle of Max Bauhaus, Walter G. It was built in 1881 and is the permanent home of the Jewish department of the Berlin Museum, plus host to several temporary exhibitions. It's an ideal space for large-scale exhibitions, like a recent study of Japan opening up to the west or the pace-setting Metropolis and Zeitgeist shows. The Berlinische Galerie, part of the Gropius-Bau, usually exhibits contemporary art.

### Museum Haus am Checkpoint Charlie

*Friedrichstraße 44, Kreuzberg, 10969 (251 10 31). U6 Kochstraße.* **Open** 9am-10pm daily. **Admission** DM7.50; DM4.50 concs for groups of ten or more.

An essential trip for anyone interested in the Wall. The muse-um opened not long after the GDR government constructed the Berlin Wall in 1961 with the purpose of documenting the grisly events that were then taking place. The exhibition charts the history of the Wall, and gives details of the ingenious ways people escaped from the GDR – as well as exhibiting some of the contraptions that were used, such as suitcases and a car with a propeller. There's a display about non-violent revolutions – including information on Mahatma Gandhi, Lech Walesa and the 1989 upheaval in East Germany – plus an excellent exhibition of art by people from all over the world, showing what the Wall meant to them.

### Museum für Verkehr und Technik (Museum of Transport and Technology)

*Trebbiner Straße 9, Kreuzberg, 10963 (25 48 40). U1, U7 Möckernbrücke.* **Open** 9am-5.30pm Tue-Fri; 10am-6pm Sat, Sun. **Admission** DM4; DM3 concs; DM1 groups of ten or more.

Opened in 1983 in one of the workshops of the once thriving Anhalter Bahnhof (train station), this is a quirky collection of industrial objects. On view are exhibitions on the industrial revolution; street, rail and air traffic; computer technology and printing technology. Oddities, such as vacuum cleaners from the twenties and a large collection of sextants, make this a fun spot for implement enthusiasts.

### Topographie des Terrors

*Stresemannstraße 110, Kreuzberg, 10963 (25 48 67 03). S1, S2 Anhalter Bahnhof.* **Open** 10am-6pm Tue-Sun. **Admission** free.

The Topography of Terror is a piece of waste ground where once stood the Prinz Albrecht Castle, headquarters of the Gestapo. It was from here that the Holocaust was directed, and where the Germanisation of the east was dreamt up. You can walk around – small markers explain what was where – before examining the fascinating exhibit documenting the history of Nazi state terror. This is housed in what used to be some cells in the basement of the Gestapo complex. The catalogue (DM10 and available in English) is excellent.

## Tiergarten

### Kunstgewerbe (Museum of Applied Art)

*Matthäikirchplatz, Tiergarten, 10875 (266 29 02). U1 Kurfürstenstraße.* **Open** 9am-5pm Tue-Fri; 10am-5pm Sat, Sun. **Admission** DM4; DM2 concs.

Opposite the Philharmonie, the Kunstgewerbe holds a collection of European arts and crafts from the Middle Ages to the present day. The top attractions are the ecclesiastical goldsmith works from the eleventh to the fifteenth century.

### Musikinstrumenten Museum

*Tiergartenstraße 1, Tiergarten, 10785 (25 48 10). Bus 129, 148, 248, 341.* **Open** 9am-5pm Tue-Fri; 10am-5pm Sat, Sun. **Admission** DM4; DM2 concs; free children under 12; free Sun.

Over 2,200 string, keyboard, wind and percussion instruments dating back to the 1500s are crammed into this small museum next to the Philharmonie. The place comes alive during tours, when guides play such obsolete instruments as the Kammerflugel (Bach played one in the court of Friedrich The Great). Concerts are held on the first Saturday of the month.

### Neue Nationalgalerie

*Potsdamer Straße 50, Tiergarten, 10785 (266 26 51). U1 Kurfürstenstraße.* **Open** 9am-5pm Tue-Fri; 10am-5pm Sat, Sun. **Admission** DM4; DM2 concs.

The modern building, designed in the sixties by former Bauhaus president Ludwig Mies van der Rohe, houses German and international paintings from the twentieth century. It's strong on German expressionists and surrealists, like Max Beckmann, Otto Mueller, Ernst Ludwig Kirchner,

Paul Klee and Max Ernst. The Neue Sachlichkeit is also well represented by George Grosz and Otto Dix. The Germans aside, many major twentieth-century artists are featured: Picasso, de Chirico, Léger, Munch, Wols, Dubuffet and Dali, to name a few. However, the pleasure of the gallery really is in discovering lesser known artists like Ludwig Meidner, whose post WWI apocalyptic landscapes exert the great, garish power of the most action-packed Marvel comic centrefold. NB: its nineteenth-century exhibits have been moved to the **Alte Nationalgalerie** on the **Museumsinsel** (*see above*).

# Elsewhere in the West

## Allied Museum

*Outpost, Clayallee 135, Zehlendorf, 14195 (813 41 61)* U1 Oskar-Helene-Heim **Open** 10am-6pm Tue-Sun, 10am-8pm Wed. **Admission** free.
The Allied forces arrived as conquerors and left many Berliners with tears in their eyes when they went home. Housed in what used to be a cinema for US forces, this museum opened with a temporary exhibition about the changing role of the military. At time of writing, it was clear that the Allied Museum would continue to exist, but precisely where and in what form were still open to question. It'll probably stay here, but check before setting out.

## Bauhaus Archiv-Museum für Gestaltung

*Klingelhöferstraße 13-14, Tiergarten, 10785 (25 40 02-0). Bus 109, 116, 124, 129.* **Open** 10am-5pm Mon, Wed-Sun. **Admission** DM4; DM2 concs.
Walter Gropius, founder of the Bauhaus school, designed this modern white building, located just across the canal from the Grand Hotel Esplanade. The museum presents furniture, ceramics, metal objects, prints, sculptures, photographs and sketches created in the Bauhaus workshop from 1919-1933. Designs and models by Gropius, Ludwig Mies van der Rohe and paintings and drawings by Paul Klee, Georg Muche, Wassily Kandinsky and Oskar Schlemmer are also on show. A computer exhibition in German and English provides a useful context to the museum. There's a café, plus a library with Bauhaus documents (open 9am-1pm Mon-Fri).

## Bröhan-Museum

*Schloßstraße 1a, Charlottenburg, 14059 (321 40 29). U2 Sophie-Charlotte-Platz/U7 Richard-Wagner-Platz.* **Open** 10am-6pm Tue-Sun. **Admission** DM4; DM2 concs.
The Bröhan Museum, across from the Egyptian Museum, offers a welcome break for those weary of tourist traps. This quiet, private museum contains three levels of Art Nouveau and Art Deco pieces that businessman Karl Bröhan began collecting in the sixties. The wide array of paintings, furniture, porcelain, silver, vases and sculptures dates from 1890-1939. Hans Baluschek's paintings of social life in the twenties and thirties, and Willy Jaeckel's series of portraits of women, are the pick of the bunch.

## Deutsches Rundfunkmuseum (German Broadcasting Museum)

*Hammarskjöldplatz 1, Charlottenburg, 14055 (302 81 86). U2 Theodor-Heuss-Platz.* **Open** 10am-5pm Mon, Wed-Sun. **Admission** DM3; DM1.50 concs.
Located at the base of the Funkturm (radio tower), this museum tells the history of radio and television in Germany. Most compelling are the radio reports of Hitler's appointment as Chancellor in 1933 and his speeches to the German people. While you're there, take a ride up the Funkturm for a view of Berlin (DM5; DM3 students). A restaurant on a lower level provides an expensive view of the city.

## Gedenkstätte Haus der Wannsee-Konferenz

*Am Grossen Wannsee 56-58, Zehlendorf, 14109 (80 500125). S1, S3, S7 S-Bahnhof Wannsee, then bus 114.* **Open** 10am-6pm Tue-Fri; 2-6pm Sat, Sun. **Admission** free.
On January 20, 1942, a gruesome collection of prominent Nazis – Heydrich and Eichmann among them – gathered at this villa on the Wannsee to draw up plans for the Final Solution. Today, it has been converted into a place of remembrance, with a standing photo-exhibition about the conference and its consequences. Call in advance if you want to join an English-language tour, otherwise all information is in German.

## Georg-Kolbe-Museum

*Sensburger Allee 25, Charlottenburg, 14055 (304 21 44). Bus 149, 105; or a 15-minute walk from U2 Theodor-Heuss-Platz.* **Open** 10am-5pm Tue-Sun. **Admission** DM3; DM1.50 concs.
Georg Kolbe's former studio in a quiet neighbourhood of Charlottenburg has been transformed into a showcase for his work. The Berlin sculptor, regarded as Germany's best in the twenties, mainly focused on naturalistic human figures. The museum features examples of his earlier, graceful pieces, as well as his later sombre and larger-than-life works created in accordance with the ideals of the Nazi regime. One of his most famous pieces, *Figure for Fountain*, is outside in the sculpture garden.

## Käthe-Kollwitz-Museum

*Fasanenstraße 24, Wilmersdorf, 10719 (882 52 10). U3 Uhlandstraße.* **Open** 11am-6pm Wed-Sun. **Admission** DM6; DM3 concs.
Käthe Kollwitz's powerful work embraces the full spectrum of life, from the joy of motherhood to the pain of death. Charcoal sketches and sculptures by this Berlin artist (1867-1945) are housed in a beautiful four-storey villa on one of Berlin's most elegant streets. Guided tours on request.

## Postmuseum Berlin

*An der Urania 15, Schöneberg, 10787 (21 71 17 17). U1, U2 Wittenbergplatz or U4 Nollendorfplatz.* **Open** 9am-4.30pm Mon-Thur; 10am-4.30pm Sat, Sun. **Admission** free.
A potentially boring subject is presented in a captivating manner at the Postmuseum. Using several short videos, exhibits and displays for kids to push, pull and turn, the museum traces the Prussian-German postal system from the late nineteenth century to the present day. The videos of Berlin's city life in the past century are intriguing and provide an insightful glimpse into the city's pre-war history. Who said stamp-collecting was dull?

## Reichstag

*Platz der Republik, Tiergarten, 10557 (397 70). S1, S2 Unter den Linden.* **Open** 10am-5pm Tue-Sun. **Admission** free.
The Reichstag was the main government building before World War II. Until the government returns (which it still plans to do), it's still home to an exhibition chronicling German history from 1848 to the present, entitled *Questions on German History*. Historical documents, photographs, dioramas – even old radio programmes – knit together the story of modern Germany. Since the annotation and broadcasts are in German, be sure to borrow a headset that provides an English commentary. There are also booklets in English available (DM6).

## Zucker Museum

*Amrumer Straße 32, Wedding, 13353 (31 42 75 74). U9 Amrumer Straße.* **Open** 9am-5pm Mon-Wed; 11am-6pm Sun. **Admission** DM4; DM2 concs.
Any museum devoted to the chemistry, history and political importance of sugar would have problems thrilling the punters. But the Zucker does have a very unusual collection of sugar paraphernalia. Most interesting is a slide show on the slave trade, on which the sugar industry was so dependent. Something to ponder on over a coffee.

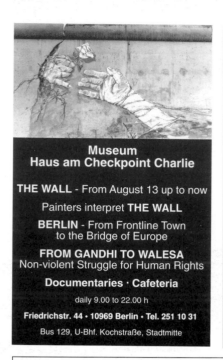

# Arts & Entertainment

# Media

*Germany has no national media centre, but the communications scene in Berlin is vibrant, varied and vociferous.*

Berlin is Germany's greatest newspaper city, rivalling London in the number of daily and weekly papers published within its borders. But thanks mostly to the Cold War and partly to Germany's postwar passion for spreading the wealth and busting up power bases, Berlin is no real media centre. Not like it was in the twenties and thirties, anyway. Broadly speaking, film is in Munich, TV is in Cologne, magazine publishing is in Hamburg, and advertising agencies are in Frankfurt am Main. Still, because Berlin has the country's largest urban population and, arguably, its most politicised, the media sector in Berlin is vibrant, varied and vociferous.

In newspaper publishing, Axel Springer's quality daily *Die Welt* has moved publishing operations from Bonn to Berlin. The move was more symbolic than substantive, as the paper continues to provide a conservative, turgid read on national and international news. In film and TV, the historic DEFA studios south of Berlin in Potsdam have been overhauled and are attracting production budgets on big international projects. Also in TV, a Berlin-based, all-news cable channel called n-tv is recording weak audiences and big losses, in spite of co-ownership by US media giants CNN and Time-Warner.

The arrival of the government by the end of the decade will swell the ranks of correspondents here, and already membership of Berlin's foreign press association has reached a postwar high. International editions of British and American news weeklies and newspapers are readily available in most downtown newsagents, particularly those near the Zoo and Friedrichstraße railway stations. As far as local English-language publications go, there is *Checkpoint Berlin*, a monthly listings magazine published in partnership with *Time Out* and *Zitty*, a German-language fortnightly.

## Newspapers

### National

#### BILD
Germany's answer to Britain's *The Sun*. For over 40 years this broadsheet has done its best to give the gutter press ('yellow' or 'boulevard' press in German) an even worse reputation than it already has, with sensationalist, heavily biased (right-wing) reporting. In the sixties *BILD*, and its owners Springer Verlag, became the targets of left-wing protesters.

It is still seen as thoroughly politically incorrect to be caught catching up on the latest Windsor tattle from the the pages of *BILD*. But despite recent setbacks (it has yet to take off in east Germany), it remains far and away the country's biggest -selling newspaper, with a circulation of over four million. Its main editorial offices are in Hamburg, although Berlin editions are tailored for the local readership.

#### Die Welt
Conceived to be the quality flagship daily of the Springer publishing empire, *Die Welt* is Germany's only thoroughly national daily, in the sense that it has no real hometown. Its recent move of editorial offices to Berlin was supposed to be accompanied by a full-fledged relaunch designed to stem a dwindling readership. So far, the broadsheet hasn't caused much damage on the local press scene, probably because its readers remain concentrated around Bonn.

#### Frankfurter Allgemeine Zeitung (FAZ)
Dry, thorough and conservative, the *FAZ* is the daily read for the well-educated (you need to be to plough through its articles) and the powerful. If you want to find out what's on the minds of the people who govern Germany, read the *FAZ*.

#### Frankfurter Rundschau
The left-liberal bible of the 1968 generation of radicals still maintains a presence on the national newspaper scene. Although, just as its readers have aged and settled down, so the *Rundschau* reads more and more like a journal for teachers and lecturers. It's good on long, in-depth pieces and for amusing foreign coverage.

#### Süddeutsche Zeitung
Based in Munich, the *Süddeutsche* is required reading for the liberal chattering classes of southern Germany and, as a result, not so popular in northerly Berlin. The light-hearted and sarcastic *Streiflicht* column on the front page is an unusual journalistic treat in a country which normally adopts a heavy-handed approach to journalism. The paper is much praised for its foreign coverage.

#### Handelsblatt
Germany's business and financial daily, *Handelsblatt* is very good on up-to-date company information and profiles, though probably too stolid for anyone but the most committed economic or market analyst.

### Local

#### BZ (Bild Zeitung)
*BILD*'s stablemate is Berlin's most popular read. If the *BZ* were to take human form, it would be a middle-aged, male bigot, who spends most of his time sitting in the pub inflicting his opinions on anyone within earshot. Whether readers are attracted by its slightly dated, saucy editorial content, its politician-bashing leaders or the numerous pages of adverts for call-girls is unclear.

#### der tageszeitung (taz)
Set up in the late seventies as an alternative paper, the *taz* is the house journal of the dissenting, ecologically aware left

*Billion-dollar German media conglomerate*
**Axel Springer** *keeps the presses rolling.*

and anyone who walks around with a dog on a string and ponces money at underground stations. Numerous financial crises later, the *taz* survives as a genuinely original, though often annoyingly shrill voice in the cluttered newspaper world. But it's very good on local Berlin feature stories.

### Der Tagesspiegel

The 'old aunt' of the Berlin newspaper scene. Independently owned until recently, the *Tagesspiegel* rejoices in always being just slightly boring and just slightly behind the times with its well-meaning, liberal coverage of events. In the years preceding the fall of the Wall, the *Tagesspiegel* was the last local refuge for readers fleeing a market dominated by Springer, which then sold 74 per cent of all papers in the city. Since reunification it has made a partially successful bid to become more cosmopolitan and authoritative. A bid to recover its postwar national readership has so far failed; it's having enough trouble keeping its previously loyal readership from straying to the *Berliner Zeitung*.

### Berliner Morgenpost

Nicknamed the 'Mottenpost' – the moth ball post – this is another Springer title. It caters for a middlebrow, conservative audience in west Berlin and, because of its professionalism in local news-gathering, never quite manages to shake off a provincial feel. Its Sunday classified section is the prime source for finding flats, provided you're at the head of the queue at the newsagents when it's delivered in the wee hours.

### Berliner Zeitung

Once an organ of the East German Communist Party, the *Berliner Zeitung* was sold to Robert Maxwell and west German publishers G&J, who also produce *Stern*. When the Big Man went overboard, G&J quickly snapped up his share. Now the paper is one of the city's top broadsheets, though it owes this largely to subscribers in east Berlin. The

journalists, however, are mostly western. Its liberal editorial policy has already won it a new readership in the west, among those who excuse its sometimes sloppy reporting habits in a show of solidarity with east Berliners.

## Weekly

### Die Zeit

A heavyweight read for the liberal intelligentsia. Former Chancellor Helmut Schmidt is one of *Die Zeit's* publishing directors. Pertinent and well written, but difficult to finish before the next issue lands on the newsstands with a thud on Thursday morning.

### Die Woche

A new, lighter version of *Die Zeit*. Slimmed down, with four-colour and snappier graphics, *Die Woche* specialises in in-depth treatment of a title story theme, plus analysis of the week's events. Like newcomer newsweekly *Focus*, *Die Woche* seems to be proving to German readers that less can be more.

## Magazines

### Focus

This is the upstart news weekly which most said would never fly in Germany: a short, snappy read, colourful pictures, and useful, easy-to-understand charts and graphics. Focus covers the same news but comes to a point much more quickly than its verbose, established rival *Der Spiegel*, making it more suitable for a day and age where there's (sadly) little leisure time left over for extensive reading.

### Prinz

A monthly, glossy Berlin mag aimed at young scene wannabes, with listings and reviews of events in the city, as well as features and a gossip column. Actually, a regional edition of the same *Prinz* magazine in other German cities.

### Der Spiegel

A weekly current affairs magazine which, since it was set up after WWII, has been required reading for anyone interested in German politics. Its success (over a million copies sold each week) has led to its tone becoming increasingly arrogant and cynical. Nearly all its readers complain about the sweeping, smart-arse style and say they will stop taking it – before heading off to buy the latest issue on Monday.

### Stern

The embarrassing saga in the early eighties of the faked 'Hitler Diaries' still hangs over *Stern*, which serves up a colourful mix of reportage and picture-stories linked to politics and current affairs. Because of its deep pockets, it's still good at paying for the Big Story, although it often ruins this with sloppy attention to factual detail. *Stern* sells nearly a million copies every Thursday.

## Listings Magazines

### Berlin Programm

This monthly compendium of what's on in Berlin is useful even if you can't read German. It is exhaustive in its coverage of main events, shows and exhibitions, while being more clearly organised for the first-time reader than other listings magazines. No journalism though, and only PR photos.

### Checkpoint Berlin

The city's only English-language monthly is a mix of features and listings. It includes a useful City Guide with maps and tips for getting around Berlin and is available at English-language bookshops, downtown newsagents and hotels. Backed by *Time Out* and *Zitty*.

### Tip

A colourful fortnightly which covers most events in Berlin. *Tip*'s features are often good, and it's generally considered a little more upmarket (read: less socially concerned) and mainstream than *Zitty*. Its strengths are music and film, and it appears every second Wednesday.

### Zitty

Also fortnightly, but appears in alternate weeks to *Tip*. The coarser paper, rare use of colour and deliberate slap-dash editorial tone go towards giving *Zitty* a rough-and-ready feel which belies its success as Berlin's best-selling listings mag. *Zitty* is known for its campaigning style of journalism. Both *Zitty* and *Tip* have settled into a comfortable middle age along with their original readers. One consequence: neither is seen as meeting the needs of the teenage market.

## Television

In the mid-eighties Berlin became one of the first German cities to be cabled. Today, some 900,000 households are plugged into the system and can receive up to 30 channels. Non-subscribers and east Berliners have to make do with aerial reception (six channels) or get a satellite dish.

On the whole, German TV is lamentable. In the late eighties, media laws changed allowing private ownership of TV channels, and when these arrived they brought with them truckloads of old US sitcoms and drama series. They also introduced 'strip programming', meaning they broadcast shows of interest to bored housewives during the day, family fare after dinner, and cartoons on Saturday morning for the kids. The private channels became an instant hit, and advertisers took notice. After decades of treating both advertisers and viewers with the kind of arrogance that accompanies monopoly status, the politicised public networks, **ARD** and **ZDF**, scrambled to maintain audiences. Today the situation has stabilised somewhat, but, in general, German TV has taken a sloppy dive from the ten-metre platform into the mass market.

Sender Freies Berlin (**SFB** or Radio Free Berlin) is the local affiliate of national network ARD. It trades its own programming to other ARD members throughout the country, and broadcasts its own daily programme on the **B1** channel. A highlight is its nightly round-up of local news, *Abendschau*, at 7.25pm. National nightly news on ARD is called the *Tagesschau* and is broadcast at 8pm. At 10.30pm comes news analysis on *Tagesthemen*. ZDF's nightly news, *heute*, starts at 7pm, followed by analysis at 9.45pm on *heute-journal*.

The two private TV channels which 'revolutionised' the medium in Germany (because they made audience ratings a factor in both the advertising price and programming equation) are **RTL** and **Sat 1**. Both specialise in what the masses want to see most: sport, action, thrillers, porn and talk shows where people bite each other's heads off. There's lots more on Berlin TV. **1A** is a novelty. The first private, regional TV channel in the country, it's low budget but close to its downmarket audiences. **n-tv** is Germany's answer to **CNN**, and **arte**, on cable, broadcasts first-rate cultural stuff from all over Europe. Also on cable are plenty of English-language services, including CNN, **NBC-Super Channel** (which carries *NBC Nightly News* from the States, and the *Financial Times Business Today* show from London), and **MTV Europe**.

## Radio

Berlin is home to the most competitive and largest regional radio market in the country. Already cluttered airwaves have now become completely jammed, leaving everyone a smaller slice of the advertising pie. The result: low-budget radio becomes no-budget radio. One arrival on the ether last year, **Radio JFK**, doesn't even bother with disc jockeys: it's all pre-recorded swing music and soft jazz. Other stations to have joined the maelstrom are **Radio Energy**, **Rock Radio 2**, **Klassik-Radio**, **RTL** and **Kiss FM**; they're now competing with stalwarts such as the broadcaster SFB (public channels spanning classical to rock, and a new Radio MuliCulti channel) and the eastern **Berliner Rundfunk** (the old East German radio station which now has a blend of music, news and general interest programmes with an eastern bias). Market leader is private radio **Hundert, 6** which makes no claim to be anything other than a broadcast version of Berlin's lowbrow but immensely popular *BZ* tabloid. There are some musically tuned-in jocks with enlightened shows on some stations, but they are rare fish in a vast sea of mediocrity. Overall audiences are dwindling, in spite of the proliferation of stations.

**BBC World Service** comes in on 90.2, and the **Voice of America Europe** can be found via cable only on 106.50.

# FM Radio Frequencies

**BBC World Service** 90.2
**Berliner Rundfunk** 91.4
**Deutsche Welle**
**(foreign language)** 106.95
**Deutschlandradio** 89.6
**Fritz** 102.6
**Hundert, 6** 100.6
**Kiss FM** 98.45
**Klassik-Radio** 101.3
**Radio B Zwei (SFB)** 92.4
**Radio Energy** 103.4
**Radio JFK** 98.2
**RTL** 104.6

# Cabaret

*From glitter to gloss, Berlin is a boom-town for the Popular Art.*

Despite more than half a century's dramatic shifts in cultural climes, the notion persists of a Sally Bowles Berlin replete with decadent dandies and notorious night-time naughtiness. It really isn't like that any more. But though the Kit Kat Klub may be no more than a Hollywooden memory, the tradition of Kabarett in this, the city of its Golden Age, is alive and well and flourishing.

A diverse assortment of venues houses shows that vary from the usual glitz and feathered fare you can find in the tourist traps of any major city to political pastiche and alternative comedy in tiny storefront bars. At every level, Varieté is back with a vengeance. Expect clowns and comedians, acrobats and illusionists, conjurors and can-can.

We've organised the venues below according to how established they are. Though the traditional venues hold their own, and since 1991 a new wave has become a solid presence on the scene, right now the spotlight shines brightest on the city's alternative horizon. That's how Berlin is right now. And it may just be that we are entering our second Golden Age.

## Old Guard

These are venues featuring the more traditional kinds of revue: ie lots and lots of dancing girls. Most serve drinks and the tab can be high.

### Chez Nous
*Marburger Straße 14, Tiergarten, 10789 (213 18 10). S3, S5, S6, S7, S9/U2, U9 Zoologischer Garten.* **Open** 7.30pm-1am daily. **Shows** 8.30pm and 11pm daily. **Admission** DM15 (DM35 minimum drinks bill). **No credit cards.**
Chez Nous's rather mild drag (or Travestie) revue still gives you the feeling you've glimpsed a little of Berlin's saucy nightlife. The only established drag cabaret left in the city.

### Friedrichstadtpalast City Lights Show
*Friedrichstraße 107, Mitte, 10117 (23 262 474). S2, S3, S5, S6, S7, S9/U6 Friedrichstraße.* **Open** box office noon-7pm daily. **Shows** 8pm Tue-Sun; *matinées* 4pm Sat. **Admission** DM14-DM77. **No credit cards.**
A dinosaur of dazzle and kitsch – sort of East Vegas – this enormous theatre stages some of the most spectacular showstoppers in Berlin.

### Friedrichstadtpalast Kleine Revue
*Friedrichstraße 107, Mitte, 10117 (23 262 474). S2, S3, S5, S6, S7, S9/U6 Friedrichstraße.* **Open** 6pm-4am Tue-Sat. **Shows** 10.30pm. **Admission** DM20-DM70. **No credit cards.**
War-horse of the former GDR's privileged classes (and small-

er sibling to the upstairs mainstage – *see above*); the goings-on can get rather tacky.

### Kleine Nachtrevue
*Kurfürstenstraße 116, Tiergarten, 12105 (218 89 50). U1, U2, U3 Wittenbergplatz.* **Open** 9pm-4am Mon-Sat. **Shows** lasting for 40 minutes on and off throughout the evening, Sat two longer shows starting at 10.30pm and 12.30am. **Admission** DM10 Mon-Thur; DM20 Sat. **Credit** AmEx, DC, V.
A gem. Opened by Sylvia Schmid, a talented *chanteuse* who also appears in the show, the club is intimate, sexy and as close to Old Berlin as one can get.

### La Vie en Rose
*Europa-Center, Tiergarten, 10789 (323 60 06). S3, S5, S6, S7, S9/U2, U9 Zoologischer Garten.* **Open** box office 10am-midnight Tue-Sun. **Shows** 9pm Sun-Thur; 10pm Fri-Sat. **Admission** DM25-DM60. **Credit** AmEx, D, EC, V.
This small nightclub in the bowels of the Europa-Center offers a polished revue in a lesser Vegas vein.

## Vanguard

Established venues offering a more creative approach to cabaret. Prices are generally cheaper, though, again, any alcohol can up the ante.

### Bar Jeder Vernunft
*Spiegelzelt at the Freien Volksbühne, Schaperstrasse 24, Wilmersdorf, 10719 (883 15 82). U1, U9 Spichernstraße.* **Open** box office 11am-6pm daily. **Shows** 8.30pm daily; 11pm Fri, Sat. **Admission** DM14-65. **Closed** Sept. **No credit cards.**
Bar Jeder Vernunft occupies this splendid mirrored tent venue and serves up top-notch Varieté with a free late show on the weekends. Very popular and justifiably so.

### BKA (Berliner Kabaret Anstalt)
*Mehringdamm 34, Kreuzberg, 10961 (251 01 12). U6, U7 Mehringdamm.* **Open** box office noon-8.30pm Thur-Sun. **Shows** 8pm Thur-Sun. **Admission** DM19-DM35. **No credit cards.**

*Drag yourself along to* **Chez Nous**.

This comfortable first-floor venue has a fine reputation, with new shows every two to three weeks. Could be anything from a drag act to a satirical revue. BKA also runs a tent venue next to the Neue Nationalgalerie which offers similar fare and a disco on Saturday nights.

### Kartoon
*Französische Straße 24, Mitte, 10117 (29 99 305). U6 Französische Straße.* **Open** 6pm-late Tue-Sun. **Shows** 9pm. **Admission** DM25; DM10 concs. **No credit cards.**
Now in its twentieth year, Michael Fülle's friendly club is the homestead of political cabaret and social satire. Probably not much fun, though, unless you're fluent in German and well-versed in local politics.

### Wintergarten-Varieté
*Potsdamerstraße 96, Tiergarten, 10785 (262 70 70). U1, U15 Kurfürstenstraße.* **Open** 7.30pm-midnight daily. **Shows** 8pm Mon-Sat; 3.30pm and 8.30pm Sun. **Admission** DM39-DM73. **No credit cards.**
The best of Old World-style Varieté (in keeping with the original Wintergarten of Mistinguett fame), a magical, red-plush revue with slick international performers. The waitresses are dressed twenties-style, the waiters wear rouge and the walls of this 600-seat theatre are lined with memorabilia from the golden age of Varieté. Booking recommended.

## Avant-Garde

These venues offer what is new and most exciting. Quality varies but surprise is guaranteed and the stars of tomorrow shine here.

### Chamäleon Varieté
*Rosenthaler Straße 40/41, Mitte, 10178 (282 7118). S3, S5, S6, S7, S9 Hackescher Markt.* **Open** for information 10am-6pm Mon-Fri; entrance from 7.30pm, closes 4am. **Shows** evening show begins 8.30pm Wed-Sun; entry to midnight show from 11.30pm. **Admission** DM28 Wed, Thur, Sun; DM32 Fri, Sat; midnight show DM18. **No credit cards.**
Undisputedly Berlin's most prestigious venue for Off-Kabarett and Varieté, the still young Chamäleon is casual, friendly and classy. New artists perform at the two midnight shows on Friday and Saturday. You can drink at the tables but smoking is not allowed.

### Famagusta
*Holsteinische Straße 48, Steglitz, 12163 (793 1129). U9 Walter-Schreiber-Platz.* **Shows** 7.30pm Sat. **Admission** DM5-12. **No credit cards.**
A café-cum-gallery-cum-crafts school that offers a cabaret night on Saturdays. Low key and strictly a local crowd.

### Scheinbar
*Monumentenstrasse 9, Schöneberg, 10829 (784 5539). U7/S1, S2 Yorckstraße.* **Open** 7pm Wed-Mon; box office 5pm Wed-Mon. **Shows** 8pm Mon, Wed, Thur; 9pm Fri-Sun. **Admission** DM15-25. **No credit cards.**
A tiny store-front theatre that presents Varieté at its popular best.

### Theater im Keller
*Weserstraße 211, Neukölln, 10247 (623 1452). U7, U8 Hermannplatz.* **Open** 8-10pm Fri, Sat. Phone for reservations. **Admission** DM30. **No credit cards.**
A minute corner theatre in the unexpected regions of Neukölln. The fare is often a drag revue and loads of fun.

### UFA Fabrik
*Viktoria Straße 10-18, Tempelhof, 12105 (75 50 30). U6 Ullsteinstraße.* **Open** *information* 10am-7pm daily. **Shows** between 8pm and 9.30pm. **Admission** prices vary, call for details. **No credit cards.**
Formerly the UFA Film Studios, now home to a colourful complex of theatres, cafés and galleries. There's always something interesting on and sometimes high-quality Varieté performances are staged.

*Those crazy folk at the* **Chamäleon Varieté**.

# Clubs

*Go bonkers in Gestapo bunkers or clatter about the pots and pans in old communist kitchens – the club scene may not be big but it's wild.*

For all that it's the legendary city of nightclubbing, bright white clubbing, Berlin actually doesn't have as many clubs as you might expect – partly because much of the action happens in bars. If you want to drink late in this town, you don't have to pay an entrance fee and go somewhere there's a dancefloor. Indeed, until a few years ago, it was difficult to find an interesting place to go dancing.

All that has changed since the fall of the Wall coincided with the arrival of acid house from the UK, and the Berlin techno scene exploded into spaces left over by the dismantling of border defences and the collapse of east German industry. **Tresor**, in the old safe deposit room of a long-demolished department store, deep under the wasteland of Potsdamer Platz, was the first important club. Later came **Planet**, in an old chalk factory on the Spree river, organised by the people who now run **E-Werk**.

In those days a whole new energy was sparking up the unifying city. A generation of young east Germans were free, for the first time, to take

their fill of sex, drugs and the new electronic music that was beginning to displace rock 'n' roll. What better sounds to celebrate the end of history than techno's throbbing soundtrack of self-conscious futurism, wrapped up in an apocalyptic beat?

Berlin's mood is different now, but techno has never stopped expanding. The annual Love Parade (*see chapter* **Berlin By Season**) in 1994 drew 120,000 people out to dance along the Ku'damm. Every weekend, all weekend, thousands of people party in old power stations, bunkers and factories. From Friday night through Monday morning you can go from club to club to club. Though perhaps past its peak, techno is an exciting scene and a living one – the DJs here don't just play the records, they often make them too.

Smaller, but also happening, is the hip hop, jazzy, funky scene. More and more places are opening up to serve rap and acid jazz to an increasingly enthusiastic public. In this area, and on the techno scene, the biggest and most important clubs are only open at weekends, while members

*Two Sundays a month, Gay T-Dances are held at Schöneberg's **Metropol**. See page 178.*

*The Glo chill-out party at **Tresor/Globus** winds on through Sunday to 5am. See page 175.*

of the same crowds will congregate at assorted bars during the week. For this reason, in those parts of this chapter organised by scene, we've included a bar or two among those venues which could more properly be described as clubs. Those places listed under 'Discos' each have a scene of their own.

Many clubs don't have a set closing time, and in those cases we've just listed the hour that they open. Bear in mind that many places, especially at the weekends, don't get going until well into the night. If you turn up at opening time you may well be the only person there. Where it seemed to make sense, we have also noted the hours when a given club peaks.

Finally, be warned. Like Berlin itself, the club scene is in a constant state of flux – particularly because it occupies so many odd spaces left behind by history that will soon be swallowed up by encroaching property development. By the time you read this, many of the clubs listed may have closed down, moved on or changed their names. It's best to check with the local listings press before setting out.

## Club & Party Information

Look for flyers littered around the clubs, or at record shops. *Very Important!* is a directory of the club scene which comes out occasionally and can be picked up free at clubs and shops. Watch out also for 1000 Clubzine, a free monthly broadsheet with party listings.

## Techno & House

### Bunker
*Corner of Albrechtstraße/Reinhardtstraße, Mitte, 10117 (no phone). U6 Oranienburger Tor.* **Open** from 11pm Fri, Sat; peaks midnight-6am. **Admission** DM15.
Don't be fooled by appearances: this forbidding Nazi bunker houses all manner of throbbing, decadent nightlife. Two floors of this reinforced concrete labyrinth are open every weekend. On the first floor you can strobe out to techno and breakbeats. Upstairs you can relax in the dim and misty ambient chambers. One Saturday a month, the fourth floor opens for Bunker's justly notorious Fetish & Fantasy parties. Dress code: skin, leather and PVC (further information from Boutique Hautnah, *Uhlandstraße 170, Charlottenburg, 10719 tel 882 3434*). The DM15 entrance includes access to the Ex-Kreuz Club next door (*see below*).

### Drama
*Oranienstraße 169, Kreuzberg, 10999 (614 5356). U2 Kottbusser Tor.* **Open** 9pm-5am daily. **Admission** free.
Small gay bar on Kreuzberg's main drag that's packed at the weekends, bustly on week nights, but still finds room to cram in the odd house DJ for their 'Drama Dance Events'. A good bet in midweek.

### Dubmission at Café Moskau
*Karl-Marx-Allee 34, Mitte, 10178 (279 6070). U5 Schillingstraße.* **Open** from 10pm-10am Fri; peaks 3am-7am. **Admission** DM10.
This former communist restaurant complex (also home to Saturday night's Plush – *see chapter* **Gay & Lesbian**) on Friday nights opens two floors to fun-seeking ravers, with a bar and dancefloor on each and a chill-out foyer in between. There are five DJs a night – three up and two down – and occasional live performances. Dubmission generally represents the lighter, more accessible end of Berlin Techno and the crowd is fairly young. Most of the night, it's heaving.

## Elektro

*Mauerstraße 15, Mitte, 10117 (no phone). U6
Stadtmitte.* **Open** Thur-Sun from 11pm. **Admission**
free.
People wander over from nearby E-Werk and Tresor to
take a break in this tiny bar/club. It's an insider place with
a family feel to it – get 20 in here and it's crowded. They
mostly play house and techno and on Sunday nights it's full
of DJs, who take turns at the turntables.

## E-Werk

*Wilhelmstraße between Leipziger Straße and
Zimmerstraße, Mitte, 10117 (rave line: 251 2012). S1,
S2 Potsdamer Platz.* **Open** from midnight
Sat; peaks 1am-5am Fri, 3am-8am Sat. **Admission**
DM15 Fri, DM20 Sat.
A former power station turned post-industrial pleasure
dome, E-Werk is the perfect party in no-man's location.
Berlin techno didn't start here; Tresor (*see below*) was the
first important club. But E-Werk is where techno has reached
its apotheosis and the club takes its place in the pantheon of
legendary scene-defining venues such as Manchester's
Haçienda, New York's Paradise Garage or London's Heaven
in their heydays. It's an impressive place. The main hall is
cavernous and white-tiled, with a large dancefloor, a sound
system good enough to exploit the acoustics and different
optical installations every week. There are also four bars
(including one serving coffee, tea and guarana), a mezzanine
bar restricted to club cardholders, and various comfortable
corners, with assorted pieces of old power station machinery scattered about. One drawback: no chill-out area. The
techno thud can only be escaped in the courtyard outside,
which is fine in summer but pretty miserable the rest of the
year. Fridays are Front Page parties, with international DJs.
Twirl on Saturdays is older, gayer and fuller and the music
veers from house to hardcore.

## Ex-Kreuz Club

*Albrechtstraße (cnr Reinhardtstraße), Mitte, 10117 (no
phone). U6 Oranienburger Tor.* **Open** from 10pm Wed-
Sat; from 10pm Sun. **Admission** DM10-DM15.
This small bar and club next door to and accessible from
within Bunker (*see above*) serves weird cocktails, has occasional Wednesday night performances and hosts fetish
parties every Saturday (these last, be warned, are difficult
to get into without an invite – look right, and be in front of
the door before 11pm. For further information, see the
listing for Bunker above). From 10am Sunday, Ex-Kreuz
is the Red Hot Chillout bar, an ideal place to cool down after
partying all night.

## Kitchen

*Fischerinsel 12, Mitte, 10179 (no phone). U2
Spittelmarkt.* **Open** from 11pm Fri. **Admission** DM10.
Weekly Fantasy World parties swing out of control in the
enormous kitchen of a former communist restaurant complex – look for the angular, pointy building on the corner of
Leipziger Straße. Ravers get seriously spaced out and cavort
among huge shiny metal tubs, once used for preparing hundreds of portions of cabbage and boiled potato. And you
never know, one of these days someone might get round to
starting a club in the old GDR nuclear bunker downstairs.

## Nautilus

*Görlitzer Straße 71, Kreuzberg, 10997 (618 7026). U1
Görlitzer Bahnhof.* **Open** 9am-5am daily. **Admission**
free.
A lovingly decorated ambient bar/café on two floors. Downstairs there's a chill-out area with submarine decor, comfy
beanbags and occasionally a DJ playing trance and ambient
music. Upstairs there's a bar that serves reasonably priced
drinks and guarana cocktails and another chill-out area in
the back. Sometimes they have special performances on
Sunday mornings, when everyone decants from the clubs.

## Tresor/Globus

*Leipziger Straße (cnr Wilhelmstraße), Mitte, 10117 (229
23 46). S1, S2 Potsdamer Platz.* **Open** from 10pm Wed;
from 11pm Fri-Sun. **Admission** free Wed, DM10 Fri-
Sun.
The first no-man's land techno club, Tresor opened in 1991
in a building on the surface that had once been a part of the
Globus bank, connecting via stairs and corridors to the sub-
terranean former safe deposit room of the pre-War Wertheim
department store. The prison-like metal bars, bunker atmosphere and harsh acoustics suited Techno in its early,
apocalyptic phase. But while these days it's still hardcore
downstairs, the larger Globus dancefloor offers lighter house
sounds, there's a quieter bar in the back, and outside there
are tables, with lights strung among the shrubbery and food
served from the grill. In summer DJs play outdoors from
around midday and all year round the Glo chill-out party on
Sunday evenings, where various DJs come to finish their
weekends, winds down through to 5am.

## Turbine Glogau

*Glogauer Straße 2, Kreuzberg, 10999 (782 4779). U1
Görlitzer Bahnhof.* **Open** 10pm-6am Wed-Sat; 6pm-6am
Sun. **Admission** DM5-DM10.
This smallish friendly club in the depths of Kreuzberg
(best accessible from round the corner in Wiener Straße –
take the entrance that leads through several interlocking
courtyards) creeps into the techno section for its Friday night
acid techno events, and its trance chill-out parties on
Sundays, which is where many die-hards choose to end
their weekends. Otherwise they offer S&M events on Wednesday nights, disco on Thursdays and soul and acid jazz
on Saturdays.

## Vereinsheim '1893'

*Michael-Kirch-Straße 19, Mitte, 10179 (no phone). U8
Heinrich-Heine-Straße.* **Open** from 11pm Fri; from 6am
Sat to around 5am Mon. **Admission** DM10.
This L-shaped former communist clubhouse on two floors
has a dancefloor and small bar downstairs, a bar and café
upstairs, and couches here and there. Friday night is house
music. The Saturday through Monday stretch is known as
Fade Out, which is what you'll do if you stay long enough.
It peaks between 5pm and midnight on Sunday. Two Thursdays a month, 1893 hosts the Kit Kat Club from 11pm, where
sexual fantasy outfits are the order of the night.

# Hip Hop/Acid Jazz/Rare Groove

## A-Bar

*Adalbertstraße 31, Mitte, 10179 (no phone). U8
Heinrich-Heine-Straße.* **Open** 11pm-5am Wed, Fri; peaks
1-3am. **Admission** free.
In the scruffy tiled basement of a squatted house, just north
of where the Wall used to separate Mitte from Kreuzberg,
A-Bar has a small dancefloor but beefy sound system and a
bar serving dirt-cheap drinks. A very underground kind of
place. There's no sign outside so look for the homies hanging out on the street, or listen for the beats from within.
On Wednesdays it's hip hop, on Fridays raggamuffin and,
increasingly, a bit of jungle techno.

## Boogaloo Groove Station

*Corner of Heinrich-Heine/Köpenicker Straße, Mitte,
10179 (279 1974). U8 Heinrich-Heine Straße.* **Open**
from 11pm Fri, Sat; peaks 1-3am. **Admission** DM10.
Entered from an unobtrusive door just inside the U-Bahn
station, Boogaloo was once the heart of Berlin hip hop.
Though past its heyday, it's still a lively place, with black
and chrome decor, a small dancefloor and various chill-out
corners. Fridays is hip hop and mellow beats; Saturdays
the sound is funky. There are also occasional live shows by
acts in the hip hop, jazzy, funky field. There's a relaxed

# Time Out

# City Guides

The essential guides to the world's most exciting cities

# AmsterdamBerlinLondon
# MadridNewYorkParis
# PragueRome

Available from February 1996
# Budapest & San Francisco

*DJ Mec Beth (left) unmasked at Kreuzberg's friendly* **Turbine Glogau***. See page 175.*

atmosphere and a nice bar, which seems to be mostly staffed by French people. And in Berlin, places where a lot of foreigners work are usually a good bet.

### Delicious Doughnuts Research

*Rosenthaler Straße 9, Mitte, 10119 (283 3021). U8 Weinmeisterstraße.* **Open** 10pm-5am Tue-Sun; peaks 1-3am Tue-Thur, Sun; 1-6am Fri, Sat. **Admission** DM5-8.
On the periphery of Mitte's nightlife district and one of the few clubs in this field with an adequately sized dancefloor and DJs all through the week. There's also a stage with some sofas and chairs and a small bar out the front, perhaps a little expensive for this part of town – and yes, they do sell doughnuts. The music is strictly funk, jazz and soul, with a tendency to push the envelope in a rarer-than-thou direction. This is a friendly, comfortable place, but get a hundred in and it's crowded.

### Friseur

*Kronenstraße 3, Mitte, 10117 (no phone). U2, U6 Stadtmitte.* **Open** 11pm-5am Fri, Sat; peaks midnight-4am. **Admission** DM5.
An old hairdresser's (some of the fittings remain) converted into a small jazz and hip hop club. There's a bar out front and a tiny dancefloor in the back, with the world's most primitive light show (one white light with a blue and red filter on a piece of string – someone gives it a spin from time to time). There are DJs only on Saturdays. On Fridays it's just a small, friendly bar.

### Schnabelbar

*Oranienstraße 31, Kreuzberg, 10999 (no phone). U1 Kottbusser Tor.* **Open** 10pm-5am daily. **Admission** free.
A happening bar with a small dancefloor that has DJs all through the week. Monday it's reggae and ragga, Tuesday

funk and soul. It's called Cosmic Jam on Wednesdays, which means a mix of house, hip hop and world music. Thursday is hip hop, reggae and a bit of jungle techno. Every Friday there's a different DJ. On Saturday expect to hear poppy hip hop, and jazz-funk aficionados should turn up on Sundays. It's heaving at the weekends but people still dance, a doorperson keeps the local crazies and winos at bay, and the frozen margaritas are excellent.

### Yam

*Former bus depot at Eichenstraße, Treptow, 12435 (no phone). U1 Schlesisches Tor.* **Open** 11pm-5am Fri, Sat; peaks 1-3am. **Admission** DM10 (more when there's a live act).
This huge old bus depot was a happening place in summer 1994, especially on Sundays from midday, when people played basketball outside or chilled to reggae and ragga and ate Jamaican food. On Saturdays there was hip hop, funk and the occasional live gig. At time of writing, though, its future was in doubt. Check local press for details.

## Discos

### 90°(Neunzig Grad/Ninety Degrees)

*Dennewitzstraße 37, Tiergarten, 10785 (262 89 84). U1 Kurfürstenstraße.* **Open** from 11pm Thur-Sun; peaks 1am-5am. **Admission** DM10.
90° has a large dancefloor room with a big bar, a small bar in the back where conversation is possible, and decor that changes frequently. Last time we looked it was giant architectural sketches on the walls of the main room. Fridays are soul and house and Saturdays just about anything apart from house and techno. On these nights there's a young, straight, well-heeled crowd. Dress smart. Thursdays and Sundays are gay nights, when house beats are interspersed with the occasional performance or talent contest.

### Abraxas

*Kantstraße 134, Charlottenburg, 10625 (312 94 93). U7 Wilmersdorfer Straße.* **Open** from 10pm Tue-Sun. **Admission** DM10.
A dusky, relaxed club where you don't have to dress up to get in and where unemployed academics, ordinary people and left-wingers populate the floor. Flirtation rules. Dance to funk, soul, Latino and jazz – like techno never happened.

### Afro Negro

*Waitzstraße 23, 10629 (323 1513). U7 Adenauerplatz.* **Open** 11pm-6am Tue-Sun. **Admission** DM10-DM15.
The scene from the old Orpheuo (*see below*) seems now to have moved to this newish club, which is trying to be the happening place of the Ku'damm area. It's kind of chic, frequented by many Africans and Afro-Americans, and the music is soul, funk and hip hop, often with someone rapping at the mike. There are two bars and a circular dancefloor. On Thursdays strange entertainment takes to the stage.

### Blue Note

*Courbièrestraße 13, Schöneberg, 10787 (214 12 37). U1 Nollendorfplatz.* **Open** from 10pm Tue-Sun. **Admission** free.
A successful mix of night café, bar and disco, where the mirrored wall enlarges one of Berlin's tiniest dancefloors and the light interior reveals designer clothes. Modern soul and dance music.

### bronx

*Wiener Straße 34, Kreuzberg, 10999 (611 84 45). U1 Görlitzer Bahnhof.* **Open** from 10pm daily. **Admission** DM5.
If the bronx ever dies the Kreuzberg that everyone knows and loves will have passed away. The police have tried to close this club several times because of drug problems, but

*Try Saturday's Pop Club at the **Knaack Club**.*

somehow it has survived. The same old records by the same old bands fill the dancefloor: the Rolling Stones, The Doors, Nina Hagen, even Alex Harvey. The world of the alternative, freaky hippy crowd would fall apart if the DJ ever dared to play Madonna.

### Eimer
*Rosenthaler Straße 68, Mitte, 10119 (282 7440). U8 Weinmeisterstraße.* **Open** *from 11pm Fri, Sat.* **Admission** DM10.
First-floor club with a dancefloor room, bar and chill-out corner in the back – all of it decorated with rambling, spiny sculptures and squiggly day-glo paintings that sit somewhat oddly as background for mostly soul and funk sounds. A lively place with strange toilets.

### Far Out
*Kurfürstendamm 156 (Lehniner Platz), Wilmersdorf, 10709 (32 00 07 23). U7 Adenauerplatz.* **Open** *from 10pm Tue-Sun.* **Admission** DM5.
A huge illuminated picture of Bhagwan Rajineesh watches over dancers at Far Out. A happy, youngish crowd dances the night away at this clean and bright no-smoking disco. The music is far from far out: a curious mix of German pop, soul and bland English/American rock and pop. Nowhere else do DJs remind dancers to put their glasses down safely.

### Fou-Na-Na
*Bachstraße 475, 10555 (391 2442). S3, S5, S6, S7, S9 Tiergarten.* **Open** *from 11pm.* **Admission** DM5-DM10.
Occasional reggae concerts are held at this club in the arches under the S-Bahn line. Otherwise most of the music is African, like the clientèle, mixed with reggae, pop and jazz.

### Franz-Club
*Schönhauser Allee 36-39, Prenzlauer Berg, 10435 (442 82 03). U2 Eberswalder Straße.* **Open** *9pm-5am daily.* **Admission** varies.
Bar, disco, summer garden, CD and postcard shop and live music every single day of the year: it's all here at the Franz-Club, a favoured gathering place for east Berliners.

### Golgatha
*Auf dem Kreuzberg, Kreuzberg, 10965 (785 24 53). U7, S2 Yorckstraße.* **Open** *Apr-Sept 10pm-6am daily.* **Admission** free.
Find your way through Viktoriapark by going through the Katzbachstraße gate and heading west. Sit on benches in the beer garden, or dance to mainstream music from the seventies, eighties and nineties, plus every Prince song ever. It's cosy and comfortable, and you don't have to be stylish to get in – which means it's sometimes not very stylish at all.

### Knaack Club
*Greifswalder Straße 224, 10405 (426 23 51). S8, S10, S85, S86 Greifswalder Straße.* **Open** *from 10pm.* **Admission** DM4.
A three-storey venue whose assortment of interlocking spaces offers a stage for live acts (usually indie-rock), several bars, one sitting room, and a disco for a variety of different dance nights (try Saturday's 'Pop Club' with bonkers English DJ Trevor Wilson). The drinks are cheap and the crowd is young, scruffy and enthusiastic.

### Metropol
*Nollendorfplatz 5, Schöneberg, 10777 (216 41 22/216 27 87). U1, U4 Nollendorfplatz.* **Open** *from 9pm Fri, Sat.* **Admission** DM10; *happy hour* 9-10pm.
A gigantic disco for teenagers and visitors to Berlin is held in this renovated art nouveau theatre every week. If you like anonymous bars and dancefloors, try the Diskothek in Perfektion with a choice of six different bars with names such as West Side Bar and Champanger Bar. Two Sundays a month from 8pm-1am they hold a Gay T-Dance here. Expect high-energy, house and lots of fun.

### Mingus
*Basement of Weltrestaurant Markthalle, Pücklerstraße 34, Kreuzberg, 10977 (617 5502). U1 Görlitzer Bahnhof.* **Open** *from 10pm.* **Admission** varies.
Undergoing renovation as we went to press, Mingus is a comfortable cellar bar and club in the basement of the popular Weltrestaurant Markthalle, through which it is entered (take the unobtrusive wooden door opposite the one you come in by). There are plans for soul, funk and jazz DJs at the weekends, various comedy and cabaret-type things during the week and an ambient night on Mondays. Check local listings press for details.

### Orpheuo
*Marburger Straße 2, Charlottenburg, 10789 (211 64 45). U1 Kurfürstendamm.* **Open** *from 11pm Wed-Sun.* **Admission** DM10.
Not as hip as it used to be, this small sweaty and stylish club offers a mix of modern soul, funk, house and mainstream dance music. At the time of going to press, it wasn't opening Mondays and Tuesdays, but this will probably change.

### Sophienclub
*Sophienstraße 6, Mitte, 10178 (282 45 52). U8 Weinmeisterstraße.* **Open** *from 9pm daily.* **Admission** varies.
A maze of several small rooms on different storeys. There's a tiny disco on the ground floor that gets packed at the weekend. Often heavy on acid jazz.

### Trash
*Oranienstraße 40-41 (first floor), 10999 (614 23 28). U7 Kottbusser Tor.* **Open** *from 11pm Thur-Sat.* **Admission** DM5.
Mix with the typically trashy side of Kreuzberg: tacky leather jackets, long hair with bandanas, torn black jeans, biker boots and lots of tattoos. In a small lounge you can pull out your ear-plugs and recover from the hard and heavy rock that shakes this black cave of a club.

# Dance

*There is no shortage of opportunities to watch or perform – the next step must be to upgrade the quality, in spite of the lack of cash.*

Berlin has the largest independent dance scene in Germany and, with some 70 dance schools, offers more training opportunities than any other German city. It also has some of the grandest venues and most innovative companies. But the city is still lagging behind its old-time European competitors, London and Paris.

A look around Berlin's independent dance scene shows the potential for international competition. Companies such as Jo Fabian's example dept., TanzTheater Skoronel, Detektor and TanzFabrik Berlin all present innovative programmes that are worth watching out for. But funding for fringe groups is meagre and, in the present economic climate, unlikely to increase. Both the opera houses' ballet companies and independent dance groups have felt the reunification squeeze. In 1994 there were just under 300 applications from independent theatre and dance groups for a piece of the Senate's DM6.8 million funding pie. About 50 groups got it, 13 of which were dancers.

Dance has been out of the city's cultural limelight since the thirties. Back then, the capital was home to such names as Anita Berber, and was a hotbed of New German Dance, a form linked to Expressionism. While many dancers joined the flood of emigrating artists after the rise of the Nazis, artists at the forefront of the movement such as Mary Wigman, Rudolph von Laban and Gret Palucca were blinded by the excitment of receiving government support for their work.

That support didn't last long. Although these artists were involved in the 1936 Berlin Olympics, the Nazis soon saw the inherent freedom of expression in their work as a threat. Laban's Olympics choreography was banned and he fled to the UK where he founded the Laban Centre at Goldsmiths' College. Fascism checked the development of Expressionist dance, imposing restrictions on its teaching and performance.

After the War, interest shifted to modern ballet – Hilter had labelled work by Prokofieff and Stravinsky as degenerate. Efforts by Wigman and others to take up their work again proved difficult. Their initial cooperation with the fascists was held against them, and their art, with its strong emphasis on individual experience, did not fit into Germany's new, dependable image. What counted now were measurable values like the length of legs or number of pirouettes.

In the German Democratic Republic the emphasis remained on classical Russian ballet. Standards at the state ballet school in East Berlin were high, but the rigidity of communist rule left little opportunity for dancers to develop individual forms of expression. West Berlin followed the general trend in Germany towards generous subsidies for drama but little for dance, making it almost impossible for private, experimental dance groups to survive. Members of Motion, an off-shoot of the Wigman school, emigrated to the US in the early sixties.

Still, creativity flourished during Berlin's island life. The Hinterhofkultur (courtyard culture) of abandoned Kreuzberg factories during the seventies, and the 'live together-work together' credo of the early eighties squatting movement, generated fertile ground from which the huge Freie Tanzszene (independent dance scene) sprang.

The question today is how to upgrade the quality of this quantity. Representatives of Berlin's public and private dance companies and organisations who have been meeting at round table discussions since 1990 believe the answer lies in higher educational standards and better working conditions for dancers in united Berlin. Their concept for a professional dance centre, modelled on The Place in London, Théâtre Contemporain de la Danse in Paris, and Dansens Hus in Stockholm, has Senate support. But this Tanzhaus will not come cheap and in these cash-strapped times there is scant likelihood of it opening in the near future.

## Venues

### Deutsche Oper
*Bismarckstraße 34-37, Charlottenburg, 10627 (34 38 1). U2 Deutsche Oper.* **Box office open** 11am-7pm Mon-Sat; 10am-2pm Sun, and one hour before performances. **Tickets** DM13-DM76; *premières* DM18-DM135. **Credit** AE, DC, EC, V.

When Peter Schaufuss, the former head of the ballet company at West Berlin's opera house, was offered the direction of the Royal Danish Ballet, he packed up and left the Deutsche Oper before the season ended. US-born Spanish choreographer Ray Barra from the Stuttgart Ballet took his place in January 1994. While the company is no star among Europe's corps de ballets, it does tour frequently. Opened a few weeks after the Wall went up in 1961, the opera building itself is a sixties architectural nightmare devoid of glamour or romance. The dance programme is usually pleasing, if not particularly exciting or innovative, with classical or contemporary ballet scheduled for between four and seven nights a month. The ballet direction says it is keen to feature world premières of modern dance, but doesn't do so very often. *See chapter* **Music: Classical & Opera.**

## Hebbel Theater

*Stresemannstraße 29, Kreuzberg, 10963 (251 0144). U1 Hallesches Tor.* **Box office open** 3-7pm Mon-Sun. **Tickets** DM13-DM45. **No credit cards.**
This 600-seat Kreuzberg theatre is noted for international avant-garde theatre and dance. Since the Hebbel opened in 1989, director Nele Herling has concentrated on featuring top contemporary dance companies such as Trisha Brown from New York or Anne Teresa de Keersmaeker's Rosas from Belgium. Tanz im August and February's Tanz im Winter are three-week blocks of performances highlighting current developments in modern dance. Although the narrow portal of the classical Italian-style stage is less than ideal for dance, Nele says someone has to offer Berlin a glimpse of world-class dance. Not that it's such a dirty job – Hebbel's dance programmes draw some of its greatest crowds.
*Four spaces for wheelchairs available.*

## Komische Oper

*Behrenstraße 55-57, Mitte, 10117 (220 2761). U6 Französische Straße.* **Box office open** 11am-7.30pm Mon-Sat; 11am-7pm Sun. **Tickets** *for performances with orchestra* DM8-DM70; *without orchestra* DM5-DM45. **Credit** EC.
The 'dance-theatre' tradition at this neo-baroque opera house was founded by Tom Schilling in 1966 and was under his experimental direction until he retired in 1993. The new administrative director is Marc Jonkers, former head of the Holland Festival. His compatriot Jan Linkens is chief chore-ographer, a position he was offered following the success of his two Schilling-commissioned choreographies. Schilling's work remains an important part of the Oper's repertoire. His modern ballet choreographies garnered international atten-tion in the seventies and gave the company its experimental reputation. The company's openness to experimentation has continued under the two Dutchmen.

## Staatsoper Unter den Linden

*Unter den Linden 7, Mitte, 10117 (203 540). U6 Französische Straße/bus100.* **Box office open** noon-6pm Mon-Sat; 2-6pm Sun. **Tickets** DM6-DM125; *premières* DM25-180. **No credit cards.**
East Berlin's elegant opera house celebrated its 250th anniversary in 1992 by launching an ambitious opera agen-da under its new director Daniel Barenboim. After he settled in, Barenboim made it his business to find a new ballet direc-tor who could infuse fresh life into the company's unimagi-native classical repertoire. In a united city blessed with three ballet ensembles, the company needed a new profile. Michaël Denar, the star soloist at the Paris Opera, arrived in Berlin in autumn 1993 to take up a position as ballet director for the first time. The programme already reflects Denar's deep roots in French style. One of the first things he did was to commission French choreographer Roland Petit for the mod-ern ballet 'Dix'. Denar also has his eyes on the local inde-pendent scene – he commissioned Berlin choreographer Helga Musial for 'Wozzeck-Reflexe', an out-of-house pro-duction in spring 1994. All this at last does justice to the tal-ent in the company's dancing ranks.

## Theater am Halleschen Ufer

*Hallesches Ufer 32, Kreuzberg, 10963 (251 0941). U1/U7 Möckernbrücke.* **Box office open** 30 minutes before performance. **Tickets** DM20; DM15 concs. **No credit cards.**
Although this venue is generally considered to have the most suitable stage for modern dance productions in Berlin, the Senate has been reluctant to surrender to pressure from the independent dance scene and turn it into a dance-only venue. This is partly because the theatre has been home to fringe

theatre groups since 1962. The Senate cleared the house of resident theatre group Theater Manufaktur – which was funded on condition that it schedule 22 weeks of dance a year – and put it under new direction in early 1993. The pro-gramme now is divided up fairly between theatre and dance, the latter mainly featuring productions by local independent groups and soloists.

## Theater unterm Dach

*Dimitroffstraße 101, Prenzlauer Berg, 10405 (420 0610 ext 73). S8, S10 Ernst-Thälmann-Park.* **Box office open** 30 minutes before perfomance. All performances begin 8pm. **Tickets** DM5-DM10. **No credit cards.**
Theater unterm Dach was the first venue in eastern Berlin to devote itself to contemporary dance. The small theatre within the Ernst-Thälmann-Park community cultural centre opened in 1986 with a mixed theatrical progamme. A new concept for a 'movement and dance theatre' was introduced in spring 1992 under the artistic direction of two east Berliners: experimental theatre director Jo Fabian, and the young choreographer Thomas Guggi, who directs his own dance-drama group. Jo Fabian's seven-member group 'exam-ple dept.' have garnered national acclaim, and in 1994 became the first independent dance group ever to be asked to the annual Berlin Theater Treffen. While there are guest performances from the west Berlin independent dance scene, the theatre concentrates on work by eastern artists.

# Classes & Information

## Die Etage

*Hasenheide 54, Kreuzberg, 10967 (691 2095). U7 Südstern.* **Open** 9am-9pm Mon-Sat; 10am-4pm Sun.
Courses in modern dance, jazz, tap, pantomime, acrobatics, juggling and flamenco cost DM18 for one-hour and half-hour classes; DM70 per month. The school also conducts a three-year state-recognised dance education with a grounding in classic and modern disciplines.

## Maison de la Danse

*Pestalozzistraße 60, Charlottenburg, 10627 (323 2043). U7 Wilmersdorfer Straße.* **Open** 9.30am-1pm, 2-6pm, Mon-Fri; 9.30am-1pm Sat. **No credit cards.**
Leotards, leg warmers and tutus, jazz, tap and pointe shoes, and almost anything else you might need to waltz your way around Berlin, is on sale at this house of dance.

## Schokofabrik

*Naunynstraße 72, Kreuzberg, 10997 (615 5391). U1 Kotbusser Tor.* **Open** noon-4pm Tue, Fri; noon-6pm Wed. **No credit cards.**
A former factory, now converted into a women's centre, com-plete with a café, crèche and Turkish bath, and two floors for dance and sport. Weekend workshops at DM90 (DM72 concessions), in Argentinian tango, pantomime, belly danc-ing, mambo or flamenco.

## Staatliche Balletschule Berlin und Schule für Artistik

*Erich-Weinert-Straße 103, Prenzlauer Berg, 10409 (424 4028). S8, S10 Ernst-Thälmann-Park.* **Open** 8am-4pm Mon-Fri.
The former GDR's state ballet school was founded in 1951 and – like all schools in East Berlin – absorbed into the west-ern school system after reunification. The eight-year educa-tion focuses on classical Russian ballet, but also includes Limon, Graham, jazz and folk. Academic subjects also form part of the curriculum. The ballet school admits children from the age of ten, and about 15 per cent of its 200 students come from abroad. The state school for artistry, which was merged with the ballet school after reunification, has 40 students who begin training from the age of 15.

## TanzFabrik Berlin

*Möckernstraße 68, Kreuzberg, 10965 (786 5861). U7, S1, S2 Yorckstraße.* **Open** 10am-noon, 5-8pm, Mon-Thur. **No credit cards**.

Berlin's largest contemporary dance school, with about 50 classes a week and 600 students. The school was set up in 1978 by a US modern dancer and a Berlin sports student. Over the years the school has moved away from its dance/sport curriculum to embrace a variety of techniques. Although the emphasis is still on Limon, classes include jazz, ballet, contact improvisation, new dance, tai-chi, African and Afro-Brasileiro. Bartenieff fundamentals, developed by former Laban student Irmgart Bartenieff, and Feldenkrais technique, are also instructed. The TanzFabrik's company was established at the same time. Today it's made up of ten dancers, seven of whom choreograph. Performances combining elements of Limon/new dance/contact improvisation are given regularly on the tiny in-house stage of its 100-seat theatre, but in recent years the pieces have grown larger and included more dancers, so the ensemble often now appears at larger venues.

## Tanz Initiative Berlin e.V.

*Gottschedstraße 4, Wedding, 13357 (462 6812). U9 Nauener Platz.* **Open** 10.30am-noon weekdays, phone first. Set up in 1988 by an enterprising group of contemporary dancers, choreographers and teachers to establish a focus and voice for Berlin's lively modern dance scene, this association acts as an information centre and festival organiser. Its bi-monthly newsletter, *Parkett,* keeps independent dancers informed on all the latest developments and job opportunities.

## Tanz Tangente

*Kuhligkshofstraße 4, Steglitz, 12165 (792 9124). U9 Rathaus Steglitz.* **Open** 3-9pm Mon-Fri.

Former Wigman student Leanore Ickstadt set up this school 20 years after she first arrived in Berlin in 1961 on a Fulbright scholarship. Today Ickstadt only teaches children, but adult classes are held in modern dance, awareness through movement, tap, Feldenkrais and ballet. Visitors to Berlin can take part in five lessons of their choice with a DM110 guest ticket. Those staying longer can register for four-month blocks of one 90-minute class a week: it costs DM75 a month (DM65 concessions). Professional training in classical ballet is offered from Monday to Friday. Ickstadt's six-member company, Dance Berlin, disbanded shortly after a split with her choreography partner Joseph Tmimm. He went on to found the Tolada Dance Company and his high-energy productions can be seen at Theater am Halleschen Ufer (*see above* **Venues**).

*Opened weeks after the Wall went up, the **Deutsche Oper** reflects the spirit of the time.*

# Film

*If your favourite movie got panned at Cannes or died a death in Venice, stop grizzling, it could win a Golden Bear in Berlin. Bitte? No thanks, I'll have a lager, as Michael Caine once said.*

Cinemas are among Berlin's main attractions, and not only in February when the International Film Festival takes place. There are over 130 screens (including those in multi-screen centres) throughout the city and a huge variety of films being shown. The cinemas in the Ku'damm area show the usual Hollywood stuff that dominates screens all over Germany. But more interesting forms of cinematic life can be discovered in the smaller houses off Ku'damm or in the often very small off-off cinemas, known as Programm-Kinos. The majority of the latter are in the Kreuzberg, Prenzlauer Berg and Mitte areas.

Most mainstream foreign-language films and many of the more obscure variety are dubbed rather than subtitled. However, at any given time at least five or six films will be playing somewhere in their English-language versions. Three first-run cinemas specialise exclusively in English-language films, the largest and oldest being the Odeon in Schöneberg. The Babylon in Kreuzberg nearly always shows one film in English, and quite often devotes both of its screens to English films in their original versions. Likewise, the Kurbel just off the Ku'damm almost always has one, and often two, of its three screens showing English-language fare. Programm-Kinos such as Arsenal, Eiszeit, Checkpoint, Babylon (Mitte) and Moviemento will normally also be showing more obscure films in English.

Always check for the notation OF or 'OV' (Originalfassung or Original Version), OmU (Original mit Untertitel – original with German subtitles), or even OmE (Original with English subtitles) in the adverts. There is also a monthly listing of films playing in English in *Checkpoint*, the English-language city guide.

Videos of movies in the original English are available for rental from The (Original Version), Incredibly Strange Video, Videodrom and The British Council (*see below* **Video Rental**).

## Berlin Film Festival

Berlin's most important annual event for cineastes is the Berlinale, the second biggest film festival in the world after Cannes. More than 800 films are shown over 12 days each February. This excess of

celluloid is divided into seven sections, the most important of which are the following. *See also chapter* **Berlin by Season**.

### The International Competition

The International Competition attracts the world's major film companies to Berlin, proffering their best new movies to be judged for the prestigious Gold and Silver Bear awards. Big films are presented in the large cinemas in the Ku'damm area (which are often sold out), and premières take place in Germany's largest cinema, Zoo-Palast 1. The films are also shown the following day at the Urania, between Wittenbergplatz and Nollendorfplatz. The presence of Hollywood stars – both promoting films and on jury panels – makes the Competition the most glamorous part of the festival. There are annual complaints about how the big US companies with their big-budget productions dominate the contest and diminish the artistic range, and yet year after year these are also the films that attract the largest audiences.

### The Panorama

The Berlinale Panorama was originally conceived as a mere supplement to the International Competition, presenting films that didn't make it into the more glamorous contest. But during the eighties it began to attract increased attention and is now an important festival for international independent film-makers, and (semi-officially) a main event for international gay and lesbian cinema.

### The International Forum of Young Cinema

The first Forum was inaugurated in 1971, with the intention of opening the festival to avant garde and progressive developments in world cinema that had until then been neglected. Nowadays, this section of the Berlinale is widely regarded as the most interesting by hardcore film buffs. Its main venue, the restored Delphi, gives premières a slightly incongruous touch of luxury and glamour. The films are also shown at the Akademie der Künste, one U-Bahn station north of the Zoo at Hansaplatz; at the Arsenal, one U-Bahn station east, about a five-minute walk from Wittenbergplatz; and at cinemas in the east, lately the Zeughaus Kino and the Centre Culturel Français. During the festival, difficult and never-to-be-seen-again films from countries in Africa, eastern Europe or the Far East play here to enthusiastic admirers of the offbeat.

### Retrospectives

The Berlinale Retrospective focuses every year on a particular aspect of film production. It was originally conceived in the fifties as a forum to show neglected work by German directors who were forced into internal exile during the Nazi period. Lately, the retrospective has divided itself neatly into two sections – one devoted to an aspect of film history, such as the films of Erich von Stroheim, Cinemascope, say, or films from the Babelsberg Studio; the other to honour a 'living legend', who usually appears in person to receive an honorary Golden Bear for lifetime achievement and add a little glitz to the proceedings. Those recently honoured include Robert Mitchum, Gregory Peck and Sophia Loren. The Haus der Kulturen der

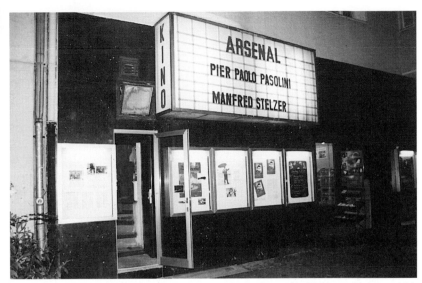

The **Arsenal** *in Schöneberg – much less boring than the Arsenal in Highbury. See page 184.*

Welt in the Tiergarten, where the press centre is located, also has screenings of films from the Panorama and Forum of Young Film open to the public. Accredited participants can use the shuttle service from the Zoo. Others must either drive, go to S-Bahn station Lehrter Bahnhof and walk ten minutes, or go by bus 100 (not recommended in rush hour).

### Internationale Filmfestspiele Berlin (Administration)

*Budapester Straße, Tiergarten, 10787 (254 890/fax 254 89 249). U2, U9/S3, S5, S7,S75,S9 Zoologischer Garten.* **Open** 10am-5pm Mon-Fri.
These are the people who organise the festival, as well as other film events throughout the year.

### Berlinale Shop

*Budapester Straße 48, Tiergarten, 10787 (254 89 254). U2, U9/S3, S5, S7, S75, S9 Zoologischer Garten.* **Open** noon-6pm. **Dauerkarten** (season tickets) DM250 approx.
This is the place to buy Dauerkarten (season tickets) for the film festival. For approximately DM250 (you'll also need two passport-size photos), you gain entry to the following: all films at the Zoo Palast (before 4pm); films that are part of the competition, and evening screenings of the Panorama films and Retrospectives (screened at the Filmpalast Berlin and the Urania-Humboldtsaal); and films shown at the Delphi-Filmpalast, the Akademie der Künste and the International. Dauerkarten can be obtained by writing to the Berlinale Shop the December before the festival, or three days before the festival begins at the same address. Tickets for individual screenings can be bought three days in advance (four days for repeat showings) at the ticket office on the first floor of the Europa-Center and in the International (*see below* for both). On the day of screening, tickets are available only at the box office of the relevant cinema. Tickets go very fast, and the queues can be enormous. A three-hour wait is not unusual. Get there before 10am to beat the crowds and be sure to bring eating and reading materials. Tickets for some theatres, notably the Arsenal and those in the east, must be bought at the theatre box offices

themselves. Prices range from DM7-DM25, but most screenings are DM10-DM16. Every year the administration will tinker with this or fine-tune that, so it is always best to pick up a programme from the Europa-Center or Berlinale Shop to get the lowdown on the latest developments. Posters, catalogues and paraphernalia can also be found at both places.

### Europa-Center

*Breitscheidplatz 5, Charlottenburg, 10787 (3 48 00 88). U2, U9/S3, S5, S7, S75, S9 Zoologischer Garten.* **Open** 11.30am-6.30pm, from three days before Berlinale begins.

### International

*Karl-Marx-Allee 3 (corner of Schillingstraße), Mitte, 10178 (242 58 26). U5 Schilling Straße.* **Open** noon-7pm, from three days before festival starts.

## DEFA Studio Babelsberg

Whatever you want to say about World War I and its effects on Germany as a whole, it was the best thing that ever happened to the German film industry. First, the war wiped out Italy, the main European competition. Then, in the twenties, spurred on by the phenomenal successes of Ernst Lubitsch, Fritz Lang, FW Murnau and such films as *The Cabinet of Dr Caligari*, the German film industry was Hollywood's only real competition. Because films were silent, language was no barrier and the rich visual style of the Germans made their films highly exportable. Hollywood fought back by buying off Germany's greatest talents. Lubitsch and Murnau made the trip across the Atlantic, as well as such superstars as Emil Jannings and Pola Negri. Even with the advent of sound in the late 1920s, German films were still extremely popular abroad.

Nazism, however, finished off whatever chance Germany had of capturing the international markets, not only forcing established talents such as Lang into exile, but sending budding talents such as Fred Zinnemann, Billy Wilder and Max Ophüls to America. But in the pre-Nazi era Berlin was the film-making capital of Europe, and Babelsberg, in Potsdam, was its largest studio.

Guided tours (in German, but also in English by prior arrangement) are run around the 36-hectare (89-acre) site, taking in 80 years of film-making. During the tour, devotees can kiss the floor upon which Marlene Dietrich took her first big step to stardom in 1929, when she played the showgirl Lola in Josef von Sternberg's *Der Blaue Engel*, and can see mock-ups for such early special effects extravaganzas as *The Golem* and Fritz Lang's *Die Niebelungenlied*.

When the Nazis came to power, Babelsberg and the German film industry became an arm of the Nazi propaganda machinery, churning out not only pro-Nazi (see *Hitlerjunge Quex*) and anti-Semitic (see *Jud Süß*) horrors, but also relentlessly 'apolitical' pure entertainment films to bolster morale on the home front. The most famous of these is a version of *The Adventures of Baron Münchausen*, a Technicolor superproduction made in 1943 that stands up well to Terry Gilliam's version.

After 1945, Babelsberg found itself in East Germany and became the DEFA (Deutsche Film AG). Babelsberg was converted to socialist realism. Few of the nearly 700 feature films that came out of former East Germany's film factory dared to take any risks at all; the most successful genre internationally being children's films. Since reunification, many suppressed films have come to light, resulting in at least one classic: *Spur der Steine*, unseen for 25 years, is a psychologically complex story of a doctrinaire Party secretary, an unorthodox construction foreman and a woman engineer. The film is quite daring in its feminist attitudes, and although it is certainly no attack on socialism, that the characters question the system at all could not be tolerated by the East German authorities.

Babelsberg was recently bought by a French company, who plan to carry on making movies there, while turning much of it into a theme park and renting out certain other facilities. Such films as *The Neverending Story III* and *The Innocent* have been among its most recent productions and much TV work is done there, too. *See also chapter* **Trips out of Town**.

### DEFA-Studio Babelsberg
*August-Babel Straße 26-53, entrance on Großbeerenstraße, Potsdam, 14482 (0331 965 27 50 reservations, 965 27 55 information). S3 Griebnitzsee, then bus 693 direction Bahnhof Rehbrücke or 20 minutes' walk.* **Open** *Mar-Oct* 10am-6pm daily; *Nov-Feb* 10am-4pm. Entrance up to 90 mins hours before close. **Tickets** DM16; DM12 children, students, unemployed. Special rates for groups.
The large park area allows you to wander around various pavilions devoted to aspects of the behind-the-scenes work that goes into a film, such as costumes, make-up, stunts and special effects. There's even a mini-zoo for animals used in productions. A tour (in German) leaves every hour to visit the prop warehouse and sets currently in use. Considering the complications and cost involved, this is something of a disappointment and not really worth a special trip if you have only limited time and resources.

## Cinemas

### Arsenal
*Welserstraße 25, Schöneberg, 10777 (218 68 48). U1, U15, U2 Wittenbergplatz, U4 Viktoria-Luise-Platz. Bus 119, 129, 146, 185, 249.* **Tickets** DM9; DM7 members.
The excellent small cinema is run by the Freunde der Deutschen Kinemathek (Friends of German Cinema) who organise the Forum section of the Berlin Film Festival. It shows anything and everything from prime thirties Hollywood, through avant garde Third World début films, to classic Russian silents. Their programmes are often around themes, ranging from retrospectives of directors to the colour

blue. Often a film-maker will be in attendance. Another regular feature is classic silent films with live piano accompaniment, which almost always attract near sell-out crowds. Many films are in English or with English subtitles.

### Babylon A & B (Kreuzberg)
*Dresdener Straße 126, Kreuzberg, 10999 (614 63 16). U1, U15, U8 Kottbusser Tor. Bus 247.* **Tickets** DM11; DM8.50 Tue, Wed.
This two-screen cinema shows first-run films in English, often on both screens.

### Babylon (Mitte)
*Rosa-Luxemburg-Straße 30, Mitte, 10178 (242 50 76). U2 Rosa-Luxemburg-Platz. Bus 140, 147, 157, 240. Tram 15 17, 63, 71.* **Tickets** DM8; DM7 students, children, pensioners.
East Berlin's counterpart to the Arsenal (*see above*) was built in the twenties by the architect Hans Poelzig (who, besides working for Max Reinhardt, created the sets for German expressionist films such as *The Golem* and *Wie Er In Die Welt Kam*). Recently restored, it is now divided into a Foyer and a Grüne Salon. Its ambitious retrospective programmes are somewhat more conventional than the Arsenal's, and less likely to be in English.

### Balazs 1 & 2
*Karl-Liebknecht-Straße 9 im Haus Ungarn, Mitte, 10178 (242 57 24). U & S Banhof Alexanderplatz. Bus 140, 142, 157, 240. Tram 11, 15, 18.* **Tickets** DM9; DM7 students, children, pensioners.
The Balazs is a new cinema which opened in the Hungarian

*The **Babylon** often shows films in English.*

Cultural Center and devotes itself to films from and about eastern Europe, or by eastern European directors, whether at home, abroad or in exile. Many hard-to-see films make their way to its screens.

## Checkpoint

*Leipziger Straße 55, Mitte, 10117 (208 29 95). U2, U6 Stadtmitte. Bus 129, 142.* **Tickets** DM7; DM5 Thur.
Just a few minutes' walk away from the old frontier, this tiny theatre is tucked away on the first floor of an ugly modernist building. Checkpoint screens trash films for the youth of east Berlin. If you are interested in the lesbian vampire movie genre or the early works of John Waters, join the queue. The intimate atmosphere makes this a real gem, and even if the movie isn't in English, you can still sit at the bar in the back and quaff a few.

## Eiszeit

*Zeughofstraße 20, Kreuzberg, 10997 (611 60 16). U1, U15 Görlitzer Bahnhof.* **Tickets** DM9; DM5 children.
A crucial venue for Berlin's avant garde, the Eiszeit is a place where the screening of an obscure underground film may well turn into an Event. It started illegally in the early eighties in a squatted house in Schöneberg and has since moved to a Kreuzberg loft. Although the cinema is now sponsored by cultural authorities, some aesthetic extremism persists. The regular, strongly US-orientated programme features independently made films in the original versions. Every summer the Eiszeit hosts the Horror and Fantasy Film Festival, with most films in their original versions.

## fsk

*Segitzdamm 2, Kreuzberg, 10969 (611 70 10). U1, U8, U15 Kottbusser Tor.* **Tickets** DM9.
Formerly located in the back of the fsk bar on Wiener Straße, the new fsk kinos opened in November 1994. The mini-kino is the old fsk with its comfy aeroplane-style seats. The larger 100-seat theatre has enabled the fsk to expand its repertoire. The programme is still far from conventional with everything from tacky cult B-movies to artistically challenging new films that need cinemas like these to reach the audience they deserve.

## Kurbel I, II, III

*Giesebrechtstraße 4, Charlottenburg, 10629 (883 53 25). U7 Adenauer Platz. Bus 101, 109, 119, 129, 204, 219.* **Tickets** DM11-DM13; DM7 Tue, Wed.
The name means crank, a reference to a now outmoded appendage of early film cameras. This cinema dates back to 1947 and screened the German première of *Gone With The Wind*. If you crave the comfort of typical Multi-Plex viewing, this is the closest you'll come in Berlin, complete with air-conditioning, plush seating and no opportunity spared to get you to spend a fortune at the concession stand. Screens I and II are large cinemas, while III is rather small, and sloped so steeply that every seat is a good one.

## Moviemento 1-3

*Kottbusser Damm 22, Kreuzberg, 10967 (692 47 85). U8 Leinestraße, U7 Hermannplatz. Bus 141, 144, 241.* **Tickets** DM9-DM10; DM12 double features; DM14 allnighters; DM5 children before 3pm weekends; DM7 Wed.
Opened in 1907 (with a name that afterwards became the German word for vintage movies: Kintopp), Moviemento is the oldest surviving cinema in Berlin. Yet it doesn't look a bit like a museum. A youthful Kreuzberg audience crowds into three small rooms (232 seats altogether) to watch an off-beat mix of films: forgotten early work of now famous actors or directors; very late-night shows (for example, the five Star Trek films starting at midnight), and low-budget offerings from promising new German directors. In fact, manager Thomas Tykwer made quite a splash of his own in 1993 with his début film *Die Tödliche Maria*. Usually one of the six or seven films shown every day is in English.

## Odeon

*Hauptstraße 116, Schöneberg, 10827 (781 56 67). U4 Innsbrucker Platz, S45, S46 Innsbrucker Platz, Schöneberg.* **Tickets** DM11; DM8.50 Tue, Wed.
The only one-screen cinema to have an exclusively English programme. The Odeon shows the newest productions from Hollywood and mainstream films from the UK.

## Sputnik 1 (Wedding)

*Reinickendorfer Straße 113, Wedding, 13347 (465 87 69). U6 Reinickendorfer Straße. Bus 127, 227, 248.* **Tickets** DM10; DM7.50 Wed, Thur.
Founded a decade ago by ambitious Bavarian Berliners, the Sputnik enterprise started in the dull western district of Wedding in a run-down fifties cinema that soon became the city's most happening film venue. The programme balanced the most brilliant with the most bizarre films (sometimes revealing secret connections between both), but didn't attract enough viewers until a German sixties SF series called *Raumschiff Orion* was screened. It proved to be an instant cult hit and made enough money for a second Sputnik to be launched in Kreuzberg (*see below*). The cinema at Wedding has now been restored to its original fifties look, and its programme has become more mainstream.

## Sputnik 2 (Südstern)
## Sputnik 3 (Kulturrevolution)

*Hasenheide 54, Kreuzberg, 10967 (694 11 47). U7 Südstern. Bus 241, 242.* **Tickets** DM9; DM6 children.
Sputnik's filmic experiments continue at its smaller Südstern cinema. The programme, including many films in English, is worth the effort of climbing five floors. The Kulturrevolution is a tiny cinema which screens the latest cult hits.

## Xenon

*Kolonnenstraße 5, Schöneberg, 10827 (782 8850). U7 Kleistpark.* **Tickets** DM9, DM7.50; DM6 children.
A small, cosy cinema offering a varied programme of schlock horror movies and recent commercial hits. There are frequent midnight screenings at weekends.

## Zoo Palast

*Hardenbergstraße 29a, Charlottenburg, 10623 (261 15 55). S3, S5, S7, S75, S9/U2, U9 Zoologischer Garten. Bus 100, 109, 145, 146, 149, 219, 245, 249, X9.* **Tickets** DM10-DM13; DM7.50 Tue, Wed.
A nine-screen cinema, Leicester Square in one building. Newly renovated, it only shows English-language fare during the Berlinale. Otherwise, the programme is in German.

# Video Rental

## The British Council Video Club

*Hardenbergstraße 20, Charlottenburg, 10623 (31 10 99 10). U2, U9/S3, S5, S7, S75, S9 Zoologischer Garten. Bus 100, 109, 145, 146, 149, 219, 245, X9.* **Open** noon-7pm Mon-Fri. **Membership** DM20, students/teachers free.
The British Council has a selection of British films and TV programmes, to be hired out on a weekly basis. Depending on the video, it will cost you between DM2.50-DM7.

## Incredibly Strange Video

*Eisenacher Straße 115, Schöneberg, 10823 (215 17 70). U7/Eisenacher Straße.* **Open** 2-10pm Mon-Sat.
If your life was changed by *Pink Flamingos* or if your taste in movies runs towards the 'psychotronic', or even if you understand the term, this is the video rental place for you. The selection of over 2,000 titles lives up to its name in a store that would do any English city proud. Video rentals are DM8 per night for the first one and DM6 for each additional one. You must bring personal ID, and either police registration or enough money for a deposit.

## The (Original Version)

*Sesenheimer Straße 17, Charlottenburg, 10627 (313 76 22). U2, U7 Bismarckstraße/U2 Deutsche Oper. Bus 101.* **Open** noon-9pm Mon-Sat.

A friendly, American-owned establishment which stocks a large selection of US and UK films in the original English version. All are on PAL format and cost between DM5-DM7 for one day. The one-off membership fee is DM50. Take your passport and proof of address. Second-hand books in English also bought and sold.

## Videodrom

*Mittenwalder Straße 11, Kreuzberg, 10961 (692 88 04). U7/Gneisenaustraße. Bus 140, 341.* **Open** 3pm-midnight Mon-Sat.

Videodrom's selection of over 3,000 titles easily makes it the largest English-language video store in Berlin. With titles ranging from the ultra-conventional to the ultra-weird, everyone should be able to find something to please. Video rental costs DM7.50 per night. You'll need personal ID and police registration.

# Berlin in Film

1. **One, Two, Three** *(US, 1961, Billy Wilder)*
The Wall went up while this comedy was being filmed in Berlin. A replica of the Brandenburg Gate had to be built in Munich to complete it. By the time it came out, German audiences found it about as funny as, well, the Berlin Wall, and for almost a quarter of a century it remained unseen. Now, it plays constantly in Berlin cinemas. They've even turned it into a stage musical. James Cagney is brilliant as the Pepsi executive whose bodacious daughter falls in love with Communist Horst Buchholz. The torture scene involving 'Itsy Bitsy Teeny Weeny Yellow Polka Dot Bikini' is one of the high points of screen comedy.

2. **Cabaret** *(US, 1972, Bob Fosse)*
This dazzling movie may be the last great musical ever to come out of Hollywood. Let's face it, Liza Minnelli was born to play Sally Bowles. Once you've seen her, the part is unimaginable with anyone else. When it's over, you feel as if you've been singing and dancing for two and a half hours and you wish you could have been in Berlin in the twenties, even though you know no place on earth could ever have been so magical.

3. **The Spy Who Came In From The Cold** *(UK, 1965, Martin Ritt)*
This adaptation of the Le Carré classic features brilliant acting by Burton, Claire Bloom, Oskar Werner and Peter van Eyck, intense atmosphere and just enough plot switches to keep you in the dark without becoming annoying. After 30 years of imitations, this remains the best Cold War spy movie ever.

4. **A Foreign Affair** *(US, 1948, Billy Wilder)*
Wilder again, but if anyone can be called a Film Deity in Berlin it's Billy Wilder, and this film is one reason why. Although it's wildly uneven, with jokes that were old before World War I and a Hollywood ending that even Hollywood must have found contrived, it provides an extraordinary look at Berlin right after WWII – a devastated, wide open town. And it's got Marlene!

5. **Taxi Zum Klo** *(W Germany, 1980, Frank Ripploh)*
The title means 'Taxi to the Toilet', which gives you an idea of how, um, forthright, this Confessions of an Exhibitionist is. It has become an international cult film, and with good reason. Ripploh spares neither himself nor the audience in this XXX-rated look at his extremely egotistical and relentless pursuit of an orgasm. By turns hilarious and gross, but always honest, this film brings new meaning to the phrase 'in yo' face'.

6. **Berlin Alexanderplatz**
*(W Germany, 1979, Rainer Werner Fassbinder)*
Made as a TV mini-series, but released as a film overseas, this 15-and-a-half-hour marathon is best viewed on video, where it can be broken up. Based on the novel by Alfred Döblin and as much a chronicle of the obsessions of Germany's greatest post-WWII director as it is of post-WWI Berlin, this film is a staggering achievement,

especially the censor-bating final hour, where the entire preceding 14 hours are brought together in a monumental cataclysm that leaves you wanting to see the whole thing over again.

7. **Westler** *(W Germany, 1985, Wieland Speck)*
This gay romance between a West Berliner and an East Berliner was obviously made on a shoestring budget, so director Speck had to make do with truth, charm, sweetness and honesty. Without resorting to melodrama or preachiness, everything you need to know about the tragedy of the Wall is contained in one checkpoint strip-search scene.

8. **Olympia** *(Germany, 1937, Leni Riefenstahl)*
Germany's greatest Nazi director was given unlimited resources to film the 1936 Olympics in Berlin. As a historical record it is invaluable, but time has not been kind. It's not just the Nazi ideology, which here is pretty subtle. It's also that technology has caught up with her, and what required such painstaking effort in 1936 is part and parcel of almost any modern TV sportscast.

9. **It's Not The Homosexual Who Is Perverse But The Situation In Which He Lives**
*(W Germany, 1973, Rosa von Praunheim)*
Rosa is one of Berlin's biggest local celebs, whether showing up to Berlin Film Festival opening nights in flamboyant drag, outing big stars on national television, or tirelessly promoting his latest films. Maybe you'll even see him on the streets, or talk to him on the phone. He's listed in the book, and if at home will even answer it himself. This is the best of his many films, a laundry list of the follies of the gay population of Berlin, and the direction the movement should take. Ahead of its time then, and the world still hasn't caught up.

10. **Wings Of Desire (Der Himmel Über Berlin)**
*(W Germany, 1987, Wim Wenders)*
Magnificent photography, nifty aerial views of Berlin and some wonderful subplots just can't compensate for one of the most boring films ever made. Really folks, Berlin is not nearly as dull as this film would have you believe.

# Music: Classical & Opera

***Boasting no fewer than three opera houses, two major concert halls and myriad smaller venues and churches, Berlin is a Mecca for top-flight performers from around the world.***

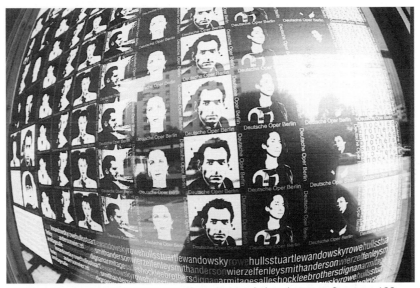

The **Deutsche Oper** attracts more stars than you can shake a baton at. See page 188.

The classical music scene here is in a state of flux, indeed crisis. Because the city is teetering on the edge of bankruptcy, the Berlin Senate has made drastic cutbacks in arts funding. This hasn't, however, prevented Berlin's major musical establishments from continuing to offer an almost year-round abundance of the finest names in the field. Still in the process of exorcising the ghost of Herbert von Karajan, the Berlin Philharmonic, now under the musical directorship of Claudio Abbado, is simply not the orchestra it once was and faces stiff competition from its arguably now better rival, the Deutsches Sinfonie-Orchester (formerly the Berlin Radio Symphony Orchestra), led by Vladimir Ashkenazy. Also not to be sneezed at is the increasingly accomplished Berliner Sinfonie-

Orchester, which is based at the Konzerthaus (formerly the Schauspielhaus).

Aside from July and August, when most of the resident orchestras pack up for the season and few visiting orchestras are in town, there is a tremendous amount of choice. The German-language fortnightly guides *Tip* and *Zitty*, as well as the English-language monthly *Checkpoint*, all carry listings of what's on and where.

The Deutsche Staatsoper, Komische Oper and Konzerthaus are situated within an easy stroll of one another, near or on east Berlin's grand boulevard, Unter den Linden and, while they rarely attract the megastars of the classical music circuit, they offer a generally excellent standard of performance that is noticeably cheaper than, say, the

Berlin Phil or the Deutsche Oper in the city's western half. Nevertheless, concert-going in the east is not the bargain it once was. Prices have risen sharply in the past few years and show every sign of continuing to do so as the eastern-based opera companies and ensembles scramble to stay afloat with vastly reduced subsidies.

Naturally, most classical music fans want tickets for the Berlin Philharmonic Orchestra at the Philharmonie. Be warned, however, that these concerts are often booked up months in advance and it may simply be impossible to get tickets. If you desperately want tickets at the last minute, make yourself a sign saying 'Suche eine Karte' ('seeking a ticket') and stand outside the building. With any luck, someone whose companion needed to work late will approach you with a sign reading 'Karte zu verkaufen' ('ticket for sale'). Be warned: there may be ticket sharks.

If you can't get tickets to see the Berlin Phil, don't despair; tickets are usually to be had for a concert by the Deutsches Sinfonie-Orchester, which is coming astonishingly close to usurping the crown of 'Berlin's finest'.

If you have time to buy tickets for special concerts when they first go on sale, be prepared for a strange bit of German orderliness organised by fans of the orchestra. Early on the day tickets are first offered, these fans appear outside the box office, handing out numbered slips of paper, representing your place in the queue. Equipped with your number, you can take off for breakfast and return when the box office opens.

The major Berlin music festival is the Berliner Festwochen. Started in 1950, this brings to Berlin the crème-de-la-crème of the world's soloists and orchestras and spans the month of September.

The contemporary music festival, the Biennale (every other year in March), as well as the presence of Berlin's première group for modern music, the Ensemble Modern, assures that those who want more challenging fare than Bach, Beethoven and Brahms are fairly well looked after. Smaller, less high-profile modern ensembles are starting to come to the fore, among them the highly accomplished Ensemble Oriol.

For details of the Biennale, as well as other music festivals, *see chapter* **Berlin by Season**.

## Ticket Agencies

Tickets are sold at the concert hall box offices or through ticket agencies, Theaterkassen. At the box offices, seats are generally sold up to an hour before the performance. You can also reserve by telephone. The Theaterkassen provide the easiest means of buying a ticket, but be prepared to pay for the convenience: commissions run as high as 17 per cent. Some take credit cards, but most accept only Eurocheques or cash.

Below are details of some of the major Theaterkassen in central Berlin. For details of the 50 or so other ticket agencies, look in the *Gelbe Seiten* (Yellow Pages) under Theaterkassen.

### Hekticket

*Rathausstraße 1, Mitte, 10178 (242 67 09). S3, S5, S6, S7, S9/U2, U5, U8 Alexanderplatz.* **Open** 4-8pm daily. **No credit cards.**
Hekticket offers discounts of up to 50 per cent on theatre and concert tickets, so it should be your first choice if using an agency. For a DM2 commission, staff will sell tickets for the same evening's performance. Tickets for Sunday matinées are available on Saturday.

### Kant-Kasse

*Kantstraße 54, Charlottenburg, 10627 (313 45 54). S5, S6, S9/U7 Wilmersdorfer Straße.* **Open** 10am-6.30pm Mon-Fri; 10am-2pm Sat. **No credit cards.**

### Kartenhaus im Berliner Congress Center

*Märkisches Ufer 54, Mitte, 10179 (27 58 41 90). S3, S5, S6, S7, S9, S10/U8 Jannowitzbrücke.* **Open** 10am-6pm Mon-Fri. **No credit cards.**

### Konzertkasse

*Oranienstraße 29, Kreuzberg, 10999 (615 88 18). U1, U8 Kottbusser Tor.* **Open** 9am-6pm Mon-Fri; 9am-1pm Sat. **No credit cards.**

### Tele-Card

*Birkbuschstraße 14, Steglitz, 12167 (834 40 73). U9, S1 Rathaus Steglitz.* **Open** 10am-6pm Mon-Fri; 10am-1pm Sat. **Credit** AmEx, DC, EC, MC, V.

## Major Venues

## Deutsche Oper

The Deutsche Oper attracts the biggest names of all Berlin's three opera houses as far as singers are concerned, but it still doesn't have the funding to import the biggest names of all. Whilst it rarely gives poor performances, most are rather uninspired. Occasionally, however, the Deutsche Oper can pull a truly remarkable rabbit out of its hat.

Designed by Fritz Bornemann and built in 1961, the theatre's interior is certainly pleasant enough, although its exterior, an enormous tranche of granite, has led to Berliners nicknaming it, with their irrepressible wit, 'Sing-Sing'.
**Deutsche Oper Berlin**
*Bismarckstraße 34-37, Charlottenburg, 10585 (box office 34 381). U2 Deutsche Oper.* **Open** box office 11am-6pm Mon-Sat. **Tickets** DM190-DM15. **Credit** AmEx, DC, EC, V.

## Deutsche Staatsoper

The Deutsche Staatsoper has a longer and grander history than the Deutsche Oper. It was founded as Prussia's Royal Court Opera for Frederick the Great in 1742, and designed along the lines of a

**Opposite:** *the sublime* **Berlin Philharmonie.** *See page 190.*

The **Berliner Congress Center** *has a useful, central ticket agency. See page 188.*

Greek temple – one of many Greek-inspired buildings which earned Berlin the name 'Athens on the Spree'. Although the present building dates from 1955, the façade faithfully copies that of Knobelsdorff's original, twice destroyed in World War II (in 1941 and 1945). The elegant interior gives an immediate sense of the house's past glory, with huge chandeliers and elaborate wall paintings. Its relatively small size lends performances a certain intimacy. But the Staatsoper is still feeling the effects of the Cold War. Because it was politically isolated from arts in the West, it finds it difficult to attract internationally known artists. This is changing slowly, but very slowly. Daniel Barenboim now divides his time between being music director of this house and music director of the Chicago Symphony Orchestra and is striving to instill new life into its performances and repertoire. One drawback is that many of their productions are embarrassingly dated in their staging, but the flip-side is that some productions, particularly the more recent ones directed by Ruth Berghaus, are as exciting as anything to be seen in any opera house in the world. Chamber music is performed in the small, ornate Apollo Saal, housed within the main building.

**Deutsche Staatsoper**
*Unter den Linden 5-7, Mitte, 10109 (200 47 62/200 43 15). U6 Französische Straße.* **Open** *box office* noon-6pm Mon-Sat; 2-6pm Sun. **Tickets** DM125-DM8. **No credit cards**.

## Komische Oper

The Komische Oper means, ostensibly, one thing: Harry Kupfer. Kupfer, artistic director and one of the few 'Ossis' whose career has not just continued but taken off since reunification, runs a tight

ship here, ably assisted by his young Russian-American musical director Yakov Kreizberg. Kupfer, one of the star directors on the German opera scene, is nothing if not bold; his radical but usually gripping interpretations of modern works and bread-and-butter fare virtually guarantee a stimulating evening's worth of opera. And what's more, it's half the price of the Deutsche Oper.

**Komische Oper**
*Behrenstraße 55-57, Mitte, 10117 (229 25 55). U6 Französische Straße.* **Open** *box office* 11am-7pm Mon-Sat; 1pm-half an hour before perf Sun. **Tickets** DM75-DM10. **Credit** EC, MC, V.

## Philharmonie

Berlin's most famous concert hall, home to the world-renowned Berlin Philharmonic Orchestra, is also its most daring architecturally – a joyous and playful piece of organic modernism. It's such a fine, witty, beautiful design, it's hard to see why so many people revile it. The hall, with a golden, reconstructionist vaulting roof, was designed by the architect Hans Scharoun in 1963, and has been nicknamed the 'Karajani Circus'. Its reputation for superb acoustics is accurate – but this depends very much on where you sit; behind the orchestra the acoustics are appalling, but in front (where you will empty your wallet to sit, *if* you can get tickets) the sound is heavenly. Same goes for the smaller Kammermusiksaal, contained in the same complex. The Berlin Philharmonic Orchestra was founded in 1882 and has been led by some of the world's finest conductors. Its greatest fame came under the baton of the late Herbert von Karajan, and current director Claudio Abbado has his work cut out. This is an orchestra that has for far too long rested on its laurels, and its quality has decreased markedly in recent years. They're still top-notch, but they're getting too smug for their own good, both in the quality of their playing and the insufferable, almost exclusively nineteenth-century safeness of their repertoire. The Philharmonic gives about 100 performances in Berlin between August-June, with another 20-30 concerts worldwide. Plan ahead if you want tickets: performances sell out months in advance. Tickets for visiting orchestras are usually easier to come by.

**Philharmonie**
*Matthäikirchstraße 1, Tiergarten, 10785 (25 48 8 132). U1 Kurfürstenstraße.* **Open** *box office* 3.30-6pm Mon-Fri; 11am-2pm Sat, Sun. **Tickets** DM115-DM12; half-price for students for some concerts 30 mins before perf. **No credit cards.**

## Konzerthaus

The Konzerthaus (formerly the Schauspielhaus), an 1821 architectural gem by Friedrich Schinkel, was all but destroyed in the war. Lovingly restored, it was reopened in 1984. There are two main spaces for concerts, the Großer Konzertsaal for orchestras, and the Kammermusiksaal (not to be confused with the one at the Philharmonie) for chamber music. Organ recitals in the large concert hall are a wonderful treat, played on a massive organ at the back of the stage. Danish conductor Michael Schønwandt is the new musical director of the Berliner Sinfonie-Orchestra, based here. This house has some of the most imaginative programming in Berlin; recent series have included Nietzsche as composer and his influence on the music of his time, as well as an extraordinary group of concerts in 1994 to mark the centenary of the birth of Paul Dessau. In terms of year-round programming, a healthy mixture of the old, the new and the rediscovered, the Konzerthaus is a wonderful venue for concert-goers. The Deutsches Sinfonie-Orchester, one of the finest in the land, is also based here, and their performances, particularly of contemporary music, are not to be missed.

**Konzerthaus**
*Gendarmenmarkt (Platz der Akademie), Mitte, 10117 (Konzertsaal 20 30 9-21 or 4/Kammermusiksaal 20 30 9-21 or 5). U6 Französische Straße.* **Open** *box office* 2-6pm Tue-Sat. **Tickets** DM70-DM5; half price for students and pensioners for some concerts 30 mins before perf. **Credit** AmEx, EC, MC, V.

## Other Venues

Many churches offer regular organ recitals. It's also worth enquiring whether concerts are to be staged in any of the castles or museums in the area, especially in the summer or around holidays. Telephones are often erratically staffed, so check *Zitty*, *Tip* or *Checkpoint* for listings.

### Akademie der Künste
*Hanseatenweg 10, Tiergarten, 10557 (39 00 738/30 00 70). U9 Hansaplatz.* **Open** *box office* 10am-6pm Mon-Fri for enquiries, and one hour before performance. **Tickets** DM12-DM10. **No credit cards.**

The Academy of Arts offers visitors everything from art exhibitions, through literary readings, to music, specialising in performances of compositions from the twentieth century. Concerts are either in the large (507 seats) or the small (205 seats) hall. Acoustics in both rooms of the 1960 building are reasonable. Wander through an exhibition before the performance to put yourself in the right frame of mind.

### Ballhaus Naunynstraße
*Naunynstraße 27, Kreuzberg, 10997 (25 88 66 44). U8 Moritzplatz.* **Open** *box office* Reserve by leaving a message on the answering machine. Pick up tickets up to one hour before perf. **Tickets** DM15-DM10. **No credit cards.**

Don't expect to hear anything ordinary at this Kreuzberg cultural centre; a varied assortment of western and oriental music is on the menu. A café sells drinks and snacks after performances. The long, rectangular hall, which seats 150, has ideal acoustics for classical music.

### Berliner Dom
*Lustgarten, Mitte, 10117 (246 90). S3, S5, S6, S9 Hackescher Markt.* **Open** *enquiries* 10am-6pm Mon-Fri. **Tickets** DM5. **No credit cards.**

Berlin's cathedral, having been almost fully restored from its war-damaged state, now houses some rather fine concerts, usually of the organ or choral variety.

### Hochschule der Künste
*Hardenbergstraße 33, Tiergarten, 10623 (31 85 23 74). U2 Ernst-Reuter-Platz.* **Open** *box office* 3-6.30pm Tue-Fri; 11am-2pm Sat. **Tickets** free for student concerts; DM50-DM20 for guest performers. **No credit cards.**

Berlin's wannabe musical luminaries study in the adjacent building. A grotesquely ugly but thoroughly functional hall plays host to both student soloists and orchestras, as well as lesser known, underfunded professional groups. There's a great deal of variety here, and the fact that it doesn't attract the best known artists is certainly no reason to avoid it.

### Kesselhaus der Kulturbrauerei
*Knaackstraße 12, Prenzlauerberg, 10405 (441 92 69). U2 Eberswalder Straße.* **Open** *enquiries* 10am-6pm Mon-Sat. **Tickets** DM30-DM20. **No credit cards.**

Situated, as its name implies, in the boiler house of a converted brewery, which also houses art galleries and a rather overpriced courtyard bar, this small theatre is rapidly establishing a reputation amongst Berlin's black-clad culture vultures who come to see occasional opera or music-theatre pieces. Look out for new productions by the Neue Opern- und Theaterbühne Berlin, whose recent productions have included the first Berlin performance in over a decade of Benjamin Britten's chamber opera masterpiece *The Turn of the Screw*.

### St Matthäus-Kirche
*Matthäikirchplatz, Tiergarten, 10785 (261 36 76). U2, S1, S2 Potsdamer Platz.* **Open** *box office* 2-4pm Mon-Fri. **Tickets** DM35-DM15; discount tickets DM30-DM12. **No credit cards.**

Organists and small ensembles play in this small brick Charlottenburg church, which is sited snugly between the Philharmonie and Neue Nationalgalerie. It's a fine spot to relax in after pondering the art next door. You can usually count on a Thursday night concert, with others at weekends.

### Staatsbibliothek-Otto Braun Saal
*Potsdamerstraße 33, Tiergarten, 10785 (266 1). U2, S1, S2 Potsdamer Platz.* **Open** *enquiries* 10am-1pm Mon-Fri; *box office* one hour before perf. **Tickets** DM25-DM15; DM12-DM8 concs. **No credit cards.**

The Staatsbibliothek is everything to anyone looking for a bit of culture: exhibitions, historical archives and music are all on the programme. Smaller ensembles provide the lion's share of the music in this chamber of the state library.

# Podewil

arts & experiments

MUSIC
THEATRE
DANCE

...and a cup of coffee

Klosterstrasse 68-70
10179 Berlin (Mitte)
Phone 24749-777

# Music: Rock, Folk & Jazz

**Techno has redrawn Berlin's musical map, but live music continues to thrive in concert halls, stadia and dives.**

Base-camp for Brecht and Weill, backdrop for Liza Minelli as Sally Bowles, host to David Bowie and hometown to Einstürzende Neubauten – Berlin's reputation as music city out on the dark and decadent edge of things goes back a long way. As far back as Marlene Dietrich, in fact. Hold that reputation up to the light, though, and it begins to look a little threadbare.

Sure, there's plenty of live music. Germany's biggest and most cosmopolitan city offers concert venues of every shape, size and degree of discomfort. Almost every European tour, be it indie-cult band or international mega-star, makes a point of stopping here. There are also scores of local bands, thriving jazz, dance and world music scenes and a city government still keen, though with vastly reduced funds, to subsidise the whole mess.

Yet, despite a clutch of interesting and innovative independent labels, Berlin does not really have much of a music industry. And for all the city's reputation as a hotbed of extremism and experimentation, don't expect to find some radical new rock concept on every street corner. Even so, the city is still a place where the unusual has space to happen. And on certain street corners, you might just stumble on a techno rave that is harder and heavier than anything in your wildest dreams. Or nightmares.

## THE MYTH

Think of things beginning with a 'D', as in 'decadence'. There's deviant sex, doomed romance, drag, drugs and dabbling with the dark side of things. And Dietrich, of course.

For any music city, the myth is as important as the music itself – attracting people who then fuel it with their own dreams and expectations. The Berlin myth began with Marlene as Lola-Lola and arrived at Minelli as Sally Bowles. The intervening 12 years of poncing around in Nazi uniforms followed by several decades of Cold War division did little to scotch the city's reputation for darkness and degeneracy.

The Berlin myth drew Bowie here, in the dodgiest and druggiest phase of his career. The experience provided both him and Iggy Pop with the two best albums of their careers, while simultaneously feeding back into the nightclubbing, bright white clubbing myth which had been their inspiration.

Others who have consulted the Berlin muse include Lou Reed (his harrowing *Berlin* album), Nick Cave (who stayed here for a dark and druggy yet prolific stretch) and Depeche Mode (who recorded a series of albums in the city). More recently, U2 not only made *Achtung Baby* here, but also based their whole campaign for the album around the Trabant car, Zoo Station and other Berlin icons.

Oh yes, both Depeche Mode and U2 took to wearing black leather trousers. These lamentable fashion items, a hardy perennial in Kreuzberg and related districts are, along with skull rings and death's-heads daubed on jackets, the very things in which the dark, decadent (and – as often as not – dull, dull, dull) myth of Berlin survives.

## THE REALITY

In the late twenties, working with Bertolt Brecht on musicals like *Die Dreigroschenoper* or *Happy End*, Kurt Weill spruced up songs in the German varieté tradition by adding a jazzy, American influence. The results were so successful and enduring that the idiom has been translated back into American by everyone from Louis Armstrong through Bobby Darin to Jim Morrison and Tom Waits. This was a trick few Germans, and fewer Berliners, have managed to pull off since.

Long before satellite media began to exert their continent-wide, homogenising influence, the output of British and American forces radio, which accompanied the post-War Allied military presence, meant Germans, and especially Berliners, were better placed than most mainland Europeans to catch on to the sound of anglophone pop and rock. Perhaps too well placed. A paradoxical result has been that while outsiders have often looked to Berlin for inspiration, many of the locals are stuck in some corny version of the American myth – usually either an Austin, Texas or else a Lower East Side of the imagination. They might get the general idea right but most miss out on cultural nuance and sense of humour.

The fall of the Wall in 1989 didn't open the west to east German influence. Under the communist regime, culture had atrophied around Brecht and Weill, yet revivals of their music was still a more palatable option than the state-approved strain of musicianly progressive rock. Very late on, some GDR groups, such as new wave satirists Pankow, did manage gingerly to sidestep restrictions with a modicum of credibility intact. But whatever underground East Berlin had was too deeply buried to exert any musical or moral pressure on its western equivalent.

## LANGUAGE PROBLEMS

Stray into German-language music and it's easy to be snobbish about the serviceable if often ordinary song-orientated rock that satisfies the home market, such as that from Berlin bands Element of Crime or Die Ärzte. Yet most of it lacks that extra something special necessary to win the ear of non-Germans.

Tough as it is on guitar-toting Germans who like playing nice tunes, German music raises two expectations either. To exert some influence it must be either noisily avant-garde (Can, Neu, Neubauten) or else electronic. Kraftwerk were from Düsseldorf and Giorgio Moroder worked in Munich, but Berlin has contributed the guitar/electronic trance group Ashra Tempel, Tangerine Dream and now techno.

The noise end of Berlin music might not mean much in body count terms, but its influence has been deep and lasting. Observe the continuing international fascination with Einstürzende Neubauten. After Kraftwerk, they remain the best known German group abroad, both despite and because of the way they've literally battered away at the very limits of rock music using an arsenal of junk metal, jackhammers and drills. Sadly, they've left for dead many of the bands they started out with in the early eighties – bands such as Düsseldorf exiles DAF (who recorded the definitive version of the classic Berlin song 'Kebabträume'), techno precursors Liaisons Dangereuses, Malaria and others on the Zensor and Monogam labels.

Even so, the same people in different combinations intermittently produce Berlin's most absorbing music. Militant rock guitar classicists Die Haut, for example, after a decade of wasted opportunities, are now producing consistently strong records and performances. The highly innovative guitarist Caspar Brötzmann is one of the few (newish) names to watch out for.

More recently, techno has picked up Berlin's baton for electronics, experiment and noise and carried it deeper into the heart of the crowd than any Berlin music that has gone before.

## TECHNO AND BEYOND

It's perhaps no accident that Berlin's shift from rock music towards dance has coincided with the end of the Cold War. Dance music has traditionally been expert at breaking down barriers and Berlin techno is where it all comes together. The noise underground meets dance pop meets electronics. Clubbers from the east meet clubbers from the west – usually in post-industrial spaces left over by the collapse of the eastern economy and sometimes quite literally in no-man's land.

Techno has been the biggest thing in Berlin music for a decade and perhaps the most influential ever. Having gone through a period where the music was stripped down to little more than the tyrannical rhythm, techno has also spawned 'trance' – a less brutal form of electronic music where dreamy, ambient textures that hark back to the likes of Tangerine Dream merge with the monstrous rhythm of the nineties. Many of the best examples can be found on Berlin's MFS label. For more on techno, *see chapter* **Clubs**.

## Venues

## Rock

### Deutschlandhalle

*Messedamm 26, Charlottenburg, 14055 (303 8 0/4444).* U2 Kaiserdamm. **Open** *for information* noon-6pm daily. Great big aircraft hangar of a venue that lacks atmosphere and comfort but is capacious enough for all but the very biggest of big groups.

### Franz

*Schönhauser Allee 36-39, Prenzlauer Berg, 10435 (442 82 03). U2 Eberswalderstraße.* **Open** 9pm-5am daily. Boasting 365 concerts a year, from blues and R&B to folk and rock, Franz also runs a record store, a disco and, in good weather, a garden café.

### Huxley's Neue Welt

*Hasenheide 108-114, Kreuzberg, 10967 (621 10 28). U7 Hermannplatz.* **Open** *box office* 11am-6pm Mon-Fri. A former roller-skating rink that contains stages both large and small (Huxley's Junior). Good middle range venue for mainstream and not-so-extreme alternative, plus the occasional gangsta rapper and any German band with enough pulling power.

### Knaack Club

*Greifswalder Straße 224, Prenzlauer Berg, 10405 (442 70 61). S8, S10, S86 Greifswalder Straße.* **Open** from 10pm. Knaack's adventurous booking policy covers alternative and jazz, and there's billiards and the occasional movie, too. Handily located in Berlin's new Bohemia.

### KOB

*Potsdamer Straße 157, Schöneberg, 10783 (215 20 60). U2 Bülowstraße.* **Open** from 9pm Fri, Sat. An anarchistic institution dating from when Schöneberg was as much a squatter area as neighbouring Kreuzberg. Punky, but don't be fooled by the pose – they're sweeties really.

### Loft

*In the Metropol, Nollendorfplatz 5, Schöneberg, 10777 (215 54 63). U1, U2, U4 Nollendorfplatz.* **Open** *box office* 11am-6pm Mon-Fri; 9.30am-2pm Sat.

**Sun Electric** – *kitchen hands of distinction.*

Still the best small-to-medium concert venue in Berlin. This has little to do with the space, which is low-ceilinged and bleak, or the acoustics, which are poor, and everything to do with a sharp booking policy. If they're still smallish but you've read about them in the *NME*, then they'll turn up here sooner or later.

### SO36
*Oranienstraße 190, Kreuzberg, 10999 (615 26 01/fax 614 78 46). U1 Görlitzer Bahnhof.* **Open** times vary; phone for details between 10am and 6pm.
Legendary punk and atonal venue which these days feeds the local appetite for an unending slurry of ska and hardcore. They also let in bands such as Hamburg's postpunk perennials Abwärts, so it's worth scanning their concert lists.

### Tacheles
*Oranienburger Straße 53-56, Mitte, 10117 (312 10 77). U6 Oranienburger Tor.* **Open** phone for details.
Struggling against closure as we go to press, this odd, anarchic venue represents a distinct phase in Berlin's history: post-Wall and pre-property development. There are several stages, a café and a basement disco in which all kinds of musical events take place.

## Folk & World Music

Compared to London or Paris, with their huge immigrant populations, the world music scene in Berlin, which has many Turks but no other foreign communities of any consequence, is small. Berliners generally, though, are well travelled and the audience for world music is enthusiastic and receptive. The Berlin Senate is keen to support world music events, particularly the Heimatklänge festival. For up-to-date information on world music events stop off at Canzone Record Store (*see chapter* **Shopping**), tune to world promoters Piranha's Kiss FM slot (Tue 8-10pm) or scan the listings in *Tip* and *Zitty*.

### Café Global
*Haus der Kulturen der Welt, John-Foster-Dulles-Allee 10, Tiergarten, 10557 (397 005 66). S3, S5, S6, S7, S9 Bellevue, bus 100.* **Open** live music from 10pm Fri, Sat. **Admission** free.
A world music disco that occasionally also features bands, in a café overlooking the Spree river.

### Haus der Kulturen der Welt
*John-Foster-Dulles-Allee 10, Tiergarten, 10557 (397 87 0) S3, S5, S6, S7, S9 Bellevue, bus 100.* **Open** box office and information 10am-8pm Tue-Sun.
Important venue for the 'high art' end of world music – Indian classical music, for example.

### Slumberland
*Goltzstraße 24, Schöneberg, 10781. U1, U2, U4 Nollendorfplatz.* **Open** 9am-4am daily.
A bar that's seen better days, but its regular flow of world music makes it a good place to meet fellow fans. Sand on the floors and vaguely tropical decor.

### Trommelfieber
The name means 'drum fever' and this is a club night run by Senegal's Abdourahmane Diop & Griot Music Company which takes place at changing venues across the city. Lots of musicians turn up and spontaneous jam and jazz sessions are a feature.

## Irish Pubs

Most of Berlin's many Irish pubs put on folk music. Here are a few of the better ones. You'll find others in the local listings press.

### Irish Harp Pub
*Giesebrechtstraße 15, Charlottenburg, 10629 (882 66 41). U7 Adenauerplatz.* **Open** 11am-2am daily; music from 8pm Fri, Sat. **Admission** free.
Big, rowdy pub in the middle of Charlottenburg. Music at night and fry-up breakfasts in the mornings.

### Irish Pub
*Europa-Center, Tiergarten, 10787 (262 1634). U2, U9, S3, S5, S6, S7, S9 Zoologischer Garten.* **Open** from 11.30am-3pm; bands from 9pm Mon-Fri, 6pm Sat, Sun. **Admission** free.
The biggest and most central of Irish bars, this place is well-frequented by tourists. A bit of a meat market.

### Oscar Wilde
*Friedrichstraße 112a, Mitte, 10117 (282 8166). U6 Oranienburger Tor.* **Open** 11am-2am daily, to 3am Fri, Sat. Live music 10.30pm Thur-Sat.
Guinness, egg and chips, construction workers, and music at the weekends.

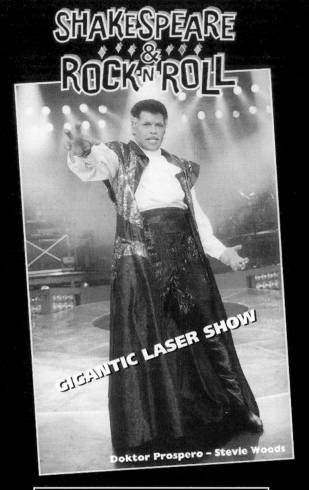

## Jazz

Berlin's jazz scene is neither the best nor the worst in Germany (the best almost certainly being Cologne's), but it is large and encompasses everything from jam sessions in small pubs to major international festivals in po-faced classical music venues (*see below* **Festivals**).

Be warned: Germans take jazz seriously. Some might say too seriously. There is no chance, for example, of jazz ever regaining its original status as dance music and woe betide you if you talk through the band. Even in small places, the appreciation of jazz is usually intense and often eerily intellectual.

If you want your head cleared of all musical prejudices keep a look out for the Berlin-based FMP (Free Music Production) label's concerts, often featuring some of the world's best improvisors, specially if they involve FMP founder Peter Brötzmann, an extremely physical baritone sax player. They're sometimes free when the sessions are being recorded. For concerts, check listings magazines, look out for fliers in shops such as Gelbe Musik (*see chapter* **Shopping**), and see Total Music Meeting under **Festivals** (*below*).

### A-Trane
*Pestalozzistraße 105, Charlottenburg, 10623 (313 25 50). S3, S5, S6, S9 Savignyplatz.* **Open** *box office from 9.30pm, music from 10pm, daily.*
Swanky attempt at a New York-style jazz bar. Expensive, but when it promotes the likes of free jazz pianist Alexander von Schlippenbach playing Monk you can hear past the yuppy trimmings.

### Flöz
*Nassauische Straße 37, Wilmersdorf, 10717 (861 1000). U7 Berliner Straße.* **Open** *box office from 8pm, bands from 9pm, daily.*
A dark and woody cellar bar in the old Berlin style where the players, usually local groups, blast out a little bebop.

### Junction Bar
*Gneisenaustraße 18, Kreuzberg, 10961 (694 66 02). U6, U7 Mehringdamm.* **Open** *music daily, differing start times, usually after 10.30pm.*
Jazz in all its varieties – swing, Latin, contemporary, jazz poetry – but not all on the same night. Occasionally blues and rock here, too.

### Parkhaus (Kulturhaus Treptow/Jazzkeller)
*Puschkinallee 5, Treptow, 12435 (272 79 52). S6, S8, S10, S46 Treptower Park.* **Open** *box office from 7.30pm, music from 10pm, Thur-Sat.*
A club that with Senate support puts on a jazz programme in the cellar of an old villa. The oldest jazz venue in Berlin.

### Podewil
*Klosterstraße 68-70, Mitte, 10179 (247 49 777). U2 Klosterstrasse.* **Open** *box office 2-6pm Tue-Fri.*
Former headquarters of the FDJ (*Freie Deutsche Jugend* – the Communist youth organisation) and 'music-vetting' centre of the GDR. Jazz is one of the more conservative options in Podewil's imaginative programmes, which might range across Free music meetings, themed concert/arts/theatre seasons, contemporary music and related movies.

### Quasimodo
*Kantstraße 12a, Charlottenburg, 10623 (312 8086). U2, U9, S3, S5, S6, S7, S9 Zoologischer Garten.* **Open** *box office from 5pm, concerts from 10pm.*
A small and successful club in the centre of west Berlin and a stopping-off point for many American groups on tour. The programme is mainly jazz but also includes roots and blues. Non-smokers take note: this is notoriously the smokiest venue on Europe's jazz club circuit, a fact which performers often bemoan.

## Festivals

Berlin's Senate is highly supportive of the Berlin music scene, particularly when it comes to keeping Berlin's musicians in work. In conjunction with the public, music business and the media, all of them invited to vote for Berlin's best bands, the City is establishing Metrobeat as a two-day festival for the established and the new in a number of venues across the city in January and February each year. Check with Tourist Information and Berlin press for more up-to-date information. For more seasonal events, *see chapter* **Berlin By Season**.

### Heimatklänge (World Wide Festival of Urban Roots and Dance Music)
*At the Tempodrom, In den Zelten, Tiergarten, 10557 (313 4081/fax 394 61 73). S3, S5, S6, S9 Lehrter Stadtbahnhof.* **Dates** *July/Aug; phone for details.* **Admission** *free.*
Heimatklänge is Berlin's biggest world music event. The Tempodrom tent-venue in the Tiergarten hosts a procession of acts from all corners of the globe. *See also chapter* **Berlin By Season**.

### Jazz Across The Border
*Haus der Kulturen der Welt, John-Foster-Dulles-Allee 10, 10557 (397 870).* **Tickets** *available from May; phone for details.*
Over June and July, around 15 different groups play five weekends of concerts at the Haus der Kulturen der Welt (*see above under* **Folk & World Music**).

### Jazzfest Berlin
*At various venues around Berlin: information on 254 890.* **Dates** *Oct.* **Admission** *varies.*
A four-day event that aims to present a cross-section of international jazz along with some local groups and examples of new influences. Usually around 25 bands play, most of them at the Philharmonie but some (when there's money) at the Delphi cinema on Kantstraße. The Total Music Meeting, a free jazz and improvised music event, runs alongside the more mainstream JazzFest. The concerts take place mostly at Podewil. *See also chapter* **Berlin By Season**.

### Love Parade
*For information contact Kati Schwindt on 618 7353.*
Like a cross between a political demonstration and a techno mardi gras, on the first Saturday of every July tens of thousands of ravers mass and party through the city centre behind a series of floats blasting house and techno. There are also various huge raves over the weekend. In 1994 120,000 people turned up and it seems the event has got too big and crazy for the authorities to allow the traditional route up and down the Ku'damm. This excellent event will certainly continue, though, in some shape or form – keep an eye on local press.

# Berlin on Record

From Brecht to Bowie, Tangerine Dream to techno, we list, in alphabetical order, 19 essential Berlin albums and one vital Berlin single. All were available at the time of writing.

**Als die Partisanen Kamen** *(Monogam/Zensor)*
CD compilation of great Berlin underground 'hits' from 1980-83, including Neubauten, Mania D and Rainy Day Women.

**Ashra Tempel VI: Inventions For Electric Guitar** *(Spalax)*
Influential pre-techno trance from the early seventies by Berlin waveform guitarist Manuel Göttsching.

**David Bowie: Heroes** *(EMI)*
Perhaps both Berlin's and Bowie's best album, even though 'Neuköln' is spelt wrongly.

**Ernst Busch: Lieder der Arbeiterklasse/Lieder aus den Spanischen Bürgerkrieg** *(Pläne)*
Nobody sang socialist standards about tractors and solidarity with as much conviction as Ernst Busch. Shame his versions of Brecht are currently unavailable, though.

**Cabaret: Music From The Original Soundtrack** *(MCA)*
Life is a cabaret, old chum: the very definition of the Berlin myth.

**Nick Cave: From Her To Eternity** *(Mute)*
The Australian expat in typically Berlinisch debauched and desperate mode, with a title track later featured in *Wings Of Desire*.

**DAF: Kebabträume** *(Mute)*
'We are the Turks of tomorrow': this single both summed up and satirised the paranoia of early-eighties Berlin.

**Marlene Dietrich: On Screen, Stage And Radio** *(Legend)*
From 'I Am The Sexy Lola' through 'Ruins Of Berlin', the sultry Schöneberg songstress embodies the mood of decadent Berlin.

**Einstürzende Neubauten: Strategies Against Architecture Parts I & II** *(Mute/Some Bizarre)*
A three-CD history of how Berlin's most important group

**David Bowie** – *could do with a gazetteer.*

augmented guitars with pneumatic drills and raised manic destruction to fine art.

**Die Haut: Head On** *(What's So Funny About)*
Militant guitar classicism plus guest vocals from Debbie Harry, Lydia Lunch, Blixa Bargeld, Alan Vega and others.

**Der Klang der Familie** *(Tresor/Mute)*
The first Berlin techno compilation documents the scene in its early, apocalyptic, camoflage-and-smoke-machine phase.

**Lotte Lenya: Happy End** *(Sony)*
Including Surabaya-Johnny and the Bilboa-Song, this is Brecht and Weill at their most accessible.

**Malaria!: Revisited** *(Danceteria)*
The Berlin version of the girl group: dark, suffocating, passionate and unforgettable.

**Iggy Pop: Lust For Life** *(Virgin America)*
Listen to 'The Passenger' while riding the S-Bahn and check the way Iggy caught the intensity and sardonic cheer of the city at ground level.

**Sun Electric: Kitchen** *(R&S)*
Berlin techno unfolds brilliantly into international ambience.

**Tangerine Dream: Zeit** *(Jive Electro)*
Where cosmic consciousness and electronic minimalism first met by the Wall.

**Die Tödliche Doris: Die Unsichtbare 5. LP Materialisiert Als CD** *(Die Tödliche Doris Records)*
Charming fringe performance trio present puckish Berlin Dada, mid-eighties style.

**3Phase: Straight Road** *(Tresor)*
A fine example of late Berlin techno: six raw versions of one huge-sounding club stomp. *Time Out Berlin Guide* office turntable favourite.

**Tranceformed From Beyond** *(MFS)*
The compilation that defined Berlin trance. The segued selection includes Cosmic Baby, Microglobe, Effective Force and others.

**U2: Achtung Baby** *(Island)*
It took the Wall coming down to inspire the U2 album for people who don't like U2.

*Ride and ride the S-Bahn with* **Iggy Pop**.

# Sport & Fitness

**The city might have failed in its Olympic bid, but it's not the winning, it's the taking part that counts – and Berlin has lots of opportunities for doing just that.**

Berlin is not a major sporting city. It has the world's fifth largest women's tennis championship and the third largest marathon. It has the giant Olympiastadion, where every alternate winter Saturday the 600 or so fans of Hertha BSC huddle together to keep warm and fail to cheer Berlin's best-known football team out of the second division. Berlin also lost out to Sydney in its bid to host the Olympic Games in the year 2000.

Part of the point of that Olympic bid was to build up Berlin's sporting infrastructure. Without the games, Berlin's sporting facilities are suffering from the same cash-draining circumstance as everything else in the city – reunification.

If you want to play sports, though, there are plenty of opportunities. Berlin is amply equipped with parks for jogging, cycling or playing football; also with lakes for ice-skating in the winter, swimming, sailing or wind-surfing in the summer. Squash, tennis and fitness centres are scattered all over the city and there are clubs dedicated to just about every sport you can think of. Here's how to make the most of them.

## Information

The cheapest way to do sports is to be a member of a club. These are highly organised. Almost every sporting discipline has its own club and governing body (known as a Verband). These associations are affiliated to the Landessportbund Berlin, general overseer of sporting activity in the city. If you have plenty of time in Berlin, contact the relevant Verband and ask staff to send you their latest directory (Verzeichnis) of clubs and events in Berlin. The Verband is always the best place to start, as staff can give you impartial information on the best clubs, the cheapest courses, and so on.

### Landessportbund Berlin

*Jesse-Owens-Allee 2, Charlottenburg, 14053 (30 00 20).* **Open** 8.30am-4.30pm Mon Fri.
If you want a general overview of sporting events throughout the year in Berlin, as well as a list of sporting organisations by area, ask the Landessportbund for a copy of their Freizeitsportkalender.

### Sportsphone

*(011 63).* **Open** 24 hours daily.
Recorded sports news.

## Sports Centres

### SEZ (Sport und Erholungszentrum)

*Landsberger Allee, Friedrichshain, 10249 (42 28 33 20). S6, S8, S10, S85 Landsberger Allee.* **Open** 9am-9pm daily. **Admission** two hours DM7; DM3.50 children, students.
Since it first opened in March 1981, close to 30 million visitors have passed through the SEZ's doors. This huge complex includes indoor and outdoor swimming pools, plus wave-, cascade- and jet-pools. Even divers are catered for, and there is a multi-purpose pool for people with disabilities. The centre also has saunas, a solarium, a weight-training room, and a 'Polarium' (indoor rink) for ice-skating (open Oct-Mar), roller-skating (May-Sept), and a 16-lane bowling alley. Other activities range from badminton to aerobics, tae kwon-do to dance. In summer the centre runs outdoor sports in its park – volleyball, badminton, table-tennis, bowls and mini-golf. There are also seven restaurants.

## Sport Club Siemensstadt Berlin

*Rohrdamm 61-64, Siemensstadt, 13629 (38 00 20). U7
Rohrdamm.* **Open** office 7.30-8.30pm daily. **Admission**
DM7; DM3.50 concessions.
A smaller project than the SEZ, but with more or less the
same facilities. It also puts on many club activities in vari-
ous disciplines, including tennis.

## Athletics

### Leichtathletic-Verband

*Glockenturmstraße 1, Charlottenburg, 14053 (305 72
50). U2 Olympia-Stadion.* **Open** 8.30am-5pm Mon, Tue;
8.30am-7pm Thur; 8.30am-2pm Fri.
Contact this office for information about events, tracks and
clubs in Berlin.

### Olympiastadion (Olympic Stadium)

*Charlottenburg, 14053 (30 06 34 30). U2 Olympia-
Stadion.* **Open** *winter* 9am-8pm; *summer* 9am-3.30pm
daily, except event days. **Admission** DM1.
Built between 1934-36 for Hitler's 1936 Olympic Games (an
attempt at Aryan propaganda that was gloriously sunk by
Jesse Owens and other black US athletes breaking records
and winning medals which in some cases the Führer refused
to present – in Owens' case he simply wasn't in the stadium
because of prior engagements), the 76,000-seater Olympia-
stadion still hosts football matches and athletics meetings,
as well as rock concerts. For DM1 you can get in and have
a look around on days when there's nothing on. *See also
chapter* **By Area.**

## Basketball

### Berliner Basketball-Verband

*Bismarckallee 2, Grunewald, 14193 (891 95 10). Bus 119
Hagenplatz.* **Open** 10am-noon Mon, Tue; 4-7pm Thur.
Phone for details about local basketball clubs.

### Basketball Supercup

The international competition will take part in Berlin up to
the year 2000. **Date:** early July. **Admission** DM10-DM25
for a one-day ticket, which inludes two games. Information
(891 95 10).

## Billiards

Many Berlin bars have billiard tables. At halls, an
hour's pool or Carambolage (a billiards-type game
played on a table with no pockets) costs from
DM10-DM20.

### Billard-Landesverband Berlin
### (Berlin Billiards Association)

*Blumberger Damm 67, Marzahn, 12685 (258 76 24).*
**Open** 8am-6pm Mon-Fri.

### Billard Centrum

*Nollendorfplatz 3-4, Schöneberg, 10777 (216 33 61). U1,
U2, U4 Nollendorfplatz.* **Open** noon-1am daily.

### Billardparadies

*Immanuelkirchstraße 14, Prenzlauer Berg, 10405 (442
82 70). U2 Eberswalderstraße.* **Open** noon-4am Mon-
Thur, Sun; 24 hours Fri, Sat.

### Frank's Billard Halle

*Oranienstraße 40-41, Kreuzberg, 10999 (615 65 66).
U1, U8 Kottbusser Tor.* **Open** 2pm-4am daily.

## Canoeing

Berlin and the surrounding countryside are
streaked with lakes, rivers and canals on which
canoeing is possible. Renting a canoe costs from
DM10 an hour to DM50 a day and DM180 a week.

### Kanu Connection

*Köpenicker Straße 9, Kreuzberg, 10997 (612 26 86). U1
Schlesisches Tor.* **Open** *Apr-Oct* 10am-6pm Mon-Fri; 10am
2pm Sat; *Nov-Mar* 10am-6pm Wed-Fri; 10am-2pm Sat.
Kanu Connections has four landing places in Berlin, from
which you can set off on a guided day- or weekend tour on
the waterways of former East Germany. For a weekend you
pay DM130; a day will cost about DM60.

### Der Bootsladen

*Brandensteinweg 8, Spandau, 13595 (362 56 85). U2
Theodor-Heuss Platz, then bus 149 Pichelswerder.*
Take a trip through Klein Venedig (Little Venice) as
Berliners call the canal system in the western part of Berlin.
Prices are similar to the those at Kanu Connection.

## Chess

### Berliner Schachverband

*Blumenweg 17, Mariendorf, 12105 (705 66 06). S2
Mariendorf.* **Open** 10am-2pm Mon, Tue, Thur, Fri; 2-6pm
Wed.
Contact for details of forthcoming matches, or local leagues.

### Café Belmont

*Kurfürstenstraße 107, Schöneberg, 10787 (218 63 65).
U1, U2, U3 Wittenbergplatz.* **Open** 24 hours daily.
The best place to get into the Berlin chess scene. Most of the
hours this place is open you'll find a cosmopolitan crowd
playing and talking chess.

## Cycling

### Berliner Radsport-Verband

*Priesterweg 3, Schöneberg, 10829 (781 17 12/784 57
53). S2 Priesterweg.* **Open** 11am-6.30pm Mon-Fri.

### Internationale 4 Etappen Fahrt
### (International 4 Stage Race)

*Information (781 17 12 /784 57 53).*
A 600km race through Berlin. Begins in front of the
Kaiser-Wilhelm-Gedächtniskirche, Tauentzien, Charlottenburg, U1, U2 Zoologischer Garten. Date early May. Phone
for details.

### City-Night Rundkurs

*Information (781 17 12 /784 57 53). U1, U2
Zoologischer Garten.* **Date** early September. Phone for
details. **Time** 7-9pm.
A mixture of amateur and professional cyclists speed around
the Kaiser-Wilhelm Gedächtniskirche for a couple of hours
in a tight 1km circle, just for the merry hell of it. Cycling
freaks gather to goggle in Breitscheidplatz. Saddle up for
a fun event.

### Fahrradstation

*Möckernstraße 93, Kreuzberg, 10963 (216 91 77). S1,
S2 Anhalter Bahnhof or bus 248.* **Open** 10am-6pm Mon-
Fri; 10am-2pm Sat. **Prices** DM25/24 hours; DM20/day.
A bike shop that rents machines as well as sells them.
They're good ones, both city bikes and trekking bikes.
Fahrradstation also provides information and organises city
tours in groups of up to eight.

## Fitness Studios

### Jopp Frauen-Fitness Berlin
*Tauentzienstraße 13, Wilmersdorf, 10789 (21 01 11).*
*U1, U2, U15 Wittenbergplatz.* **Open** 7am-11pm Mon-
Thur; 7am-10pm Fri; 10am-5pm Sat, Sun. **Credit** EC, V.
Olympic winners such as Katarina Witt and Franziska van
Almsick say they train at this fitness centre – one of four for
women only. Large studios with friendly trainers.

### Oasis
*Stresemannstraße 74, Kreuzberg, 10963 (262 6661). S2*
*Anhalter Bahnhof.* **Open** 10am-11pm Mon-Fri; 10am-
8pm Sat; 10am-4pm Sun. **No credit cards.**
Oasis is well equipped, for both men and women, with a great
swimming pool.

## Football

Football is Berlin's most popular sport. If you want
to join in a weekend game, go to the Tierpark and
tag on to one of the many games.

### Berliner Fußball-Verband
*Humboldtstraße 8a, Grunewald, 14193 (896 99 40-*
*47/48). S6, S9 Westkreuz.* **Open** 8am-4.30pm Mon-Thur;
8am-7pm Fri.
Phone for details and ask for a list of local football clubs.

### Hertha BSC
*Reichsstraße 17, Charlottenburg, 14052 (305 50 01). U1*
*Neu-Westend.* **Open** office 9am-1pm, 2-5pm, Tue-Fri.
None of Berlin's football teams is represented in the Erste
Bundesliga. Hertha BSC spent a solitary season there in
1990-91, but promptly dropped back down into their natur-
al habitat – the second division. The club is not expected to
bounce back.

### Türkiyem Spor
*Friedrich-Ludwig-Jahn Sportpark Cantianstraße,*
*Prenzlauer Berg, 10437. U2 Eberswalderstraße.*
*Information (615 74 07).*
A Turkish team that regularly tops the local league and has
a loyal and vociferous following lending a lot of atmosphere
to their matches. Up to a 1,000 people can turn up to see their
Sunday afternoon games, which is more than Hertha draw
to the enormous Olympiastadion.

## Horse Racing

### Galloprennbahn-Hoppegarten
*Goetheallee 1, Dahlwitz-Hoppegarten, 15366 (559 61 02).*
*S5 Hoppegarten.*
Berlin's race-course is just outside the city limits to the north-
east. Races take place between April and October. The bet-
ting system in Germany is run pretty much like the English
Tote (and is computerised).

## Trotting

Trotting is popular in Germany. Otherwise known
as harness racing, it entails riders pelting along in
modern-day chariots.

### Trabrennbetrieb-Karlshorst
*Treskowallee 129, Karlshorst, 10318 (509 08 91). S3*
*Karlshorst.*
Meetings are held throughout the year on Saturdays at
2.30pm. Races also take place on Tuesday evenings at
6.30pm.

### Trabrenn Verein-Mariendorf
*Mariendorfer Damm 222, Mariendorf, 12107 (740 12*
*12). U6 Alt-Mariendorf, then bus X76, 176, 179*
*Trabrennbahn.*
Race meetings are held Sun at 2pm and Wed at 6.30pm.

## Ice Sports

These are the best ice-skating rinks in the city:

### Eislauf an der Glocke
*Glockenturmstraße, Charlottenburg, 14055 (305 50 20).*
*U2 Theodor-Heuss-Platz, then bus 149 Stößenseebrücke.*
**Open** from mid-November to end of February; 10am-
noon Mon-Sat; 3-5pm, Tue-Fri; 10am-noon, 2-4pm, 4.30-
6.30pm, Sat, Sun; 10.30am-12.30pm Sun. **Admission**
DM4 for two hours; DM2.50 concs.

### Eisstadion Berlin Wilmersdorf
*Fritz-Wildung-Straße 9, Wilmersdorf, 14199 (824 10*
*12). U1 Heidelberger Platz.* **Open** Oct to mid-March 9am-
6.30pm, 7.30-10pm, Mon, Wed, Fri; 9am-5.30pm, 7.30-
10pm, Tue, Thur; 9am-9.30pm Sat; 9am-5pm Sun.
**Admission** DM3 for two hours, DM1.50 concs.

## Sailing & Surfing

Sailing and surfing have become very popular.
The two biggest lakes are the Müggelsee in the
east and the Wannsee in the west.

### Berliner Segler-Verband
### (Berlin Sailing Association)
*Bismarckallee 2, 14193 Charlottenburg, 14193 (891 50*
*15). S3, S6, S9 Westkreuz.* **Open** 3-5pm Tue-Thur.
If you want to sail or surf on the lakes, you need to be able
to pronounce the term Amtlicher Sportbootführerschein-
Binnen. That's a sailing licence. To get one you must pass a
theoretical and practical course administered by this association. If you think you have enough practical experience
to pass, register for the six-day theoretical course (to learn
the rules and regulations on Berlin's waterways). It costs
DM116. Write for an application form.

## Squash

An hour on a squash court costs about DM20. You
can hire a racket for DM5 from larger sports centres.

### Squash-City-Club Berlin
For membership details, phone Gene Scites (803 789 59). The
club plays at Tennis and Squash City (*see below*).

### Tennis and Squash City
*Brandenburgische Straße 53, Wilmersdorf, 10707 (87 90*
*97). U7 Konstanzer Straße.* **Open** 7am-midnight daily.
Apart from seven tennis courts and 11 squash courts, this
centre has four badminton courts (DM25 per hour) and a
small driving range (DM10 for 30 min). There's also a sauna,
solarium and restaurant. Training is given in all games.

## Swimming

## Indoor Swimming Pools

All the swimming pools listed below are open
throughout the year. Almost every Berlin district
has at least one swimming pool. Pools will be

either Normale Bäder (the water temperature will be at or below 26°C/78.8°F) or Warmbäder (above 27°C/80.6°F).

### Schwimmhalle
*Rudolf-Seiffert-Straße 3, Lichtenberg, 10369 (972 70 06/91 69). S8, S10 Storkower Straße.* **Open** 6.30-9am Mon, Wed, Thur, Fri; 8am-5.30pm Sat; 8am-1.30pm Sun. **Admission** DM2.50; DM1.50 concs.

### Schwimmhalle Fischerinsel
*Fischerinsel 11, Mitte, 10179 (242 54 49). U2 Märkisches Museum.* **Open** 6.30-9am Mon, Tue, Thur, Fri; 5-9.30pm Tue, Fri. **Admission** DM2.50; DM1.50 concs.

### Stadtbad Charlottenburg
*Krumme Straße 6a-8, Charlottenburg, 10585 (34 30 32 41). U2 Deutsche Oper.* **Open** 2-8pm Mon, Tue, Fri; 2-5pm Wed; 2-4pm Thur. **Admission** DM3.50; DM2 concs.

### Stadtbad Kreuzberg
*Wiener Straße 59, Kreuzberg, 10999 (25 88 58 13). U1 Görlitzer Bahnhof.* **Open** 8am-10pm daily; *women only* 2-7pm Mon. **Admission** DM3.50; DM2 concs.

## Open-air Swimming

The following pools are open from early- or mid-May to September. A swim costs about DM3.50 for adults and DM2 for children.

### Freibad Halensee
*Königsallee 5a, Charlottenburg, 14193 (891 17 03). S3, S6, S9 Westkreuz.* **Open** 8am-8pm daily.

### Kombiniertes Bad Seestraße
*Seestraße 80, Wedding, 13347 (455 94 99). U8, U9 Seestraße.* **Open** 8am-8pm daily.

### Olympia Schwimmstadion
*Olympischer Platz, Charlottenburg, 14053 (300 633). U2 Olympia-Stadion.* **Open** 7am-7pm daily.

### Seebad Friedrichshagen (lake)
*Müggelseedamm 216, Friedrichshagen, 12587 (645 57 56). S3 Friedrichshain.* **Open** 9am-6pm daily.

### Sommerbad am Insulaner
*Munsterdamm 80, Steglitz, 12169 (79 04 24 32). S2 Priesterweg, Bus X76, 176 Priesterweg.* **Open** 8am-7pm daily.

### Sommerbad Kreuzberg
*Gitschiner Straße 18-31, Kreuzberg, 10969 (25 88 54 16). U1 Prinzenstraße.* **Open** 8am-7pm daily.

### Sommerbad Neukölln
*Columbiadamm 160, Neukölln, 10965 (68 09 27 75). U7, U8 Hermannplatz. Bus 104.* **Open** 7.30am-7.30pm daily.

### Sommerbad Wilmersdorf
*Forckenbeckstraße 14, Schmargendorf, 14199 (86 41 25 31). U1 Heidelberger Platz.* **Open** 7am-8pm daily.

### Strandbad Müggelsee (lake)
*Fürstenwalder Damm 838, Rahnsdorf, 12589 (645 18 26). S3 Rahnsdorf.* **Open** 8am-10pm daily. With nudist colony.

### Strandbad Wannsee (lake)
*Wannseebadweg, Nikolassee, 14129 (803 54 50). S1, S3 Nikolassee.* **Open** 7am-8pm daily.

## Table Tennis

### Berliner Tisch-Tennis Verband
*Bismarckallee 2, Charlottenburg, 14193 (892 91 76). S3, S6, S9 Westkreuz.* **Open** 10am-noon Wed, Fri; 3-6pm Thur.
Information about table tennis clubs and events in Berlin.

### Lux Tischtennis Zentrum
*Lobeckstraße 36, Kreuzberg, 10969 (614 90 15). U8 Moritzplatz.* **Open** 10am-6pm Mon-Fri; 10am-2pm Sat.
Meet all your table tennis needs at this shop. It's also a good place to go for advice about which club to join.

## Tennis

Tennis is expensive in Berlin. At the cheapest time (mornings) it will cost you DM26-DM32 for one hour on an indoor court. *See also above* **Tennis and Squash City** *under* Squash.

### tsf (tennis, squash, fitness)
*Richard-Tauber-Damm 36, Marienfelde, 12277 (742 10 91). U6 Alt-Mariendorf.* **Open** 7am-11pm daily.

### tsf
*Galenstraße 33-45, Spandau, 13597 (333 40 83). U7 Rathaus Spandau.* **Open** 7am-11pm daily.

## Windsurfing

### Vereinigte Windsurfing Schule Berlin (office)
*Holtzendorffstraße 1, Charlottenburg, 14057 (321 18 33). S6 Charlottenburg.* **Open** 9am-6pm Mon-Fri; 9am-1pm Sat.
The best-equipped windsurfing school in Berlin. You can rent equipment at reasonable prices (DM18 for an hour with fully equipped board and wetsuit, or DM120 for three days), take theoretical and practical courses, and take advantage of Berlin's reliable winds on a great stretch of water.

### Am Grossen Fenster (boat house)
*Bootshaus Irmgard, at Schwanenwerder close to Wannsee Grunewald, 14129 (803 66 34). S1, S3, S7 Nikolassee, then bus 218 Großes Fenster.* **Open** mid-Apr-Oct 10am-7.30pm daily.

## Women's Sports

There is a special organisation attached to the Landessportbund (*see above* **Information**) catering for and promoting women's sports. Information can be obtained from:

### Landesausschuss Frauensport
*Jesse-Owens-Allee 2, Charlottenburg, 14053 (300 02 0). U2 Olympia-Stadion.* **Open** 9am-3pm Mon-Fri; 9am-2pm Fri.

### Women's Run
*Contact: Berlin Marathon, Waldschulallee 34, Charlottenburg, 14055 (302 53 70).* **Date** May. **Admission** DM12.
Starting and finishing point for this 10km run through the Tiergarten is Straße des 17 Juni.

### Dina's Bodystyling
*Bismarckstraße 98, Charlottenburg, 10625 (312 11 10). U2 Ernst-Reuter Platz.* **Open** 4-9.30pm Mon, Wed, Fri;

# Sporting Calendar

Below we list the major sporting events taking place in Berlin through the year. More details are printed in the Freizeitsportkalender, available from the **Landessportbund Berlin** (*see* **Information**). *See also chapter* **Berlin By Season**.

## Winter

### Berliner New Year Fun Run
*Begins at the Soviet Monument, Straße des 17 Juni, on January 1. Bus 248/100.* **Information** *(302 53 70).*

## Spring

### Berlin Half-Marathon
*Contact: Berlin Marathon, Waldschulallee 34, Charlottenburg, 14055 (302 53 70).* **Date** first Sun in April. **Admission** participants DM30 for German residents; DM40 for foreign residents, free spectators. Starting point is the wide, majestic Karl-Marx-Allee; finishing point is Alexanderstraße (S-/U-Bahn Alexander Platz).

### Gay and Lesbian Run Berlin
*Volkspark Rehberge. U6 Rehberge.* **Information** *(782 51 94).* **Date** early May. **Admission** DM25.
This 10km run is the most important component of a lesbian and gay athletics event that also includes high- and long-jumping, shorter runs and a 10km wheelchair race. It's like a tiny version of the gay games in New York.

### German Open (International Women's Tennis Championships)
*LTTC Rot Weiss, Gottfried-von-Cramm-Weg 47-55, Grunewald, 14193 (826 22 07). S3 Grunewald or bus 119, 186 Hagenplatz.* **Dates** nineteenth week of the year, in May. **Admission** DM30-DM100 for seats, DM25 for day-ticket with access to all courts except centre court.
The world's fifth largest international women's tennis championship. Tickets with access to all eight courts except centre court are affordable and available during the first few days of the tournament.

## Summer

### German Football Association Cup Finals
*Olympiastadion, Charlottenburg, 14053 (300 633). U2 Olympia-Stadion.* **Information** *(305 04 25).* **Tickets** Reserve in writing at Berliner Fußball Verband, Humboldtstraße 8A, 14193 Berlin. **Dates** May, June. **Admission** DM20-DM90.
Reserve tickets as early as possible. The Olympic Stadium fills up for the German equivalent of the FA Cup Final.

### ISTAF Track and Field Meet
*Olympiastadion, Charlottenburg, 14053. U2 Olympia-Stadion.* **Information** *(238 42 51/52).* **Date** late Aug. **Admission** DM10-DM60. **Tickets** Kant-Kasse (313 45 54).
Established a year after the 1936 Berlin Olympics, this international one-day tournament is now one of the four venues in the light athletics grand slam. Some 250 athletes from 50 nations compete.

### American Bowl
*Olympiastadion, Charlottenburg, 14053. U2 Olympia-Stadion.* **Date** one Sunday in August. **Admission** DM25-DM100; DM300 for VIPs, whoever they are. For VIP tickets phone 069-530 99 35. Unimportant people call 81 07 50.
The Bears, the Broncos, the Dolphins and other American football teams have been touching down in Berlin since 1989. The National Football League chooses two NFL teams for this guest game, complete with cheerleaders, hamburgers and beer. The summer event's massive popularity shows the extent to which this sport is finding a following among German slaves to urban American fashion.

## Autumn

### Berlin Marathon
*Finishing point at Kaiser Wilhem Memorial Church, Breidscheidplatz. U2 Zoologischer Garten.* **Information** *Berlin Marathon, Waldschulallee 34, Charlottenburg, 14055. S3, S6, S7, S9, S45, S46 Westkreuz then bus 219.* **Date** last Sunday in Sept. **Admission** participants DM55 German residents, DM60 foreign residents; spectators free.
The world's third largest marathon, after New York and London. Runners are led past most of Berlin's landmarks on their 42km (26-mile) trek through ten districts, including the Brandenburg Gate, Unter den Linden, the Berlin Cathedral, Philharmonie and Kaiser Wilhem Memorial Church. About 20,000 take part.

### International ADAC Avus Auto Race
*Avus race course, at the Funkturm next to the AMK Trade Fair Grounds, Messedamm 22, 1/19 (86 86 285/6). U2 Kaiserdamm.* **Date** end Sept. **Admission** DM15-DM70.
The most important race in the German Touring Car Championships speeds along a 2.64km (1.6-mile) portion of the Autobahn towards Wannsee. It's also held in May.

11am-9.30pm Tue, Thur; 11am-4pm Sat. Fitness, aerobics, stretching, sauna, solarium.

### Seitenwechsel – Women/Lesbian Sportsclub
*Chaussseestraße 34/35 Aufgang B, Zimmer 309, Mitte, 10115 (288 32 62). U2 Zinnowitzerstraße.* **Open** 11am-1pm Mon; 11am-3pm Thur.
Seitenwechsel organises a gay and lesbian athletics event. Write for information about courses.

### Schokosport/Schoko-Fabrik
*Office: Naunynstraße 72, Kreuzberg, 10997 (615 53 91) U1, U8 Kottbusser Tor, Bus 129 Heinrichplatz.* **Open** noon-4pm Thur, Fri; noon-8pm Wed.
The best place for women's sports. In this former chocolate factory turned Kreuzberg neighbourhood centre, you'll find self-defence courses, dance, movement and exercise classes. A course will cost from DM10-DM50. Apart from the sports centre the Schoko-Fabrik has a Turkish bath, café and more (*see* **Women's Berlin**).

# Theatre

**Subsidised theatre may be under pressure, but new alternative companies are sprouting almost daily in the fringe.**

More than 150 established theatres and performance spaces in Berlin compete for a dwindling audience, while the state subsidies which had so generously supported them (especially in the West) have all but dried up. One sign of the times was the closure of the Schiller Theater's resident company, formerly one of Berlin's premier subsidised groups. These days the Schiller is hired out to commercial companies touring stage musicals. Safe, commercial fare is these days the norm in Berlin, with only an occasional spark on the fringe – or Off-Theater, as it's called in German.

But there is hope. Alternative venues seem to crop up almost daily, mainly in the East where cheaper space is still more readily available. Most notable of these is the **Kulturbrauerei** in Prenzlauer Berg. Even as unlikely a spot as the infamous Ex 'n' Pop in Schöneberg (*see* **Cafes & Bars**) now hosts a regular performance series, mostly in English, on Thursday nights.

Though productions in English are rare, there are a few well-established fringe groups who perform regularly: among them, the Berlin Play Actors and the Out To Lunch Theater Co. These companies stage two to three productions a year.

Unless otherwise indicated, all box offices are open one hour before a performance to sell tickets for that performance only. Tickets can cost as little as DM5 for an informal performance piece or DM75 for the best seats at major venues. Concessions for students and pensioners are available on production of identification, but as a rule only from the theatre one hour before curtain-up, and almost never from commercial theatres. Audioloops for the hard of hearing and full or limited wheelchair access (ring ahead to book places) are indicated when they are available.

## Ticket Agencies

Ticket agencies charge a booking fee of between DM2 and DM5. Advance booking is usually limited to a maximum of between two and five weeks. *See also chapter* **Survival** for last-minute, half-price tickets.

### Theatershop am Alex
*in S-Bahnhof Alexanderplatz, Mitte, 10178 (241 50 87). S3, S5, S6, S7, S9/U2, U8 Alexanderplatz.* **Open** 9am-7pm Mon-Fri; 10am-4pm Sat. **Credit** AmEx, DC, EC, MC, V. Booking charge 15 per cent of ticket price.

Bookings can be made here not only for all Berlin theatres, but also for venues as far afield as Vienna and Paris, and up to one year in advance of the performance.

## Civic Theatres

### Berliner Ensemble
*Am Bertolt-Brecht-Platz 1, Mitte, 10117 (282 31 60). S1, S2, S3, S5, S6, S7, S9/U6 Friedrichstraße.* **Open** 11am-6pm Mon-Sat; 3-6pm Sun, public holidays.
Brecht, whose 'Threepenny Opera' premièred here in 1928, returned to post-war Berlin by invitation of the GDR to run the Berliner Ensemble. After his death, his widow Helene Weigel took over, presiding over decades of unimaginative revivals of his work. Writer/Director Heiner Müller is now attempting to rejuvenate the company.
*Wheelchair access and audioloop.*

### Deutsches Theater and Kammerspiele des Deutschen Theaters
*Schumannstraße 13a, Mitte, 10117 (2844 1225). S1, S2, S3, S5, S6, S7, S9/U6 Friedrichstraße.* **Open** noon-6.30pm Mon-Sat; 3-6.30pm Sun.
The Main House (1850) and the smaller Kammerspiele (1906), beautifully restored, function as a 'national theatre', showing a hugely varied repertoire of German and international classics and modern plays performed by a large company. The small experimental stage, Baracke, is located in an adjacent hut where tickets for popular productions sell out fast.
*Wheelchair access (enquiries 287 12 21).*

### Hansa Theater 'Berliner Volkstheater'
*Alt-Moabit 48, Tiergarten, 10555 (391 44 60). U9 Turmstraße.* **Open** 11am-6pm Mon; 11am-7pm Tue-Sat; 3-6pm Sun.
Theatre for the locals. If your German is good and you can cope with dialect and in-jokes, you'll enjoy the amiable, lighthearted nonsense trotted out here.
*Audioloop and limited wheelchair access.*

### Hebbel Theater
*Stresemannstraße 29, Kreuzberg, 10963 (251 01 44). S1, S2 Anhalter Bahnhof/U6, U15 Hallesches Tor or U7, U15 Möckernbrücke.* **Open** 3-7pm Mon-Fri, Sun; noon-7pm Sat.
The Hebbel was almost derelict when then unknown director Peter Stein moved his company here for a handful of performances. The critics loved him, the public swarmed and the New German Theatre was born. The building, with its 1907 wood-panelled auditorium, was restored in 1988 and reopened to host short appearances by top-notch companies from all over the world. If you can get tickets, you're almost guaranteed a fascinating night's theatre.
*Limited wheelchair access.*

### Maxim Gorki Theater and Studiobühne
*Am Festungsgraben 2, Mitte, 10117 (208 27 83/48). S1, S2, S3, S5, S6, S7, S9/U6 Friedrichstraße.* **Open** 1-6.30pm Mon-Sat; 3-6.30pm Sun.
As you'd expect, a lot of Gorki and northern European playwrights feature in this small baroque theatre. Writer-direc-

*Since the closure of its resident company, the **Schiller Theater** is hired out for musicals.*

tor George Tabori, an Austrian Jew whose family fled to America before the war, was briefly at the helm here, but its most recent productions have been decidedly lacklustre.
*Audioloop.*

### Metropol Theater
*Friedrichstraße 101-102 (entrance in courtyard), Mitte, 10117 (203 640). S1, S2, S3, S5, S6, S7, S9/U6 Friedrichstraße.* **Open** 10am-6pm Mon-Sat.
Berlin's longest-running musical revue theatre features an almost daily changing menu of musicals, operetta and revues, enjoyed by a loyal and mostly eastern audience. It's a light-hearted, trivial, but undemanding night out.
*Limited wheelchair access.*

### Schaubühne am Lehniner Platz
*Kurfürstendamm 153, Charlottenburg, 10709 (89 00 23). S3, S5, S6, S7, S9 Charlottenburg/U7 Adenauerplatz.* **Open** 11am-6.30pm Mon-Sat; 3-6.30pm Sun, public holidays.
Erich Mendelsohn's 1926 design was restored as a permanent home for the company which since 1981 has given it its name. Robert Wilson is a familiar guest director, helping to perpetuate the tried and trusted programme of Russian classics, French comedy, Greek tragedy and contemporary plays.
*Audioloop and limited wheelchair access.*

### Schloßpark Theater
*Schloßstraße 48, Schöneberg, 12165 (793 15 15). S1/U9 Rathaus Steglitz.* **Open** 9am-noon Mon-Sat.
After a hard day's shopping at Forum Steglitz, unwind in a country house-style theatre, be gently entertained and mildly provoked by German and international warhorses.
*Audioloop and wheelchair access.*

### Volksbühne
*Rosa-Luxemburg-Platz, Mitte, 10178 (230 87 46 61/2). U2 Rosa-Luxemburg-Platz.* **Open** noon-6pm Mon-Sat; 11am-6pm Sun; after 6pm tickets sold for that night's performance only.
Under the direction of angry and youngish ex-GDR man Frank Castorf, this large 1906 theatre is now the venue for the most provocative and exciting programme of re-interpreted classics and contemporary works in town. After the play you can catch a rock band (Fri), a reading (Sat), or a video (Sun) in the Roter Salon (Red Salon).
*Limited wheelchair access.*

## Commercial Theatres

### Komödie
*Kurfürstendamm 206, Charlottenburg, 10719 (882 78 93). U15 Uhlandstraße.* **Open** 10am-7pm Mon-Sat; 3-7pm Sun.
A diet of light comedies and farces, packed with 'names' from German TV, attracts a mostly tourist audience.
*Audioloop.*

### Theater am Kurfürstendamm
*Kurfürstendamm 209, Charlottenburg 10719 (882 37 89). U15 Uhlandstraße.* **Open** 10am-7pm Mon-Sat; 3-7pm Sun.
The main house offers light comedies and farces with star casts, while the smaller Magazin (882 10 72) caters for the slightly older and less demanding fringe audience. The entrance to Magazin is via Ku'damm Karree arcade.
*Audioloop and wheelchair access.*

### Theater des Westens
*Kantstraße 12, Tiergarten, 10623 (882 28 88). S3, S5, S6, S7, S9/U2, U9 Zoologischer Garten.* **Open** box office 10am-6pm Mon-Fri; 10am-3.30pm Sat; reservations noon-6pm Tue-Sat; 3-6pm Sun.
Now restored to its original glittering glory, this kitsch palace is deservedly famous for its camp revivals of musicals, operettas and revues, overseen by Helmut Baumann. Berlin's most successful independent theatre has felt the financial pinch along with everyone else, but looks like surviving to churn out its delightfully vapid entertainment for many years to come.
*Wheelchair access.*

## Off-Theater (Fringe)

Berlin has an enormous number of fringe companies, perhaps 200 at any given time, of which half may be recently formed ensembles grabbing whatever performance space they can (in these hard times often settling for a percentage of the box office, rather than a booking fee). The rest are more or less established under their own roofs, usually with a loyal and enthusiastic following.

The opening times and working methods of individual box offices are liable to wide variation. Most box offices are usually open around 30 to 60 minutes before curtain-up and do not accept credit cards. Where telephone numbers are given, reservations may often be made on a (German-speaking) answering machine and collected half an hour before the performance.

## BAT

*Belforter Straße 15, Prenzlauer Berg, 10405 (442 79 96). U2 Senefelderplatz.* **Open** 9am-4pm daily.
The studio theatre of the Ernst Busch High School of Dramatic Art, formerly the leading theatre school of the GDR and still said by many to be the best German-speaking drama academy, presents regular performances by students, plus appearances by professional Berlin theatre groups.

## Brotfabrik

*Prenzlauer Promenade 3, Prenzlauer Berg, 13086 (471 40 01). S8, S10 Prenzlauer Allee, then tram 1, 13, 23.*
Far out in the sticks, but inly worth the journey, is this small, cosy, budget-priced alternative arts centre. It's housed in a former bakery and packed with new and interesting attractions, particularly its theatre. There's also a cinema, a bar, an art gallery and you can sit in the garden in summer.

## Ensemble Theater am Südstern

*in first courtyard, Hasenheide 54, Schöneberg, 10967 (692 32 39). S7 Südstern.*
Not to be confused with several other groups based at this address (such as the dependable Stükke), this theatre forms part of a multi-purpose complex. There's a high standard of production, but the crowd and unique atmosphere are what make the plays work.

## Friends of Italian Opera

*Fidicinstraße 40 (entrance in the courtyard), Kreuzberg, 10965 (691 1211). U6 Platz der Luftbrücke.*
Despite the name, you will find no opera here. Instead this small, cosy venue plays host to some of Berlin's best solo performers and English language theatre.

## Kulturbrauerei

*Schönhauser Allee 36-39 (entrance at Knaackstraße 97), Prenzlauer Berg, 10435 (441 9269). U2 Eberswalderstraße.*
This former Schultheiss brewery now provides a venue for a variety of international performance events throughout the year, including the occasional chamber opera. The courtyard is a pleasant place for a drink before the show.

## Tacheles

*Oranienburger Straße 53-56, Mitte, 10969 (282 61 85). U6 Oranienburger Tor.*
Tacheles, a Yiddish word which roughly translates as 'straight talk', is the name for the ruins of a bombed department store which houses an unsubsidised co-operative. Occasional presentations feature visiting groups and in-house co-productions. Both have a good reputation.

## Theater am Ufer

*in second courtyard, Tempelhofer Ufer 10, Kreuzberg, 10963 (251 31 16). U1, U7, U15 Möckernbrücke.*
Resident company Theater Kreatur play infrequently but to packed houses. Their style is 'physical theatre': lots of poses and few words – easy to understand.

## Theater ON Am Kollwitzplatz

*im Atelier Werdin, Knaackstraße 45, Prenzlauer Berg, 10435 (422 11 46). U2 Senefelderplatz.* **Open** 30 minutes before curtain-up.
The Theater Ohne Name (Without Name) is an entirely unsubsidised 60-seater, one of many east Berlin companies to

have survived the 1989-90 upheavals, staging a mixture of house and guest productions: children's theatre on midweek mornings and weekend afternoons; adult theatre in the evenings. There are also marionette shows.

## Theater Zerbrochene Fenster

*Fidicinstraße 3, Kreuzberg, 10965 (694 24 00). U6 Platz der Luftbrücke or U7 Gneisenaustraße.*
Afflicted, like numerous smaller companies, by uncertain local government funding, the well-heeled avant-garde 'broken window' company is tending to give way to more guest productions, including some from non-German-speaking groups (the English-language Berlin Play Actors are worth catching if performing). The theatre's in a converted factory; the entrance is at the rear, via *Schwiebusser Straße 16.*

## Theater zum Westlichen Stadthirschen

*Kreuzbergstraße 37-38, Kreuzberg, 10965 (785 70 33 answering machine). S1, S2/U7 Yorckstraße.* **Open** office 2-5pm Tue, Thur.
The theatre is not quite as monumental as its entrance portal might suggest, but its excellent reputation is substantial, based on a stimulatingly erratic programme of new works from the house and visiting companies. Worth catching, if you can get a ticket.

## Unart

*Oranienstraße 163, Kreuzberg, 10969 (614 20 70). U8 Moritzplatz.*
An alternative-style, multi-purpose performance and exhibition space which occasionally features drama. Provocative.

## Vaganten Bühne

*Kantstraße 12a, Charlottenburg, 10623 (312 45 29). S3, S5, S6, S7, S9/U2, U9 Zoologischer Garten or U15, U9 Kurfürstendamm.* **Open** 10am-4pm Mon; 10am-7pm Tue-Fri; 5-7pm Sat, public holidays.
The original experimental impulse behind the 'vagrants' stage' had long succumbed to the stifling comfort of generous subsidy and an undemanding public, but the tide is changing. Recent productions have marked its serious return to classic drama.

## Zan Pollo Theater

*Rheinstraße 45, Schöneberg, 12161 (852 20 02). U9 Walter-Schreiber-Platz.*
In darkest Steglitz, otherwise a cultural desert, this oasis of enlightenment bubbles with the continuing success of a company which has been thriving since 1976. A rich variety of German and international works are performed in the recently renovated 100-seat theatre.

# Festivals

## Berliner Festspiele

*Budapester Straße 50, Charlottenburg, 10787 (25 48 90). S3, S5, S6, S7, S9/U2, U9 Zoologischer Garten.* **Open** 10am-6pm Mon-Thur; 10am-4pm Fri.
Advance information about all festivals presented by the city of Berlin can be obtained from this office.

## Theater Treffen Berlin (Berlin Theatre Meeting)

Usually the first three weeks in May see the largest gathering of productions by German-speaking companies. In addition to the dense programming of performances, there are talks, interviews, exhibitions and even films.

## Berliner Festwochen (Berlin Festival)

A general arts festival running during August and September. It includes a good proportion of theatrical productions, designed in part to bridge the gap left by the summer vacations of Berlin theatres.

# After Hours

**What to do and where to do it in the city that never shuts up shop.**

Forget New York, Berlin is the city that never sleeps. Some pallid locals rarely ever emerge during the daytime, and when they do, they can be seen blinking in the unexpectedly bright light.

While shopping hours are rigorously enforced, nightlife in Berlin remains more or less unregulated. It's hard to get a pint of milk after 6.30pm, but you can party around the clock. Even on a Tuesday, many places stay open so late that after hours begins to shade into rush hours.

For bars and clubs, see their respective chapters. Here, to help you make it through the night, we list some late-night services, all-night transport, and a few locations for both small-hour dining and the very earliest of breakfasts.

## Changing Money

The banks listed below have the longest hours of any in Berlin, including those at the airports. If you have the Visa symbol on your bank card you can withdraw money from your UK account at the machine outside this bank and at many others throughout the city.

### Deutsche Verkehrsbank
*Zoologischer Garten, Hardenbergplatz, Charlottenburg, 10623 (881 71 17). U2, U9, S3, S5, S6, S7, S9 Zoologischer Garten.* **Open** 7.30am-10pm Mon-Fri; 8am-7pm Sun, public holidays.

### Deutsche Verkehrsbank
*In Hauptbahnhof, Friedrichshain, off Stralauer Platz, 10243 (428 70 29). S3, S5, S6, S7, S9 Hauptbahnhof.* **Open** 7am-10pm Mon-Fri; 7am-6pm Sat; 8am-4pm Sun, public holidays.
The Wechselstuben of the Deutsche Verkehrsbank offer among the best rates of exchange in the city, as well as the longest opening hours.

## Shopping

If you absolutely must stock up with food after 6pm, go to one of the following. It would probably be cheaper to eat out, though. Many 24-hour petrol stations (*see below*) also stock equally expensive basic groceries.

### Edeka
*in Schloßstraße Station, Steglitz, 12163 (794 40 45). U9 Schloßstraße.* **Open** 3-10pm Mon-Fri; 1-10pm Sat; 10am-8pm Sun, public holidays. **No credit cards.**

### Metro
*in Fehrbelliner Platz Station, Wilmersdorf, 10707 (861*

*70 10). U2, U7 Fehrbelliner Platz.* **Open** 11am-10.30pm daily. **No credit cards.**

### Metro
*in Kurfürstendamm Station, Charlottenburg, 10719 (883 41 41). U3, U15 Kurfürstendamm.* **Open** 11am-11pm Mon-Fri, Sun; 11am-midnight Sat. **No credit cards.**

## Chemists

A list of pharmacies offering Sunday and evening services should be displayed at every pharmacy. For information, phone:

### Emergency Pharmaceutical Services (Apotheken Notdienst)
*(0 11 41).* **Open** 24 hours daily.

## Transport

Maps of the night line network (Nachtliniennetz) are available free from the grey-uniformed Customer Assistance personnel who can be found in most of the larger U-Bahn and S-Bahn stations.

The bus, tram and U-Bahn routes marked on this map make most areas of the city accessible after hours. The network operates between 1-4am. The rest of the time, regular timetables apply. So stay out late enough and you won't have to worry about a thing – except perhaps early shop closing hours on Saturday.

If you need a taxi, you should be able to hail one or find a few waiting at a stand. At most bars and restaurants, the staff will call a cab for you. Otherwise, call *26 10 26* for a 24-hour taxi service.

## Petrol

Most petrol stations in the city centre are open 24 hours and sell basic groceries, snacks, soft drinks and cigarettes. A small selection:
**BP** *Kurfürstendamm 128, Wilmersdorf, 10711.*
**BP** *Dudenstraße 9, Kreuzberg, 10965.*
**BP** *Yorckstraße 38, Schöneberg, 10965.*

## Eating

*See also chapter* **Restaurants**.

### Athener Grill
*Kurfürstendamm 156, Charlottenburg, 10709 (892 10 39). U7 Adenauerplatz.* **Open** 11am-4am Mon-Thur; 11am-5am Sat, Sun. **Credit** AmEx, MC, V.
A fairly ordinary self-service Greek fast food and pizzeria joint that's heavy on grease, but handy for late nights.

## Café November

*Husemannstraße 15, Prenzlauer Berg, 10435 (442 8425). U2 Eberswalder Straße.* **Open** 10am-2am at least. **No credit cards.**

Handily situated in one of the most happening parts of the new east, this lively café feeds into the main action, and feeds it until midnight. Breakfasts daily from 10am-6pm.

## El Burriquito

*Wielandstraße 6 (corner of Kantstraße), Charlottenburg, 10625 (312 99 29). S3, S5, S6, S7, S9 Savignyplatz.* **Open** 7pm-5am daily. **No credit cards.**

A lively Spanish tapas bar/restaurant where you can stuff yourself with tapas at a ridiculous hour in the morning, or perch at the bar and work up a serious hangover.

## Jimmy's Diner

*Pariser Straße 41, Wilmersdorf, 10707 (882 31 41). U1 Hohenzollernplatz.* **Open** noon-3am Sun-Thur; noon-6am Fri, Sat. **No credit cards.**

A re-creation of a fifties diner serving American beers and the usual Tex-Mex staples. Chilli, burgers, ribs and fries make up the bulk of the menu. Useless for veggies.

## Presse Café

*Corner Hardenbergstraße/Joachimstalerstraße, Charlottenburg, 10623 (312 2644). U2, U2, U3, S5, S6, S7, S9 Zoologischer Garten.* **Open** 24 hours daily. **No credit cards.**

Just opposite Bahnhof Zoo train and bus stations, the Pressecafé has a decidedly transient ambience. A good place to wait for the U-bahn to start up again.

## Schwarzes Café

*Kantstraße 148, Charlottenburg, 10623 (313 8038). S3, S5, S6, S7, S9 Savignyplatz.* **Open** 24 hours daily except Tue. **No credit cards.**

The 'distressed' walls and darklit interior give the Black Café a fashionably forbidding aura that is undermined by its young and friendly, if occasionally overstretched service and its mixed clientèle. Good coffee and cheesecake round the clock.

## Titanic

*Winsstraße 30, Prenzlauer Berg, 10405 (442 0340). U2 Eberswalder Straße.* **Open** 9am-2am daily. **No credit cards.**

This rough, rustically decorated and popular bar serves food until it closes. Lots for vegetarians, too.

## Voltaire

*Stuttgarter Platz 14, Charlottenburg, 10627 (324 63 17). U7 Wilmersdorfer Straße.* **Open** 24 hours daily. **No credit cards.**

A light friendly café. The relaxed feel is augmented by a fountain.

*Dine all night at Charlottenburg's* **Voltaire.**

## XII Apostoli

*Bleibtreustraße 49 (Savigny Passage), Charlottenburg, 10623 (312 1433). S3, S5, S6, S9 Savignyplatz.* **Open** 24 hours daily. **No credit cards.**

Popular upmarket pizzeria and croissanterie. If you want a DM200 bottle of wine at six in the morning, this is the place for you. *See also chapter* **Restaurants.**

## Zwiebelfisch

*Savignyplatz 7-8, Charlottenburg, 10623 (312 73 63). S3, S5, S6, S7, S9 Savignyplatz.* **Open** noon-6.30am daily. **No credit cards.**

Greet the morning German-style with a plate of salami and great German Pils. Otherwise, just drink the superb coffee and wander home through Savignyplatz.

# Imbiß & Fast Food

## Freßco

*Oranienburger Straße 47, Mitte, 10117 (282 9647). U6 Oranienburger Tor.* **Open** *winter* noon-midnight daily; *summer* noon-2am daily.

Soups, salads, baguettes, tapas, doughnuts, pasta, Calzone – this Imbiß opposite Tacheles has it all, in both carnivorous and veghead versions. Be prepared to queue a while: this place is understandably popular.

## Habibi

*Goltzstraße 24, Winterfeldtplatz, Schöneberg, 10781 (215 33 32). U1, U4 Nollendorfplatz.* **Open** 11am-3am Mon-Fri, Sun; 11am-5am Sat.

Arab specialities are served in this favourite stop for ravenous night owls. Handily located for Schöneberg's bars, cafés and clubs.

## Imbiß am Holst

*Corner of Hardenbergstraße/Joachimstalerstraße across the street from Bahnhof Zoo, Charlottenburg, 10623. U2, U2, S3, S5, S6, S7, S9 Zoologischer Garten.* **Open** 24 hours daily.

Neither salubriously located nor particularly nice-looking, but fine if you need something hot while waiting for the next night bus from the bus station opposite.

## Traube

*Dimitroffstraße 24, Prenzlauer Berg, 10405 (441 7447). U2 Eberswalder Straße.* **Open** 24 hours daily.

Excellent Turkish Imbiß off the Kollwitzplatz that offers salads and vegetarian snacks as well as kebabs and chicken.

## Post Office

The main post office in Zoo Station is open to midnight, operating all services. You can also phone long distance, fax, and collect your post restante. Workaholics who need late-night copying, binding, faxing and translation work can use:

## Trigger

*Pohlstraße 69, Tiergarten, 10785 (261 60 37). U1 Kurfürstenstraße.* **Open** 9am-2am Mon-Fri; 1pm-2am Sat, Sun. **No credit cards.**

## Video

Most video shops have no films in English: the best place to go is The (Original Version) on Sesenheimer Straße, open until 9pm Mon-Sat (*see chapter* **Shopping**).

# In Focus

# Business

**Berlin's unification boom has gone bust, but by the turn of the century, things could look a lot different.**

Because of its isolation, Berlin was never really a direct participant in Germany's fabled Economic Miracle. But it did enjoy nearly five decades of uninterrupted growth – on both sides of the Wall. Now, after a mini boom in 1990-91, Berlin's united economy is in a shambles. No other German city has been hit as hard by the financial burden of unification. Berlin is labouring under a record deficit, causing its net debt to soar from DM18 billion in 1990 to a projected DM51.5 billion for 1996.

Costs for raising the standards of amenities in east Berlin to western levels have been huge. And generous tax breaks and subsidies which kept industries alive in West Berlin throughout the Cold War are expiring, driving large employers out of the city. With them go jobs and tax revenues.

It wasn't supposed to happen this way. After converting their worthless East Mark savings to powerful Deutsche Marks at generous rates, east Berliners went on a two-year spending spree in which the local economy boomed. For two years after the Wall was breached in 1989, Berlin was touted as the perfect launching pad for exploiting emerging markets in Central and eastern Europe.

As it turns out, many east Berliners found themselves unemployed after their savings were spent. And most investors by-passed Berlin to set up in Poland, Hungary or the Czech Republic.

Also, foot dragging in Bonn about a final commitment to re-install the government in Berlin scared off other money interests. This issue has finally been settled. But Bonn's incessant belly-aching about moving to Berlin has soured the investment climate. If the German government isn't enthusiastic about Berlin, why should private investors be? The private economy has been hit by declining disposable incomes and rising prices for retail rents. Many small shops are being replaced by chain stores, travel agencies or other shops offering marginally useful products with high profit margins, such as designer opticians.

Berlin still has only a very insular business culture. A handful of successful real estate moguls, auto dealers and furniture store owners who became rich in West Berlin still make up its hard core. Still, there is promise. Three full city blocks of retail development on Friedrichstraße in east Berlin are opening in the spring of 1995. The shopping malls, known as the Friedrichstadt Passages, will draw thousands of shoppers downtown daily.

Sony is moving its European headquarters to Potsdamer Platz, in the same construction complex where Daimler-Benz will be locating its Debis computer services division. The buildings will be finished by the year 2000, and both companies will spawn dozens of firms supplying them. Berlin is scheduled to merge administratively and politically with the surrounding state of Brandenburg within the next few years, making economic development promotion more efficient and effective.

## PRODUCTION LINE

Despite the Cold War years during which Berlin lost much of its manufacturing base as companies fled to West Germany, Berlin remains Germany's largest industrial city. Its GDP in 1992 was DM130 billion – larger than some European countries. Electrical and mechanical engineering, pharmaceuticals, print and publishing are still represented by the big names – Siemens, AEG, Schering, Springer. Light manufacturing and food production are further mainstays of the local economy.

During the decades when the Wall stood, subsidies and tax breaks doled out by Bonn encouraged inward investment. Millions were spent on developing West Berlin's excellent R&D base and there are now over 300 technical and scientific institutions in the city. Capitalising on this, Berlin has embarked on a campaign to lure high-tech businesses to set up shop.

Another beneficial relic of Cold War planning was the policy of attracting more business visitors through the development of the huge International Congress Centre (ICC) in west Berlin. Trade fair business linked with the ICC was also heavily subsidised, but this now appears to be paying its own way; a restructured trade fair company, now called Messe Berlin, is expanding the Berlin exhibition grounds to attract even bigger fairs. Dozens of major trade fairs take place at the Berlin exhibition grounds annually, attracting business people from all over the world. The Funkausstellung International Consumer Electronics Fair, for example, takes place here every two years and draws crowds of nearly 450,000 visitors.

A less beneficial element of Berlin's Cold War heritage is that its service sector is underdeveloped. One result was that prices for scarce office space were high after the Wall was breached. Construction surged to meet the demand. In the gold-digger atmosphere of 1990-92, many investors miscalculated, leaving plenty of affordable, brand new offices on the market today.

### BANK ON IT

The home of German banking is Frankfurt. That said, all the domestic banks have upgraded their Berlin operations since 1989. In addition to the prospect of doing business in Berlin itself, they used the city to expand into eastern Germany. Foreign banks, which never had any real presence in the city, have followed. The Senate has raised the city's profile by merging three municipally owned banks: now the Bankgesellschaft Berlin AG ranks among Germany's top ten largest banks.

There are no deals left in east Berlin. Berlin's Treuhand agency, charged in 1990 with privatising the GDR's bankrupt nationalised economy, is closing shop after organising some 14,000 company and property sales and 3,000 liquidations. Genuine business opportunities, such as they existed, were snapped up quickly by fast-moving companies from West Germany.

### SLOWLY BUT SURELY

German efficiency is not based on speed, but on method. So do not expect things to happen fast. Instead, nearly everything – from requesting a telephone to transferring money – will be done methodically, but slowly. The good news is that when things get done, they get done properly.

Inevitably this all leads to a lot of paperwork. So be prepared for form-filling. If you are signing any contracts you will need to have them notarised by a state-approved notary. By law you are required to be able fully to comprehend the terms of the contract which, if you cannot understand German, means it will need to be professionally translated. One way of avoiding this expense is to give your right of signature to a trusted German-speaking colleague or lawyer.

The same diligence is applied to the working week – arrive on time (early) and leave on time (early). Germans, despite their reputation as a nation of workaholics, now work fewer hours than anyone else in Europe. Watch for lunch-hours that devour afternoons, and get used to the fact that on Fridays few people are at their desks after 3pm.

Finally, foreigners are often surprised at the extent of graft and corruption that accompany even small transactions in Berlin: another reason to be sure you work through a reputable law firm when doing business here.

## Stock Exchange

### Berlin Stock Exchange
### Börsenverwaltung (Administration)

*Fasanenstraße 3, Charlottenburg, 10623 (311 09 10; fax 31 10 91 78/79). S3, S5, S6, S9/U2, U9 Zoologischer Garten.* **Open** 8am-5pm Mon-Fri.
Groups wanting to be shown round the **Börsengebäude** (*see below*) should arrange tours at these offices beforehand.

### Börsengebäude (Stock Exchange)

*Hardenbergstraße 16-18, Charlottenburg, 10623 (31 51 00). S3, S5, S6, S9/U2, U9 Zoologischer Garten.* **Open** 10.30am-1.30pm Mon-Fri.
Located at the site of the Berlin Chamber of Commerce (Industrie und Handelskammer/IHK). Individuals and small groups are allowed access to the visitors' gallery during operating hours.

## Banks

The following are the head offices for the major banks in Berlin.

### Berliner Bank

*Hardenbergerstraße 32, Charlottenburg, 10623 (310 90; fax 31 09 25 48). U2, U9 Zoologischer Garten.* **Open** 8.30am-1.30pm Mon, Wed, Fri; 8.30am-6pm, 3-6pm, Tue, Thur.

### Berliner Commerzbank

*Potsdamer Straße 125, Schöneberg, 10783 (265 30; fax 265 90 37). U1 Kurfürstenstraße.* **Open** 9am-1.30pm Mon, Wed; 9am-1.30pm, 3.30-6.30pm, Tue, Thur; 9am-1pm Fri.

### Deutsche Bank

*Otto-Suhr-Allee 6-16, Charlottenburg, 10585 (340 70; fax 340 727 88). U2 Ernst-Reuter-Platz.* **Open** 9am-3.30pm Mon, Wed; 9am-6pm Tue, Thur; 9am-12.30pm Fri.

Take stock of the **Börsengebäude**.

### Dresdener Bank

*Uhlandstraße 9-11 (corner of Kantstraße), Charlottenburg, 10623 (3153 0; fax 312 40 41). U15 Uhlandstraße.* **Open** 8.30am-2pm Mon, Wed, Fri; 8.30am-6pm Tue, Thur.

### IKB Deutsche Industriebank

*Bismarckstraße 105, Charlottenburg, 10625 (31 00 90; fax 31 009 109). U2 Deutsche Oper, Sophie-Charlotten-Platz.* **Open** 8am-5pm Mon-Fri.

## Government Organisations

### Berlin Economic Development Corporation (Wirtschaftsförderung Berlin)

*Hallerstraße 6, Charlottenburg, 10587 (3 99 89 0; fax 3 99 80 2 39). U2 Ernst-Reuter-Platz.* **Open** 8.30am-5pm Mon-Fri.
Help for foreign investors settling in Berlin.

### Brandenburg Economic Development Corporation (Wirtschaftsförderung Brandenburg)

*Stadt Verwaltung, Neuendorferstraße 90, 14770 Brandenburg. Amt für Wirtschaftsförderung (03381 530 690; fax 03381 530 274).* **Open** 9am-noon, 2-4pm, Tue; 9am-noon Thur.
Advice on investment in Brandenburg.

## Embassies & Agencies

### American Embassy Commercial Department

*Neustädtische-Kirchstraße 4-5, Mitte, 10117 (238 51 74; fax 238 62 90). S1, S2, S3, S5, S6, S9/U6 Friedrichstraße.* **Open** 8.30am-5.30pm Mon-Fri.

### American Chamber of Commerce

*Budapester Straße 29, Tiergarten, 10787 (261 55 86; fax 262 26 00). S3, S5, S6, S9/U2, U9 Zoologischer Garten/U2, U3 Wittenbergplatz.* **Open** 9am-5pm Mon-Fri.

### Berlin Chamber of Commerce

*Hardenbergstraße 16-18, Charlottenburg, 10623 (31 51 00; fax 315 10 31). S3, S5, S6, S9/U2, U9 Zoologischer Garten.* **Open** 9am-5pm Mon-Fri.

### Brandenburg Ministry of Economics (Wirtschaftsministerium Brandenburg)

*Heinrich-Mann-Allee 107, 14467 Potsdam (0331 8660).* **Open** 9am-4pm Mon-Fri.
Advice and assistance on investing in Brandenburg.

### British Embassy Commercial Department

*Unter den Linden 32/34, Mitte, 10117 (220 24 31; fax 201 84 157). S1, S2 Unter den Linden.* **Open** 9am-noon, 2-4pm, Mon-Fri.
Assistance and advice for British business looking to set up in Berlin.

### Senatsverwaltung für Wirtschaft und Technologie (Senate for Economics and Technology)

*Martin-Luther-Straße 105, Schöneberg, 10820 (78 31; fax 783 35 70/68). U4 Rathaus Schöneberg.* **Open** 9am-3pm Mon-Fri.
Advice and guidelines for investors.

## Business Services

## Accountants & Consultants

The major international accountants and consultants are represented in Berlin. The Gelbe Seiten (Yellow Pages) are not quite complete in this respect, so look them up by name in the normal telephone book.

### Arthur Andersen and Co

*Tauentzienstraße 9, Charlottenburg, 10789 (25 47 10; fax 254 71 34). S3, S5, S6, S9/U2, U9 Zoologischer Garten.* **Open** 8am-7pm Mon-Fri.

### Bossard Consultants

*Bleibtreustraße 38, Charlottenburg, 10623 (88 59 42 0; fax 883 6958).* **Open** 8.30am-5pm Mon-Fri.

### McKinsey and Company

*Kurfürstendamm 185, Charlottenburg, 10707 (88 45 20). U7 Adenauer Platz.* **Open** 8.30am-5.30pm Mon-Fri.

### Price Waterhouse Consulting

*An der Mühle 3, Reinickendorf, 13507 (782 04 44). U6 Alt-Tegel.* **Open** 8am-7pm Mon-Fri.

## Conference Facilities

### Aktiver Büroservice

*Mommsenstraße 28, Charlottenburg, 10629 (323 75 88; fax 324 96 38). U7 Adenauerplatz.* **Open** 8am-5pm Mon-Fri.
Office services and conference organisers.

### HeMo Büro-Service GbR

*Münstersche Straße 12, Wilmersdorf, 10709 (893 13 51; fax 893 15 08). U7 Adenauerplatz.* **Open** 8am-5pm Mon-Thur; 8am-4pm Fri.
Office space to let short-term and for conferences.

### Messe Berlin

*Messedamm 22, Charlottenburg, 14055 (3038 0; fax 3038 23 25).* **Open** 9am-3pm Mon-Fri.
The city's official trade fair and conference organisation, which can advise on setting up small professional seminars and congresses, or big trade fairs.

### Regus Business Centre

*Kurfürstendamm 11, Charlottenburg, 10719 (88 44 19; fax 88 44 15 20). S3, S5, S6, S9/U2, U9 Zoologischer Garten.* **Open** 8.30am-6pm Mon-Fri.
Offices for short-term rent, multilingual secretarial services and conference facilities in a central location.

### Schunack and Löllke

*Schloßstraße 48a, Steglitz, 12165 (792 30 98; fax 7 92 30 01). U9 Rathaus Steglitz.* **Open** 8am-6pm Mon-Thur; 8am-4pm Fri.
Office, secretarial and conference facilities.

## Couriers

A package 1kg (2.2lbs) or under, within Berlin, will cost about DM15-DM30. These companies use both motorbike and cycle couriers.
**Berliner Kurier** *(23 27 66 60).* **Open** 24 hours daily.
**Messenger** *(31 10 93 11).* **Open** 24 hours daily.
**Moskitos** *(426 41 72).* **Open** 7am-5pm Mon-Fri.
Prices vary for national and international deliveries, but in general a package under 1kg (2.2lbs)

delivered within Germany costs about DM60, to America about DM150. It might be worth going to the post office and using their express service.

### DHL
*Kaiserin-Augusta-Allee 16-24, Charlottenburg, 10553 (347 8511/20 96 25 98). U9 Turmstraße.* **Open** 8am-6pm Mon-Fri. **No credit cards.**

### Federal Express
*Friedelstraße 34, Neukölln, 12047 (6244700; fax 623 44 81). U8 Schöleinstraße.* **Open** 8am-6pm Mon-Fri. **No credit cards.**

### World Courier
*Pariser Straße 35, Wilmersdorf, 10707 (881 70 15; fax 882 58 24). U1, U9 Spichernstraße.* **Open** 24 hours daily. **No credit cards.**

### XP Express Parcel Systems
*Gewerbehof 1-9, Spandau, 13597 (33 08 93 30; fax 33 08 93 33). R5 Spandau.* **Open** 8am-6pm Mon-Fri. **No credit cards.**

## Estate Agents

Agents listed will do business with you in English.

### Burotel
*Kurfürstendamm 180, Charlottenburg, 10707 (882 70 31; fax 882 66 44). U7 Adenauerplatz.* **Open** 9am-5pm Mon-Thur; 9am-4pm Fri.

### Healey and Baker
*Mommsenstraße 68, Charlottenburg, 10629 (882 57 24; fax 882 56 70). U15 Uhlandstraße.* **Open** 9am-5.30pm Mon-Fri.

### Saddelhoff Deutschland
*Kempinski Plaza, Uhlandstraße 181-183, Charlottenburg, 10623 (88 48 50; fax 883 41 59). U15 Uhlandstraße.* **Open** 8.30am-6pm Mon-Fri.

## Lawyers

The British Embassy (*see chapter* **Survival: Consulates & Embassies**) will provide a list of English-speaking lawyers. We list three that specialise in Commercial law and speak English.

### Guentsche und Partner
*Hr Johann Peter Sieveking, Hubertusbader Straße 14a, Wilmersdorf, 14193 (825 2085; fax 825 2080). S3 Grunewald.* **Open** 9am-6.30pm Mon-Fri.

### Mayer, Brown & Platt
*Spreeufer 5, Mitte, 10178 (240 7930; fax 240 79344). U2 Klosterstraße.* **Open** 9am-6pm Mon-Fri.

### Peter Evers
*Ludwigkirchstraße 3, Wilmersdorf, 10179 (882 79 33; fax 882 79 34). U1, U9 Spichernstraße.* **Open** *for consultation* 9am-noon Mon-Wed; 2pm-6pm Thur-Fri.

## Office Equipment

### Büroorganisation
*Müggelseedamm 207, Köpenick, 12587 (645 18 86). S3 Friedrichshagen.* **Open** 8am-1pm, 2-5pm, Mon-Fri. **No credit cards.**
Everything you could want to organise your office.

### Engels
*Ollenhauerstraße 105-106, Reinickendorf, 13403 (41 77 83 0; fax 41 77 83 77). U6 Kurt-Schumacher-Platz.* **Open** 8am-4.30pm Mon-Thur; 8am-2.30pm Fri. **No credit cards.**
A large selection of office furniture, typewriters and supplies.

### L and W
*Weitlingsstraße 70, Lichtenberg, 10317 (525 39 87; fax 525 25 77). U5 Lichtenberg.* **Open** 10am-6pm Mon-Fri. **No credit cards.**
Furniture, office software and communications technology.

### Pärschke Bürobedarf
*Potsdamer Straße 98, Tiergarten, 10785 (264 91 30; fax 26 49 13 26). U1 Kurfürstenstraße.* **Open** 9am-6pm Mon-Fri. **Credit** EC, V.
A large supply of office essentials, stationery and gimmicks.

## Relocation Services

The following business offers assistance in looking for homes and schools, and will help you deal with residence and work permits.

### Relocation Services Grönlund Alsing
*Schinkelstraße 2, Wilmersdorf, 14193 (891 1393). S46 Halensee.* **Open** 8am-9pm Mon-Fri. **Credit** AmEx, DC, EC, JCB, V.
They help you through the maze of bureacracy if you're settling in Berlin; they also help you get out if need be.

## Staff Hire Agencies

Below we list temp agencies specialising in technical and sales personnel. A secretary will cost about DM25 an hour.

### City Büro
*Wexstraße 1 (on Innsbrucker Platz), Schöneberg, 10825 (854 10 94; fax 854 10 97). U4 Innsbrucker Platz.* **Open** 8am-4.30pm Mon-Fri.

### Personal Partner
*Tauentzienstraße 18a, Schöneberg, 10789 (213 10 51; fax 2 13 25 27). U1 Wittenbergplatz.* **Open** 8am-4.30pm Mon-Fri.
This agency places multi-lingual secretarial staff.

## Translators & Interpreters

*See also* 'Übersetzungen' in the Gelbe Seiten (Yellow Pages). A thousand words will cost about DM500 at professional translation rates.

### Scharpe & Arend Simultaneous Translations
*Claudiusstraße 12, Tiergarten, 10557 (392 9010; fax 393 0766). U9 Hansaplatz.* **Open** 9am-5pm Mon-Fri.

### Übersetzerteam
*Nestorstraße 58, Wilmersdorf, 10711 (881 67 46). U7 Adenauerplatz.* **Open** 9am-4pm Mon-Fri.
English-language business, technical and legal documents.

### Übersetzungsdienst
*Innsbrucker Straße 58, Schöneberg, 10825 (781 75 84; fax 782 26 80). U4, U7 Bayerischer Platz.* **Open** 9am-4pm Mon-Fri.
Interpreters for Italian, English, Spanish, French and Arabic. Specialists in legal, technical and business documents.

# Children

**With one of the biggest zoos in the world and no shortage of playgrounds and parks, Berlin offers hours of delight for tiny terrors.**

Although Berlin is not known as a particularly child-friendly city, there's still more for families to do than most visitors – or residents – ever get around to. Young visitors will love to board the trains at the **Museum for Transport and Technology**, visit one of Berlin's two excellent zoos, visit the animals at one of the children's farms or museum villages, or take in a current puppet show, musical, or open-air.

Forewarned is forearmed: part of getting on happily in Berlin – especially when travelling with children – is perfecting the ability to brush off occasional critical scowls, comments and stares from older natives and Prussian museum guards. Don't let these intrusions affect you in the slightest: smile blandly, blink slowly, ignore and enjoy.

## THE GERMAN FAMILY

Since the end of World War II, German families have tended to be small. Berlin, in particular, had relatively few young families during the Cold War. There are excellent social benefits for families with children: free education and healthcare, and monthly government stipends for parents of young children. In theatres, cinemas and so on, you should get reduced rates for school-age and younger children. Children under six years of age are usually free. Also watch for special family prices at various attractions.

The structure of most German households is still very traditional and many mothers do not work outside the home. This is at least partly because children have short and erratic school hours and frequent holidays, wreaking havoc with a working mum's schedule. Children are sometimes considered a luxury in Germany, and toys and children's clothes and accessories are correspondingly wonderful and expensive.

## TRANSPORT

Berlin is a large, decentralised city, and the best way to get around is by bus, S-Bahn or U-Bahn. The above-ground transport is best for sightseeing, while the S- and U-Bahn system is best for covering longer distances quickly. For a kid-friendly and economical tour, hop on the 100 bus in front of Bahnhof Zoo and try to get a seat in the first row on the top deck. From there you'll have a great view as you pass the President's palace,

Kongresshalle, and Reichstag, go right through the Brandenburg Gate, and up Unter den Linden past the opera, state library, parliament and Humboldt University to Alexanderplatz. You can return to the Zoo station on the S-Bahn. For a different bargain tour, catch the 129 bus on the Ku'damm and ride it along the canal, past the National Gallery and main library, past Checkpoint Charlie and into Kreuzberg. Transfer to the U-Bahn when you've seen enough.

All buses have a back entrance where baby buggies can be lifted on to the bus; some even have a special 'lift' which comes down to assist you (these buses have a button near the back entrance, marked with a picture of a pram). Negotiating the U- or S-Bahn with a pushchair is another matter: few stations have lifts, so you will just have to struggle with your buggy. At least, the majority of U-Bahn stations are not far below ground.

Children under age 15 qualify for reduced fares on Berlin's transport network, and travel free until they are six (age 19 if the child has a valid Schüler-ausweis, an identity card stating that the child is at school). On weekends and holidays, family cards are often the cheapest way to travel on public transportation.

## Shopping for Children

All necessities are quite easily found in any shopping district. For recreational shopping, look for beautiful traditional clothing, wooden toys and wonderful puppets. Imaginative toys can be found in toy shops in all the nicer shopping districts. *See also chapter* **Shopping**.

### Kaufhaus des Westens (KaDeWe)
*Wittenbergplatz, Charlottenburg, 10789 (212 10). U1, U2, U12 Wittenbergplatz.* **Open** 9.30am-6.30pm Mon-Fri; 9.30am-8.30pm Thur; 9am-2pm Sat. **Credit** AmEx, DC, EC, JCB, V.
KaDeWe has an extensive but expensive children's wear department, a wonderful toy section with many model trains, a food emporium on the sixth floor, and a no-smoking cafe-teria in the new rooftop atrium.

### Drospa
*Kurfürstendamm 200, Wilmersdorf, 10719 (88 50 06 94). U15 Uhlandstraße.* **Open** 9am-6pm Mon-Fri; 9am-2pm Sat. **Credit** AmEx.
A well-priced drugstore chain with all the basics for babies and children. Branches all over town.

## Prenatal

*Tauentzienstrasse 1, Charlottenburg, 10789 (211 7340).*
**U1, U2, U12** *Wittenbergplatz.* **Open** 9.30am-6.30pm
Mon-Fri; 9.30-8.30 Thur; 9.30am-2pm Sat. **Credit** AmEx,
EC, JCB, V.
A nice range of wonderful but expensive baby and children's
wear.

## Baby-sitters

If you want to experience night-time Berlin, you
may be able to arrange a baby-sitter through your
hotel. If not, two university student employment
agencies can help. It's best to book as early as possible, and state that you wish to have an experi-
enced baby-minder. Both have English-speakers
available, but the person answering the phone may
not speak English. Both services charge DM15 to
DM20 per hour, with a DM60 minimum.

### Heinzelmännchen (Freie Universität)

*(831 6071).* **Open** 7am-6pm Mon, Tue, Thur; 7am-5pm
Wed, Fri.

### TUSMA (Technische Universität)

*(308 546).* **Open** 8.30am-5.30pm Mon-Fri.

## Attractions

## Museums

In addition to the museums listed below, also keep
the following in mind: the **Pergamon Museum's**
Greek altar and Babylonian Ishtar Gate awe children as well as adults, and a quick tour of the
museum's highlights (English tape tour available)
is free on Sunday. The **Egyptian Museum's** bust
of Cleopatra and sarcophagi appeal even to pre-
schoolers. The **Natural History Museum**
(Naturkundenmuseum) has the world's largest
dinosaur skeleton and a lovely mineral collection.
Cars used to smuggle people through the Wall at
the **Checkpoint Charlie Museum** appeal to
kids eight and above. The Citadel Spandau has an
interpretive museum and a tower to climb to get a
view of the sixteenth-century fortress and environs. *See chapter* **Museums**.

### Museum für Verkehr und Technik (Museum of Transport and Technology)

*Trebbiner Strasse 9, Kreuzberg, 14193 (254 840).* **U1,
U7, U15** *Möckernbrücke.* **Open** 9am-5.30pm Tue-Fri;
10am-6pm Sat, Sun. **Admission** DM4; DM2 children.
The Transport Museum has been happily installed in the old
Anhalter Bahnhof roundhouse. Not surprisingly, the best
and biggest part of the exhibition is concerned with trains.
They are massive, sitting on the original tracks, and include
engines and passenger and freight cars from the eighteenth
century to the present. There's even an old miner's cart which
children can push back and forth on its tracks. The museum
also has demonstrations of early machines, and computers
and gadgets to play with. It is known as one of Berlin's most
child-friendly museums and is great on a rainy day. Don't
miss the outside exhibits, or the Spectrum annex (included
in admission ticket) where there are 200 interactive devices
and experiments.

### Museum für Völkerkunde (Ethnological Museum)

*Lansstraße 8, Zehlendorf, 14195 (830 1226).* **U1**
*Dahlem-Dorf.* **Open** 9am-5pm Tue-Fri; 10am-5pm Sat,
Sun. **Admission** DM4; DM2 students, children.
Among the masks, totems and tools from the South Seas
(well displayed, with lots to see at child's-eye level) stands a
large wooden clubhouse which children may enter and run
around in. Children may also board a catamaran-type replica of an eighteenth-century wooden boat from the Tonga
Islands. Check with a guard to make sure you've found
the right one. In the basement of this building (which also
houses the Dahlem picture galleries) is a small Junior
Museum, with exhibits designed for young people.

## Museum Villages & Farms

### Domäne Dahlem

*Königin-Luise-Straße 49, Zehlendorf, 14195 (832 5000).*
**U1** *Dahlem-Dorf.* **Open** 10am-6pm daily except Tue.
**Admission** DM3; DM1.50 children, students.
On this working farm, children can see how life was lived
in the seventeenth century. Craftspeople, including black-
smiths, carpenters, bakers and potters, preserve and teach
their skills. It is best to visit during one of several festivals
held during the year, when children can ride ponies, tractors
and hay-wagons. Also open during the week to commune
with the animals. Phone for information on weekend events.

### Jugendfarm Lübars

*Quickborner Strasse, Reinickendorf, 13469 (415 7027).*
**S1** *Wittenau, then bus 221.* **Open** 9am-7pm Tue-Fri,
Sun. **Admission** free.
Lübars was at the very north-eastern edge of West Berlin,
bordering the GDR. The working farms in the charming old
village and expansive fields provided a haven from the bustle of the city, and although West Berliners are no longer
hemmed in, Alt Lübars is still a wonderful place to go. In the
nearby children's farm (Jugendfarm Lübars) you can see
farm animals, watch craftspeople at work, and have a bite
to eat at the restaurant in the Hof. Adjacent is a great playground, and a hill of World War II rubble to climb.

### Museumdorf Düppel

*Clauertstraße 11, Zehlendorf, 14163 (802 6671).* **U1**
*Oskar-Helene-Heim, then bus 115.* **Open** *mid-Apr to
mid-Oct* 3-7pm Thur; 10am-5pm Sun and public holidays.
**Admission** DM3; DM1.50 children, students.
A fourteenth-century village, reconstructed based on schol-
arly archeological excavations on the site, surrounded by the
Düppel Forest. Workers demonstrate handicrafts, medieval
technology, and farming techniques. Some products of their
labours are for sale. Ox cart rides for kids. Small snack bar
at exit. A very quiet type of outing.

## Zoos

### Berlin Zoologischer Garten (Zoo) and Aquarium

*Hardenbergplatz 8, Tiergarten, 10623 (254 010).* **U1,
U2, U12, U9, S3, S5, S6, S7, S8** *Zoologischer Garten.*
**Open** 9am-6pm daily except Christmas Eve. **Admission**
*zoo only* DM10, DM5 children; *aquarium only* DM9,
DM4,50 children; *combined admission* DM15, DM7,50
children.
At the edge of the Tiergarten and one block from the
Ku'damm, West Berlin's zoo boasts more species (1,500) than
any zoo in the world. The grounds are nice with a good playground, many snack stands and a restaurant. Highlights
include a children's petting zoo, nocturnal house, and giant
pandas. The aquarium has tropical fish, lizards, alligators
and an insect zoo. There's also a snack bar.

### Tierpark Friedrichsfelde

*Am Tierpark 125, Friedrichsfelde, 10319 (515 310). U5 Tierpark.* **Open** 9am-7pm (ticket office closes 6pm) daily. **Admission** DM9; DM4,50 children.

The zoo in east Berlin is larger and more spacious but has fewer animals than its western counterpart. It's great for long walks and views of grassland animals (giraffes, deer) in wide-open spaces. Facilities for children include a petting zoo where goats, monkeys and other animals can be fed, a children's playground, and snack stands.

## Entertainment

### Children's Films

Most films shown in Berlin are in German but check the fortnightly magazines *Tip* and *Zitty* listings for the notation OF (Originalfassung – original version) or OmU (subtitled); American or English movies so noted have English soundtracks. The city's annual film festival in February (*see chapter* **Film**) features several movies for children, many of which are in English.

### Parks & Playgrounds

Parks abound in Berlin. The vast **Grunewald** (*see chapter* **Trips Out Of Town**) is great for long walks, as is the more centrally located **Tiergarten** (*see chapter* **Sightseeing**). Paddle and rowing boats can be hired near the Cafe am Neuer See (Thomas-Dehler-Straße) in the Tiergarten, and just south of the S1 Schlachtensee station in the Grunewald. You can rent bicycles at the Grunewald S-Bahn station. **Treptower Park** (*see chapter* **Sightseeing**), across the road from the Treptow Soviet war memorial and on the Spree River, has lovely flowers and trees and standard German food.

For a playground paradise, head to the **Volkspark** on the east side of Bundesallee near Berliner Straße in Wilmersdorf. There are myriad slides and playground paraphernalia, as well as a horizontal ski-lift ride. Nearby you'll find a pond with ducks. At the **Freizeitpark Tegel**, trampolines, table-tennis and paddle-boats are available and the Humboldt Schloß can be visited at the same time. **Viktoria Park** in Kreuzberg has a great hill for climbing (and for tobogganing), Berlin's only waterfall, a small children's zoo and a good playground.

Further afield, the **FEZ Köpenik** (south-eastern corner of Berlin) is a great place for a day out with the kids. Facilities include a swimming pool, park and miniature railway, plus other amusements to keep the little 'uns happy. **Peacock Island** (Pfaueninsel) is a nice place to spend a quiet afternoon in the south-western part of the city. Peacocks roam this island nature reserve near Wannsee, accessible by a short ferry ride. There's also an unusual castle built by Friedrich Wilhelm II with a small museum inside. There are places

*All aboard in Kreuzberg's Viktoria Park.*

to go swimming or paddling nearby, as well as plenty of boat trips leaving from the Wannsee Harbour, which has a spider's web-type jungle gym for restless children. *See chapter* **Trips out of Town**.

If swimming is what you're after, the **BLUB** is popular all year. The name translates as 'Berlin's air and water paradise': the BLUB has pools, a water-slide, waterfalls, a sauna and restaurants. A much less expensive alternative is **SEZ** in east Berlin. There you'll find public facilities, plus a gym, weight room, and ice skating rink. All Berlin districts have public pools but most are crowded. For summer swimming, the **Strandbad Wannsee** is west Berlin's famous beach (playground adjacent); the Muggelsee is the east's equivalent.

### BLUB (Berliner Luft und Badeparadies)

*Buschkrugallee 64, Neukölln, 12359 (606 6060). U7 Grenzallee.* **Open** 10am-11pm daily. **Admission** all day DM26; DM23 students; DM21 children. Lower rates during the summer and for briefer visits.

### Freizeitpark Tegel

*Schlosspark Tegel, Tegel, 13507. U6 Alt-Tegel.*

### FEZ (Freizeit und Erholungszentrum) Köpenik

*An der Wuhlheide 250, Köpenik, 12459 (635 1833). S3 Wuhlheide.* **Open** 1-5pm Sat; 10am-5pm Sun-Fri; and until 6pm daily in summer. **Admission** free.

### SEZ (Sport und Erholungszentrum) Friedrichshain

*Landesberger Allee 77, Friedrichshain, 10249 (42 28 33 20). S8 Landesberger Allee.* **Open** 3-9pm Mon; 9am-9pm Tue-Sun. **Admission** DM7; DM3.50 children.

### Volkspark

*Wilmersdorf. U7, U9 Berliner Straße.*

### Viktoria Park

*Kreuzberg. U6 Platz der Luftbrücke.*

## Theatre & Circus

For current theatre listings, check *Tip* and *Zitty*. Visiting circuses hang their posters around town. There's also a permanent circus show at the **UFA-Fabrik** (*Viktoria Straße 13, Tempelhof; phone 752 8085*). Because of the language problem, theatre may not generally be ideal, but Berlin has several puppet theatres and, around Christmas, ballet productions such as *The Nutcracker* and *Cinderella*, to appeal to non-German speakers.

### Berliner Figuren Theater

*Yorckstraße 59, Kreuzberg, 10965 (786 9815). S1, S2, S5 Yorckstraße.* **Open** phone for details.
West Berlin's oldest and possibly best puppet theatre. Its traditional repertoire of fairy tales and adventure stories is aimed at a very young audience, and played by a company of exquisitely hand-crafted dolls.

### Grips Theater

*am Hansaplatz, Altonaer Straße 22, Tiergarten, 10557 (391 4004). U9 Hansaplatz.* **Open** phone for details.
The runaway success of the original German musical *Linie 1* proved the Grips to be more than a children's theatre, but the majority of its morning and evening programming remains targeted at young theatre-goers. The plays (all in German) often mix a moral with wit and fantasy. *See chapter* **Theatre**. Wheelchair access.

### Klecks

*Schinkestraße 8/9, Neukölln, 12047 (693 7731). U8 Schönleinstraße.* **Open** phone for details.
A puppet theatre with hand-puppets, marionettes and stick figures, along with lashings of audience participation. A good choice for non-German speakers.

## Restaurants

Most Berlin restaurants do not make special provisions. Those with very young children might wish to avoid nicer German restaurants altogether, but if you make a point of asking if children are welcome before sitting down, the waiting staff are more likely to be helpful. Italian, Greek, Turkish or Asian (*see chapter* **Restaurants**) restaurants and those on the Kurfurstendamm are generally quite friendly to children. Or you could take the path of least resistance and go to McDonald's (*Bahnhof Zoo, Ku'damm 34, Karl-Liebknecht-*

*Strasse 13 in Mitte*, and other locations), or Burger King (*Ku'damm 202 and 224, Tauentzienstrasse 13*, and other locations). For a really memorable evening, teens enjoy the all-evening medieval dinners served at the Citadel Spandau, with period entertainment (*see chapter* **Restaurants**).

### Restaurant am Grunewaldturm

*Havelchaussee 62, Wilmersdorf, 14193 (304 1203). S1, S3, S7 Nikolasse, then bus 218.* **Open** 10am-10pm daily. **Average** DM50. **No credit cards.**
The food is German and unexceptional, the setting – in the middle of the Grunewald – pleasant. German families fill the place, and in good weather there are tables in the garden. There's space for children to run around outside, but first run them to the top of the tower for a great view over the region. No-frills mini-golf also nearby. Book for weekends.

### Churrasco

*Kurfürstendamm 170, Wilmersdorf, 10707 (883 4900). U7 Adenauerplatz.* **Open** 11.30am-midnight daily. **Average** DM30. **Credit** AmEx, DC, EC, JCB, V.
A steak-and-potatoes chain with outlets throughout Berlin. Children's menus, high-chairs, and a relaxed atmosphere.

### Hard Rock Cafe

*Meinekestrasse 21, Wilmersdorf, 10719 (884 620). U1, U2, U12, U15 Kurfürstendamm.* **Open** noon-midnight daily. **Average** DM25. **Credit** AmEx, DC, EC, JCB, V.
Famous American chain with excellent hamburgers, sandwiches and milkshakes, and a fun decor of rock 'n' roll memorabilia. Children of all ages generally love the place, are well treated and are given colouring books.

### Maredo

*Kurfürstendamm 48, Wilmersdorf, 10707 (883 6752). U15 Uhlandstraße.* **Open** 11.30am-midnight daily. **Average** DM25. **Credit** AmEx, DC, EC, V.
Much like **Churrasco** (*see above*), this steakhouse chain has branches throughout the city. It also has high-chairs and children's menus and a no-smoking section.

### Mövenpick

*1/30 Europa-Center, Charlottenburg, 10789 (262 7077). U1, U2, U9, U12, S3, S5, S6, S7, S8 Zoologischer Garten.* **Open** 8am-midnight Mon-Fri; 8am-1am Sat, Sun. **Average** DM28. **Credit** AmEx, DC, EC, V.
Located in the Europa-Center, Mövenpick has a small play area, no-smoking section, children's menu, and colouring books for young diners. The menu consists mainly of hearty Swiss and German specialties, and you get a view of the Memorial Church and busy Breitscheidplatz below. The place is usually packed and can be slow, but the ice cream is great and the early hours and central location make it good for brunch before a zoo visit.

### Pizza Hut

*Kurfürstendamm 146, Wilmersdorf, 10707 (893 2326). U7 Adenauer Platz.* **Open** 11am-midnight Mon-Thur; 11am-1am Fri; noon-midnight Sat, Sun. **Average** DM20. **No credit cards.**
The food is predictable, but you could do a lot worse. High-chairs, a children's menu and very tolerant staff.

### TGI Friday's

*Karl-Liebknecht-Straße 5, Mitte, 10178. S3, S5, S6, S9/U2, U8 Alexanderplatz.* **Open** noon-midnight daily. **Average** DM25. **Credit** AE, DC, EC, V.
Located across the river from the Berliner Dom, TGI Friday's has a great view, an extensive menu of good American multi-ethnic international food and great desserts. Menus in English or German. The very friendly staff all speak English and they welcome children. No-smoking section.

Where else can you see
over 250 films in a week
for only £1.50?

**Time Out**

Every detail. Every week.

# Gay & Lesbian

**A tour round Berlin's bars, clubs, shops, saunas and dark rooms.**

In the 1920s Berlin became the first city in the world to have what we might recognise as a large-scale gay community. The club Eldorado (now a Plus supermarket in Schöneberg's Motzstraße, still an important gay street) attracted Marlene Dietrich, Ernst Roehm, leader of the Nazi SA, and Christopher Isherwood, who lived nearby at Nollendorfstraße 17 and whose novels about the era were later turned into the movie *Cabaret*. Under the Nazis, gays were persecuted and forced to wear the Pink Triangle in concentration camps, where 100,000 died. They are commemorated on the plaque outside Nollendorfplatz U-Bahn station.

Since the late sixties, Berlin has resumed its role as one of the world's gay Meccas. In the seventies a wave of politicisation swept homosexual women and men on to separate paths and today the only real crossover between lesbians and gays in Berlin is here and there on the eastern scene.

The Berlin gay and lesbian scenes are big, with scores of different bars, clubs and organisations, but mostly they're concentrated in the same fairly small areas – northern Schöneberg, Kreuzberg and Prenzlauer Berg around Schönhauser Allee. This lends something of a village atmosphere. There's more going on in the west, but the home-grown and still more politicised attractions of the east make an illuminating contrast.

The point where everybody comes together is at the Christopher Street Day Parade (the Saturday nearest June 27) a flamboyant annual event commemorating the Stonewall riots. Lately, though, because of political disputes, there have been two different parades, one for the more radical element and one for everyone else. Earlier in June the area around Motzstraße (just off Nollendorfplatz) is closed off for three days for an extremely popular gay street fair (straights and others welcome, too). The annual Love Parade, one week after Christopher Street Day, also has a large gay contingent among the techno music fans.

## Gründerzeit Museum

*Hultschiner Damm 133, Hellersdorf, 12623 (527 83 29). S5 Mahlsdorf, turn right and walk 500m through village and across main road, museum is in an old farmhouse on right.* **Open** 1-5pm Sun (guided tours only).
A famous private museum, founded and still managed by Charlotte von Mahlsdorf, half-Jewish survivor of the Third Reich and the late GDR's most notorious transvestite. The

*The colourful **Christopher Street Day Parade** takes place on the Saturday nearest June 27.*

museum is set in an old farmhouse and each room is decorated in the 1870-1910 style. In the basement is a re-creation of a gay bar. Every spring the museum opens its garden for a lesbian and gay garden party, which as recently as 1991 was disrupted by an attack by neo-Nazis.

### Mitfahrzentrale für Schwule und Lesben
*Yorckstraße 52, Kreuzberg, 10965 (216 40 20). U7/S1, S2 Yorckstraße.* **Open** 8am-8pm Mon-Fri; 10am-8pm Sat, Sun.
The cheapest way to travel is by car and the various Mitfahrzentralen (ride-sharing services) offer clearing-houses for both those offering rides and those looking for them. This one caters specifically to a gay and lesbian clientèle, but there are many others to choose from if you can't find what you're looking for here. Those requesting a ride pay a small fee to the agency and a (very reasonable) set fee to the driver depending on the destination. If you need a travelling companion or help with expenses in your car trip, this is very safe and reliable. Highly recommended for travel within Germany, especially between the larger cities. Rides are also available to almost anywhere in Europe.

# Gay

The visibility of gay businesses and venues throughout the city is a good indication of the upfront, bold face the Berlin Schwulenszene has today. You don't need to look for the gay scene in Berlin. It'll find you in about ten minutes. Bars, clubs and shops, saunas and dark rooms – the choice is so wide and varied you'll find it practically impossible to experience everything on the one visit, or even to choose which facet of the scene to check out first. Since 1993, the age of consent has been 16 – the same as for everyone else. Making contact with other gays in public is rarely a matter of interest to passers-by. Nevertheless, bigots do exist, and the scale of anti-gay violence has increased over the past few years. In the west it tends to be from gangs of Turkish teenagers, and in the east the most dangerous groups are the right-wing skinhead Germans. The most dangerous areas are Kreuzberg in the west and Lichtenberg in the east. The latter should be kept in mind because of its train station, which might be where you arrive in Berlin. The attitude of the authorities is equivocal. However, if you see police hanging around they are likely to be there for your protection.

The scene here is constantly shifting, so much of that which is listed below may have changed or disappeared by the time you read it. Mann-O-Meter (*see below*) is the best place to go for up-to-the-minute information.

## Advice & Information

### Berliner AIDS Hilfe (BAH)
*Meinekestraße 12, Charlottenburg, 10719 (883 30 17). U1, U15, U9 Kurfürstendamm.* **Open** 24 hours daily.
Berlin has one of the most advanced and integrated approaches to HIV in the world. The BAH runs a 24-hour phone service where advice and information is given on all questions relating to HIV and AIDS. Staff speak English.

### Mann-O-Meter
*Motzstraße 5, Schöneberg, 10777 (216 80 08). U1, U15, U2, U4 Nollendorfplatz.* **Open** 3-11pm Mon-Sat; 3-9pm Sun.
An efficient and helpful information drop-in centre and phone line with an exhaustive computer database. Regularly updated wall displays detail weekly events in the political, cultural and frivolous spheres. Cheap stocks of safer sex materials are available, and stacks of listings magazines and newspapers adorn the cosy bar in the back. English spoken. This should be your first stop when you arrive.

## Publications

*Gay Express, Pink Power* and *Siegessäule* are all monthly freebie papers widely available at most venues in Berlin. Although in German, the vital information is simple to follow. *Siegessäule* is especially recommended. If you can read some German, it's worth having a look at the monthly national *Magnus* (DM8). The guide *Berlin von Hinten* (DM16.80) also has some illuminating articles. And don't ignore the *Spartacusgay* guide to the world.

### Schwules Überfalltelefon
*c/o Mann-o-Meter (216 66 36).* **Open** 6-9pm daily.
A phone helpline for victims and witnesses that opened in response to the growing wave of anti-gay violence. Counselling and assistance are offered. Based at Mann-O-Meter (*see above*), where you can also go in person for advice. English spoken.

### Schwules Museum
*Mehringdamm 61, 2nd Courtyard, Kreuzberg, 10961 (693 11 72). U6, U7 Mehringdamm/119, 140 bus.* **Open** 2-6pm Wed-Sun; guided tours Sat only at 5pm; library and archive open 2-6pm Wed-Sun.
Regular exhibitions of gay history in Berlin. Archive of gay publications from Germany and around the globe.

## Accommodation

Most hotels realise how important gays are to the health of the city's tourist industry and are courteous and efficient. An accommodation service is run from Mann-O-Meter (*see above* **Advice & Information**). For a charge of DM5, staff will find you a variety of places to stay (including sleeping on floors or waterbeds), from gratis to a top rate of about DM50 per night. You must negotiate the price with your host.

### Arco
*Kurfürstendamm 30, Charlottenburg, 10719 (882 63 88). U7 Adenauerplatz.* **Rates** *single* DM90 per night, DM110 w/shower; *double* DM135 per night, DM155 w/shower.
An inexpensive establishment, with 20 rooms, in an excellent location. The owner and staff are gay.

### Club 70 Pension
*Eberstraße 58, Schöneberg, 10827 (784 17 86). U4/S45, S46 Innsbrucker Platz.* **Rates** *single* DM75; *double* DM110, breakfast and shower included.
The cheapest gay hotel in town and very popular with male visitors. The rooms are upstairs; downstairs is a bar and sex shop.

## Le Moustache

*Gartenstraße 4, Mitte, 10115 (281 7277). U6
Oranienburger Tor/U8 Rosenthalerplatz.* **Rates** *single*
DM50 per night; *double* DM80 per night.
There are some basic rooms (five doubles, one single) in the
pension above the bar (*see below* **Bars: Leather**) and the
atmosphere is friendly and less hectic than in west Berlin.

## Tom's House

*Eisenacherstraße 10, Schöneberg, 10777 (218 55 44).
U1, U15, U2, U4 Nollendorfplatz.* **Rates** *single* DM130
per night; *double* DM155 per night.
An eccentric and unpredictable establishment, with seven
double rooms and one single. Great buffet brunches are
served from 10am-1pm. Some of the leather-clad guests are
actually awake at that hour to enjoy them.

# Eating Out

Specifically gay eating places are thin on the
ground in Berlin, but there are many places
which are either gay-run or where you will just
feel at home. Basically, Berliners have accepted
gays as part of the scenery, and restaurants, especially in the areas around the gay bars, are only
really interested in whether you've brought
enough money to cover the bill. *See also chapter*
**Restaurants**.

## Le Bistrot

*Rheinstraße 55, Schöneberg, 12159 (852 49 14). U9
Friedrich-Wilhelm Platz.* **Open** 7pm-5am daily. **Average**
DM50. **Credit** AE, DC, EC, JCB, MC, V.
A favourite with better-off Berlin gays, and no wonder.
Terrific French and German food at reasonable prices.

## Offenbach Stuben

*Stubbenkammerstraße 8, Prenzlauer Berg, 10437 (448
41 06). S8, S10 Prenzlauer Allee.* **Open** 7pm-2am daily.
**Average** DM25. **No credit cards.**
For a long time this was considered the most desirable place
in which to be seen eating in Prenzlauer Berg. The cuisine is
traditional German (roasts and the like); the décor is 1950s-
style. Book to avoid disappointment.

## Regenbogenfrühstück, BAH

*Meinekestraße 12, Wilmersdorf, 10719 (883 30 17).
U15, U9 Kurfürstendamm.* **Open** 10am-1pm Mon. **No
credit cards.**
For DM3 you can enjoy a relaxed and nourishing breakfast
alongside people with HIV and AIDS, friends and staff.

# Bars

## Anderes Ufer

*Hauptstraße 157, Schöneberg, 10827 (784 15 78). U7
Kleistpark.* **Open** 11am-2am daily.
A good starting point for an exploration of Berlin. A relaxed
café with a youngish, mixed bag of habitués, mostly men
with an eye for trends and an ear for good conversation.
Occasional art shows, live entertainment and special parties
add to the attraction.

## Andreas Kneipe

*Ansbacherstraße 29, Schöneberg, 10777 (218 32 57).
U1, U15, U2 Wittenbergplatz.* **Open** 11am-4am daily.
One of the oldest bars in Berlin; you can breathe tradition
from the moment you set foot across the threshold. If you
want real Berlin atmosphere and to get away from the
tourists, this is the place to go.

## Zum Burgfrieden

*Wichertstraße 69, Prenzlauer Berg, 10439 (449 98 01).
U2, S8, S85, S86, S10 Schönhauser Allee.* **Open** 7pm-
3am daily.
Although it now attracts its clientèle from the whole city,
the former flagship of the east Berlin gay scene has changed
little since reunification. The arrival of various other bars in
the area has somewhat diluted its centrality to the eastern
scene, but not its charm. Leathermen stand and locals sit in
the front bar, students and the unemployed sit in the larger
side room, and fashion victims pack into the black and white
bar in the back.

## Café Anal

*Muskauerstraße 16, 10997 (618 7064). U1,
U15 Görlitzerbahnhof.* **Open** 5pm-4am Mon-Sat;
3pm-2am Sun.
The crucible of autonomous Kreuzberg: Tuntenbarock ('fag-
got-baroque') décor – lawdy it's gaudy – and indolent
drinkers, laced with a tasteful fringing of political correct-
ness. Punks, skinheads, students, artists and drop-outs feel
at home here. Women-only Mon, men-only Tue.

## Café Ecke Schönhauser (Café Peking)

*Kastanienallee 2, Prenzlauer Berg, 10435 (448 33 31).
U2 Eberswalderstraße.* **Open** 2pm-midnight Mon-Sat.
A good stop for coffee and cake in the afternoon or a cocktail in the evening. Like most bars in east Berlin, it was
recently renovated. Old leather seating has been replaced by
black wooden tables and chairs.

## Café PositHIV

*Großgörschenstraße 12, Schöneberg, 10829 (782 03 54).
U7 Kleistpark, S1 Großgörschenstraße.* **Open** 5-11pm
Tue-Sat; 3-10pm Sun.
A café for people affected by HIV and AIDS; mainly gay
men. There is communal cooking and eating every Thursday
lunchtime and there are regular art and craft classes.

## Café Savigny

*Grolmanstraße 53/54, Charlottenburg, 10623 (312 81
95). S3, S5, S6, S7, S9 Savignyplatz.* **Open** 10am-1am
Mon-Fri; 11am-1am Sat-Sun.
It may be slightly outside the more popular gay stomping
grounds, but the Café Savigny provides the perfect setting
for a classy rendezvous. Its Mediterranean atmosphere
and upscale clientèle are genteel without in any way being
obnoxiously swank.

## Connection Café & Bistro

*Martin-Luther-Straße 19, Schöneberg, 10777
(213 11 36). U1, U15, U2, U4 Nollendorfplatz.*
**Open** 2pm-2am daily.
Earthenware tiles, pot plants, mirrors and chrome furnish
this friendly, glitzy bar frequented by a cross-section of well-
dressed men. Club-style music makes it an ideal kicking-off
place for a night on the town.

## Coxx Café

*Nürnburgerstraße 17, Charlottenburg, 10789 (213 61
55). U1, U15, U2 Wittenbergplatz.* **Open** summer 5pm-
2am Mon-Fri, 1pm-3am Sat, 6pm-2am Sun; winter 2pm-
2am Mon-Sat, 4pm-2am Sun.
A cool and airy long bar, Coxx Café is perfect for relaxing in
in the middle of west Berlin's shopping district. Best in the
afternoon, as it's very quiet at night.

## Drama

*Oranienstraße 169, Kreuzberg, 10999 (614 53 56). U1,
U8 Kottbusser Tor.* **Open** 9pm-5am daily.
Hot and happening bar on Kreuzberg's main drag, popular
with the house and techno crowd. Live DJs on Wednesday
and Sunday.

**Café Ecke Schönhauser** – see page 221.

### Hafen
*Motzstraße 19, Schöneberg, 10777 (211 41 18).*
*U1, U15, U2, U4 Nollendorfplatz.* **Open** 8pm-4am (or later) daily.
A red plush and vaguely psychedelic bar. Popular with the fashion- and body-conscious, especially at weekends, when it provides a safe haven from nearby heavy cruising dens.

### Hudson American Bar
*Eßholzstraße 10, Schöneberg, 10781 (216 16 02). U7 Kleistpark.* **Open** 8pm-2am Thur-Sun.
Style is more crucial than purpose with the good-looking crowd that soaks in the atmosphere of this shiny, brilliant cocktail bar.

### Kleine Philharmonie (Bei Wanda)
*Schaperstraße 4, Wilmersdorf, 10719 (883 11 02). U9 Spichernstraße.* **Open** 5pm-3am Mon-Fri; 8pm-3am Sat.
Wanda plays hostess to guests who appreciate the chintz comfort of her umbrella-ceilinged parlour. Popular with staff and visitors to the BAH (*see above* **Eating Out**) around the corner. Wanda is an indefatigable fundraiser for charity.

### Lenz
*Eisenacher Straße 3, 10777 (217 78 20/217 77 29). U1, U15, U2, U4 Nollendorfplatz.* **Open** from 8pm.
An ultra-trendy bar where the élite meet to greet each other and it's stuffed to the gills with wall-to-wall chicness every night of the week. Consider yourself warned.

### Mister X
*Graefestraße 11, Kreuzberg, 10967 (691 50 96). U8 Leinestraße.* **Open** 10pm-5am daily.
A bizarre and sleazy bar with a south German flavour: wooden chairs with heart-shaped backs, candles on the tables, beer in litre mugs, and the oldest working Wurlitzer in town. Regular orgasm parties are held, usually Fri, Sun. Mixed ages. Ring for entry.

### Neue Busche
*Warschauerstraße/Strahlauerallee 48, Friedrichshain, 10243 (no phone). S3, S5, S6, S7, S75, S9 Warschauerstraße.* **Open** 9pm-5pm Fri-Sun. **Admission** DM5.
A popular new seventies-style disco for gays and lesbians housed in an old red-brick building that was formerly the canteen of the Narva lightbulb factory.

### Schall und Rauch
*Gleimstraße 23, Prenzlauer Berg, 10437 (448 92 26). U2/S8, S85, S86, S10 Schönhauser Allee.* **Open** 2pm-2am daily.
One of the newest editions to the eastern scene, this modern café/bar has been an instant hit. The clientèle is trendy without being as out of hand as in many similar western establishments. Perfect for a drink or an evening of hanging out.

### Stiller Don
*Erich-Leinert-Straße 67, Prenzlauer Berg, 10439 (449 36 51). U2, S8, S10 Schönhauser Allee.* **Open** 6pm-2am daily.
Formerly home to the avant garde of Prenzlauer Berg, this is now the place where just about everyone from all over comes to see and be seen when in the east.

### Tom's Bar
*Motzstraße 16, Schöneberg, 10777 (213 45 70). U1, U15, U2, U4 Nollendorfplatz.* **Open** 10pm-6am Mon-Thur.
Described by *Der Spiegel* as climax, or crash-landing of the night, Tom's wide appeal is undiminished with the passage of time. The front bar is fairly chatty, but the closer you get to the steps down into Berlin's busiest dark room, the more intense things become. A huge video screen plays an abstract mix of porn, Care Bears cartoons and MTV. There's a DM5 door charge on Fridays and Saturdays which will buy you any one drink. Men only.

### Valentino
*Auguststraße 21, Mitte, 10117 (208 94 84). S1, S2 Oranienburger Straße/U6 Oranienburger Tor.* **Open** 6pm-2am Mon-Fri; 2pm-2am Sat; 10am-3am Sun.
One of east Berlin's newest, post-revolution cafés. The pale interior makes for an elegantly relaxed choice for a beer, hot chocolate laced with rum or ice cream. It attracts a pleasantly subdued mix of younger, fashion-conscious men and women, mainly from the east.

## Leather Bars

Some of the best leather-wear designers work and sell their wares in Berlin, wielding great influence over the look of the scene. In fact, they might as well get it over with and declare leather the official fabric of Berlin. There are also plenty of fascinating places in which to show off your animal hide, including the eternally popular Leather Meeting over the Easter week holidays. Full information from MSC (Motorsports and Contacts) Berlin (*see below* **Knast**).

### Knast
*Fuggerstraße 34, Schöneberg, 10777 (218 10 26). U1, U15, U2 Wittenbergplatz.* **Open** 9pm-5am daily.
The name means jail, and this leather bar has chains, helmets, bars and riot sticks galore: so much diversion that the porn videos go almost unnoticed. A small backroom exists although little happens there. The weekend is busiest and cruisiest. The home of MSC (Motorsports and Contacts) Berlin.

### Le Moustache
*Gartenstraße 4, Mitte, 10115 (281 72 77). U6 Oranienbuurger Tor/U8 Rosenthaler Platz.* **Open** 9pm-3am daily.
A combination hotel, bar and café, Le Moustache is the leather establishment for all your basic needs. *Also see above* **Hotels**.

### New Action
*Kleiststraße 26, Schöneberg, 10787 (211 82 56). U1, U15, U2, U4 Nollendorfplatz.* **Open** from 8.30pm Mon-Sat; from 1pm Sun.
This atmospheric and custom-designed bar features a pool table, porn videos, and a backroom. The friendly staff sell a huge selection of condoms as well as drinks. A bizarre collection of parties and events are held.

## Spike Connection

*Motzstraße 25, Schöneberg, 10777 (213 85 80).*
*U1, U15, U2, U4 Nollendorfplatz.* **Open** 10pm-7am
Sun-Thur.
An otherworldly emporium where fantasy runs riot: military
camouflage, motorcycles, US licence plates, barrels and bolt
holes, slings and arrows of love. The action in the cellar is
late and heavy. Open every other Saturday for a rubber
party. Jack-Off Party every last Monday of the month.

## Clubs & One-Nighters

### 90°

*Dennewitzstraße 18, Tiergarten, 10785 (262 89 84). U1,*
*U15 Kurfürstenstraße, U2 Bülowstraße.* **Open** 11pm-
5am Thur, Sun. **Admission** DM10.
This extremely popular one-nighter (well okay, two-nighter)
gets so packed you can hardly move in time to the hard,
heavy house spun by well-informed DJs. Although also open
on Fridays and Saturdays, the Thursday and Sunday Gay
Days nicely top and tail the long Berlin weekend.

### Bunker

*Albrechtstraße 24-25, Mitte, 10117 (87 40 97). U6*
*Oranienburger Tor.* **Open** 11-6am Fri, Sat. **Admission**
DM15.
A highly atmospheric and unforgettable club housed in a
former air-raid shelter. Different sounds in different rooms
are enjoyed by a young, mainly male, east Berlin set.

### Connection

*Welserstraße 24, Schöneberg, 10777 (24 14 32). U1,*
*U15, U2 Wittenbergplatz.* **Open** 10pm-5am Fri, Sat.
**Admission** DM10 (includes drink ticket).
Although by next week things may be different, this is currently Berlin's most popular gay disco. A hot mixture of the
esoteric and Top 40 sounds ensure that Connection's dancefloor is constantly packed. There's a small leather and jeans
cellar bar with back room. Men only.

### Disco Doppelfenster

*Ackerstraße 12 HH, Mitte, 10115 (no phone). S1, S2*
*Nordbahnof.* **Open** from 9pm Tue, Fri. **Admission**
DM3.50.
To get a good idea of the differences between east and west,
this is a great place to start. The upstairs (ground floor) looks
like a gay bar somebody set up in their dad's rec room – even
the glasses look suspiciously like old jam jars. The basement
has a very small dancefloor and a long bunker-like room next
door for conversation. As for novelty, this disco has come up
with a new gimmick – friendly people.

### E-Werk

*Wilhelmstraße (near Leipziger Straße, entrance across*
*from Treuhandanstalt), Mitte, 10117 (no phone). U2*
*Mohrenstraße.* **Open** from 11pm Fri-Sat. **Admission**
DM15-20.
This former power station is one of Berlin's biggest and best
discos. The crowd is mixed although the atmosphere does
not get particularly gay until around 3am. The house people
could stand a tad less attitude but the hardcore techno, elaborate light shows and brilliant decor all combine to make a
night at the E-Werk worth the visit to Berlin. On the third
Sunday of every month, top house DJs are flown in for the
Faggots At The Ranch one-nighter.

### Erotic Party, AHA (Allgemeine Homosexuelle Allianz)

*2nd floor, stairs from courtyard, Mehringdamm 61,*
*Kreuzberg, 10961 (692 36 00). U5, U7 Mehringdamm.*
**Open** from 9pm 2nd Fri in month. **Admission** DM9.
Leave your shoes and as much of the rest of your clothes as
you want at the cloakroom, drink at the bar with a number

to run up your bill, sit and relax at tables and explore the
veiled and comfortable backrooms with beds, armchairs and
porn videos. Popular with a young and friendly crowd. A
café opens here every Sunday from 3-8pm.

## HIV-HIV-Hurra Party, BAH

*Meinekestraße 12, Wilmersdorf, 10719 (883 30 17). U3,*
*U9 Kurfürstendamm.* **Open** 8pm-2am every last Friday
in month.
A monthly party, with a bar, free buffet, music, cabaret and
dancing for anyone affected by HIV and AIDS.

## Lipstick

*Richard-Wagner-Platz 5, Charlottenburg, 10585 (342 81*
*26). U7 Richard-Wagner-Platz 145, N45 bus.* **Open**
10pm-4am Tue, Thur, Sun. **Admission** DM3.
Europe's largest lesbian club opens its doors to a predominantly male mixed crowd three days a week, pulling the silk-
shirt set from Charlottenburg and drawing other beautiful
people on to the small, mirrored, stainless-steel dancefloor.

## Plush at Café Moskau

*Karl-Marx-Allee 34, 10178 (no phone). U5*
*Schillingstraße.* **Open** from 11pm Sat. **Admission** DM10.
The crowd from 90° basically packs up and heads on out to
the east side on Saturday nights. The accommodation is a
little bit more luxurious, but it's sweating room only once
the crowds arrive in force around 2am.

## SchwuZ

*second rear courtyard, stairs under arch, Hasenheide 54,*
*Kreuzberg, 10967 (694 10 77). U7 Südstern.* **Open**
10pm-6am Fri, Sat. **Admission** DM5 after midnight
Fri; DM3 Sat.
The Schwulen Zentrum (gay centre) is perched on the fifth
floor of an old factory building, and retains a decayed urban
charm, with a small dancefloor and wildly variable music.
A basic bar offers the cheapest drinks in (west) clubland, and
there's a non-smoking lounge. Friday nights are oldies discos, sometimes dedicated to the usual culprits (Abba, Connie
Francis, Abba, the Supremes, and on occasion Abba). Mainly
for young men, although women are not made to feel unwel-
come. Occasional special events are held, including the Safer
Sex Party (DM12, including refundable DM10 for towel hire;
leave your clothes at the door and pick up a towel).

## Saunas

Saunas are popular places with all kinds of people
and you may have to queue, especially on cheaper days. After disrobing, shower and wash thoroughly before getting into the flow. Furthermore,
traditional practice in a dry sauna is to put your
towel between as much of your body and the
wooden interior as you can. In-house bills can be
run up on your locker or cabin number and settled
on leaving. Penalties for lost keys.

## Apollo City Sauna

*Kurfürstenstraße 101, Tiergarten, 10787 (213 24 24).*
*U1, U15, U2 Wittenbergplatz.* **Open** 1pm-7am daily.
**Admission** DM20 a day (two for price of one Mon).
Short-term cabin reservation.
Busy and at times almost hectic, the Apollo has both dry and
damp saunas and is favoured by younger men. The regularly announced Slivovicz Aufguss massage (where the alcohol is poured on to hot coals to create a heady atmosphere)
is a special feature. There are miles of corridors around the
cabins, each of which contains a bed, mirror and TV. The
premises also house a porn video den, a TV lounge, sunbeds,
weights room and bar.

### Steam Sauna

*Kurfürstenstraße 87, Tiergarten, 10787 (218 40 62).*
*U1, U15, U2 Wittenbergplatz.* **Open** 11am-7am Mon-
Thur; 11am Fri to 7am Mon continuously. Short-term
cabin reservation, except Fri-Mon. **Admission** DM27;
DM20 Wed, Sat (after 1pm).
Smaller than the Apollo, the Steam Sauna is more laidback
and visited by all ages, as well as the more macho set. There's
both a dry and a damp sauna. A Jacuzzi operates every hour
on the hour for 30 minutes. Each cabin has a bed and mirror
(there are three free cabins, which, however, should not be
monopolised). You'll also find a large porn video den, a TV
lounge and a bar. The maximum duration of a visit is ten
hours before renewal.

### Treibhaus Sauna

*Schönhauser Allee 132, Prenzlauer Berg, 10437 (448 45
03/449 34 94). U2 Eberswalder Straße.* **Open** 3pm-6am
Mon-Thur; 3pm Fri to 6am Mon continuously.
**Admission** DM20; DM17 students, unemployed; DM17
Tue, Thur everyone.
Tucked back in the first courtyard (buzz for entry), this
has fast become a big favourite, especially with students,
although the clientèle runs the gamut of ages. Facilities
include both a dry and a damp sauna, whirlpool, cycle jet,
solarium and massage room. Cabins equipped with TV &
VCR are on a first-come first-served basis. There's also a TV
room, a bar and Imbiß.

## Shopping

Berlin is well served with gay shops and the majority of them can also provide you with routine
information. Most places selling videos offer
reasonably priced hire services, as well as good
supplies of condoms.

### Bruno's

*Kurfürstendamm 227 (Ku'damm Ecke), 1st Floor,
Charlottenburg, 10719 (882 42 90). U1, U15, U9
Kurfürstendamm.* **Open** 10am-10pm Mon-Sat.
Conveniently located smack dab in the middle of downtown,
Bruno's offers an excellent selection of reading materials and
videos for sale and rent. Postcards and CDs also.

### Condomi

*Kantstraße 38, Charlottenburg, 10625 (313 50 51). S3,
S5, S6, S7, S9 Savignyplatz.* **Open** 10am-6pm Mon-Fri;
10am-3pm Sat.
Condoms galore, with multiple lubricants, served in an extraordinary variety of packagings. All your safer sex needs
catered for – and more.

*Out on the town – scene but not heard.*

### Connection Garage

*Fuggerstraße 33, Schöneberg, 10777 (218 14 32).
U1, U15, U2, U4 Nollendorfplatz.* **Open** 10am-1am
Mon-Sat; 2pm-1am Sun.
The folks from Connection Disco here bring their expertise
to the rubber novelty, chains 'n' thangs, T-shirt, magazine,
and, well, you-name-it-they've-got-it market. These folks
have gone for comprehensiveness and to provide you with
everything you think you need and lots of stuff to put a new
idea or two into your head. Be sure to bring extra cash – you
never know what you might fancy.

### Galerie Janssen

*Pariser Straße 45 and Pfalzburgerstraße 76,
Wilmersdorf, 10719 (881 15 90). U3 Uhlandstraße.*
**Open** 11am-6.30pm Mon-Sat.
Primarily an art gallery, which with some books, Galerie Janssen
has regularly changing art exhibitions, plus reproductions,
posters and cards.

### Horsts Laden

*Rankestraße 14, Charlottenburg, 10789 (881 39 29). U3,
U9 Kurfürstendamm.* **Open** 11am-6.30pm Mon-Fri;
11am-2pm Sat; 11am-4pm first Sat of month.
Long-established outfitters for leather, rubber, sports clothing, chaps, harnesses, handcuffs, military gear and the
like. Prices at Horsts Laden are reasonable and the service
is friendly and helpful.

### Marc & Bengels

*Grünewaldstraße 92, Schöneberg, 12165 (784 84 64).
U7 Kleistpark.* **Open** noon-6.30pm Mon-Wed, Fri; noon-
8pm Thur; 10am-2pm Sat; 10am-4pm first Sat in month.
Big range of underwear of all shapes, sizes, styles and
designer labels.

### Man's World

*Hauptstraße 8, Schöneberg, 10827 (784 84 64). U7
Kleistpark.* **Open** 10am-6pm Mon-Fri; 10am-3pm Sat.
Friendly and attentive staff sell a small but very stylish selection of menswear and accessories. There's also a branch
at Mommsenstraße 15.

### Prinz Eisenherz Buchladen

*Bleibtreustraße 52, Charlottenburg, 10623
(313 99 36). S3 Savignyplatz.* **Open** 10am-6pm
Mon-Fri; 10am-1pm Sat.
One of the finest lesbian and gay bookshops in Europe,
including, among its large English-language stock, many
titles that aren't always available in Britain. There's a good
art and photography section, plus magazines, postcards and
news of book readings and other events.

### Walters Leder Boutique

*Martin-Luther-Straße 45, Schöneberg, 10779
(211 18 97). U4 Viktoria-Luise-Platz.* **Open** 10.30am-
1.30pm, 2-6pm, Mon-Fri; 10am-1.30pm Sat.
Leather clothing is made and sold at this specialist shop.
There's a good made-to-measure service. Opening hours are
sometimes unpredictable.

## Sport & Sunshine

The Continental climate in the summer months
brings out all of the city's finery, creating new
meeting places. There is no taboo attached to
nudity in large parks or large groups. The most
popular places to go are Strandbad Wannsee (*S1,
S3 to Nikolassee, then walk or take Bus 157*); and
the Tiergarten (*Liegewiese between double gravel
path and west of Hofsagerallee*).

## Apollo Sports Studio

*Hauptstraße 150, Schöneberg, 10827 (784 82 03). U7*
*Kleistpark.* **Open** 11am-9.30pm Mon-Fri; 1-5pm Sat;
11am-3pm Sun.
A well-equipped fitness studio that is well patronised by
gays. Facilities at Apollo Sports Studio include a weights
room, a bar and a sauna.

## Manuel Sportstudio

*first courtyard, Joachim-Friedrich-Straße 37,*
*Wilmersdorf, 10711 (892 20 80). U7 Adenauerplatz.*
**Open** 9am-10pm Mon-Fri; 9am-6pm Sat, Sun.
The clientèle is predominantly gay at this discreet fitness
studio. Aerobics, a small sauna, a bar and a good weights
room are among the facilities.

## Stadtbad Wilmersdorf II

*Heidelberger Platz, Wilmersdorf, 14197 (864 10). U2*
*Heidelbergerplatz.* **Open** 9am-9pm Mon-Fri; 9am-5pm
Sat; noon-5pm Sun.
Berlin's public swimming pools are enthusiastically patronised by those seeking relaxation, health, a suntan (DM2,
for eight minutes) or new friends. Standard adult admission
for 75 minutes is DM3. Concessions with identification. This
cruisy and sociable pool is known as the Tuntenaquarium
('faggot aquarium').

# Lesbian

Berlin is a paradise for lesbians. A tolerant city by
any standards, it also boasts a huge network of
cultural and political activity and a wide variety
of bars and clubs (*see below*). The scenes are
markedly different between east and west, though,
and seem to be getting even more so as time goes
by. In the east the scene only really came into being
around 1983, and lesbians there remain closer to
gay men than in the west. Nevertheless, many lesbian bars and clubs in the west also admit men
some nights of the week – it would be uneconom-
ic for them not to do so. Most of Berlin's women-
only venues can only afford to remain so because
they are subsidised by the Senate.

The listings here concern specifically lesbian
activities and services. For more general information about **Women's Berlin**, see the chapter
of that name, or consult Berlin's monthly women's
magazine *Blattgold*. This costs DM5, can be found
at many of the places below and lists everything.
There's also a monthly east Berlin lesbian magazine, *Schnepfe*, which costs DM3 and has listings.

## Help and Information

### Lesbenberatung

*Kulmerstraße 20a, Schöneberg, 10783 (217 27 53,*
*helpline 215 20 00). U7 Yorckstraße, S1*
*Großgörschenstraße.* **Open** 4-8pm Mon, Tue, Thur.
Founded in 1988, this centre offers counselling, as well as
workshops, self-help groups, courses and cultural events.

### Berlin Exclusiv für Sie und Sie (Map of Berlin for lesbians)

**Phone** (787 51 10).
An advertising-financed free map giving a general overview

of lesbian life in east and west. You can pick one up at the
**Lesbenberatung** (*see above*) or at many of the places listed below and in the chapter **Women's Berlin**.

## Cultural Centres

### Araquin

*Bülowstraße 54, Schöneberg, 10783 (215 12 95). U1*
*Kurfürstenstraße.* **Open** *office* 5-7pm Tue.
Once a flat occupied by a group of lesbian artists, since 1989
Araquin has been a cultural centre offering exhibitions,
workshops, movies and lectures. There is also a small café.

### Cnemidophorus Uniparens – Künstlerinnenhaus

*Knaackstraße 92, Prenzlauer Berg, 10435*
*(442 7847 or 421 3891). U2 Eberswalderstraße.*
**Open** *office* 3-8pm Wed.
Named after a desert lizard which procreates by self-insem-
ination, this multicultural project (where most of the workers also live) hosts the Porto Femmes gallery, studios for
artists, a silk-screen printing workshop and other facilities
for the use of the female public. The irregular workshops
are listed in Blattgold. The **Whistle Stop Café** (*see below*)
is just next door.

### Pelze Multi Media

*Potsdamer Straße 139, Schöneberg, 10783 (216 2341).*
*U2 Bülowstraße.* **Open** from 9pm Fri. Closed summer;
phone to check.
Since 1981 this former fur shop has been a meeting place,
exhibition space, stage, gallery and night café for international, experimental women and lesbian artists. Men not
admitted. Call for current events or check listings in *Blattgold*.

## Cafés, Bars & Restaurants

Most of the venues listed below are women-only
and the vast majority of the customers are lesbians. Some places admit men because, as one
lesbian bar-owner explained: 'One heterosexual
couple spends more money in an evening than a
whole week of lesbian customers.' All the women-
only venues in Berlin, apart from the **Whistle
Stop Café** and **Dinelo**, survive as such through
Senate subsidy. For more cafés *see also chapter*
**Women's Berlin**.

### Café Seidenfaden

*Dircksensstraße 47, Mitte, 10178 (283 27 83). S2, S5,*
*S7, S9 Hackescher Markt.* **Open** 11am-9pm Tue, Fri;
11am-6pm Sat, Sun.
This place is run by women from a rehabilitation and therapy group of former addicts. You'll find it packed at lunchtime and quiet in the evenings. There are cultural events,
readings, a monthly exhibition and no drugs at all.

### Golden Girls

*Zietenstraße 8, Schöneberg, 10783 (262 59 33). U1, U2*
*Nollendorfplatz.* **Open** 4pm-1am Mon, Wed, Fri; men
admitted from 3pm Sat-Mon.
An upmarket restaurant frequented by trendy, thirtysomething lesbians with money and style. Can be a bit snobby,
mind. There are monthly exhibitions.

### Whistle Stop Cafe

*Knaackstraße 94, Prenzlauer Berg, 10178 (442 78 47).*
*U2 Eberswalder Straße.* **Open** from 6pm Mon-Sat; from
10am Sun.
In the middle of an area full of alternative cultural projects

*Open after 6pm – the* **Whistle Stop Cafe.**

and right next door to **Cnemidophorus Uniparens** (*see above*) the Whistle Stop Café opened in May 1994. It is the only unsubsidised women-only café in east Berlin. It's furnished like a snack bar and offers cheap and tasty vegetarian food, exhibitions and monthly classical concerts.

## Clubs

*See also chapter* **Women's Berlin.**

### Die 2 am Wasserturm

*Spandauer Damm 168, Charlottenburg, 14059 (302 52 60). Bus 145.* **Open** from 7pm Mon-Sun; disco from 9pm Wed, Sat, Sun.
A romantic garden promises wonderful summer nights. Inside they play oldies like *La Vie En Rose* and *Sex Machine.* A very easy-going atmosphere.

### Doppelfenster mitNichten

*Ackerstraße 12, Mitte, 10115 (208 74 18). U2 Rosenthaler Platz.* **Open** 9pm-2pm Tue; 9pm-2am Wed; 10pm-4am Fri. Women only Wed.
The café of Lambda, a counselling service for young gays and lesbians, hosts a women-only disco on Wednesday nights. The thirtysomething clientèle dance to every kind of music except techno – because the 'sound system isn't strong enough'. A mixed crowd inhabits the café on Tuesday and Friday.

### Ex-Kreuz-Club

*Albrechtstraße 24/25, Mitte, 10117 (no phone). S3, S5, S7, S9 Friedrichstraße.* **Open** from 10pm Sat only.
This smallish annex to Bunker (*see chapter* **Clubs**) hosts a small S&M party every Saturday at which lesbians are welcome. Newcomers to the 'rubber, leather and fantasy' event should turn up at the dooor from 10-11pm. Nobody gets in after that. Take your best outfit – the dress code is, of course, strict. Further information, accessories etc can be had from Boutique Hautnah, *Uhlandstraße 170, Charlottenburg, 10719 (882 34 34).*

### Lipstick

*Richard-Wagner-Platz 5, Charlottenburg, 10585 (342 8126). U7 Richard-Wagner-Platz.* **Open** from 10pm Tue-Sun; men admitted Tue, Thur, Sun and first Fri of month.
Frequented by young, trendy lesbians and some straight women, Lipstick is well established and a must at weekends. Mainstream disco-beats, hip hop, soul and oldies.

### Pour Elle

*Kalkreuthstraße 10, Schöneberg, 10777 (245 57 33). U4 Viktoria-Luise-Platz.* **Open** 9pm-5am daily; men admitted Mon, Wed.
Berlin's oldest lesbian bar/club has existed since 1973. The kitsch plush gold décor can be a little overpowering.

### Reitzbar

*Urbanstraße 70, Kreuzberg, 10967 (694 4975). U8 Hermannplatz.* **Open** from 10pm Tue, Wed, Fri-Sun; women only Thur.
Very popular with students. At weekends there's a joint lesbian and gay event, and sometimes disco, soul and acid jazz.

## Lesbian Centres

See also the list of Women's centres in *chapter* **Women's Berlin**. Most of them have special events for lesbians.

### biz-café im Sonntags-Club

*Rhinower Straße 8, Prenzlauer Berg, 10437 (449 75 90). S8, S10 Schönhauser Allee.* **Open** 4-10pm Mon-Thur; 6-midnight Fri-Sun.
The Sonntags-Club is an association of lesbians, gays, bisexuals, and transsexuals. At the biz-café they offer events, exhibitions, poetry readings, discussions, psychological and social counselling. Once a month there's a women-only disco including a dark room.

### Café Rosa

*At Lambda Berlin, Ackerstraße 12, Mitte, 10115 (282 79 90). U2 Rosenthaler Platz.* Call for details.
Don't be fooled by the name: Café Rosa is actually an umbrella name for a selection of events every second Tuesday that are organised at the above address but take place in various venues. There are discussions, theatre workshops, videos, readings and so on. On Wednesdays it does, however, become a café from 4pm at Lambda. This later segues into the disco mitNichten (*see above*) at the same address.

## Lesbian Studies

### Spinnboden Archiv zur Entdeckung und Bewahrung von Frauenliebe

*Burgsdorfstraße 1, Wedding, 13353 (465 2021). U6 Wedding.* **Open** 1-8pm Wed, Fri.
An exhaustive lesbian archive. From video films, photos and magazines to personal letters and manuscripts, Spinnboden has been collecting multimedia material and books on lesbian life since 1973.

## Conferences

### Berliner Lesbenwoche

*c/o Literaturfrauen e V, Kurfürstenstraße 21-22, Tiergarten, 10785 (262 0087).*
From beginnings in 1985 as a conference for Berlin lesbians, this week-long event has been steadily acquiring a more international perspective. Workshops and discussions take place in a variety of venues every October, and centre on a single topic (in 1994, racism). Call the above number for details, but remember that to attend you have to register by around mid-August.

## Shopping

### Birotic, biank – brillant

*Schlüterstraße 30, Charlottenburg, 10623 (324 96 20). S3, S5, S6, S7, S9 Savignyplatz.* **Open** noon-6.30pm Mon-Fri; 11am-3pm Sat.
A gallery and shop selling exclusive designer jewellery and erotic toys. The fascinating selection includes everything from gold and silver geisha-balls to unique body jewellery. If you feel like splashing out on a gift for a loved one (the cheaper pieces cost around DM800), this may be the place.

# Students

**Student life has its hardships after reunification, but there are still cheap places to eat, sleep and buy books.**

There are over 160,000 students in Berlin: some 120,000 in the west and about 45,000 in the east, spread between the three universities and 17 subject-specific colleges (Fachhochschulen).

Throughout the sixties, West Berlin's students fought for democratic structures in the universities and for freedom of speech on campus. The last powerful student protest was in the winter of 1988/9, when students fought against the Berlin Senate's plans to restructure universities and cut their budgets. The Senate promised to provide more money for universities and colleges. But since reunification and the selection of Berlin as Germany's new capital, rents have risen, libraries and lecture halls have become congested, while the budget is eaten up by reunification programmes.

*Mensae – self-service student restaurants.*

## The Universities

### Freie Universität Berlin (FU)

*Kaiserswertherstraße 16-18 (central administration), Dahlem, 14195 (8381). U2 Dahlem-Dorf.*

The Free University was founded by a group of students in 1948, after the Humboldt was taken over by East German authorities. What is now Germany's biggest university started out with a few books, a villa provided by the US military and a constitution which gave students a vote. Today, the student committee elected by the student parliament has no decision-making powers and the financial situation is getting worse – more students, fewer books and professors.

### Humboldt Universität zu Berlin (HUB)

*Unter den Linden 6, Mitte, 10117 (20930). S3, S5, S6, S9/U6 Friedrichstraße.*

The Berliner Universität, Berlin's first university, was founded by the humanist Wilhelm von Humboldt in 1810. From the mid-thirties until 1945, the university was dominated by the Nazi government. Books were burned, students and professors expelled and murdered. When the Soviets reopened the university in 1946, there were hopes of a fresh start. But the Humboldt University, renamed in 1949, was stifled by the GDR. After 1989, students fought, with partial success, against the plans of the united German government to close some faculties. Jobs are the priority today.

### Technische Universität Berlin (Technical University, TU)

*Straße des 17 Juni 135, Tiergarten, 10623 (314 1). U2 Ernst-Reuter-Platz.*

The TU started life as a mining, building and gardening academy in the eighteenth century. Its remit was expanded in 1946 to include social sciences, philosophy, psychology, business studies, computers and analytical chemistry. With 40,000 students, the TU is one of Germany's ten largest universities. There are special supplementary classes and a Language and Cultural Exchange Programme for foreigners, where you can take language courses, join conversation

groups, attend seminars and apply for exchange partnerships. The SKB services are open to students at any Berlin university. For further information, contact **Sprach-und Kulturbörse an der TU Berlin**, *Franklinstraße 28-29, room 3012, Charlottenburg, 10587 (31 42 27 30, fax 31 42 11 17). U2 Ernst-Reuter-Platz.* **Open** 2-7pm daily.

## Information

### Studentenwerk Berlin

*Hardenbergstraße 34, Charlottenburg, 10623 (3112 313/203). U2 Ernst-Reuter-Platz.* **Open** 9am-3pm Mon-Fri.

The central organisation for student affairs, Studentenwerk Berlin runs hostels, student restaurants and job agencies.

## Accommodation

It's difficult for students to find an affordable room or flat in Berlin. Waiting lists for student hostels are long, but if you have enrolled at one of Berlin's universities you may apply at the Studentenwerk (student affairs office) that maintains the hostels (*see above* **Information**). Student visitors should try the numerous Mitwohnzentralen (flatshare agencies, *see chapter* **Accommodation**) or the student hostels listed below. Book well in advance.

### Studentenhotel Wohnheim Hubertusallee

*Delbrückstraße 24, Grunewald, 14193 (891 97 18). S3, S5 Grunewald.* **Open** *enquiries* 7am-10pm daily (Apr-Oct); 9-11pm daily (Nov-Mar).

Between April and October, the hostel rents out its single rooms for DM45 a night.

### Studentenhotel

*Meininger Straße 10, Schöneberg, 10823 (784 67 20). U7 Eisenacher Straße.* **Open** 24 hours daily.

A private student hotel with accommodation including two- and four-bed rooms. A night in a four-bed room costs DM35, including breakfast.

## Bookshops

There are many second-hand and half-price bookstalls in front of the main building of the HUB (*see above* **Universities**) and in front of the Freie Universität, Mensa II (*see below* **Eating Out**). The following bookstores are close to the three universities and stock a good range of academic volumes. *See also chapter* **Shopping: Bookshops**.

### Akademische Buchhandlung am Gendarmenmarkt
*Markgrafenstraße 36, Mitte, 10117 (200 41 52). U6 Französische Straße.* **Open** 8.30am-6pm Mon-Fri; 9am-2pm Sat.
Subjects from law to philosophy, fiction and natural sciences are covered here. It's two minutes' walk from the HUB.

### Kiepert
*Hardenbergstraße 4-5, Charlottenburg, 10623 (311 00 90/fax 31 10 09 20). U2 Ernst-Reuter-Platz.* **Open** 9am-6.30pm Mon-Fri; 9am-2pm Sat.
Huge general bookshop close to the TU.

### Tell
*Thielallee 34, Dahlem, 14195 (832 40 51). U2 Thielplatz.* **Open** 9am-6pm Mon-Fri; 10am-1pm Sat.
Humanities is the speciality at Tell, round the corner from the Rostlaube, one of the largest Freie Universität buildings.

## Cut-Price Tickets

Your student identity card allows you cheaper admission to most theatres, as well as some museums and exhibitions. Otherwise, the last-minute ticket agency Heckticket (*see chapter* **Services**) at Alexanderplatz, sells reduced-price tickets for shows at private theatres. For listings *see chapter* **Theatre**. Most cinemas sell cheaper seats on Tuesdays and/or Wednesdays (*see chapter* **Film**).

## Eating Out
## Cafés & Bars

### Assel
*Oranienburger Straße 21, Mitte, 10178 (281 44 90). S6 Oranienburger Straße.* **Open** 9am-3am Mon-Fri; 9am-late Sat, Sun.
Join psychology students from the HUB assessing each other over breakfast (served 9am-1pm Mon-Fri), in this cosy cellar café. At night students are joined by a fashionable crowd.

### Café Campus
*Marchstraße 6-8, Villa Bel, Charlottenburg, 10587 (312 91 61). U2 Ernst-Reuter-Platz.* **Open** 10am-midnight Mon-Fri; 11am-midnight Sat, Sun.
Stylish and ecologically sound restaurant founded by students of the Technical University in April 1993.

### Luise
*Königin-Luise-Straße 40, Dahlem, 14195 (832 84 87). U2 Dahlem-Dorf.* **Open** 10am-1am daily.
A great, rustic bar and restaurant, all wooden floors and dark

walls – one room even has a tree in it. In summer the beer garden gets packed with up to 700 students, tutors and professors from the nearby Freie Universität.

### Der UNIverselle Club
*Universitätsstraße 4, Mitte, 10117 (208 28 83). S1, S2, S5, S6, S9/U6 Friedrichstraße.* **Open** 8.30am-noon Mon, Tue, Thur; 8.30-3am Wed; 8.30am-4pm, 10pm-5am, Fri; 10pm-5am Sat.
The UNIverselle was founded by students from the FDJ (Free German Youth) in 1976. It includes a (non-smoking) cafeteria for breakfast and afternoon coffee and a beer bar with wooden benches, where hot savouries are served.

## Mensae

If you think you can cope with balancing a tray through seething crowds of starving students, it's worth eating at one of Berlin's many self-service mensae (student restaurants). Run by the governing Studentenwerk, they enjoy substantial subsidies: a three-course meal costs around DM3.50; main courses cost DM2 or less. If you want the food warm, avoid the rush between 11.45am and 1.45pm. To get food at the student price you will usually need ID (ISIC will do).

### Freie Universität, Mensa 1
*Van't-Hoff-Straße 6, Dahlem, 14195 (830 02 52). U2 Thielplatz.* **Open** noon-2.30pm Mon-Fri.
Every year nearly 5 million meals are sold at all FU mensae.

### Hauptmensa and Säulemensa
*Main Building, Unter den Linden 6, Mitte, 10117 (209 30). S1, S2, S5, S6, S9/U6 Friedrichstraße.* **Open** *Hauptmensa* 11am-2.30pm Mon-Fri; *Säulemensa* 8am-6pm Mon-Thur; 8am-3pm Fri.
Two choices of hot meals are cooked every weekday in the small and over-crowded Hauptmensa in the left wing of the building. Buy food tickets first. The Säulemensa is in the right wing and is more like a cafeteria, with hot meals and a salad bar. Tables outside in summer.

### Technische Universität: Mensa TU
*Hardenbergstraße 34, Charlottenburg, 10623 (311 22 41). U1 Ernst-Reuter-Platz.* **Open** 11.10am-2.30pm Mon-Fri; *cafeteria* 8am-4pm, 4.30-8pm, Mon-Fri.
The only mensa in Berlin that serves evening meals. The location makes it handy for tourists, but you can't ignore the queues of slavering students and the functional atmosphere.

## Language Schools

### Goethe-Institut
*Hardenbergstraße 7, Charlottenburg, 10623 (31 58 40/fax 312 42 25). U2 Ernst-Reuter-Platz.* **Open** 10am-12.30pm, 3-5pm, Mon-Fri.
Well-organised, solid and reliable, the facilities include a cultural extension programme (theatre, film and museum visits), accommodation for students, and a media centre with computers. Evening and intensive courses last eight weeks and cost DM1,200 and DM2,830 respectively.

### Tandem
*Lychener Straße 7, Prenzlauer Berg, 10437 (441 30 03/fax 791 90 00). U2 Eberswalderstraße.* **Open** 11am-1pm Tue, Fri; 4-6pm Mon, Thur.
For a fee of DM30 Tandem will put you in touch with three German speakers who want to learn English, and are prepared to teach you German.

# Women's Berlin

*From salon culture to the chocolate factory, Berlin has seen changes in women's lives like any major city – well, like any major city with a bloody great wall running through it.*

As capital cities go, Berlin, though getting more dangerous, is still among the safest. Lone women can travel around late at night and go into bars and cafés without too many problems.

The influence of women on Berlin's culture and development is barely recognised in official histories. Those who want to discover the whole truth can visit **The Hidden Museum** (*listed under* **Art & Museums**), which redresses the balance.

When women's rights were severely restricted, they found other ways to influence the cultural and political landscape. The salon was one. Henriette Herz founded the first literary salon in 1780. Other salons followed, hosted by Elsa Lasker-Schüler, Fanny Lewald and Bettina von Arnim, all helping to advance Berlin as a city of science and art throughout the nineteenth century.

Later, women made more of a mark on the political scene. Rosa Luxemburg is, of course, the most famous. She and Karl Liebknecht founded the left-wing, revolutionary Spartakus party. She spent much of her life in jail and was murdered, with Liebknecht, on January 15, 1919 by the Freikorps.

The fight for women's suffrage was eventually won in 1919 and 41 women were elected members of the first parliament of the Weimar Republic. In 1945, the Trümmerfrauen (rubble women) were given the task of clearing the city of its hundreds of thousands of tons of rubble. There were very few men left for the work.

A more radical women's movement emerged in 1969. The protests of the early seventies were aimed mainly at the restrictive abortion legislation of Paragraph 218. After a more liberal abortion law was passed in mid-1992 – similar to that in the former GDR – Bavaria challenged its constitutionality. A final decision is still pending and abortion laws remain different in west and east.

On the surface, women in the GDR seemed to be more integrated in the political, economic and cultural life of society. Most women were employed full-time and more held higher positions than in the West. But it was still women who carried the main burden of housework and bringing up children. Sounds familiar?

The women's scene in Berlin today is huge compared to other German cities, but also small in that if you hang around in town for a while, you're bound to start bumping into the same old faces. After the radical seventies, things have settled down a little.

We have listed places that are women-only, but there are dozens of bars and cafés throughout the city where you can go without being eyed up, chatted up or touched up – unless, of course, you want to be. *See chapter* **Cafés & Bars** for details. Certainly not recommended, though, are corner *Kneipes* – the equivalent to a dodgy English pub. For lesbian bars, clubs and information, *see chapter* **Gay Berlin**.

## Help & Information

The monthly German-language women's calendar and magazine *Blattgold* (DM5) will help you negotiate the bewildering number of women's events in Berlin. It's on sale at most of the cafés *listed below under* **Bars, Cafés & Restaurants**.

### Fraueninfothek
*Dircksenstraße 47, Mitte, 10178 (282 3980/fax 208 53 64). S3/5/6/9 Hackescher Markt.* **Open** 10am-6pm Mon-Fri.

Whether you want to contact women artists in Berlin, are planning a trip to Brandenburg, need to know about computer classes for women, or are in desperate need of a babysitter, the Fraueninfothek can help. Phone or visit the office, which is near the S-Bahn station at Hackescher Markt. There are 15 women involved in this Senate-funded project. They hold a huge number of useful leaflets, booklets and addresses, while on the leaflet stall at the entrance you'll find flyers and lists of events. The Fraueninfothek even provides a mail service: write to them, detailing your interests and plans for your Berlin trip, and they can arrange the whole thing, from finding accommodation to organising meetings with women's groups. Write at least four weeks in advance to give them enough time. All services are free, except for hotel reservation which costs DM10. Fraueninfothek produces a women's guide to Berlin, *Women's City*, available in English at DM3.

### Frauenkrisentelefon (women's helpline)
*(615 4243).* **Open** 10am-noon Mon, Tue; 7-9pm Wed, Fri; 5-7pm Sat, Sun.

The women's helpline receives over 1,000 calls a year and offers help, advice or information.

### Notruf (rape crisis phone line)
*(251 2828).* **Open** 6-9pm Tue, Thur; noon-2pm Sun; answering machine at other times.

Advice and help on rape and sexual harassment, as well as help dealing with the police and doctors.

**Das Verborgene Museum** *rescues female artists from historical oblivion. See page 231.*

## Health

### Berliner Aids-Hilfe
*Meineckestraße 12, Wilmersdorf, 10719 (883 3017/24-hour helpline 19 411). U3, U9 Kurfürstendamm.* **Open** 24 hours daily.
The Berlin equivalent of the Terrence Higgins Trust has a special service for women. Female counsellors can help and inform on AIDS-related problems. There's also a self-help group for HIV-positive women.

### Feministisches Frauengesundheitzentrum (FFGZ)
*Bamberger Straße 31, Schöneberg, 10777 (213 9597). U4, U7 Bayerischer Platz or Spichernstraße.* **Open** 11am-2pm Tue; 11am-2pm, 5-7pm, Thur.
Founded in 1974, this project offers courses and lectures on menstruation, natural contraception, pregnancy, cancer, abortion, AIDS, migraines and sexuality. Self-help and prevention are stressed. Information on gynaecologists, health institutions and organisations. The FFGZ's archive holds an international collection of books, magazines and articles.

## Accommodation

### artemisia
*Brandenburgische Straße 18, Wilmersdorf, 10713 (873 63 73/873 89 05/fax 861 8653). U7 Konstanzer Straße.* **Rates** *single* DM159; *double* DM220. **Credit** AmEx, DC, EC, V
An old, shabby elevator brings you to the fourth floor of this central, art nouveau building near the Ku'damm, where Germany's first and Berlin's only women-only hotel opened its doors in 1989. The artemisia is comfortable and bright. Each room is dedicated to a famous woman from Berlin's history. The breakfast buffet on the first floor is a treat. There are two conference rooms, and the hotel welcomes groups and business women. Further extras: a roof terrace, a small bar and a Queen's Suite.

### Fraueninfothek
The women's information centre (*see above*) helps find women-friendly and safe accommodation in Berlin and Brandenburg, whether it's a hotel room, a private room, or bed and breakfast – at reasonable prices. Write at least four weeks in advance so they can find a suitable place; but if you're stranded at the airport they won't let you sleep under a bridge.

## Art & Museums

### allgirls gallery
*Kleine Hamburger Straße 16, Prenzlauer Berg, 10115 (no phone). S1, S2 Oranienburger Straße.* **Open** 3-6pm daily.
Despite the name, the allgirls gallery is not strictly a women's gallery. The place is run by three women, but men are both admitted and their work exhibited.

**artemisia** – *Berlin's only women-only hotel.*

## Kunstpraxis/ Künstlerinnenprojekt

*Dirckenstraße 47, Mitte, 10178 (282 2235). S3, S5, S7, S9 Hackescher Markt.* **Open** *office* 10am-5pm Tue.
If you want to contact women artists working in and around Berlin, or if you plan to join the Berlin art scene yourself, then this organisation of east and west Berlin women can help. Any information, or even an individual consultation, is free. The Kunstpraxis also organises discussions on topics concerning women and the art market. Call for details.

## Das Verborgene Museum (The Hidden Museum)

*Schlüterstraße 70, Charlottenburg, 10625 (313 3656). S3, S5, S7, S9 Savignyplatz.* **Open** 3-7pm Thur, Fri; noon-4pm Sun.
The amount of art by women that is rotting unseen in Berlin's museum cellars is alarming. With temporary exhibitions and lectures, the Hidden Museum tries to rescue female artists from historical oblivion.

## Baths & Massage

### Hamam Turkish Bath for Women

*Schoko-Fabrik, Naunynstraße 72, Kreuzberg, 10997 (615 1464). U1 Kottbusser Tor.* **Open** 5-10pm Mon; 1-10pm Tue-Sun. Closed July/Aug. **Admission** call for details.
Daylight filters through the glass cupola of the main hall, where women sit in small annexes, bathing in the warm water of the baths – a perfect place for relaxation and a soothing sense of well-being. Enjoy Turkish tea and a reviving massage afterwards. The bustle of Berlin seems miles away. *See also below* **Women's Centres**.

## Bookshops

### Lilith

*Knesebeckstraße 86-87, Charlottenburg, 10623 (312 3102). U2 Ernst-Reuter-Platz.* **Open** 10am-6.30pm Mon-Fri; 10am-2pm Sat.
Located in Knesebeckstraße, *the* street of bookstores in Berlin, Lilith stocks around 5,000 titles by women. There's a selection of British and American lesbian fiction and the current issue of *Off Our Backs* (an American magazine for lesbians, priced DM16). Noticeboards and piles of leaflets are near the entrance.

### Marga Schoeller Bücherstube

*Knesebeckstraße 33, Charlottenburg, 10623 (881 1112/22). S3, S5, S5, S9 Savignyplatz.* **Open** 9am-6.30pm Mon-Wed, Fri; 9am-8.30pm Thur; 9am-2pm Sat. **Credit** AmEx, EC, V.
A co-operatively owned general bookstore which has a wide selection of English-language titles by women: feminist and lesbian fiction, biography, history and culture. There are also women's books in German and many other books in English.

## Business

### Weiberwirtschaft

*Anklamerstraße 38, Mitte, 10115 (282 11 80).*
In October 1992 the Weiberwirtschaft leased a building complex at Anklamer Straße 38 from the Treuhand, where 5,000 square metres (5,980 square yards) can be used as a business space for women. Companies owned and run by women can meet and liaise here, both profit- and non-profit-making organisations.

**Begine** *boasts a café and cultural centre.*

## Cafés, Bars & Restaurants

All venues listed below are women-only. *See also below* **Women's Centres** for cafés. The lesbian/ gay Café Anal, *Muskauer Straße 15, Kreuzberg (618 7064),* is women-only on Mondays from 3pm; *see chapter* **Gay Berlin**.

### Begine

**Café und Kultur Zentrum für Frauen (Café and Cultural Centre for Women)**
*Potsdamer Straße 139, Schöneberg, 10783 (215 4325). U2 Bülowstraße.* **Open** 6pm-1am daily.
This café and cultural centre is named after the *Beginen*, women who shared a common social and economic network in the Middle Ages. There's always something going on, from an African women's band, an actress reading poetry, to a scientific lecture. A popular meeting place for all kinds of women. Hot snacks, soups and salads are available.

### Dinelo

*Vorbergstraße 10, Schöneberg, 10823 (782 2185). U7 Eisenacherstraße.* **Open** 6pm-midnight Tue-Sun.
A red-flagged floor, wooden and cane furniture and palm-trees add to the rustic, relaxing atmosphere where you can have small dishes and drinks. There's a billiard table.

### Extra Dry Café und Treff für Frauen

*Pariser Straße 1, Wilmersdorf, 10719 (885 22 06).* **Open** noon-11pm Tue-Thur; noon-midnight Fri; 11am-midnight Sat; 11am-11pm Sun.
A modern bar-café that is run by women from a rehabilitation and therapy group for ex-addicts. Taste one of the superb non-alcoholic cocktails. There's a small range of hot snacks and breakfasts available. The Extra Dry also organises dancing and Tai-Chi classes, small concerts, and provides a separate room for groups, lectures and parties.

### Schoko-Café

*Mariannenstraße 6, Kreuzberg, 10997 (615 15 61). U1 Kottbusser Tor.* **Open** 1pm-midnight Tue-Sun.
Part of the women's centre Schoko-Fabrik (*see below* **Women's Centres**), this beautiful, factory-style café is mostly frequented by the women who participate in the many courses and activities, or who finish their afternoon in the Turkish bath. Cakes, soups and hot snacks are served. Occasional dancing-parties are held: call for details.

# Travel

## Frauen Unterwegs

*Frauenreisen, Potsdamer Straße 139, Schöneberg, 10783 (215 1022/fax 216 98 52). U2 Bülowstraße.* **Open** noon-6pm Mon; 5-8pm Wed.

If you want to take a trip out of Berlin, you can book a women-only cultural tour with this association (Frauen Unterwegs means 'women on the way'). Staff will organise tours for small groups, which may involve meeting local people and retracing the steps of important women, as well as city trips, sporting and walking vacations, language holidays, workshops.

# Women's Centres

## EWA Frauenzentrum

*Prenzlauer Allee 6, Prenzlauer Berg, 10405 (426 3233/427 7157).* **Open** *office* 10am-6pm Mon-Fri; *café, centre and gallery* 4-11pm Mon-Fri; 9pm-3am Sat; *library* 4-7pm Tue; 3-6pm Thur.

EWA stands for Erster Weiblicher Aufbruch (first feminine awakening); essentially, it's a meeting place for women from the former GDR. Women at the centre offer legal advice and counselling, but you can also just pop in for breakfast. Other courses cover computers, sport, foreign languages and art. The collection of the library and archive Hex Libris charts the development of women's groups in the GDR.

## Frieda Frauenzentrum und Frauencafe (Frieda Woman's Centre and Café)

**Frieda Frauenzentrum**
*Grünberger Straße 24, Friedrichshain, 10243 (707 4053). U5 Rathaus Friedrichshain.* **Open** 8.30am-11pm Mon, Wed-Fri; 4-6pm Tue.

**Frieda Frauencafe**
*Proskauer Straße 7, Friedrichshain, 10247 (no phone). U5 Rathaus Friedrichshain.* **Open** 10am-11pm Tue-Fri; 7-11pm Sat.

The founding women's group (belonging to the New Forum) first met in 1989. Three years later, in August 1992, this new communication centre and café opened. The monthly programme includes exhibitions and poetry readings, as well as political debates. There's a disco twice a month and weekly meetings of self-help and conversational groups, plus a variety of courses and advisory services.

## Schoko-Fabrik (Chocolate Factory)

*Naunynstraße 72, Kreuzberg, 10997 (615 2999). U1 Görlitzer Bahnhof.* **Open** *office* 10am-4pm Mon-Wed; 10am-1pm Fri.

In 1981 this old chocolate factory in Kreuzberg was squatted and turned into the Kreuzberg neighbourhood centre for Turkish and German women. On the first floor you can listen to the buzz of a joinery; women practise self-defence on the second floor. There's a fifth floor where cultural events take place and a garden on the roof. And we haven't even mentioned the Turkish Bath Hamam (*see above* **Baths & Massage**), the café, kindergarten, private flats and the office.

# Women's Studies

*See also* **EWA** under **Women's Centres** for library.

## FFBIZ

*Frauenforschungs, -bildungs, und Informationszentrum Danckelmannstraße 47 and 15, Charlottenburg, 14059 (322 1035). U1 Sophie-Charlotte-Platz.* **Open** *archive, library and telephone advice* 2-6pm Tue; 10am-1pm Thur; 3-10pm Fri; *additional phone service* 10am-noon Mon-Fri.

A women's research, education and information centre. The huge archive files contain leaflets, press cuttings, badges, posters, exam papers and documents. The centre offers an extensive programme of historical walks, lectures, poetry readings, exhibitions and courses.

## Zentraleinrichtung zur Förderung von Frauenstudien und Frauenforschung

*Freie Universität, Königin-Luise-Straße 34, Dahlem, 14195 (838 6254/5/6/838 3044). U2 Dahlem-Dorf.* **Open** *information and library* 3-5pm Tue; 1-4pm Wed; 10am-noon Fri.

Literally, the department of promotion of women's studies and women's research at the Free University. Twice a year, the department publishes a brochure listing current projects and interdisciplinary seminars relating to women's studies.

## Zentrum Interdisziplinäre Frauenforschung (ZIF)

*Humboldt Universität zu Berlin, Mittelstraße 7-8, Mitte, 10117 (2093 2135). S3, S5, S6, S9/U6 Friedrichstrasse.* **Open** *information and documentation* 9am-noon Mon-Fri.

This department of east Berlin's Humboldt University organises seminars and lectures, provides a computer pool and courses for women, and stores information for research.

*The converted* **Schoko-Fabrik** *in Kreuzberg.*

# Trips Out of Town

# Getting Started

*The city's surroundings retain a lot of the history and natural beauty Berlin itself has lost. Some tips to get you off the Ku'damm.*

Berlin is a city in the middle of nowhere. For miles around, fields, lakes and dense woods are scarcely interrupted by small towns and villages. Chancellor Adenauer, travelling to Berlin from Bonn, pulled down the blinds after Hannover because, as he put it, 'there begin the Steppes of central Asia'.

The hard details about what is to be seen, when and for how much, are available from central tourist offices, usually in or near main railway stations. Most of them keep up-to-date supplies of inexpensive or free tourist maps and leaflets and are indefatigable promoters of themselves and other towns and points of interest within reach. English is widely spoken in the west and printed information is often available in translation. This is changing slowly in the former GDR.

## Information

Before leaving your home country, it is advisable to speak to the nearest German Tourist Office. In Germany itself, the places to look out for are the Verkehrsamt or Informationszentrum, usually marked on maps and signposts with an 'i'. These places are concerned specifically with the town or region in which they are situated. If you want to find out about places outside their jurisdiction, they will direct you to the nearest travel agency which will be able to help. Berlin has several to choose from, and the Potsdam office is also a good place for information about the Brandenburg area.

### German National Tourist Office
*Nightingale House, 65 Curzon Street, London W1Y 7PE (071 495 3990).* **Open** 10am-5pm Mon-Fri.

### German National Tourist Office
*747 Third Avenue, New York, NY 10017 (212 308 3300). 44 S Flower Street, Suite 220, Los Angeles, CA 90017 (213 668 7332).*

### German National Tourist Office
*Place Bonaventure, Montréal, Québec H5A 1B8 (514 8778 9885).*

### Berlin Tourist Information (Verkehrsamt)
*Europa-Center, Budapester Straße, Tiergarten, 10787 (262 60 31). U2, U9, S3, S5, S6, S7, S9 Zoologischer Garten.* **Open** 8am-10.30pm Mon-Sat; 9am-9pm Sun.

### Touristenzentrale am Alten Markt
*Friedrich-Ebert-Straße 5, 14467 Potsdam (0331 29 11 00/0331 29 33 85).* **Open** *Apr-Oct* 9am-8pm Mon-Fri; 9am-6pm Sat, Sun, public holidays. *Nov-Mar* 10am-6pm Mon-Fri; 11am-3pm Sat, Sun, public holidays.

### Verkehrsamt im Bahnhof Zoo
*Main Hall, Zoologischer Station, Hardenbergplatz, Charlottenburg, 10623 (313 90 63). U2, U9, S3, S5, S6, S7, S9, Bahnhof Zoo.* **Open** 8am-11pm Mon-Sat.

### Verkehrsamt am Flughafen Tegel
*Main Hall, Tegel Airport (4101 31 45). U7 Jacob-Kaiser-Platz, then bus 109, X9 or both buses run direct from Bahnhof Zoo.* **Open** 8am-11pm daily.

## Using the Train

The S-Bahn system is integrated with the DB network (Deutsche Bahn), reaching about 40km (25 miles) beyond the city boundary. Any BVG (Berliner Verkehrsbetrieb Gesellschaft) ticket is valid for unlimited distances within the system – there are maps at most stations and in all train carriages (*see chapter* **Getting Around**). A single ticket

*Get around above ground on the* **S-Bahn**.

must be used within two hours of being franked, so a multiple (DM12, DM7.80 concs), 24-hour (DM13, DM6.50 concs), or monthly ticket (DM82, DM38 students) may be better. (These prices were current at the time of going to press – BVG tariffs are set to rise in 1995 by about 7 per cent.) Once the two-hour ticket has been stamped you can get on and off as many times as you like within two hours. Travelling without a valid ticket can land you with an instant DM60 fine.

The welding together (sometimes literally) of the eastern and western rail systems into the new Deutsche Bahn often creates changes in services. Information about timetable alterations is displayed on affected platforms. At popular times of the year – Christmas, Easter, Whitsun – longer-distance trains can be fully booked well in advance. You should also book a seat at weekends.

## Travelling by Coach

There are a number of regular, fast coach links between Berlin and some other destinations in Germany. The main company is:

### Berlin Linien Bus
*Mannheimerstraße 33-34, Wilmersdorf, 10713 (8600 9692). U1, U7, Fehrbelliner Platz.* **Open** 9am-6pm Mon-Fri.

## Travelling by Car

Inside Berlin, the long, straight AVUS (Allgemeine Verkehrsübungsstrecke – General Transport Testing Strip) was built by Mercedes-Benz to test its vehicles, and was then incorporated into the city's motorway system. The German highway code gives drivers precedence over pedestrians and German drivers are only too aware of this fact. If you own, borrow or hire a car, make sure you are well briefed before setting out. Speed limits are ruthlessly enforced: in built-up areas it's usually 30kmph (19mph); 50kmph (31mph) is customary on main arterial roads; the Schnellstrecke – dual carriageway – functions in all but name as a motorway, with a limit of 100- or 120kmph (62-75mph); and on the motorway there is, as yet, no speed limit, although Bonn still talks of imposing one, much to German drivers' horror.

The motorway system of the old GDR is being quickly brought up to western standards, although traffic jams are still more prevalent in the East. The BAB, Bundesautobahn (federal motorway), now presides over an increasingly efficient network which makes road travel around the country very fast. There are regular service and filling stations which are all listed in free maps issued by the **ADAC** (German automobile association) and available at any of their outlets. Most filling stations have shops, usually open 24 hours, providing everything from beer to microwaveable snacks;

*Get out of town by* **bike** *– plus U- or S-Bahn.*

some cafeterias are also open continuously, although the provision of hot meals may be restricted; larger stations usually have a children's playground. Information on car transport can be obtained from the German motoring association:

### ADAC Berlin-Brandenburg
*ADAC Haus, Bundesallee 29-30, 10717 (information and advice 8686-0; 24-hour breakdown and accident assistance 01802 22 22 22).*

## Shared Lifts

The well-established national network of lift-sharing was founded in the sixties and was originally used mainly by students. Each city or town has at least one office, advertised in the phone book or Yellow Pages (Gelbe Seiten) under **Mitfahrzentrale**. Passengers can call the office, or visit in person, to find out if there are any drivers seeking companions. Usually a small fee is charged by the agent (about DM15). Theoretically, each agent recommends a fixed number of pfennigs per kilometre, but in practice the deal travellers strike up with each other is more important.

Once, lifts could be arranged a matter of hours in advance; now you should allow two or three days' warning. Very long jaunts (say, Berlin to London) are not as common as short ones; you should prepare at least a week in advance and be flexible. *See also chapter* **Survival**.

### City-Netz
*3rd floor of Ku'damm Eck, Kurfürstendamm 227, Charlottenburg, 10719 (19 444). U9, U15 Kurfürstendamm.* **Open** 8am-9pm daily.
City-Netz has branches in every major German city. Their DM2 insurance covers a taxi to the nearest station and a train to your destination in case of breakdown.

*Berlin is flanked by lakes, rivers and canals – these boats are pictured at Treptower Park.*

### Mitfahrzentrale am Alex
*Alexanderplatz U-Bahn, in the hall between lines 8 and 2, Mitte, 10178 (24 15 82 0). S3, S5, S6, S9/U2, U8 Alexanderplatz.* **Open** 8am-8pm Mon-Fri; 8am-6pm Sat; 10am-6pm Sun, public holidays.

## Hitching

Hitch-hiking is still widely used in Germany, mostly by the young. Inner-city hitching, especially at night, has almost disappeared and been replaced by a much improved night bus system and two 24-hour tube lines at the weekend. Asking around at lorry parks and filling stations on the main routes out of the city can be a good way to cut your travelling expenses.

If you are heading to Hamburg take bus 224 direction Henningsdorf and get off at Heiligensee. The bus stop is 150 metres from the car and lorry park known as the Trämperparkplatz.

If you are heading in the direction of Hannover, Leipzig or Nürnberg take the S1, S3 or S7 to Wannsee; exit towards Potsdamerchaussee, then walk 300m to the slip road leading to the lorry park and petrol station (known as Raststätte Dreilinden). Standing on the hard shoulder is illegal and you may be moved on – not arrested – by the police. But this is still a busy spot, so arrive early and – as ever when hitching – carry a clearly marked sign. *See chapter* **Survival**.

## Bicycles

Cycling is a popular way to get about. Especially in fine weather, it is common for Berliners to pack their bikes on to the train and head off into the countryside. On the U-Bahn, there is a limit of two cycles at the end of carriages which have a bicycle sign on them. More may be taken on to S-Bahn carriages, but in each case a fare of DM2.10 must be paid per bike. With a yearly, monthly, Berlin or Kombi-Tageskarte ticket you can take your bicycle for free. For bicycle hire shops, *see chapter* **Getting Around**.

## Travelling by Air

Internal European air fares are notoriously expensive. However, if time is of the essence, then the shuttle flights between Berlin, Hamburg and Leipzig are worth trying. Last-minute cheap offers by the main companies based in Tegel are also possible. Bucket shops advertise in the classifieds of *Tip* and *Zitty*, and other companies can be contacted via their offices in town or at the airports:
*Tegel (41 01 23 06).*
*Tempelhof (69510).*
*Schönefeld (60910).*

## Travelling by Water

Berlin is flanked to the east and west by an interconnecting series of lakes, rivers and canals. These waterways are served by impressive fleets of pleasure barges, ferries and private and hired boats.

All ferries which lie within the BVG tariff zone are treated the same as any other public transport. Private companies have ports of call dotted along their routes. The main harbour is at Tegel, from where very reasonably priced voyages along the Havel, to Potsdam, into the Spreewald, and even up the Elbe to Dresden, depart on a regular basis. For ferry companies, *see chapter* **Getting Around: Boat Trips**.

# Trips in Berlin

**Berlin may conjure up the quintessential urban landscape, but you don't have to go far from the Ku'damm before you hit the countryside.**

Gone are the days when an ordinary Berliner might spend an entire life within the immediate neighbourhood (the Kiez), with perhaps an annual outing to Kurfürstendamm. Nowadays, everybody seems to seize almost any opportunity to escape into the forests, towns and lakes clustered around Berlin's periphery.

## Tourist Information

All the following are within Berlin's city boundaries. To obtain up-to-the-minute information about them, speak to any of the Verkehrsämte listed in the *chapter* **Getting Started**.

## Grunewald

The largest of Berlin's forests is also its most visited; on a fine Sunday afternoon, its lanes and paths are as packed as the Kurfürstendamm, but with walkers, runners, cyclists, horse-riders and dog-walkers.

A favourite starting – or finishing – point is S-Bhf Grunewald. There are several restaurants next to the station, and on the other side of the motorway at Schmetterlingsplatz, open during the season (from April to October). Follow Schildhornweg (past the Sandgraben, from which high-quality Berlin sand was dug for building and to supply its glass industry) to Teufelssee, a tiny lake packed with bathers (mostly naked hippies) in summer.

The nearby Teufelsberg is a product of wartime devastation: a railway was laid from Wittenbergplatz, along Kurfürstendamm, to carry rubble from the city centre for depositing in a great pile at the terminus here. There are great views from the summit, on which sits a now-disused American electronic listening post.

To the south, there are kiosks for sausages, drinks and ice-creams at the Großer Stern or Hüttenweg (also an exit from the motorway) in the summertime. It's a busy pitstop for the hundreds of cyclists who pelt up and down the paths, Kronprinzessinweg and Königsweg, both parallel to the road.

At Grunewaldsee, the **Jagdschloß** (hunting lodge) is a good example of hundreds of such buildings which once maintained the country life of the Prussian Junkers (landed gentry). Built by Kurfürst Joachim II von Brandenburg in 1542, he described it as 'zum grünen Wald' ('in the green wood') thus coining the name of the forest in which it stands. Considerably altered by Graf Rochus zu Lynar and Frederick the Great (1770), much of the Renaissance façade was pulled down and thrown into a nearby pit.

Later excavations unearthed this pit and recently the building has been restored to its original sixteenth-century appearance. There is bathing by the lake in the summer, including a nudist section; for some reason, it is also a favourite promenade for chic dogs and their owners, who like to refresh themselves in the deer-horn-bedecked **Forsthaus Paulsborn.**

A kilometre east through the woods, **Chalet Suisse** is an over-the-top Swiss-themed restaurant popular with families because of its playground and petting zoo. A ten-minute walk takes you to the **Allied Museum** (*see chapter* **Museums**). Also nearby, the **Brücke Museum** (*see chapters* **Sightseeing, Museums**) houses surviving works by the influential Brücke group (including Kirchner, Heckel and Schmidt-Rottluff), known for their impressionistic views of Berlin.

Krumme Lanke and Schlachtensee are attractive urban lakes (along the south-eastern edge of Grunewald – take the U1 to Krumme Lanke or the S1 to Schlachtensee), perfect for a picnic, swimming and rowing. And **Siedlung Onkel Toms Hütte** (1926-32) is a good example of a modern housing development, with detatched, semi- and terraced homes by Bruno Taut, Hugo Häring and Otto Rudolf Solvisberg.

Half way up the Havelchaussee, the **Grunewaldturm** (Grunewald Tower), built in 1897 in memory of Wilhelm I (aka 'Kaiser-Wilhelm-Turm'), has an observation platform 105 metres (115 yards) above the lake with views on a clear day as far as Spandau and Potsdam. There is a restaurant at the base, the **Ausflugsrestaurant am Grunewaldturm,** and another restaurant on the other side of the road, **Waldhaus Wildspezialitäten,** both with garden terraces. A short walk along Havelufer brings you to the ferry to Lindwerder Island, which also boasts a restaurant in the form of the **Lindwerder Insel Restaurant**.

### Getting there

**By train** is the quickest method: the S-Bahn runs direct from Bahnhof Zoo, Friedrichstraße (S3/S5 Grunewald) or anywhere intersected by S-Bahn lines 3 and 5.
**By bus** take Bus 219 to Schmetterlingplatz; 218 to anywhere along Havelchaussee; or 700 parallel to the AVUS. There are many bus and U-Bahn connections to the parts of the forest bordering the built-up areas of Wilmersdorf and Zehlendorf.
**By car** take Kantstraße to Messedamm and then Eichkampstraße to the car park at Schmetterlingplatz.

### Allied Museum

*Outpost, Clayallee 135, 14195 Berlin (813 4161) U1 Oskar-Helene-Heim.* **Open** 10am-6pm Tue, Thur-Sun; 10am-8pm Wed. **Admission** free.

### Ausflugsrestaurant am Grunewaldturm

*Havelchaussee 62, Grunewald, 14193 (304 12 03). S3, S5 Grunewald.* **Open** *Oct-Mar* 9.30am-7pm daily; *Apr-Sep* 9.30am-midnight daily. (Closing times vary according to weather and season.) **Average** DM35. **Credit** EC, V.
Honest German cuisine eaten by tourists.

### Chalet Suisse

*Im Jagen, Zehlendorf, 14195 (832 63 62). U1 Dahlem Dorf.* **Open** 10.30am-11.30pm daily. **Average** DM45. **Credit** AmEx, DC, EC, JBC, MC, V.
Extensive wine list, and some excellent, if slightly odd, Swiss dishes: mountain goat, anyone?

### Forsthaus Paulsborn

*am Grunewaldsee, Zehlendorf, 14193 (8 13 80 10). S3, S5 Grunewald.* **Open** *Apr-Sept* 11am-11pm Tue-Sat; 9.30am-11pm Sun; *Oct-Mar* 11am-6pm Tue-Sat; 9.30am-6pm Sun. **Average** DM30. **Credit** AmEx, DC, EC, MC, V.
Dine amid a turn-of-the century hunting-lodge atmosphere on typical German dishes at Forsthaus Paulsborn, which also contains a few hotel rooms.

### Jagdschloß Grunewald

*On the shore of the Grunewaldsee, Zehlendorf, 14193 (813 35 97). S3, S5 Grunewald.* **Open** 10am-5pm Tue-Sun. **Admission** DM2.50; DM1 students, children.

### Lindwerder Insel Restaurant

*Lindwerder Island, Havelsee, 14193 (803 65 84). Bus 218.* **Open** noon-9pm Tue-Sun. **Average** DM30. **No credit cards.**
If you happen to be on Lindwerder Island then you might like to try this restaurant's fish dishes.

### Siedlung Onkel Toms Hütte

*Argentinische Allee. U1 Onkel-Toms-Hütte.*

### Waldhaus Wildspezialitäten

*Havelchaussee 66, 14193 (304 05 95). S3, S5 Grunewald.* **Open** 10am-8pm Tue-Sat; 9am-8pm Sun, public holidays. **Average** DM25. **No credit cards.**
Catering to a very mixed public of tourists and Berliners. The Waldhaus specialises in game dishes.

### Wannsee, Pfaueninsel & Glienicke

Boats, beaches and windsurfing in summer, islands, castles and forests through the year – these are the highlights of the 'Berlin Riviera'.

### Getting there

**By train** take the S-Bahn (S1/S3/S5) to Nikolassee or Wannsee; journey time from Bahnhof Zoo about 30 minutes. From both S-Bahn stations there are bus connections: 513 to Strandbad Wannsee (or ten minutes' walk); 116 to Glienicke; 216 and 316 to Pfaueninsel.
**By car** take the AVUS to Wannsee and then Königsallee to Glienicke; and either Nikolskoer Weg or Pfaueninselchaussee to Pfaueninsel.

## Wannsee

Strandbad Wannsee is the largest inland beach in Europe. Between May and September it is the most popular resort in Berlin, with service buildings housing showers, toilets, cafés, shops and kiosks. There are boats and pedaloes and hooded, two-person wicker sunchairs for hire (enquire about all these at the entrance), a children's playground and separate sections for nudists and the severely disabled. The waters of the Havel are extensive and in summer are warm enough to make swimming comfortable; there is a strong current, so do not stray beyond the floating markers. The rest of the open water is in constant use by ferries, speed- and sailing boats and waterskiers.

Just beyond the Strandbad lie the Wannseeterrassen, a couple of rustic lanes on the slopes of the hill, at the bottom of which private boats and yachts are moored. There is a good view from the restaurant **Wannseeterrasse**, but less remarkable food. A small bridge takes you across to Schwanenwerder, once the exclusive private island retreat of Goebbels and now home to the international think-tank, the Aspen Institute.

The town of Wannsee to the south is clustered around the bay of the Großer Wannsee and dominated by a long promenade, Am Großen Wannsee, which is scattered with hotels and fish restaurants. Also here is the **Gedenkstätte Haus der Wannsee-Konferenz** (Memorial House of the Wannsee Conference). Here, in January 1942, a meeting of Nazis chaired by Reinhard Heydrich laid out plans for the extermination of the Jewish race – the 'Final Solution'. The house, an elegant Grunderzeit mansion, is now a museum documenting the Holocaust (*see chapter* **Museums**).

A short distance from S-Bhf Wannsee along Bismarckstraße is a little garden in which the German dramatist Heinrich von Kleist shot himself in 1811; the beautiful view of the Kleiner Wannsee was the last thing he wanted to see. On the other side of the railway tracks is Düppler Forst, a little-explored forest including a nature reserve at Großes Fenn at the south-western end. Travelling on the S-Bahn to Mexikoplatz and then the 629 Bus to Krummes Fenn brings you to **Museumsdorf Düppel**, a working reconstruction of a medieval Brandenburg village. *See chapter* **Children.**

*Take the S-Bahn (S1/3/5) to Nikolasse or Wannsee, then hop on a 116 bus to* **Glienicke.**

### Gedenkstätte Haus der Wannsee-Konferenz

*Am Grossen Wannsee 56-58, Zehlendorf, 14109 (80 500125). S1, S3, S7 S-Bahnhof Wannsee, then bus 114.* **Open** 10am-6pm Tue-Fri; 2-6pm Sat, Sun. **Admission** free.

### Museumsdorf Düppel

*Clauertstraße 11, Zehlendorf, 14163 (802 66 71). Bus 115, 211.* **Open** *May-Sept* 3-7pm Thur; 10am-5pm Sun and public holidays. **Admission** DM3; concs DM1.50.

### Wannseeterrasse

*Wannseeterrasse 35, Zehlendorf, 14129 (803 40 24). S3, S5 Nikolassee.* **Open** *May-Sept* 9am-midnight Wed-Mon; *Oct-Apr* 10am-6pm Wed-Mon. **Average** DM30. **Credit** AmEx, DC, EC, JBC, V.

## Pfaueninsel

On the far side of the Berliner Forest from Wannsee, the shortest private ferry ride in the city takes you to the car-free, music-free, picnic-free and non-smoking island of Pfaueninsel (Peacock Island).

The island was inhabited in prehistoric times, but wasn't mentioned in archives until 1683. Two years later the Grand Elector presented it to Johann Kunckel von Löwenstein, a chemist who experimented with alchemy and produced instead 'ruby glass', examples of which are on view in the castle. But it was only at the start of the Romantic Era that the island's windswept charms began to

attract more serious interest. In 1793, Friedrich Wilhelm II purchased it and built a Schloß for his mistress, Wilhelmine Encke. But he died in 1797 before they had a chance to move in. Its first residents were the happily married couple, Friedrich Wilhelm II and Queen Luise.

The island was later added to and adorned. A huge royal menagerie was developed, with enclosed and free-roaming animals (most of which were moved to the new Tiergarten Zoo in 1842). Only peacocks, pheasants, parrots, goats and sheep remain. Surviving buildings include the Jakobsbrunnen (Jacob's Fountain), a copy of a Roman temple; the Kavalierhaus (Cavalier's House), built in 1803 from an original design by Schinkel; and the Swiss cottage, also based on a Schinkel plan. All are linked to each other by winding, informal paths laid out in the English manner by Peter Joseph Lenné. A walk around the island, with its extreme quiet, its monumental trees and rough meadows, and its breathtaking views of the waters of the Havel and the 'mainland' beyond, provides one of the most complete sensations of escape from urban living to be had within the borders of Berlin.

Back on the mainland, just a short walk south along the bank of the Havel is the **Blockhaus Nikolskoe**, a re-creation of a huge wooden chalet, built in 1819 by Friedrich Wilhelm II for his daughter Charlotte, and named after her husband, the future Tsar Nicholas of Russia. There is a magnificent view of the Havel from the terrace, where you can also enjoy an excellent choice of mid-price Berlin cuisine, or just coffee and cakes in the afternoon. The nearby Kirche St Peter und St Paul (Church of St Peter and St Paul) dates from 1834-37 and has an attractive interior.

### Pfaueninsel (Peacock Island)

*in der Havel, Zehlendorf, 14109 (805 30 42). Bus 216 or 316 to ferry at Nikolskoer Weg.* **Ferries** run hourly from 8am-6pm daily.

### Schloß Pfaueninsel

**Open** *Apr-Sept* 10am-5pm daily; *Oct* 10am-4pm daily. Guided tours every hour.

### Blockhaus Nikolskoe

*Nikolskoer Weg, Wannsee, 14109 (805 29 14). S1, S3, S5 Wannsee, then bus 216.* **Open** 10am-10pm Mon-Wed, Fri; 9am-10pm Sat, Sun (10am-8pm *Nov-Apr*); last orders for the kitchen 7pm.

## Glienicke

The centre of this park (now a conference centre) and its outbuildings, which are being restored, is a hunting lodge designed by Schinkel for Prinz Carl von Preußen, who quickly became notorious for his ban on all women visitors. On at least one occasion, Prinz Carl's wife was turned away at the gate by armed guards. The Prinz adorned the walls of the gardens with ancient relics collected on his holidays around the Mediterranean, and decided to simulate a walk from the Alps to Rome in the densely wooded park, laid out by Pückler between 1824-50. The summerhouses, fountains and follies are all based on original Italian models, and the woods and fields surrounding them make an ideal place for a Sunday picnic, since this park is little visited. Close by, the suspension bridge over the Havel (1909), was named Brücke der Einheit (Bridge of Unity) because it joined Potsdam with Berlin; the name continued to be used even when, after the building of the Wall, it was painted different shades of olive green on the east and west sides and used only by Allied soldiers and for top-level exchanges (Anatoly Scharansky was one of the last in 1986).

### Schloß & Park Glienicke (Glienicke Palace & Park)

*on the Königstraße, Zehlendorf, 14109 (805 30 41). Bus 116.* The Schloß is currently closed to the public, but you can view it from the park.

### Restaurant 'Schloß Glienicke'

*Königstraße 36, 14109 (805 4000). Bus 116.* **Open** noon-6pm Wed-Sun. **Average** DM35; menu at DM52. **No credit cards.** Created by the former proprietors of the famed Bamberger Reiter restaurant, this fancy new place with a large terrace serves gourmet lunches to fuel visitors for an exploration of the property.

## Spandau

Berlin's western neighbour and eternal rival; the home of Rudolf Hess, the city's last Nazi chieftain, until 1987; a little Baroque town which seems to contradict everything about the city of which it is now, reluctantly, a part: Spandauers still talk about 'going into Berlin' when they head off to the rest of the city.

The original charter of the town lies in the **Stadtgeschichtlichesmuseum** in the **Zitadelle** and dates from 1232, a fact which Spandauers have relied on ever since to assert their legitimacy before Cölln and Berlin to be the historical heart of the capital. The oldest building here (and the oldest secular building in Berlin) is the **Juliusturm**, probably dating back to an Ascanian (*see chapter* **History**) water fortress from about 1160; the present tower, with 154 steps and walls measuring up to 3.6 metres (4 yards) thick, was home until 1919 to the 120 million Goldmark reparations, stored in 1,200 boxes, which the French paid to Germany in 1874 after the Franco-Prussian War. In German financial circles, state reserves are still referred to as 'Juliusturm'.

The adjacent **Palas**, which now houses the museum, has stones in its cellar dating back to 1200; the base of the south front contains Jewish tombstones from 1244-1347, when Spandau was the only place guaranteeing safety for Jewish graves, but these can only be seen on the twice-daily guided tour.

The bulk of the Zitadelle, however, was designed in 1560-94, in the style of an Italian fort; its purpose was to dominate the confluence of the Spree and Havel rivers. Since then it has been used as everything from garrison to prison to laboratory. Today, most of the huge 300m (328yd) by 300m site (except for the museums and a few galleries and ateliers) is under restoration and archaeological excavation and not accessible to the public.

The old town centre of Spandau is mostly pedestrianised, with two- and three-storey eighteenth-century townhouses interspersed between the Burger Kings and department stores. One of the prettiest examples is the former Gasthof zum Stern in Carl-Schurz-Straße; older still are the houses in Kinkel- (until 1933, Juden-) and Ritterstraße; but perhaps the best preserved district is across Am Juliusturm in the area bounded by Hoher Steinweg, Kolk and Behnitz. Steinweg contains a fragment of the old town wall from the first half of the fourteenth century; Kolk has the Catholic garrison church (Alte Marienkirche dating from 1848); and in Behnitz, at number 5, stands the Heinemannsche Haus, perhaps the finest late-Baroque townhouse in Berlin. And at Reformationsplatz, the brick nave of the Nikolaikirche dates from 1410-1450, the west tower having been added in 1468, and with further additions by Schinkel. All these landmarks, of course, had to be thoroughly restored after the last war.

One of the best times to visit the town is in the weeks before Christmas, when the market square houses a life-size Nativity scene with real sheep. The Konditorei (bakery/café) on Reformationsplatz is excellent.

The most notorious of Spandau's recent residents was Rudolf Hess, Hitler's deputy, imprisoned in the Allied Gaol after the Nuremberg Trials, where he remained (alone after 1966) until his suicide on August 17, 1987. Once he'd gone, the nineteenth-century brick building at Wilhelmstraße 21-24 was demolished to make way for a supermarket for the British Forces – who have now left the city. Hess's story has attracted controversy for decades, but, until the official documents are released by the British government, there's still little evidence to contradict the official version: that Hess parachuted into Scotland in 1940 in a private attempt to negotiate an end to the war with Britain.

### Getting there

**By train** take the U7 to Zitadelle, Altstadt Spandau or Rathaus Spandau; journey time from Adenauerplatz is about 25 minutes.
**By bus** bus 145 from Bahnhof Zoo, about 45 minutes.
**By car** from Jakob-Kaiser-Platz take Siemensdamm and then follow this main road through to Spandau.

### Stadtgeschichtlichesmuseum Spandau (Museum of Local History)

*Am Juliusturm, Spandau, 13599 (3391 264). U7 Zitadelle.* **Open** 9am-5pm Tue-Fri; 10am-5pm Sat, Sun. **Admission** DM1.50; DM1 children, students, pensioners. Combined with Juliusturm/Palas ticket.

### Zitadelle (Juliusturm, Palas)

*Am Juliusturm, Spandau, 13599 (339 11). U7 Zitadelle.* **Open** 9am-5pm Tue-Sun. **Admission** *to Juliusturm, Palas & Stadtgeschichtlichesmuseum* DM1.50; DM1 children, students, pensioners. **Tours** noon & 3pm daily, DM5; DM3 children, students, pensioners.

## Köpenick

The name Köpenick is derived from the Slavonic *copanic*, meaning place on a river. The Altstadt (old town) stands at the confluence of the Spree and Dahme, and having escaped bombing, decay and, worse, development by the GDR, still maintains much of its eighteenth-century character.

The imposing Rathaus (Town Hall) is a good example of Wilhelmenisch civic architecture (late Victorian). It was here, in 1906, two years after the building's completion, that Wilhelm Voigt, an unemployed cobbler who'd spent half his life in jail, disguised himself as an army captain and ordered a detachment of soldiers to accompany him into the Treasury, where they

confiscated the town coffers. He instantly entered popular folklore as the Hauptmann von Köpenick (Captain of Köpenick), and was pardoned by the Kaiser because he had shown how obedient Prussian soldiers were.

His theft is re-enacted every year during the Köpenicker Sommer festival (late June), when a parade of locals in period costume march to the Town Hall steps. There they are presented with a box containing a list entitled Mach-Mit-Wettbewerb (the 'Get Involved Competition'): the winners of the annual competition for the best charitable or social work in the community.

Köpenick, of all the areas of east Berlin, was and still is the most sought after, with handsome and increasingly affluent shops, cafés and restaurants clustered around the old centre, the Kiez. With its old buildings and extensive riverfront, it's a fine place for a Sunday afternoon Bummel, or wander – a great Berlin tradition.

On the Schloßinsel island stands Köpenick's **Schloß**, with its medieval drawbridge, Renaissance gateway and Baroque chapel. Occasional open-air concerts are held here in summer, and the late-medieval and classical-style **Kunstgewerbemuseum (Museum of Applied Art)** houses a collection of porcelain, glass, gold and splendid Berlin Iron. It was also here in the Weapons Room in 1730 that Friedrich Wilhelm I ordered the trial for desertion of his son (the future Frederick the Great) who had attempted to flee to England with his friend (also, probably, his lover) Lieutnant von Katte. The couple were betrayed by a third man involved in the escape attempt. The courtmartial sentenced them both to two years' imprisonment, but the King then altered the verdict, forcing his son to watch von Katte's decapitation from his cell.

A few minutes' walk from the castle is the Kiez. It stands on the site of a fishing community founded by Slavonic Wendish settlers a thousand years ago, and fishing weirs are still set in the river today. The poky little streets, lined with narrow, cramped houses, are currently being restored and taken over by the new east Berlin Schickeria, or trendies. There's now a good choice of art galleries and antique dealers.

### Getting there

**By train** take the S3 to Köpenick and then walk down Bahnhofstraße, turning left at Lindenstraße, or take Tram 62, direction Wendenschloß, and get off at Schloßplatz; journey time from Bahnhof Zoo is about 45 minutes.
**By car** drive east along Karl-Marx-Allee to Friedrichsfelde, turn right into Am Tierpark, and then follow Waldow Allee as far as Köpenicker Allee and turn left into Lindenstraße. A vast reconstruction project, however, makes public transport your best bet.

### Schloß and Kunstgewerbemuseum

*Schloßinsel, Köpenick 13507 (657 26 51). Tram 60, 61, 62 Schloßplatz.* **Open** 9am-5pm Tue-Sun. **Admission** DM4; DM2 children; free Sun and holidays.

# checkpoint

## BERLIN IN ENGLISH

# Checking into Berlin?

....................................................

*Check out Checkpoint!*

....................................................

There's more to Berlin than meets the eye. If you don't read German, let CHECKPOINT be your crash course on what's happening in the new German capital.

Each issue includes programme listings, news, trends, columns and features, all in English, and all for only three marks!

Our City Guide section contains everything you need find your way around town 24 hours a day, including a useful street map to show where you're going, and a public transport map to help you get there.

Check out CHECKPOINT today! Ask for us at large downtown newsagents that stock international magazines and newspapers, or send us five marks for the next three issues.

A publishing partner of

# Day Trips

*Berlin's immediate surroundings provide opportunities for fascinating excursions that help put the city itself into context – and can have you breathing something other than the famous Berliner Luft.*

## Potsdam

### Getting there

**By train** direct link S-Bahn (trains S1/R3, R4 to Potsdam Stadt) runs three times an hour from the centre of Berlin; journey time about 45 minutes from Bahnhof Zoo.
**By bus** bus 116 from S-Bhf Wannsee across Glienicke Brücke; then Tram 93 into Potsdam centre.
**By car** take the AVUS as far as the Drewitz turn-off, then turn right into Großbeerenstraße and follow it until Babelsberg and then Potsdam.

## Tourist Information

### Touristenzentrale am Alten Markt

*Friedrich-Ebert-Straße 5, 14467 Potsdam (0331 29 11 00/0331 29 33 85).* **Open** *Apr-Oct* 9am-8pm Mon-Fri; 9am-6pm Sat, Sun, public holidays; *Nov-Mar* 10am-6pm Mon-Fri; 11am-3pm Sat, Sun, public holidays.
A 'Potsdam Billett' is available for DM7.50 that allows 24 hours' free travel on public transport, as well as reductions on museum entry fees, concessions on theatre and cabaret tickets, and much else. It is available at both tourist offices, as well as from the VIP (Potsdam Transport Company) ticket offices in the Platz der Einheit and Luisenplatz. The DM1 map available here is good value, showing the main attractions and how to move between them on public transport.

### Potsdam Information

*Brandenburger Straße 18, 14467 Potsdam (0331 29 30 38).* **Open** 10am-6pm Mon-Fri; 10am-2pm Sat.

Potsdam is capital of the state of Brandenburg and Berlin's closest and most beautiful neighbour. In 1993 it celebrated its one thousandth anniversary, by which time it had once again become a chic exurb of Berlin, with burgeoning shops, restaurants and cafés. The main permanent attraction is the grandiose collection of palaces and outbuildings in Park Sanssouci. This in itself would take a whole day to see. There is plenty to fill another whole day in the Baroque town centre, as well as nearby Babelsberg.

Large parts of Potsdam town centre were destroyed in a single bombing raid on April 14, 1945, which claimed 4,000 lives. The vagaries of postwar reconstruction produced a ghastly 'restoration' of Schinkel's **St Nikolaikirche**, whose dome can be seen for miles, as well as acres of featureless blocks which crowd out Platz der Einheit (Square of Unity) and the surrounding streets.

The unusual, mid-eighteenth-century Palladian-style Rathaus (Town Hall) is worth admiring, particularly for its round tower, which until 1875 was used as a prison. It is now an arts centre (**Kulturhaus**). The Hans-Otto-Theatre, resembling a nuclear plant or a Midwestern Toyota parts warehouse, was intended to be part of the millennium festivities and finished with diminished funds after the *Wende*. The park at the Alter Markt here covers the ruins of the first Stadtschloß, and a square of stones marks its oldest tower, dating from 1200.

Yorck- and Wilhelm-Raab-Straße retain their Baroque architecture: the Kabinetthaus, a small palace at Am Neuen Markt 1, was the birthplace of Friedrich Wilhelm II (the only Hohenzollern to have both been born and die in the royal residence of Potsdam). The Baroque heart of the town, originally intended as a quarter to house people servicing the court, is bounded by Schopenhauer-, Hebbel-, Charlottenstraße and Hegel Allee. The dwellings were built between 1732 and 1742, at the behest of Friedrich Wilhelm I; the best of them can be seen running west along the pedestrianised Brandenburgerstraße. Potsdam's Brandenburg Gate (by Gontard 1733), at the Sanssouci end of Brandenburger Straße, is a delightfully happy contrast to Berlin's.

The Holländisches Viertel (Dutch Quarter) is between Gutenberg-, Friedrich-Ebert-, Hebbel- and Kurfürstenstraße, and takes its name from the Dutch immigrant workers that Friedrich Wilhelm I, the inveterate builder, invited to the town. He ordered 134 gable-fronted redbrick houses to be built, most of which fell into neglect after the last war, but the survivors, particularly along Mittelstraße at the junction with Benckerstraße, are being scrubbed into shape now that the squatters have been evicted and private money has been poured into them.

The best museum in town is the **Filmmuseum**, with an excellent documentation of the history of German cinema from 1895 to 1980. Indeed, it's one of the finest of its kind anywhere. Contained in the elegant former Marstall (royal stables), which were given their current appearance by Knobelsdorff during the eighteenth century, it has rooms full of famous props, costumes, set-designs and projection screens showing clips. There's also a good café and a large, comfortable cinema with an art-house programme rivalling anything on offer in Berlin. Ask about talks and special events.

The extensive gardens of **Sanssouci** (French was the language of the Prussian court in the eighteenth century, and this means 'without care') were begun by the francophile Friedrich Wilhelm II in 1740. They were intended to be in stark contrast to the style favoured by his detested father – German history is littered with examples of one generation doing the precise opposite of its predecessor. The first palace to be built, and the one which gives the park its name, forms a semi-circle at the top of a terrace on whose slopes symmetrical zig-zag paths are interspersed with vines and orange trees. It houses a collection of paintings.

Voltaire was brought to live in a suite here between 1750 and 1753, supposedly to oversee the library. But he devoted most of his time to his own writing, an act of defiance which brought the relationship with his patron to an acrimonious end. The abundant attractions include Friedrich Wilhelm II's huge Neue Palais, built 1763-69 to celebrate the end of the Seven Years' War. So many statues were needed for the roof that they had to be mass-produced in a factory. The last occupant, Kaiser Wilhelm II, took its contents with him in 60 railway carriages when he fled into exile in Holland in 1918, where most of the items remained in boxes, unopened until they were returned to fill the restored palace in the 1980s. Also worth visting in Sanssouci are: the gigantic Orangerie, in Italian Renaissance style; the Spielfestung (toy fortress), built for Wilhelm II's sons, complete with toy cannon which can be fired; the Chinesisches Teehaus (Chinese Teahouse), with its collection of Chinese and Meissner porcelain; the Römischer Bäder, an imitation Roman villa by Schinkel and Persius; and Schloß Charlottenhof, with its extraordinary blue-glazed entrance hall and Kupferstichzimmer (copper-plate engraving room) adorned with reproduction Renaissance paintings; and the Drachenhaus (Dragonhouse), a pagoda-style coffee shop with great cakes. If you want to see them all, take a stout pair of walking shoes.

While the park is open all the year round, much of the statuary – as is customary in this part of the world – is protected from the harsh winter by being encased in wooden boxes. For this reason, it's best to visit between April and October, a fact which is well known by vast crowds of tourists. Arrive early on a weekday.

Outside Sanssouci Park is Alexandrowka (between Puschkinallee and Am Schragen), a fake Russian village built in 1826 by Friedrich Wilhelm III to house Prussian musicians and their families who came into Prussian hands as prisoners of war during the Napoleonic campaigns. The houses were arranged in the form of a St Andrew's cross and

designed to look like log cabins. They still carry the names of the original tenants in inscriptions on their fronts, some in cyrillic. The icon-filled Alexander Newski Kapelle, constructed three years later at the top of the densely wooded Kapellenberg hill, is named – strangely – after the celebrated Russian hero who defeated the medieval Teutonic Knights.

In the Neuer Garten (New Garden), at the end of Johannes-Dieckmann-Allee, the **Marmorpalais** (Marble Palace), overlooking the beautiful Heiliger See, was where Friedrich Wilhelm II died. Nearby, **Schloß Cecilienhof**, the last royal addition to Potsdam's palaces, was begun in 1913 and completed four years later: its English-country-house style was unaffected by the war with Britain.

It was here that the Potsdam Conference (July 17-August 2, 1945) took place, and where Stalin, Truman and Attlee signed the Potsdamer Abkommen, the treaty which divided postwar Germany. The conference room, including the specially fashioned round table (so none of 'The Big Three' would take precedence) were left untouched. The room was damaged in an arson attack in 1990, presumably by neo-Nazis. One wing was converted into a hotel in 1960, and remains an expensive place to stay or dine.

### Altes Rathaus: Kulturhaus Potsdam
*Am Alten Markt, 14467 Potsdam (0331 29 31 75).* **Open** 10am-6pm Tue-Sun.

### Besucherservice (Information Centre of Park Sanssouci)
*Zur Historisches Mühle, 14469 Potsdam (0331 969 4202).* **Open** 8.30am-4pm daily.
The visitors service arranges tours around the parks and palaces of Sanssouci. Phone or write in advance.

### Filmmuseum
*Breite Straße, 14467 Potsdam (0331 29 36 75).* **Open** 10am-5pm Tue-Fri; 10am-6pm Sat, Sun, public holidays. **Admission** DM6; DM4 children.

### Marmorpalais
*In the Neuer Garten on the shore of the Heiligen See.* **Closed** at present with no scheduled reopening date; contact tourist office for information.

### St Nikolaikirche
*Am Alten Markt, 14467 Potsdam (0331 2 16 82).* **Open** *Mar-Oct* 10am-5pm Mon-Sat; *Nov-Feb* 2-5pm Mon-Sat. **Admission** free (tours by prior arrangement).

### Sanssouci
*(0331 969 4202).* **Open** *for tours* (every 20 mins) 9am-5pm daily; *park* until dusk daily. **Admission** *palace and exhibition buildings* DM8; DM4 children, students; *park* free. **Note:** Each of the various outbuildings has its own closing days each month, and some are only open 'during the season' of mid-May to mid-Oct. If you have a particular interest, call the number above for full information as to opening.

### Schloß Cecilienhof
*Am Neuen Garten, Potsdam 14469 (0331 96 94 244).* **Open** 9am-5pm daily (closed every second and fourth Mon in month). **Admission** DM4; DM3 children, students, pensioners.

**Babelsberg Film Studios** – *take a bus down Großbeerenstraße and get off by S-Bhf Drewitz.*

## Babelsberg

### Getting there

By train from Potsdam take the S3, S5 or R4 from
Potsdam Stadt to Griebnitzsee; journey time ten minutes.
By bus from Platz der Einheit in Potsdam take the 693
bus; journey time ten minutes.

## Tourist Information

### Touristenzentrale am Alten Markt

*Friedrich-Ebert-Straße 5, 14467 Potsdam (0331 29 11
00/0331 29 33 85).* **Open** *Apr-Oct* 9am-8pm Mon-Fri;
9am-6pm Sat, Sun, public holidays; *Nov-Mar* 10am-6pm
Mon-Fri; 11am-3pm Sat, Sun, public holidays.

Across the Lange Brücke, Albert-Einstein-Straße
leads past the state parliament building (known as
the Kreml, or Kremlin, during the GDR) on to the
Telegrafenberg (Telegraph Hill). In 1832 one of the
mechanical telegraph stations linking Berlin to
Koblenz was built here. When electrification made
it obsolete, an astronomical observatory was erected, whose futuristic tower by Erich Mendelsohn,
the Einsteinturm, was added in 1920: Albert
Einstein attended experiments here to test his
Theory of Relativity.

From Lutherplatz, a bus down Großbeerenstraße runs along the south side of the **Babelsberg Film Studios**, whose entrance is just before
you reach S-Bhf Drewitz. The first studio was
opened here in 1912 by the Berlin production company Bioscop. But it was not until 1917, when the
German General Staff decided that the war effort
was suffering because of their inferior propagan-

da, that the Universum Film AG (UFA) was founded with the financial support of the Deutsche Bank.

By the twenties the studio had become the
largest in the world outside Hollywood, making as
many as 100 films a year, including the Expressionist *The Cabinet of Dr Caligari*, the futurist
*Metropolis* and the decadent *The Blue Angel* (the
young Marlene Dietrich was so convinced she
would not be eligible for the role of Lola that she
came to her audition without a song to sing). A
mixture of success, the Depression and the rise of
the Nazis saw most of the studios' talent leave for
America, or the concentration camps.

During World War II, films such as the anti-
Semitic *Jew Süß* and the colour, escapist fantasy
*The Adventures of Baron Münchhausen* were
made. Renamed Deutsche Film AG (DEFA) in the
GDR, film-making resumed and included *Der
Untertan* (The Subject), possibly the best study of
German totalitarianism ever made. It was banned
after its première in 1952 – a common fate.

The rediscovery, and sometimes reconstruction,
of 'lost' DEFA films continues at a time when the
studios have ceased feature film production, prior,
some suspect, to disappearing for ever.

Sadly, the sections of the studio open to the public have been transformed into a cheap and crud-
dy theme park where the product placement of
international soft drink sponsors overshadow the
exhibits on display. Avoid, unless you're turned
on by inflatable Coca-Cola bottles. A walk by
the pretty Griebnitzsee is a far more appealing
prospect – even in the rain.

### DEFA-Studio Babelsberg

*August-Bebel-Straße 26-53, 14482 Potsdam (0331 72 27
55 information; 965 27 50 reservations). S3
Griebnitzsee, then bus 693 direction Bahnhof Rehbrücke
or 20 minutes' walk.* **Open** *Mar-Oct* 10am-6pm daily;
*Nov-Feb* 10am-4pm. **Tickets** DM16; DM12 children,
students, unemployed; special group rates.

## Spreewald

This filigree network of tiny rivers, streams and
canals, dividing dense patches of deciduous forest
interspersed with market garden farmland, is one
of the most spectacular, and most touristy excursions out of Berlin. The area is extremely crowded
in season, and particularly at weekends, giving the
lie to its otherwise justified claim to be one of the
most perfect areas of wilderness in Europe.

### Getting there

Located 100km (62 miles) to the south-east of Berlin, the
Spree bisects the area in **Unterspreewald** and
**Oberspreewald**. For the former, Schepzig or Lübben
are the best starting points; for the latter go 15km further
on the train to Lübbenau. **Journey time by car** 90
minutes approximately.

## Tourist Information

### Spreewald Information

*Ehm-Welk-Straße 15, Lubbenau, 03222 (035 42 36 68).*
**Open** 10am-6pm Mon-Fri; 10am-2pm Sat.

The character of both sections is very similar.
The Oberspreewald is perhaps better, for its 500
sq km (193 sq miles) of territory contains more
than 300 natural and artificial channels, called
Fliesse. You can travel around these on hand-
propelled punts – rent your own or join a larger
group – and take out kayaks. Motorised boats
are forbidden. Here and there in the forest are
restaurants and hotels.

Theodor Fontane described the Spreewald as
resembling Venice more than 1,500 years ago. The
local population belongs to the Sorbisch Slavonic
minority, with their own language much in evidence in street names, newspapers and so on.

## KZ Sachsenhausen

Many Nazi concentration camps (Konzentrations-
lager) have been preserved and opened to the
public as memorials to what happened and how.
Sachsenhausen is the one nearest to Berlin.

### Getting there

**By train** take the S1 from Friedrichstraße to
Oranienburg, journey time about 45 minutes. After that
it's a 15-minute walk: east along Straße des Friedens, left
into Straße der Einheit, and finally along Straße der
Nationen to the camp entrance.

### KZ Sachsenhausen

*Straße der Nationen 22, Oranienburg, 16515 (033 01 80
37 15).* **Open** 8.30am-6pm Tue-Sun. **Admission** free.

Upon coming to power, Hitler set about rounding
up and interning his opponents. From 1933-35 an
old brewery on this site was used to hold them.
The present camp received its first prisoners in
July 1936 (coinciding with the Berlin Olympics).
It was designated with cynical euphemism as a
Schutzhaftlager (Protective Custody Camp). The
first Schutzhäftlings were political opponents of
the government: communists, social democrats,
trade unionists. With time, the number and variety of prisoners widened to include anyone guilty
of 'anti-social' behaviour (for instance, petty theft),
homosexuals and, of course, Jews.

About 6,000 Jews were forcibly brought here
after Reichskristallnacht. It was here that some
of the first experiments in organised mass
murder were made: tens of thousands of prisoners
of war from the Eastern Front were killed at the
neighbouring Station Z, where the cells for
Prominenz (high-class detainees) housed Pastor
Martin Niemöller, a decorated World War I U-Boot
captain and one-time supporter of the Nazis.

The SS evacuated the camp in 1945 and began
to march 33,000 inmates to the Baltic, where they
were to be packed into boats and sunk. Some 6,000
died during the Todesmarsch (Death March) before the survivors were rescued by the Allies. A
further 3,000 prisoners were found in the camp
hospital when it was captured on April 22, 1945.

But the horror did not end here. After the German capitulation, the Russian secret police, the
MVD, reopened Sachsenhausen as Camp 7 for the
detention of war criminals; in fact it was filled with
anyone they suspected of opposing them. Following the fall of the GDR, mass graves were 'discovered', containing the remains of an estimated
10,000 prisoners.

On April 23, 1961, the partially restored camp
was opened to the public as Nationale Mahn- und
Gedenkstätte Sachsenhausen, a national monument and memorial. As far as the GDR was concerned, it was absolved of all complicity in the
actions of the Hitler regime, whose rightful successors, they claimed, could be found across the
border in the Federal Republic. There is a watch-
tower, with some once-electrified fencing to either
side of it; the inscription over the entrance, 'Arbeit
Macht Frei' ('Work Sets You Free'), could be found
over the gates of all concentration camps.

The parade ground, where morning roll-call was
taken, and from where inmates were required to
witness executions on the gallows, stands before
two remaining barrack blocks. One is now a museum and the second a memorial hall and cinema,
where a film about the history of the camp is
shown hourly, on the hour. The scale and the gris-
liness of the horror remembered here can be very
disturbing; but it is worth noting that there are
some people today who would like to pretend that
none of it ever happened.

# Longer Excursions

***Travel a couple of hours from Berlin in any direction – Leipzig, Weimar, the Baltic Coast, the Polish border, Dresden or Hamburg.***

*Leipzig's* **Altes Rathaus** *has the longest building inscription in the world. See page 248.*

If you've time to spare, try sampling the east German hinterland, exploring the Polish border region, or surrendering to the allure of Hamburg.

It is possible to get to and from the following destinations within one day, and, given the dearth of affordable hotel accommodation in the former GDR cities, it might be best to treat them as day trips – albeit arduous ones for inveterate museum-goers. All but Hamburg are within the five new federal states, where the economic, political, social and cultural base is of an entirely different character, not only from the west, but also from eastern Berlin, which enjoyed a comparatively favoured position in the former Eastern Bloc. Federal subsidies for rebuilding have been eagerly seized, and construction is rampant, meaning some landmarks, particularly neglected churches, may be closed or clad with scaffolding.

Most services, such as transport, restaurants and particularly hotel accommodation, are seriously underdeveloped by west German standards.

Furthermore, such services as there are can be strangely priced, or prone to sudden and unpredictable changes in ownership and style of management, mostly in the form of moving upscale.

Nevertheless, a longer excursion into the east German hinterland affords an unrepeatable experience, as the continent of Europe continues to move into a new era.

## Leipzig

One of Germany's most important trade centres and former second city of the GDR, Leipzig is both Bach's city and the place where the Wende, or 'change', started. Once one of Germany's biggest industrial strongholds, specialising in new technologies and manufacturing, trade fairs are its bread and butter these days. The recent influx of western businesspeople (plus spouses) has resulted not only in the scrubbing clean of the city, but in a proliferation of pricey shops and boutiques.

## Getting there

All forms of transport between Berlin and Leipzig are liable to be overcrowded or fully booked during important Messen (trade fairs); ask at a tourist information office for details. The advantage of taking a slower train is that it enables you to make stops en route (perhaps Wittenberg, former home of Martin Luther and a pretty, medieval town). Another sight which cannot be overlooked by train is the gigantic chemical works at Leuna. The factories were built in the early 1900s for the conglomerate IG Farben, which produced the poison gas used on the Western Front during World War I and the Zyklon B nerve gas for the Nazi Vernichtungslager (extermination camp) gas chambers.

A trip to Leipzig by car takes about two and a half hours down the motorway, but be prepared for considerable traffic jams as you approach the city; a good road map of Leipzig and its environs will help you make time-saving diversions.

**By train** direct from Berlin-Hauptbahnhof eight times daily; journey time about two and a half hours. Or from Berlin-Lichtenberg 15 times daily; journey time about two and a half hours.
**By car** via the AVUS to the Berliner Ring, then take the A9.

## Tourist Information

### Tourist Information Leipzig

*Sachsenplatz 1, 04199, Leipzig (0341 710 40).* **Open** 9am-7pm Mon-Fri; 9.30am-2pm Sat, Sun.

The compact town centre is surrounded by the **Ring**, a wide road built on the site of the old city wall (torn down in the last century). Most things worth seeing are within this ring. Leipzig was heavily bombed during the war and restoration has been piecemeal, if not chaotic. But several examples of grand, turn-of-the-century civic pomp survive dotted among the Communist blandness.

The **Neues Rathaus** (New Town Hall), on Martin-Luther-Ring 2, dates from the end of the last century, and competes well with the University skyscraper for ugliness. At Dimitroffplatz, opposite, the **Reichsgerichtsmuseum** with the **Museum für Bildende Künste** (Museum of Arts) is worth a visit just to look at the building. Further along the Ring is the **Runde Ecke**, where the dreaded Stasi had their headquarters. It now houses a museum about their activities.

Across the park and back south is the **Thomaskirche**, where Bach spent the last 27 years of his life as Kapellmeister (music director). He is buried in the choir, and fans won't want to miss the **Bach Museum**, located in the Bosehaus behind the church, or the small monument in the park, which was erected by another Leipziger, Friedrich Mendelssohn, in Bach's honour. Continue down Thomaskirchhof as it turns into Grimmaische Straße and you reach the **Altes**

**Rathaus,** which dates from the Renaissance and has the longest building inscription in the world. It also houses the town history museum. The covered Galerie Mädler Passage across the street has been completely rebuilt, attracting expensive shops and boutiques. In its basement is **Auerbachs Keller**, one of Germany's most famous restaurants. Goethe came here regularly to eat, and especially to drink, and used it as a location for a scene in his epic drama *Faust*. Two bronze models at the entrance and paintings inside depict scenes from the drama. The restaurant, which is over 300 years old, was refurbished in 1911.

Reichstraße leads past the **Alte Börse**, sparkling with its new gilding, to Sachsenplatz, the city's main outdoor market. But turn just before the market to see the **Nikolaikirche**, Leipzig's proud symbol of its new freedom. This medieval church, with its Baroque interior featuring columns that imitate palm trees, is the place where regular free-speech meetings started in 1982. These evolved into the Swords to Ploughshares peace movement, which led to the first anti-GDR demonstration on Monday, September 4, 1989 in the Nikolaikirchhof. (Today, there is the excellent Kulturcafé in the church's former school.)

By November 6, 1989, the Monday Demonstrations had swelled into 600,000-strong rallies in Augustusplatz (formerly Karl-Marx-Platz) just down the street by the University. The crowd chanted *Deutschland Einig Vaterland* and *Wir Sind Das Volk* and listened to speakers such as Kurt Masur, chief conductor of the Leipziger Gewandhaus Orchester (housed in the brown glass-fronted buildings on the south side). Augustusplatz was a project of GDR Communist party leader Walter Ulbricht, himself a Leipziger, and the staggeringly ugly skyscraper is supposed to represent an open book. Be sure to catch the inscription memorialising the Universitätskirche, a medieval building destroyed to make way for this eyesore. On the north side of the square stands the **Opernhaus Leipzig** (opera house, opened in 1960), which also has an excellent reputation.

Wandering through the city centre, you can see many of the handsome, prosperous homes of Leipzig's industrialists that survived the ravages of recent history. Now some of the stores in the city centre built to cater for this elite are fast being restored. As a contrast, visit the offices of the Universität Leipzig, Augustusplatz, which have an impressive bronze bas-relief of Marx urging workers of the world to unite.

### Auerbachs Keller

*Mädlerpassage, Grimmaischestraße 2-4, 04109 Leipzig (0341 21610 40).* **Open** 11am-3pm, 5pm-midnight daily. **Average** DM35. **Credit** AmEx, DC, EC, JBC, V.
The menu and especially the wine list are of excellent quality at Auerbachs. Specialities include Leipziger Allerlei, a dish of steamed mixed vegetables and mushrooms with crayfish.

*Weimar – the* **Residenz-Schloß Thüringen**.

### Johann-Sebastian-Bach-Museum and Archive

*Thomaskirchhof 16, 04109 Leipzig (0341 7866).* **Open** 10am-5pm daily. **Tickets** DM2; DM1 students, pensioners.

### Leipziger Gewandhaus Orchester

*Augustusplatz 8, 04199 Leipzig (0341 12700/127080).* **Open** 1-6pm Mon; 10am-6pm Tue-Fri; 10am-2pm Sat. **Admission** varies.

### Museum für Bildende Künste

*Dimitroffplatz 1, 04107 Leipzig (0341 216990).* **Open** 9am-5pm Tue, Thur-Sun; 1-9.30pm Wed. **Tickets** DM5; DM2.50 students, pensioners.

### Museum in der Runden Ecke

*Dittrichring 24, 04199 Leipzig (0341 29 44 05).* **Open** Wed-Sun 2-6pm.

### Opernhaus Leipzig

*Augustusplatz 12, 04199 Leipzig (0341 12610).* **Open** box office 10am-6pm Mon-Fri; 10am-1pm Sat. **Admission** varies.
Call for information about tours of the building.

## Weimar

Weimar lies 50km (31 miles) to the south-west of Leipzig across the state border in Thüringen (Thuringia). If you travel by car, you will be able to explore the stunning Saale valley on the way.

### Getting there

**By train** there are eight departures daily from Berlin-Hauptbahnhof; journey time four and a half hours.
**By car** as for Leipzig (*above*), but continue on the E4055.

## Tourist Information

### Tourist Information

*Markt 10, 99421 Weimar (03643 240020).* **Open** Apr-Oct 9am-7pm Mon-Fri, 9am-4pm Sat, 10am-4pm Sun; Nov-Mar 9am-6pm Mon-Fri, 9am-1pm Sun.

Known as Kulturstadt Deutschlands (Home of German Culture), Weimar is a small provincial town stuffed to the gunnels with monuments to the country's literature, music and other arts. Goethe and Schiller both lived and worked here. The town was bombed heavily in the war, but after

decades of work most of it has now been restored. Apart from writing, directing the State Theatre and working on scientific theories, Goethe also held various posts in the government of Weimar. His house is now a museum, and the office where he did much of his writing has been preserved intact – complete with original desk, quills and paper at the ready.

Not very far off is the considerably more modest house (also now a museum) of Schiller, the first German to make a career out of playwriting.

Both Schiller and Goethe had their plays performed at the Nationaltheater. The building was the assembly point of the 1919 conference which drew up Germany's first republican constitution, thereafter known as the Weimar Republic. Weimar was also the first German town to elect a Nazi-dominated council.

Bach lived here and worked at the **Stadtkirche St Peter und Paul** on Herderplatz. The church is also known under the name Herder Kirche; it was built in 1498 in late Gothic style and renovated in early baroque style. In the mid-nineteenth century, when the Abbé Liszt arrived, music became a focal point of town life. Today, regular concerts by the Hochschule für Musik Franz Liszt, the music school of which Liszt was the first director, are of the highest quality. The Hochschule is at the *Platz der Demokratie 2-3 (03643 652 41)*. Ticket prices vary.

The castle and former home of the court of Thüringen (Thuringia) is now a Museum, beside a large, handsome park. And the town square houses an open-air market selling local specialities such as the celebrated Thüringer Rostbratwurst sausage. The **Ratskeller** has a good selection of inexpensive regional dishes. But for a choice of bars and cafés, your best bet is to explore the pedestrianised section of the town, especially near the Schillerhaus.

### Castle and Museum: Die Kunstsammlung zu Weimar

*Burgplatz 4, 99423 Weimar (03643 618 31).* **Open** 10am-6pm Tue, Wed, Fri-Sun; 10am-8pm Thur. **Tickets** DM8; DM4 students, unemployed, pensioners; free children under six.

### Deutsches Nationaltheater

*Theaterplatz, 93401 Weimar (03643 75 50; telephone ticket service 03643 755 334).* **Open** box office 2-6pm Mon; 10am-1pm, 4-6pm, Tue-Fri; 10am-noon, 3-6pm, Sat. **Tickets** DM9-DM40; half-price students, unemployed, pensioners.

### Goethe House and Museum

*Am Frauenplan, 4 (03643 54 50).* **Open** 9am-5pm Tue, Fri-Sun; 9am-7pm Wed, Thur. **Tickets** DM8; DM6 students, unemployed, pensioners.

### Ratskeller

*Markt 10, 99420 Weimar (03643 641 42).* **Open** 11.30am-midnight daily. **Average** DM30. **Credit** AmEx, EC, V.

*The **Baltic coast** – two hours from Berlin.*

### Schiller House and Museum
*Schillerstraße, (03643 54 50).* **Open** 9am-5pm Fri-Mon; 9am-7pm Wed, Thur. **Tickets** DM8; DM6 students, unemployed, pensioners.

## The Baltic Coast

Along the coastline of the quiet, virtually land-locked Baltic Sea (Ostsee), you'll come across old Hanseatic towns and miles of deserted beaches.

### Getting there
**By train** from Berlin-Lichtenberg to Rostock there are nine trains daily; journey time is about three hours. There are 13 trains daily to Stralsund; journey time three hours. **By car** drive north to the Berliner Ring and then follow the A24 to Rostock (about two hours); continue on the B105 to Stralsund and Rügen. The motorway to Rostock affords easy access on the way to the many inland lakes and forests.
**By ferry** there are regular links between Rügen and the mainland, as well as the Danish island of Bornholm.
**By coach** from Omnibusbahnhof am Funkturm to Usedom on the eastern German Baltic coast (Saturdays, Mar-Oct only); journey time about four hours.

## Tourist Information

### Fremdenverkehrsverband 'Insel Usedom'
*Bäderstraße 4, 17459 Ueckeritz (038375 7693).* **Open** 8am-4pm Mon-Fri.

### Fremdenverkehrsverband Rügen
*August-Bebel-Straße 12, 18592 Ostseebad Sellin (038303 1470/1).* **Open** 8am-4.30pm Mon-Fri .

### Regionalverband Mecklenburgische Ostseebäder
*Goethestraße 1, 18203 Bad Doberan (038203 21 20).* **Open** 8am-5pm Mon-Thur.

### Rostock Information
*Schnickmannstraße 13-14, 18055 Rostock (0381 4925260).* **Open** *May-Sept* 10am-6pm Mon-Fri, 10am-2.30pm Sat, Sun; *Oct-Apr* 10am-5pm Mon-Fri, 10am-2.30pm Sat.

The Baltic Coast was the favoured holiday destination of the ordinary GDR citizen; post-reunification it is now the most easily accessible seaside resort for all Berliners. The coast forms the northern boundary of the modern state of Mecklenburg-Vorpommern. Bismarck said of the area: 'When the end of the world comes, I shall go to Mecklenburg, because there everything happens a hundred years later.'

The large island of Rügen is gradually resuming its rivalry with Sylt in the North Sea – both islands claim to be the principal north German resort. In July and August especially it can get very crowded indeed, and the amenities to support this great surge of tourists are still inadequate. Rügen's meagre handful of restaurants and lack of late-night bars mean visitors are early to bed and early to rise. Go out of season instead and enjoy the solitude.

Rostock was one of the founder-members of the medieval Hanseatic League, and until wrecked by bombing in the last war was an attractive port full of grandiose, gabled merchants' houses and seamen's cottages. The GDR did a good job of putting Rostock back together and, though it is no longer the vital trading link it once was, it is a quietly attractive, if slightly melancholy town, especially off-season.

Much of the past flavour can be found around the waterfront, where cafés, restaurants and hotels have recently opened. But Rostock's reputation has not yet recovered from the ugly racial incident in 1992, when people and police alike stood around and watched as neo-Nazis stormed and fired a hostel for asylum seekers.

Forty kilometres (25 miles) to the east of Rostock is Peenemünde, site of secret weapons development in the closing years of World War II. Here, a group of engineers and technicians produced the Vergeltungswaffen (revenge weapons) V1 and V2, and several rockets were fired from the island. Part of the complex has been preserved as a museum, and examples of the rockets are on display. After the war, both the Americans and Russians were quick to requisition the services of the scientists responsible for the rockets' creation. One of the boffins, Werner von Braun, became the leading expert of NASA's Apollo programme.

## The Polish Border

The Polish border region is a must for World War II buffs, since it is the place where the Russians finally broke through the German lines to start the final assault on Berlin. But it is also a place of peaceful countryside dotted with relatively untouched villages that are quite unlike anything in western Germany. For anything but a day trip to Frankfurt-Oder, a car and a detailed map are essential, since transport in this part of the country is severely underdeveloped and the places referred to below are way off the usual routes.

### Getting there

**By train** there are 21 departures daily from Berlin-Hauptbahnhof to Frankfurt-Oder; journey time one and a half hours.

**By car** take Frankfurter Allee straight out to Münchenberg, heading from there either to Frankfurt-Oder or to Seelow; journey time about one hour.

## Tourist Information

### Frankfurt-an-der-Oder Verkehrsverein

*Karl-Marx Straße 8a, Frankfurt-an-der-Oder 510230 (0335 325216).* **Open** 10am-noon, 12.30pm-6pm Mon-Fri; 10am-12-30pm Sat; *summer only* 10am-1pm Sun.
If their phone manner's anything to go by, don't expect an excess of help here. Otherwise, no centralised tourist information bureau exists, although most towns have small information centres.

The central metropolis of the border region is Frankfurt-an-der-Oder, a thirteenth-century market town that was almost completely destroyed during the War. It has little to recommend it, since the GDR reconstruction was along the usual Socialist architectural lines, and its chief virtue is as a jumping-off point to Poland to the east. A bridge across the river leads to the Polish town of Slubice, where flea-markets depressingly reminiscent of those on the US/Mexican border sell cigarettes, meats, cheese, horrid clothing and knick-knacks.

Seelow, just to the north of Frankfurt, is another thirteenth-century town that suffered horrible wartime devastation. The battle for the Eastern Front is commemorated at the **Gedankstätte Seelower Höhen**, a hill topped with a statue of a Russian soldier. Until 1990, no mention was made of the 12,000 German soldiers, mostly old men and boys from the Hitler Youth, who perished here, but today, the museum pays homage to both sides, and a slide presentation (available in English) with a light-up map and a rather tendentious narration will explain the struggle to break through and take Berlin.

Going back south from Seelow, you'll find an even grimmer reminder in the recent German Military Cemetery in Lietzen, where so far 890 graves have been installed. Few of the inhabitants are over 20.

A drive through the villages near Seelow, in the area known as the Oderbruch, will turn up a Russian war memorial in every village square. Neu Hardenburg has a Schinkel church, built as part of the reconstruction of the village after a disastrous fire, a project overseen by the teenage genius who was one of his first projects.

The Schloß was the family home of the Graf von Hardenburg, one of the plotters against Hitler, and it was here that he was captured by the SS and taken to Sachsenhausen. The Oderbruch was a special project of Friedrich the Great after his release from prison in Kostryzn across the Polish border, and he built a huge levee on what

*The Glockenturm,* **Dresden** *– see page 252.*

is now the German side of the river to control the flooding so that the area could be settled for agriculture.

Wilhelmsaue has the area's only windmill, which is sometimes open as a museum. North of Seelow, Neutrebbin was a village personally founded by the king, and today it is a gem which hardly looks touched by the twentieth century, let alone the GDR. The statue of Frederick in the town square is brand new, a replica of one melted down by the GDR authorities in 1953. The one in the town square at nearby Letschin, however, is original, albeit restored, and the centre of a hilarious story involving the innkeeper at the nearby Zum Alten Fritz and several of his buddies, who hid the statue in a cow stable and managed to drag it out as far as the bus-stop one drunken night in 1986.

The steeple in the town's centre is all that remains of one of Schinkel's first churches, the only one he did in red brick. The innkeeper, Wolfgang Bartsch, frequently conducts tours of the area for the German Army with a military theme, but is also possessed of an encyclopaedic knowledge of the whole Oderbruch, and will be happy to negotiate a tour of the area in German for interested tourists. Accommodation is available in several Gäststätte in surrounding villages, and there is a small motel in Seelow.

### Gedenkstätte Seelower Höhen

*Küstriner Straße 28a, 15306 Seelow (03346 597).* **Open** 9am-4.30pm Tue-Sun. **Admission** DM2; DM1 students, pensioners.

### Zum Alten Fritz

*Karl-Marx Straße 1, 15324 Letschin (033475 223).*
**Open** 10am-6pm Tue; 10am-11pm Wed, Thur, Sun;
10am-midnight Fri, Sat. **Average** DM12. **No credit
cards.**
Mammoth portions of typical Oderbruch cuisine in a fine
family-run inn typical of the area. Ask to see the Frederick
the Great room, with souvenirs of the notorious battle to
rehabilitate the statue.

## Dresden

Destroyed twice and rebuilt one and a half times,
the capital of Saxony currently looks like one huge
building site. But among the tower cranes can be
found one of Germany's best art museums and
numerous historic buildings.

### Getting there

**By train** there are seven departures daily from Berlin-
Zoologischer Garten and Berlin-Hauptbahnhof to
Dresden (journey time about two hours) and ten
departures from Berlin-Lichtenberg to Dresden (journey
time two hours). Book a ticket to Dresden-Hauptbahnhof,
not Dresden Neustadt.
**By car** take the AVUS to the Berliner Ring and then the
A16. Journey time about 90 minutes.
**By water** a number of cruises are offered up the Spree
and the Elbe; if you've time to spare, this is a peaceful,
but expensive way to journey to the city. Try to go in
spring when the route is festooned with blossom (*see
chapter* **Getting Around: Boat Trips**).

## Tourist Information

### Dresden Tourist Information

*Prager Straße 10, 01069 Dresden (0351 495 50 25).*
**Open** *Nov-Feb* 9am-6pm Mon-Fri; 9am-2pm Sun, public
holidays; *Mar-Oct* 9am-8pm Mon-Sat; 9am-2pm Sun,
public holidays.
*Neustädter Markt, 01097 Dresden (0351 53539).* **Open**
9am-6pm Mon-Fri; 9am-4pm Sat; 11am-4pm Sun, public
holidays.

Modern Dresden is built on the ruins of its past. A
fire consumed Altendresden on the right bank of
the Elbe in 1685, provoking a wave of rebuilding
throughout the city. On the night of February 13,
1945, the biggest of Sir Arthur 'Bomber' Harris's
raids caused huge fire storms killing 30,000 or
100,000 people, mostly refugees from the Eastern
Front. After the war, Dresden was twinned with
Coventry, and Britten's *War Requiem* was given
its first performance in the Hofkirche by musicians
from both towns and soloists from Britain, Germany and the Soviet Union. Reconstruction of the
old buildings under the GDR was erratic, but the
maze of cranes and scaffolding now in place is
evidence that Dresden is making up for lost time.

Dresden's greatest attraction remains the buildings from the reign of Augustus the Strong (1670-
1733): notably, the Hofkirche cathedral, Am
Theaterplatz 1, the Zwinger, a pleasure-garden
containing a complex of museums which starts at
Theaterplatz, and the Grünes Gewölbe (Green
Vault) a collection of Augustus's over-the-top

jewels and gem-encrusted knick-knacks in the
Albertinium, still give a flavour of the city's
baroque exuberance. You get to them by leaving
the Hauptbahnhof's Prager Straße exit and walking through the pedestrianised mall that competes
with Alexanderplatz for the title of ugliest GDR
public space.

Building was continued by Augustus's successor, Augustus III, who then lost badly to Prussia
in the Seven Years War (1756-63). Frederick the
Great destroyed much of the city in this war,
although not the Brühlsche Terrassen in the old
part of the city. A victorious Napoleon ordered the
demolition of the city's defences in 1809. In 1985
the **Semperoper** (opera house), named after its
architect Gottfried Semper (1838-41), was fully
restored to its earlier glittering rococo elegance.
Tickets are notoriously hard to come by (you can
try to get them from the central theatre box office
in Schinkel's Altstädter Wache – also known as
Schinkel Wache – on the main square). The
**Gemäldegalerie Alte Meister** in the Zwinger
has a superb collection of Old Masters, particularly Italian Renaissance and Flemish, including
Raphael's *Sistine Madonna*, that belonged to
Augustus (check the AR monogram on the frames)
and there are exhibitions of porcelain from nearby Meißen, and fascinating collections of armour,
weapons, clocks and scientific equipment.

The industrialisation of Dresden heralded a new
phase of construction that produced the **Rathaus**
(town hall, built 1905-10) at Dr Külz-Ring, the
**Hauptbahnhof** (1892-95) at the end of Prager
Straße, the exotic **Yenidze cigarette factory**,
designed in the shape of a mosque (1912), in the
Könneritzstraße, and the grandiose **Landtags-
gebäude** (completed to plans by Paul Wallot,
designer of Berlin's Reichstag, in 1907) at Heinrich-
Zille-Straße 11. The finest example of inter-war
architecture is Wilhelm Kreis's **Deutsches
Hygienemuseum** (1929) at Lingner Platz 1, built
to house the German Institute of Hygiene.

The **Frauenkirche** (Church of Our Lady) at
the Neumarkt is, with the Schloß, one of the last of
the bombed buildings to be reconstructed. Plans
are underway to have the entire Altstadt reconstructed by the city's one thousandth anniversary
in 2006. The nearby Müntzgasse, with its pricey
Hilton hotel, cafés and restaurants, is wryly
referred to by locals as Wessistraße.

In the GDR days, this part of the country, behind
the Saxon hills, could not receive western television or radio broadcasts and was called Tal der
Ahnungslosen (Valley of the Clueless). Today's
Dresden is catching up quickly, with a vibrant
alternative scene in the Neustadt, particularly in
the bars and cafés on and around Alaunstraße
such as Schaune Café, Café 100, Planwirtschaft
and Raskalnikov.

The **Striezelmarkt** (named after the savoury

pretzel you will see everyone eating) is held on Altstädtermarkt during December every year. This Christmas market is one of the most colourful events of the year. Dresden is also home to the best Stollen, a sweet yuletide pastry.

### Albertinium (including Grünes Gewölbe)

*Georg-Treu-Platz, 01067 Dresden (0351 4953056).* **Open** 10am-6pm Fri-Wed. **Admission** DM7; DM3.50 concs. For details about museum Tageskarte *see below* **Gemälde Galerie Alte Meister**.

### Altstädter Wache

*Theaterplatz, 01067 Dresden (0351 484 23 23).* **Open** *box office for the Semperoper* noon-5pm Mon-Fri; 10am-1pm Sat. **Tickets** DM5-DM65; DM8 students (occasionally), available half an hour before performance. **No credit cards.**

### Gemäldegalerie Alte Meister

*in the Zwinger at the Theaterplatz, 01067 Dresden (0351 484 01 20).* **Open** 10am-6pm Tue-Sun. **Admission** DM7; DM3.50 students, pensioners, unemployed. If you intend to see several of the local museums, a better alternative is a Tageskarte, DM10, DM5 students, pensioners, unemployed, which will also get you into the armour collection, porcelain collection, the Schloß, the Albertinium complex, and several other museums.

### Mathematisch-Physikalischer Salon

*in the Zwinger at the Theaterplatz, 01067 Dresden (0351 495 1364).* **Open** 9.30am-5pm Wed-Mon. **Admission** DM3, in two instalments for the instrument and clock collections.

### Semperoper

*Theaterplatz 2, 01067 Dresden (0351 484 20).* **Open** *box office see* **Altstädter Wache**.

## Hamburg

Germany's largest port was the most important city of the medieval Hanseatic League and is home to the flourishing Reeperbahn red-light district, the elegant villas of the Elbchaussee and most of Germany's major publishing houses.

### Getting there

**By train** there are eight departures a day from Berlin-Hauptbahnhof and Berlin-Zoologischer Garten to Hamburg-Hauptbahnhof; journey time three hours; three hours 20 minutes to Hamburg-Altona.
**By bus** there are four departures daily from Berlin-Omnibusbahnhof am Funkturm to Hamburg-Hauptbahnhof; journey time about three hours.
**By car** drive north from Jakob-Kaiser-Platz along Kurt-Schumacher-Damm to the A24; journey time two hours.
**By air** there are nearly 20 flights daily, mostly from Berlin-Tempelhof and some from Tegel; journey time about one hour.

## Tourist Information

### Tourismus-Zentrale Hamburg

*Burchardstraße 14, 20095 Hamburg (040 30 05 10).* **Open** 8.45am-5.15pm Mon-Fri.

The Freie- und Hansestadt Hamburg (Free and Hanseatic City of Hamburg), has an important place in German history. The Hanseatic League was founded here as a protected trade zone stretching along the North Sea and Baltic coasts.

The legacy of mercantile independence continues to give Hamburg its unique character: Chancellor Helmut Schmidt turned down the Bundesverdienstkreuz (highest honour of the Federal Republic) because Hamburgers do not accept 'foreign' honours. Hamburg has always been a wealthy city: today perhaps 1 per cent of the population are millionaires. At the same time, there is a long history of social democracy and the SPD has a virtual monopoly of power in the Burgschaften (city parliament).

Hamburg is built on the lower reach of the Elbe, where the river is joined by the waters of the Binnen- and Aussenalster lakes (a fine view of both can be seen from the Kennedy Brücke bridge). The city has more canals than Venice, although most are in the harbour area.

Much of Hamburg was destroyed during World War II, but subsequent restoration has created a generally attractive appearance. In winter, the city, located on the flat northern expanse that stretches from the Dutch coast to the Asian steppes, can be both bleak and bitterly cold. But in spring and summer, it is transformed by the abundant greenery lining its lakes and boulevards. Spend the days lazing on the water or in the parks recuperating from heavy club nights in Saint Pauli.

The nineteenth-century **Hauptbahnhof**, constructed to resemble a fortress, may be your first view of the town; try the roast mushrooms, a local delicacy, sold from the gallery above the platforms.

Nearby are a number of good, reasonably priced hotels; as well as the **Deutsches Schauspielhaus** which has a programme of everything from classics to musicals, with occasional live, large-screen video relays shown in the square. Within walking distance is the **Kunsthalle** (Art Gallery) on Glockengießerwall, which has a very good collection of German medieval, nineteenth-century, Impressionist and Brücke (a form of German Expressionism) artists.

North-east from the station is the area of St Georg. Along Lange Reihe are many good cafés, restaurants and ice cream parlours. Cut through leafy Danzigerstraße on to Steindamm and then to Adenauer Allee for a more commercial atmosphere; in among the concrete and steel are several good nightclubs.

Parts of the old town centre are pedestrianised with numerous street cafés and frequent al fresco music and cabaret performances (particularly at the Alter Markt).

On May 7 is Überseetag (Overseas Day), a city holiday commemorating Frederick Barabarossa giving Hamburg the right to trade freely on the lower Elbe in 1189. A variety of events fill the week either side of this day, including the music festival, when all available spaces are occupied with open-air and usually free concerts by rock, folk, jazz and classical groups from around the world. The weather in May is usually particularly good, and the best time to experience the city.

In among the array of department stores and specialist shops are a large number of dealers in English antiques, especially around Gänsemarkt.

In complete contrast, the **Reeperbahn** on the far western side of the town is unrivalled in Germany for its permissiveness. A long, broad boulevard running practically to the harbour which provided the Reeperbahn with its original pleasure-hungry seagoing clientèle, it is packed with over 300 venues. They include raucous drinking bars, where bands in sailor uniforms blast out popular melodies, cheap (and not so cheap) restaurants and kebab bars, and bordellos. The Star Club – where The Beatles played in their infamous Hamburg days – was situated at Große Freiheit 39, just off the Reeperbahn. Today the same street reverberates with post-punk noises from the Große Freiheit rock club and sleazy cabaret sounds oozing out of sex bars and dubious oriental cafes. There's also the infamous side street, Herbertstraße, hidden by a metal barrier, through which women and US military personnel are forbidden to pass. The street is eerily quiet, with men wandering around gaping at the women of varying age and beauty sitting in illuminated bay windows.

At the harbour end of the Reeperbahn lies Hafenstraße, once the scene of pitched territorial battles between squatters, punks, anarchists and riot police. Some oddly interesting, transient bars and clubs can sometimes be found in gone-to-seed stripjoints. There's also **Harry's Hamburger Hafenbasar** (*Bernhard-Nocht-Straße 63, 20359 Hamburg, tel 040 31 24 82*): a musty, bizarre junk shop where sailors come to offload sharktooth necklaces, stuffed armadillos and other weird souvenirs picked up on their travels. Behind its deceptively small shopfront is a maze of rooms packed with fascinating rubbish. Expect to pay a small admission fee refundable against any purchase.

Rather quieter but no less interesting is the traditional workers' district of St Pauli (with the celebrated football team) just north of the Reeperbahn. In its network of narrow streets and small houses, clustered round the main road, Schulterblatt, you can find good, cheap Italian, Greek and Turkish food.

Altona was originally a separate community described in old Plattdeutsch (Low German) as *all to nah* (all too near). Follow the Elbchaussee, lined with handsome villas and rows of smaller cottages built for merchant marine officers in the last century. Explore the **Rosengarten** (Rose Garden) en route to the Altonaer Balkon hill, where you can get a good view across the Elbe. Its sandy shore is a favoured bathing spot in good weather.

The gigantic harbour (Hafengelände) occupies 10 per cent of the city's area. Completely rebuilt and modernised after the last war it is now second only to Rotterdam as Europe's chief container port. Fascinating dockyard tours (Hafenrundfahrt) are run by HADAG, Hafen-Dampf Schiffarts AG; the ticket office is at *St Pauli Landungsbrücke 4*. Boats leave half-hourly daily from 9am-6pm.

If you can get up early enough, join the throngs at the market at **Landungsbrücke** around 6am Sundays in time for the fishermen landing their hauls. Other sights include the **Binnenalster**, a lake in the centre of Hamburg which has a beautiful tall fountain (illuminated at night); and the Rathaus Markt (town square), which has a memorial to the wartime destruction and a handsomely rebuilt nineteenth-century **Rathaus** (town hall). Immediately south of here, the **Hohe Brücke** (High Bridge) over the Nikolai Fleet affords a view of old warehouses and boats on the canal bend.

The south-eastern shore of the Aussenalster, An der Alster, is greener and a busy beach in summer (although bathing is not allowed), and home to the pricey hotels Vier Jahreszeiten (Four Seasons) and Atlantic. To the north is the luxuriant Volkspark. Closer to the centre, Planten und Blumen (Plants and Flowers) Park and the Botanischer Garten (Botanical Garden) next to it also feature music concerts in summer and a *son et lumière* fountain display every evening (10pm; 9pm out of season).

Hamburg also has one of the oldest breweries in the world, Gröningers, serving its dark and light beers as well as food in the claustrophobic lower ground floor rooms.

Hamburg is a good base from which to venture further afield to Friedrichsruh, where Bismarck's family home has been turned into a museum. Off the coast to the north, the long, thin island of Sylt can be reached by train, bus or car, and has a beach stretching the length of its North Sea shoreline. It's a favourite destination for holidaymakers in and out of season.

### Deutsches Schauspielhaus
*Kirchenallee 39, 20099 Hamburg (040 24 87 13).* **Open** box office 10am-6pm Mon-Sat; 10am-1pm Sun, holidays. **Tickets** prices vary. **Credit** AmEx, DC, EC, JBC, MC, V.

### Gröningers Brewery
*Gröninger Braukeller, Ost-West-Straße 47, 20457 Hamburg (040 33 13 81).* **Open** 11am-midnight Mon-Fri; 5pm-midnight Sat. **Average** (meal) DM35.

### Kunsthalle
*Glockengießerwall, 20095 Hamburg (040 24 86 26 12).* **Open** 10am-6pm Tue-Sun. Tickets DM8; DM4 students, pensioners.

### Friedrichsruh Bismarck Museum
*Am Museum, 21521 Friedrichsruh (04104 24 19). Transport from Hamburg S-Bahn to Aumühle, walk 20 mins through woods.* **Open** *Apr-Sept* 2-6pm Mon, 9am-6pm Tue-Sun; *Oct-Mar* 9am-4pm Tue-Fri; 10am-5pm Sat, Sun. **Admission** DM4.50; DM2 under-14s; DM3.50 students.

Survival

# Survival

*How to cope in Berlin: everything you need to know about surviving in the city.*

## Embassies & Consulates

Before visiting an embassy or consulate it's advisable to phone and check opening hours; you may also need to make an appointment. All are closed on German public holidays; many are closed on the public holidays of their own country. We list below the British, Irish and US embassies. You can obtain a full list from the Verkehrsamt (tourist information office) in Zoo Station, or look under 'Botschaften' in the Gelbe Seiten (Yellow Pages).

### British Embassy
*Unter den Linden 32/34, Mitte, 10117 (220 24 31, fax 201 84 157). S1, S2 Unter den Linden.* **Open** 9am-noon, 2-4pm, Mon-Fri.

### Irish Consulate
*Ernst-Reuter-Platz 10, Charlottenburg, 10587 (34 80 08 22/348 00 80). U2 Ernst-Reuter-Platz.* **Open** 10am-1pm Mon-Fri.

### US Embassy
*Clayallee 170, Zehlendorf, 14169 (832 40 87). U2 Oskar-Helene-Heim.* **Open** *visa enquiries* 8.30-10.30am Mon-Fri; *consular enquiries* 8.30am-noon Mon-Fri.

## Gas & Electricity

Electricity in Germany runs on 220V. To use British appliances (which run on 240V), simply change the plug or use an adaptor (available at most electrical goods shops). American appliances run on 110V; to use one in Germany you'll need to buy a converter, which will be expensive.

Gas and electricity are supplied by state- and region-owned companies that vary in name according to where you are living. In Berlin gas is now supplied by a single company, Berliner Gaswerke (GASAG). Electricity, however, is supplied by Bewag (Berliner Kraft-und Licht AG) in the west and EBAG (Energieversorgung Berlin AG) in the east, though there are plans to bring the two services together under one umbrella.

### Berliner Gaswerke (GASAG) Service
*Torgauer Straße 12-15, Schöneberg, 10829 (7872-0; emergency/Störungsdienst 787229). S1 Schöneberg.* **Open** 24 hours daily.

### Berliner Kraft-und Licht (Bewag) AG Service
*Stauffenbergstraße 26, Tiergarten, 10730 (267-0; emergency/Störungsdienst 267 12525/heating 267 27106). U1 Kurfürstenstraße.* **Open** 24 hours daily.

### EBAG (Energieversorgung Berlin AG) Service
*Luisenstraße 35, Mitte, 10117. (295400 emergency/ Störungsdienst 295 4099/heating 295 45 98).* **Open** 24 hours daily.

## Health

Should you fall ill in Germany, take a completed form E111 to the AOK (Local Sickness Fund) and staff will exchange it for a Krankenschein (medical certificate) which you can present to the doctor treating you, or to the hospital in an emergency. For details on obtaining form E111 and the AOK, *see chapter* **Essential Information: Insurance**.

If you require non-emergency hospital treatment, the doctor will issue you with a Notwendig-

*If you fall ill in Berlin, fill out form E111.*

keitsbescheinigung (need certificate) which you must take to the AOK. They in turn will give you a Kostenübernahmeschein (cost transferral certificate) which will entitle you to hospital treatment in a public ward.

All hospitals have an emergency ward open 24 hours daily. Otherwise, it is customary in Germany for patients to be admitted to hospital via a practising physician. For a complete list of hospitals in and around Berlin, consult the Gelbe Seiten (Yellow Pages) under Krankenhäuser/Kliniken.

### AOK Auslandsschalter (Foreign Section AOK)

*Hohenzollerndamm 183, Wilmersdorf, 10713 (86 30 20). U2, U7 Fehrbelliner Platz.* **Open** 8am-3pm Mon, Wed; 8am-6pm Tue, Thur; 8am-noon Fri.

## Complementary Medicine

There is a very long tradition of alternative medicine (Heilpraxis) in Germany and your normal medical insurance will usually cover treatment costs. For a full list of practitioners in Berlin, look up 'Heilpraktiker' in the Gelbe Seiten (Yellow Pages). You'll find a complete list of chiropractors, osteopaths, acupuncturists and homoeopaths. Homoeopathic medicines are harder to get hold of and much more expensive than in the UK, and it's harder to find osteopaths and chiropractors.

### Bund Deutscher Heilpraktiker (Federation of German Alternative Medical Practitioners)

*Bifröstweg 4, Reinickendorf, 13465 (401 82 43/401 82 43). Bus 120.* **Open** 10am-5pm Mon-Fri.
This organisation answers queries concerning all branches of alternative medicine. Staff will be happy to find someone who can speak English to you.

## Contraception & Abortion

Family planning clinics are thin on the ground in Germany, and generally you have to go to a gynaecologist (Frauenarzt). Although it's different in other parts of Germany, abortion is available on demand in Berlin. It's expensive, though, and involves a lot of bureaucracy. The following agency can advise you of your rights:

### Pro Familia

*Ansbacher Straße 11, Schöneberg, 10787 (213 90 13). U1, U2 Wittenbergplatz.* **Open** *consultations without appointment* 3pm-6pm, Mon, Thur; *arranging an appointment* 10am-1pm Mon, Tue, Thur, 1-4pm Wed.
Free advice about sex, contraception and abortion. Best to call for an appointment. Staff speak English.

## Doctors & Dentists

If you don't know of any doctors or are too ill to leave your bed, phone the Emergency Doctor's Service/Ärztlicher Notdienst (*31 00 31*), which specialises in dispatching doctors for house calls. Charges vary according to treatment.

# Emergencies

The following emergency services are all open 24 hours daily.
**Ambulance**/*Krankenwagen (112)*.
**Fire Service**/*Feuerwehr (112)*.
**Police**/*Polizei (110)*.
**ADAC Auto Assistance**/*ADAC-Stadtpannendienst (01802 22 22 22)*.
**Emergency Dental Service**/*Zahnärztlicher Notdienst (0 11 41)*.
**Emergency Doctor's Service**/*Ärztlicher Notdienst (310 031)*.
**Emergency Pharmaceutical Services**/*Apotheken Notdienst (0 11 41)*.
**Emergency Veterinary Care**/*Tierärztlicher Notdienst (0 11 41)*.
**Poisoning**/*Giftnotruf (302 30 22)*.

## Emergency Repairs

There are very few 24-hour emergency repair services dealing with plumbing, electricity, heating, locks, car repairs and carpentry. If possible, get your landlord to fix the problem, as calling out private firms will be expensive. They usually charge a minimum of DM40 call-out charge and DM25 per hour labour, plus parts. The companies listed below are open 24 hours daily.

### Water, Gas & Heating

*See also above* **Gas & Electricity**.
**Meisterbetrieb** *(703 50 50/51)*.
**Kempinger** *(628 90 00)*.
**Rohrbruch-Express** *(745 91 59)*.

### Lock-Opening & Repairs

For a local locksmith, look in the Gelbe Seiten (Yellow Pages) under Schlösser. The following firms provide emergency assistance 24 hours daily:
**Schlossdienst** *(834 22 92)*.
**Hüwe** *(46 71 04 50)*.

In Germany you choose your doctor according to his or her speciality. You don't have to get a referral from a GP. The **British Embassy** (*see above* **Embassies & Consulates**) will provide you with a list of English-speaking doctors, but many doctors can speak some English. They will all be expensive, so either have your E111 at hand or your private insurance document. The following are English-speaking doctors and dentists:

### Dentists

**Mr Pankaj Mehta** *Schlangenbader Straße 25, Wilmersdorf, 14197 (823 30 10). U1 Rüdesheimerplatz.* **Surgery hours** 9am-noon, 2-6pm, Mon, Tue, Thur; 8am-1pm Wed, Fri.
**Dr John Jarvis-Walters** (private practitioner) *Kurfürstendamm 210, Charlottenburg, 10719 (882 67 67). U3 Uhlandstraße.* **Surgery hours** 9.30am-noon, 2-6pm, Mon-Fri.

### General Practitioners

**Frau Dr I Dorow** *Rüsternallee 14-16, Charlottenburg, 14050 (302 46 90). U2 Neu-Westend.* **Surgery hours** 9-11.30am Mon-Fri; 5-7pm Mon, Thur; 4-6pm Tue.
**Herr Dr U Beck** *Bundesratufer 2, Moabit, 10555 (3 91 28 08). U9 Turmstraße.* **Surgery hours** 9.30am-noon, 4-6pm, Mon, Tue, Thur; 9am-noon Wed, Fri.
**Dr Christine Rommelspacher** *Gotzkowskystraße 19, Moabit, 10555 (392 20 75). U9 Turmstraße.* **Surgery hours** 4-7pm Mon-Fri.

### Gynaecologists

**Dr Lutz Opitz** *Tegeler Weg 4, Charlottenburg, 10589 (344 40 01). U7 Mierendorffplatz.* **Surgery hours** 8am-2pm Mon-Fri; 8am-noon, 3.30-6pm, Tue; 8am-noon Wed; 3-7pm Thur.
**Dr H Wendorff** *Rheinstraße 29, Friedenau, 12161 (852 56 34). U9 Walther-Schreiber-Platz.* **Surgery hours** 10am-noon, 3-6pm, Mon; 3-6pm Tue, Wed, Fri; 3-7pm Thur.

## Pharmacies

Prescription and non-prescription drugs (including aspirin) are sold only at pharmacies (Apotheken), while household goods, toiletries, and cosmetics are available more cheaply at Drogerien or department stores. You can recognise pharmacies by a red 'A' outside the front door. A list of pharmacies offering Sunday and evening services should be displayed at every pharmacy. For information, phone: **Emergency Pharmaceutical Services**/*Apotheken Notdienst (0 11 41).* **Open** 24 hours daily.

## Sexually Transmitted Diseases

### Berliner Aids-Hilfe (BAH)

*Büro 15, Meineckestraße, Wilmersdorf, 10719 (883 30 17; advice line 194 11). U9, U15 Kurfürstendamm.* **Open** noon-6pm Mon-Thur, Fri; noon-4pm.
The BAH runs a 24-hour advice line; information is given on all aspects of HIV and AIDS. Free consultations; supplies of condoms and lubricant also provided. Staff speak English.

### Deutsche Aids-Hilfe (DAH)

*Dieffenbachstraße 33, Kreuzberg, 10967 (690 08 70; 24-hour advice line 194 11). U8 Schönleinstraße.* **Open** 11am-5pm Mon; 10am-5pm Tue-Fri.
The Germany-wide version of the **BAH** (*see above*), which will also provide information on other sexual diseases.

## Help Lines & Agencies

### Alcohol & Drugs

#### Alkoholkranken-Beratung (Alcoholic Advice Centre)

*Gierkezeile 39, Charlottenburg, 10585 (348 00 90). U7 Richard-Wagner-Platz.* **Open** (for advice) 3-6pm Mon; 2pm-4pm Tue, Thur. 10am-noon Thur. Outside of consultation hours, by appointment only. Telephone manned from 9am-noon, 1-6pm, Mon-Fri.
This organisation provides advice and free information on self-help groups.

#### Drogen Notdienst (Emergency Drug Service)

*Ansbacher Straße 11, Schöneberg, 10787 (19 237). U1, U2 Wittenbergplatz.* **Open** *for advice* 8.30am-9pm Mon-Fri; 2-9.30pm Sat, Sun, public holidays.

The centre is open 24 hours daily for emergency cases, with overnight stays possible. No appointments are necessary if you are coming for advice.

## Emotional Counselling

### KUB (Crisis & Advice Centre)

*Apostel-Paulus-Straße 35, Schöneberg, 10823 (781 85 85). U7 Eisenacher Straße.* **Open** 6pm-midnight Mon-Thur; 10pm-8am Fri-Sun.
Free and confidential advice for people in need of emotional counselling.

### Psychiatrischer Notdienst (Emergency Psychiatric Help)

*Horstweg 2, Charlottenburg, 14059 (32 20 20). U2 Sophe-Charlotte-Platz.* **Open** 6pm-midnight Mon-Thur; 3pm-midnight Fri-Sun, public holidays.
Staff will be able to put you in touch with your local psychiatric clinic.

### Help & Advice Line

*(111 01).*
A crisis telephone line for the depressed and suicidal. The staff speak English.

## Financial & Legal Help

The local Finanzämter (tax offices – listed at the back of the Gelbe Seiten/Yellow Pages) will provide help on tax legislation, claims etc. For non-German speakers, the British Embassy (*see above* **Embassies & Consulates**) is the best bet. The Embassy also has pamphlets on working in Germany, insurance, taxation and the like.

If you run out of cash you can get money wired to you within four hours from the UK. Ask someone in the UK to contact the local branch of Western Union (central office phone number *0800 833 833*) from where money can be wired to your bank account or to any post office that has a fax.

If you get into legal difficulties and cannot afford a lawyer, contact your local Sozialamt (social services office, listed in the back of the telephone book). If you can afford a lawyer, the **British Embassy** (*see above* **Embassies & Consulates**) can provide a list of English-speaking lawyers in Berlin.

## Gay

### Schwules Überfall Telefon (Gay Crisis Telephone)

*(216 33 36).* **Open** 6-9pm daily.
This telephone service is run from the offices of **Mann-O-Meter**, Berlin's information centre for gays. *See also chapter* **Gay**.

## Racism

### Antirassistische Initiative

*Yorckstraße 59, Kreuzberg, 10965 (785 72 81). U7/S2 Yorckstraße.* **Open** 5.30-7pm Mon; 4-7pm Tue; 2.30-5.30pm Fri.
A non-profit-making organisation defending the rights of ethnic minorities.

# Women

*See also chapter* **Women**.

### Fraueninfothek
### (Women's Information Centre)
*Dircksenstraße 47, Mitte, 10178 (282 39 80). U2 Kloster Straße.* **Open** 10am-6pm Mon-Fri.
Besides organising crêches and providing career and training advice for women in Berlin, the Fraueninfothek will help you find accommodation, organise tours and generally point you in the right direction. Staff are willing to help tourists.

### Frauenkrisentelefon
*(615 42 43).* **Open** 10am-noon Mon, Thur; 7-9pm Tue, Wed, Fri; 5-7pm Sat, Sun.
A crisis line for women in need of help and advice.

### Notruf (Rape Crisis Help Line)
*(251 2828).* **Open** 6-9pm Tue, Thur; noon-2pm Sun; answering machine at other times.
Advice and help on rape and sexual harassment, as well as help dealing with police and doctors.

## Libraries

There are dozens of Bibliotheken (public libraries) and Büchereien (ditto) in Berlin. To borrow books from them, you will need your stamped Anmeldungsformular (certificate of registration, *see chapter* **Essential Information: Visas**) and your passport. There will be a small joining fee.

### Amerika-Gedenkbibliothek
*Blücherplatz 1, Kreuzberg, 10961 (690 50). U1, U6 Hallesches Tor.* **Open** 3-7pm Mon; 11am-7pm Tue-Sat.
This library has a collection of English/American literature.

### Amerika-Haus Library
*Hardenbergstraße 22-24, Charlottenburg, 16023 (31 00 01 22). U2, U9, S3, S5, S6, S7, S9 Bahnhof Zoo.* **Open** 1-5.30pm Mon, Wed, Fri; 1-8pm Tue, Thur.
To borrow books you need your police registration and your passport.

### British Council
*Hardenbergstraße 20, Charlottenburg, 10623 (31 10 99 10). U2, U9, S3, S5, S6, S7, S9 Bahnhof Zoo.* **Open** 2-6pm Mon, Wed, Fri; 2-7pm Tue, Thur.* **Membership** DM50 per year; DM10 for students or teachers.

### Staatsbibliothek
*Potsdamer Straße 33, Tiergarten, 10772 (266 22 35). U1 Kurfürstenstraße.* **Open** 9am-9pm Mon-Fri; 9am-5pm Sat.
Books in English on every subject are available at this branch of the State Library.

### Staatsbibliothek
*Unter den Linden 8, Mitte, 10102 (20 15-0). U6 Französische Straße.* **Open** 9am-9pm Mon-Fri; noon-5pm Sat.
This branch has a smaller range of English books than the above, but is still very much worth a visit. The café is a good place to get into conversation with Berliners.

## Lost or Stolen Property

If your belongings are stolen, you should go to the police station nearest to where the incident occurred (listed in the Gelbe Seiten/Yellow Pages

under Polizei), report the theft and fill in report forms for insurance purposes. If you can't speak German, the police will call in one of their interpreters at no cost.

If you've lost a credit card, phone one of the emergency numbers listed below. All lines are open 24 hours daily.
**Access/Mastercard/EC**
*(069 79 330).*
**American Express**
*(069 72 00 16).*
**Diners' Club**
*(069 260 30).*
**Visa**
*(069 79 201 333).*

### BVG Fundbüro
*Lorenzweg 5, Tempelhof, 10773 (*lost property 751 80 21; customer services 752 70 20). U6 Ullsteinstraße.*
**Open** 9am-3pm Mon, Tue, Thur; 9am-6pm Wed; 9am-2pm Fri.
Contact this office with any queries about lost property on Berlin's public transport system.

### Zentrales Fundbüro
### (Central Lost Property Office)
*Platz der Luftbrücke 6, Tempelhof, 12101 (69 90). U6 Platz der Luftbrücke.* **Open** 7.30am-4pm Mon, Tue; noon-6.30pm Wed.

## Post Offices

### Main Post Office
*Postamt 120, Charlottenburg, 10612. At Zoologischer Bahnhof, Hardenbergplatz, (313 97 99). U2, U9, S3, S5, S6, S7, S9 Zoologischer Bahnhof.* **Open** 6am-midnight Mon-Sat; 8am-midnight Sun.
If your mail is urgent, send it from here and it should get to the UK in about three to four days. Letters to the States will take about seven or eight days. Letters for poste restante should also be sent to this post office, addressed: (recipient's name) Postamt 120, 10612 Postlagernd. They can be collected from the counter marked Postlagernde Sendungen. Take your passport. **Fax and Telex** facilities are also available here, and at many modern hotels and some copyshops. Most other post offices (Post in German) are open from 8am-6pm Monday to Friday, and 8am to noon on Saturday. **Stamps** are sold at all post offices. Letters and cards can be deposited in yellow mail boxes throughout the city. For non-local mail, be sure to use the Andere Richtungen (other destinations) slot as opposed to the Berlin slot. Letters of up to 20 grams (7oz) to anywhere in Germany and the EC need DM1 in postage. Postcards require 80pfg. A 20g airmail letter anywhere else costs DM3; postcards cost DM2.

## Public Toilets & Baths

Using public toilets is not a very pleasant experience in Berlin, but recently the authorities have been trying to clean them up. Unfortunately their design (underground, near the entrance to the U-Bahn stations) means they are dark and not particularly safe. The loos in main stations are looked after by an attendant and are relatively clean. Restaurants and cafés have to let you use their toilets by law and legally they can't refuse you a glass of water – though they may get stroppy about it.

Public baths nowadays generally include swimming pools as well and will cost about DM2-DM3 entrance, usually cheaper for students by about a mark. Opening times often change weekly. *See also chapter* **Sport**.

### Stadtbad Tiergarten (Indoor Pool)
*Seydlitzstraße 7, Tiergarten, 10557 (39 05-40 13). S3, S5, S6, S9 Lehrter Stadtbahnhof.* **Open** 9am-11.15am, 2-6pm, Mon; 2-6.15pm Tue, Thur, Fri; 9am-1.45pm, 4-8.15pm, Wed; 9am-4.15pm Sat; 9am-12.15pm Sun.

### Schwimmhalle Fischerinsel
*Fischerinsel 11, Mitte, 10179 (242 54 49). U2 Märkisches Museum.* **Open** 6.30-9am Mon, Tue, Thur, Fri; 5-9pm Tue, Fri; 8am-4pm Sat; 8am-2pm Sun.

# Religion

At the time of going to press, the English-language churches, or those providing English services, had not yet fully reorganised themselves after the departure of the British and US forces, who, with their families, formerly made up most of their congregations in Berlin. For up-to-date information on English-language services, contact the British Embassy. The Verkehrsamt (Tourist Office, *see chapter* **Essential Information**) publishes an extensive list of churches, synagogues and mosques in Berlin.

### The American Church in Berlin
*Alte Dorfkirche, Zehlendorf, corner of Clayallee and Potsdamer Straße, 14169 (813 20 21). U2 Oskar-Helene-Heim, then bus 110. Mailing address: Onkel-Tom-Straße 93, 14169 Berlin.* **Services** 11am Sun. **Holy Communion** 11am first and third Sun in month. **Sunday school** 9.30am Sun.
International ecumenical congregation. All services are conducted in English.

### International Baptist Church
*Rothenburgstraße 13, Steglitz, 12165 (774 46 70). U9 Rathaus Steglitz.* **Services** noon Sun. **Sunday school** 10.45am Sun. **Prayer service** 7pm Wed. **Singles Bible study** 7pm.
All services are conducted in English.

### Catholic
*St Hedwigs-Kathedrale, Bebelplatz, Mitte, 10117 (203 48 10). U6 Hausvogteiplatz.* **Services** 8am, 10am, 11.30am, 6pm Sun; 7am, 6pm weekdays; 7pm Sat.
Services in German. In Latin first Sunday of the month.

### Islamic
*Die Moschee-Islamische Gemeinde (Moshee Islamic Community), Brienner Straße 7-8, Wilmersdorf (87 57 03). U2 Fehrbelliner Platz.* **Friday service** 1.30pm.
Services are conducted in English (prayers in Arabic). All religions welcome.

### Jewish
**Central Information Office**, *Fasanenstraße 75-80, Charlottenburg, 10623 (88 42 03 30). U2, U9, S3, S5, S6, S7, S9 Zoologischer Garten.* **Open** 8am-3pm Mon-Thur; 8am-1pm Fri.
The Information Office issues a monthly calendar of events listed on an information sheet and advertised every month in *Zitty* and *Tip*.

# Telephones

While it has been tricky obtaining phone lines in the east, and sometimes phoning between east and west, modernisation of the eastern phone system is due to be completed in 1995. The eastern phone network will then reputedly be more advanced than that in the west.

### Phone Boxes
Phone boxes in the east are slowly improving. Your best bet is to try the post office, where there'll be both coin- and card-operated phones. Phonecards can be bought there for DM12 or DM50; you will save time if you have one as, particularly in the west, practically all phone boxes are card only. (You can sometimes find a coin-operated phone in a bar or café, though.) The minimum fee for a call from a phone box within Berlin is 30 pfennigs for six minutes, between 8am and 6pm on weekdays, and 30 pfennigs for 12 minutes, between 6pm and 8am and at weekends. If you're here for a while, the DM50 card works out cheaper in the long run by 5 pfennigs per call. Look for phone boxes marked *international* and with a ringing-bell symbol – you can be called back on them. The post office at Zoo Station (*see above* **Post Offices**) is your centre for telecommunications. Here you can send telexes, faxes and use the metered pay phones.

### Dialling Codes
If you have any difficulty with codes, ring directory enquiries (*see below* **Operator Services**). Dialling within Berlin, no code is necessary.

### International Calls
To phone Berlin from abroad, dial the international code (in the UK it's 010) then 49 30. To phone out of Germany dial

*To call the police in an emergency, dial 110.*

00, then the appropriate country code: **Australia** 61; **Canada** 1; **Ireland** 353; **New Zealand** 64; **United Kingdom** 44; **United States** 1. For calls to the UK and Ireland, **International charges** start at DM0.92 per minute from 6pm to 8am Monday to Friday and at weekends, rising to DM1.15 per minute during the day. Calls to the US and Canada cost DM2.07 per minute and to Australia DM3.22 per minute at all times.

## Phone Books

Phone books for public use are found in all post offices. The Telefonbuch (which runs to three volumes) lists names of people and businesses alphabetically. The Gelbe Seiten (Yellow Pages, two volumes) lists businesses under category headings. The initial pages of the first volume give international dialling codes, telephone services and a useful list of services (such as administrative offices, social and recreational services).

## Operator Services

All these services are open 24 hours daily.
**Operator assistance/***Telefonauskunft*, German directory enquiries *(011 88)*.
**International directory enquiries** *(001 18)*.
**Alarm calls/***Weckruf (011 41)*.
**Engineers/***Störungsannahme*, for phone repairs *(11 70)*.
**Financial markets/***Börsenachrichten (*national *011 68;* international *0116 08)*.
**Telegram/***Telegrammaufnahme (0 11 31)*.
**Theatre and concert booking/***Theater- und Konzertveranstaltungen (0 11 56)*.
**Time/***Zeitansage (0 11 91)*.
**Traffic news/***Straßenzustandberichte (0 11 69)*.
**Travel advice/***Fahrplanhinweise (*national and international *(19419)*.
**Weather/***Wettervorhersage (011 64)*.

## Transport

For car hire firms look under Autovermietung in the Gelbe Seiten (Yellow Pages) and be sure to shop around. Look in the back of the listing magazines *Tip* and *Zitty* (*see chapter* **Media**) under Reisen for a list of companies offering bargains in air and coach travel. The following reputable agents have some good deals. *See also chapter* **Trips Out Of Town**.

## Air Travel

### Express Travel

*Giesebrechtstraße 18, Charlottenburg, 10629 (324 94 20)*. *U7 Adenauerplatz*. **No credit cards**.
Extremely helpful English-speaking staff search out best deals on Berlin-UK flights.

### Minar

*Bülowstraße 30, Schöneberg, 10783 (216 39 23, 215 12 81; fax 215 61 21)*. *U2 Bülowstraße*. **No credit cards**.
Aside from its cheap worldwide flights, Indian-run Minar is a nice place. Free cups of tea while you wait.

## Coach Travel

### Alternativ Bus Reisen

*Zossener Straße 7, Kreuzberg, 10961 (69 50 00 00)*. *U7 Gneisenaustraße*. **Open** 11am-6.30pm Mon-Fri. **No credit cards**.
Tickets to destinations throughout Europe can be arranged

by this bus travel company, which specialises in competitively priced holidays for young people.

### Gulliver's

*Eberstraße 70, Schöneberg, 10827 (78 10 21)*. *U4 Innsbrucker Platz*. **Open** 9am-6pm Mon-Fri; 9am-1pm Sat. **Credit** MC, V.
Gulliver's runs cheap one-way and return trips to major cities throughout Europe.

## Hitch-Hiking

Germany, unlike many other countries in Europe, is hitch-hiker-friendly, although you should still follow the obvious rules of safety: avoid hitching alone, don't get in the back of a two-door car, and so on. Even in a city as large as Berlin it is not unusual to see people hitching their way up the street. Outside Berlin, hitching will be more difficult as the former citizens of East Germany are much less accustomed to it. On major routes out of the city heading westwards, you should have no trouble getting a ride, though. *See chapter* **Trips Out Of Town**.

Mitfahrzentrale are companies that match car drivers to prospective travellers for a small fee. This is a safe and cheap method of travel; the companies listed below are the most popular.

### Mitfahrzentrale am Alex

*Alexanderplatz U-Bahn, in the hall between lines 8 and 2, Mitte, 10178 (24 15 82 0)*. *S3, S5, S6, S9/U2, U8 Alexanderplatz*. **Open** 8am-8pm Mon-Fri; 8am-6pm Sat; 10am-6pm Sun, public holidays.

### Mitfahrzentrale am Zoo

*Zoo Station U-Bahn, platform of line 2 (Vinetastraße), Zoologischer Garten, Hardenbergplatz, Charlottenburg, 10623 (297 613 41)*. *U2, U9, S3, S5, S6, S7, S9 Zoologischer Garten*. **Open** 8am-8pm daily.

## Parking

Parking is free in the side streets of Berlin, but spaces are hard to find. If you park illegally (pedestrian crossing, loading zone, bus lane and so on), you risk getting your car clamped or towed away. There are no meters.

If you've travelled to Berlin by car, it might be a good idea to park on the outskirts of the city and then use public transport, which is very efficient (*see chapter* **Getting Around**).

Long-term car parks are located at Schönefeld and Tegel airports (*see below*). Otherwise there are numerous Parkgaragen and Parkhäuser (multistorey and underground car parks) around the city. They're open 24 hours and will charge about DM3 an hour.

### Schönefeld Airport Car Park

*(60 91 55 82)*. **Cost** *one day* DM15; *one week* DM39; *two weeks* DM140. **Credit** EC, Avis.

### Tegel Airport Car Park

*(41 01 33 77)*. **Cost** *one day* DM15-DM18; *more than seven days* DM189-DM390 per week. **No credit cards**.

## 24-Hour Petrol

Most 24-hour stations have shops selling rudimentary groceries, chocolates and cigarettes.
**BP** *Kurfürstendamm 128, Wilmersdorf, 10711.*
**BP** *Dudenstraße 9, Kreuzberg, 10965.*
**BP** *Yorckstraße 38, Schöneberg, 10965.*
**Esso** *Tempelhofer Damm 20, Tempelhof, 12101.*

## Car Breakdown

The following garages offer 24-hour assistance. As with most German businesses, they are credit-card shy. The minimum call-out charge will be about DM100.

### Eichmanns Autodienst
*Rothenbachstraße 55, Weissensee, 13085 (471 05 70).*

### Abschleppdienst Kunze
*Wolburgsweg 39, Spandau, 13589 (373 51 22).*

## Travellers With Disabilities

Only some U- and S-Bahn stations in the west have wheelchair facilities; the full map of the city (the **Liniennetzplan**) indicates which ones. There are even fewer in the east, but work is proceeding rapidly and has given the authorities the impetus to improve facilities in the west as well. You may prefer to take advantage of the **Telebus**, a bus service for disabled people.

The **Verkehrsamt** (tourist information office, *see chapter* **Essential Information**) can give details on which of the city's hotels have disabled access, but if you require more specific information, try the **Berliner Behindertenverband** or the **Touristik Union International**.

### Berliner Behindertenverband (Berlin's Centre for the Disabled)
*Märkisches Ufer 28, Mitte, 10179 (274 14 46).* U2 *Märkisches Museum.* **Open** 8am-6pm Mon-Fri.
Information, legal and social advice, together with a transport service and travel information, are provided by the Centre.

### Blisse 14 Sozial Therapeutisches Zentrum und Café
*Blissestraße 14, Wilmersdorf, 10713 (821 10 91, fax 821 56 73).* U7 *Blissestraße.* **Open** noon to 11pm Mon-Fri; 10am-5pm Sun. **Closed** Sat. **Office** 9am-1pm Mon-Fri.
The café-bar at this social therapy centre, designed for disabled people, is popular with a mixed clientèle.

### Gästehaus der Fürst-Donnersmarck-Stiftung
*Wildkanzelweg 28, Frohnau, 13465 (40 69 0).* S1 *Frohnau.* Call for prices.
This is Berlin's only hostel that has been specially adapted for disabled people.

### Telebus-Zentrale
*Esplanade 17, Pankow, 13187 (478 820).* U2 *Vinetastraße.* **Open** (office hours) 9am-3pm Mon-Fri.
The Telebus is available to tourists if they contact this organisation in advance. A pass has to be issued for each user, so give plenty of notice. *See also chapter* **Getting Around**.

### Touristik Union International (TUI)
*Postfach 610280, 30602 Hannover (0511 56 70).* **Open** 9am-6pm Mon-Fri. Call or write for appointment.
The TUI provides information on accommodation and travel throughout Germany for disabled people.

## Working in Berlin

Berlin remains one of the most liberal and open cities in Germany and offers a wealth of opportunity for people wanting to stay and work. However, the price of accommodation is soaring and even German economic growth is slowing.

The small ads of the magazines *Zitty*, *Tip* and *Zweite Hand* (*see chapter* **Media**) are good places to start the search for work, but jobs are filled quickly, so move fast. Teaching English is a popular choice: there is always a demand for native English speakers. Look for adverts around the city.

If you're a student studying in Berlin, try the **Studentische Arbeitsvermittlung** (student job service). You'll need your passport, student card and a Lohnsteuerkarte (tax card), available from your local Finanzamt (tax office – listed in the Gelbe Seiten/Yellow Pages under Finanzämter). Your tax is reclaimable: get details from the tax office. Students looking for summer work lasting between two and four months can contact the **Zentralstelle für Arbeitsvermittlung**.

The British/German Chamber of Commerce publishes a list of English companies who have associates in Germany. There's a copy in the commercial department of the **British Embassy** (*see above* **Embassies & Consulates**).

The German equivalent of the Job Centre is the Arbeitsamt (employment service). There are very few private agencies. In effect, this makes looking for a job less hassle, as you only have one office to deal with. To find the address of your nearest office in Germany, look in the Gelbe Seiten (Yellow Pages) under Arbeitsämter.

EC nationals have the right to live and work in Germany without a work permit. UK nationals working in Germany have the same rights as German nationals with regard to pay, working conditions, access to housing, vocational training, social security and trade union membership. Families and immediate dependants are entitled to join them and have similar rights. For information about registration in Germany and residence permits *see chapter* **Essential Information: Visas**.

### Studentische Arbeitsvermittlung (TUZMA)
*Wilhelmstraße 64, Mitte, 10117 (308 546).* U2 *Mohrenstraße.* **Open** 8am-6pm Mon-Fri.

### Zentralstelle für Arbeitsvermittlung (ZAV)
*Feuerbachstraße 42-46, 60325 Frankfurt am Main (069 711 12 75).* **Open** 9am-noon Mon-Fri; 4-6pm Thur.

# Further Reading

We've chosen these books for quality and interest as much as for availability. Most are currently in print, but some will only be found in libraries or second-hand shops. The date given is that of the first publication in English.

## Fiction

**Deighton, Len**: *Berlin Game, Mexico Set, London Match* (London 1983, 1984, 1985)
Epic espionage trilogy with labyrinthine plot set against an accurate picture of eighties Berlin.
**Deighton, Len**: *Funeral In Berlin* (London 1964)
Perhaps the best of Deighton's sixties novels.
**Döblin, Alfred**: *Berlin-Alexanderplatz* (London 1975)
Devastating Expressionist portrait of the inter-war underworld in working class quarters of Alexanderplatz.
**Eckhart, Gabriele**: *Hitchhiking* (Lincoln, Nebraska 1992)
Short, evocative stories viewing East Berlin through the eyes of street cleaners and a female construction worker.
**Grass, Gunther**: *Local Anaesthetic* (New York 1970)
The Berlin angst of a schoolboy who threatens to burn a dog outside a Ku'damm café to protest the Vietnam War is firmly satirised, albeit in Grass's irritating schoolmasterly way.
**Harris, Robert**: *Fatherland* (London 1992)
Alternative history and detective novel set in a 1964 Berlin as the Nazis might have built it, had they won the War.
**Isherwood, Christopher**: *Mr Norris Changes Trains, Goodbye To Berlin* (London 1935, 1939)
Isherwood's two Berlin novels, the basis of the movie *Cabaret*, offer finely drawn characters and a sharp picture of the decadent city as it tipped over into Nazism.
**Johnson, Uwe**: *Two Views* (New York 1966)
Love story across the great East-West divide, strong on the mood of Berlin in the late fifties and early sixties.
**Kerr, Philip**: *March Violets* (London 1989)
Bernie Gunther is a private detective in a tension-filled Nazi Berlin. Two further novels follow the character's fortunes.
**Le Carré, John**: *The Spy Who Came In From The Cold* (London 1963)
The primal shot-going-over-the-Wall thriller.
**Markstein, George**: *Ultimate Issue* (London 1981)
Stark novel of political expediency that leads to an uncomfortably likely conclusion about why the Wall went up.
**McEwan, Ian**: *The Innocent* (London 1990)
Fascinating tale of naive young Englishman recruited into Cold War machinations with tragi-comic results.
**Müller, Heiner**: *The Battle* (New York 1989)
By the East Berlin playwright and successor to Brecht at the Berliner Ensemble, a collection of plays and pieces strong on the grimness of the Stalinist fifties, failing utopias and the false temptations broadcast from the West.
**Nabokov, Vladimir**: *The Gift* (New York 1963)
Written and set in twenties Berlin, where an impoverished Russian émigré dreams of writing a book very like this one.
**Royle, Nicholas**: *Counterparts* (London 1993)
Bizarre tale of Doppelgängers, split personalities and tightrope-walkers, set against the fall of the Wall.
**Schneider, Peter**: *The Wall Jumper* (London 1984)
Somewhere between novel, prose poem and artful reportage, a meditation on the madhouse absurdities of the Wall.

## Children

**Kästner, Erich**: *Emil And The Detectives* (London 1931)
The classic children's story is set mostly around Berlin's Zoo Station and Nollendorfplatz.

## Biography & Memoir

**Baumann, Bommi**: *How It All Began* (Vancouver, 1977)
Frank and often funny account of the Berlin origins of West German terrorism, by a former member of the June 2nd Movement.
**Benjamin, Walter**: *One Way Street And Other Writings* (New York 1978)

First published in the late twenties, the title piece is a collage of reflection and analyses triggered by city signs and graffiti. Also contains his Berliner Childhood memoir.
**Bielenberg, Christabel**: *The Past Is Myself* (London 1968)
Fascinating autobiography of an English woman who married a German lawyer and lived through the War in Berlin.
**F, Christiane**: *H – Autobiography Of A Child Prostitute And Heroin Addict* (London 1980)
Stark account of life in the housing estates and on the heroin scene of seventies West Berlin. Later filmed as *Christiane F.*
**Friedrich, Ruth Andreas**: *The Berlin Underground 1938-45* (New York 1947)
A few courageous souls formed anti-Nazi resistance groups in Berlin. The journalist-author's diaries capture the day-to-day fear of the knock on the door in the night.
**Millar, Peter**: *Tomorrow Belongs To Me* (London 1992)
Memoir of a Prenzlauer Berg local pub by a former East Berlin Reuter's correspondent.
**Rimmer, Dave**: *Once Upon A Time In The East* (London 1992)
The collapse of communism from ground level – strange and hilarious tales of games between East and West Berlin and travels through assorted East European revolutions.
**Schirer, William L**: *Berlin Diaries* (New York 1941)
A foreign correspondent in Berlin from 1931-1941 bears appalled witness to Europe's plunge into Armageddon.

## History

**Farr, Michael**: *Berlin! Berlin!* (London 1992)
Lightweight history, concentrating on cultural life and colourful characters.
**Garton Ash, Timothy**: *We The People* (London 1990)
Instant history of the 1989 revolutions, as witnessed in Warsaw, Prague, Budapest and Berlin.
**Gelb, Norman**: *The Berlin Wall* (New York 1986)
Gripping narrative history of how the Wall went up.
**McElvoy, Anne**: *The Saddled Cow* (London 1992)
Lively history of East Germany by a former Berlin *Times* correspondent.
**Masur, Gerhard**: *Imperial Berlin* (London 1971)
Berlin in the days of the Kaiser, from the proclamation of empire in 1871 to the end of World War I.
**Read, Anthony and Fisher, David**: *Berlin – The Biography Of A City* (London 1994)
Probably the best single-volume history of Berlin.
**Schirer, William L**: *The Rise And Fall Of The Third Reich* (New York 1960)
Still the most readable history of Nazi Germany.
**Tusa, Ann & John**: *The Berlin Blockade* (London 1988)
Absorbing account of the 11 months when the Allied sector was fed from the air and not just Berlin, but Germany and Europe also, proceeded to fall into two.

## Architecture

*Berlin-Brandenburg – An Architectural Guide* (Berlin 1993)
Berlin by building, with quirky text in both English and German.

## Miscellaneous

**Alacevich, Francesco & Alessandro**: *The Lost Graffiti Of Berlin* (Rome 1991)
Full-colour photos of graffiti paintings that once covered the Wall. Introductory text in English.
**Bertsch, Georg C & Hedler, Ernst**: *SED* (Cologne 1990)
Over 200 illustrations of the kind of crazy East German consumer product design that has now completely disappeared from the shops. Text in German, French and English.
**Friedrich, Thomas**: *Berlin – A Photographic Portrait Of The Weimar Years 1918-1933* (London 1991)
Superb photographs of lost Berlin, its personalities and its daily life, with a foreword by Stephen Spender.
*Semiotext(e) 11 – The German Issue* (New York 1982)
A special issue of the philosophical periodical, packed with absorbing interviews, focusing on the Wall and division.

# Area Index

*See chapter* **Berlin by Area** for maps and information on each area.

## Charlottenburg

**ACCOMMODATION:** Hotel Palace, p16; Berlin Plaza Hotel, p19; Hotel Bremen, p19; Hotel Consul, p19; Curator Hotel, p19; Hecker's Hotel, p19; Alpenland Hotel, p20; Hotel Bogota, p20; Hotel California, p20; Hotel Pension Castell, p20; Hotel Charlot am Kurfürstendamm, p20; Hotel Clausewitz, p20; Hotel-Pension Elba, p20; Hotel-Pension Funk, p20; Hotel-Pension Großmann, p21; Pension Kettler, p21; Hotel Heidelberg, p21; Pension Silvia, p21; Pension Viola Nova, p21; Hotel-Pension Waizenegger, p21; Hotel Westerland, p22; Hotel-Pension am Lehniner Platz, p22; Hotel-Pension Bialas, p22; Hotel-Pension Charlottenburg, p23; Hotel-Pension Elfert, p23; Hotel-Pension Imperator, p23; Pension-City Galerie, p23; Jugendgästehaus am Zoo, p25; Arco, p220.

**CAFES & BARS:** Aschinger, p116; Café Aedes, p117; Café Bleibtreu, p117; Café Hardenberg, p117; Café Konditerei Richter, p117; Café Kranzler, p117; Café Möhring, p117; Café Savigny, p117; Dicker Wirt, p117; Diener, p117; Dollinger, p117; Dralle's, p117; Gasthaus Lentz, p117; Klo, p117; Ku'dorf, p117; Leysieffer, p118; Rosalinde, p118; Rost, p118; Schwarzes Café, p118; Wintergarten im Literaturhaus, p118; Zillemarkt, p118; Zwiebelfisch, p118; Café Savigny, p221; Coxx Café, p221; Café Campus, p228.

**MUSEUMS:** Ägyptisches Museum, p163; Antiken Museum (Museum of Greek and Roman Antiquities), p163; Museum für Vor und Frühgeschichte (Primeval and Early History Museum), p164; Schloß Charlottenburg, p164.

**RESTAURANTS:** Bovril, p102; Don Camillo, p102; Florian, p102; Lubitsch, p102; Lutter & Wegner, p102; Paris Bar, p104; Shell, p104; Toto, p104; Astir's, p105; Ax Bax, p105; Carpe Diem, p105; Hard Rock Café, p105; Hardtke, p105; Heinrich, p105; Hitit, p105; Istanbul, p106; Kien-du, p106; Kyoto, p106; Marjellchen, p106; Meyhane, p106; Petit Chinois, p106; XII Apostoli, p111; Angkor, p111; Athener Grill, p111; Café Hardenberg, p112; La Culinaria, p112; Luisen-Bräu Brauerei, p112; Mahachai, p112; Ashoka, p114; Joseph Lange, p115; Vietnam Imbiß, p115; Mövenpick, p217.

**SHOPPING:** *fashion* Biscuit, p127; Blue Moon, p127; Bramigk Design, p127; Brown's, p127; Durchbruchp 127; Ermenegildo Zegna, p128; Evento, p128; Max Mara, p128; Ozone, p128; Patrick Hellmann Pour Elle, p128; Patrick Hellmann Sport, p128; Ralf Setzer Fashion for Women, p128; Seven Ups, p129; Skoda Attendance, p129; Toni Gard, p129; Windsurfing Chiemsee and Friends, p129; Esprit, p140; Hallhuber, p140; H & M (Hennes und Mauritz), p140; Kookai, p140; Mey & Edlich, p140; *vintage/second hand clothes* Spitze, p129; *shoes* Birkenstock Shop, p129; Bleibgrün, p131; Bree, p131; Brilliant, p131; Budapester Schuhe, p131; Chapeau Claudette!, p131; Kaufhaus Schrill, p131; Rio, p131; Mandarina Duck, p131; Zoé, p131; Birotic, biank – brillant, p226; *handmade jewellery* Feinschmiede, p131; Treykon Schmuckwerkstatt, p132; *antiques* Flea Market on Straße des 17 Juni, p132; Zille Hof, p132; Klaus Rachner Raumausstattung, p132; Salon Art Deco, p132; Schöne Alte Spitzen, p133; Ubu, p133; Wolfgang Haas, p133; *books* Bücherbogen am Savigny Platz, p133; Kiepert, p133; Kohlhaas & Co, p133; Marga Schoeller Bücherstube, p133; The (Original Version), p133; One World Books, p133; Antiquariat Kiepert, p135; Antiquariat Senzel, p135; Das Arabische Buch, p135; Düwal, p135; Kiepert, p227; Lilith, p231; Marga Schoeller Bücherstube, p231; *children* Berliner Zinnfiguren Kabinet, p135; Heidi's Spielzeugladen, p135; Klein-Holz, p135; Modellautos, p135; Tam-Tam, p136; Übermuth, p136; Prenatal, p215; *cosmetics* Condomi, p136; Friseur Bedarf von Malachinski, p136; Harry Lehmann, p136; Mekkanische Rose, p137; Rosewater's, p137; *design/household* Antik und Kerzen, p137; Depot, p137; Galerie Extra, p137; Genious-Group, p137; Magazin, p137; Seidlein & Seidlein, p137; Wohnart, p137; *glass/ceramics* Galerie Glaswerk, p138; Glasklar Glaeser, p138; Galerei Theis, p138; *food* Brotgarten, p138; Fuchs Rabe, p138; Leysieffer, p139; Mekong, p139; Salumeria, p139; The Old Empire, p139; *CDs/records* Canzone Importschallplatten, p139; Delirium, p139; FNAC, p141; *stationery* Art Store, p141; Washi, p141; *supermarkets* Bolle, p141; *department stores* Hertie, p141; Karstadt, p141; Wertheim, p141; Woolworth, p141.

**SIGHTSEEING:** Bahnhof Zoo/Zoo Station, p32; The Kurfürstendammp 32; Savignyplatz, p34; Charlottenburg Museums, p37; Europa-Center, p37; Funkturm, p39; Gedenkstätte Plötzensee (Plötzensee Memorial), p40; Kaiser-Wilhelm-Gedächtniskirche (Kaiser-Wilhelm-Memorial-Church), p40; Olympiastadion (Olympic Stadium), p42; Schloß Charlottenburg, p44.

## Kreuzberg

**ACCOMMODATION:** Hotel Riehmers Hofgarten, p19; Hotel Transit, p23; Pension Kreuzberg, p23; Jugend Zentrale, p25.

**CAFES & BARS:** Anton, p118; Bar, p118; Bierhimmel, p118; Café Altenberg, p118; Café Bar Morena, p119; Café Übersee, p119; Elefant, p119; Der Goldene Hahn, p119; Henne Alt-Berliner Wirtshaus, p119; Madonna, p119; Maureen Bar, p119; Max und Moritz, p119; Milchbar, p119; Mini Café, p119; Morgenland, p119; Die Rote Harfe, p119; Schnabelbar, p119; Wiener Blut, p119; Arcanoa, p119; Café Adler, p119; Café Anfall, p119; Café Atlantic, p119; Café Milagro, p120; Café Mistral, p120; Café Mora, p120; Café Rampenlicht, p120; Café Turandot, p120; Ex, p120; Golgotha, p120; Kookaburra, p120; Malheur, p120; Niagara, p120;

Yorckschlößchen, p120; Drama, p221; Mister X, p222; Schoko-Café, p231.

**MUSEUMS:** Martin-Gropius-Bau, p164; Museum Haus am Checkpoint Charlie, p164; Museum für Verkehr und Technik (Museum of Transport and Technology), p164, p215; Topographie des Terrors, p164.

**RESTAURANTS:** Abendmahl, p101; Altes Zollhaus, p101; Franzotti, p102; Café Addis, p105; Café Restaurant Jolesch, p105; Merhaba, p106; Osteria No 1, p108; Primo, p108; Publique, p108; Ristorante Chamisso, p108; Thürnagel, p109; Trattoria da Enzo, p109; Tres Kilos, p109; Ambrosius, p111; Chandra Kumari, p112; Großbeerenkeller, p112; Noodle Company, p113; Weltrestaurant Markthalle, p113; Kulinarische Delikatessen, p114; Pagoda, p115.

**SHOPPING:** *fashion* New Noise/Scenario, p128; Colours, Kaufrausch, p129; Checkpoint, p129; *handmade jewellery* Schmuckgalerie Fritz & Fillmann, p131; *antiques* Knopf Paul, p132; *books* Bücherbogen, p133; Fair Exchange, p135; Grober

Unfug, p135; *design & household goods* Galerie Weinand, p137; Katakomben, p137; Ceramica Atelier, p138; *records* Hardwax, p141; Logo, p141
**SIGHTSEEING:** The Kreuzberg, p42.

## Mitte

**ACCOMMODATION:** Berlin Hilton, p16; Maritim Grand Hotel Berlin, p16; Hotel Metropol, p17; Radisson Plaza Hotel, p17; Berliner Congress Center, p19; Berlin Hilton Krone, p19; Hotel Luisenhof, p20; Hotel Unter den Linden, p20; Hotel Berolina, p22; Hotel Fischer Insel, p22; Hotel Märkischer Hof, p22; Spreehotel, p22; Le Moustache, p221.

**CAFES & BARS:** Bärenschänke, p121; Boudoir, p121; Café Beth, p121; Café Silberstein, p121; Hackbarths, p121; Ici, p121; Öbst & Gemüse, p121; Opern Café, p121; Oscar Wilde, p121; Tacheles, p121; Village Voice, p121; VEB OZ, p121; Valentinop 222; Le Moustache, p222; Café Seidenfaden, p225; Assel, p228; Der UNIverselle Club, p228; Hauptmensa and

Säulemensa, p228; Technische Universität: Mensa TU, p228.

**MUSEUMS:** Brecht-Haus, p162; Deutsches Historisches Museum, p162; Museum für Naturkunde (Museum of Natural History), p163; Postmuseum, p163; Zille Museum, p163.

**RESTAURANTS:** Französischer Hof, p102; La Riva, p102; Opern Palais, p102; Café Oren, p105; Ginetun, p105; Kellerrestaurant im Brecht Haus, p106; Reinhard's, p108; Skales, p109; TGI Friday's, p109, p217; Turmstuben, p109; Zur Nolle, p111; Brazil, p111; Café Clara, p111; Café Orange, p112; Freßco, p114; McKebap City, p115.

**SHOPPING:** *fashion* Karl Faktor, p128; Lisa D, p128; Nix, p128; Fiona Bennett, p131; *antiques* Berliner Antik & Flohmarkt, p132; *books* The British Bookshop, p133; Akademische Buchhandlung am Gendarmenmarkt, p227; *food* Kolbo, p139; *department stores* Kaufhof, p141.

**SIGHTSEEING:** Alexanderplatz, p31; Gendarmenmarkt, p32; Oranienburger Straße, p32;

Museumsinsel (Museum Island), p32; Unter den Linden, p34; Berliner Dom (Berlin Cathedral), p34; Berliner Rathaus (Berlin Town Hall), p34; Brandenburger Tor (Brandenburg Gate), p37; Checkpoint Charlie, p37; Fernsehturm (TV Tower), p37; Friedrichswerdersche Kirche, p37; Karl-Marx-Allee, p40; Marx-Engels Platz, p42; The New Synagogue, p42; Nikolaiviertel, p42; Palast der Republik (Palace of the Republic), p42; Stadtmauer (City Wall), p46.

## Prenzlauer Berg

**CAFES & BARS**: Bibo Ergo Sum, p121; Bla-Bla, p121; Café Anita Wronski, p122; Café November, p122; Café Westphal, p122; Galerie-Café Eisenwerk, p122; Kommandatur, p122; Krähe, p122; Lampion, p122; Metzer-Eck, p122; Tantalus, p122; Seife und Kosmetik, p122; Titanic, p122; Torpedo Käfer, p122; Zum Burgfrieden, p221; Café Ecke Schönhauser (Café Peking), p221; Schall und Rauch, p222; Stiller Don, p222; Whistle Stop Cafe, p225.

**MUSEUMS**: Friseurmuseum (Hairdressing Museum), p162; Museum Berliner Arbeiterleben (Museum of Berlin Working-Class Life), p162.

**RESTAURANTS**: Offenbach-Stuben, p106; Restauration 1900, p108; Santiago, p108; Altberliner Bierstuben, p111; Dodge, p112; Pasternak, p113; Konnopke's Imbiß, p114; Mr Hot Dog, p115; Offenbach Stuben, p221.

**SHOPPING**: *books* Antiquariat, p135.

## Schöneberg

**ACCOMMODATION**: Hotel Berliner Hof, p19; Jugendgästehaus, p25; Deutscher Camping Club, p25; Alexanderplatz, p31; Club 70 Pension, p220; Tom's House, p221; Studentenhotel, p227.

**CAFES & BARS**: Belmundo, p122; Café Berio, p122; Café Kleisther, p122; Café M, p123; Ex 'n' Pop, p123; Fischlabor, p123; Mutter, p123; Pinguin Club, p123; Screwy Club, p123; Strüdel, p123; Turbine Rosenheim, p123; Zoulou Bar, p124; Anderes Ufer, p221; Andreas Kneipe, p221; Café PositHIV, p221; Connection Café & Bistro, p221; Hafen, p222; Hudson American Bar, p222; Tom's Bar, p222; Knast, p222; New Action, p222; Spike Connection, p223; Golden Girls, p225; Begine, p231; Dinelo, p231.

**MUSEUMS**: Postmuseum Berlin, p165.

**RESTAURANTS**: Bamberger Reiter, p101; Dschungel, p102; Hakuin, p102; Sabu, p104; Café

Aroma, p105; Candela, p105; India Haus, p106; Storch, p109; Tandoory, p109; Tuk Tuk, p109; Wohlbold, p111; Petite Europe, p113; Habibi, p114; Le Bistrot, p221.

**SHOPPING**: *fashion* Biscuit, p127; Mike's Laden, p128; Schwarze Mode, p129; Wicked Garden, p129; Marc & Bengels, p131; Zapato, p131; *antiques* Das Alte Bureau, p132; Jukeland, p132; *books* Dharma Buchladen, p133; Wiens Laden & Verlag, p133; Schropp, p135; *children* Michas Bahnhof, p135; Ria's Kinderstube, p136; Vom Winde Verweht, p136; *cosmetics & healthcare* Calla, p136; *design & household goods* Fingers, p137; Firlefanz, p137; Lichthaus Mösch, p137; *food* KaDeWe (Kaufhaus des Westens), p138; Winterfeldt Market, p139; *records* Mr Dead and Mrs Free, p141; *stationery* Papeterie, p141; *supermarkets* Aldi, p141; Kaiser's, p141; Penny Markt, p141; Plus, p141; Reichelt, p141; *Department Stores* KaDeWe, p141.

**SIGHTSEEING**: Kaufhaus des Westens (KaDeWe)p 40.

## Tiergarten

**ACCOMMODATION**: Grand Hotel Esplanade, p16; Hotel Inter-Continental, p16; Hotel Schweizerhof Berlin, p16.

**CAFES & BARS**: Bar am Lützowplatz, p124; Café Einstein, p124; Caracas, p124; Harry's New York Bar, p124; Kumpelnest 3000, p124.

**MUSEUMS**: Kunstgewerbe (Museum of Applied Art), p164; Musikinstrumenten Museum, p164; Neue Nationalgalerie, p164.

**RESTAURANTS**: Café Einstein, p102; Paris Moskau, p104; Café Nola, p112; Tiergarten Quelle, p113; Spätzle, p115; Die Tofuerei, p115.

**SHOPPING**: *fashion* Garage, p129; Made in Berlin, p129; *antiques* Bücherbogen der Nationalgalerie, p133; *design & household goods* KPM (Königliche Porzellan Manufaktur), p137.

**SIGHTSEEING**: Gedenkstätte Deutscher Widerstand (Memorial of the German Resistance), p39; Haus der Kulturen der Welt, p40; Philharmonie, p44; Reichstag, p44; Shell House, p45; Siegessäule, p45; Sowjetisches Ehrenmal im Tiergarten (Soviet War Memorial), p46; Tiergarten, p46; Zoologischer Garten (Zoo), p46, p215.

## Wedding

**ACCOMMODATION**: Jugendberge Ernst Reuter, p25; artemisia, p230.

**MUSEUMS**: Zucker Museum, p165.

**SHOPPING**: *antiques* Flea Market Am Humboldthain, p132.

## Wilmersdorf

**ACCOMMODATION**: Hotel Alexander, p17; Hotel Pension München, p23; Hotel-Pension Trautenau, p23; Pension Finck, p23; Studentenhotel Hubertusalle, p23.

**CAFES & BARS**: Berlin Bar, p124; Café Kronenbourg, p124; Galerie Bremer, p124; Zur Weißen Maus, p124; Kleine Philharmonie (Bei Wanda), p222; Extra Dry Café und Treff für Frauen, p231.

**MUSEUMS**: Käthe-Kollwitz-Museum, p165.

**RESTAURANTS**: Biberbau, p101; Diekmann, p102; Restaurant am Fasanenplatz, p104; Mesa, p106; Thai Palace, p109; Jimmy's Diner, p112; Marché, p112; Restaurant Jagdhütte, p113; Tegernseer Tönnchen, p113; Ku'damm 195, p114; Kwang-Ju-Grill, p115; Sushi, p115; Regenbogenfrühstück, BAH, p221; Restaurant am Grunewaldturm, p217; Churrasco, p217; Hard Rock Cafe, p217; Maredo, p217; Pizza Hut, p217.

**SHOPPING**: *fashion* Anna von Griesheim, p127; Falbala, p129; Les Dessous, p131; Escada, p140; Harvey's, p140; Jil Sander, p140; Kramberg, p140; Ralf Setzer Men's, p140; Gianni Versace, p140; Yves St Laurent, p140; *antiques* Flea Market on Fehrbelliner Platz, p132; Kontor für Antike Öfen, p132; *children* Spiele Shop, p136; Spiel Vogel, p136; Drospa, p214; *florist* Eberhard Bohnstedt, p138; *records* Gelbe Musik, p141.

**SIGHTSEEING**: The Kurfürstendamm, p32.

# Index

# Berlin Guide
## Advertiser's Index

Please refer to the relevant sections for addresses/telephone numbers

# TimeOut Maps

From Classic Movie Stars to your
Favourite Looney Tunes Characters:
Discover Berlin's Newest Shopping Experience!

# WARNER BROS. STUDIO STORE
## TAUENTZIENSTRASSE 9 • EUROPA CENTER • BERLIN

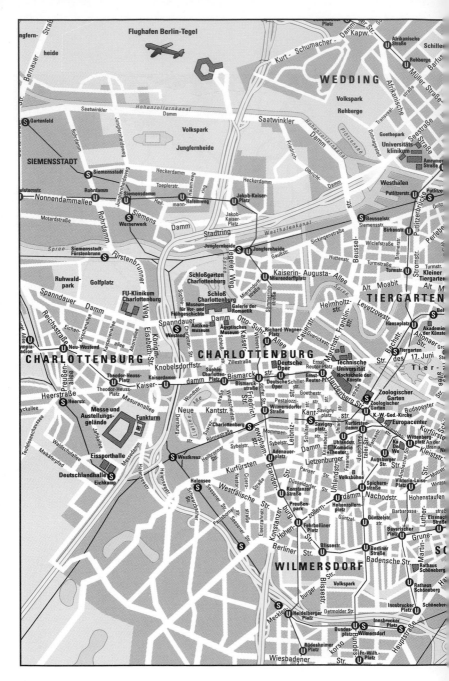

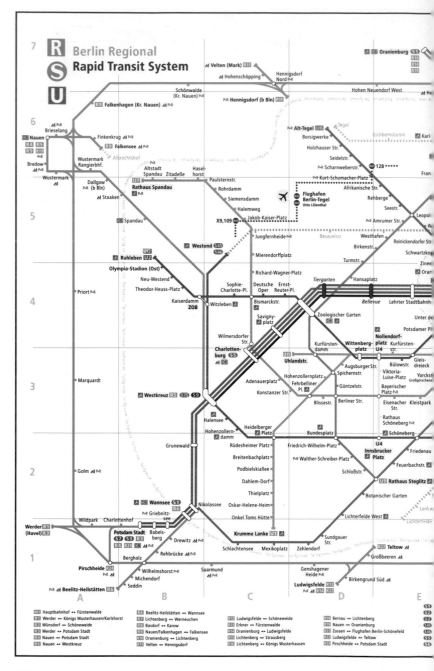

# R Berlin Regional
# S Rapid Transit System
# U

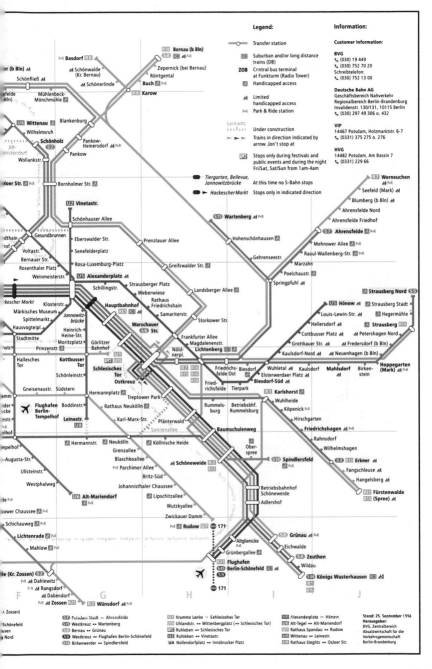

**Legend:**

- ═○═ Transfer station
- DB Suburban and/or long distance trains (DB)
- ZOB Central bus terminal at Funkturm (Radio Tower)
- ♿ Handicapped access
- ♿ Limited handicapped access
- P+R Park & Ride station
- ••••• Under construction
- ►► Trains in direction indicated by arrow 'Jon't stop at
- U12 Stops only during festivals and public events and during the night Fri/Sat, Sat/Sun from 1am-4am
- ● *Tiergarten, Bellevue, Jannowitzbrücke* At this time no S-Bahn stops
- ●► *Hackescher Markt* Stops only in indicated direction

**Information:**

Customer Information:

**BVG**
☎ (030) 19 449
☎ (030) 752 70 20
Schreibtelefon:
☎ (030) 752 13 00

**Deutsche Bahn AG**
Geschäftsbereich Nahverkehr
Regionalbereich Berlin-Brandenburg
Invalidenstr. 130/131, 10115 Berlin
☎ (030) 297 49 306 o. 432

**VIP**
14467 Potsdam, Holzmarktstr. 6-7
☎ (0331) 375 275 o. 276

**HVG**
14482 Potsdam, Am Bassin 7
☎ (0331) 229 66

G7 Potsdam Stadt ↔ Ahrensfelde
S7S Westkreuz ↔ Wartenberg
S8 Bernau ↔ Grünau
S9 Westkreuz ↔ Flughafen Berlin-Schönefeld
S10 Birkenwerder ↔ Spindlersfeld

U1 Krumme Lanke ↔ Schlesisches Tor
U15 Uhlandstr. ↔ Wittenbergplatz (↔ Schlesisches Tor)
U12 Ruhleben ↔ Schlesisches Tor
U2 Ruhleben ↔ Vinetastr.
U4 Nollendorfplatz ↔ Innsbrucker Platz

U5 Alexanderplatz ↔ Hönow
U6 Alt-Tegel ↔ Alt-Mariendorf
U7 Rathaus Spandau ↔ Rudow
U8 Wittenau ↔ Leinestr.
U9 Rathaus Steglitz ↔ Osloer Str.

Stand: 25. September 1994
Herausgeber:
BVG, Zentralbereich
Absatzwirtschaft für die
Verkehrsgemeinschaft
Berlin-Brandenburg

# Berlin Districts

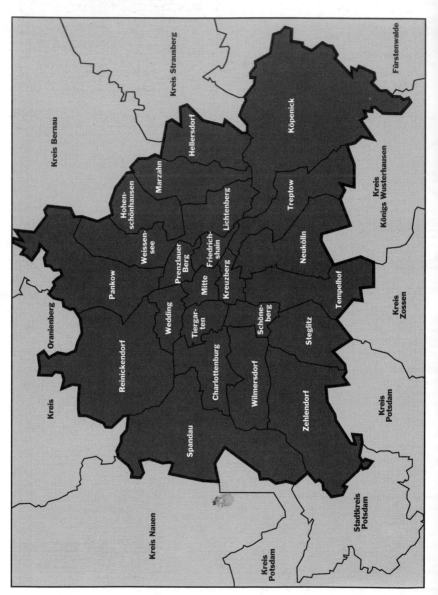

Kreis Strausberg

Fürstenwalde

Kreis Bernau

Köpenick

Hellersdorf

Hohen-schönhausen

Marzahn

Kreis Königs Wusterhausen

Lichtenberg

Treptow

Friedrich-shain

Weissen-see

Prenzlauer Berg

Neukölln

Pankow

Mitte

Kreuzberg

Kreis Zossen

Oranienberg

Wedding

Tiergar-ten

Schöne-berg

Tempelhof

Reinickendorf

Steglitz

Kreis

Charlottenburg

Wilmersdorf

Zehlendorf

Kreis Potsdam

Spandau

Kreis Potsdam

Kreis Nauen

Stadtkreis Potsdam

Kreis Potsdam

# Time Out Berlin Guide Reader's Report

Name: _____

Address: _____

Telephone: _____

Age: up to 19 ☐  20-24 ☐  25-29 ☐  30-34 ☐  35-44 ☐  45+ ☐

Occupation: _____

Did you travel to Berlin:

|  | Alone? ☐ | With partner? ☐ |
|  | As part of a group? ☐ | With children? ☐ |

How long is your trip to Berlin:?

Less than 3 days ☐          3 days-one week ☐

One week-two weeks ☐      Over two weeks (please specify) ☐

Are you a *Time Out* magazine reader?  Yes ☐  No ☐

Have you bought other *Time Out* guides? If so, which ones?

| Amsterdam Guide | ☐ | Paris Guide | ☐ |
| London Guide | ☐ | Prague Guide | ☐ |
| Madrid Guide | ☐ | Rome Guide | ☐ |
| New York Guide | ☐ | Eating and Drinking in London Guide | ☐ |
|  |  | London Visitors Magazine | ☐ |

Would you like to receive information about new titles?  Yes ☐  No ☐

How often did you consult the following sections:

|  | before arrival? | once? | daily? | never? |
| --- | --- | --- | --- | --- |
| Accommodation | ☐ | ☐ | ☐ | ☐ |
| Sightseeing | ☐ | ☐ | ☐ | ☐ |
| Berlin by Area | ☐ | ☐ | ☐ | ☐ |
| History | ☐ | ☐ | ☐ | ☐ |
| Eating & Drinking | ☐ | ☐ | ☐ | ☐ |
| Galleries & Museums | ☐ | ☐ | ☐ | ☐ |
| Arts & Entertainment | ☐ | ☐ | ☐ | ☐ |
| In Focus | ☐ | ☐ | ☐ | ☐ |
| Survival | ☐ | ☐ | ☐ | ☐ |
| Trips Out Of Town | ☐ | ☐ | ☐ | ☐ |

Is there anything you'd like us to cover in greater depth?

_____

_____

Please use the space below to tell us about places that you think should be included in the Guide:

_____

_____

_____

_____

_____

_____

AFFIX
STAMP
HERE

Time Out Magazine
Universal House
251 Tottenham Court Road
London
United Kingdom
W1P OAB